EYEWITNESS *TRAVEL GUIDES*

CALIFORNIA

DORLING KINDERSLEY

LONDON • NEW YORK • STUTTGART • MOSCOW

A DORLING KINDERSLEY BOOK

Produced by Duncan Baird Publishers
London, England

MANAGING EDITOR Louise Bostock Lang
MANAGING ART EDITOR Clare Sullivan
EDITORS Slaney Begley, Joanne Levêque, Zoë Ross
EDITORIAL ASSISTANT Leo Hollis
DESIGNERS Christine Keilty, Susan Knight,
Jill Mumford, Alison Verity
PICTURE RESEARCH Lindsay Hunt, Susannah Stone
DTP DESIGNER Rhona Green

Dorling Kindersley Limited
MANAGING EDITORS Vivien Crump, Helen Partington
DEPUTY ART DIRECTOR Gillian Allan
DEPUTY EDITORIAL DIRECTOR Douglas Amrine
SENIOR EDITOR Fay Franklin
MAP CO-ORDINATORS Emily Green, David Pugh
PRODUCTION David Proffit

MAIN CONTRIBUTORS Jamie Jensen, Barry Parr,
Ellen Payne, J Kingston Pierce, Rebecca Poole Forée,
Nigel Tisdall, John Wilcock, Stanley Young

MAPS
Kim Bushby, Jane Hanson, Phil Rose, Jennifer Skelley
at Lovell Johns Ltd, Oxford, UK
Gary Bowes, Fiona Casey, Anna Nilsson at
ERA-Maptec Ltd, Dublin, Ireland
Street Finder Maps based upon digital data, adapted with
permission from original survey by ETAK INC 1984–1994

PHOTOGRAPHERS
Max Alexander, Peter Anderson, John Heseltine, Dave
King, Neil Lukas, Andrew McKinney, Neil Setchfield

ILLUSTRATORS
Arcana Studios, Joanna Cameron, Stephen Conlin, Dean
Entwhistle, Nick Lipscombe, Lee Peters, Robbie Polley,
Kevin Robinson, John Woodcock

•

Film outputting bureau Creative Text Limited (London)
Reproduced by Colourscan (Singapore)
Printed and bound by Graphicom (Italy)

First published in Great Britain in 1997
by Dorling Kindersley Limited
9 Henrietta Street, London WC2E 8PS

Copyright 1997 © Dorling Kindersley Limited, London

Visit us on the World Wide Web at http://www.dk.com

A CIP CATALOGUE RECORD IS AVAILABLE FROM THE BRITISH LIBRARY.

ISBN 0-7513-0403-4
•

Every effort has been made to ensure that the information in this
book is as up-to-date as possible at the time of going to press.
However, details such as telephone numbers, opening hours,
prices, gallery hanging arrangements and travel information are
liable to change. The publishers cannot accept responsibility for
any consequences arising from the use of this book.

We would be delighted to receive any corrections and
suggestions for incorporation in the next edition. Please write to:
Deputy Editorial Director, Eyewitness Travel Guides,
Dorling Kindersley, 9 Henrietta Street, London WC2E 8PS.

THROUGHOUT THIS BOOK, FLOORS ARE REFERRED TO IN ACCORDANCE WITH
AMERICAN USAGE, IE THE "FIRST FLOOR" IS AT GROUND LEVEL.

CONTENTS

Volleyball on Pismo Beach

LOS ANGELES

EYEWITNESS *TRAVEL* *GUIDES*

CALIFORNIA

THE NORTH
Pages 426–437

WINE COUNTRY
Pages 438–449

**GOLD COUNTRY AND
THE CENTRAL VALLEY**
Pages 450–465

**NORTH CENTRAL
CALIFORNIA**
Pages 482–501

THE HIGH SIERRAS
Pages 466–481

LOS ANGELES
Pages 54–183

HIGH
SIERRAS

Independence

Fresno

Death
Valley

THE MOJAVE
DESERT

Bakersfield

SOUTH
CENTRAL

SOUTHERN
CALIFORNIA

Santa
Barbara

LOS
ANGELES

Los
Angeles

San
Bernardino

Anaheim
ORANGE
COUNTY

Palm
Springs

THE INLAND
EMPIRE AND
LOW DESERT

SAN DIEGO
COUNTY

San
Diego

Half Dome in Yosemite National Park

State Capitol
building in
Sacramento

HOW TO USE THIS GUIDE

THIS GUIDE helps you to get the most from your stay in California. *Introducing California* maps the whole state and sets it in its historical and cultural context. The ten regional chapters, plus *Los Angeles* and *San Francisco and the Bay Area*, describe important sights with maps, pictures and illustrations, as well as introductory features on subjects of regional interest.

Suggestions on restaurants, accommodation, shopping and entertainment are in *Travellers' Needs*. The *Survival Guide* has tips on getting around the state. LA, San Francisco and San Diego have their own *Practical Information* sections.

LOS ANGELES AND SAN FRANCISCO AND THE BAY AREA

The centres of the two major cities have been divided into a number of sightseeing areas. Each area has its own chapter which opens with a list of the sights described. All the sights are numbered and plotted on an *Area Map*. Information on each sight is easy to locate within the chapter as it follows the numerical order on the map.

Sights at a Glance lists the chapter's sights by category: Historic Streets and Buildings, Shops, Modern Architecture, etc.

A locator map shows where you are in relation to other areas of the city centre.

2 Street-by-Street Map
This gives a bird's-eye view of the heart of each sightseeing area.

A suggested route for a walk covers the more interesting streets in the area.

All pages relating to Los Angeles have lilac thumb tabs. San Francisco pages have grass-green thumb tabs.

1 Area Map
For easy reference, the sights are numbered and located on a map. The sights are also shown on the Los Angeles Street Finder *(see pp172–83) or the* San Francisco Street Finder *(see pp384–93).*

Stars indicate sights that no visitor should miss.

3 Detailed information on each sight
All the sights in Los Angeles and in San Francisco and the Bay Area are described individually. Addresses and practical information are provided. The key to the symbols used in the information block is shown on the back flap.

Story boxes explore specific subjects further.

1 Introduction
The landscape, history and character of each region is described here, showing how the area has developed over the centuries and what it offers to the visitor today.

NORTHERN CALIFORNIA AND SOUTHERN CALIFORNIA
Apart from San Francisco and the Bay Area and Los Angeles, California has been divided into two regions (Northern and Southern California), each of which has five separate area chapters. The most interesting towns and places to visit are numbered on a *Pictorial Map* at the beginning of each chapter.

Each area of California can be identified quickly by its own colour coding, which is shown on the inside front cover.

2 Pictorial Map
This shows the main road network and gives an illustrated overview of the whole area. All entries are numbered and there are also useful tips on getting around the region.

3 Detailed information
All the important towns and other places to visit are described individually. They are listed in order, following the numbering on the Pictorial Map. *Within each entry, information is given on the most important sights. A map reference refers the reader to the road map inside the back cover.*

For all the top sights, a visitors' checklist provides the practical information you need to plan your visit.

4 California's top sights
These are given two or more full pages. Historic buildings are dissected to reveal their interiors; museums and galleries have colour-coded floorplans to help you locate the most interesting exhibits; national parks and forests have maps showing facilities and trails.

INTRODUCING
CALIFORNIA

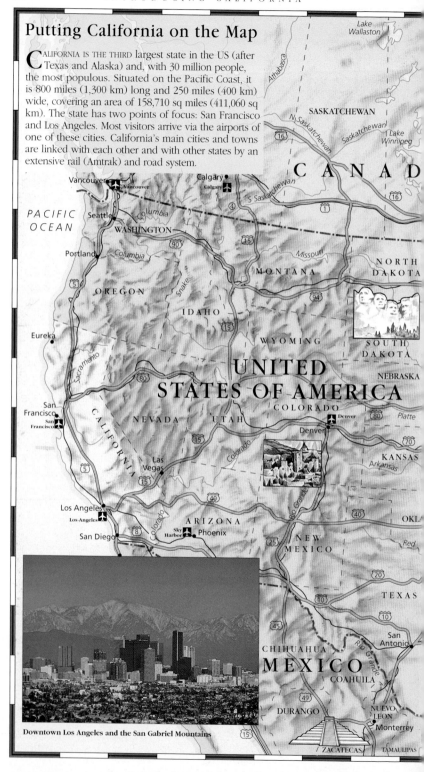

Putting California on the Map

CALIFORNIA IS THE THIRD largest state in the US (after Texas and Alaska) and, with 30 million people, the most populous. Situated on the Pacific Coast, it is 800 miles (1,300 km) long and 250 miles (400 km) wide, covering an area of 158,710 sq miles (411,060 sq km). The state has two points of focus: San Francisco and Los Angeles. Most visitors arrive via the airports of one of these cities. California's main cities and towns are linked with each other and with other states by an extensive rail (Amtrak) and road system.

Downtown Los Angeles and the San Gabriel Mountains

A

Satellite view of the San Francisco Bay Area

ATLANTIC
OCEAN

0 kilometres   500

0 miles   300

The Bahamas

KEY

☐   California

✈   Airport

━━   Freeway

━━   Major Amtrak routes

A Portrait of California

IMPRESSIVE FOR BOTH ITS SIZE *and its sway over modern culture, California symbolizes the United States' diversity and sense of prosperity. Here can be found towering forests, deserts within half a day's drive of ocean beaches, and two of the world's foremost cities, San Francisco and Los Angeles.*

Perceptions of California vary so greatly that some now joke that there are two states. The first is geographic: California is the third-largest state in the Union (after Alaska and Texas), containing its largest county, San Bernardino, which covers 20,155 sq miles (52,200 sq km) – larger than Vermont and New Hampshire combined. This California has 840 miles (1,350 km) of coastline and measures 365 miles (587 km) at its widest point. It claims the highest peak in the country (Mount Whitney) and its lowest expanse of dry land (Death Valley). More than 1,500 plant species grow here that cannot be found anywhere else on earth. Roughly one in every eight

State seal

Americans is a Californian, making this the most populous of the 50 states, represented by the largest congressional delegation.

And that other California? It is a realm of romance, formed by flickering celluloid images. Think "California" and pictures are immediately conjured up of bikini-clad beachcombers, middle-class suburban families in ranch houses, and film stars emerging from limousines into hordes of autograph-seekers. These stereotypes are perpetuated by the entertainment and tourism media.

Hollywood is only partly to blame for this blurring of fact and fiction. It goes back to Spanish legends of an exotic outpost called California, flung

Sun-worshippers on Manhattan Beach, Los Angeles

◁ Roller coaster at Knott's Berry Farm, Orange County

Joshua Tree National Park

out at the edge of the sea. Most of the world, though, knew nothing of this spot until the Gold Rush of 1849. Tales of the riches to be found encouraged thousands of would-be Croesuses to invade the region. Whether they found their fortunes or not, prospectors spread the same message: California was not as colourful or seductive as they had been told. It was even more so.

SOCIETY AND POLITICS

If the US as a whole is a melting pot of people, California is an ethnic microcosm. It receives the highest number of immigrants (more than 200,000 annually), and the racial makeup is the most diverse in the nation. The percentage of whites and African-Americans is lower than the national average, but the Asian residency is more than triple the national level. Hispanics account for more than a quarter of all Californians – three times the US average. Walk through any of the four most-populated cities

(LA, San Diego, San Jose and San Francisco), and you receive an immediate taste of this ethnic cocktail. It is still more potent during Mexican *Cinco de Mayo* (5 May) festivities, Chinese New Year bashes, and other multicultural events held around the state.

Racial prejudice has plagued the state since its early days. Abolitionists prevented California's 1849 constitutional convention from barring the entry of blacks into this land, but in the 1870s nativist orators such as Denis Kearney endorsed violence against Chinese immigrants, said to be "stealing" white jobs. Sadly, overcrowding is reigniting racial tensions today, with overpopulation also having a negative effect on law enforcement and education. It is raising already high student–teacher ratios in California's schools, which have been short of funding since property taxes, a source of revenue for both state and local governments, were cut and capped in 1978. But the most inevitable result of population growth has been an altered balance between rural and urban sectors. More people means that more land is needed for housing. The

Surfer

Golden Gate Bridge, San Francisco

Red Rock Canyon in the Mojave Desert

value of California's agricultural goods still outranks that of all other states, but its farmland has declined steadily since the 1950s. Timber workers have also had a hard time, due to conservation measures and a continuing shrinkage of the state's forests. The fastest-expanding job markets now are in service industries and high technology, which suggest a more metropolitan than pastoral future. Visitors usually come to California to see one of two cities: San Francisco or Los Angeles. In the north and south of the state respectively, these cities define the opposing sides of its character. San Francisco is older and more compact. Although California in general is recognized for its eccentricities and is still the birthplace of new trends, San Francisco is particularly proud of its nonconformity and open-mindedness. It was here that the "Big Four" railroad barons built their millionaire's mansions, but the city has since evolved into a pro-labour hotbed, with a history of activism (the Bay Area was a hub of the anti-Vietnam War movement). It also

Californian oranges

has one of the world's largest concentrations of gays and lesbians, with a substantial gay vote.

By contrast to San Francisco, LA is a sprawling city without a discernible focal point. The car rules, demanding a network of freeways that have hemmed in some of the city's historical buildings, and grind to smoggy standstills during rush hours. The façades of wealth, fame and glamour leave LA as a dimensionless creation of bright lights and conservative politics.

Wild poppies in Antelope Valley

This is not to say that the north is entirely Democrat (left wing) and the south, Republican (right wing). Hollywood is a chief sponsor of liberal causes and there are pockets of anti-government rebels in the northeast. But the conflicting power that the two cities exert on state government in Sacramento and the state's representatives in Washington, DC explains why California may appear a little schizophrenic.

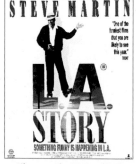

Film poster for *LA Story* (1991)

McLaughlin and Elmer Bischoff, and ceramists Peter Voulkos and Robert Arneson have all made international reputations. So have a few pioneers of photographic art, such as Imogen Cunningham and Ansel Adams. British artist David Hockney lived here for many years, capturing the state's sun-soaked image on canvas. California is also home to some of the world's finest art museums, including LACMA, the Oakland Museum, the San Francisco MOMA and the two J Paul Getty Museums.

CULTURE AND LEISURE

High- and low-brow art enjoy comparable support here. For most people, the state's contributions to culture are the many blockbusters made by Hollywood movie studios, or televised sitcoms shot on LA sound stages. This is art in unashamed pursuit of the almighty dollar, complete with tabloid scandals and giant movie billboards blotting out the Los Angeles sun. But another creativity reveals itself through the state's history of landscape painting, portraiture and 20th-century avant-garde art. Modern artists John

Victorian architecture in the Bay Area has always been a major tourist attraction, as have the many historic buildings across the state designed by Californians such as Willis Polk and Bernard Maybeck. Visiting designers Frank Lloyd Wright

Al Pacino receiving an Academy Award in 1993

and Daniel Burnham have left their

Napa Valley Train in Wine Country

El Capitán in Yosemite National Park

mark here, too. More recent influential architects include residents Frank Gehry and Joe Esherick.

The state has seen many littérateurs over the years, including Nobel prize-winner John Steinbeck and the Beat authors Jack Kerouac and Allen Ginsberg. The tradition continues with Armistead Maupin *(Tales of the City)*, detective novelist Sue Grafton and Amy Tan *(The Joy Luck Club)*, among others. Music also plays a major role, whether it is the work of the cities' orchestras or rock musicians. This is where the Beach Boys, Janis Joplin, the Grateful Dead and Cher launched their careers.

Californians love to eat out, and chefs Wolfgang Puck and Alice Waters have made their name promoting "Californian cuisine" – a blend of local ingredients and Asian preparation techniques. This, combined with a selection of local world-class wines, is proof that Californians take care of their palates.

Yet residents are also body-conscious, aware that they live among the "beautiful people" who come here with dreams of film stardom. So they become slaves to the gym or take up a sport. On any weekend, in various parts of the state, you will see cyclists, surfers, in-line skaters, even white-water rafters. Californians are eager supporters of professional baseball and football, but they like to be active themselves. Luckily, surrounded by some of the nation's most beautiful countryside and the gentlest climate, they don't have to go far to enjoy a satisfying outdoor experience.

Padres baseball stadium in San Diego

California's Landscape and Geology

CALIFORNIA'S DRAMATIC LANDSCAPE includes the highest point in the US, Mount Whitney in the High Sierras, and the lowest, Death Valley in the southern deserts. Millions of years ago, subduction of the Pacific Ocean floor beneath the North American Plate created the Coastal Range, the Central Valley and the granitic rocks of the Sierra Nevada Mountains. Later, the granites were uplifted and tilted westwards. The meeting of tectonic plates, now a lateral movement along the San Andreas Fault, is still changing the shape of California.

The Coastal Range along the Pacific Coast was created around 25 million years ago, when fragments of the ocean floor and oceanic islands were pushed up by plate movements.

HOW THE WEST WAS MADE

Over a period of 150 million years, ending about 15 million years ago, the movement of the Pacific Plate and North American Plate formed the western margin of California.

Off-shore Pacific islands

Pacific Plate

Shallow water sediment

North American Plate

Subduction zone where the two plates meet

100 million years BC

1 The North American Plate, moving westwards, sweeps up any off-shore islands.

MOUNT SHASTA 14,162 ft (4,317 m)

25 million years BC

Coastal Range

2 As the ocean floor moves north, the fragments of off-shore islands are scattered along the coast. They are then pushed up to form the Coastal Range.

San Andreas Fault

Sierra Nevada

Central Valley basin filled by sediment

Present Day

3 The boundary between the North American Plate and the Pacific Plate is marked by the San Andreas Fault (see pp20–21).

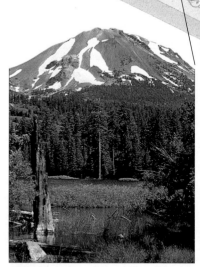

Mount Lassen *(see p437) and Mount Shasta (see p436) are part of the Cascades, a range of extinct and active volcanoes (including Mount St Helens) created by a subduction zone beneath the north-western corner of the North American Plate. Both Mount Lassen and Mount Shasta are still considered active. When young, the Sierra Nevada range must have resembled the Cascades.*

Lemon trees *flourish in central California. The highly fertile surface sediments of the flat Central Valley come from erosion of the surrounding mountains. The sediments have accumulated over the last few hundred thousand years.*

Mount Whitney *(see p479) in the High Sierras is the highest point in the continental United States, rising to 14,494 ft (4,418 m). The process that raised the Sierra Nevada Mountains began more than 50 million years ago, but peaked a few million years ago.*

NORTH PALISADE
14,242 ft (4,341 m)

MOUNT DANA
13,053 ft
(3,979 m)

MOUNT WHITNEY
14,494 ft (4,418 m)

DEATH VALLEY

BIG PINE MOUNTAIN
6,826 ft (2,081 m)

0 kilometres 100

0 miles 100

Oil wells *sprang up at a frantic pace when oil was discovered in California. The drilling was so intense that the extraction of oil and gas deflated the land. Part of Los Angeles County subsided 28 ft (8.5 m) before oil companies were required to pump sea water down the wells to replace the extracted fuels.*

Death Valley *(see pp280–83) in the Mojave Desert displays extreme height variations. Surrounded by some of the highest mountains on the continent, the valley floor lies 280 ft (85 m) below sea level. Death Valley was formed less than 15 million years ago when the North American plate began to stretch due to the northwest drag created by the Pacific Plate.*

California's Earthquakes

THE SAN ANDREAS FAULT extends almost the full length of California, some 600 miles (965 km) from the Gulf of California northwest to Cape Mendocino. It is not the only fault in California but is the line of most activity. Each year, on average, the Pacific Plate moves 1–1.6 inches (2.5–4 cm) to the northwest. Earthquakes occur when this movement is resisted. Stresses build up and eventually they are released, causing an earthquake. Many of California's major earthquakes have occurred in the northern section of the fault. The terrible fire of 1906 that destroyed San Francisco was caused by an earthquake that recorded 8.3 on the Richter Scale. More recently, the earthquake of October 1989, south of San Francisco, killed 62 people and caused at least 6,000 million dollars worth of damage *(see p489)*. In 1994, the Northridge quake, magnitude R6.7, rocked Los Angeles and was felt in Las Vegas, Nevada. Scientists now predict that the next major earthquake, the "Big One", will hit Southern California.

The San Andreas Fault *is one of the few sites on earth where an active plate boundary occurs on land.*

Hayward Fault

1989 earthquake epicentre

1989 earthquake hypocentre

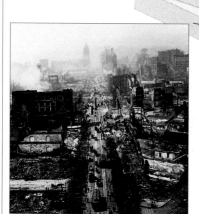

The 1906 earthquake *confounded contemporary geologists and led to the "elastic rebound" theory of earthquake formation, which is still in use today.*

The 1989 earthquake *struck the Santa Cruz Mountains in central California.*

TIMELINE

1769 Members of Portolá's expedition are first Europeans to experience an earthquake in California	**1865** San Francisco hit by its first major earthquake on 9 October and another on 23 October	**1872** Town of Lone Pine is destroyed and Sierra Nevada Mountains rise 13 ft (4m)	**1952** Kern County (R7.7) **1940** Imperial Valley (R7.1)	**1992** Yucca Valley outside LA, (R7.4) **1989** Loma Prieta (R7.1) strikes San Francisco area

1750	1800	1850	1900	1950

Don Gaspar de Portolá

1857 Fort Tejon (R8) is followed by smaller earth tremors in Bay Area	**1906** San Francisco earthquake (R8.3) causes a devastating three-day fire which leaves 3,000 dead and 250,000 homeless	**1994** Northridge (R6.7). At least 56 people killed, more than 7,000 injured and 20,000 made homeless. Anaheim Stadium and several Los Angeles freeways are badly damaged	

The 1994 earthquake caused havoc in the Los Angeles area. Collapsed overpasses closed the Santa Monica Freeway and Interstate 5 near Reseda. Fires caused further damage in the San Fernando Valley and in Malibu and Venice.

The movement of plates is most pronounced along the San Andreas Fault Zone. Friction sometimes causes the fault to "stick".

Garlock Fault

Seismically-safe housing is designed to withstand the stresses caused by the ground shaking during an earthquake. Every time a strong earthquake occurs, scientists carefully measure how various structural designs respond to earthquake motion.

Elsinore Fault

Santa Barbara •

Los Angeles

• San Diego

San Andreas Fault

S (secondary) waves travel through solid parts of the crust.

Northern American Plate

PACIFIC PLATE MEETS NORTH AMERICAN PLATE

The San Andreas Fault is a major fracture in the earth's crust. It is the result of friction where two plates meet – the Pacific Plate (consisting of most of the Pacific Ocean and the California coastline) and the North American Plate.

P waves   S waves   L waves

Pacific Plate   Hypocentre

P (primary) waves travel through the earth's core.

It is possible to calculate the magnitude of an earthquake from a seismograph recording. Printouts show the intensity of earthquake vibrations graphically. The magnitude of the earthquake is registered on the Richter Scale (R).

Earthquake energy vibrations move through the earth's crust in waves. There are three types of wave: P or primary waves, S or secondary waves and L or surface waves. The waves change as energy moves from the epicentre to the earth's surface. Surface waves cause most of the damage associated with earthquakes.

Literary California

As JOURNALIST Carey McWilliams remarked in 1946, "What America is, California is, with accents, in italics." The chance to study the nation in microcosm has been especially appealing to authors. Many, such as Robert Louis Stevenson (1850–94), have simply passed through. He arrived in Monterey in 1879 and later based scenes in *Treasure Island* on the surrounding coastline. But California has not lacked for resident wordsmiths. This, after all, is where Henry Miller (1891–1980) blended erotic and verbal inventiveness and William Saroyan (1908–81) found his eccentric rural characters. Nobel prize-winning playwright Eugene O'Neill (1888–1953) produced some of his best work at Tao House in the Ramon Valley *(see p410)*. California is also where several successful contemporary writers, such as Amy Tan (born in 1952), now chase their muse.

Mask used in plays at Tao House

Robert Louis Stevenson, author of *Treasure Island*

THE PIONEERS

Much of the very early writing about California was unsophisticated, satisfying readers who simply wanted a taste of the frontier environment. But the Gold Rush *(see pp44–5)* created a market for prose that captured the poignancy, romance and raw humour of life in the West. Bay Area literary journals such as *The Golden Era* and *The Overland Monthly* nurtured many local fiction writers. These included Bret Harte (1836–1902), the author of *The Luck of Roaring Camp*, essayist Henry George (1839–97), and bards ranging from Joaquin Miller (1837–1913) to Ina Coolbrith (the nation's first poet laureate in 1915).

The literary journals also provided an apprenticeship for San Franciscan writer Samuel Clemens (1835–1910). His 1865 publication of the Gold Country yarn, "The Celebrated Jumping Frog of Calaveras County", introduced him to a national readership as "Mark Twain".

Writer Samuel Clemens, alias Mark Twain

THE SOCIAL CRITICS

Ambrose Bierce (1842–1914) ranked among the first of many Californian writers who used their art to advocate wide-ranging political and social reforms. During the late 19th century, Bierce filled his *San Francisco Examiner* column with tirades against hypocrites and bureaucrats. His poisonous articles helped to trim the overweening influence of the vast Southern Pacific Railroad Company *(see pp46–7)*.

Frank Norris (1870–1902) attacked America's greed in his novel, *McTeague* (1899). In *The Octopus*, Norris also lashed out at the Southern Pacific, this time for its monopolistic mistreatment of ranchers in the San Joaquin Valley.

Back from the Klondike Gold Rush (setting for *The Call of the Wild*), working-class author Jack London alternated between writing adventure novels and stories – such as *The Iron Heel* – that showed his faith in Marxism.

Upton Sinclair (1878–1968) had already published *The Jungle*, his exposé of the Chicago stockyards, when he moved to California after World War I. But it was in Pasadena that he wrote most of his novels, campaigning against poverty and inequality.

Social injustice was a frequent theme for Salinas-born novelist John Steinbeck (1902–68). *Tortilla Flat* (1935), about a band of Mexican-American outcasts, was his first success. It was *The Grapes of Wrath* (1939), however, that brought him the prestigious Nobel Prize for

Jack London at his Sonoma Valley ranch

Steinbeck on the Californian coast

Literature. Steinbeck's book so powerfully portrayed the miseries endured by migratory labourers, that it was banned from public libraries in some parts of the state.

THE CRIME WRITERS

THREE CALIFORNIAN writers established the American school of private-eye fiction. The first of these was Dashiell Hammett (1884–1961), a tubercular former Pinkerton Agency detective and San Francisco resident. He began writing for *Black Mask* and other "pulp" crime-fiction magazines in the 1920s. He then went on to produce five novels, including *The Maltese Falcon* (1930). Hammett's work boasted a grim realism not found in either British whodunits or more venal tales by pulp writers lacking his investigative credentials.

Raymond Chandler (1888–1959) was less intimate with urban "mean streets", but was a more lyrical storyteller.

Poster for the film adaptation of Hammett's *The Maltese Falcon*

Chandler was an oil company executive in Los Angeles, until he was sacked for drunkenness. He went on to create the quintessential American detective – Philip Marlowe, star of seven novels, the best being *Farewell, My Lovely* and *The Long Goodbye*. But it was Ross Macdonald (né Kenneth Millar) who finally rounded off his genre's rough edges and confirmed LA as its ideal setting. Macdonald was also the most prolific of this trio. He wrote 19 novels about sleuth Lew Archer, including *The Underground Man*.

Beat writers and friends, Jack Kerouac and Neal Cassady

THE BEATS

PROTEST AGAINST the political conservatism of President Eisenhower's America, and against the conventions of society and art, combined to produce San Francisco's "Beat Movement" of the 1950s. The Beats (or "Beatniks," as *San Francisco Chronicle* columnist Herb Caen labelled them) were led by writers Allen Ginsberg (born in 1926), Jack Kerouac (1922–69) and William Burroughs (born in 1914). They extolled poetry made up of random word usages, produced stream-of-consciousness, drug-assisted narratives and shunned social, literary and sexual restraints.

The Beatniks' rebellion officially began in December, 1955, when Ginsberg gave a public reading of his poem "Howl" which was more like a shouting. Despite protests that "Howl" was obscene, it was subsequently published by San Franciscan Lawrence Ferlinghetti, poet and owner of City Lights *(see p330)*, the first paperbacks-only bookshop in the United States.

Two years later, Kerouac's novel *On the Road* spread the Beats' bohemian ethic nationwide. The most influential of the beat writers, Kerouac also wrote *Desolation Angels* and the poetry cycle, *The Dharma Bums*, both set in California. By 1960 the beat movement was waning, but not before it had paved the way for that decade's hippie movement.

THE MODERNS

TODAY, MOST best-seller lists feature at least one novel by a Californian author. The state has many distinctive young voices, such as Ethan Canin (*The Palace Thief*, 1988), Michael Chabon (*The Wonder Boys*, 1995) and Ron Hansen (*Mariette in Ecstasy*, 1991). But more established lights in the literary world, such as Joan Didion (*A Book of Common Prayer*, 1977), Amy Tan (*The Joy Luck Club*, 1989) and Alice Walker (*The Color Purple*, 1985), are still shining as brightly as ever. There are also many genre writers in California, from science fiction masters, such as Larry Niven (*Ringworld*, 1981), to Sue Grafton (*L is for Lawless*, 1995), one of many women writers currently adding new depth to detective fiction.

Novelist Amy Tan

Art in California

IN THE WAKE of the Gold Rush *(see pp44–5)*, California became both a magnet and a breeding ground for artists. They generally eschewed native folk traditions, however, in favour of European aesthetics that, while making the most of this new land and its people, were not dramatically changed by it. Only after World War II did Californians – including painter Richard Diebenkorn and photographer Imogen Cunningham – shed subservience to Old World art movements in order to develop distinctive visual trends, which then spread internationally. Since the 1950s, Los Angeles has challenged San Francisco's cultural primacy, and Californian art has become a prized source of investment.

Figure on a Porch (1959) by Richard Diebenkorn

PAINTERS

CALIFORNIA's mountain and desert landscapes and dramatic ocean shores dominated painters' attention here during the late 19th century. Thomas Hill (1829–1908) was born in England and trained in Paris. He moved to California in 1861 and began to produce epic natural panoramas, especially of the stunning Yosemite Valley *(see pp472–5)*. His work not only attracted new visitors to the West Coast, but also helped win Yosemite national park status in 1890. Even more popular was William Keith (1838–1911), a Scotsman who spent 50 years portraying the state's virgin wilderness. At

that time, cities and people may have seemed comparatively pale inspirations. Yet Gilded Age California *(see pp46–7)* could not now be fully understood without such talents as William Hahn (1829–87), a German immigrant who captured life in nascent San Francisco; Grace Carpenter Hudson (1865–1937), renowned for her portraits of coastal natives; and Irishman William A Coulter (1849–1936), who recorded maritime scenes.

As early as 1900, the state's two halves displayed stylistically disparate growth. In the north, Xavier Martinez (1869–1943) and his fellow Tonalists filled canvases with the familiar hazy light and grey-brown hues of their

environment. In the south, Guy Rose (1867–1925) led an Impressionist school that used the region's vibrant colours and brighter light to produce Monet-like effects.

Prohibition-era Los Angeles flirted with the Synchromist style of Stanton Macdonald-Wright (1890–1973). San Francisco was enchanted by Cubist Realists such as Otis Oldfield (1890–1969). Another popular artist there was the great Mexican muralist Diego Rivera, who in 1940 composed *Panamerican Mind*, an enormous fresco which can be seen at the City College.

Modernism flowered fully in California after World War II. It was at that time that David Park (1911–60), Richard Diebenkorn (born in 1922) and other members of the Bay Area Figurative School began to blend Expressionism with realistic imagery. In Southern California, Hard-Edge Abstractionists such as Helen Lundeberg and John McLaughlin (1898–1976) drew critical acclaim with their large-scale geometric shapes.

What is remarkable about contemporary Californian painters is not simply the worldwide recognition that they have earned, but their stylistic breadth. They range from Pop Artist Ed Ruscha (born in 1937) and urban landscapist Wayne Thiebaud (born in 1920), to cutting-edge British émigré David Hockney (born in 1937) and Arthur Carraway (born in 1927), whose work celebrates his African-American heritage.

Afternoon in Piedmont (Elsie at the Window) by Xavier Martinez

Two Callas by Imogen Cunningham

PHOTOGRAPHERS

MANY EARLY Californian photographs were either portraits or straightforward documentary scenes done by surveyors. Some photographers, however, such as Eadweard James Muybridge (1830–1904), found photography no less powerful than painting in depicting nature. Others preferred to focus on human subjects. Allegorical nudes and other images by Anne Brigman (1869–1950) found fans even in New York City. Arnold Genthe (1869–1942) studied the Bay Area's Asian community, producing (with writer Will Irwin) a 1913 volume called *Pictures of Old Chinatown*.

In 1932 an Oakland group called "f/64" mounted a major exhibition at the MH de Young Memorial Museum in San Francisco *(see pp362–3)*. Members of f/64, among them Ansel Adams (1902–84), Imogen Cunningham (1883–1976) and Edward Weston (1886–1958), believed photography should emphasize realism. This approach was riveting when used in close-ups of plants, or as Dorothea Lange (1895–1965) applied it in her portraits of Californians during the Great Depression.

The range of approaches now includes the snapshot aesthetics of Judy Dater (born in 1941) and photographs of Weimaraner dogs by William Wegman (born in 1942).

SCULPTORS

GERMAN-BORN Rupert Schmid (1864–1932) arrived in San Francisco in the 1880s. He soon became famous for figurative works employing western themes, such as *California Venus* (1895), his life-size female nude adorned with Californian poppies. More important still was Douglas Tilden (1860–1935), a sculptor from Chico who created impressive civic monuments. Arthur Putnam (1873–1930) also won notoriety with his sensual representations of wild animals.

Schmid's *California Venus*

Californians have been expanding the parallel fields of sculpture and ceramics since the early part of this century. Peter Voulkos (born in 1924) experimented in large-scale fired clay sculptures. Robert Arneson (born in 1930) abandoned more traditional vessel aesthetics to pursue startling and amusing Pop Art ceramics, while Bruce Beasley (born in 1939) and Michael Heizer (born in 1944) have created pieces that take on different dimensions depending on the weather.

ART PATRONAGE IN CALIFORNIA

Private and public patronage have been essential to the vitality of Californian culture since the late 19th century. Had it not been for railway baron Henry Huntington's money and interest in art treasures, there would today be no Huntington Library, Art Galleries and Botanical Gardens in Pasadena *(see pp154–7)*. The public would not have access to that institution's collection of 18th-century British art, including Thomas Gainsborough's *The Blue Boy* (c.1770) and many other masterpieces. Multimillionaire J Paul Getty brought together the world-famous collection of Greek and Roman antiquities housed in the J Paul Getty Villa in Malibu *(see p82)* and the painting, sculpture and decorative arts collection occupying the new J Paul Getty Center in Brentwood *(see pp78–9)*. Another multimillionaire, Norton Simon, amassed the renowned selection of Goyas, Picassos, Rembrandts and Van Goghs and now on public display in the Norton Simon Museum *(see pp152–3)*.

Public financing, too, has enriched the state's art offerings. In the 1930s, the New Deal paid artists to paint the frescoes in San Francisco's Coit Tower *(see p321)* and embellish public structures up and down the state. More recently, city funds have been used to make Los Angeles one of the most important centres of mural art in the world.

Henry Huntington

Architecture in California

CALIFORNIA'S ARCHITECTURAL history began with the
arrival of the Europeans in the 18th century *(see
pp42–3)*. Many of the Spanish missions of the late 18th
and early 19th centuries were adaptations of Mexican
baroque architecture and the Spanish-Mexican influence continued to dominate Californian buildings
until the middle of the 19th century. Later, the population influx caused by the Gold Rush led to this Hispanic
vernacular merging with styles imported by settlers
from the eastern United States and Europe. Architects
such as Henry Cleaveland, S & J Newsom and
Bernard Maybeck were all influential in creating the
state's unique Victorian style.

**Hale House in Heritage Square,
Los Angeles**

MISSION

Franciscan missionaries
arriving in California from
Mexico, established a chain
of 21 missions, from San
Diego to Sonoma, as centres
from which to colonize the
state. They were all designed
to be within a day's journey
of their nearest neighbours.
These provincial versions of
Mexican churches and their
communal buildings were
designed by friars and built
of adobe bricks and timber
by unskilled Native American labourers. Over the years
their crude constructions
decayed and were shaken by
earthquakes, but many have
been carefully restored in
the 20th century. Distinctive
features include massive
walls covered with white
lime cement, small window
openings, rounded gables
and tiered bell towers.

**Distinctive rounded bell tower
at Carmel Mission**

Mission San Luis Rey *(1811–51) was the 18th
mission to be established and was so architecturally
impressive that it was often referred to as a "palace".*

MONTEREY

In the 1850s and 1860s, East
Coast settlers flooded into
the newly declared 31st state,
bringing with them styles
that were already going out
of fashion on the East Coast,
such as Greek Revival. Monterey, the state capital under
Mexican rule, gave its name
to an architecture that is, in
essence, a wooden Greek
temple wrapped around a
Mexican adobe. Features
include two-storey wooden
porticoes supported by slim
square posts, wood shingle
roofs and a chaste symmetry
of plan and elevation.

**Monterey-style Rancho
Los Cerritos, Long Beach**

Larkin House *(1837), built by Thomas Larkin, was the first
Monterey-style house, with its two storeys of adobe brick.*

VICTORIAN

Three major styles emerged in California during the Victorian era: Italianate, most popular in San Francisco *(see pp290–91)*, Queen Anne and Eastlake. The two latter styles achieved a pinnacle of exuberance in California during the 19th century when they were brought to the state by migrants from the East Coast. The restrained Eastlake style, with its geometrically patterned façades and ornamentation, was often combined with the more extravagant Queen Anne style, notable for its gables, turrets, wraparound porches and splendidly confused anthology of classical details.

Turret

Decorative gable

Decorative window on a Victorian house in Napa

Wraparound porch

Carson Mansion in Eureka (1886) was built by S & J Newsom, who were masters of the Queen Anne style. Now a private club, the house may be California's ultimate Victorian folly.

ARTS AND CRAFTS

Pioneered by William Morris and Charles Voysey in England, the Arts and Crafts movement flourished briefly in California in the early 20th century. Also known as Craftsman style, its leading proponents included Bernard Maybeck and Charles and Henry Greene. Its emphasis is on simplicity and refinement on the outside and in the handcrafted interiors.

Characteristic beamed roof at Gamble House, Pasadena

Clapboard wall

Shady porch

The First Church of Christ Science in Berkeley (1907) is the finest example of Bernard Maybeck's Arts and Crafts designs.

MISSION REVIVAL

The Spanish-Mexican style was dormant during the second half of the 19th century. Decorative or pared-down versions were then enthusiastically revived in the early 20th century. The style is distinguishable by its rounded arches, harmonious proportions and its absence of ornamentation.

Red-tiled roof at the Beverly Hills Hotel

White stucco wall

Red-tiled roof

Rounded arch

The Women's Club (1913) in La Jolla was designed by Irving Gill, a pioneer of modernism who used poured concrete and stucco to create elegant versions of the Mission style.

Twentieth-Century Californian Architecture

IN THE EARLY 20TH CENTURY an architecture distinctive to California emerged, after a brief return to the state's Hispanic roots and an Art Deco style imported from Europe. This Californian style borrowed post-and-beam construction and wide porches from traditional Japanese buildings. Later, during the postwar building boom of the 1950s, the whole of the US was influenced by Cliff May's Californian ranch house, with its fusion of indoor and outdoor living. In more recent years, many architects, such as Craig Ellwood and Frank Gehry, have helped to make LA a centre of modern architectural innovation *(see pp68–9)*.

San Francisco Museum of Modern Art (1995)

SPANISH COLONIAL

ORNATE VERSIONS of traditional Spanish architecture were first given wide currency by the Panama-California Exposition in San Diego in 1915 *(see pp246–7)*, where many buildings were decorated in this style. Simplified versions became the popular style for houses and public buildings throughout the 1920s. Distinguishing features included ornamental wood, stone and ironwork, used to set off expanses of white stucco, red pantiled roofs and lush gardens.

George Washington Smith, the Montecito-based architect, was a master of the style, creating abstracted Andalusian-style villages, such as **Ostoff House** (1924) in San Marino and Casa del Herrero (1925), a private house in Montecito. Another striking example of this style is William Mooser's **Santa Barbara County Courthouse** (1929), with its hand-painted ceilings, murals and sunken gardens.

STREAMLINE MODERNE

ART DECO made a brief appearance in California at the end of the 1920s, with jazzy reliefs and tile façades. It was superseded by Streamline Moderne, in which sleek, rounded forms are animated by ribs, canopies and reliefs. Its inspirations were machine-age imagery. The style is best seen in cinemas, such as the **Academy Cathedral** (1939) in Inglewood and the **Paramount Theater** in Oakland (Miller & Pflueger, 1931).

PWA MODERNE

THIS MOVEMENT was named after the Public Works Administration, established in the 1930s to fund public buildings. It is a marriage of Beaux-Arts formality and the simplicity of Modernism. It is notable for its stone façades, pilasters and carved ornamentation. A good example is the **Monterey County Courthouse** (1937) in Salinas.

CONTEMPORARY

A DIVERSITY of approaches by leading architects has resulted in some striking contemporary buildings. Among the notable achievements of recent years are the ground-hugging, barn-like structures of **Sea Ranch**. This ecologically friendly holiday home community on the Northern Californian coast began as a cluster of condominiums by Moore Lyndon Turnbull Whittaker in 1965. In sharp contrast is the **Salk Institute**, in La Jolla (Louis Kahn, 1959–65). State-of-the-art laboratories in poured concrete flank a bare travertine-paved plaza – a symbolic meeting place that links the continent and the ocean.

The **San Francisco Museum of Modern Art** (1995) by Swiss architect Mario Botta is both a civic symbol and an indoor plaza. A cylindrical skylight reaches up from stacked, top-lit galleries clad in precast panels of plain and angled bricks, to light an expansive foyer.

POST-MODERNISM

REACTING to the impersonality of corporate towers, architects such as Michael Graves, Venturi Scott-Brown

George Washington Smith's Casa del Herrero in Montecito (1925)

and Robert Stern popularized a more decorative approach to Modernism in the 1970s. Buildings such as **The Library** (1984) by Robert Stern in San Juan Capistrano make playful use of historical elements (columns, pediments and pergolas) while employing colourful palettes.

Jon Jerde scrambles colours and architectural references with even greater abandon in his popular shopping centres, most notably **Horton Plaza** (1989) in San Diego. This multilevel outdoor shopping mall with domes and tilework echoes local Spanish-style buildings.

Programmatic Donut Hole in La Puente, east of Los Angeles

Post-Modern Horton Plaza

PROGRAMMATIC BUILDINGS

THE AUTOMOBILE began to reshape California as early as the 1920s and there was fierce competition to attract the attention of passing motorists on the commercial strips that linked scattered communities. An exuberant roadside architecture developed, in which travellers were invited to sleep in Wigwam motels or have their shoes repaired inside a huge shoe (Doschander's Shoe Repair Shop, Bakersfield, 1947). Most of these fantasies have been demolished, but a few remain in outlying areas, notably the drive-thru **Donut Hole** (1958) in La Puente and the **Tail o' the Pup** hot dog stand (1946) in West Hollywood.

FRANK LLOYD WRIGHT

Born in Wisconsin, Frank Lloyd Wright (1867–1959) lived in California in the 1920s and continued throughout his career to design buildings in the state. He began with **Hollyhock House** (1917–20) in Hollywood, and ended with the **Marin County Civic Center** in San Rafael, north of San Francisco, completed in 1972. Other notable buildings are the old VC Morris store (1949), now the **Circle Gallery** in San Francisco, and several LA "textile block" houses, inspired by Mayan temples.

Frank Lloyd Wright's Hollyhock House in Hollywood

WHERE TO FIND THE BUILDINGS

Multicultural California

Japanese sign

CALIFORNIA IS the most ethnically diverse state in the Union. In the 19th century, the discovery of gold, silver and oil each brought an influx of migrants of many nationalities to California and the landscape and climate still attract farmers, fishermen and vintners from all over the world. By the 21st century, many believe California will be a hybrid of cultures, with no clear ethnic majority. The concentration of races varies statewide: a greater number of Hispanics reside in the south, while the Silicon Valley and northern farmlands have attracted Asians and Europeans. Most ethnic communities still celebrate their cultures with festivals *(see pp32–5).*

San Francisco's Chinatown

entire areas of cities. Although many of the younger Chinese have now moved to middle-class areas, the Chinatowns of LA and San Francisco still attract tourists to their traditional shops and restaurants.

Mexican street musicians in Los Angeles

THE NATIVE AMERICANS

CALIFORNIA has more resident Native Americans than any other state. The indigenous population grew in the 1960s when they gained more political rights. A few Native Americans still live on reservations, but the majority have opted for integration throughout the state.

Girl in Native American dress

THE HISPANIC-AMERICANS

YOU CANNOT go far in California without becoming aware of the state's Hispanic heritage. Spanish explorers who arrived in the 17th and 18th centuries *(see pp42–3)* established many of today's cities. As early as the 1940s the state was home to the largest population of Mexicans outside their own country. Political and economic troubles in Central and South America have continued to fuel Hispanic immigration. Today, almost every city has Mexican influences in its architecture, cuisine and art. The Hispanics are also responsible for some of the brightest fiestas, including the extravagant *Cinco de Mayo* (5 May) *(see p32).*

THE CHINESE

CHINESE IMMIGRANTS first arrived in California during the Gold Rush *(see pp44–5).* A further influx escaped the economic problems of their homeland in the 1860s to work as cheap labour building the transcontinental railroad *(see pp46–7).* Following its completion, they remained in California, setting up laundries and other businesses, but were met with racial violence by activists claiming they were stealing "white jobs". In the 1880s Congress severely limited Chinese immigration, a law that was not repealed until as late as 1943.

Such antipathy resulted in ghetto-like Chinese communities, which dominated

THE AFRICAN-AMERICANS

AFRICAN-AMERICANS have been present in California since the days of Mexican rule. It was the increase in heavy industry during World War II, however, that led to the largest influx from the poorer southern states. In the

Rotchev House at Fort Ross

years that followed, low social standing and racism resulted in the growth of urban ghettos. Racial problems still persist, but many African-Americans are beginning to make their mark in government, entertainment and business. Cities like Oakland *(see pp406–9)* continue to celebrate traditional festivals.

THE JAPANESE

THE JAPANESE arrived in California in the early 20th century. The majority of them were farmers who literally sowed the seeds of the state's agricultural industry. During World War II, however, Japanese-Americans were considered a risk to national security and were interned for the duration of the war. The succeeding generation has overriden these events and Japanese businesses have continued to grow since the 1980s property boom.

THE ITALIANS

ITALIANS, predominantly fishermen, arrived in California in the late 19th century, and settled in North Beach, San Francisco *(see pp330–33)*. The climate and soil also tempted Italian vintners, who founded what is now a highly respected wine industry.

THE RUSSIANS

FUR-TRAPPERS from Russia and Alaska were among the first European settlers in California, arriving in the early 1800s. For a short time, they established a successful settlement at Fort Ross *(see p444)* and today there is a Russian population of some 25,000 in and around San Francisco. The *Russian Times* is printed five days a week.

THE IRISH

FEWER PEOPLE of Irish descent reside on the West Coast than on the East Coast and there are no distinct Irish districts in California. The Irish have largely integrated into a multicultural way of life, but their presence is still felt in the many Irish city bars, and particularly during the statewide parades on St Patrick's Day *(see p32)*.

Santa Monica
English pub sign

THE MELTING POT

OVER THE LAST few decades there has been a steady rise in immigrants from Asia. Long Beach has the largest population of Cambodians outside Cambodia and the district is known as "Little Phnom Penh". Wars in Korea and Vietnam brought natives of these countries to the liberal atmosphere of California in the 1950s and 1970s. Made to settle in the poorer areas of inner cities, they have now turned many of these into thriving communities. Fresno *(see p500)* has the second largest Hmong population outside Laos in the world.

The technological opportunities of Silicon Valley *(see p412)* have continued to attract Indians and Pakistanis to the region since the 1970s. Santa Monica is home to a large British contingent, complete with "authentic" pubs *(see pp72–3)*. The town of Solvang *(see p209)* was founded by immigrants from Denmark in 1911 and retains its Danish heritage. California also has the second largest Jewish community in the US, two thirds of whom live in LA.

Danish windmill in Solvang

CALIFORNIA
THROUGH THE YEAR

CALIFORNIA generally enjoys a moderate climate (see pp36–7), which explains how residents can schedule annual fêtes without concern for the weather. The size of the state, however, means that a range of activities can be pursued in different locations: winter can be spent skiing in the north or soaking up the sun in the warmer south. Californians love to celebrate and the calendar is full of parades and festivals. Many are related to the state's agricultural heritage; others have been inspired by its social history, such as the Gold Rush, or its ethnic diversity. There are also cultural events, including jazz and film festivals, and national sporting fixtures.

Runners in the Los Angeles Marathon

SPRING

THERE'S A CLEAR sense of re-emergence in spring, when wildflowers carpet California's coastal headlands, grey whales swim north with their newborn offspring and people start searching frantically for the sunglasses they tucked away the previous October. Cinco de Mayo (5 May) celebrations in Los Angeles and San Francisco, Hollywood's glamorous Academy Awards ceremony, baseball games and San Francisco's Bay-to-Breakers run are all familiar elements of the season.

MARCH

Return of the Swallows (19 Mar), San Juan Capistrano. Crowds gather to see the birds fly back to the mission gardens from their winter homes in Argentina (see pp230–31).

Los Angeles Marathon (first Sun).
Snowfest (first two weeks), Tahoe City. The winter carnival features ski competitions, a "polar bear" (cold water) swim and live music.
St Patrick's Day Parade (Sun nearest 17 Mar), San Francisco. A parade down Market Street is usually followed by Irish coffee in the city's Irish bars.

St Patrick's Day shamrock

Swallows returning to Mission San Juan Capistrano

Redwood Coast Dixieland Jazz Festival (end Mar), Eureka. Some of the world's finest Dixieland bands gather for this annual event.

APRIL

Academy Awards Ceremony (Apr), Los Angeles. Hollywood's finest gather to honour the year's top films and actors.
Major League Baseball (Apr–Sep). The San Francisco Giants, Oakland Athletics, LA Dodgers and San Diego Padres begin their season.
Toyota Grand Prix (mid-Apr), Long Beach. The biggest street race in the US.
Agua Cahuilla Indian Heritage Festival (mid-Apr), Palm Springs. Festivities honour the Native Americans who discovered the therapeutic properties of the local hot springs.
Cherry Blossom Festival (mid-Apr), San Francisco. Japanese dancing and martial arts displays are all part of this traditional annual event (see p342).
Anniversary of the 1906 Earthquake (18 Apr), San Francisco. Survivors gather around Lotta's Fountain, at Kearny and Market Streets, to remember the earthquake.
San Francisco International Film Festival (mid-Apr–early May). Independent films from around the world.
Red Bluff Round-Up Rodeo (third weekend). The largest two-day rodeo in the US.

MAY

Raisin Festival *(early May)*, Selma. A parade, art competitions and the Raisin Queen.
Cinco de Mayo *(5 May)*, LA and San Francisco. The state's largest Mexican celebrations feature folk dancing and mariachi music.
Bay-to-Breakers *(third weekend)*, San Francisco. The world's largest fun run is 7.5-miles (12.5-km) from the Embarcadero to Ocean Beach.
Calaveras County Fair *(mid-May)*, Angels Camp. The famous frog jumping contest *(see p463)* and a rodeo.
Mainly Mozart Festival *(end May–early Jun)*, San Diego. Leading orchestras perform Mozart masterpieces.
Carnaval *(last weekend)*, San Francisco. The Mission District turns Latin American, with salsa and reggae bands.
Sacramento Jazz Jubilee *(last weekend)*.

Mexican dancer at the *Cinco de Mayo* festival in Los Angeles

SUMMER

At no other time of year are the clichés of California so evident. Beaches are crowded with tanned, muscled bodies and daredevil surfers, and colourfully dressed gays and lesbians parade through San Francisco streets in June. Tourists flood into the state, attending its many outdoor music events, Wild West celebrations (such as Old Miners Days in Big Bear Lake), and the renowned annual Gilroy Garlic Festival.

Lesbian and Gay Pride parade in San Francisco

JUNE

Lesbian and Gay Pride Day *(Sun in late Jun)*, San Francisco. The largest gay parade proceeds down Market Street.
Lumber Jubilee *(end Jun)*, Tuolumne. Logging competitions recall the history of California's timber industry.
Monterey Blues Festival *(end Jun)*. Star blues performers draw crowds annually.
Juneteenth *(end Jun)*, Oakland. An African-American cultural celebration, featuring jazz and gospel music.

JULY

International Surf Festival *(whole month)*. Body boarding and surfing events take place at various beaches.
Fourth of July Fireworks Particularly good displays are at Disneyland and on Santa Monica Pier.
Mammoth Lakes Jazz Jubilee *(first weekend after 4 Jul)*. Some dozen world-class jazz bands perform.
Obon Festival *(mid-Jul)*, San Jose. Taiko drummers and dancers join in this Japanese-American party.
Carmel Bach Festival *(mid-Jul–early Aug)*. Bach concerts and classes.
Gilroy Garlic Festival *(end Jul)*. This food festival serves garlic in all kinds of dishes.
San Francisco Marathon *(mid-Jul)*.
Old Miners' Days *(end Jul–mid-Aug)*, Big Bear Lake. The Gold Rush is recalled with a chilli cook-off and a liars' contest.
Festival of the Arts *(Jul–Aug)*, Laguna Beach.

AUGUST

Native American Powwow *(early Aug)*, Costa Mesa. A celebration of Native American food and culture.
Old Spanish Days Fiesta *(early Aug)*, Santa Barbara. Spanish markets, a carnival and dancing.
Nisei Week *(early Aug)*, Japanese festival in LA's Little Tokyo.
Pebble Beach Concours d'Elegance *(mid-Aug)*. Classic automobile show.
California State Fair *(mid-Aug–early Sep)*, Sacramento. Everything from star-studded entertainment to pig races.
Bigfoot Days *(end Aug)*, Willow Creek. A parade and an ice cream social at this homage to Northern California's legendary hermit.

Native American dancers at the Costa Mesa Powwow

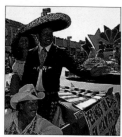
Mexican Independence Day parade in Santa Monica

AUTUMN

I N THE HIGH SIERRAS, leaves of deciduous trees turn stunning shades of red and yellow. The Napa Valley wineries *(see pp446–7)* invite visitors to help celebrate their grape harvests with wine tastings and live music. All over the state, Oktoberfests serve up foamy mugs of beer and the "oom-pah-pah" of German bands, while rodeos dramatize California's frontier past.

SEPTEMBER

Pro Football *(Sep–Dec)*. The San Francisco '49ers, Oakland Raiders and San Diego Chargers take to the field.
Los Angeles County Fair *(whole month)*, Pomona. This vast county fair includes horse races.

American football

Oktoberfest *(early Sep–end Oct)*, Torrance. The largest German beer festival in Southern California.
Mexican Independence Day *(16 Sep)*. Mexican dancing, music and food in Santa Monica, Calexico and Santa Maria.
Monterey Jazz Festival *(third weekend)*. The world's oldest continuously-held annual jazz festival.
Danish Days *(end Sep)*, Solvang. Danish food stalls and parades *(see p209)*.
San Francisco Blues Festival *(last weekend)*. Two-day event at Fort Mason.

OCTOBER

Sonoma County Harvest Fair *(early Oct)*, Santa Rosa. A grape stomp and a 6-mile (10-km) run are highlights of this annual fair.
US National Gold Panning Championship *(early Oct)*, Coloma. The 1849 Gold Rush is remembered with a gold panning competition.
Mountain Man Rendezvous *(early Oct)*, Bridgeport. Shooting contests and a barbecue re-create an 1840s get-together of mountain guides and trappers.
Black Cowboy Heritage Invitational Parade and Festival *(early Oct)*, Oakland. Commemorating the part African-Americans played in settling the American West.
Columbus Day Parade *(Sun nearest 12 Oct)*, San Francisco. Bands and floats proceed down Columbus Avenue to Fisherman's Wharf.
San Francisco Jazz Festival *(end Oct–early Nov)*. All-star jazz performances throughout the city.
Pumpkin Festival *(mid-Oct)*, Half Moon Bay. The World Heavyweight Pumpkin Championship, pumpkin carving and pumpkin dishes are served in every edible variety.
International Festival of Masks *(last Sun)*, Los Angeles. Originally part of Hallowe'en, this mask parade now celebrates LA's ethnic diversity.

Hallowe'en *(30–31 Oct)*, San Francisco. Costumed residents parade through the city streets.
Grand National Rodeo *(end Oct–early Nov)*, Daly City. Lassooing mustangs and a livestock exposition are part of this traditional event.
Butterflies *(end Oct–mid Mar)*, Pacific Grove. Thousands of monarch butterflies migrate here annually *(see p494)*.

Costumed participants in Pasadena's Doo Dah Parade

NOVEMBER

Día de los Muertos/Day of the Dead *(2 Nov)*. Festivities in LA's El Pueblo and San Francisco's Mission District highlight this Mexican religious festival, in which the souls of the dead are said to visit their surviving relatives *(see p122)*.
Death Valley '49ers Encampment *(mid-Nov)*. Fiddlers' competitions, cowboy poetry and gold panning are all featured.
Doo Dah Parade *(mid-Nov)*, Pasadena. Costumed merchants parody the approaching holiday and current events.

Mexican musicians at the *Día de los Muertos* festival

Grey whale approaching a boat off Baja California

PUBLIC HOLIDAYS

New Year's Day (1 Jan)
**Martin Luther King, Jr
Day** (3rd Mon in Jan)
Presidents' Day (3rd
Mon in Feb)
Memorial Day (last Mon
in May)
Independence Day (4 Jul)
Labor Day (1st Mon
in Sep)
Veterans' Day (11 Nov)
Thanksgiving (4th Thu
in Nov)
Christmas Day (25 Dec)

WINTER

CALIFORNIANS LOVE bright
lights, and this is most
apparent at Christmas, when
every building and public
square seems to be draped
in twinkling bulbs. Churches
resound with carols, while
film stars take part in seasonal
parades. As Lake Tahoe's ski
season gets underway, highways jam up with avid skiers
travelling north.

DECEMBER

**Hollywood Christmas
Parade** (first Thu after
Thanksgiving), Los Angeles.
Hollywood and Sunset
Boulevards are crowded with
this celebrity-heavy extrava-
ganza, held since 1931.
**Russian Heritage Christmas
Celebration** (weekends,
whole month), Guerneville.
Costumes, food and music
recall the area's early 19th-
century Russian influences.

Christmas decorations in
Carmel Plaza

**International Tamale
Festival** (early Dec), Indio.
Mexican dancing accompanies
the *tamale* (spicy corn husk
parcels) gluttony.
Whale-watching (end Dec–
Apr). Californian grey whales,
migrating south annually
from the Bering Strait to Baja,
can be sighted along the
coast or from whale-watching
boats out of many coastal
cities (see p580).

Float at the Tournament of Roses
Parade in Pasadena

JANUARY

Bald Eagles (Jan–Feb),
Mount Shasta. Bird-watchers
come to see bald eagles that
nest here (see pp420–21).
**Tournament of Roses
Parade** (1 Jan), Pasadena. A
pageant, followed by the Rose
Bowl inter-collegiate football
game (see p151).
**Palm Springs International
Film Festival** (early–mid
Jan). Screenings and awards.
Gold Discovery Day (24
Jan), Coloma. Gold-panning
demonstrations take place
on the anniversary of the
first gold discovery (see p459).

**AT&T Pebble Beach Pro-
Am Golf Tournament** (end
Jan–early Feb). Pros and
celebrities play golf together.

FEBRUARY

Dickens Festival (early
Feb), Riverside. Writer Charles
Dickens' life is celebrated in
a re-creation of a mid-19th-
century London marketplace.
**Napa Valley International
Mustard Festival** (mid-Feb),
Calistoga. Hundreds of mus-
tards are available for tasting.
**Riverside County Fair and
National Date Festival**
(mid–late Feb), Indio. Date
dishes and camel and ostrich
races (see p249).
Chinese New Year Festival
(mid-Feb–early Mar), San
Francisco. The nation's largest
Chinese New Year festival
includes a Golden Dragon
parade through the Financial
District and Chinatown.

Chinese New Year celebrations
in San Francisco

The Climate of California

APART FROM the extremes of the North and the deserts, the state's climate is neither oppressive in summer nor too cold in winter. The Northern Coastal Range is temperate, although wet in the winter. To the east, rain turns to snow on the Sierra Nevada Mountains. Central California and the Central Valley has a Mediterranean climate. The weather becomes drier and warmer towards the south with soaring temperatures in the desert during summer.

•Eureka

•Redding

Chico

Tahoe City•

Santa Rosa

•Sacramento

•Stockton

San Francisco

•Modesto

•San Jose

•Monterey

•San Luis Obispo

THE NORTH

° C

	Apr	Jul	Oct	Jan
max	16	17	16	12
min	9	11	9	5
sun %	55	52	49	42
rain mm	73	3	68	142

Average monthly maximum temperature

Average monthly minimum temperature

Average monthly sunshine during daylight hours (%)

Average monthly rainfall

WINE COUNTRY

° C

	Apr	Jul	Oct	Jan
max	21	28	25	14
min	6	12	9	3
sun %	75	85	80	52
rain mm	40	1	42	137

SAN FRANCISCO AND THE BAY AREA

° C

	Apr	Jul	Oct	Jan
max	17	20	22	14
min	10	12	13	8
sun %	73	66	70	56
rain mm	33	1	32	103

GOLD COUNTRY

° C

	Apr	Jul	Oct	Jan
max	19	33	23	12
min	4	13	7	0
sun %	70	89	78	54
rain mm	77	5	58	171

NORTH CENTRAL CALIFORNIA

° C

	Apr	Jul	Oct	Jan
max	24	37	27	12
min	9	18	10	3
sun %	85	96	88	51
rain mm	25	0	13	50

SOUTH CENTRAL CALIFORNIA

° C

	Apr	Jul	Oct	Jan
max	21	28	25	16
min	7	12	9	2
sun %	83	97	87	46
rain mm	28	18	8	75

HIGH SIERRAS

°C

| | 10 | 25 | 15 | 5 |
| -3 | 7 | 0 | -7 |

	65%	82%	70%	50%
	51 mm	8 mm	52 mm	143 mm
month	Apr	Jul	Oct	Jan

MOJAVE DESERT

°C

| | 26 | 38 | 28 | 16 |
| 9 | 19 | 11 | 0 |

	91%	93%	91%	81%
	5 mm	8 mm	5 mm	13 mm
month	Apr	Jul	Oct	Jan

LOS ANGELES

°C

| | 22 | 29 | 22 | 20 |
| 13 | 18 | 16 | 10 |

	70%	67%	80%	76%
	31 mm	5 mm	10 mm	70 mm
month	Apr	Jul	Oct	Jan

ORANGE COUNTY

°C

| | 21 | 28 | 25 | 19 |
| 12 | 17 | 15 | 9 |

	70%	67%	80%	76%
	21 mm	0 mm	6 mm	63 mm
month	Apr	Jul	Oct	Jan

PALM SPRINGS

°C

| | 31 | 43 | 33 | 21 |
| 12 | 24 | 15 | 6 |

	94%	91%	92%	84%
	3 mm	5 mm	5 mm	25 mm
month	Apr	Jul	Oct	Jan

SAN DIEGO

°C

| | 21 | 25 | 24 | 19 |
| 14 | 19 | 16 | 10 |

	66%	67%	70%	72%
	20 mm	0 mm	10 mm	46 mm
month	Apr	Jul	Oct	Jan

Independence

sno

Death
Valley

ersfield

Santa
Barbara

Los
Angeles

San
Bernardino

Anaheim

Palm
Springs

San
Diego

The History of California

AN EARLY 16th-century chivalric Spanish novel, *Las Sergas de Esplanadían (The Exploits of Esplanadían)*, first gave the name *California* to a mythical island, plump with natural wealth and ruled by a pagan queen called Calafía. By 1542, when the Portuguese navigator Juan Rodríguez Cabrillo sailed north from Mexico on Spain's behalf and discovered what he believed to be an island, the name California was already familiar enough for him to use it in his journal. Two centuries would pass, however, before Spain made a real claim on the land, sending Father Junípero Serra in 1769 to establish Franciscan missions along the length of California.

State seal

THE GOLD RUSH

Still, the territory remained remote until 1848; the same year that Mexico ceded California to the US, gold was found in the Sierra Nevada foothills. By 1849, hordes of fortune seekers had arrived in Northern California.

The Gold Rush, followed by silver finds in the western Sierras and the completion of the transcontinental railroad in 1869, brought prosperity to the whole state. But the changes caused social rifts: whites charged Chinese immigrants with "stealing" their jobs, and by the beginning of the 20th century, economic divisions left over from the time of plenty had helped to create powerful labour unions.

20TH-CENTURY CALIFORNIA

San Francisco's earthquake in 1906 convinced many that California's heyday was over. However, during the next 90 years, Hollywood drew international attention with its moviemaking. Oil wells serviced the needs of increasingly car-dependent residents and by 1937 orange groves had become a symbol of the state's fertile future. When the UN charter was signed in San Francisco in 1945, it was clear that California, once considered at the edge of civilization, was finally a player at centre stage.

Early map of the United States, showing California as an island

◁ **Mural at the Santa Barbara County Courthouse showing Cabrillo's landing in California**

Early California

Early basketry

IT IS ESTIMATED that, at the time of European discovery, between 100,000 and 275,000 natives lived in California. They were not warlike, nor did they have much in the way of government. Only on the Colorado River did they practise agriculture; most relied on hunting, fishing or the gathering of staples such as acorns for food. Their religion and medical beliefs were bound together in the person of a shaman, said to be in direct communication with the spirit world. They congregated in villages of 100 to 150 inhabitants, generally living in conical or dome-shaped dwellings. Social classes were almost nonexistent, but there were great language divisions between different tribes.

Tcholovoni People
Various tribes, including these Tcholovoni people, settled in small villages on the shores of San Francisco Bay.

Money Box
Natives of Northern California used dentalium shells for money, held in ornately carved boxes.

Jewellery
This necklace, made of abalone and clam shells, is thought to be one of the earliest artifacts of Native Californian life.

Gift baskets such as this Miwok example, were often decorated with beads.

Quail feathers and geometric dancers decorate this basket of the Yokut people.

Eel trapper

BASKETRY
Basket-weaving was the primary native activity. They used a wide range of materials which were twined or coiled into imaginative or symbolic designs. Baskets were used in all walks of life, including hunting, storage, cooking and eating.

Headdresses
This headpiece, made out of black and white magpie feathers, derives from the native Miwok people.

TIMELINE

3,400,000 BC Volcanic ash from Mount St Helena creates the Petrified Forest at Calistoga *(see p445)*

200,000 BC Early inhabitants, possibly predecessors of *Homo sapiens*, live near what is now Calico *(see p275)* — *Early flint stone tool*

3,400,000 BC	2,000,000 BC	200,000 BC

3,000,000 BC Plate movements form Redrock Canyon in Death Valley *(see pp280–83)*

2,000,000 BC Mammoths, tigers and other Pleistocene epoch creatures are trapped in Los Angeles' La Brea Tar Pits

Mammoth skeleton from La Brea Tar Pits

Kule Loklo People
These early Bay Area inhabitants were depicted by Anton Refregier in his mural in the foyer of the Rincon Center (see p307).

WHERE TO SEE EARLY CALIFORNIA

The George C Page Museum of La Brea Discoveries *(see p114)* includes fossil reconstructions of creatures recovered from the nearby tar pits. The Chumash Painted Cave State Historic Park *(p209)* has rare pictographs executed by the Chumash people. LA's Southwest Museum *(p149)* and the California Academy of Sciences in San Francisco *(pp360–61)* both feature Native American artifacts.

***Painted caves** dating back thousands of years have been carefully preserved in the Chumash Painted Cave State Historic Park in Southern California.*

Storage baskets were made in a variety of shapes, designs and materials.

Water basket

Ladles were tightly woven to hold a large amount of water.

Woodpecker traps were made out of willow branches.

Ceremonial Costumes
Aprons made of cat skins and tails were worn by participants in the traditional White Deerskin Dance.

10,000 BC	6,000 BC	2,000 BC		AD 100
	8,000 BC Climate is warm enough to support cone-bearing trees	**2,000 BC** Ubehebe Crater formed in Death Valley *(see pp280–81)*	*Native American dwelling*	
10,000–8,000 BC Pleistocene epoch (Ice Age) ends. First Indians settle in California area	**6,000 BC** Climate is warm enough to support deciduous trees		**AD 100** Devil's Golf Course in Death Valley formed by an evaporated lake *(see pp280–81)*	

The Colonial Period

Mission statue

A̲LTHOUGH THE SPANISH "discovered" California in 1542, they did not colonize the area until the 18th century. Their rule was enforced through a trio of institutions – the mission (church), the *presidio* (fort) and the *pueblo* (town). Of these, the mission was the most influential. Beginning at San Diego in 1769, Franciscan friars founded 21 missions at approximately 30-mile (48-km) intervals along *El Camino Real* ("the Royal Road"). Missionaries wanted to bring religion to the "benighted Indian"; but they also used natives as cheap labour. European colonists committed a more serious crime, by spreading diseases that would reduce the native population to about 16,000 by 1900.

- San Francisco de Solano *(1823)*
- San Rafael Arcangel *(1817)*
- San Francisco de Asis *(1776)*
- San Jose *(1797)*
- Santa Clara de Asis *(1777)*
- Santa Cruz *(1791)*
- San Juan Bautista *(1797)*
- Nuestra Señora de la Soledad *(1791)*
- San Carlos Borromeo de Carmelo *(1770)*
- San Antonio de Padua *(1771)*
- San Miguel Arcangel *(1797)*
- San Luis Obispo de Tolosa *(1772)*
- La Purisma Concepcion *(1787)*
- Santa Ines *(1804)*
- Santa Barbara *(1786)*
- San Buenaventura *(1782)*

El Camino Real

Sir Francis Drake
The English navigator landed in California in 1579 to make repairs to his ship, the Golden Hind. He named the land "Nova Albion" and claimed it for Queen Elizabeth I.

Father Junípero Serra
Originally from the Spanish island of Majorca, Father Junípero Serra led the Franciscan expedition to establish a chain of missions in California.

Jedediah Smith
In 1828, a fur-trapper, Jedediah "Strong" Smith, was the first white man to reach California overland across the Sierra Nevada Mountains, from the eastern United States.

TIMELINE

1524 Hernán Cortés, Spanish conqueror of Mexico, encourages King Charles V to seize control of the "California Islands"

1579 English privateer Francis Drake anchors his *Golden Hind* near Point Reyes *(see pp396–7)*

| 1500 | 1600 | 1650 |

1542 Juan Rodríguez Cabrillo sails north from Mexico to San Diego harbour, making him the official discoverer of California

Juan Rodríguez Cabrillo

1595 Portuguese navigator Sebastián Rodríguez Cermeño discovers Monterey Bay

1602 Spanish merchant-adventurer Sebastián Vizcaíno sails up the Californian coast, naming landmarks as he goes – including San Diego, Santa Barbara, Point Concepcion and Carmel

Mission San Gabriel Arcángel
Ferdinand Deppe's 1832 work is thought to be the first painting of a mission. It depicts the central role of the mission in the community, surrounded by Native American dwellings.

WHERE TO SEE COLONIAL CALIFORNIA

Restored living quarters *are on show at the Santa Barbara Mission Museum.*

Mission-era artifacts can be found at San Francisco's Mission Dolores (*see p351*), the Oakland Museum of California (*pp408–409*), the Mission San Carlos Borromeo in Carmel (*pp496–7*) and the Mission Santa Barbara (*pp212–13*). Most of the 21 missions offer public tours.

US Victory
On 9 July 1846, 70 US sailors and marines marched ashore at San Francisco (then Yerba Buena) and claimed it for the US.

Mission Artifacts
The Franciscan friars brought many items from Spain and Mexico to California. As well as decorative objects, some, such as these prayer bells, had practical purposes.

• San Fernando Rey de España *(1797)*

• San Juan Capistrano *(1776)*

• San Gabriel Arcangel *(1771)*

• San Luis Rey de Francia *(1798)*

• San Diego de Alcalá *(1769)*

EL CAMINO REAL
The 21 missions along El Camino Real, from San Diego to Sonoma, were planned so that each was one day's journey on horseback from the next.

1701 Father Eusebio Francesco Kino proves that Baja California is a peninsula, not an island

1781 Pueblo of Los Angeles founded

1776 Captain Juan Bautista de Anza reaches San Francisco and sites a new presidio (*see pp366–7*)

1835 William Richardson founds Yerba Buena, later renamed San Francisco

1822 Mexican Revolution ends Spanish rule of California

| 1700 | 1750 | 1800 |

1769 Gaspar de Portolá discovers San Francisco Bay. California's first mission is founded at San Diego (*see p250*)

1804 California's first orange grove is planted at San Gabriel Mission

John C Frémont

1846 John C Frémont leads Bear Flag Revolt (*see p448*). US troops claim California from Mexico

18th-century presidio cannon

1777 Monterey becomes capital of Mexican California

The Rush For Riches

I N 1848 newspaperman Sam Brannan brandished nuggets that had been found in the Sacramento Valley, shouting "Gold! Gold! Gold from the American River!". Most of the prospectors who thereafter stampeded California's Mother Lode did not find fortune. But the gold-seeking hordes changed the area forever – especially San Francisco. Between 1848 and 1850, the town's population shot from 812 to 25,000. Food and property prices skyrocketed and crime thrived. In 1859, after the Gold Rush had ended, silver ore (the Comstock Lode) was exposed on the eastern Sierras, and Northern California boomed again.

Nugget of Californian gold

Forty-Niners
Gold prospectors from all over the US travelled to California in 1849, hence their name. They carried tools, weapons and food provisions on their journey.

Pickaxes were used to loosen hard rock ready for the sluice.

Barbary Coast Saloon
Gambling and prostitution were rife in San Francisco's Barbary Coast region, and men were often pressed into naval service.

State Capital
Once little more than farmland, Sacramento grew into a bustling city within two years of the Gold Rush. It became the state capital in 1854.

The sluice was a long trough with wooden bars. As water was flushed along, gold particles were trapped behind the bars.

TIMELINE

1848 California is annexed by the US. Gold discovered at Sutter's Mill *(see p459)*

Sign from the Flying Cloud clipper ship

1854 Sacramento becomes California state capital

1849 Almost 800 ships leave New York, full of men bound for the gold fields

1848	1850	1852	1854

John Sutter (1802–1880)

1850 California becomes 31st state of the Union

1851 San Francisco vigilante movement hangs several lawbreakers. Clipper ship *Flying Cloud* sails from New York to San Francisco in a record 89 days

1853 Levi Strauss lands in the Bay Area and begins selling his canvas trousers *(see p333)*

Count Agoston Haraszthy
The Hungarian was the first vintner to plant European grapevine cuttings in California.

Hydraulic mining blasted away rock with water to uncover gold underneath.

WHERE TO SEE THE ERA OF RICHES

Many of the settlements that were once thronged with gold miners have since disintegrated into ghost towns, such as Bodie *(p478)* and Calico *(p275)*. But you can still get a feel for the times at Columbia State Historic Park *(pp464–5)*, a restored Mother Lode town. The Wells Fargo History Museum in San Francisco *(p304)* has mementos of the Gold Rush. The Jackson Square Historical District *(p304)* was once part of the Barbary Coast.

Old schoolhouse at Calico ghost town

Comstock Lode Silver
Between 1859 and the mid-1880s, 400 million dollars worth of silver was extracted from mines in the High Sierras.

Gold panning involved swirling dirt and water around a flat-bottomed pan until only gold residue remained.

Emperor Norton
Self-proclaimed Emperor of the United States and Protector of Mexico, the eccentric Joshua Norton printed his own currency and gave advice to Sacramento legislators.

GOLD MINING TECHNIQUES
As the rush for gold increased, ways of extracting the ore became more sophisticated. What began as an adventure became a highly developed industry.

1855 Vigilante justice is enforced in Los Angeles	**1856** Street-murder of newspaper publisher James King of William sparks San Francisco's second vigilante uprising; William T Sherman leads militia campaign to restrain them	**1859** Prospector James Finney discovers silver deposits, the Comstock Lode	**1860** Bankrupt grain merchant Joshua Norton declares himself Norton I, Emperor of the United States until his death in 1880

1856	1858	1860

San Francisco vigilante medal

1857 Agoston Haraszthy, father of California's wine industry, founds the Buena Vista estate in the Sonoma Valley *(see p449)*

1861 California swears allegiance to the Union. The first oil well is drilled

Humboldt County oil well

The Gilded Age

FOR CALIFORNIA'S *nouveaux riches*, the smartest address during the late 19th century was on Nob Hill in San Francisco *(see p320)*, where grand mansions were built. This was a time of ostentation, but also of expansion, thanks to train connections with the east and south. Californian oranges could now be exported easily to New York markets. Taking the return trip were European immigrants and others hoping for a better life on the West Coast. Land prices increased in LA County, and by 1900 San Francisco's population exceeded 300,000.

Victorian Décor
Windows in the Winchester Mystery House (see pp414–15) are typically ornate.

Gold pocket watch

Transcontinental Railroad
On 12 May 1869, the final spike was driven for the new railroad, linking the East and West Coast.

Bathroom, with original bath tub and tiles

Front parlour

Dining room

The "Big Four"
Charles Crocker, Leland Stanford, Collis Huntington and Mark Hopkins made millions investing in the transcontinental railroad.

TIMELINE

1863 Construction begins on the Central Pacific Railroad

1871 Racial violence in LA leaves about 20 Chinese dead

1873–5 Orange planting begins in Riverside

1876 Southern Pacific Railroad reaches Los Angeles

Californian oranges

1884 Sarah Winchester embarks on her 38-year house-building project in San Jose *(see pp414–15)*

1870   1875   1880

1869 Transcontinental railroad is completed

1873 Andrew Hallidie tests San Francisco's first cable car

San Francisco's first cable car

1877 San Franciscans torch Chinese stores and laundries to protest against cheap labour

1882 US Congress passes the Chinese Exclusion Act, limiting Chinese immigration

Sutro Baths
The largest swimming pool in San Francisco stood from 1896 until the 1960s.

Yosemite National Park
Made a national park in 1890, Yosemite also became California's first tourist attraction and a popular image for advertisers.

The California State Railroad Museum is a celebration of rail travel on the West Coast.

The sitting room was originally the master bedroom.

Porch

Hall, with Victorian corner sofa

Chinese Immigrants
The "coolies" who helped build the transcontinental railroad stayed and set up businesses such as laundries and restaurants, but were met with racisim.

HAAS-LILIENTHAL HOUSE
Grocer William Haas built this elaborate Queen Anne-style house in 1886, one of many in San Francisco. Today it is a museum, and shows how a wealthy family would have lived at the end of the 19th century *(see p338).*

1890 Yosemite wins national park status *(see pp472–5)*

Stanford University seal

1893 San Andreas Fault discovered by University of California geologist Andrew Lawson

1896 Comstock tunnel builder Adolph Sutro opens the world's largest indoor saltwater swimming centre in San Francisco

1885 | 1890 | 1895

1888 Hotel del Coronado opens in San Diego *(see p245)*

1891 Stanford University opens *(see p411)*; future president Herbert Hoover is in the first graduating class

1894 West Coast's first world fair is held in San Francisco's Golden Gate Park

1897 San Franciscan merchants prosper by outfitting gold miners travelling to Canada's Klondike River

The Rise of Hollywood

IN 1887, KANSAS PROHIBITIONIST Harvey Henderson Wilcox wanted to call his farm and the LA suburb surrounding it "Figwood", after his chief crop. His wife chose instead a name she had overheard on a train: "Hollywood". By the 1920s, the film industry was making the town famous and offering Americans entertainment to help them escape the reality of World War I, Prohibition and, later, the Great Depression. Silent film stars such as Mary Pickford and Charlie Chaplin were succeeded by icons of a more glamorous Hollywood, such as Mae West and Errol Flynn. Wall Street bankers were quick to realize their potential and invested heavily in the film industry.

Oscar statuette

Panama Canal
Two world fairs celebrated the completion of the canal in 1915.

Clara Bow, dubbed the "It" girl, was one of Hollywood's first sex symbols.

San Francisco Earthquake and Fire
After the 1906 disaster, many buildings had to be demolished.

Actors were chosen for their looks and often had little stage experience.

Los Angeles Aqueduct
The vast aqueduct was built at a cost of $24.5 million to irrigate the arid south with melted snow from the High Sierras.

HOLLYWOOD'S SILENT ERA
The movie industry grew rapidly and soon large corporate studios emerged. Hundreds of silent movies were made each year, such as *Mantrap* (1927).

TIMELINE

1905 Tobacco magnate Abbot Kinney opens his many-canaled resort of Venice (*see p76*), west of LA. Excavations begin on La Brea Tar Pits (*see p115*)

1907 San Francisco political "boss" Abraham Ruef pleads guilty to extortion and brings down Mayor Eugene Schmitz

1913 Opening of Owens Valley–Los Angeles aqueduct improves LA's access to water

1900	1905	1910

1901 A three-month waterfront labour strike affects San Francisco business; four men die and 300 are injured in hostilities

1906 San Francisco is struck on 18 April by the worst ever US earthquake, at an estimated 8.3 on the Richter scale: 3,000 die and 25,000 are left homeless

Early Hollywood film camera

1911 *The Law of the Range*, shot by William and David Horsley, is the first film made in Hollywood

Prohibition *(1920–33)*
Los Angeles became a popular port of entry for smugglers bringing illegal alcohol into the United States from Mexico during the nationwide ban.

WHERE TO SEE CLASSIC HOLLYWOOD

The likenesses of numerous movie stars are displayed at the Hollywood Wax Museum *(p105)*. The Hollywood Studio Museum *(p108)*, once Cecil B De Mille's offices, now exhibits movie mementos. Some 200 stars have cemented their fame in front of Mann's Chinese Theatre *(p106)*.

Mann's Chinese Theatre *has hand-prints, footprints and autographs of film stars cemented in its forecourt.*

Paramount Studios *are the only studios now located in Hollywood and still attract would-be stars* (p109).

Studios operated like factories, filming different movies on adjacent sets.

Cameramen used 35 mm cameras, operating at 24 frames per second.

Directors also found fame and fortune in the new industry.

Orchestras were often hired to play in the background of a scene during filming to create the right mood for the actors.

Aimee Semple McPherson
The controversial evangelist and spiritualist opened her Angelus Temple in LA in 1923, where she held regular spiritual revivalist meetings.

1916 The Lockheed brothers start building aeroplanes in Santa Barbara

WR Hearst

1924 LA eclipses San Francisco as the most important port on the West Coast

1929 Stock exchange crash causes national depression. Actor Douglas Fairbanks, Sr hosts the first Academy Awards presentation

1915

1920

1925

1915 San Francisco and San Diego both hold Panama-Pacific Expositions

1917 The US enters World War I

1919 WR Hearst begins construction of his magnificent castle at San Simeon *(see pp202–205)*

Norma Talmadge

1927 Actress Norma Talmadge is the first star to cement her footprints at Mann's Chinese Theatre *(see p106)*

1928 Cartoonist Walt Disney creates character of Mickey Mouse

The Californian Dream

CINEMA AND THE NEW MEDIUM of television made
California *the* symbol of America's postwar
resurgence – suddenly everybody wanted the
prosperous middle-class existence they believed
was common here. The aeroplane industry, ship-
yards and agriculture had burgeoned during the
war, and a sense of prosperity lasted through the
1950s. Suburbs sprang up to meet the needs of
returning soldiers, while new highways were laid
to make them accessible. Yet at the same time,
state schools lacked funds, African- and Mexican-
Americans faced discrimination and violence, and
Hollywood found itself attacked by politicians as
a hotbed of Marxist Communism.

Olympic Games 1932
*Los Angeles won the bid to hold the
1932 games and built Exposition
Park for the event (see pp160–61).*

Kitchen units
became more
practical,
with formica
worktops.

Longshoreman's Strike
*On 5 July 1934, police opened
fire on dockers striking for
better conditions, killing two.*

Hoover Dam
*In 1936 the Hoover Dam was built on
the Colorado River to supply electricity.*

Household appliances
became more widely
available, easing
domestic duties.

TIMELINE

1930	1935	1940

1932 LA hosts its first Olympic Games

1934 Alcatraz Island becomes a maximum security penitentiary (*see* pp28–9)

1936 Hoover Dam begins supplying Southern California with much-needed electricity

1940 Los Angeles opens its first freeway – Arroyo Seco Parkway

1942 Japanese-Americans sent to relocation camps for "war security reasons" (*see p479*)

1933 Prohibition ends. "Sunny Jim" Rolph, a popular San Francisco mayor turned California governor, shocks supporters by praising a lynch mob in San Jose

"Sunny Jim" Rolph

1937 The Golden Gate Bridge opens

1939 San Francisco's third world fair, the Golden Gate Exposition, is held on Treasure Island

1941 Japan attacks US fleet at Pearl Harbor

1943 California becomes nation's leading agricultural state

Golden Gate Bridge
On 28 May 1937 an official convoy of black limousines were the first vehicles to cross the bridge, which linked San Francisco with Marin County.

WHERE TO SEE THE CALIFORNIAN DREAM

LA's Petersen Automotive Museum celebrates California's love affair with the car *(see p114)*. At the Treasure Island Museum in San Francisco, memorabilia from the Golden Gate International Exposition is displayed *(p396)*. A trip to the Sleeping Beauty Castle in Disneyland is the ultimate Californian Dream experience *(p223)*.

The Petersen Automotive Museum
displays many classic models. This 1959 Cadillac epitomizes Californian cars.

Land of Plenty
California's agricultural industry boomed in the 1940s, and its farmland was the most productive in the US.

Large refrigerators, stocked with food, were a symbol of the Californian "good life".

THE CALIFORNIAN HOME

Eduardo Paolozzi's image is a pastiche of California's white, middle-class lifestyle in the 1950s. Nuclear families, ranch houses and outdoor living were all part of the "dream".

San Francisco Giant
Willie Mays was part of the first team to bring professional baseball to California in 1958.

1945 End of World War II. International delegates meet at San Francisco 25 April–25 June to found the United Nations

1955 Disneyland opens in Anaheim. Actor James Dean, aged 24, dies in a car accident near Paso Robles

James Dean

1945	1950	1955

United Nations flag

1953 Beginning of Cold War is a boost to Californian defence industry

1958 New York Giants baseball team moves to San Francisco, finally bringing major-league baseball to the West Coast

California Today

SINCE 1962, when California surpassed New York as the most populous state in the Union, it has become the focus of many of the country's most significant issues. UC Berkeley was home to America's Free Speech Movement during the 1960s, and Haight Ashbury in San Francisco was the mecca for the "hippie" movement. Silicon Valley has led high-tech development in the US, and California benefits commercially from its proximity to the Far East. On a darker note, the state is still at risk from earthquakes; San Francisco has a high proportion of the country's AIDS cases; and racial tension, marked in LA, has led to riots.

1978 Apple Computer produces its first personal computer

1976 French judges award California the top two prizes for wine at a blind tasting

1968 Democratic presidential candidate Robert Kennedy is assassinated at LA's Ambassador Hotel on 5 June after announcing his victory in the California primary

1962 Actress Marilyn Monroe dies in Hollywood, aged 36, from an overdose of sleeping pills

1967 Haight Ashbury is swamped by half a million young people celebrating the "Summer of Love" *(see p349)*

1970s Huey Newton, a founder of Oakland's Black Panther Party, is arrested in 1967 and becomes a symbol of resistance during the 1970s

1960	1970
1960	1970

1960 Winter Olympic Games are held at Squaw Valley near Lake Tahoe

1966 LA becomes the most populous county in the nation, with more than 7 million inhabitants

1978 San Francisco Mayor George Moscone and his deputy Harvey Milk are assassinated at City Hall on 27 November by former policeman Dan White

1963 Surfing becomes a popular sport in California

1969 American Indian Movement occupies Alcatraz Island *(see pp328–9)* to publicize its differences with the Bureau of Indian Affairs

1968 Richard Nixon becomes the first native-born Californian to be elected President of the United States. Discredited, Nixon retired to San Clemente in 1974 *(see p228)*

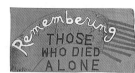

1991 AIDS becomes San Francisco's number one killer of men

1989 The Bay Area endures its second worst earthquake, measuring 7.1 on the Richter Scale; 67 people die, another 1,800 are left homeless

1992 Fires in the Oakland hills kill 26 people and destroy 3,000 homes

1996 After 15 years as the speaker of the California Assembly, Democrat Willie Brown is sworn in as San Francisco's first black mayor

1981 Ronald Reagan, one-time film actor and former Californian governor, is sworn in as President of the United States

980   1990

980   1990

1987 Film director Steven Spielberg starts his own studio, Dreamworks

1995 The America's Cup yacht race, in which five countries compete, is held in San Diego from January to May

1984 LA hosts its second Olympic Games

1992 Riots in LA follow the acquittal of four white police officers who were videotaped beating a black motorist, Rodney King

1994 An earthquake measuring 6.8 on the Richter scale strikes LA, killing more than 60 people, injuring 9,000 and destroying freeways

LOS ANGELES

Los Angeles at a Glance

GREATER LOS ANGELES is made up of 80
different towns, with a total population of more than 8.5 million and covering
more than 460 sq miles (1,200 sq km). In
this book, LA has been divided into six
areas. Downtown is a cultural melting pot,
juxtaposing Hispanic El Pueblo, Chinatown, Little Tokyo and the Business District. The glamour of the movies is just
one aspect of Hollywood and West Hollywood, which today is a vibrant area of
museums and galleries. Beverly Hills, Bel
Air and Westwood are still the playground
of the stars. Beaches and ports in the
coastal regions of Santa Monica Bay, Palos
Verdes and Long Beach show the importance of the sea to Angelenos. Around
Downtown covers some of the outlying
districts of the city, including Pasadena.

AROUND DOWNTOWN
(See pp136–61)

**BEVERLY HILLS,
BEL AIR AND
WESTWOOD**
(See pp84–95)

SANTA MONICA BAY
(See pp70–83)

Sunset Boulevard (see
pp98–103) *is one of the
most famous roads in the
world. Lined with clubs
and hotels, the section
known as Sunset Strip is
the centre of LA's nightlife.*

0 kilometres   5

0 miles   5

**The J Paul Getty Museum
at the Getty Center** (see
pp78–81) *is situated on
a hill and has stunning
views across Los Angeles
and the Santa Monica
Mountains. Included in its
world-class collection is
Joseph Nollekens' marble
statue of* Venus *(1773).*

LACMA (see pp110–13) *has
been sited in Hollywood's
Hancock Park since 1965.
The five museum buildings
house a remarkable
collection of European,
American, Asian, Middle
Eastern and Japanese art.*

At Universal Studios (see pp142–5), *just north of Hollywood, visitors can see working film sets on the Backlot Tram Tour. A series of thrilling rides, based on the studios' movies, includes Jurassic Park – The Ride.*

The Huntington Library, Art Collections and Botanical Gardens (see pp154–7) *in Pasadena have a wealth of treasures. The North Vista is one of the gardens' most lovely aspects.*

HOLLYWOOD
AND WEST
HOLLYWOOD
(See pp96–115)

DOWNTOWN
LOS ANGELES
(See pp116–25)

AROUND DOWNTOWN
(See pp136–61)

El Pueblo (see pp122–3), *in the heart of Downtown Los Angeles, is the site of the city's first settlement. The area's Mexican population throngs its churches, plaza and colourful markets, especially at festival time.*

The Queen Mary (see pp130–31), *one of the most famous liners in the world, is now permanently docked in Long Beach. The ship is still in use as a tourist attraction and luxury hotel. Many of her Art Deco features remain intact.*

LONG BEACH AND
PALOS VERDES
(See pp126–35)

The Shape of Los Angeles

THE CITY OF LOS ANGELES sits in a broad, flat basin, facing the Pacific Ocean and enclosed by mountains. The San Gabriel Mountains and the Traverse Range come from the north, meeting the Santa Ana Mountains east of the city. The Santa Monica Mountains and the Hollywood Hills in the northwest split the basin, dividing the city centre from the San Fernando Valley in the north. The shoreline varies from the rocky cliffs of Palos Verdes, to the sands of Santa Monica Bay. Downtown, with the impressive skyscrapers of the Financial District, sits in the centre of the basin. Hollywood, Beverly Hills and Santa Monica lie to the west.

Hollywood (see pp96–115) *is the birthplace of the modern film industry. Its famous sign* (see p141) *stands out like a beacon above Tinseltown.*

The San Fernando Valley *(see p140)*, the city's great suburban sprawl, is home to the Mission San Fernando Rey de España.

Malibu *(see pp82–3)* is an area of fine surfing beaches, wildlife havens and private beach colonies nestled below rugged mountains.

Santa Monica (see pp72–5), *perched on palm-lined bluffs overlooking beautiful beaches, boasts stunning coastal views. It is LA's oldest and largest beach resort, with all the traditional seaside attractions, such as a pier and funfair. Santa Monica is also known for its excellent restaurants, one-off shops, exciting nightlife and vibrant arts scene.*

Beverly Hills (see pp84–93) *is home to the rich and famous of Los Angeles. Their lifestyle is epitomized by the exclusive shops that line Rodeo Drive.*

Pasadena (see pp150–57) *is an affluent community, with an ornate city hall. It grew up as a winter retreat for wealthy Easterners in the 19th century. Site of the Rose Bowl stadium, it has fine museums as well as excellent shopping and dining.*

Downtown Los Angeles *is a diverse area* (see pp116–25). *Attractions range from the skyscrapers of the Business District to the ethnic delights of Little Tokyo and Chinatown.*

Watts, a deprived area, has the Watts Towers *(see p159)*.

VERDUGO MOUNTAINS

SAN RAFAEL HILLS

MONTEREY PARK

PUENTE HILLS

5

DOWNEY

605

The City of Long Beach has a strong nautical tradition *(see pp128–31)*.

BALDWIN HILLS

42

105

INGLEWOOD

COMPTON

710

405

DOMINGUEZ HILLS

SIGNAL HILL

110

TORRANCE

S A N

P E D R O

SAN PEDRO

B A Y

S A N T A

M O N I C A

B A Y

PALOS VERDES HILLS

Los Angeles International Airport, *known simply as LAX, lies along the coast. It is well placed for easy access to most areas of the city, and near major freeways leading out of town.*

Point Fermin lighthouse *is a Victorian landmark among the green rolling hills of Palos Verdes* (see pp134–5).

North Los Angeles Coastline

EACH YEAR MORE than 30 million people visit the beaches around Los Angeles, making them the most popular destination on the West Coast. The Malibu headland, from Point Dume to Malibu Lagoon, alternates between rocky shorelines and beaches. Further along, the shoreline becomes a long sandy strand leading to the renowned beaches at Santa Monica and Venice. Inland, the terrain of the Santa Monica Mountains is rugged and largely unspoilt, with plenty of hiking trails leading to panoramic views of the Pacific Ocean. The waters off the Malibu Pier, Leo Carillo and Topanga state beaches are considered to be the best for surfing.

Castro Crest *is characterized by large areas of exposed reddish-purple sandstone and oak woodland. The park's hiking trails offer magnificent views inland of the Santa Susana mountains and, offshore, of the Channel Islands.*

Cold Creek Canyon Preserve *was set up in 1970 to protect the rich diversity of fauna and flora found in the Santa Monica Mountains, including the bobcat, the Pacific tree frog and the stream orchid.*

★ **Leo Carillo State Beach** ①
At low tide it is possible to explore the wide variety of life in the rock pools around Sequit Point.

★ **Surfrider County Beach** ⑤
One of California's finest surfing beaches, Surfrider has featured in many surfing films. Malibu Pier is a good place from which to watch the action.

Zuma County Beach ②

The white sands of Malibu's largest beach are very popular during the summer. There is good surfing and swimming, but care must be taken with the hazardous rip tides.

Point Dume County Beach ③

Surf fishing, diving, sunbathing and exploring the rock pools beneath Point Dume are all popular activities on this sandy sheltered beach.

Paradise Cove ④

This privately owned cove was featured in the TV series *The Rockford Files*. The pier is a good place for surf fishing, while the beach is ideal for sunbathing and swimming.

Topanga State Beach ⑥

This narrow sandy beach is popular with windsurfers. It is divided in two by the mouth of Topanga Creek.

Marina del Rey Harbour ⑩

This is one of the world's largest artificial harbours *(see p76)*. The quaint Fisherman's Village, next to Basin H, has shops, cafés and restaurants.

LOCATOR MAP KEY

▬	Freeway
▬	Major road
▭	Minor road
▭	River
⋇	Viewpoint

★ Venice City Beach ⑨

Backed by picturesque Venice *(see p76)*, Venice City Beach offers an eclectic mix of street performers, skaters and body builders, working out on Muscle Beach.

★ Will Rogers State Beach ⑦

Named after the Hollywood actor *(see p77)*, this is a good beach for body surfing.

★ Santa Monica State Beach ⑧

This is one of Santa Monica's *(see pp72–5)* most popular beaches. The group of houses at the western end of the beach are known collectively as "the Gold Coast".

South Los Angeles Coastline

THE COAST BETWEEN Dockweiler State Beach and
Torrance County Beach boasts shallow waters and
wide stretches of sand that are ideal for families. The
two main communities, Manhattan Beach and Redondo
Beach, have some of the cleanest waters off LA. Further
down the coast, the rocky bluffs of the Palos Verdes
Peninsula shelter coves with rock pools teeming with
marine life. Beyond Worldport LA, the coastline turns
into a vista of white sand and rolling waves bordering
Long Beach, the second largest city in LA County.
Belmont Shores is popular with anglers. Windsurfers,
sea kayakers and jet-skiers frequent Alamitos Bay, home
to the man-made canals and islands of Naples.

★ **Manhattan State Beach** ②
Backed by the coastal cycle path, this long wide
beach is good for swimming, surfing and fishing.

★ **Hermosa City Beach** ③
This family beach is ideal for all types of
beach sports, as well as being popular with
anglers who fish the surf for perch.

*Worldport LA, with its 28 miles
(45 km) of waterfront, includes an
oil terminal and cargo port. It is
also home to the country's second
largest fishing fleet.*

★ **Torrance County Beach** ⑤
Popular with surfers,
swimmers, anglers and divers
alike, this beach marks the end
of the Santa Monica Bay coastal
cycle path (*see p168*).

★ **Redondo State Beach** ④
A bronze bust commemorates George
Freeth, who introduced surfing to
California in 1907 at Redondo Beach.

*HOLLYWOOD
BEVERLY HILLS*

*SANTA
MONICA*

42

1

405

Vista del Mar Boulevard

Sepulveda Boulevard

1

105

Manhattan Blvd

②

Artesia Blvd

③

107

TORRANCE

Torrance Blvd

④

⑤

1

N7

Palos Verdes

**Palos
Verdes
Peninsula**

Drive

Dockweiler State Beach ①

The north end of Dockweiler, beyond the harbour entrance, includes a nesting area for the rare California least tern.

Cabrillo Beach ⑥

Split in two by the breakwater, Cabrillo has a fishing pier on the ocean side and a protected stretch of sand within San Pedro Bay.

Long Beach City Beach ⑦

At the western end of Long Beach Strand, as it is also known, stands the old, clap-board lifeguard headquarters, now a lifeguard museum.

Belmont Shores ⑧

Belmont Pier, situated at the northern end of the beach, is used by anglers fishing for halibut, bonito and perch. It is also a roosting site for the endangered California brown pelican. The beach stretches south as far as the mouth of the San Gabriel River.

LOCATOR MAP

Alamitos Bay ⑨

Windsurfing, water-skiing and swimming are all popular activities in the protected waters of the bay.

DOWNTOWN LOS ANGELES

DOWNTOWN LOS ANGELES

405

110

213

710

405

Alameda Street

Long Beach Blvd

WILMINGTON

103

LONG BEACH

Ocean Blvd

ANAHEIM

SAN PEDRO

Worldport LA

HUNTINGTON BEACH

Point Fermin

0 kilometres 5

0 miles 5

KEY

━━ Freeway

━━ Major road

╌╌ Minor road

〰 River

�� Viewpoint

Palos Verdes Peninsula rises 1,300 ft (400 m) above the rocky shoreline, which is home to many wading birds. Steep trails connect the shore to the clifftop with its panoramic views.

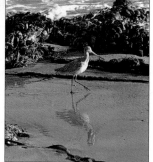

The Movies in Los Angeles

Hollywood street sign

W HEN PEOPLE refer to Los Angeles as an "industry town", they invariably mean the movie industry. Its great fantasy factories employ more than 60,000 people and pump about $4 billion into the LA economy every year. Hollywood Boulevard has sadly lost much of its glamour over the years, and some film companies have decamped to cheaper movie-making venues. But the air of Hollywood as a dream-maker, a place where a secretary named Ava Gardner or college football player John Wayne could be "discovered" and go on to earn million-dollar salaries, still persists.

Film crews *shooting location scenes for various Hollywood movies are a regular sight on Los Angeles' streets.*

The Griffith Observatory (see p146) was the setting for the teenage school trip and dramatic car race at the climax of the legendary film Rebel Without A Cause *(1955). The film catapulted James Dean to stardom, but he was to die in a car crash later the same year.*

WRITERS IN HOLLYWOOD

Hollywood novels have been a literary feature since the 1930s. Some writers, such as Nathanael West and F Scott Fitzgerald, worked in Hollywood, only to turn against the town and publish novels that exposed its shallow and often cruel sides. West's *The Day of the Locust* (1939) is still considered the classic literary put-down of the film industry. Fitzgerald's posthumous *The Last Tycoon* (1941) sentimentalizes the career of Irving Thalberg, one of the most influential producers during Hollywood's "Golden Age". More recent is Michael Tolkin's *The Player* (1988), a murder mystery that satirizes stereotypical Hollywood executives.

F Scott Fitzgerald

The Last Action Hero, *Arnold Schwarzenegger's 1993 blockbuster, filled this LA street with the excitement of controlled explosions, car chases and stuntmen flying through the air.*

LA LOCATIONS

As well as utilizing the man-made sets erected on the backlots of the major studios in the 1940s and 1950s, film directors now regularly turn to the local landmarks of Los Angeles as locations for their films, often disguising them as other towns and cities. As a consequence, many of these places have become familiar to moviegoers all over the world.

Million-dollar contracts *have been a feature of Hollywood since Charlie Chaplin's eight-picture deal in 1917. Two-time Oscar winner Tom Hanks now demands as much as $20 million a picture – ten times as much as the salary of the US President. Also in the eight-figure category are Robin Williams, Julia Roberts and Harrison Ford. Studio executives justify these salaries by saying that big stars bring in a large enough audience to recoup the high production costs.*

Julia Roberts   **Harrison Ford**

The Venice district *(see p76) saw actress Sarah Jessica Parker dancing around Steve Martin, in his 1991 hit film* LA Story. *The colourful buildings and characters of the area make it a popular film location.*

TOP GROSSING FILMS

Critics gush over *Citizen Kane* (1941), a spin on the life of WR Hearst *(see pp202–205)*, and *Casablanca* (1943) is the most popular Hollywood love story ever made. Yet neither of these films appears on trade paper *Variety*'s list of the American film industry's top ten money-makers:

1. *E.T., The Extra Terrestrial* (1982)
2. *Jurassic Park* (1993)
3. *Star Wars* (1977)
4. *The Lion King* (1993)
5. *Forrest Gump* (1993)
6. *Home Alone* (1990)
7. *Return of the Jedi* (1983)
8. *Jaws* (1975)
9. *Batman* (1989)
10. *Raiders of the Lost Ark* (1981)

The only films made before 1960 on the top 50 list are *Gone With the Wind* (1939), at No. 20, and *Snow White and the Seven Dwarfs* (1937), at No. 27.

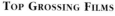

Film poster for *E.T., The Extra Terrestrial*

Santa Monica Pier *(see p74) should be familiar to fans of the gangster film* The Sting *(1973), starring actors Robert Redford and Paul Newman.*

Star-gazing *is enjoyed by both visitors and locals in LA's many glamorous venues. Good opportunities to spot actors, directors and film executives can be found at Wolfgang Puck's trendy Spagos (see p550) and the Polo Lounge at the Beverly Hills Hotel (see p508).*

Los Angeles's Best: Museums and Galleries

THE MUSEUMS of LA reflect the great diversity of the city. Collections ranging from natural history to Native American artifacts and from cowboy heritage to the history of the Holocaust educate and inspire the visitor. The city also contains many museums of art. Some of these display the private collections of the wealthy, such as Norton Simon, J Paul Getty and Henry and Arabella Huntington, and feature internationally acclaimed Old Masters, Impressionist paintings and European and Asian works of art. "Museum Row" on Wilshire Boulevard is home to five museums, including the renowned LACMA.

Ceci n'est pas une pipe.

LACMA *is one of the top US art museums. Its collection includes* La Trahison des Images (Ceci n'est pas une Pipe), *painted by René Magritte in around 1928. (See pp110–13.)*

Around Downtown

Santa Monica Bay

J Paul Getty Museum *has recently relocated most of its holdings to the Getty Center in the Santa Monica Mountains.* La Promenade *(1870) by Pierre-Auguste Renoir is just one of the extraordinary paintings in this collection. (See pp78–81.)*

The Museum of Tolerance *aims to promote understanding between peoples. This sculpture of President Sadat of Egypt, with President Carter of the United States and Prime Minister Begin of Israel, illustrates that aim. (See p89.)*

0 kilometres   5

0 miles   5

The Southwest Museum
*exhibits thousands of artifacts of the
native cultures of the Americas,
including this ceramic jar, which
was produced around 1900 by
the Acoma people. (See p149.)*

**The Autry Museum
of Western Heritage** *is
dedicated to preserving
the history of the Amer-
ican West. This wax model
of outlaw Billy the Kid is
one of the exhibits on
display. (See p147.)*

Norton Simon Museum of Art *was
built in 1969. It houses a superb
collection of European, Indian and
Southeast Asian art that spans more
than 2,000 years. (See pp152–3.)*

Hollywood
and West
Hollywood

Downtown
Los Angeles

**The Huntington
Library, Art
Collections and
Botanical Gardens**
*are sited in Pasadena.
Roger van der Weyden's
15th-century Madonna
and Child is one of
the many works of
art on display.
(See pp154–7.)*

**Natural History Museum of Los
Angeles County** *is one of three museums in
Exposition Park. The exhibits include this
eight-million-year-old skeleton of a short-
legged rhinoceros. (See p160.)*

Contemporary Architecture in Los Angeles

Fᴏʀ ᴍᴏʀᴇ ᴛʜᴀɴ ᴀ ᴄᴇɴᴛᴜʀʏ after it was founded in 1781, LA remained a small town of modest adobe buildings. It was not until the late 19th century that settlers from the East and Midwest introduced the Victorian styles of building that they had grown up with. When the trans-continental railroad reached LA in 1887 there was a building boom, and the city has been expanding ever since. In the 20th century, LA's finest contributions to architecture have been the inventive reworkings of past styles. In recent years, archi-tects have remodelled dilapidated commercial buildings to create lively, fashionable venues.

Kate Mantilini's *(1985)*
This building-within-a-building restaurant is typical of LA's avant-garde deconstructivism (see p544).

2 Rodeo *(1990)*
This pastiche of European architecture, including a replica of Rome's Spanish Steps, is part of the renowned shopping district (see p90). The car park has Victorian-style streetlamps and a cobblestoned floor.

Around Downtown

Beverly Hills, Bel Air and Westwood

Santa Monica Bay

Eames House *(1949)*
This steel-framed house and studio were designed by Charles and Ray Eames as one of 36 projects commissioned by Arts & Architecture *magazine.*

Chiat/Day Advertising Agency *(1991)*
Frank Gehry, the leading LA architect, designed this striking building (see p74).

Disney Studio Office Building *(1991)*
Michael Graves' Post-Modern Disney building in Burbank includes a classically inspired pediment supported by 19-ft (5.7-m) statues of the Seven Dwarfs. Inside, chairs incorporate Mickey Mouse in their design (see pp140–41).

Ennis House *(1924)*
The base, plan and textured interiors of this house are typical of Frank Lloyd Wright's "textile block" houses.

Gamble House
(1908)
This is the finest example of Charles and Henry Greene's turn-of-the-century Arts and Crafts bungalows. Its expansive eaves, outdoor sleeping porches and elegant interior are characteristic of the brothers' style (see p150).

Hollywood and West Hollywood

Downtown Los Angeles

Eastern Columbia Building *(1930)*
This Art Deco building, designed by Claude Beelman, is one of the most impressive of its kind in LA.

Union Station *(1939)*
The last of the great American railway terminals, the vaulted concourse, arches, waiting room and patios combine Mission Revival and Streamline Moderne styles (see p124).

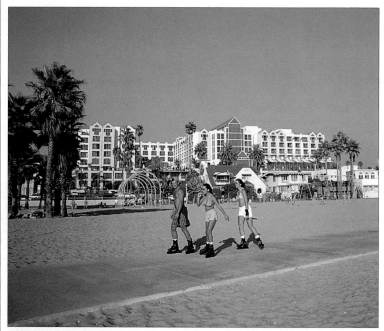

In-line skaters on Venice Beach boardwalk

*PACIFIC
OCEAN*

SIGHTS AT A GLANCE

Districts
Malibu Colony ⓫
Marina del Rey ❸
Santa Monica pp72–5 ❶
Venice ❷

Museums
Adamson House and Malibu
    Lagoon Museum ❾
*J Paul Getty Museum at the
    Getty Center pp78–81* ❺

J Paul Getty Museum at the
    Getty Villa ❽
Museum of Flying ❹

Parks and Beaches
Malibu Creek State Park ⓬
Malibu Lagoon State
    Beach ❿
Topanga State Park ❼
Will Rogers State
    Historic Park ❻

KEY

	Street-by-Street map
	See pp72–3

0 kilometres   2

0 miles   2

SANTA MONICA BAY

WITH ITS WARM SUN, cool sea breezes, miles of sandy beaches, excellent surf and world-class museums, Santa Monica Bay epitomizes the best of California. The area was inhabited by the Chumash and Tongva/Gabrielino peoples for 2,500 years before the arrival in 1542 of the Spanish explorer Juan Cabrillo (see p42). In the early 19th century, Santa Monica Bay was divided into several land grants, including Rancho San Vicente y Santa Monica and Rancho Topanga Malibu Sequit. In 1875, Nevada senator John Percival Jones bought control of the former, hoping the port of Los Angeles would be built there. Thankfully, that honour went

Bather in Venice Beach

to San Pedro (see pp134–5) and the beach resorts of Santa Monica and Venice were developed in its place. These areas have remained two of the most attractive and lively parts of Los Angeles.

Further along the coast, the Rancho Topanga Malibu Sequit was bought in 1887 by Frederick and May Rindge. The Rindge family fought with the state for many years to keep their property secluded. Eventually failing, they sold much of Malibu to the rich and famous. Large areas of Santa Monica Bay have remained undeveloped, however. The vast Topanga and Malibu Creek state parks help to improve Los Angeles's air quality and offer miles of hiking trails.

GETTING THERE

Santa Monica lies at the end of the Santa Monica Freeway (I-10) and is linked to Malibu by the Pacific Coast Highway. Santa Monica and Venice are well served by the Santa Monica Blue Bus Company. Possibly the best way to see the area is by hiring a bicycle and taking the coastal cycle path (see p168).

Street-by-Street: Santa Monica ❶

SANTA MONICA'S fresh sea breezes, mild climate (on average, the sun shines here 328 days a year) and pedestrian-friendly streets make it one of the best places in LA to go for a stroll. The city is perched on a high yellow cliff, overlooking Santa Monica Bay and miles of broad, sandy beach. Running along the cliff edge is palm-shaded Palisades Park, a narrow, 26-acre (10-ha) garden offering spectacular views, especially at sunset. A stairway leads down to Santa Monica's famous beach and pier. A few blocks inland from the hotel-lined seafront is Third Street Promenade – a great place to sit outside a café or restaurant and people-watch.

Street entertainer

View from Palisades Park
The cliff top park offers pano-ramic views of Santa Monica Bay. Looking northwards, you can see all the way to Malibu.

★ Third Street Promenade
Metal and topiary fountains, shaped like dinosaurs, decor-ate these three lively blocks. This is one of the best outdoor shopping areas in LA.

Hotels line the seafront.

★ Palisades Park
This narrow strip of park-land, planted with mature palm trees, is a good place to walk, jog or sit on a bench and admire the view. In the evening, many people come here to watch the sun go down.

STAR SIGHTS
★ Palisades Park
★ Santa Monica Pier
★ Third Street Promenade

KEY

– – – Suggested route

0 metres   200

0 yards   200

Santa Monica Place
This lively shopping mall was designed by architect Frank Gehry in 1979. The first floor food hall offers a variety of reasonably priced meals. The shops on the upper two storeys range from chain stores to one-off boutiques.

LOCATOR MAP

★ **Santa Monica Pier**
Since 1908, Angelenos and visitors alike have flocked to this landmark pier. With its long boardwalk, arcades and fishing areas, it still has plenty to offer. A new amusement area, Pacific Park, has a Ferris wheel, roller coaster and bumper cars.

Tourist information

Beach
Following the success of the television series Baywatch, *Santa Monica's beach is famous throughout the world.*

Exploring Santa Monica

Statue in Bergamot Station gallery

SANTA MONICA has been the star of LA's coastline since the 1890s, when trams linked it to the city, and beach parties became the rage. In the early days, it lived a dual life as a sleepy coast town and the headquarters for offshore gambling ships. In the 1920s and 1930s, movie stars such as Cary Grant and Mary Pickford bought land here, creating "the Gold Coast". The beach and pier are still major attractions, but the city is now also famous for its restaurants *(see p548)*. With the cleanest air in LA, Santa Monica offers many outdoor shopping areas and an active arts scene. Bergamot Station and the Edgemar complex on Main Street have a range of galleries.

Frank Gehry's innovative design for the Chiat Day Mojo Advertising Agency

Around Santa Monica

Grassy parks dot the city's landscape, with none quite as beautiful or revered as **Palisades Park** on the bluff overlooking the ocean. Stretching 1.5 miles (2.5 km) along the cliff's edge, this narrow, well-manicured park is one of the best spots to watch the sun go down. For the quintessential California experience, take a walk or jog along the paths, with the ocean as a backdrop and the towering palms overhead. The landscaping is beautiful, with semitropical trees and plants. At the northern end, the aptly named Inspiration Point has great views of the bay, stretching from Malibu to Palos Verdes.

Inland, between Wilshire Boulevard and Broadway, is **Third Street Promenade**. Once a decaying shopping street, this boulevard has undergone a major face-lift and is now one of the liveliest places in Los Angeles. Its three pedestrianized blocks are lined with shops, coffee houses, restaurants, bookshops and cinemas. At night the mood is especially festive. Street performers entertain passersby with music, dance, puppet shows and magic tricks. Nearby, on Arizona Avenue, a farmers' market on Saturdays and Wednesdays is one of the best in the city.

Santa Monica's other important shopping area is **Main Street**, which runs south towards Venice *(see p76)*. At the turn of the 20th century, Main Street was the commercial district for Pacific Ocean Park, an amusement park, baths and pier on the seafront. By the early 1970s, however, the majority of the neighbourhood's attractions had been demolished and Main Street itself had become a slum.

Today, this revitalized street abounds with a wide range of

Chain Reaction by Paul Conrad

shops, superb restaurants and first-rate art galleries.

There are many examples of public art displayed along Main Street. Sculptor Paul Conrad's *Chain Reaction* (1991) is a stainless steel and copper link chain statement against nuclear war. It stands next to the Civic Auditorium. *Ocean Park Pier* (1976), a mural by Jane Golden and Barbara Stoll, is situated at the junction with Ocean Park Boulevard and depicts the Pacific Ocean Park in the early 1900s.

A lovely example of Spanish Colonial architecture remains at the northwest corner of Main Street and Pier Avenue. Nearby, the Chiat Day Mojo Advertising Agency building, designed in 1991 by Frank Gehry and shaped like a giant pair of binoculars, dominates the street *(see p68)*.

🚋 Santa Monica Pier

Colorado & Ocean aves. 📞 *(310) 458-8900.* ⏰ *daily.* **Carousel** ⏰ *May–Sep: 10am–5pm Tue–Sun; Oct–Apr: 10am–5pm Sat & Sun.* ♿

This popular 1908 landmark is the West Coast's oldest pleasure pier. All the usual seaside attractions are here, such as popcorn, candyfloss, bumper cars and an amusement arcade. At the western end, rides in Pacific Park include a roller coaster and a Ferris wheel rising to the height of an 11-storey building. Nearby, the 1922 Looff Carousel, similar to that in Santa Cruz *(see p490)*, with 44 handcrafted horses, was featured in George

Beach apartments along the front of Palisades Park

Roy Hill's 1973 film *The Sting* *(see p65).* No permit is necessary to fish from the balconies on the pier's lower deck. On Thursday evenings during the summer, there is free dancing and live music *(see p163).*

🏛 Bergamot Station

2525 Michigan Ave. ☎ *(310) 829-5854.* ◯ *10am–5:30pm Tue–Fri; 11am–5:30pm Sat; 12 noon–5pm Sun.* ⬤ *public hols.*
Bergamot Station is a 5.5-acre (2-ha) arts complex that stands on the site of a disused Red Line tram station. The crude buildings are constructed from aluminium siding, with an added touch of high-tech styling. More than 20 galleries showcase the latest works in contemporary and radical art, including painting, sculpture, photography, furniture and glass, as well as collectibles and African art. Bergamot Station also houses a number of artists' studios.

Cuban political poster on display in Bergamot Station

🏛 California Heritage Museum

2612 Main St. ☎ *(310) 392-8537.* ◯ *11am–4pm Wed–Sat; noon–4pm Sun.* ⬤ *1 Jan, 4 Jul, Thanksgiving, 25 Dec.* 🏷 ♿
The Queen Anne museum building was built in 1894 by architect Sumner P Hunt as the home of Roy Jones, son of the founder of Santa Monica *(see p71).* On the first floor, the rooms depict the lifestyle of various periods in Southern California history: a Victorian dining room, an Arts and Crafts living room and a 1930s kitchen. Upstairs,

Victorian façade of the California Heritage Museum

there are changing exhibitions on topics such as surfing *(see pp188–9),* the Hollywood Western, quilts and Monterey Rancho-style furniture.

🏛 Santa Monica Museum of Art

2437 Main St. ☎ *(310) 399-0433.* ◯ *11am–6pm Wed–Sun (until 10pm Fri).* ⬤ *1 Jan, 4 Jul, Thanksgiving, 25 Dec.* **Donation**.
The Santa Monica Museum of Art is dedicated to contemporary and modern art. Its main

aim is to publicize the work of living artists, particularly performance and multimedia art. Although the museum has no permanent collection, the Edgemar complex, in which it is housed, is itself a work of art. Originally built in 1908 as an ice factory, the warehouse eventually became the egg-processing plant of Edgemar Farms. In 1988, the innovative architect Frank Gehry *(see p68)* transformed the building and the adjoining property into a mixed-use complex, with shops, restaurants, galleries and the museum.

RAYMOND CHANDLER

Novelist and screenwriter Raymond Chandler (1888–1959) set several of his works wholly or partly in Santa Monica, a city that he loathed and which he thinly disguised as sleazy Bay City in *Farewell, My Lovely.* There was some truth in Chandler's portrayal of Santa Monica. Corruption and vice in the 1920s and 1930s are well documented. Illegal gambling ships were anchored offshore, including the *Rex,* 5 miles (8 km) out in Santa Monica Bay, called the *Royal Crown* in *Farewell, My Lovely.*

Chandler's novels *Farewell, My Lovely, The Big Sleep, The High Window, The Little Sister* and *The Long Goodbye* were made into films that portrayed the shadowy side of LA. With an elegant, dark style, he wrote vivid dialogue in the voice of the common man. His character Philip Marlowe was the definitive detective. A loner with a hard-boiled veneer often hiding a soft heart, Marlowe uttered tough one-liners, played by the rules and usually didn't get the girl.

Film poster for *The Big Sleep* (1946)

Venice ❷

Road map inset A. ℹ️ *2904 Washington Blvd, Suite 100 (310 827-2366).*

SINCE ITS INCEPTION, Venice has attracted a bohemian society, from the rowdy crowd who frequented its dance hall and bathhouse in the 1910s to beatniks in the 1950s. Today, the town has a large population of artists, whose studios line the streets.

The community was founded in 1900, by tobacco magnate Abbot Kinney as a US version of Venice, Italy. Hoping to spark a cultural renaissance in Southern California, he built a system of canals and imported gondolas and gondoliers to punt along the waterways. Unfortunately, Kinney did not take the tides into consideration when designing Venice, and the area was constantly dogged by sewage problems.

Today, only a few of the original 7 miles (11 km) of canals remain, the rest having been filled in during 1927. The roundabout at Windward Avenue was the main lagoon, and Grand Boulevard, which runs southeast from there, was the Grand Canal. The best place to see the remaining canals is on Dell Avenue, where old bridges, boats and ducks grace the waterways.

Over the years, the circus atmosphere of Venice Beach has never faltered. On the boardwalk during weekends, semi-clad men and women whiz past on bicycles and skates, while a zany array of street performers captivates the crowds. Other spectacles have included chain saw jugglers and one-man bands. Muscle Beach, where film star Arnold Schwarzenegger used to work out, still attracts body builders.

While Venice Beach is safe to explore on foot by day, it is best avoided at night.

Yachts in the harbour at Marina del Rey

Marina del Rey ❸

Road map inset A. ℹ️ *4111 Via Marina (310 821-0555).*

COVERING AN AREA of just 1.3 sq miles (3.4 sq km), approximately half of which is water, Marina del Rey has the world's largest artificial small-craft harbour. Those attracted to this town tend to be young and single or with families and enjoy outdoor activities such as skating, cycling and water sports. Everything from paddle boats to yachts can be hired, or you can charter boats for deep-sea fishing or a luxury cruise.

Fisherman's Village, on Fiji Way, resembles a New England fishing town. It has a variety of shops, restaurants and cafés, many of which offer beautiful views of the harbour.

Museum of Flying ❹

2772 Donald Douglas Loop N, Santa Monica. **Road map** inset A. 📞 *(310) 392-8822.* 🕙 *10am–5pm Wed–Sun.* ⬤ *1 Jan, 4 Jul, Thanksgiving, 25 Dec.* 🖼️ ♿ 📷

THE FIRST AEROPLANE to fly around the world, the 1924 *New Orleans*, is on display at this fascinating museum of aviation history. Other highlights of the collection of 40 aircraft are P-51 Mustangs and Spitfires, the victorious fighter planes of World War II. Interactive exhibits explain the complexities of aircraft design and there are workshops for children, who can take part in a variety of related activities. Some of the vintage aircraft remain airworthy and visitors

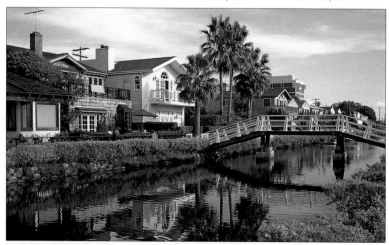

Man-made canal in Venice

can watch them take off from and land at the adjacent Santa Monica Airport. Classic aviation films are also shown.

Yellow Peril Boeing Sherman at the Museum of Flying

J Paul Getty Center ❺

See pp78–81.

Will Rogers State Historic Park ❻

1501 Will Rogers State Park Blvd, Pacific Palisades. **Road map** inset A. 📞 *(310) 454-8212.* ⭕ *8am–sunset daily.* ⚫ *1 Jan, Thanksgiving, 25 Dec.* 🏷 ♿ *lawn area.* 📷

WILL ROGERS (1879–1935) started life as a cowboy and went on to become a film star, radio commentator and newspaper columnist. Called the "Cowboy Philosopher", he was famous for his homespun humour and shrewd comments on current events, usually made while performing rope tricks. His show business career lasted from 1905 until his death. When his widow, Betty, died in 1944, she deeded the house and the surrounding 186 acres (75 ha) of land to the state. Her will stipulated that nothing in the house be changed and that polo matches be held at weekends (Rogers was an avid polo player).

Hiking trails lead up from the ranch, many of them originally cut by Rogers. The lawn just east of the house is an ideal setting for a picnic. Tours of the house include the living room, where Rogers used to practise his roping skills.

THE WILDLIFE OF SANTA MONICA BAY

Among the marine mammals that inhabit the waters of Santa Monica Bay are harbour seals, California sea lions and bottle-nosed dolphins. From December to February grey whales can be seen migrating from Alaska to Baja California to calve. One of the best places in Los Angeles for whale-spotting is Point Dume. In the mountains, the range of wildlife is exceptional. The rare mountain lion can reach a size of 7 ft (2 m) in length and tends to live in the rockier, more remote areas. Its cousin the bobcat is smaller, with tufts of hair on the ends of its ears. Coyotes come out at dusk, often preying on the pets of people living in the hills. The bold, intelligent raccoon raids camp sites even when people are present. Mule deer, desert cottontail and striped skunk also abound. Birds seen here include golden eagles and red-tailed hawks.

Raccoon (Procyon lotor)

Topanga State Park ❼

20825 Entrada Rd, Topanga. **Road map** inset A. 📞 *(310) 455-2465 & (805) 488-8147 for fire conditions in summer & autumn.* ⭕ *8am–sunset daily.* 🏞 ♿

TOPANGA STATE PARK stretches from the Pacific Palisades to the San Fernando Valley *(see p140).* Topanga is thought to be an Indian term meaning "the place where the mountains meet the sea". The area was inhabited by the Tongva/ Gabrielino and Chumash Indians 5,000 years ago. Today, its groves of sycamore and oak trees attract people seeking an alternative way of life.

The marked entrance to the 10,000-acre (4,000-ha) park lies just north of Topanga village, off Hwy 27 on Entrada Road. Most of the land falls within the LA city boundary, making it the largest city park in the US. As such, it vastly improves the region's air quality and provides ample space for hiking and riding.

As you ascend the Santa Monica Mountains, canyons, cliffs and meadows give way to vistas of the ocean and the San Fernando Valley. Four trails begin from the park's headquarters at Trippet Ranch: a 1-mile (1.6-km) self-guided nature trail; the Dead Horse Trail; Musch Ranch Trail (which leads to a camp site); and East Topanga Fire Road, which connects with Eagle Junction. The 2.5-mile (4-km) Eagle Rock/Eagle Spring Trail from Eagle Junction is one of the most popular.

Bicycles are allowed on the park's dirt fire roads and horses on all but one of the trails.

Hiking trails crossing the Santa Monica Mountains in Topanga State Park

J Paul Getty Museum at the Getty Center ❺

THE NEW GETTY CENTER holds a commanding position both physically and culturally in the city. Situated amid the wild beauty of the Santa Monica Mountains, next to the San Diego Freeway (I-405), the centre will open in December 1997. The complex houses not only the museum but also the Getty's research, conservation and education institutes, dedicated to art and cultural heritage. Getty made his fortune in the oil business and became an ardent collector of art. He wanted his collection, which focuses on European art from the Renaissance to Post-Impressionism, to be open to the public without charge. Greek and Roman antiquities are displayed at the Getty Villa in Malibu *(see p82)*.

LOCATOR MAP

Illustrated area

Research, conservation, education, administration, restaurant, café and auditorium buildings

Tram station

★ **Irises** *(1889)*
This work was painted by Vincent Van Gogh while he was in the asylum at St-Rémy. Its graphic style reveals the influence of artists such as Paul Gauguin (1848–1903) and the Japanese printmaker Hokusai (1760–1849).

East Pavilion

Hispano-Moresque Deep Dish
This elaborately decorated earthenware dish was made in Valencia, Spain, in the mid-15th century. The use of lustrous colours was a speciality of Moorish potters at that time.

North Pavilion

Courtyard

Entrance

STAR PAINTINGS

★ **Wheatstacks, Snow Effect, Morning by Claude Monet**

★ **The Abduction of Europa by Rembrandt**

★ **Irises by Vincent Van Gogh**

Cabinet on Stand

Attributed to the French master craftsman A-C Boulle, this 17th-century cabinet was made to celebrate the victories of Louis XIV.

VISITORS' CHECKLIST

1200 Getty Center Drive. **Road map** inset A. [ ] *(310) 440-7300.*
[ ] *from December 1997, Tue–Sun, parking reservations required.*
[ ] *1 Jan, 4 Jul, Thanksgiving, 25 Dec.* [symbols]

South Pavilion

West Pavilion

South Promontory

Korean Man
(c.1617)
This drawing in black and red chalk is by the Flemish artist Peter Paul Rubens. He used the red chalk to highlight the fine detail of the subject's face.

★ Wheatstacks, Snow Effect, Morning *(1891)*
This is one in a series of works by Monet that shows the same landscape at different times of the day and year.

Temporary exhibitions
and the museum café are housed in this building.

★ **The Abduction of Europa** *(1632)*
One of Rembrandt's few landscapes, this depicts the Roman god Jupiter, disguised as a bull, kidnapping Europa, princess of Tyre.

GUIDE TO THE GETTY CENTER
From below, the Getty Center may look like a fortress, but once on top, the scale is intimate, with fountains, walkways, courtyards and niches. An electric tram brings visitors from the car park to the complex. The museum has a tall, airy foyer that opens onto a central courtyard. From here radiate five two-storey pavilions, which contain the art collections. The Conceptualist artist Robert Irwin has created a central garden to the west of the museum. Across the main plaza from the tram station there is a café and restaurant. Another café and a bookshop are located within the museum.

Exploring the Getty Museum

J PAUL GETTY (1892–1976) amassed a remarkable collection of European painting, sculpture and decorative arts, focusing on pre-20th-century artistic movements. He was a bold collector who enjoyed the pursuit of an object almost more than the possession of it. Since his death, the Getty Trust has strengthened the museum's holdings by purchasing works of the highest quality to complement the existing collection. New departments in related areas such as drawings and manuscripts have also been added. Since the move to the Getty Center in 1997, the museum can now display twice as much of its collection as at the Getty Villa *(see p82).*

Man with a Hoe, painted between 1860 and 1862 by Jean-François Millet

EUROPEAN PAINTINGS AND SCULPTURE

THE MUSEUM boasts a superb collection of European paintings, dating from the 13th century to the late 19th century. Italian works from the Renaissance and Baroque periods include *The Adoration of the Magi* (c.1495–1505) by Andrea Mantegna and *View of the Dogana, Venice* (1744) by Canaletto. Rembrandt's *The Abduction of Europa* (1632) is a highlight from the Flemish and Dutch collections, which also include an oil sketch by Peter Paul Rubens (1577–1640) and a portrait by Anthony Van Dyck (1599–1641).

Of the French artworks on display, *The Race of the Riderless Horses* (1817) is an important painting by the Romantic painter Théodore Géricault. In *Still Life with Apples* (1900) by Paul Cézanne, the artist's preoccupation with gradations of light and colour reveals the progression in the late 19th century from the old, realistic style of painting, to a more modern, abstract approach. This painting, along with

Claude Monet's *Wheatstacks, Snow Effect, Morning (see p79)* and Vincent Van Gogh's *Irises (see p78),* has helped to elevate the museum's collection of Impressionists and Post-Impressionists.

European sculptures in the Getty span from the 16th century to the end of the 19th century. Pier Jacopo Antico's *Bust of Marcus Aurelius* (c.1520) was created at the end of the High Renaissance in Italy. The elongated body favoured by the Mannerists can be seen in Benvenuto Cellini's *Satyr* (c.1542). Fine examples of Baroque sculpture are *Pluto Abducting Proserpine* (c.1693–1710) by François Girardon and Gian Lorenzo Bernini's *Boy with a Dragon* (c.1614). Neo-Classical works include three statues by Joseph Nollekens': *Venus, Juno* and *Minerva* (1773).

DRAWINGS

THE PURCHASE in 1981 of Rembrandt's red chalk study of *Nude Woman with a Snake* (c.1637) marked the beginning of the museum's drawings collection. Today, the collection contains more than 400 works in a wide range of media, spanning the 15th to the late 19th century. *The Stag Beetle* (1505) by Albrecht Dürer is an exquisitely detailed illustration in watercolour and gouache. By contrast, Leonardo da Vinci's *Three Sketches of a Child with a Lamb* (c.1503–6), is a looser pen-and-ink study.

Peter Paul Rubens' *Korean Man (see p79)* is one of several portrait drawings. The *Self-Portrait* (c.1857–8) by Edgar Degas, executed in oil on paper and showing the young artist on the threshold of his extraordinary career is another.

PHOTOGRAPHS

THE MUSEUM launched its photographic department in 1984 with the purchase of several major private collections, including those of Bruno Bischofberger, Arnold Crane and Samuel Wagstaff. The holdings focus on European and American photography up to the 1950s. Exceptionally rich in works from the early 1840s, the collection features

Columbia River, Oregon (1867) by Carleton E Watkins

many of the pioneers of photography. In daguerreotypes, the identity of the sitter was often more important than that of the maker. The museum has one portrait of Louis-Jacques-Mandé Daguerre himself, taken in 1848 by Charles R Meade.

Englishman William Henry Fox Talbot (1800–1877) was the first to make prints from negatives. A lovely example of his work is *Oak Tree* (c.1845). Other early practitioners on exhibition include Hyppolyte Bayard (1801–87), portraitist Julia Margaret Cameron (1815–79), war photographer Roger Fenton (1819–69), Gustave Le Gray (1820–82) and Nadar (1820–1910).

Among the important early 20th-century artists represented are Edward Weston (1886–1958), who created beautiful still lifes, and Walker Evans (1903–75), who was a pivotal influence in American documentary photography.

Renaissance chalcedony, or agate, glass bowl, made in Venice, Italy, in around 1500

APPLIED ARTS

Applied arts in the museum encompass pre-1650 European pieces and works from southern Europe from 1650 to 1900. They have been chosen to complement the Getty's extensive holdings of French decorative arts.

Highlights include glass and earthenware from Italy and Spain; metalwork from France, Germany and Italy; and highly decorated furniture. An extravagantly inlaid display cabinet from Augsburg in Germany (c.1620–30) falls into this last category. All four of the piece's sides open to reveal numerous drawers and compartments for collectables.

Sèvres porcelain basket, dating from the mid-18th century

DECORATIVE ARTS

Decorative arts were Getty's first love as a collector, after he rented a New York penthouse furnished with 18th-century French and English antiques. Originally, his collection focused on furnishings from the reign of Louis XIV to the Napoleonic era (1643–1815), encompassing the Regency, Rococo and Empire periods.

The age of Louis XIV saw the development of French furniture reach great artistic heights, in which appearances mattered more than function. The premier craftsman during that time was André-Charles Boulle (1642–1732), who was noted for his complex veneers and marquetry. The museum has several pieces attributed to Boulle from the French royal household. Two coffers on stands (c.1680–85), made for the Grand Dauphin, son of Louis XIV, probably held jewellery and valuable objects.

Several of the tapestries in the collection have remained in excellent condition, with their colours still vibrant. They include one woven by Jean de la Croix (active 1662–1712) for Louis XIV. The holdings also include ceramics, silver and gilded objects such as chandeliers and wall lights.

In recent years, pieces from Germany, Italy and northern Europe have been added. A Neo-Classical roll-top desk (c.1785), made by the German David Roentgen, has a weight-operated, concealed writing stand. This type of elaborate mechanical feature was Roentgen's trademark.

MANUSCRIPTS

The museum began collecting illuminated manuscripts in 1983 with the purchase of the Ludwig Collection of 144 works, which emphasized German and Central European texts. Tracing the development of illumination from the 6th to the 16th century, the collection today has masterpieces from the Byzantine, Ottonian, Romanesque, Gothic and Renaissance periods.

Illuminated manuscripts were written and decorated entirely by hand. Initially, most were produced in monasteries, which were then the centre of European intellectual life. Later, in the 12th century, they were also made in the growing number of universities. Most books contained religious material, but some also preserved the philosophy, history, literature, law and science of Western civilization. Kings, nobles and church leaders commissioned these richly painted books, some of which were decorated with jewels and precious metals.

The manuscripts are exhibited on a rotating basis during the year. Highlights include an Ottonian Gospel lectionary from either Reichenau or St Gall (950–75); an English Gothic Apocalypse (c.1250); two Byzantine Gospel books; *The Visions of Tondal* (1474), in the Flemish holdings; and the *Hours of Simon de Varie*, illuminated by French artist Jean Fouquet in 1455.

Portrait of St John (c.1120–40) from the German Abbey of Helmarshausen's Gospel book

J Paul Getty Museum at the Getty Villa ❽

17985 Pacific Coast Hwy. ☎ *(310) 458-2003. ◷ until summer 1997, 10am–5pm Tue–Sun (limited parking, visitors should book at least 2 weeks in advance). ● public hols.* 🈲 🚻 📷

THE J PAUL GETTY MUSEUM is currently housed in the Getty Villa in the hills above Santa Monica Bay. This fascinating building, completed in 1974, is a reconstruction and adaptation of the Villa dei Papiri, the country estate of a Roman consul. The original was in Herculaneum, a resort town near Pompeii in Italy. It was buried by the eruption of Mount Vesuvius in AD 79.

The gardens of the villa are planted with seeds and bulbs imported from Italy. The Main Peristyle Garden is particularly spectacular, with its large pool bordered by bronze statuary. The buildings combine authentic Roman detailing with modern technology.

In summer 1997, the Getty Villa will close and most of the museum's holdings will be transferred to the Getty Center *(see pp78–81)*. It will reopen in the year 2000 as a centre for the display, study and conservation of ancient art.

Decorative façade and grounds of Adamson House

Adamson House and Malibu Lagoon Museum ❾

23200 Pacific Coast Hwy. **Road map** inset A. ☎ *(310) 456-8432. ◷ 11am–3pm Wed–Sat. ● 1 Jan, 4 Jul, Thanksgiving, 25 Dec.* 🈲 🚻 📷 *last tour 2pm.*

ADAMSON HOUSE was built in 1929 for husband and wife, Merritt and Rhoda Adamson. Rhoda was the daughter of Frederick and May Rindge, the last owners of the Rancho Malibu Spanish land grant. Until 1928, the family owned 24 miles (39 km) of Malibu coastline. Situated on the beach, the idyllic house and its 6 acres (2.5 ha) of gardens overlook Malibu Pier and Malibu Lagoon. The house was designed by Stiles

Intricate tile detail in Adamson House

Clements. The Spanish Colonial style building is covered with vivid tiles from the Malibu Potteries – a ceramics firm that was started by May Rindge and owned by the family. These tiles, each one individually designed, are featured throughout the house and grounds. The floors, walls, doorways and fountains are all intricately decorated. The house's original 1920s furnishings are also on display.

Located in the converted garage of Adamson House is the Malibu Lagoon Museum, which is devoted to the history of Malibu. Artifacts, documents and photographs tell the story not only of the Rindge family, but also of the early Chumash population and José Tapia, who in 1802 became Malibu's first Spanish landowner.

Malibu Lagoon State Beach ❿

Road map inset A. ☎ *(818) 880-0350. ◷ 8am–sunset daily.* 🈲 🚻

THE CHUMASH people built Humaliwo, their largest village, on the shores of this lagoon. By the 16th century, about 1,000 people had their home here, making it one of the most populated Native American villages north of what is now Mexico.

The estuary supports a wide range of marine life and is an important feeding ground for up to 200 species of migratory and native birds. To the east of

The Getty Villa's Main Peristyle Garden

Exclusive beach houses in Malibu Colony

the lagoon, the 35-acre (14-ha) Surfrider County Beach is devoted to surfers; swimming is prohibited. With its rare point break, Malibu is one of the finest surfing spots in Southern California. The area closest to the pier is thought to have the best waves for longboarding in the world. Volleyball courts are also located on the beach.

View across Malibu Lagoon to the Santa Monica Mountains

Malibu Colony ⓫

Road map inset A. 🚍 🛈 *23805 Stuart Ranch Rd, Suite 100 (310 456-9025).*

Iᴺ 1928, to raise money for an ongoing battle to keep Malibu in the family, May Rindge sold this section of shoreline to film stars such as Bing Crosby, Gary Cooper and Barbara Stanwyck. Today, the colony is a private, gated compound, still favoured by people working within the entertainment industry. There is no public access to the beach, but stars can often be spotted in the Malibu Colony Plaza, which is located near to the entrance.

Malibu Creek State Park ⓬

Road map inset A. 🚻 *(818) 880-0367, (818) 880-0350 or (800) 444-7275 for camp site reservations.* 🕐 *daily.* 🎫 ♿ 🚻

Tʜɪs 10,000-ᴀᴄʀᴇ (4,000-ha) park was inhabited by the Chumash Indians until the mid-19th century. A varied landscape of forests, meadows and rocky outcrops create the illusion of a vast wilderness, miles from civilization.

Some 2,000 acres (800 ha) of the park were once owned by 20th-Century Fox, who made it a favourite location for movie-making *(see pp64–5).*

M*A*S*H (1970), *Butch Cassidy and the Sundance Kid* (1969), and *Planet of the Apes* (1968) were all filmed here. The state bought the land back from the film company in 1974.

The information centre is close to the car park and has exhibits on the area's history, flora and fauna. The stunning Gorge Trail starts from the centre of the park and leads to a rock pool, which was used as a pseudo-tropical location to film the movies *South Pacific* (1958) and *Tarzan* (1959).

Off Crags Road, the marshy Century Lake harbours catfish, bass, bluefish, red-winged blackbirds, buffleheads, coots and mallards. In spring the meadows are a riot of colourful wildflowers. Groves of live and valley oaks, redwood and dogwood trees are scattered throughout the park.

Within the park there are 20 trails for hiking, cycling or horse riding, a nature centre and many picnic areas.

Malibu Creek State Park, near Castro Crest *(see p60)*

BEVERLY HILLS, BEL AIR AND WESTWOOD

EVERLY HILLS is a city, independent of Los Angeles and with its own laws and regulations. Since the early 1920s it has been the entertainment industry's favourite residential address. Beverly Hills' Golden Triangle is the West Coast's answer to New

City limits sign

York's Madison Avenue, with its array of restaurants, shops and coffee bars. South of Bel Air's shady canyons, youthful Westwood brims with UCLA students. In the business-minded Century City, high-rises crowd the skyline. Together, these areas are known as the Westside.

SIGHTS AT A GLANCE

Historic Buildings
Beverly Hills Civic Center ❶
Beverly Hills Hotel ❽
Hotel Bel-Air ⓫

Parks and Gardens
Greystone Park and Mansion ❼
Virginia Robinson Gardens ❾

Shopping Areas
Century City ❻
Rodeo Drive p90 ❸
2 Rodeo ❹

Tours
Tour of the Stars' Homes
pp92–3 ❿

Museums
Museum of Television and
Radio ❷
Museum of Tolerance ❺

Universities
UCLA and Westwood
Village ⓬

GETTING THERE

A car is essential when visiting this area, which has a lot of car parks. From the San Diego Freeway (I-405) take Wilshire or Sunset boulevards east to Westwood, Bel Air and Beverly Hills. There is a limited DASH bus service in Westwood.

0 kilometres 1
0 miles 0.5

KEY

Street-by-Street map
See pp86–7

Illustrated tour
See pp92–3

◁ **Distinctive tower of Beverly Hills City Hall, part of the Civic Center**

Street-by-Street: The Golden Triangle

THE AREA BORDERED by Santa Monica Boulevard, Wilshire Boulevard and North Crescent Drive, known as the "Golden Triangle", is the business district of Beverly Hills. The shops, restaurants and art galleries lining the streets are some of the most luxurious in the world. Cutting through the middle is Rodeo Drive, where many international designer boutiques are to be found. On Wilshire Boulevard, the cream of American department stores offer a heady mix of style and opulence. To the north are the beautifully manicured Beverly Gardens, the elegant Civic Center with its landmark City Hall and the recently opened Museum of Television and Radio.

★ **Museum of Television and Radio**
The latest addition to the Golden Triangle, this museum gives a comprehensive history of broadcasting ❷

The Electric Fountain was built in 1930. The statue on the top is of a Native American praying for rain. Scenes from Californian history are depicted on the base frieze.

Saks Fifth Avenue is one of the four major department stores along Wilshire Boulevard.

The Creative Artists Agency was built in 1989 by architect IM Pei. Its curving mirrored glass and marble walls anchor Santa Monica and Wilshire boulevards.

★ **Beverly Hills Civic Center**
*The 1932 Spanish Renaissance
City Hall has recently been
restored and a series of new
administration and
public buildings
added* ❶

LOCATOR MAP
See Street Finder, map 5

Anderson Court
was designed by
Frank Lloyd Wright
in 1953.

2 Rodeo
*When built in 1990,
this centre included
the first new street in
Beverly Hills since
the city established
independence
from LA in
1914* ❹

The MGM Building was
built in the 1920s by Louis
B Mayer. The white and
gold Art Deco structure
was the headquarters of
the newly formed
Metro-Goldwyn-
Mayer film studios.

The Beverly Theatre, a
Moorish-style building built
in 1925, was the site of
many film premieres in the
1920s and 1930s. It is now
the Israeli Discount Bank.

0 metres	100
0 yards	100

KEY

‒ ‒ ‒ ‒ Suggested route

Rodeo Drive
*The three blocks of Rodeo
Drive are one of the most
famous shopping areas
in the world* ❸

**The Regent Beverly Wilshire
Hotel** first opened in 1928. In
1970 a second wing was added
to the original Beaux-Arts building. A private, cobbled street
links the two wings (*see p508*).

STAR SIGHTS

★ **Beverly Hills
Civic Center**

★ **Museum of
Television and Radio**

Beverly Hills Civic Center with City Hall in the background

Beverly Hills Civic Center ❶

455 N Rexford Drive. **Map** 5 F3.
☎ (310) 285-1000. ◯ 7:30am–
5:30pm Mon–Thu; 8am–5pm Fri.
● public hols. ♿

THE SPANISH COLONIAL City Hall, with its majestic tower capped by a tiled cupola, was designed in 1932 by local firm Koerner and Gage. Over the years it has become a symbol of the elegant, European-inspired city of Beverly Hills.

In 1990, architect Charles Moore linked the building to a new Civic Center by a series of diagonal landscaped and pedestrianized courtyards. On the upper levels, balconies and arcaded corridors continue the Spanish Colonial theme. The sympathetic modern addition houses a beautiful public library as well as the local fire and police stations.

Billboards are banned in the area, and a height restriction of three storeys or 45 ft (14 m) was imposed on any new buildings, leaving City Hall to dominate the skyline.

Museum of Television and Radio ❷

465 N Beverly Drive. **Map** 5 F3.
☎ (310) 786-1000. ◯ noon–5pm
Wed–Sun (until 9pm Thu). ● public
hols. ♨ ♿ ☑

VISITORS TO the Museum of Television and Radio may watch and listen to news and a collection of entertainment and sports programmes from the earliest days of radio and television to the present.

Pop music fans can see footage of the early Beatles or a young Elvis Presley making his television debut. Sports enthusiasts can relive classic Olympic competitions.

Visitors can select up to four extracts from the library's computerized catalogue at any one time. These are then played on small private consoles. The museum also has a 150-seat theatre, which hosts

major exhibitions, seminars and screenings on specialized subjects and selected actors or directors.

The collection of more than 75,000 television and radio programmes, includes such timeless classics as *I Love Lucy* (see p145) and *Sergeant Bilko*. Favourite television and radio commercials, encompassing the industry's advertising history, are also available.

The holdings duplicate those of New York's highly successful Museum of Television and Radio, which was created in 1975 by the late William S Paley, when he was the head of CBS Television.

Rodeo Drive ❸

See p90.

2 Rodeo ❹

Map 5 F3. 🛈 239 South Beverly
Drive (310 271-8174).

DEVELOPED IN 1990 on the corner of Rodeo Drive (see p90) and Wilshire Boulevard, 2 Rodeo is one of the most expensive retail centres ever constructed. It looks a little like a Hollywood film set of a European shopping street, complete with a public square and Victorian-style streetlamps. Exclusive shops such as Cole Haan and Charles Jourdan

Lucille Ball, the most popular television star during the 1950s

Spanish Steps leading to 2 Rodeo

line Via Rodeo, the cobbled lane that bisects the centre. Via Rodeo meanders to the Spanish Steps, which descend to Wilshire Boulevard.

Museum of Tolerance ❺

9786 W Pico Blvd. **Map** 5 F5.
📞 (310) 553-8403. ⬤ 10am–4pm Mon–Thu, 10am–3pm Fri (Nov–Mar: 10am–1pm), 11am–5pm Sun.
⬤ 1 Jan, Thanksgiving, 25 Dec and all major Jewish holidays. 🎦 ♿

THIS MUSEUM is dedicated to the promotion of respect and understanding among all people. Its two primary areas of focus are the history of racism and prejudice in the United States and the European Holocaust experience, examined in both historical and contemporary contexts.

The museum tour begins in the Tolerancenter, where visitors are challenged to confront racism and bigotry within their own environments through interactive exhibits. "The Other America" is a computerized wall map that locates and gives information on more than 250 known racist groups in the US. A 16-screen video wall depicts the 1960s civil rights struggle in America. Interactive video monitors ask visitors for their personal profiles and then challenge them on questions of responsible citizenship and

social justice. They also offer footage of the LA riots of 1992 *(see p53)*, with follow-up interviews. One of the most hard-hitting exhibits is the 15-ft (4.5-m) "Whisper Gallery", in which visitors hear racial and sexual taunts.

At the beginning of the Holocaust section, each visitor is given the details and photograph of a child whose life was in some way altered by that period. Throughout the tour, the child's history is updated and, at the end, his or her fate is revealed. During the tour visitors become a witness to events in Nazi Germany. Wax models in an outdoor café scene, set in pre-war Berlin, seem to discuss the impending Nazi takeover of Germany. In a re-creation of the Wannsee Conference, the Third Reich leaders decide on the "The Final Solution of the Jewish Question". Videotaped interviews with concentration camp survivors tell of their harrowing experiences in the "Hall of Testimony". Artifacts on display include Anne Frank's original letters and memorabilia from the camps.

The upper floors of the museum house special exhibits, films and lectures. There is also a multimedia learning centre with interactive computers containing additional information on World War II topics. Some of the exhibits may not be suitable for children under the age of ten.

History of racial prejudice at the Museum of Tolerance

Century City ❻

Map 5 D5. 🏢 2049 Century Park E, Suite 460, Century City (310 553-2222).

THIS SITE used to be part of 20th-Century Fox's backlot. It was sold in 1961 to the developers of Century City, who designed a high-rise complex of offices, shops and homes on the 180 acres (73 ha).

Today lawyers, agents and production companies fill the office blocks. Despite this, the area has never developed a community feel and at night the streets are empty.

The Century City Shopping Center, however, is a notable success. This outdoor complex has more than 120 shops, some 20 restaurants, and a 14-screen cinema.

Century City Shopping Center

Greystone Park and Mansion ❼

905 Loma Vista Drive. **Map** 5 F1.
📞 (310) 550-4654. **Park** ⬤ 10am–5pm daily. ⬤ 1 Jan, 25 Dec.
♿ terrace & lower grounds.

IN 1928 Edward L Doheny, an oil millionaire, built this 55-room mock-Tudor manor house for his son. Just three weeks after moving in with his family, Doheny's son was found dead in his bedroom with a male secretary, an apparent murder-suicide. His wife and children soon moved out, and since then the mansion has often been vacant.

Now owned by the city of Beverly Hills, Greystone is used in films, music videos and commercials. The house is closed to the public, but visitors can walk or picnic in the beautiful 18-acre (7-ha) terraced gardens, which offer views across Los Angeles.

Rodeo Drive ❸

T HE NAME RODEO DRIVE is derived
from *El Rancho Rodeo de las
Aguas* ("the ranch of the gathering of waters"), the name of an
early Spanish land grant that
included Beverly Hills. Today, Rodeo
Drive is one of the most celebrated
and exclusive shopping streets in the
world, with Italian designer boutiques, the best of French fashion,
world-class jewellers and some
of the leading LA retailers. For
those who enjoy celebrity-spotting,
Rodeo Drive is a prime area.

Rodeo Drive's *wide pavements,
bordered by trees, help create a
pleasant shopping environment.*

Barakat *sells
fine jewellery
but also has
an impressive
collection of
pre-Columbian
and ancient
Greek artifacts.
Barakat is located in the
group of shops known as
the Rodeo Collection, under
an atrium, at No. 421.*

• 421

BRIGHTON WAY

Gucci,
*at No. 347, is
a leading
Italian boutique.
Best known for its
leather accessories and
colourful scarves, it also
produces furnishings,
such as this cushion.*

• 347

• 317

VAN CLEEF & ARPELS

DAYTON WAY

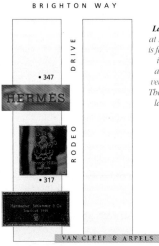

Lalique,
*at No. 317,
is famous for
its Art Deco
and Art Nou-
veau glassware.
The shop's frosted
lamps are typical
of Lalique's style.*

Fred Hayman Beverly Hills,
*at No. 273, is a fashion bou-
tique with a fireplace and bar.*

• 273

• 230

Christian Dior, *at No.
230, is one of the leading
names in French* haute
couture. *The founder of
the house was responsible
for the 1950s "New Look".*

0 metres   50

0 yards   50

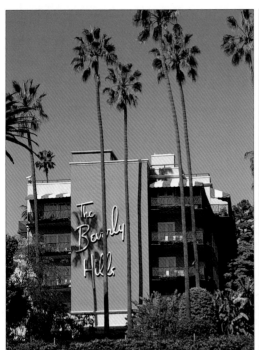

The landmark Beverly Hills Hotel

Beverly Hills Hotel ❽

9641 Sunset Blvd. **Map** 5 D2.
🕿 *(310) 276-2251.* ⬜ *daily.* ♿
See **Where to Stay** *p508.*

Dubbed "the Pink Palace", this extravagant Mission Revival-style hotel was built in 1912 by developer Burton E Green, to attract people to Beverly Hills. The hotel's 21 secluded bungalows, set in 12 acres (5 ha) of landscaped gardens, have been romantic hideaways for film stars such as Marilyn Monroe, Clark Gable, Richard Burton and Elizabeth Taylor.

Recently, the Beverly Hills Hotel has undergone a $100 million programme of renovations, reviving the style of Hollywood's heyday. Its legendary pool and cabanas have remained one of the places to be seen and heard in Los Angeles, and its renowned restaurants, The Polo Lounge and Polo Grill, are once more at the centre of the movie industry's deal-making.

Virginia Robinson Gardens ❾

1008 Elden Way. **Map** 5 D1.
🕿 *(310) 276-5367.* ⬜ *Tue–Fri.*
⬤ *public hols.* 📷 ♿ 🎫 *obligatory* *10am & 1pm Tue–Thu, 10am Fri. Advance reservations required.*

In 1908 department-store heir Harry Robinson and his wife, Virginia, bought a plot of land in Beverly Hills. Three years later they completed the city's first house here and

planted 6 acres (2.5 ha) of landscaped gardens set amid terraces, ponds and fountains.

Bequeathed to LA County, the gardens were opened to the public in 1982. One of the most impressive sights is the 2.5-acre (1-ha) palm forest, where you can see the largest king palms outside Australia.

The organized tour includes part of the house, which still has its original furnishings.

Tour of the Stars' Homes ❿

See pp92–3.

Hotel Bel-Air ⓫

701 Stone Canyon Rd. **Map** 4 A1.
🕿 *(310) 472-1211.* ⬜ *daily.* ♿
See **Where to Stay** *p508.*

Considered one of the best hotels in the US, Hotel Bel-Air is located in a heavily wooded canyon, giving it an air of privacy and tranquillity. The 1920s Mission Revival-style buildings are set in 11 acres (4.5 ha) of beautiful gardens, interspersed with fountains and intimate courtyards.

Among the trees and shrubs rarely seen in Southern California are coastal redwoods, white-flowering bird of paradise trees and a floss silk tree – the largest of its kind outside its native South America. The gardens are fragrant with roses, gardenias, jasmine and the blossom from peach, apricot and orange trees. In fact, the Bel-Air is so perfect that one guest stayed for 40 years.

Pool at Hotel Bel-Air, surrounded by attractive gardens

Tour of the Stars' Homes ⑩

Security
guard sign

IN LOS ANGELES, image is everything, and Beverly Hills has long been the symbol of success for those in the entertainment industry. When, in 1920, Mary Pickford and Douglas Fairbanks built their mansion, Pickfair, at the top of Summit Drive, everyone else followed – and stayed. Sunset Boulevard divides the haves from the havenots: people who live south of it may be rich, but it is those who live to the north of the road who are considered to be the super-rich. Houses come in almost every architectural style. Some are ostentatious, others are surprisingly modest.

Jimmy Stewart's former home at No. 918 Roxbury Drive ⑬

South of Sunset

Start at No. 714 Palm Drive, the elegant home of Faye Dunaway ①, who starred with Warren Beatty in *Bonnie and Clyde* (1967). Continue south and turn right on Elevado Avenue. The former home of Rita Hayworth ② is situated on the corner at No. 512 Palm Drive.

At Maple Drive, turn right. No. 720 is the white and green New England-style home of the late George Burns and Gracie Allen ③. Continue north and just before Sunset Boulevard make a sharp left onto Lomitas Avenue. Go two blocks and turn left onto Foothill Road. On the corner, at No. 701, is the unassuming house of Carroll Baker ④. This blonde-haired beauty made her debut in *Giant* (1956) with James Dean. At one time she was being groomed to be the next Marilyn Monroe.

Turn right onto Elevado Avenue, take the next right onto Alpine Drive, left onto Lomitas Avenue and left at Crescent Drive. Doris Day's modest house ⑤ is barely

visible at No. 713, hidden behind a tall hedge and gate.

Turn right on Carmelita Avenue and right again at Cañon Drive. The pretty house ⑥ where Robert

Wagner and Natalie Wood once lived can be seen through the low wall at No. 603. Continue north to the junction with Elevado Avenue. Just across the road, at No. 707 Cañon Drive, lush palm trees in the front mark the beginning of Kirk Douglas's walled and gated property ⑦.

Turn left onto Elevado Avenue. As you cross Rodeo Drive, look to your right. The lovely home of the late Gene

Kelly ⑧ is at No. 725 Rodeo Drive. This renowned Hollywood icon performed in such classics as *An American in Paris* (1951) and

Singing in the Rain (1952).

Continue along Elevado Avenue, then turn right on Bedford Drive. The comedian and actor Steve Martin ⑨ has a home at No. 721. A modern block structure, it has no front windows and can only be partially glimpsed behind a bougainvillea hedge. Lana Turner's scandal-ridden house ⑩ at No. 730, on the

KEY

— — —	Tour route

Faye Dunaway's house at No. 714 Palm Drive ①

Jayne Mansfield's Pink Palace at No. 10100 Sunset Boulevard ⑭

LOCATOR MAP
See Street Finder, map 5

His former neighbours at No. 1000 Roxbury Drive were Lucille Ball and Desi Arnaz ⑫. Their successful show *I Love Lucy (see pp88 and 145)* is still shown daily on television. Nearby, at No. 918, is the mock-Tudor former home of the much respected Jimmy Stewart ⑬.

At Sunset Boulevard, turn right. Jayne Mansfield's Pink Palace ⑭ is at No. 10100, on the southwest corner of Sunset Boulevard and Carolwood Drive. When Mansfield moved in, she put in a heart-shaped pool with the inscription "I love you Jaynie" written on the bottom.

Turn right onto North Carolwood Drive. Just to the right, at No. 144 Monovale Drive ⑮, is one of rock-and-roll king Elvis Presley's former homes. Only the tennis courts can be seen from the street.

Continue along Carolwood Drive. Barbra Streisand ⑯ lives at No. 301 on a heavily guarded estate. The actress won an academy award in 1969 for her role as Fanny Brice in the musical *Funny Girl*. The late Walt Disney, who captured the imagination of the world with his cartoon characters, used to live just north of here at No. 355 Carolwood Drive ⑰. His house is on a bend, behind a gate.

North of Sunset
Cross Sunset Boulevard, taking the street furthest to the left, which is now Benedict Canyon Drive. On the corner is the Beverly Hills Hotel, *(see p91)*, long a celebrity rumour mill. The private bungalows behind its pink façade saw many a romantic tryst, including, it is said, those between Marilyn Monroe and John and Robert Kennedy.

At Roxbury Drive, turn left and curve south with the road. At No. 1002 is the late Jack Benny's traditional-looking brick house ⑪, which he occasionally used in his shows.

Walt Disney's mailbox ⑰

corner of Bedford Drive and Lomitas Avenue, was where her gangster-lover Johnny Stompanato was stabbed to death with a kitchen knife by her daughter, Cheryl Crane.

Turn right onto Lomitas Avenue, then make a sharp left on Cañon Drive.

TIPS FOR DRIVERS

Tour length: 5 miles (8 km).
Warning: Film stars' homes or former residences. Do not attempt to trespass or you may be arrested.

University of California, Los Angeles and Westwood Village ②

A LARGE UNIVERSITY with a first-rate reputation, UCLA has a wide range of academic departments and professional schools, including the respected UCLA Hospital. Sited on 419 acres (170 ha), with more than 35,000 students, it is a city within a city. The original campus was designed in 1925 to resemble the Romanesque towns of southern Europe. The first four buildings followed this theme, but as the university expanded more modern architecture was favoured. The disappointing mix of bland structures which resulted is redeemed by the beautiful landscaped grounds.

Romanesque-style façade of UCLA's Royce Hall

Exploring UCLA and Westwood Village

Since it was first developed in 1928, Westwood Village has been one of the most successful shopping districts in Southern California. For years, the pleasant streets south of UCLA were the most popular weekend destination in the city. People still enjoy the pedestrian-friendly avenues, the productions at the Geffen Playhouse (see p164) and the large number of cinemas that often preview the latest films. However, cheap modernization of some of the shopfronts has disrupted the overall cohesiveness of the village's Spanish Colonial design.

Detail of ceiling in Royce Hall

🐦 Royce Quadrangle
Dickson Plaza. 📞 (310) 825-2101. ☐ daily.
The four buildings that make up the Royce Quadrangle are the oldest on UCLA's campus in Westwood. Built of red brick in the Italian Romanesque style, Royce, Kinsey and Haines halls and Powell

Library far surpass the other buildings at UCLA in beauty. The best of them all is Royce Hall, which is based on the basilica of San Ambrogio in Milan, Italy. Its auditorium hosts professional music, dance and theatre shows throughout the year. Next door, Powell Library's grand rotunda was modelled on San Sepolcro in Bologna, Italy.

🏛 UCLA at the Armand Hammer Museum of Art and Cultural Center
10899 Wilshire Blvd. 📞 (310) 443-7000. ☐ 11am–7pm Tue, Wed, Fri, Sat; 11am–9pm Thu; 11am–5pm Sun. ● 4 Jul, Thanksgiving, 25 Dec. 🎟 free 6–9pm Thu. ♿ 📷
The museum presents selections from the collection of businessman Armand Hammer (1899–1990). Works are largely Impressionist or Post-Impressionist by artists such as Mary Cassatt (1845–1926), Claude Monet (1840–1926), Camille Pissarro (1830–1903), John Singer Sargent (1856–1925) and Vincent Van Gogh (1853–90).

Exhibits from the Armand Hammer Daumier and Contemporaries Collection are also shown on a rotating basis and include paintings, sculptures and lithographs by the 19th-century French artist Honoré Daumier and his contemporaries. Displays are also drawn from the UCLA Grunwald Center for the Graphic Arts, which holds more than 35,000 works on paper dating from the Renaissance to the present day.

♣ Franklin D Murphy Sculpture Garden
📞 (310) 443-7041. ☐ daily.
This is the largest sculpture garden on the West Coast with more than 70 20th-century sculptures. The highlights

UCLA AND WESTWOOD VILLAGE

KEY

 Bus terminus

 Tourist information

P Parking

Entrance to UCLA at the Armand Hammer Museum of Art

Automne (Autumn, 1948) by Henri Laurens

include Henry Moore's *Two-Piece Reclining Figure, No. 3* (1961) and Jacques Lipchitz's *Baigneuse* (*Bather*, 1923–5).

🍁 Mildred E Mathias Botanical Garden

📞 (310) 825-1260. ⏰ 8am–5pm Mon–Fri, 8am–4pm Sat & Sun. ● public hols. ♿

Tucked away in a small shady canyon, this serene garden contains almost 4,000 rare and native species. Divided into 13 thematic sections, the gardens feature both subtropical and tropical plants. The trees are spectacular and include some outstanding Australian eucalyptus and some extremely rare dawn redwoods.

🏛 Fowler Museum of Cultural History

📞 (310) 825-4361. ⏰ noon–5pm Wed–Sun (until 8pm Thu). ● public hols. 🎫 free Thu.

This university museum is committed to enriching the community's understanding of other cultures. Its exhibitions focus on the prehistoric, historic and contemporary societies of Africa, Asia, the Americas and Oceania. The collection of 750,000 artifacts makes it one of the nation's leading university museums.

✝ Westwood Memorial Park

1218 Glendon Ave. 📞 (310) 474-1579. ⏰ 8am–5pm daily. ♿

Off the beaten track, this small cemetery is located behind the Avco Center cinemas and car park. The tranquil grounds are now the final resting place for celebrities such as Dean Martin, Peter Lorre, Buddy Rich, Natalie Wood and Marilyn Monroe. For several decades after her death, Monroe's second husband, Joe DiMaggio, used to have six red roses placed on her tomb every week.

Tranquil Westwood Memorial Park, shaded by trees

MARILYN MONROE

Born Norma Jean Baker in the charity ward of Los Angeles General Hospital, Marilyn Monroe (1926–62) was placed in foster care by her mother when she was two weeks old. Her first marriage, at the age of 16, lasted four years, before she gave it up to pursue her dream of being an actress. In 1950, her career took off with *The Asphalt Jungle* and *All About Eve*. With films such as *The Seven-Year Itch* (1955) and *Some Like It Hot* (1959), she became the biggest sex symbol Hollywood has ever seen. In the latter part of her life, she struggled to escape the narrow confines of her on-screen persona.

Marilyn Monroe's memorial plaque

MARILYN MONROE
1926 – 1962

0 metres   500

0 yards   500

BEVERLY HILLS
HOLLYWOOD

SUNSET   BOULEVARD

WEST

NORTH

CIRCLE DRIVE EAST

HILGARD AVENUE

①

②   ③

HILGARD AVENUE

④

CIRCLE DRIVE SOUTH

WESTWOOD PLAZA

TIVERTON DRIVE

CONTE   AVENUE

HILGARD AVENUE

WEYBOURN AVENUE

LINDBROOK DR

ROXTON AVENUE

⑤

WESTWOOD   BOULEVARD

TIVERTON

WILSHIRE

SANTA MONICA

AYLEY   AVENUE

⑥

⑦

BOULEVARD

GLENDON AVENUE

ASHTON AVE

WELLWORTH   AVENUE

ROCHESTER   AVENUE

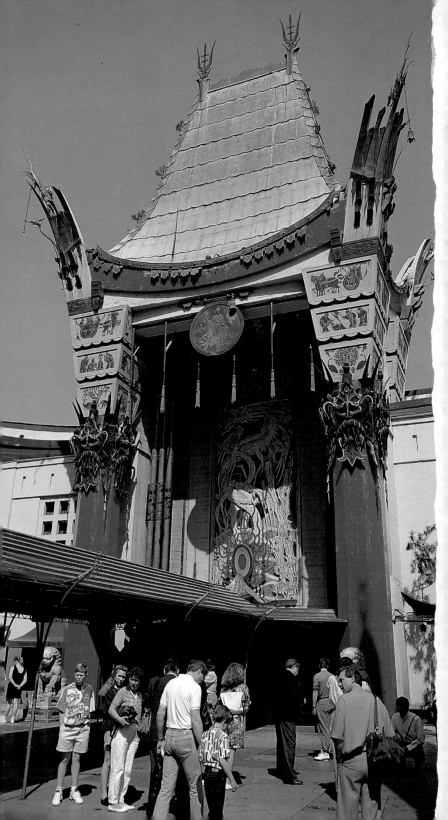

HOLLYWOOD AND WEST HOLLYWOOD

In 1887, Harvey Henderson Wilcox and his wife, Daeida, set up a Christian community, free of saloons and gambling, in a Los Angeles suburb and called it Hollywood. It is ironic that the movie business with all its decadence came to replace their Utopia. The takeover started in 1913, when Cecil B De Mille filmed *The Squaw Man* in a rented barn at Vine and Selma. For the next several decades the studios were based here, generating wealth and glamour. In recent years the area fell into decline, and today only a handful of landmarks recall its Golden Age. Sunset Boulevard has now become the focal point for nightlife in Los Angeles. West Hollywood, with its large gay community, is also a lively area for dining and shopping.

Hollywood's Walk of Fame

SIGHTS AT A GLANCE

Museums
Craft and Folk Art Museum 17
George C Page Museum of La Brea Discoveries 16
Hollywood Studio Museum 7
Los Angeles County Museum of Art pp110–13 12
Museum of Miniatures 15
Petersen Automotive Museum 14

Historic Streets and Buildings
Hollywood Bowl 6
Miracle Mile 13
Paramount Studios 10
Roosevelt Hotel 1
Walk of Fame 4

Cemeteries
Hollywood Memorial Park 9

Cinemas and Theatres
El Capitan Theatre 3
Mann's Chinese Theatre 2
Pantages Theater 8
Wiltern Theatre 18

Shops and Markets
Farmers Market 11
Frederick's of Hollywood 5

See pp104–5
See pp101–3
See pp98–100

0 kilometres 2
0 miles 1

GETTING THERE
The Metro Red Line currently runs from Downtown's Union Station to Wilshire Boulevard at Western Avenue. Bus services from Downtown include: No. 1 (along Hollywood Boulevard), No. 2 (Sunset Boulevard), No. 4 (Santa Monica Boulevard), No. 10 (Melrose Avenue) and Nos. 20, 21 and 22 (Wilshire Boulevard). Freeway 101 runs through Hollywood from Downtown and on to Ventura.

KEY
■ Illustrated areas
Ⓜ Metro Red Line station

◁ **Mann's Chinese Theatre, a lavish remnant of Hollywood's Golden Age**

A View of Sunset Boulevard: Sunset Strip

Sunset Boulevard curves westwards for 26 miles (42 km) from Downtown LA to the Pacific Coast Highway. Sunset has been associated with the movies since the 1920s, when it was a dirt track linking the burgeoning film studios in Hollywood with the hillside homes of the screen stars. Today, much of the boulevard is still lined with the mansion houses of the rich and famous *(see pp92–3)*. Sunset Strip is the liveliest and most historically rich stretch, filled with restaurants, luxury hotels and nightclubs. The 1.5-mile (2.4-km) section was first paved in the mid-1930s. Its lack of local government made it a magnet for gambling and bootlegging. Famous nightclubs included the Trocadero, Ciro's and the Mocambo – where young Margarita Cansino met studio boss Harry Cohen, who renamed her Rita Hayworth. Sunset Strip is still the centre of LA's nightlife today.

Sunset Strip and the Santa Monica Mountains from Crescent Heights

Rainbow Bar & Grill
The walls of this restaurant, at No. 9015, are lined with wine casks and gold records. Formerly the Villa Nova, Vincente Minnelli proposed to Judy Garland here and, eight years later in 1953, Marilyn Monroe met Joe DiMaggio here on a blind date.

The Original Spago
Wolfgang Puck, who is regarded by many as the founder of Californian cuisine, had his first LA restaurant at No. 8795. During the 1970s and '80s Oscar night parties were held here, hosted by the legendary Hollywood agent Irving "Swifty" Lazar.

The Roxy
This trendy nightclub, at No. 9009, occupies the site of the old Club Largo.

The Viper Room, at No. 8852, is a popular live music venue *(see p164)*, part-owned by the actor Johnny Depp. In October 1993 young film star River Phoenix, having taken a lethal cocktail of drugs, collapsed and died on the pavement outside.

The Roxbury Club, behind the big billboard to the west of the Chateau Marmont hotel, is currently popular with the stars of teenage TV shows. It stands on the site of the Players Club, owned in the 1940s by movie director Preston Sturges.

Chateau Marmont
The hotel at No. 8221 (see p513) was modelled on a Loire Valley château. When it opened in 1929, it attracted actors such as Errol Flynn and Greta Garbo. Among today's regulars are Christopher Walken and Winona Ryder.

The Trocadero nightclub, at No. 8610, had Nat "King" Cole as its pianist in its heyday. Only three steps remain of the old building.

Directors' Guild of America
This is one of the many offices on Sunset Boulevard connected with the entertainment industry.

Schwab's
The former drugstore was a popular meeting place for film stars and columnists. A Virgin Megastore now occupies the site. Across Crescent Heights was the legendary Garden of Allah apartment complex whose residents included F Scott Fitzgerald and Dorothy Parker.

BILLBOARDS

The most visible pieces of art along Sunset Strip are the huge, hand-painted billboards, produced by some of Hollywood's finest artists and designers to advertise new films, records and personalities. They are often three-dimensional, a technique introduced in 1953 when Las Vegas's Sahara Hotel rented a billboard, erected a real swimming pool and filled it with swimsuited models. During the 1960s the billboards were dominated by the music industry, with advertising space along Sunset Strip even being written into some rock stars' contracts. Despite LA's well-known antipathy towards smoking, the massive board outside the Chateau Marmont is devoted to the Marlboro cowboy.

Marlboro and tequila billboards on Sunset Strip

View of Sunset Boulevard: Old Studio District

URING THE FIRST HALF of the 20th century, this 2-mile (3-km) stretch of Sunset Boulevard was the centre of Hollywood's film industry. Major studios, including 20th-Century Fox, RKO, Warner Bros, Paramount and United Artists, were all in the vicinity and the streets were filled with directors, actors and would-be film stars. In the area known as Gower Gulch, low-budget outfits churned out westerns by the score. There are still some studios here, but most have relocated. Of the major studios, only Paramount *(see p109)*, on Melrose Avenue to the south, remains.

Sunset Boulevard during its heyday in the 1940s

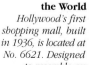

A & M Records
These mock-Tudor buildings, stretching from the southeast corner of Sunset Boulevard down La Brea Avenue, were constructed by Charlie Chaplin as homes for workers at his studio.

Crossroads of the World
Hollywood's first shopping mall, built in 1936, is located at No. 6621. Designed to resemble an ocean liner, with a globe-topped tower on its prow, it has now been converted into offices.

Hollywood High School
A long list of famous alumni have attended Hollywood High School, at No. 6800, including Lana Turner. The actress was first discovered in 1936 by director Mervyn LeRoy, sipping a soda in the now-defunct Top Hat Malt Shop – its site, opposite the school, is today occupied by a garage.

Hollywood Athletic Club
Film stars of the 1930s and 1940s exercised here. Flash Gordon *star Buster Crabbe trained in the swimming pool before winning a gold medal at the 1932 Olympics.*

Cinerama Dome
The distinctive dome of No. 6360 was the first wide-screen cinema on the West Coast.

The Cat and Fiddle
This British-style pub, at No. 6530, is built around an attractive Mediterranean-style patio. British beers are served along with pub food, such as bangers and mash. There is a dartboard inside.

TIME CAPSULE

In 1954 the Los Angeles Chamber of Commerce decided to preserve the history of Hollywood with a time capsule. A copy of Bing Crosby's hit record "White Christmas", released that year, a script of the most successful film made to date, *Gone With the Wind,* and various contemporary radio and television tapes were deposited under the pavement at the famous intersection between Sunset Boulevard and Vine Street. The time capsule is planned for retrieval 50 years after is was planted, in 2004.

A pavement plaque marking the site notes that the legend of Hollywood was born here in 1913 with the making of the first feature-length film, *The Squaw Man,* by Cecil B De Mille and Jesse Lasky. In fact, the actual location of their barn studio, now preserved on North Highland Avenue *(see p108)*, was further up the block at No. 1521 Vine Street. Hollywood had also been incorporated as a town ten years earlier and numerous short films had been made here during that decade.

Singer Bing Crosby

Poster of Gone With The Wind (1939)

Hyatt Hotel
*Visiting rock stars
regularly book in
to this hotel, at No.
8401 (see p513).
Jim Morrison
stayed here when
he played with The
Doors at the nearby
Whisky A Go Go.*

Argyle Hotel
*This hotel is an Art Deco high-rise. In Holly-
wood's heyday it was an apartment block
and home to Jean Harlow, Clark Gable
and other luminaries. (See p513.)*

The Source, at
No. 8301, is the
restaurant where
Woody Allen rants
about LA in his film
Annie Hall (1977).

The Comedy Store
*This is a world famous venue for
stand-up comedy, often enjoying
television coverage. It stands on the
site of the 1940s nightclub, Ciro's.*

0 metres   100

0 yards   100

**The Mondrian
Hotel**, at No. 8440,
is decorated with
stripes in primary
colours, as a tribute
to artist Piet Mon-
drian *(see p513).*

Sunset Plaza
*This area is lined
with chic shops
and cafés. It is a
good section to
explore on foot.*

The House of Blues
*This tin-roofed blues bar, at No.
8430, has been transported from
Clarksdale, Mississippi. It is part-
owned by the actor Dan Ackroyd,
who co-starred with John Belushi
in the 1980 cult movie* The Blues
Brothers *(see p164).*

Hollywood Palladium
Norman Chandler, of the Los Angeles Times *dynasty, built this theatre at No. 6215. It was opened by Lana Turner in 1940, when Frank Sinatra gave a concert. Big bands and musical stars still perform here.*

CBS Studios
No. 6121 was inherited from Columbia Pictures. They in turn succeeded the Nestor Film Co., who rented the site in 1911 for $40 a month.

N GORDON ST

N BRONSON AVE

HOLLYWOOD FREEWAY

GOWER GULCH

GOWER ST

TAMARIND AVE

Gower Gulch
Now a shopping mall, in the 1930s and 1940s would-be actors gathered here each morning hoping for $10-a-day jobs at the small studios shooting low-budget Westerns.

| 0 metres | 100 |
| 0 yards | 100 |

Warner Bros Studio
The first talkie, Al Jolson's The Jazz Singer *(1927), was made here at No. 5858. The following year the studio moved to Burbank (see p141). The building now houses local radio stations.*

WARNER BROS. SUPREME TRIUMPH
AL JOLSON
in **The JAZZ SINGER**

WARNING
This section of Sunset Boulevard is sadly run down and frequented by drug dealers and prostitutes. It is advisable to stay in your car, with the doors locked and valuables out of sight. If you do decide to walk around, try to look as if you know where you are going. Keep your wallet in an inconspicuous place and do not wear valuable jewellery.

Sunset Boulevard Theatre
Showman Earl Carroll's Vanities Theater originally occupied this site at No. 6220 in the 1940s. It had the world's largest revolving stage, which held 60 dancers.

A View of Hollywood Boulevard

HOLLYWOOD BOULEVARD is one of the most famous streets in the world, and its name is still redolent with glamour. Visitors wishing to recapture a Golden Age of cinema may be disappointed, however, as few vestiges of that era remain. A renewal programme has been under way for some years, with limited success. Mann's Chinese Theatre and its autograph patio live up to expectations, as does the Walk of Fame. World premieres of Disney films occur at the El Capitan Theatre and often feature a live revue by the Magic Kingdom's favourite characters. Other attractions include the Hollywood Wax Museum, the Hollywood Guinness World of Records and Ripley's Believe it or Not!®

First National Bank detail

LOCATOR MAP
See Street Finder map 2

★ **Mann's Chinese Theatre**
Stars' autographs are set in the concrete courtyard ❷

The Hollywood Galaxy houses a six-screen cinema complex and the Hollywood Entertainment Museum, which has film, television, radio and recording memorabilia.

HOLLYWOOD BOULEVARD NORTH SIDE ▶▶▶▶▶▶▶▶▶▶▶▶▶▶▶▶▶▶▶▶▶▶▶▶▶▶▶▶▶▶▶▶

★ **Walk of Fame**
Marilyn Monroe's star is embedded in the pavement at No. 6776 Hollywood Boulevard. The camera symbol below her name indicates her career as a film actress ❹

Hollywood Guinness World of Records uses models, videos and special effects to bring record-breaking achievements alive. It is housed in the area's first cinema.

Ripley's Believe It or Not!® is a museum devoted to the bizarre. The building, topped by a model tyrannosaurus rex, contains more than 300 exhibits, such as shrunken heads and two-headed calves.

HOLLYWOOD BOULEVARD SOUTH SIDE ▶▶▶▶▶▶▶▶▶▶▶▶▶▶▶▶▶▶▶▶▶▶▶▶▶▶▶▶▶▶▶▶

KEY

►►►►►► North Side walking east

◄◄◄◄◄◄ South Side walking west

STAR SIGHTS

★ **Mann's Chinese Theatre**

★ **Walk of Fame**

The Hollywood Wax Museum has life-size models of film stars, musicians and public figures. Clint Eastwood, Marilyn Monroe, Madonna, Michael Jackson, Dolly Parton and Ronald Reagan are among those on show. There is also a wax tableau based on Leonardo da Vinci's painting, *The Last Supper* (1497).

First National Bank marks the junction with Highland Avenue. Its tiered façade is decorated with stone reliefs of historical figures such as Christopher Columbus and Nicolaus Copernicus.

0 metres   200

0 yards   200

Roosevelt Hotel
An image of actor and director Charlie Chaplin (1889–1977) decorates the wall of this historic 1920s hotel ❶

El Capitan Theatre
Neon lights welcome filmgoers to this beautifully restored Art Deco cinema. Movies can be seen in old-fashioned comfort, but with state-of-the art sound ❸

The Masonic Hall now displays interactive exhibitions of Disney shows.

Sid Grauman's famous Chinese Theatre (now Mann's)

Roosevelt Hotel ❶

7000 Hollywood Blvd. **Map** 2 B4.
📞 *(213) 466-7000.* ♿ *See* **Where to Stay** *p510.*

NAMED AFTER US president Theodore Roosevelt, this hotel was opened in 1927 by joint owners Louis B Mayer, Mary Pickford, Marcus Loewe, Douglas Fairbanks, Sr and Joseph Schenk. It soon became one of Hollywood's most popular locations. Marilyn Monroe, Ernest Hemingway and Clark Gable were all visitors and, on 16 May 1929, the first Academy Awards banquet was held in the Roosevelt's Blossom Room.

Renovations in 1986 revealed the hotel's original Spanish Colonial design. The following year the swimming pool was decorated by David Hockney *(see p24).* The Hollywood Historical Review exhibition, on the mezzanine level, documents the history of the area.

Roosevelt Hotel, venue for the first Academy Awards

Mann's Chinese Theatre ❷

6925 Hollywood Blvd. **Map** 2 B4.
📞 *(213) 461-3331.* 📠 *(213) 464-8111.* ⭕ *daily.* 📷 ♿

ONE OF THE most famous sights in Hollywood has not changed much since it opened in 1927 with the gala premiere of Cecil B De Mille's *King of Kings.* The exterior is an ornate medley of Chinese temples, pagodas, lions and dragons, reflecting the keen sense of showmanship of the cinema's creator, Sid Grauman.

Besides the spectacle of the movie premiere, Grauman also thought up one of the longest-running publicity stunts in Hollywood history: inviting movie stars to impress their handprints, footprints and autographs in the cement courtyard of his cinema. There are many versions of how this custom began. One tells of silent screen star Norma Talmadge accidentally stepping in the wet cement at the gala opening *(see p49).* Another is that the French stonemason, Jean Klossner, put his hand in the wet cement for posterity. Whatever the precedent, Sid Grauman liked the idea and invited Norma Talmadge to legitimately leave her mark, along with Mary Pickford and Douglas Fairbanks, Sr, on 17 May 1927.

Anyone can visit the courtyard, but only film-goers can see the extravagant interior of the cinema. Make sure the

film is playing in the main auditorium and not in one of the additions in the east wing.

Steel tower of El Capitan Theatre

El Capitan Theatre ❸

6838 Hollywood Blvd. **Map** 2 B4.
📞 *(213) 467-9545.* ⭕ *daily.* 📷

BUILT IN 1926 as a theatre, El Capitan was later converted to a cinema. It was the venue for many film premieres, such as Orson Welles's *Citizen Kane* (1941). In 1942 the cinema was refurbished and its interior was covered up. It was renamed the Hollywood Paramount.

Disney and Pacific Theatres bought El Capitan in 1991 and restored it to its former glory. Luckily, the original Art Deco interior was found virtually intact. Today, many Disney feature animations open at the cinema, such as *The Lion King* (1994) and *Pocahontas* (1995).

Walk of Fame ❹

Map 2 B4. ℹ *6541 Hollywood Blvd*
(213 689-8822). 🆔 *(213) 469-8311.*

PERHAPS THE ONLY pavement in the city to be cleaned six times a week, the Walk of Fame is set with more than 2,000 polished marble stars. Since February 1960, celebrities from the worlds of film, radio, television, theatre and music have been immortalized on Hollywood Boulevard and Vine Street. Stardom does not come easily, however: each personality has to be sponsored and approved by the Chamber of Commerce, and pay a $7,500 installation fee. Among the most famous are Charlie Chaplin (No. 6751) and Alfred Hitchcock (No. 6506).

Frederick's of Hollywood ❺

6608 Hollywood Blvd. **Map** 2 C4.
📞 *(213) 466-8506.* 🕐 *10am–6pm Mon–Thu, Sat; 10am–9pm Fri; noon–5pm Sun.* ⬛ *1 Jan, Thanksgiving, 25 Dec.* ♿

FREDERICK MELLINGER launched his now world-renowned mail-order business in 1946, selling provocative lingerie. He believed that "fashions may change, but sex appeal is always in style". This purple and pink Art Deco building is Frederick's flagship store. As well as selling underwear, it

Garish exterior of Frederick's of Hollywood

houses a Celebrity Lingerie Hall of Fame, which includes the bra worn by Marilyn Monroe in *Let's Make Love* (1960), Tony Curtis's black lace bra from the classic *Some Like It Hot* (1959) and Madonna's infamous black bustier.

Hollywood Bowl ❻

2301 N Highland Ave. **Map** 2 B3.
📞 *(213) 850-2000.* 🕐 *late Jun–mid-Sep.* ⬛ *Labor Day.* 📷 ♿
Box office 🕐 *10am–9pm Mon–Sat; noon–6pm Sun.* ⬛ *Labor Day.*
Edmund D Edelman Hollywood Bowl Museum 📞 *(213) 850-2058.*
🕐 *Jul–mid-Sep: 10am–8:30pm Tue–Sat; mid-Sep–Jun: 10am–4:30pm Tue–Sat.* ⬛ *public hols.*

SITUATED IN a natural amphitheatre that was once revered by the Cahuenga Pass Gabrielino Indians, the Bowl has now become sacred to Angelenos. Since 1922 it has been the summer home of the LA Philharmonic *(see p121)*. Even though the acoustics are not perfect, the atmosphere cannot be beaten.

Thousands gather on warm evenings to picnic – often in high style – under the stars and listen to the orchestra. There are 13 picnic areas on the 60-acre (24-ha) site. Jazz, country, folk and pop concerts are also performed during the season.

The most popular events at the Bowl are the concert with fireworks on the Fourth of July, the Easter Sunrise Service and a Tchaikovsky Spectacular with cannons, fireworks and a military band.

Much altered over the years, the shell-shaped stage was originally designed in 1929 by Lloyd Wright, son of architect Frank Lloyd Wright. Rumour has it that the materials for the building were taken from the set of Douglas Fairbanks, Sr's movie *Robin Hood* (1922). There is seating for 18,000 people at the Bowl, including privately owned and much sought-after boxes at the front.

The Edmund D Edelman Hollywood Bowl Museum explores the rich history of the Bowl, through videos, old programmes and posters, and memorabilia of the artists who have come here, from violinist Jascha Heifetz to The Beatles. Film excerpts shot at the Bowl include William Wellman's *A Star is Born* (1937).

Hollywood Bowl, nestling in the Hollywood Hills

Mausoleum of William A Clark, Jr in Hollywood Memorial Park

Hollywood Studio Museum ❼

2100 N Highland Ave. **Map** 2 B3.
📞 *(213) 874-2276.* 🕐 *10am–4pm Sat; noon–4pm Sun. Weekdays by appt.* 🏛 ♿ ✔

IN 1913, Cecil B De Mille and the Jesse L Lasky Feature Play Company rented this barn, then located on Vine Street, just north of Sunset Boulevard. That year De Mille used the building to make *The Squaw Man*, the first feature-length movie produced in Hollywood. In 1935 the company was renamed Paramount Pictures.

The barn was moved to its present site, in the Hollywood Bowl car park *(see p107)*, in 1983. Thirteen years later a fire prompted a major renovation programme. Today the barn is a museum, displaying props, costumes, photographs and other memorabilia from the early days of film-making.

Pantages Theater ❽

6233 Hollywood Blvd. **Map** 2 C4.
📞 *(213) 468-1700.* 🕐 *daily.* 🏛 ♿

TO ATTEND A SHOW at the Pantages is to experience the glory days of the 1930s movie palaces. Built in 1929, the marble and bronze Art

Deco cinema catered to the comfort of its audience, with a spacious foyer and luxurious lounges. It opened in 1930 with *The Floradora Girl*, starring Marion Davies, the mistress of WR Hearst *(see p204)*. Between 1949 and 1959 the Academy Awards Ceremony was also held here.

Splendidly renovated in the 1980s, today Pantages is used to stage Broadway musicals. Only show ticket holders are allowed into the breathtaking interior, with its magnificent chandeliers, vaulted ceilings and columns decorated with geometric patterns.

Elegant Art Deco façade of the Pantages Theater

Hollywood Memorial Park ❾

6000 Santa Monica Blvd. **Map** 8 C1.
📞 *(213) 469-1181.* 🕐 *8am–4pm Mon–Fri; 10am–3pm Sun.* 🌑 *public hols.* ♿

A MAP OF THIS cemetery is available at the front office and reads like an early history of film. Tyrone Power has a white memorial overlooking a pond on the eastern side. Next to him, the mausoleum of Marion Davies bears her family name of Douras. Cecil B De Mille, Nelson Eddy and many others from Hollywood's heyday are also buried in this area. Douglas Fairbanks, Sr's grave has a reflecting pool and monument, reputed to have been paid for by his ex-wife, the silent film star Mary Pickford. Inside the gloomy Cathedral Mausoleum is the tomb of Rudolph Valentino, still the cemetery's biggest attraction. Every year, on 23 August, a "Lady in Black" pays her respects to the actor on the anniversary of his death.

The back of Paramount Studios forms the southern wall of the cemetery, and Columbia used to be to the north. Columbia boss Harry Cohn is said to have picked his plot so that he could keep an eye on his studio.

Paramount Studios ❿

5555 Melrose Ave. **Map** 8 C1.
[(213) 956-5575. ◗ 9am–2pm
Mon–Fri. ● 1 Jan, Easter Sun,
Thanksgiving, 25 Dec. 🎥 & ✔
**Visitors' Center and Ticket
Window** 860 N Gower St. **[** (213)
956-3488. ◗ 8:30am–4pm Mon–
Fri. ● 1 Jan, Easter Sun, Thanks-
giving, 25 Dec.

THE LAST MAJOR STUDIO still
located in Hollywood,
Paramount was also the first
in operation. Cecil B De Mille,
Jesse Lasky and Samuel Gold-
wyn joined forces with Adolph
Zukor in 1914 to form what
became known as the directors' studio. The roster of stars
was equally impressive: Gloria
Swanson, Rudolph Valentino,
Mae West, Marlene Dietrich,
Gary Cooper and Bing Crosby
all signed with Paramount.

Aspiring actors still hug the
wrought-iron gates at Bronson
Avenue and Marathon Street.
Seeking luck, they still quote
Norma Desmond's final line in
Sunset Boulevard: "I'm ready
for my close-up, Mr De Mille."

Classics such as *The Ten
Commandments, The War of
the Worlds, The Greatest Show
on Earth* and the *Godfather
Parts I, II* and *III* were all made
in Paramount's 63 acres (25 ha)
of backlot and sound stages.
A two-hour tour of the studio
provides details of its history
and gives visitors a behind-
the-scenes view of films and
television shows currently in
production *(see p165)*.

Poster for Paramount's *The War of the Worlds* (1953)

MELROSE AVENUE

Once a bland avenue, Melrose burst onto the Los Angeles
street scene in the mid-1980s with quirky shops and good
restaurants. The prime area stretches for 16 blocks between
La Brea and Fairfax avenues, providing a rare opportunity
to walk and shop outdoors in the city. From Fifties to punk
to classic, the clothing, shoe and accessory boutiques offer
a wide range of styles and goods and stay open until late
(see pp166–7). The same can also be said of the avenue's
many restaurants, which represent the diverse ethnic
flavours of Los Angeles. Mexican and Thai are two of the
favourite cuisines, but pasta and
pizza dominate the street, as they
do the rest of the city.

At the western end of Melrose, at
San Vincente Boulevard, is the huge
600-ft (183-m) high blue-glass Pacific
Design Center, known to the locals
as the Blue Whale. Designed by
César Pelli in 1975, this showcase
for interior designers and architects
is the largest on the West Coast.
Although it caters mainly to trade,
the centre also welcomes the
general public. Admission charges
and purchasing policies may vary
between individual showrooms.

**Colourful shop window
on Melrose Avenue**

Farmers Market ⓫

6333 W 3rd St. **Map** 7 D3. **[** (213)
933-9211. ◗ 9am–6:30pm Mon–
Sat; 10am–5pm Sun. ● 1 Jan, Easter
Sun, Memorial Day, 4 Jul, Labor Day,
Thanksgiving, 25 Dec. &

IN 1934, during the Great
Depression *(see p49)*, a
group of farmers began selling their produce directly to
the public in a field then at
the edge of town. Since then,
Farmers Market has been a
favourite meeting place for
Angelenos. There are stalls
selling fresh flowers, meats,

**Clock tower at entrance to
Farmers Market**

cheeses, fruit, vegetables and
breads. There are also more
than 100 shops which sell
everything from antiques to
T-shirts and garden supplies.
Among the best of the numerous cafés and restaurants are
Bob's Donuts, where some of
the finest doughnuts in town
can be sampled; Kokomo Café,
which fills up quickly with a
fashionable crowd, hungry
for strawberry pancakes or
black bean-filled omelettes
(see p546); and The Gumbo
Pot, where the traditional
Cajun food is spicy and the
beignets (dough fritters) are
sweet *(see p546)*.

Los Angeles County Museum of Art ⑫

THE LARGEST ENCYCLOPEDIC ART MUSEUM west of Chicago, the Los Angeles County Museum of Art (LACMA) has one of the finest collections in the country. Founded in 1910, the museum moved to its present site in prestigious Hancock Park in 1965. The five-building complex offers a wide selection of European and American art, including burgeoning 20th-century and photograph collections. Also impressive are the museum's Asian and Middle Eastern works and its group of pre-Columbian artifacts. To display its internationally acclaimed holdings of Japanese art, including the Shin'enkan and Bushell collections, LACMA added the spectacular Pavilion for Japanese Art in 1988.

★ **In the Woods at Giverny**
This work of 1887, subtitled "Blanche Hoschedé at her easel with Suzanne Hoschedé reading", depicts the daughters of Monet's mistress.

★ **Mother about to Wash her Sleepy Child** (1880)
Mary Cassatt was a leading American Impressionist artist, who promoted that movement keenly in the United States. Nearly one third of the works that she produced are domestic scenes, such as this intimate portrait.

Third level

Second level

Flower Day (1925)
In this canvas Diego Rivera depicts various religious influences in Mexico. The stance of the lily seller is part-shaman, part-Christian.

Plaza level

Entrance

MUSEUM GUIDE

European and American works of art are displayed in the Ahmanson and Hammer buildings. The limestone, terracotta and glass-brick Anderson Building, completed in 1986 by Hardy Holzman Pfeiffer, holds the museum's 20th-century art collection. Beside it, the Sculpture Garden has a number of bronzes by Auguste Rodin. The Pavilion for Japanese Art, designed by architectural maverick Bruce Goff, combines Japanese elements with 1950s American styling. The museum's Plaza Café is located in the Bing Center.

STAR EXHIBITS

- ★ **In the Woods at Giverny by Claude Monet**

- ★ **Mother about to Wash her Sleepy Child by Mary Cassatt**

- ★ **Mulholland Drive by David Hockney**

Lower level

AHMANSON BUILDING

★ **Mulholland Drive** *(1980)*
British artist David Hockney has made his home in LA. This painting of one of the city's most famous roads (see p140) follows the route to his studio.

Second level

Plaza level

Entrance

HAMMER BUILDING

Third level

Second level

Second level

Plaza level

PAVILION FOR JAPANESE ART

Entrance

Plaza level

Entrance

Plaza level

BING CENTER

Main entrance

ANDERSON BUILDING

Sculpture Garden

Japanese Plate
This 17th-century glazed porcelain plate forms part of the museum's exceptional collection of Japanese art.

KEY TO FLOORPLAN

- American art
- European painting, sculpture and decorative art
- Modern and Contemporary art
- Photography, prints and drawings
- Ancient and Islamic art
- Indian and Southeast Asian art
- Far Eastern art
- Costumes and textiles
- Temporary exhibitions
- Non-exhibition space

MUSEUM PLAN

- Ahmanson Building
- Anderson Building
- Hammer Building
- Bing Center
- Pavilion for Japanese Art

Exploring LACMA

A TOUR OF LACMA offers a comprehensive survey of the history of art throughout the world. The museum has more than 250,000 objects that represent many cultures, dating from prehistoric to modern and contemporary periods. Ancient art treasures encompass pre-Columbian finds as well as the largest Islamic art collection in the western United States. Decorative arts, which include European and American pieces from medieval times to the present, are exhibited alongside paintings and sculpture from the same period. The museum also has a superb collection of costumes and textiles. A programme of world-class travelling exhibitions complements the permanent collection.

Standing Warrior

Magdalen with the Smoking Flame (c.1640) by Georges de la Tour

AMERICAN ART

THE COLLECTION of paintings traces the history of American art from the 1700s to the 1940s. Dating from the Colonial period are John Singleton Copley's *Portrait of A Lady* (1771) and Benjamin West's *Cymon and Iphigenia* (1773).

In the mid-1800s American artists such as Edwin Church (1826–1900), Winslow Homer (1836–1910) and Thomas Moran (1837–1926), turned from portrait painting and Classical subjects to landscapes of the New World. Notable Impressionist works include Mary Cassatt's *Mother about to Wash her Sleepy Child (see p110)* and Childe Hassam's *Avenue of the Allies* (1918). *Flower Day (see p110)* by Diego Rivera forms part of the Latin American collection.

Decorative arts range from Chippendale and Federal-style furniture to lamps by Louis Comfort Tiffany (1848–1933).

Monument to Balzac, sculpted in the 1890s by Auguste Rodin

EUROPEAN PAINTING, SCULPTURE AND DECORATIVE ART

THE COLLECTION of European works of art spans the 12th to early 20th centuries, beginning with medieval religious objects. Fine portraits by Lucas Cranach (1472–1553) and Hans Holbein (1497–1543) represent the Northern Renaissance.

Religious paintings by Fra Bartolommeo (1472–1517) and Titian (c.1490–1576) date from the Italian Renaissance.

One of the European collection's strengths is its 17th-century Dutch and Flemish canvases. Rembrandt's *The Raising of Lazarus* (c.1630) and Anthony Van Dyck's *Andromeda Chained to the Rock* (1637–8) are among the highlights. Works displayed from the French and Italian schools include Georges de la Tour's *Magdalen with the Smoking Flame,* painted around 1640, and Guido Reni's *Portrait of Cardinal Roberto Ubaldino,* which dates from before 1625. The French collections from the 18th and 19th centuries are also impressive, with works by Eugène Delacroix (1798–1863) and Camille Corot (1796–1875). The sculpture collection concentrates mostly on 19th-century French artists, with more than 40 works by Auguste Rodin (1840–1917).

Impressionist and Post-Impressionist works are hung in the Hammer Building. Two of the highlights are *In the Woods at Giverny* by Claude Monet *(see p110)* and Edgar Degas' *The Bellelli Sisters* (1862–4). Others include paintings by Pierre Auguste Renoir (1841–1919), Vincent Van Gogh (1853–90) and Paul Cézanne (1839–1906).

Among the finest decorative arts pieces are a Venetian enamelled and gilded blue glass ewer, dating from around 1500, and a mid-16th-century Limoges plaque that depicts Psyche and Cupid.

The Cotton Pickers (1876) by Winslow Homer

MODERN AND CONTEMPORARY ART

HOUSED IN the Anderson Building, the 20th-century collection has examples of every significant movement of modern art. The second floor presents works dating from 1900 to 1970, including Pablo Picasso's *Portrait of Sebastian Juñer Vidal* (1903) and René Magritte's *La Trahison des Images (see p66)*. German Expressionists are well represented, with works from both *Die Brücke* (The Bridge) and *Der Blaue Reiter* (The Blue Rider) groups.

Post-1970 paintings, sculptures and installations are displayed on the first floor, and include David Hockney's *Mulholland Drive (see p111)*.

PHOTOGRAPHY, PRINTS AND DRAWINGS

THE MUSEUM'S outstanding photography holdings give a rare overview of the medium. Exhibits range from early 19th-century daguerreotypes and albumen prints to abstract mixed media images. A large group of works by Edward Weston (1886–1958) is filled with texture and sensuality.

LACMA's holdings of prints and drawings includes the Robert Gore Rifkind Collection of German Expressionist works. Erich Heckel's woodcut, *Standing Child* (1910), is just one of its outstanding prints.

ANCIENT AND ISLAMIC ART

THE ANCIENT ART of Egypt, western Asia, Iran, Greece and Rome is displayed on the first floor of the Ahmanson Galley. There are massive carved stone panels from a 9th-century BC Assyrian palace; a rare Egyptian bronze from the 25th Dynasty; and delicate Iranian figures, some dating from 3,000 BC. The Islamic art collection spans almost 1,400 years. Its Iranian and Turkish holdings are particularly strong.

Carved stone objects and ceramic vessels and statues from Central America and Peru comprise the pre-Columbian holdings. *Standing Warrior* (100 BC–AD 300), a Mexican effigy, is the largest known work of its kind.

INDIAN AND SOUTHEAST ASIAN ART

WITH MORE than 5,000 works dating from the 3rd century BC, the museum has one of the most comprehensive collections outside Asia. It is especially strong in Indian arts, from splendid sculpture to intricate watercolours on cloth and paper. There are manuscripts and *thankas* (paintings on cloth) from Tibet and Nepal, and stone and bronze sculptures from Indonesia, Thailand, Sri Lanka, Cambodia and Burma.

***Pair of Officials* (618–907), from the Tang dynasty, China**

FAR EASTERN ART

THIS SECTION includes ceramics, sculpture, screens and scrolls from China, Japan and Korea. The highlight, however, is the Shin'enkan Collection in the Pavilion for Japanese Art. The collection's 200 screens and scroll paintings from the Edo period (1615–1868) are considered the most outstanding in the Western world. Masterpieces include Ito Jakuchu's 18th-century hanging scroll, *Rooster, Hen and Hydrangea*, and Suzuki Kiitsu's 19th-century *Seashells and Plums*. The Bushell Collection of *netsukes* (carved toggles used to secure a small container), ceramics, sculpture and woodblock prints is also impressive.

COSTUMES AND TEXTILES

AN ENCYCLOPEDIA of clothing and textiles, the collection boasts some 55,000 artifacts that represent more than 300 of the world's cultures. The oldest pieces are embroidered Peruvian burial shrouds that date from 100 BC and an Egyptian Coptic tunic from the 5th century AD. One of the most important pieces is the early 16th-century Iranian "Ardebil" carpet, named after a shrine in northwest Iran for which it was commissioned. A French noblewoman's gown, made from silk, gold and silver, is one of only two complete 17th-century dresses in the US.

***Dunes, Oceano* (1936) by Edward Weston**

Miracle Mile ⑬

Wilshire Blvd between La Brea &
Fairfax Aves. **Map** 7 D4. 🚇 *685
S Figueroa St (213 689-8822), 6541
Hollywood Blvd (213 689-8822).*

1932 Duesenberg Model J roadster at the Petersen Automotive Museum

I<small>N</small> 1920, developer AW Ross
bought 18 acres (7.2 ha) of
land along Wilshire Boulevard
and built a shopping district
aimed at the wealthy families
living in nearby Hancock Park.
With its Art Deco and Streamline Moderne buildings, wide
pavements and roads built for
cars rather than carriages, it
earned the nickname, "Miracle
Mile". The suburban department stores were designed
with car parks, a convenience
that attracted hordes of shoppers from the city. It was the
start of LA's decentralization.

Today, this stretch of boulevard is a shadow of its former
self, dotted with grocery shops
catering to various ethnic communities. At the eastern end, a
few Streamline Moderne relics
survive, such as the small gold-
and-black building at No. 5209,
a smaller version of the razed
Richfield Tower in Downtown.

Fortunately, the western end
of the Miracle Mile has fared
rather better. Anchoring the
corner of Fairfax Avenue, the
May Company building has a
gold and mosaic cylinder that
resembles a large perfume
bottle. With its five museums,
including LACMA *(see pp110–
13)*, the area has now become
Museum Row.

**Gold tower of the May Company
building on Wilshire Boulevard**

Petersen Automotive Museum ⑭

6060 Wilshire Blvd. **Map** 7 D4.
📞 *(213) 930-2277.* ⏰ *10am–6pm
Tue–Sun.* ● *1 Jan, Thanksgiving,
25 Dec.* 📷 🅿 💳

D<small>IORAMAS</small> and temporary
exhibitions illustrate the
evolution of the United States'
car culture *(see pp190–91)*. On
the first floor there are highly
detailed displays featuring cars
such as the 1911 American
Underslung "Stuck in the Mud"
and Earl Cooper's 1915 "White
Squadron" Stutz Racer. A 1922
Ford Model-T is shown in a
scene from a Laurel and Hardy
film and a trio of beautiful
vintage cars appear in a 1920s
street setting.

Other displays include a
1920s garage, a 1930s car
showroom, whose opulence
defied the Depression, and a
1950s drive-in restaurant.
A 1930s billboard shows how
advertising was used to boost
the popularity of the car.

Upstairs, five galleries showcase everything from hot rods
and motorcycles to vintage
classics and cars of the stars.
Vehicles that fall into the last
category are Rita Hayworth's
1953 Cadillac and Clark Gable's
Mercedes Benz.

Museum of Miniatures ⑮

5900 Wilshire Blvd. **Map** 7 E4.
📞 *(213) 937-6464.* ⏰ *10am–5pm
Tue–Sat; 11am–5pm Sun.* ● *1 Jan,
Easter Sun, 4 Jul, Thanksgiving,
25 Dec.* 📷 🅿 💳

D<small>ETAILED REPRODUCTIONS</small> by
contemporary miniaturists
of buildings, objects and
scenes are on display in this
delightful little museum. The
Kupjack Gallery exhibits
"history boxes" by the artists

Eugene and Henry Kupjack,
from a Roman banqueting hall
to a 1930s Art Deco diner. The
History Gallery contains a
collection of historical figures
by George Stuart.

Other exhibits include a
replica of London's Hampton
Court, a Biedermeier Salon
and a complete set of US first
ladies, dressed in miniature
re-creations of their inaugural
dinner ballgowns.

The museum's Petite Elite gift
shop is stocked with miniature
furniture, dolls and accessories.

Miniature Roman banquet hall

George C Page Museum of La Brea Discoveries ⑯

5801 Wilshire Blvd. **Map** 7 E4.
📞 *(213) 936-2230.* ⏰ *10am–5pm
Tue–Sun.* ● *1 Jan, Thanksgiving,
25 Dec.* 📷 *free first Tue of month.*
🅿 💳 🚻

O<small>PENED IN</small> 1976, the George
C Page Museum has a
collection of over one million
fossils that were discovered
at the La Brea Tar Pits. These
include more than 200 types
of mammals, birds, reptiles,

LA BREA TAR PITS

The tar in the La Brea Pits was formed some 35,000 years ago by oil rising to the earth's surface and gelling. Animals entering the pits to drink the water became stuck in the tar and died. Their bones were then fossilized.

For centuries the tar was used by Gabrielino Indians to waterproof baskets and boats. Later, Mexican and Spanish settlers tarred their roofs with it. In 1906 geologists discovered the largest collection of fossils from the Pleistocene Epoch ever found in one place, and the pits began to attract greater attention. The land was deeded to the county in 1916.

Models at the La Brea Tar Pits depicting how animals were trapped

plants and insects. Some of the pieces date back 40,000 years. Among the highlights are mastodons, sabre-toothed tigers, American lions and an imperial mammoth. The display of more than 400 wolf skulls shows just how much variation can occur within a single species.

The only human skeleton to have been found in the pits is that of "La Brea Woman". A hologram changes her from a skeleton to a fully fleshed person and back again.

Pit 91 has produced most of the fossils. During the summer, visitors on the viewing station can watch palaeontologists at work. Inside the museum, a glass-walled laboratory allows observation of the ongoing cleaning, identification and cataloguing of the fossils.

Craft and Folk Art Museum ⓲

5800 Wilshire Blvd. **Map** 7 E4.
((213) 937-5544. ☐ 11am–5pm Tue–Sun. ● 1 Jan, Thanksgiving, 25 Dec. 📷 ✔

THE MUSEUM'S COLLECTION has more than 3,000 folk art and craft objects from around the world, ranging from 19th-century quilts to contemporary furniture, to African masks. Those who are interested in design will enjoy the regular exhibitions on subjects such as toys, glassware and textiles.

The extensive collection of Mexican artworks includes a fine selection of the Linares family's papier-mâché pieces.

A series of exhibitions is held throughout the year and every

October the museum runs the International Festival of Masks in nearby Hancock Park.

African mask at the Craft Museum

Wiltern Theatre ⓳

3790 Wilshire Blvd. **Map** 9 D4.
((213) 380-5005. ☐ noon–6pm daily. 📷 ♿ ✔

BUILT AS A CINEMA in 1931, the Wiltern Theatre was restored in 1985 and is today a centre for the performing arts. The building's Art Deco tower and wings are faced with turquoise-glazed terracotta and its main entrance is marked by a sunburst canopy. The sun motif continues in the auditorium, where rays of low-relief skyscrapers decorate the interior ceiling.

To see inside the Wiltern Theatre visitors must buy a ticket to a show.

Mammoth skeleton at the George C Page Museum

DOWNTOWN LOS ANGELES

ONSIDERED A BACKWATER a little over a hundred years ago, Los Angeles has confounded its critics by becoming a powerful worldwide influence. The city's Spanish roots are here, at El Pueblo, where the Avila Adobe and Old Plaza Church stand as reminders of Mexican frontier days, when *rancheros* and their *señoras* strolled through the streets. To the north of El Pueblo is Chinatown, with its numerous Asian shops and restaurants. To the south, Little Tokyo is the heart of the largest Japanese-American community in North America. Downtown's business district is centred on Bunker Hill, once a wealthy neighbourhood where the city's Victorian elite lived. Today, confident office towers such as the First Interstate World Center and the Wells Fargo Center dominate the Downtown landscape. The district is also home to the Museum of Contemporary Art (MOCA) and the Music Center for the performing arts.

Detail from the Fine Arts Building on West 7th Street

SIGHTS AT A GLANCE

Historic Districts and Buildings
Angels Flight ❷
Bradbury Building ❹
Chinatown ❽
El Pueblo pp122–3 ❼
Grand Central Market ❸
Little Tokyo ❸
Los Angeles Central Library ❶
Los Angeles City Hall ⓫
Union Station ❾

Museums and Galleries
Geffen Contemporary at MOCA ⓬
Japanese American National Museum ⓮
Los Angeles Children's Museum ❿
Museum of Contemporary Art ❺

Arts Complex
Music Center ❻

GETTING THERE
The Metro Red Line stops at 7th Street/Metro Center, Pershing Square, Civic Center and Union Station. The Metro Blue Line runs between Long Beach and 7th Street/Metro Center. DASH buses also serve the district.

0 metres 500
0 yards 500

KEY
Street-by-Street map *See pp118–19*
Street-by-Street map *See pp122–3*
🚉 Amtrak station
Ⓜ Metro Red Line station
Ⓜ Metro Blue Line station

◁ **Wells Fargo Center, slicing the Downtown skyline**

Street-by-Street: Business District

Stone carving on Biltmore Hotel

THE 20TH CENTURY saw LA expand west towards the ocean, temporarily relegating Downtown to a minor role in the city. All that has changed. Today a revitalized business district has developed around Flower Street, and the pavements are once more filled with tourists and Angelenos alike. California's banking industry has its headquarters here, housed in striking skyscrapers such as the Wells Fargo Center. The revival has continued eastwards across Downtown, where jewellery, toy, food and garment wholesale industries are flourishing. A commitment to the arts has also borne fruit. The Museum of Contemporary Art (MOCA), Music Center and Los Angeles Central Library have together encouraged a thriving cultural environment that has drawn people back to the city's centre.

The Westin Bonaventure Hotel has external lifts that offer views of the business district as guests ascend to the cocktail lounge *(see p510)*.

The First Interstate World Center is a 73-storey office block, designed in 1992 by IM Pei. At 1,017 ft (310 m) it is the tallest building in Los Angeles.

Fine Arts Building

7th Street/ Metro Center

SOUTH FLOWER STREET

SOUTH HOPE STREET

WEST SIXTH STREET

WEST SEVENTH STREET

0 metres   100

0 yards   100

★ Los Angeles Central Library
The newly expanded Beaux-Arts library is decorated with carvings and inscriptions on the theme "the Light of Learning" ❶

The Oviatt Building
(1925) is a marvellous example of Art Deco styling. René Lalique made some of the glass.

The Biltmore Hotel has been one of LA's most luxurious hotels since 1923 *(see p509)*.

★ Museum of Contemporary Art
Located off California Plaza, MOCA's sandstone building was greeted with acclaim when it opened in 1986. The collection gives an exciting overview of post-1940 art ❺

LOCATOR MAP
See Street Finder, map 11

The Wells Fargo Center, the LA branch of this Californian company (*see p304*), has a museum and sculpture court, with works by artists such as Jean Dubuffet.

Angels Flight
The restored funicular runs from South Hill Street to California Plaza ❷

Pershing Square Metro station

Grand Central Market
This indoor market lies at the heart of the old theatre district ❸

Pershing Square was designated the city's first public park in 1866. The now concreted square is still a popular meeting place, and has been landscaped with trees, benches and statuary.

★ Bradbury Building
The atrium of this unassuming Victorian office block is one of the finest of its kind in the US ❹

KEY

– – – Suggested route

STAR SIGHTS

★ Bradbury Building

★ Los Angeles Central Library

★ Museum of Contemporary Art

Façade of the Los Angeles Central Library

Los Angeles Central Library ❶

630 W 5th St. **Map** 11 D4. █ *(213) 228-7000.* ◯ *10am–5:30pm Mon, Thu–Sat; noon–8pm Tue, Wed; 1–5pm Sun.* ● *public hols.* &

B UILT IN 1926, this civic treasure was struck by an arson attack in 1986. It was closed for the next seven years while a $213.9 million renovation and expansion programme was carried out. Sympathetic to the original architecture, the improvements have doubled the library's capacity to more than 2.1 million books.

The original building combines Beaux-Arts grandeur with Byzantine, Egyptian and Roman architectural elements, inscriptions and sculpture on the theme "the Light of Learning". The murals in the rotunda, painted by Dean Cornwell (1892–1960), depict the history of California and are well worth seeing.

Statue on the library wall

The attention given to detail in the new Tom Bradley wing is impressive. One example is the three atrium chandeliers, created by Therman Statom to represent the natural, ethereal and technological worlds.

The Central Library's garden is situated by the Flower Street entrance. Weary sightseers will appreciate its fountains, sculptures, shaded benches and restaurant.

A varied programme of arts events takes place within the library, including prose and poetry readings, lectures, concerts and plays.

Angels Flight ❷

Between Grand, Hill, 3rd & 4th Sts. **Map** 11 D4. █ *(213) 623-2489.* ◯ *7am–10pm daily.* ● *public hols.* 🚻 &

B ILLED AS the "shortest railway in the world", Angels Flight transported riders the 315 ft (96 m) between Hill Street and Bunker Hill for almost 70 years. Built in 1901, the funicular quickly became a familiar and much-loved method of transport. But, by 1969, Bunker Hill had sadly degenerated and was considered an eyesore. The city dismantled Angels Flight, but promised to reinstall the funicular once the area had been redeveloped. In 1996, some 27 years later, the city finally fulfilled that vow.

Grand Central Market ❸

317 S Broadway. **Map** 11 E4. █ *(213) 624-2378.* ◯ *9am–6pm Mon–Sat; 10am–5:30pm Sun.* ● *1 Jan, Thanksgiving, 25 Dec.* &

A NGELENOS have been coming to this vibrant indoor bazaar since 1917. Today, more than 40 stallholders operate inside the marketplace. Neatly arranged mounds of bargain-priced fresh fruits and vegetables line the many produce stalls, and friendly stallholders frequently offer free samples of fruit.

Almost all the signs are in English and Spanish. The market's predominantly Latin American clientele come here to buy exotic products from their home countries, such as fresh Nogales cacti and beans from El Salvador. The seafood stands are filled with an array of fish caught in the waters off Southern California. Goat heads and tripe are offered alongside the more familiar cuts of meat at the butcher stalls. Herb stands offer a range of homeopathic alternatives for minor ills. Amid all this bustle, fragrant aromas of powdered chillies, herbs and spicy foods waft through the air.

Among the many cafés and food stands in the market is China Café, which has been serving its popular chow mein since the 1930s. At Chapalita Tortilleria, visitors can enjoy watching the rickety assembly-line machine turn *masa* (corn flour dough) into tortillas and then partake of the free samples on the counter. Mexican stalls, such as Ana Maria, sell tacos and burritos, which are filled with every manner of meat and seafood.

Venturing from the market onto Broadway, you will find yourself on the main shopping street of Los Angeles's Hispanic community. Before World War II, this was the movie district, with extravagant cinemas and fashionable shops. Today, most of the cinemas have either closed down or are being used for religious meetings conducted in Spanish. The street has a great deal of energy – the feel is that of Mexico City or Lima, Peru – but tourists should be wary of pickpockets.

China Café in the market

Atrium of the Bradbury Building

Bradbury Building ❹

304 S Broadway. **Map** 11 E4.
📞 *(213) 626-1893.* 🕐 *9am–5pm daily.* ♿ *from 3rd St.*

THE BRADBURY BUILDING was designed by architectural draughtsman George Herbert Wyman in 1893. It is one of the few surviving Victorian structures in LA. Although the red façade is simple, the atrium is outstanding, with its lacework of wrought-iron railings, oak panelling, glazed brick walls, two open-cage lifts and a glass roof. It is the only office building in Los Angeles to be designated a National Historic Landmark. Visitors may get a feeling of *déjà vu* – the building is a popular film location, with Ridley Scott's *Blade Runner* (1982) just one of the movies shot here.

Museum of Contemporary Art ❺

250 S Grand Ave. **Map** 11 D4.
📞 *(213) 621-2766.* 🕐 *11am–5pm Tue–Sun (until 8pm Thu).* ⬤ *1 Jan, Thanksgiving, 25 Dec.* 🎟 *free 5–8pm Thu.* ♿

RATED BY the American Institute of Architects as one of the ten best works of architecture in the US, this museum's building makes as interesting a statement as any

piece in the collection. The Museum of Contemporary Art (MOCA) is an intriguing combination of pyramids, cylinders and cubes, designed in 1986 by Japanese architect Arata Isozaki. Its warm Indian sandstone walls, which sit on a red granite foundation, are in pleasing contrast to the cool tones of the district's surrounding skyscrapers.

The gallery area lies off the sunken entrance courtyard and is reached via a sweeping staircase. Four of the seven galleries are naturally lit from pyramid-shaped skylights that punctuate the roofline.

Founded in 1979, the Museum of Contemporary Art has quickly amassed a respected selection of post-1940 work from artists such as Piet Mondrian, Jackson Pollock, Louise Nevelson and Julian Schnabel. Added weight is given by the Panza Collection of 80 works of Pop Art and Abstract Expressionism by artists such as Robert Rauschenberg, Mark Rothko and Claes Oldenburg. In 1995, MOCA acquired the 2,100-print Freidus Collection of photographs, which traces the development of documentary photography in the United States from the 1940s through to the 1980s. The collection includes works by Diane Arbus and Robert Frank.

MOCA stands at the northern end of the 11-acre (4.5-ha)

Coca Cola Plan (1958) by Robert Rauschenberg

California Plaza. This vast development funded the creation of MOCA, donating 1.5 per cent of its budget, as stipulated by LA law, to public art. The spectacular fountain at the centre of the plaza repeats its synchronized programme every 20 minutes. The finale drops a 10,000-gal (45,500-litre) wave that washes over the fountain edge.

Music Center ❻

135 N Grand Ave. **Map** 11 E3.
📞 *(213) 972-7211.* 🎟 ♿ **Dorothy Chandler Pavilion box office** 🕐 *10am–6pm Mon–Sat.* **Mark Taper Forum & Ahmanson Theatre box offices** 🕐 *noon–8pm Tue–Sun.*

THIS PERFORMING arts complex is situated at the northern end of Bunker Hill. The Dorothy Chandler Pavilion is named after the wife of the former publisher of the *Los Angeles Times*. It is host to the annual Academy Awards ceremony, the home of the LA Music Center Opera, the LA Master Chorale and, from autumn to spring, the LA Philharmonic. The Ahmanson Theatre has moveable walls to adjust the auditorium size and stages Broadway plays. The Mark Taper Forum has won almost every theatrical prize in the US. It presents first-class plays such as Tony Kushner's *Angels in America*.

Music Center plaza and fountain leading to the Mark Taper Forum

Street-by-Street: El Pueblo ⓘ

EL PUEBLO DE LA REINA DE LOS ANGELES, the oldest part of the city, was founded in 1781 by Felipe de Neve, the Spanish governor of California. Today, El Pueblo is a State Historic Monument. The shops and stalls along Olvera Street sell colourful Mexican dresses, leather *buraches* (sandals), *piñatas* (straw animals) and snacks like *churros*, a Spanish-Mexican fried bread. During its various festivals El Pueblo is ablaze with colour and sound. The Blessing of the Animals, *Cinco de Mayo* (5 May), the Mexican Independence Day fiesta (13–15 September) and the candlelight procession of *Las Posadas* (16–24 December) are all celebrated with passion *(see pp32–5)*.

Statue of LA's founder, Felipe de Neve

★ **Old Plaza Church**
The Annunciation *(1981)*, a mosaic by Isabel Piczek, is on the façade of the city's oldest church.

Pico House
California's last Mexican governor, Pío Pico, constructed the three-storey Pico House in 1870. The Italianate building was for many years the area's finest hotel.

Site of the first cemetery in Los Angeles.

Plaza
A wrought-iron bandstand is set in the middle of the plaza. Nearby is a list of the first 44 settlers and a statue of Felipe de Neve.

NORTH MAI
NORTH LOS ANGELE
ARCADIA STREET

STAR SIGHTS

★ Avila Adobe

★ Old Plaza Church

KEY

– – – Suggested route

Firehouse

★ **Avila Adobe**
The Avila Adobe is the oldest existing house in Los Angeles. It is furnished as it would have been in the late 1840s.

LOCATOR MAP
See Street Finder, map 11

David Alfaro Siqueiros' mural, *Tropical America*, was created in 1932.

HOLLYWOOD AND WEST HOLLYWOOD

DOWNTOWN LOS ANGELES

Sepulveda House

Plaza Methodist Church

0 metres 50
0 yards 50

Olvera Steet
This pedestrianized street was preserved in the 1920s as a Mexican market-place following a campaign by local civic leader Christine Sterling.

Chinatown ❽

Map 11 F2. 🛈 *977 N Broadway, Suite E (213 617-0396).*

THE CHINESE first came to California during the Gold Rush *(see pp44–5)* to work in the mines and build the rail-ways. Confronted by prejudice, they developed tightknit com-munities. LA's first Chinatown was established in 1870 on the present-day site of Union Station *(see p124)*. It was re-located about 900 yds (820 m) northwards in the mid-1930s. Today it is the home of over 12,000 people, who live and work in this colourful district.

The ornate East Gate on North Broadway leads into Gin Ling Way and the New Chinatown Central Plaza. This pedestrian precinct is lined with brightly painted buildings that have exaggerated pagoda-style roofs. Here, import shops sell everything from exquisite jade jewellery and antiques to cheap trinkets.

In the surrounding streets, the buildings are more bland, but tantalizing restaurants offer all manner of Chinese food, from dim sum (filled, steamed or grilled dumplings, *see p540*) to spicy Szechuan dishes.

Although on a smaller scale than the celebrations in San Francisco *(see p35)*, LA has its own Chinese New Year Parade in early February. The festiv-ities include dragon and lion dancers, who snake through the district's streets accom-panied by drums, cymbals, floats and firecrackers.

Restaurant in Chinatown, topped by a pagoda

Unique blending of architectural styles on Union Station's façade

Union Station ❾

800 N Alameda St. **Map** 11 F3.
☎ *(213) 683-6979; (800) 872-7245.*
◷ *24 hours daily.* ♿

D ATING FROM 1939, this grand
railway passenger termin-
us was the last of its kind to be
built in the United States. The
exterior is a successful merging
of Spanish Mission, Moorish
and Streamline Moderne styles
(see pp26–8). The tiles edging
the interior walls, the inlaid
marble designs of the floors
and the filigree work over the
windows and doorways all
use Spanish motifs.

   The vast concourse, with its
52-ft (15.8-m) high roof, will
be familiar to any fan of 1940s
films – stars were frequently
photographed here arriving in
Los Angeles. In recent years it
has been the location for several movies, including Sydney
Pollack's *The Way We Were*
(1973) and Barry Levinson's

Bugsy (1991). Today the station
is quieter, but there are still
daily departures to Chicago,
Seattle and San Diego.

Los Angeles Children's Museum ❿

310 N Main St. **Map** 11 E4. ☎ *(213)
687-8800.* ◷ *Sep–Jun: 10am–5pm
Sat & Sun, public hols; Jul–Aug:
11:30am–5pm Mon–Fri, 10am–5pm
Sat & Sun.* ● *public hols.* 📷 ♿ 🎫

T HIS IMAGINATIVE and stimulating museum is guided
by the principle that children
learn best by doing. Opened
in 1979, it quickly became a
popular family destination.

   Some 20 hands-on activities
are linked by a series of ramps.
Called the "discovery maze",
the system was designed by
architect Frank Gehry. One of
the favourite exhibits is the

Videozone. This brings out
the performer in children, as
they sing, dance and tell
stories on video. In Sticky
City, large, brightly coloured
foam-and-Velcro blocks cling
to each other, the walls and
even the participants as they
build skyscrapers, mountains
and tunnels.

   Children between 2 and 12
years old enjoy role-playing as
the driver of a bus in the City
Streets exhibit. In the Cave of
the Dinosaurs, young visitors
can experience primitive life
in their own cave, with dinosaur sounds and holograms.

   Art activities and a range of
other events take place on a
regular basis.

Los Angeles City Hall ⓫

200 N Spring St. **Map** 11 E4. ☎ *(213)
485-2121.* ◷ *8am–5pm Mon–Fri.*
● *public hols.* ♿ *from Main St.*
🎫 *advance reservations required.*

U NTIL 1957, this 28-storey
structure was the tallest in
Downtown – all others were
limited to 12 storeys. When it
was built in 1928, sand from
every Californian county, and
water from each of the state's
21 missions, was added to the
City Hall's mortar.

   Today City Hall is dwarfed
by surrounding skyscrapers,
but its distinctive tower is still
one of Los Angeles's most

Entrance to Los Angeles Children's Museum

familiar landmarks. Among its many film and television roles it has been the location for the *Daily Planet*, Clark Kent's place of work in the television series *Superman*.

Inside, the rotunda has a beautiful inlaid-tile dome and excellent acoustics. The dome is decorated with eight figures showing the building's major concerns: education, health, law, art, service, government, protection and trust.

Organized groups who take the 45-minute tour of the City Hall can ascend to an observation area in the tower, which has been restored after damage by the 1994 Northridge earthquake *(see p53)*. From here there are panoramic views across the city.

Rotunda of LA City Hall

Geffen Contemporary at MOCA **⑫**

152 N Central Ave. **Map** 11 F4. **[** (213) 621-2766. ⬤ 11am–5pm *Tue–Sun (until 8pm Thu).* ⬤ 1 Jan, Thanksgiving, 25 Dec. ⬤ ⬤

IN 1983, this old police garage was used as a temporary exhibition space until MOCA's California Plaza facilities were

completed *(see p121)*. Frank Gehry's renovations were so successful that the warehouse became a permanent fixture of the Los Angeles art scene. Exhibitions change regularly and often include highlights from MOCA's collection.

Little Tokyo **⑬**

Map 11 E4. **🛈** 244 S San Pedro St. (213 628-2725).

LYING BETWEEN First, Third, Los Angeles and Alameda streets, Little Tokyo has more than 200,000 visitors who throng its Japanese markets, shops, restaurants and temples.

The first Japanese settled here in 1884. Today, the heart of the area is the Japanese American Cultural and Community Center at No. 244 South San Pedro Street, from which cultural activities and festivals such as Nisei Week *(see p33)* are organized. The centre's fan-shaped Japan America Theater is often a venue for performers from Japan, such as the Grand Kabuki.

The Japanese Village Plaza at No. 335 East Second Street has been built in the style of a rural Japanese village, with blue roof tiles, exposed wood frames and paths landscaped with pools and rocks. A traditional fire watchtower marks the plaza's First Street entrance. Shops include Enbun Market, one of Little Tokyo's oldest businesses, and the Mikawaya Candy Store. Off San Pedro Street, Onizuka Street offers more up-market shops.

Central Avenue entrance to the Japanese American Museum

Japanese American National Museum **⑭**

369 E 1st St. **Map** 11 F4. **[** (213) 625-0414. ⬤ 10am–5pm Tue–Sun (until 8pm Thu). ⬤ 1 Jan, Thanksgiving, 25 Dec. ⬤ ⬤ ⬤

THE FORMER Nishi Hongwanji Buddhist Temple is now a museum. In 1925, architect Edgar Cline designed a building with a dual personality. The First Street entrance has an unremarkable brick façade, but the ceremonial entrance, on Central Avenue, mixes oriental and Egyptian motifs. The concrete canopy is modelled after the gateway to a Kyoto temple, and the brick pilasters have Egyptian-style capitals made of terracotta.

The museum is committed to preserving the history of Japanese-Americans in the US and has the largest collection of Japanese-American memorabilia in the world. Because most Japanese-Americans' property was lost when they were interned during World War II, the collection has simple, everyday items, such as newspapers, luggage and clothing. An archive of camp records is available alongside camp mementos that include crafts and furniture.

Temporary exhibitions are hosted by the museum on subjects such as the "Issei Pioneers", "America's Concentration Camps" and "Japanese-American Soldiers". A series of workshops is also offered.

Onizuka Street in Little Tokyo, looking towards Los Angeles City Hall

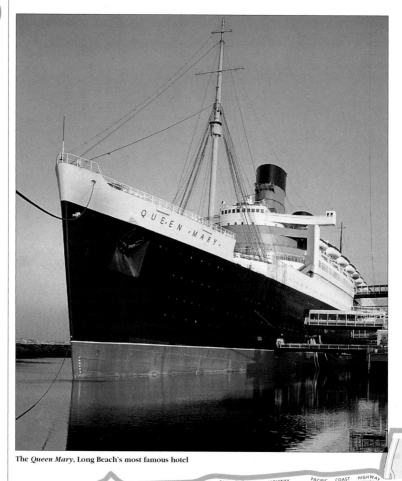

The *Queen Mary*, Long Beach's most famous hotel

LONG BEACH AND PALOS VERDES

THE OCEAN is the unifying force of this disparate region, where waves crash against the cliffs of the Palos Verdes Peninsula and tankers head for the busy ports of Los Angeles and Long Beach. The peninsula, a magnificent stretch of coastline, is an affluent area, with mansion houses and stables set amid the rolling

Statue in Ports O'Call Village

hills. On its southeastern side, working-class San Pedro is home to the Port of Los Angeles as well as generations of fishermen. The big city in the area – the fifth-largest in the state – is Long Beach. Aptly named for its 5.5-mile (9-km) expanse of white sand, this community has long attracted those who love the ocean. Its most famous landmark is the liner *Queen Mary*.

SIGHTS AT A GLANCE

Historic Ships
Queen Mary pp130–31 **5**

Districts
Long Beach **1**
Naples **4**
Ports O'Call Village **7**
San Pedro **10**

Historic Buildings
Rancho Los Alamitos **3**
Rancho Los Cerritos **2**

Modern Architecture
Wayfarers Chapel **11**

Parks and Gardens
Point Fermin Park **9**
South Coast Botanic Garden **12**

Museums
Cabrillo Marine Aquarium **8**
Los Angeles Maritime Museum **6**

GETTING THERE
The Metro Blue Line connects Long Beach to downtown Los Angeles. The busy port is well served by freeways that link it to the rest of the city. A free shuttle bus, the Runabout, makes frequent journeys between downtown Long Beach, Shoreline Village, the *Queen Mary* and the Catalina Island terminus *(see pp232–3)*. Cyclists can take the Oceanside Bike Path *(see p168)* from Long Beach to Naples.

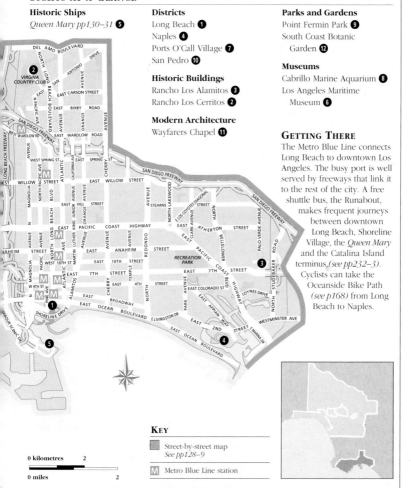

KEY

Street-by-street map
See pp128–9

M Metro Blue Line station

0 kilometres 2

0 miles 2

Street-by-Street: Long Beach ❶

Shoreline Village sign

W͟ITH PALM TREES and the ocean as a backdrop, downtown Long Beach is a mixture of carefully restored buildings and modern glass high-rises. At its heart, Pine Avenue still retains the early Midwestern charm that gave the city its nickname of "Iowa by the Sea". The trendy atmosphere attracts locals, who come to relax, enjoy a cup of espresso and sample some of the best food in the area. Nearby, Long Beach Convention and Entertainment Center was once the site of the Pike Amusement Park, famous for its roller coaster. Now the Terrace Theater's respected music and dance programmes draw the crowds. Beside the ocean, the shops and restaurants in Shoreline Village offer views of the *Queen Mary*.

Farmers and Merchants Bank Tower
When erected in 1922, this terracotta building was Long Beach's first skyscraper. Its hall is a fine example of period styling.

Transit Mall Metro station

Long Beach Municipal Auditorium Mural
This 1938 mural of a day at the beach was originally housed in the Municipal Auditorium. It was moved in 1979 when that building was demolished to make way for the Terrace Theater.

The Promenade is the site of Long Beach's farmer's market. Every Friday the street is filled with stalls selling fruit, vegetables and crafts.

The 1929 Mediterranean-style Ocean Center Building was the start of the Pike Amusement Park's Walk of a Thousand Lights.

KEY
− − − Suggested route

STAR SIGHTS
★ Pine Avenue
★ Shoreline Village

★ **Pine Avenue**
The centre of downtown Long Beach, Pine Avenue is lined with shops, cafés and restaurants. Some of these businesses are housed in historic buildings, such as the 1903 Masonic Temple at No. 230.

Convention and Entertainment Center
This newly-expanded complex includes the Terrace Theater, the home of Long Beach's symphony orchestra and opera company.

1st Street Metro station

AROUND DOWNTOWN

LONG BEACH AND PALOS VERDES

LOCATOR MAP

The Breakers (1925), an elegant former hotel, now houses senior citizens.

Planet Ocean (1992)
Recognized as the world's largest mural, artist Wyland's Planet Ocean *covers the 116,000-sq-ft (11,000-sq-m) surface of Long Beach Arena with life-size sea creatures.*

The Hyatt Regency Hotel adjoins the Convention Center *(see p511).*

★ **Shoreline Village**
This waterfront complex of restaurants and shops boasts a 1906 Looff merry-go-round. Shoreline Village is a good place to view the Queen Mary *(see pp130–31).*

The tallship *Californian* is docked at Shoreline Village. Both short and long cruises are available.

0 metres   200

0 yards   200

Rancho Los Cerritos ❷

4600 Virginia Rd. 📞 (310) 570-1755.
🕐 1–5pm Wed–Sun. ⬤ 1 Jan,
Easter Sun, Thanksgiving, 25 Dec.
♿ 📷 Sat & Sun only.

R ANCHO LOS CERRITOS was
once part of a 300,000-
acre (121,400-ha) land grant,
given between 1784 and 1790
to Spanish soldier Manuel
Nieto. Mission San Gabriel
reclaimed nearly half of the
property. The rest was left to
Nieto's children on his death
in 1804. In 1834 it was split
into five ranches.

In 1844 Los Cerritos was
bought by John Temple, who
built the adobe ranch house.
Following droughts in the early
1860s he decided to sell to the
firm Flint, Bixby & Co.

Over the years, most of the
ranch was sold, but the house
and surrounding 5 acres (2 ha)
of land remained in the Bixby
family until it was bought by
the City of Long Beach in 1955.

Today, Rancho Los Cerritos
is run as a museum, focusing
on those who lived here from
1840–1940. The Monterey-style
house (see p26) is furnished to
reflect the late 1870s.

Rancho Los Alamitos ❸

6400 Bixby Hill Rd. 📞 (310) 431-
3541. 🕐 1–5pm Wed–Sun.
⬤ 1 Jan, Easter Sun, Thanksgiving,
25 Dec. **Donation.** ♿ 📷

R ANCHO LOS ALAMITOS stands
on a mesa inhabited since
AD 500. In 1790 it formed part
of the Manuel Nieto land grant.

**Cactus Garden in the grounds of
Rancho Los Alamitos**

The house was built in 1806,
making it one of Southern
California's oldest dwellings.
It changed hands frequently
during the 19th century, until

Queen Mary ❺

Pier J, 1126 Queens Hwy. **Road
map** inset A. 📞 (310) 435-3511.
🕐 10am–6pm daily. 🍴 ♿ 📷
See **Where to Stay** p511 and **Where
to Eat** p547.

N AMED AFTER the wife of
British King George V,
this liner set new standards in
ocean travel with its maiden
voyage of 27 May 1936. The
jewel in the crown of the
Cunard White Star Line, the
Queen Mary made weekly
trips between Southampton,
England and New York City.

Although the second- and
third-class quarters may look
small next to the grandeur of

**Royal Jubilee Week, 1935 by AR Thomson,
above the bar in the Observation Lounge**

the first-class rooms, they
were considered to be chic
and spacious for their time.

On her five-day
voyages, the liner
carried an average
of 3,000 passengers
and crew members.
These used the two
swimming pools,
two chapels, syna-
gogue, gymnasium,
ballroom and child-
rens' playrooms.
Anyone who was
anyone sailed on the
Queen Mary, from
royalty to Hollywood stars.

From 1939 to 1946, the liner
was converted into a troopship

Sir Winston's
Piano Bar

Queen's Salon

Chelsea Restaurant

Sir Winston's
Restaurant

Royal
Salon

Wedding Chapel

Britannia Salon

Verandah Grill

Grand Salon

it was bought by the Bixby family in 1881. In 1906 Fred and Florence Bixby moved into the property and began to shape the house and garden.

The ranch was given to the City of Long Beach in 1968, to be developed as an historic and educational facility. Inside, the house is furnished as it was in the 1920s and 1930s. The elegant grounds are a rare example of a pioneer garden.

Naples ❹

Road map inset A. 🚂 *Long Beach.* ℹ️ *One World Trade Center, Suite 300 (310 436-3645).* **Gondola Getaway** *5437 E Ocean Blvd (310 433-9595).*

I N 1903, developer Arthur Parson began creating his own version of the city of Naples in Italy, complete with winding streets and waterways spanned by small bridges (even though the original does not have canals and gondolas).

Taking heed of the mistakes made by Abbot Kinney in Venice *(see p76)*, Arthur Parson designed his canals so that the Pacific Ocean's tidal flows would keep them clean.

Finished in the late 1920s, this most charming of Long Beach neighbourhoods is actually three islands in the middle of Alamitos Bay. An eclectic architectural mix of shingled, Mission Revival, Victorian and Arts and Crafts houses *(see pp26–9)* line the

Canal in residential Naples, with boats moored alongside the private jettys

Italian-named streets. The Rivo Alto Canal, the largest in the network, surrounds the Colonnade Park, which is in the centre of Naples. For a full exploration of the islands, meander through the streets on foot. Alternatively, book Gondala Getaway two weeks in advance for a cruise on an authentic Venetian gondola.

called the *Grey Ghost*, carrying more than 800,000 soldiers during her wartime career. At the end of the war, she transported more than 22,000 war brides and children to the US during "Operation Diaper".

In 1967, after 1,001 transatlantic crossings, the liner was bought by the City of Long Beach. She was permanently docked for use as a hotel and tourist attraction.

Detail inside the ship's Grand Salon

Today, visitors can view part of the original Engine Room, examples of the different travel accommodations and an exhibition on the war years. Many of the original Art Deco features, created by more than 30 artists, still decorate the interior. Open to the public for dining, the Grand Salon and Observation Lounge are fine examples of period styling.

Dual set of brass steering wheels in the *Queen Mary*'s wheelhouse

W6RO Amateur Radio Station

Bridge Wheelhouse

Crow's Nest

Officers' Quarters

QUEEN MARY

Promenade Café and Bar

Piccadilly Circus

Observation Lounge

Relaxing on Redondo Beach, LA *(see p62)* ▷

Los Angeles Maritime Museum ⑥

Berth 84, 6th St, San Pedro. **Road map** inset A. 🄲 *(310) 548-7618.* 🄾 *10am–5pm Tue–Sun.* ● *Thanksgiving, 25 Dec.* **Donation.** ♿

Housed in a restored ferry terminal building, the Los Angeles Maritime Museum contains an array of nautical paintings and memorabilia. A wooden figurehead of British Queen Victoria is just one of the museum's artifacts. An extensive model ship collection includes an 18-ft (5.5-m) scale model of the *Titanic*. Begun in 1971 by a 14-year-old boy, it took five years to complete. Also on display is the bow and bridge of US Navy cruiser USS *Los Angeles*. Early 20th-century Monterey fishing boats (*see p493*) can be seen in the museum's dock.

Figurehead of Queen Victoria

Ports O'Call Village ⑦

Berth 77, San Pedro. **Road map** inset A. 🄲 *(310) 831-0287.* 🄾 *11am–7pm Sun–Thu; 11am–8pm Fri & Sat.*

Ports O'Call Village is a pastiche of many different seaports from all around the world. Building styles range from a 19th-century New England fishing village, to a Mediterranean harbour, to a Mexican town.

The village's 75 shops and 15 restaurants are linked by cobblestone walkways. Street entertainers frequent this popular area during the summer. A number of fisheries supply freshly caught fish, which can be cooked and served to you on the premises. From the dockside boardwalk visitors can watch the huge cargo ships and cruise liners sail by. Daily harbour cruises tour the inner harbour, coastguard station, marina, freighter operations and scrapping yards. Tours to Catalina Island (*see pp232–3*) and winter whale-watching tours are also available.

Street scene in the picturesque Ports O'Call Village

Cabrillo Marine Aquarium ⑧

3720 Stephen White Drive, San Pedro. **Road map** inset A. 🄲 *(310) 548-7562.* 🄾 *noon–5pm Tue–Fri; 10am–5pm Sat & Sun.* ● *Thanksgiving, 25 Dec.* 🄿 *for parking only.* ♿ 🅿

Designed by architect Frank Gehry and surrounded by a geometric chain-link fence, the Cabrillo Marine Aquarium houses one of the largest collections of Southern California marine life. Sharks, moray eels and rays thrill thousands of visitors each year. The exhibition hall includes interpretive displays that explain the typical plants and animals of the region. It is divided into three environments – rocky shores, beaches and mudflats, and open ocean.

An outdoor rock pool tank contains sea cucumbers, sea anemones, starfish and sea urchins that visitors are permitted to touch. This small museum also boasts 14,150 gallons (64,400 litres) of circulating sea water, as well as a tidal tank that allows viewers to see below a wave. Another exhibit shows how human activities have altered Los Angeles Harbor.

The beautifully maintained clapboard Point Fermin Lighthouse

Point Fermin Park ⑨

Gaffey St & Paseo del Mar, San Pedro. **Road map** inset A. 🄲 *(310) 548-7756 (310 832-4444 for whale-watching tours Dec– Apr).* 🄾 *daily.*

This tranquil 37-acre (15-ha) park sits on a bluff overlooking the Pacific Ocean. Between January and March, migrating grey whales can be spotted offshore and, on a clear day, there are views of Catalina Island. The charming Eastlake-style lighthouse dates from 1874. Its bricks and timber were shipped around Cape Horn. The lighthouse originally used oil lamps that emitted approximately 2,100 candlepower. They were replaced by an electric lamp in 1925.

San Pedro ⑩

Road map inset A. ✈ *LAX, 15 miles (24 km) NW of San Pedro.* 🚌 *MTA.* ℹ *390 W 7th St (310 832-7272).*

Famous for the Worldport LA, blue-collar pride and a tradition of family fishermen, San Pedro ("San Peedro" to the locals) has a strong Eastern European and Mediterranean flavour. The harbour is the nation's busiest import-export site and an important link with the Pacific Rim. The houses are tiny compared to those in Palos Verdes, but this is a very important centre of industry.

Korean Friendship Bell in Angels Gate Park, San Pedro

In Angels Gate Park, at the end of Gaffey Street, there is a Korean Friendship Bell, given to the United States in 1976 by South Korea.

Steps leading to the hilltop Wayfarers Chapel

Wayfarers Chapel ⓫

5755 Palos Verdes Drive S, Rancho Palos Verdes. **Road map** inset A.
[(310) 377-1650. ◯ call ahead (frequently booked for weddings).
Gardens ◯ daily. 🔥

THIS GLASS and redwood-framed chapel sits on a hilltop above the ocean. From the street below, all that can be seen is a thin stone and concrete tower rising from the greenery.

When the architect Lloyd Wright (son of Frank Lloyd Wright) designed the chapel

in 1949, he tried to create a natural place of worship, surrounding it by trees. Today, its charm makes it a popular site for weddings.

The chapel is sponsored by the Swedenborgian church, which follows the teaching of Emanuel Swedenborg, the 18th-century Swedish theologian and mystic.

South Coast Botanic Garden ⓬

26300 S Crenshaw Blvd, Rolling Hills Estates. **Road map** inset A. [(310) 544-6815. ◯ 9am–5pm daily.
● 25 Dec. 🎫 🔥 🗹

THIS 87-ACRE (35-ha) garden was created on top of some 3,175,000 tonnes of waste that were dumped here from 1956 to 1960. Prior to that, the area was the location of a mine for

algae-rich diatomaceous earth. Today, gas formed underground as a result of the waste decomposing is collected and used to generate electricity.

The garden is a study in land reclamation, with an emphasis on drought-resistant landscaping. Specimens from all the continents except Antarctica are planted within the grounds.

In the Herb Garden plants are divided into three main categories: fragrant, medicinal and culinary. The Rose Garden has more than 1,600 roses, including old-fashioned and miniature roses, floribundas, hybrid teas and grandifloras.

One of the most innovative areas is the Garden for the Senses. Here, plants are chosen for their extraordinary qualities of colour, smell or touch. Some of the flowerbeds are raised, making them more accessible to those with disabilities.

Children's Garden in the South Coast Botanic Garden

AROUND DOWNTOWN

FROM THE FREEWAYS, *it is hard to appreciate the many treasures that lie within Los Angeles's sprawl. But a short drive beyond the central sights to nearby areas can be surprisingly rewarding. Up-market Pasadena, with its delightful Old Town, also has the excellent Norton Simon Museum as well as the Huntington Library, Art Collections and Botanical Gardens.*

Northeast of Downtown are the Heritage Square Museum with its historic buildings, Lummis House and the Southwest Museum, one of the finest collections of Native American artifacts in the country. Just north of Hollywood, hilly Griffith Park offers precious open spaces for picnicking, hiking and pony trekking, as well as the Los Angeles Zoo, Griffith Observatory and the Autry Museum of Western Heritage.

Nearby, Universal Studios offers tours of their film backlots as well as theme park rides. Universal is one of four major studios based at Burbank, which has replaced Hollywood as the new headquarters for the film and television industries. Further north in the broad, flat San Fernando Valley, Mission San Fernando Rey de España provides an historical insight into California's origins.

South of Downtown, the Natural History Museum of Los Angeles County and the California Museum of Science and Industry are among the top attractions at Exposition Park, along with the stately buildings of the University of Southern California.

For sheer scenic delight and outstanding views over the city and San Fernando Valley, twisting mountainous Mulholland Drive is hard to beat.

Tranquil Japanese Garden at the Huntington Botanical Gardens

◁ Monument to astronomers outside the Griffith Observatory

Exploring Around Downtown

THE OUTLYING AREAS of Los
Angeles contain a vast range
of museums, galleries, historic
buildings and parks. A little
forward planning is necessary,
however, to make the best use
of time. The Heritage Square and
Southwest museums are easily
visited on the way to Pasadena.
While Universal Studios needs a
day to itself, other studio tours in
Burbank can be combined with
a trip to Griffith Park (a good
spot to see the Hollywood sign)
or to Mission San Fernando Rey
de España. Get an early morning
start at the Flower Market before
tackling the three museums at
Exposition Park, or take a trip
east to see the Watts Towers in
between museum visits.

SIGHTS AT A GLANCE

Districts

Historic Streets and Buildings

Museums and Galleries

Parks and Gardens

Shopping Areas

Sports Venues

Film Studios

0 kilometres   5

0 miles   5

Los Angeles Memorial Coliseum and Downtown
skyline viewed from Exposition Park

View of San Fernando Valley from Mulholland Drive

San Fernando Valley ❶

Road map inset A. ✈ *Burbank-Glendale-Pasadena, 20 miles (32 km) SE of San Fernando.* 🚌 *MTA.* ℹ *519 S Branch Blvd, San Fernando (818 361-1184).*

T HE CITY OF LOS ANGELES is split into two distinct halves by the Santa Monica Mountains *(see pp58–9)*. To the north, the San Fernando Valley spreads out in a seemingly endless vista of neat houses, freeways and shopping malls, such as the Sherman Oaks Galleria *(see p166)*. Residents south of the mountains tend to dismiss "the Valley", as they call it, as it is more smoggy and noticeably hotter in the summer.

In the 19th century, the San Fernando Valley was made up of ranches, orange groves and non-irrigated farms. With the completion of the LA Aqueduct in 1913 *(see pp192–3)*, the city was ensured a plentiful water supply. As a result, the Valley was quickly developed into a mass of suburbs. Today, more than a million people live in this area of Los Angeles, which encompasses only 177 sq miles (460 sq km).

On 17 January 1994, San Fernando Valley was at the epicentre of a devastating earthquake, which measured 6.8 on the Richter Scale *(see pp20–21)*. The area was also badly damaged by the February 1971 earthquake.

Mission San Fernando Rey de España ❷

15151 San Fernando Mission Blvd, Mission Hills. **Road map** inset A. 📞 *(818) 361-0186.* ⏲ *9am–5pm daily.* ● *Thanksgiving, 25 Dec.* 🅿 ♿ *grounds only.* 📷

O NE OF THE 21 Franciscan missions in California *(see pp42–3)*, San Fernando Rey de España was founded in 1797 and named after King Ferdinand III of Spain. The present church is an exact replica of the original, which was completely destroyed in the 1971 earthquake. The *convento* (living quarters) has a 21-arch portico, and is the largest mission building still standing in California. A tour of the complex offers an insight into the early days of Spanish rule, when the monks and Native Americans worked together to make the mission self-sufficent.

Mission altar detail

Mulholland Drive ❸

Off Hwys 1 & 27, from Hollywood Fwy to Leo Carrillo State Beach. **Map** 1 C2. ℹ *Chamber of Commerce, 23805 Stuart Ranch Rd, Ste 100 (310 456-9025).*

M ULHOLLAND DRIVE, one of the most famous roads in Los Angeles, runs for nearly 50 miles (80 km) from north Hollywood to the Malibu coast *(see pp60–61)*. As it winds along the ridge of the Santa Monica Mountains, the route has spectacular views across the city, San Fernando Valley and some of LA's most exclusive houses. Its spirit was captured in David Hockney's painting of the area, which hangs in LACMA *(see p111)*.

The road was named after William Mulholland *(see p192)*. Although better known for his work on the LA Aqueduct, he oversaw the completion of Mulholland Drive in 1924.

Burbank ❹

Road map inset A. ✈ *Burbank-Glendale-Pasadena.* 🚌 *MTA.* ℹ *PO Box 8549, Universal City (818 766-7572). See **Entertainment in Los Angeles** pp164–5.*

S INCE 1915, when Universal Studios moved here *(see pp142–5)*, Burbank has been competing with Hollywood as the true centre of the Los Angeles film industry. Today there are four major studios in the area: Universal, Disney, NBC and Warner Bros.

The Disney studios are closed to the public, but the

Mission San Fernando Rey de España in the Mission Hills

Warner Bros Studios in Burbank

building, designed by Michael Graves, can be seen from Alameda Avenue. Its fanciful façade incorporates the Seven Dwarfs as pillars supporting the pediment *(see p69)*.

Next door, at NBC, *The Tonight Show* and many other television programmes are recorded before a live studio audience. Visitors are offered a 70-minute tour of the wardrobe area, production studios and *The Tonight Show* set.

Nearby, at the Warner Bros lot, small groups can take the 2-hour VIP Tour. It includes the backlot, sound stages, craft and technical areas. Visitors may also view the sets of the television series *Friends* and *ER*, subject to availability. The minimum entrance age is ten.

Universal Studios ❺

See pp142 – 5.

Hollywood Sign ❻

Mt Cahuenga, above Hollywood.
ℹ *Hollywood Visitors Information Center, 6541 Hollywood Blvd (213 689-8822).*

THE HOLLYWOOD SIGN is an internationally recognized symbol of the movie business. Set high up in the Hollywood Hills, it is now a protected historic site. It is visible for miles from many parts of Los Angeles, but it is not possible for the public to reach the sign itself as there is no legitimate trail leading up to the 45-ft (13-m) tall letters.

Erected in 1923, it originally advertised the Hollywoodland housing development of the former *LA Times* publisher Harry Chandler *(see p121)*. The "land" was removed in 1949. Nearly 30 years later, donors pledged $27,000 per letter for a new sign. It has been the scene of one suicide – that of disappointed would-be actress Peg Entwhistle, who jumped off the "H" in 1932 – and numerous prank respellings, such as "Hollyweed", acknowledging the more lenient marijuana laws of the 1970s, "UCLA" during a football game and "Perotwood" for the 1992 presidential election.

Hollyhock House ❼

4800 Hollywood Blvd. 📞 *(213) 913-4157.* ⏰ *noon– 4pm Tue –Sun (last admission 3pm).* ⬤ *1 Jan, Thanksgiving, 25 Dec.*

AMERICAN ARCHITECT Frank Lloyd Wright *(see p29)* designed a number of houses in LA. Hollyhock House was the first, and remains one of the best known. An excellent example of Wright's infatuation with pre-Columbian styles, the hilltop house resembles a Mayan temple.

It was completed in 1921 for oil heiress Aline Barnsdall, who asked that her favourite flower, the hollyhock, be used as a decorative motif throughout the building. A band of stylized hollyhocks, fashioned in concrete, therefore adorns the exterior of the house. The flowers also feature as ornamentation inside, such as on the dining room chairs. The City of Los Angeles now owns the house and is in the process of carefully restoring it to its original splendour. Some of Hollyhock House's interior furnishings, designed by Wright, remain *in situ*.

Hollywood Sign, high above Los Angeles in the Hollywood Hills

Universal Studios ❺

Logo for Universal Studios

Cᴀʀʟ ʟᴀᴇᴍᴍʟᴇ bought a chicken ranch on this site in 1915 and moved his film studio here from Hollywood. He began charging visitors 25 cents to see films being made, with the added bonus of being able to buy Uncle Carl's fresh eggs. With the advent of the "talkies" in 1927, the sets needed quiet and the visits had to stop. In 1964, Universal Studios Hollywood was launched as a behind-the-scenes tram ride. The Backlot Tram Tour has remained a major attraction, but new shows and rides such as WaterWorld – A Live Sea World Spectacular, and Jurassic Park – The Ride have added another dimension. Everything in Universal Studios is, or looks like, a film set, whether it is a Parisian courtyard, the Moulin Rouge or a Wild West town. Children can play in Fievel's Playland, an area filled with imaginatively designed slides, swings and climbing frames. Universal CityWalk is a colourful shopping street which reflects the pop culture of Los Angeles.

LOCATOR MAP

▨ *Illustrated Area*

☐ *Extent of Universal City*

Rocky and Bullwinkle Show

StarWay escalator leading to the Studio Center

Moulin Rouge

An American Tail Show

Baker Street

Entrance

★ Jurassic Park – The Ride
Visitors journey in 25-seater boats through a "prehistoric" tropical landscape. On the way they pass animatronic dinosaurs, some friendly, some fierce. The ride ends in a breathtaking water drop.

Fievel's Playland
This children's playground has a maze which resembles Swiss cheese and a slide that is shaped like a banana skin.

Moulin Rouge
A set of the Parisian nightclub is part of The Streets of the World.

STAR FEATURES

★ **Jurassic Park – The Ride**

★ **Backlot Tram Tour**

★ **Universal CityWalk**

★ Backlot Tram Tour
Over 500 outdoor sets and façades in Universal's backlot are used for locations as diverse as the Old West, New York City and Europe. Films shot here include All Quiet on the Western Front *(1930).*

VISITORS' CHECKLIST

100 Universal City Plaza, Universal City. **Road map** inset A.
📞 *(818) 508-9600.* 🚌 *424.*
⏰ *Jun–Sep: 7:30am–11pm daily; Oct–May: 9am–6pm daily.*
🔴 *Thanksgiving, 25 Dec.* 🎥 📷
♿ 🅿 ✉ 🍴 📶 🔲

Animal Actors Stage

Beetlejuice's Rockin' Graveyard Revue

Western Street

Back to the Future – The Ride

★ Universal CityWalk
Universal City's outdoor shopping mall is a fusion of pop art and kitsch. The high-energy street is lined with shops, restaurants, cafés and clubs.

Universal Amphitheatre

The Flintstone's Show

New York Street

WaterWorld – A Live Sea World Spectacular

The Wild Wild Wild West Stunt Show

Universal City Cinemas
The latest film releases can be seen in this state-of-the-art 18-screen cinema (see pp164–5).

Exploring Universal Studios

Show sign

SPREAD OVER 420 acres (170 ha), Universal is the world's largest working film and television studio. The complex is split into three areas: the Entertainment Center, Studio Center and studio lots. The entrance leads to the Entertainment Center, where visitors can stroll The Streets of the World – working sets of London's Baker Street, a Parisian Courtyard and a Western Street – or see a live action show. The Backlot Tram Tour is boarded from the Entertainment Center, and is the only way of seeing the studios' main stages and sets. The StarWay escalator leads down to Studio Center, where there are further rides and shows. Back up the hill, Universal CityWalk links the Entertainment Center and Universal City

Back to the Future Ride entrance

ENTERTAINMENT CENTER

THE ENTERTAINMENT CENTER has dozens of themed souvenir shops and restaurants. Eight spectacular shows in this area give visitors an insight into the stunts and special effects used to make a film.

Animal Actors Stage
Chimps, birds, cats and dogs display their skills in this live show. Animal "stars" include Lassie and Beethoven.

Beethoven

Beetlejuice's Rockin' Graveyard Revue
This musical revue features Beetlejuice, star of the 1988 film, and a band of ghouls and monsters, including Dracula and Frankenstein.

The Flintstone's Show
Fred and Wilma Flintstone join Barney and Betty Rubble in this rock extravaganza.

Rocky and Bullwinkle Show
Cartoon characters Bullwinkle Moose and Rocky the Flying Squirrel battle it out with Boris and Natasha in this live action revue.

WaterWorld – A Live Sea War Spectacular
From the 1995 Kevin Costner film, this thrilling show packs fire, battle scenes and wild jet-skiing in 16 minutes of daredevil action. A dive bomber crashes into the water. Fireballs

shoot into the sky and a jet-skier and water-skier catapult into the air. The set uses props from the *WaterWorld* film set.

The Wild Wild Wild West Stunt Show
This 15-minute slapstick show stars some of Hollywood's finest stuntmen and horses. The performance is packed with explosions, gunfights, horseplay and saloon bar brawls. The ultimate showdown is superbly destructive.

An American Tail Show
Young children will love the mice in this musical, in which Fievel and the Mousekewitzs (stars of the movie) journey to the Wild West in search of the American dream. An adjoining playground, Fievel's Playland, is filled with oversized objects *(see p142)*.

Back to the Future – The Ride
In an eight-seater DeLorean time-travel simulator car, guests pursue the diabolical Biff from the 1980s movie trilogy as they try to save the universe. Hurtling through the space-time continuum, the car falls down a volcanic tunnel flowing with molten lava, cascades down glacial cliffs and almost ends up as dinner for a tyrannosaurus rex. The ride uses sophisticated sound, film and hydraulics to simulate the wild chase. Not for small children or anyone with a bad back, neck or heart.

BACKLOT TRAM TOUR

VISITORS SEE the nuts and bolts of this busy studio on the ever-popular Backlot Tram Tour. If they are lucky, they may also see a film being made on the Little Europe set.

Gateway to the Backlot Tram Tour

Colourful entrance to Universal CityWalk

Passengers experience an earthquake, encounter King Kong and Jaws, and survive a collapsing bridge, flash flood and avalanche. The tour also passes the Bates Motel, used in Hitchcock's *Psycho* (1960).

STUDIO CENTER

SITUATED at the bottom of the StarWay, in the heart of Universal's working lots, the Studio Center has three thrilling rides. Other shows reveal the secrets of some of the studio's most successful films and television series.

The E.T. Adventure

Endearing E.T. takes everyone on a bicycle ride through the night sky as he tries to escape from government scientists and the police on his way home. At the end, E.T. says the name of each guest. The storyline and set are juvenile, but the magic of E.T. captures children's imagination.

Backdraft

In a re-creation of the final scene from the fire-fighting film *Backdraft* (1992), the audience can feel the heat of a blazing inferno. Beforehand, a technician explains how the scenes were created and controlled. The temperature climbs dramatically when the firestorm explodes, and the experience may be frightening for very young children.

The World of Cinemagic

Three types of special effects are explained in this fascinating look at film technology. In the *Back to the Future* section, audience members re-create a scene in the DeLorean car. Another participant dangles inches off the ground from a mock Statue of Liberty torch, showing how the falling sensation was created in the Hitchcock thriller *Saboteur* (1942). For the *Harry and the Hendersons* show, volunteers provide stormy night sound effects.

Jurassic Park – The Ride

Based on one of the most successful films of all time, Jurassic Park – The Ride takes visitors on a 5.5-minute journey through 6 acres (2.5 ha) of exotic wilderness. Sitting in yellow rafts, guests glide along a river, past lakes and waterfalls inhabited by over a dozen animatronic dinosaurs including a stegosaurus, dilophosaurus and tyrannosaurus rex. The ride culminates with an 84-ft (25-m) drop in pitch darkness.

Lucy – A Tribute

This exhibit displays memorabilia of Lucille Ball, one of the United States' favourite stage and television stars.

Actor posing as WC Fields

UNIVERSAL CITYWALK

IN 1993, architect Jon Jerde designed a fanciful assortment of façades for the shops and restaurants that line the four blocks of this promenade. A giant neon-lit baseball player swings his bat above a sports shop. On top of a toy shop, the three-dimensional face of a large bird juts from the wall. To enter an ice cream shop, visitors must walk beneath an upside-down pink convertible that has crashed through a Hollywood Freeway sign. In one area, spurts of water shoot up through the floor, fascinating young children.

BB King's Blues Club *(see p549)* is just one of many restaurants that provide music and entertainment as well as meals aimed at families. Street performers also help to give the area a festive atmosphere. Several CityWalk bookshops specialize in film-related subjects. Some of them double as cafés.

Universal CityWalk is also one of the prime areas to buy Hollywood souvenirs and memorabilia *(see p167)*. The street is anchored at one end by the 18-screen Universal City Cinemas.

Griffith Park ❽

Merry-go-round horse

G RIFFITH PARK is a 4,000-acre (1,600-ha) wilderness of rugged hills, forested valleys and green meadows in the centre of LA. The land was donated to the city in 1896 by Colonel Griffith J Griffith, a Welshman who emigrated to the United States in 1865 and made his money speculating in mining and property. Today, people come to Griffith Park to escape from the city crowds, visit the sights, picnic, hike or go pony trekking. While the park is safe during the day, it should be avoided at night.

Griffith Observatory on Mount Hollywood

Exploring Griffith Park
The ranger station, located on Crystal Springs Drive, has maps of the park showing its numerous picnic areas and miles of hiking trails and bridle paths. There are two public 18-hole golf courses on the eastern side of the park, and tennis courts on Riverside Drive and in Vermont Canyon.

In the hills just off Griffith Park Drive is a 1926 merry-go-round. Adults and children can still ride on its 66 carved horses and listen to its giant band organ. Across the street, an informal Sunday gathering of drummers has been meeting since the 1960s.

Fern Dell, at the Western Avenue entrance, is a beautiful shady glen with a flowing stream and small waterfalls.

🏛 Griffith Observatory
2800 Observatory Rd. 【 (213) 664-1181. ◯ 2–10pm Tue–Fri; 12:30–10pm Sat & Sun. ● Thanksgiving, 25 Dec. 🎫 Planetarium. ♿ limited.
Situated on Mount Hollywood, Griffith Observatory commands stunning views of the Los Angeles basin below. The Art Deco observatory is dedicated to public education and is divided into three main areas: the Hall of Science museum, the Planetarium theatre and the telescopes.

In the Main Rotunda of the Hall of Science, the Foucault Pendulum demonstrates the earth's rotation. Above the pendulum are murals on a scientific theme, painted by Hugo Ballin in 1934. Characters from Classical mythology are depicted on the domed ceiling. Below this, eight rectangular panels show important scientific concepts and figures through the ages.

Visitors to the Planetarium are taken on a journey through space and time, as some 9,000 stars, moons and planets are projected onto the ceiling. Up on the roof, the 12-in (30-cm) Zeiss Telescope is open to the public on clear nights.

🏛 Travel Town
5200 W Zoo Drive. 【 (213) 662-5874 & (213) 662-9678 for train ride. ◯ 10am–4:15pm daily. ● 25 Dec.
The spirit of the rails comes alive at this outdoor collection of vintage trains and cars. Children and adults alike can climb aboard several freight cars and railway carriages, or ride on a small train.

Just east of Travel Town, on Zoo Drive, powerful, miniature steam trains take people on rides through the hills during weekends.

1922 steam locomotive, one of 16 steam trains in Travel Town

🎭 Greek Theatre
2700 N Vermont Ave. 【 (213) 665-5857. ◯ May–Nov: 10am–6pm Mon–Fri. 🎫 for concerts.
Styled after an ancient Greek amphitheatre, this open-air music venue has excellent acoustics. On summer nights, over 6,000 people can sit under the stars and enjoy performances by leading popular, and occasionally classical, musicians. Bring a sweater as evenings can be chilly.

Flamingos at Los Angeles Zoo

✗ Los Angeles Zoo

5333 Zoo Drive. *(213) 666-4090.*
10am–5pm daily. *25 Dec.*
This 113-acre (46-ha) hilly
compound has more than
1,200 mammals, reptiles and
birds living in simulations of
their natural habitats. All the
favourite animals are here,
from lions and gorillas to
sharks and snakes.

Many newborn creatures
can be seen in the Animal
Nursery, including some from
the zoo's respected breeding
programme for rare and
endangered species.
The Koala
House is dimly
lit to encourage
the night-loving
creatures to be
active. Adventure
Island focuses on
animals and their
habitats from the
southwest.

(the visitors' checklist box)

VISITORS' CHECKLIST

Map 3 F2. ▦ 96. ◯ 5am–
10pm daily. ⓘ 4730 Crystal
Springs Drive. *(213) 665-
5188.* ▣ ♿ ◧ ◪ ◫ ◨

There are several animal shows
that are orientated towards a
young audience. Be prepared
to walk long distances, or use
the Safari Shuttle bus, which
carries visitors to the far
corners of the zoo.

🏛 Autry Museum of Western Heritage

4700 Western Heritage Way (opposite
the zoo). *(213) 667-2000.*
10am–5pm Tue–Sun.
Thanksgiving, 25 Dec. ♿
The Autry Museum of Western
Heritage explores the many
cultures that have shaped the
American West. Paintings and
sculptures by artists such
as Albert Bierstadt and
Frederic Remington
(*see pp24–5*) depict
a romantic view of
life in the region.
Tools, firearms,
tribal clothing
and religious
figurines are some of the
artifacts that show the
diversity of the people
who have lived here.

In the museum's
Discovery Center,
children can play in a
replica of a 19th-century
Mexican-American ranch
from Arizona.

Founded by the film
star Gene Autry, known as
"the singing cowboy", the
museum also houses a
superb collection of movie
and television memorabilia.

Deerskin Sioux dress

✗ Bird Sanctuary

Vermont Canyon Rd (just N
of Greek Theatre). *(213)
913-4688.* ◯ 5:30am–
10pm daily.
Many trees and
bushes have been
planted in this secluded
canyon to encourage local
birds to nest here. Although
you may not see too many
birds, you will definitely hear
their song. Depending on the
season, water may be running
in the stream, adding to the
serenity of the area.

GRIFFITH PARK

Autry Museum of Western
  Heritage ③
Bird Sanctuary ⑤
Fern Dell ⑧
Greek Theatre ⑥
Griffith Observatory ⑦
Los Angeles Zoo ②
Merry-go-round ④
Travel Town ①

0 kilometres   1
0 miles   0.5

KEY

ⓘ Tourist information

Dodger Stadium ❾

1000 Elysian Park Ave (at Stadium Way). **Map** 11 F1. ☎ *(213) 224-1491.* ☐ *for special events only.* 📷 ♿

T HIS BASEBALL STADIUM seats 56,000 spectators. Built in 1962 for the Brooklyn team, which had recently moved to LA, the stadium has a cantilevered design which ensures that every seat has an unobstructed view of the pitch.

From the stadium there are equally impressive panoramas of the city. To the south is Downtown LA, to the north and east are the San Gabriel Mountains. Around the arena are 300 acres (120 ha) of landscaped grounds, planted with more than 3,000 trees such as California rosewood, acacia and eucalyptus.

Queen Anne-style Hale House at Heritage Square Museum

Heritage Square Museum ❿

3800 Homer St, Los Angeles. ☎ *(818) 449-0193.* ☐ *10am–3pm Fri; 11:30am–4:30pm Sat & Sun.* 📷 ♿ 📶

M OST VICTORIAN buildings in Los Angeles were demolished during redevelopments, but some were saved by the Cultural Heritage Board and moved to this location. Dating from 1865–1914, they include a train depot, a church and a carriage barn. Hale House, a Queen Anne-style building *(see p27)*, has been restored in authentic colours.

Restored interior of the 19th-century Lummis House

Lummis House ⓫

200 East Ave 43, Los Angeles. ☎ *(213) 222-0546.* ☐ *noon–4pm Fri–Sun.* **Donation.** ♿ 📶

A LSO KNOWN AS "El Alisal", Spanish for "Place of the Sycamore", this house was the home of Charles Fletcher Lummis (1859–1928), who built it out of concrete and rocks from the local river bed. The structure's various design elements – Native American, Mission Revival, and Arts and Crafts – reveal the dominant influences of Lummis's life. Constructed between 1898 and 1910, mostly by his own hands, the design reveals a creative, independent thinker.

Lummis was a newspaper editor, writer, photographer, artist and historian. In 1885 he walked across the United States, from Ohio to LA, where he settled. He played a central role in the city's cultural life, editing the *LA Times*. As a co-founder of the California Landmark Club, he campaigned successfully for the preservation of the state's missions *(see pp42–3)*. His collection of Native American artifacts was the basis of the holdings at the Southwest Museum.

Today, Lummis House is the headquarters of the Historical Society of Southern California. Although few of Lummis's belongings remain in the house, there are some Native American artifacts. The built-in furnishings include a splendid Art Nouveau fireplace.

The garden was originally planted with vegetables and fruit trees. It was redesigned in 1985 and now grows drought-tolerant and native southern Californian plant species.

THE DODGERS

The Dodgers came originally from Brooklyn, New York. They used to train by dodging the trams that travelled down that city's streets, thus earning their name. Since moving to Los Angeles in 1958, they have become one of the most successful baseball teams in the United States. In 1959, they won the first of five world championships. Today, going to the Dodger Stadium is a rite of spring for Los Angeles fans.

Over the years the team has had a number of outstanding players, such as Sandy Koufax and Roy Campanella. In 1947, the Dodgers made headlines when they signed Pasadena-born Jackie Robinson, the first African-American to play in the major leagues.

Japanese star pitcher Hideo Nomo joined the Dodgers team in 1995, and created a sensation in his first season. During the playoffs, crowds brought Tokyo to a standstill as Nomo prepared to pitch on the other side of the Pacific Ocean.

Part of the victorious 1959 world championship team

Mission Revival-style Southwest Museum

Southwest Museum ⑫

234 Museum Drive, Los Angeles.
📞 *(213) 221-2164.* ⏰ *10am–5pm
Tue–Sun.* ● *1 Jan, Easter Sun,
Thanksgiving, 25 Dec.* ♿ ✓

WITH ONE of the nation's
leading collections of
Native American art and artifacts, the Southwest Museum
was the brainchild of Charles
Fletcher Lummis. During his
trek across the United States
in the late 19th century,
Lummis spent a long time in
the southwest, and became
one of the first white Americans to appreciate the history
and culture of Native Americans. Lummis donated many
of his personal holdings to
start the collection.

The museum displays tribal
objects from prehistoric
times to the present
day. Exhibits have
been drawn from
South America to
Alaska. They are
organized by their
place of origin, with
sections on the Plains,   **Sequoyah**
the Northwest Coast, the   **Indian relief**
Southwest and California.
The last two regions are the
most strongly represented, but
the museum offers an excellent
overview of Native American
heritage. The 11,000 baskets in
the collection are particularly

impressive. Tepees,
workshops, and story-
telling help to involve
children at the museum.
The Mission Revival
building *(see p27)* is set
on top of Mount Washington,
with views of Downtown Los
Angeles to the south. It has a
seven-storey tower and is surrounded by a garden planted
with indigenous species.

GALLERY GUIDE

*The galleries are situated on two floors, with
the main entrance on the upper level. Artifacts
from the Northwest Coast, California and the
Plains are displayed on this level, as are temporary exhibitions. The downstairs galleries are
dedicated to the museum's collection of baskets
and its holdings from the southwest. The shop
is also located here. Adjacent to the museum is
the Braun Research Library, dedicated to the
Native and Hispanic peoples of the Americas.*

Upper level · Entrance · Lower level

KEY TO FLOORPLAN

- ☐ The Northwest Coast
- ☐ The Southwest
- ☐ The Plains
- ☐ California
- ☐ Basketry study
- ☐ Temporary exhibitions
- ☐ Non-exhibition space

Pasadena ⑬

WITH THE COMPLETION of the Santa Fe Railroad in 1887, wealthy people from the East Coast began to spend the winter in the warmth and sunshine of Southern California. Many settled in Pasadena and were soon joined by artists and bohemians, who were also seeking the sun. This mix of creativity and wealth has resulted in a city with a splendid cultural legacy. The highlights of the area include the Huntington Library, Art Collections and Botanical Gardens *(see pp154–7)*, and the outstanding collection of old masters and Impressionist paintings at the Norton Simon Museum *(see pp152–3)*.

Rose Bowl statue

Exploring Pasadena

Just east of the Norton Simon Museum is **Old Pasadena**, once a decaying section of town. A dozen blocks of commercial buildings dating from the 1880s and 1890s have been restored and are now filled with shops, restaurants and cinemas. The mixture of Victorian, Spanish Colonial and Art Deco architecture adds to the area's pleasant environment. The stately Beaux-Arts **Civic Center**, on Union Street at Garfield Avenue, was designed by Edward Bennett in the early 1920s. It includes the city hall, police station, post office, library and civic auditorium. The neighbourhood northeast of the Gamble House has many examples of Arts and Crafts architecture *(see p27)*, most notably along tree-lined **Prospect Boulevard**.

Tiffany lamp in the Gamble House

🏟 Rose Bowl

1001 Rose Bowl Drive. 📞 *(818) 577-3100.* ⏰ *7:30am–5:30pm Mon–Fri.* ⬤ *every other Fri & public hols (except 1 Jan).* ♿

Sited in a wealthy neighbourhood, the stadium seats more than 100,000 people. It was built in 1922 for the annual Rose Bowl American football game, which matches college teams from the East and West coasts.

The first collegiate game played here was delayed for more than an hour when the visiting team was stuck in traffic, a fate that befalls many visitors today.

This is the home of UCLA's football team, the Bruins. Numerous Super Bowl games have also been played here as well as the World Cup Championships in 1994 and the 1984 Summer Olympics soccer competitions. There is also a flea market here every month.

Pasadena's city hall in the Beaux-Arts Civic Center

🏟 Gamble House

4 Westmoreland Place. 📞 *(818) 793-3334.* ⏰ *noon–3pm Thu–Sun.* ⬤ *public hols.* ♿ ▶ *obligatory.*

A masterpiece of the era, this wooden house epitomizes the Arts and Crafts movement, which stressed simplicity of design with superior craftsmanship. The dwelling was built in 1908 for David Gamble, of the Procter and Gamble Company. It is considered the crowning achievement of brothers Charles and Henry Greene, Boston-trained architects who visited Pasadena in 1893 and never left *(see p27)*.

The Gamble House was tailor-made for LA's climate. Its wide terraces and open sleeping porches, influenced by Japanese architecture, facilitate indoor-outdoor living, and broad overhanging eaves shade the house. At certain times of day, the sun illuminates the stained-glass front door, a dazzling sight.

🏛 Pacific-Asia Museum

46 N Los Robles Ave. 📞 *(818) 449-2742.* ⏰ *10am–5pm Wed–Sun.* ⬤ *public hols.* ♿

Built in 1924 to a traditional northern Chinese design, the Pacific-Asia Museum houses a collection of Far Eastern art founded by Grace Nicholson. Changing exhibitions on the arts of Asia and the Pacific Basin supplement the permanent collection. The museum's lovely courtyard garden is one of only two authentic Chinese gardens in the United States.

A packed Rose Bowl during an American football game

🍂 LA State and County Arboretum

301 N Baldwin Ave, Arcadia. **[** (818) 821-3222. ◯ 9am–4:30pm daily. ● 25 Dec. 🔳 🔳 🔳

Situated on 127 acres (51 ha) east of Pasadena, the arboretum has more than 30,000 plant species displayed according to their geographical origin. The park includes a herb garden, waterfall, lily ponds and a tropical jungle. It was used as the backdrop for all of Johnny Weissmuller's *Tarzan* films (1932–48) and

Tropical landscaping in the LA Arboretum

for some parts of Humphrey Bogart's *African Queen* (1951). Among the historical buildings in the grounds are Gabrielino Native American *wickiups* (huts), the reconstructed 1839 Hugo Reid adobe and the picturesque Queen Anne cottage.

🏛 Kidspace Museum

390 S El Molino Ave. **[** (818) 449-9143. ◯ mid-Jun–Aug: 1–5pm Sun–Thu, 10am–5pm Fri–Sat; Sep–mid-Jun: 1–5pm Wed & Sun, 10am–5pm Sat. ● public hols. 🔳

Children from 2 to 10 years old can dress up and play at this stimulating museum. They can

try on real firemen's uniforms at the Fire Station, or dress up as one of many characters in the Back Stage exhibit. Other attractions include TV Studio, Computer Room and the popular Critter Caverns, with its tree house and live animals.

THE ROSE PARADE

In 1890 the Pasadena Valley Hunt Club decided to hold the first Tournament of Roses to celebrate – and advertise – the region's balmy winters. Little did they know that their quaint parade of horse-drawn carriages draped with rose garlands would turn into a world-renowned extravaganza. Today, many of the floats have moving parts and sometimes feature people doing stunts.

Rose Parade float

PASADENA CITY CENTRE

Civic Center ④
Gamble House ②
Huntington Library,
    Art Collections and
    Botanical Gardens ⑦
Kidspace
    Museum ⑥
Norton Simon
    Museum ③
Pacific-Asia Museum ⑤
Rose Bowl ①

KEY

🔳 Tourist information

🔳 Coach terminus

0 kilometres   1

0 miles   1

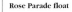

Norton Simon Museum

NORTON SIMON (1907–93) was a businessman who combined running his multinational corporation with forming an internationally acclaimed collection of works of art. From the 1950s to the 1970s, he amassed, with the genius of a connoisseur, masterpieces spanning more than 2,000 years of Western and Asian art. Within the European holdings, the Old Masters and Impressionist paintings are especially strong. Renaissance, Post-Impressionism, German Expressionism and the modern period are also well represented. Sculptures from India and Southeast Asia are among the finest outside the region, and offer an insight into the complex roles art and religion play in these cultures.

Main level

Sculpture Garden

★ **Woman with a Book** *(1932)*
Pablo Picasso, one of the great artistic forces of the 20th century, was a major influence on both the Cubist and Surrealist movements. His mistress, Marie-Thérèse Walter, was the subject of a number of his paintings in the 1930s.

Self-Portrait *(c.1636–8)*
Rembrandt painted nearly 100 self-portraits during his lifetime. This one shows the artist in his early thirties.

Lower level

STAR PAINTINGS

★ Still Life with Lemons, Oranges and a Rose by Francisco Zurbarán

★ Woman with a Book by Pablo Picasso

★ **Still Life with Lemons, Oranges and a Rose** *(1633)*
The Spanish painter Francisco Zurbarán excelled at contemplative still lifes. Many of his works were exported to the Spanish Americas, where they influenced colonial painters.

Saints Paul and Frediano *(c.1483)*
This is one of a pair of religious panels executed by Florentine artist, Filippino Lippi. It shows the influence of Lippi's more famous father, Fra Filippo Lippi, and his other mentor, Botticelli.

Spiral staircase

Main entrance

Spiral staircase

VISITORS' CHECKLIST

411 W Colorado Blvd. 🄲 *(818) 449-6840.* 🚍 *181, 182.*
◯ *noon–6pm Thu–Sun.*
● *1 Jan, 4 Jul, Thanksgiving, 25 Dec. Call ahead during summer 1997.* 🄯 📷 ♿ 🍴 🏛 🅿

GALLERY GUIDE

The museum's galleries are on two floors, linked by a spiral staircase. European paintings, prints, sculpture and tapestries, dating from the Renaissance to the 20th century, are on display on the main level. The museum bookshop is also on this level. The lower galleries showcase the Norton Simon's impressive collection of Indian and Southeast Asian works, as well as displaying special and touring exhibitions.

The galleries are currently undergoing an extensive renovation programme, which is planned for completion by autumn 1997. Asian, 19th- and 20th-century sculpture is on display in the landscaped gardens. A restaurant is being constructed in the gardens and will open in autumn 1997.

The Little Fourteen-Year-Old Dancer
(1878–81)
This bronze is one of more than 100 works by Edgar Degas in the museum. It features one of the artist's favourite subjects, the ballet.

Buddha Enthroned
This bronze was made in Kashmir in India in the 8th century. It is inlaid with silver and copper.

Huntington Library, Art Collections and Botanical Gardens

Detail from garden urn

VISITORS AND SCHOLARS alike are united in their love of the Huntington. The Beaux-Arts mansion was built between 1909 and 1911 for Henry Huntington (1850–1927), who made his fortune building a network of inter-urban trams in Los Angeles. In 1913 he married his uncle's widow, Arabella. Together they amassed one of the most important libraries and collections of 18th-century British art in the world. The key elements of the gardens were planted during Huntington's lifetime.

Mausoleum
Designed by the architect John Russell Pope, this building in the form of a Greek temple is made of Colorado yule marble.

Main entrance

Camellia Garden

Orange Grove

Breakfast in Bed *(1897)*
The Virginia Steele Scott Gallery is devoted to American art, including one of Mary Cassatt's most successful Impressionist paintings of a mother and child. The artist used this theme many times in her work (see p110).

Camellia Garden

Ikebana House

Herb Garden

Japanese House

Zen Garden

STAR FEATURES

★ **The Blue Boy by Thomas Gainsborough**

★ **Gutenberg Bible**

★ **Japanese Garden**

★ **Japanese Garden**
Designed as a place for quiet contemplation, the traditional Japanese garden always includes water, both flowing and still, often crossed by a small curved bridge, known as a moon bridge.

★ Gutenberg Bible
This Bible was printed on vellum around 1450–55 by Johannes Gutenberg in Mainz, Germany. It is the oldest printed book in the Huntington Library.

VISITORS' CHECKLIST

1151 Oxford Rd. **(** (818) 405-2100. ◐ Jun–Aug: 10:30am–4:30pm Tue–Sun; Sep–May: noon–4:30pm Tue–Fri; 10:30am–4:30pm Sat & Sun. ● public hols. ⬚ ⬚ ⬚ ⬚ ⬚ ⬚ ⬚

Jungle Garden
The palms, ferns, gingers and other plants in this garden are all typical of a tropical rainforest. Orchids and bromeliads can be seen growing high up in the trees.

Shakespeare Garden

Conservatory

Palm Garden

Desert Garden

Lily Ponds

Subtropical Garden

Australian Garden

Rose Garden

North Vista
Backed by the San Gabriel Mountains, the vista re-creates the feel of a 17th-century European garden, complete with an Italian Baroque fountain at one end.

★ The Blue Boy (c.1770)
Thomas Gainsborough's portrait of Jonathan Buttall, a merchant's son, is one of the most famous paintings in the Huntington Art Gallery.

Exploring the Huntington

In 1919 Henry and Arabella Huntington put their home and gardens into a trust, creating a non-profit research institution. Today, the Huntington plays a dual role as an educational facility and cultural centre, serving scholars and the general public. The institution comprises one of the world's great research libraries, an outstanding art collection and more than 130 acres (50 ha) of botanical gardens. The Huntington is only open to the public for a few hours each day, so plan your visit in advance.

Diana Huntress (1782) by Jean-Antoine Houdon

HUNTINGTON LIBRARY

Purpose-built in 1920, the library specializes in British and American history and literature. It attracts nearly 2,000 scholars every year. The general public can view key items and other changing exhibits in the Library Exhibition Hall.

Among the 600,000 books and three million manuscripts are a copy of the *Magna Carta* and the Ellesmere manuscript of Chaucer's *Canterbury Tales*, dating from around 1410. The vast holding of books printed before 1501 includes a Gutenberg Bible (c.1455) – one of only 12 surviving copies printed on vellum in the world.

There are also first editions and manuscripts by noted British and American authors, including Mark Twain, Charles Dickens and Lord Tennyson, and early editions of Shakespeare's plays. Letters written by George Washington, Benjamin Franklin and Abraham Lincoln are part of the collection on the Revolutionary and Civil wars.

Pilgrim from *The Canterbury Tales*

ARABELLA D HUNTINGTON MEMORIAL COLLECTION

The west wing of the main library building houses a small group of Renaissance paintings, the most important of which is the *Madonna and Child* (see p67) by Flemish artist Roger van der Weyden (c.1400–1464). The wing also displays French furniture,

Sèvres porcelain and most of the Huntington's collection of French sculpture. *Portrait of a Lady* (1777) by Jean-Antoine Houdon is considered one of the sculptor's finest busts.

HUNTINGTON ART GALLERY

The Huntingtons' mansion now houses the majority of the art collection, including British and French art from the 18th and early 19th century. The most famous works are a group of full-length portraits in the Main Gallery. They include Thomas Gainsborough's *The Blue Boy* (c.1770), *Pinkie* (1794) by Thomas Lawrence and *Mrs Siddons as the Tragic Muse* (1784) by Joshua Reynolds. Also in the Main Gallery is the *View on the Stour near Dedham* (1822) by John Constable. Other British paintings are displayed throughout the building.

The Large Library Room contains some outstanding 18th-century furnishings, which include two Savonnerie carpets made for Louis XIV, and five Beauvais tapestries.

The Small Library houses a collection of Renaissance bronzes. *Nessus and Deianira* by Italian sculptor Giovanni da Bologna (1529–1608) is a fine example of his work. In the North Passage is a collection of 15th- to 19th-century British silver. It includes John Flaxman's silver-gilt *Shield of Achilles* (1821).

European artists influential to British painting are also on show. Flemish artist Anthony Van Dyck (1559–1642) was admired by 18th-century British portraitists. While at the English court of Charles I, he produced *Anne Killigrew, Mrs Kirke* (c.1638), which hangs at the head of the stairs. There are also works by Canaletto, who had a profound effect on British landscape painting.

French furniture in the Large Library Room

VIRGINIA STEELE SCOTT GALLERY OF AMERICAN ART

OPENED IN 1984, this collection displays American art from the 1740s to the 1930s.

During the colonial period, artists such as Benjamin West (1738–1820) and Gilbert Stuart (1755–1828) were admirers of British portraitists. It was only prior to the Civil War that an American style of painting emerged. Following two visits to Ecuador, Frederic Edwin Church captured the vastness of that country in *Chimborazo* (1864). Another 19th-century highlight is Mary Cassatt's *Breakfast in Bed* (1897).

The Dorothy Collins Brown Wing houses furniture designed by the American architects, brothers Charles and Henry Greene *(see p27)*.

Desert Garden

BOTANICAL GARDENS

IN 1904, Henry Huntington hired landscape gardener William Hertrich to develop the grounds, which now contain 15 principal gardens.

The 12-acre (5-ha) Desert Garden has more than 4,000 drought-tolerant species from around the world. In the Rose Garden, a walkway traces the history of the species over 1,000 years, with 2,000 varieties. The oldest are found in the Shakespeare Garden.

One of the most popular areas is the Japanese Garden, with a moon bridge, Zen Garden and Japanese plants.

HUNTINGTON ART GALLERY

Ground floor

First floor

1 Large Library Room
2 Large Drawing Room
3 Small Drawing Room
4 Dining Room
5 North Passage
6 Main Gallery
7 Hall
8 Small Library

9 Quinn Room
10 Southeast Room
11 Wedgwood Room
12 The Adele S Browning Memorial Collection
13 The Moseley Collection
14 Southwest Room
15 Temporary exhibitions

ARABELLA D HUNTINGTON MEMORIAL COLLECTION

1 Sèvres Porcelain Room
2 French Furniture Room
3 French Sculpture Room
4 Renaissance Paintings Room
5 Temporary exhibitions

HUNTINGTON LIBRARY

1 Medieval Manuscripts and Early Printing
2 English and American Literature
3 American History

Ground floor

VIRGINIA STEELE SCOTT GALLERY OF AMERICAN ART

1 Permanent Collection
2 Dorothy Collins Brown Wing

3 Print Room (closed to the public)
4 Temporary exhibitions

Ground floor

Cowboy boot stall at El Mercado

El Mercado **⓮**

3425 E 1st St. 📞 *(213) 268-3451.*
🕐 *10am–8pm Mon–Fri; 9am–9pm
Sat & Sun.* ♿

E AST LOS ANGELES is the heart
of the Mexican-American
community *(see p30)*, and this
marketplace caters to the
locals. Its three levels bustle
with taco vendors, *mariachis*
(Mexican street musicians)
and families out for a good
meal. Unlike Olvera Street
(see p123), El Mercado is not
designed as a tourist spot.
The greatest attraction here is
the authentic Mexican food
and regional music.
    On the main floor stalls offer
everything from chillies to
snack food. A *tortillaria* sells
fresh, hot tortillas; bakeries
display traditional Mexican
breads and pastries and delicatessens have meats you may
never have seen before. To
hear the *mariachis*, go to the
mezzanine level, which is also
where the cafeteria-style restaurants are located.
    Brightly coloured Mexican
clothing, furniture and crafts
fill the shops in the basement,
along with the sounds of
Latin American salsa music.

The Lakers and Basketball

Basketball originated in Springfield, Massachusetts in 1891
as a team sport that could be played indoors during the
harsh winters. LA's cold season may be warm, but people
still love the fast-paced, high-scoring game. The city's team,
the Lakers, has a huge follow-
ing. Over the years such
illustrious players as Magic
Johnson, Wilt Chamberlain
and Kareem Abdul-Jabbar
have helped make the team
one of the most successful in
the National Basketball Association (NBA). The Lakers
started in Minnesota, a state
with hundreds of lakes, hence
their name. In 1960 they
came to LA, and became part
of the city's identity. They
won the NBA Championship
four times in the 1980s.

Magic Johnson

Flower Market **⓯**

754 S Wall St. 📞 *(213) 622-1966.*
🕐 *8am–noon Mon, Wed & Fri;
6am–noon Tue, Thu & Sat.* ♿

I N THE EARLY HOURS of the
morning, before sunrise, the
city's florists flock to this area
to buy fresh flowers and plants
wholesale for their own clients.
Warehouses lined with stalls
and shops are laden with
brightly coloured blooms that
contrast sharply with the grey
surrounding buildings. An
enormous range of flowers is
on offer, so that Californian
varieties compete with plants
from Columbia, New Zealand,
France and Holland.
    Anyone can take advantage
of the cheap prices (there are
great bargains available after
8 am). It is best, however, to
arrive early as ⁚ supplies sell
out quickly.

Exposition Park
and University
of Southern
California **⓰**

See pp160–61.

Great Western
Forum **⓱**

3900 Manchester Blvd, Inglewood.
Road map inset A. 📞 *(310) 673-
1300.* 🕐 *for events only.* 🅿 *for
events.* ♿ **Box Office** 🕐 *10am–
6pm daily.*

T HE GREAT WESTERN FORUM is
LA's most prestigious sports
arena. Situated in Inglewood,
which is well served by freeways and the international
airport, the complex is easy to
reach and has ample parking.
Seating 17,000, the Forum is

Great Western Forum in Inglewood

the home of the city's famous basketball team, the LA Lakers, and ice hockey professionals the LA Kings. It is also the venue for major boxing and tennis matches. In 1984 the Olympic Games basketball competitions took place here.

The Forum's programme is not simply limited to sporting events. It is also one of Los Angeles's major concert venues. A wide range of rock and pop stars have performed here, including Tony Bennett, David Bowie and the Artist Formerly Known as Prince.

Despite the popularity of many of the events that take place at the arena, its size means that tickets are often available if you queue.

Hollywood Park Racetrack ⑱

1050 S Prairie Ave, Inglewood. **Road map** inset A. 📞 *(310) 419-1500.* ⭘ *1–5pm Wed–Fri; 12:30–5pm Sat & Sun.* ♿ ♿

FROM APRIL to July racing enthusiasts such as Walter Matthau and Jack Klugman come to Hollywood Park to bet on the thoroughbreds. This is an elegant, nostalgic venue, beautifully landscaped with lagoons and lush trees. A large computer-operated screen relays the action from the obscured back straight, as well as showing instant replays, photo finishes and race statistics. In the North Park, the children's play area includes a merry-go-round.

Landscaped racetrack at Hollywood Park in Inglewood

Watts Towers, covered in shells, china and glass

Watts Towers ⑲

1727 E 107th St, Watts. **Road map** inset A. 📞 *(213) 847-4646.* ⭘ *10am–4pm Tue–Sat; noon–4pm Sun.* ⬤ *Thanksgiving, 25 Dec.* ♿ *Towers only.* ♿ *Arts Center only.* 📷

WATTS TOWERS is a masterpiece of folk art that embodies the perseverance and vision of Simon Rodia, an immigrant from Naples, Italy. Between 1921 and 1954, the tile-worker sculpted steel rods, pipes and whatever else he could find into a huge skeletal framework. The highest tower reaches 100 ft (30 m). Rodia adorned the cemented surface with fragments of seashell, tile, china and glass. He never gave a reason for building the towers and, upon finishing, he deeded the land to a neighbour and left Los Angeles.

Despite several attempts to have Watts Towers razed, it has now been registered as a State Historic Park. It stands as a symbol of hope in this highly deprived area that, in 1965, was the site of the worst riots that Los Angeles had ever experienced.

Situated adjacent to the monument is the Watts Towers Arts Center. This complex displays temporary exhibitions of work by African-American artists in the community.

South Central LA, which includes Watts, is a high-crime neighbourhood. Visitors should not stay in the area after dark. By day, take common-sense precautions and do not stray from the towers.

Exposition Park and University of Southern California ⓰

EXPOSITION PARK began life in the 1880s as an area of open-air markets, carnivals and horse-racing. By the end of the century, the district was rife with drinking, gambling and prostitution. When Judge William Miller Bowen's nearby Sunday school pupils began skipping church to enjoy local temptations, he pushed for the transformation of the area into a cultural landmark that today includes three museums. The Exposition Park Rose Garden in their midst contains more than 19,000 rose bushes. Across the street, the University of Southern California (USC) covers 152 acres (62 ha) and is attended by almost 28,000 students. Founded in 1880, it is the oldest and largest private university in the western United States.

Tommy Trojan statue

Bovard Administration Building

| 0 metres | 200 |
| 0 yards | 200 |

SANTA MONICA
BEVERLEY HILLS

🛗 Doheny Memorial Library

Corner of Hoover Blvd and Childs Way. ☎ *(213) 740-4039.* ◯ *daily.*
A majestic building with Italian Romanesque, Egyptian and Moorish design influences, USC's main reference library was built in 1932 in memory of Edward L Doheny, Jr, a trustee of the university. The building benefits from a monumental marble staircase at the entrance, and ornate stone and woodwork throughout. The main hall is illuminated by stained-glass windows.

🏛 Natural History Museum of Los Angeles County

900 Exposition Blvd. ☎ *(213) 744-3466.* ◯ *10am–5pm Tue–Sun.* ● *1 Jan, Thanksgiving, 25 Dec.* 🎟 *free first Tue of every month.*
This is the third largest natural history and cultural museum in the US. From dinosaur fossils to gems, a wide variety of specimens and artifacts are on show. Native American and

pre-Columbian exhibits are on the main level and include a replica of a Pueblo cliff dwelling. The Schreiber Hall of Birds, the Insect Zoo and the hands-on Discovery Center for children are further attractions.

🛗 Bovard Administration Building

Hahn Plaza. ◯ *daily.*
This Italian Romanesque structure was named after USC's fourth president, George Bovard. The former bell tower has eight sculpted figures of great men, including John Wesley, Abraham Lincoln, Theodore Roosevelt, Cicero and Plato. The restored Gothic Norris Auditorium seats 1,600 people. *Tommy Trojan*, a statue of a Trojan warrior, the university's symbol, stands outside the main entrance. It was sculpted in 1930 by Roger Nobel Burnham.

SIGHTS AT A GLANCE

Aerospace Museum ⑦
Bovard Administration Building ①
California Afro-American
    Museum ⑧
California Museum of Science
    and Industry ⑨
Doheny Memorial Library ③
Fisher Gallery ⑤
Los Angeles Memorial Coliseum ⑩
Mudd Memorial Hall ④
Natural History Museum of Los
    Angeles County ⑥
Tommy Trojan ②

Natural History Museum in Exposition Park

Los Angeles Memorial Coliseum

🏟 Los Angeles Memorial Coliseum

3939 S Figueroa St. ((213) 747-7111. ○ for events and tours. 🎟 10:30am, noon, 1:30pm Tue, Thu & Sat; call ahead (213 765-6347).

Host to the 1932 and 1984 Olympic Games, the Coliseum has also been the site of professional and USC football games, rock concerts, Pope John Paul II's mass in 1987 and John F Kennedy's acceptance speech as the Democratic candidate at the Democratic National Convention in 1960. A 40-minute walking tour of the press conference room, locker rooms and press boxes gives a history of the stadium.

🏛 California Museum of Science and Industry

700 State Drive. ((213) 744-7400. ○ 10am–5pm daily. ● 1 Jan, Thanksgiving, 25 Dec. 🎟

One of the largest of its kind in the United States, the California Museum of Science and Industry aims to make science accessible to people of all ages. The World of Life exhibit in the Kinsey Hall of Health explores how living things function, with Body Works, a 50-ft (15-m) long transparent human figure with illuminated organs, as its centrepiece. The Creative World area shows how people create what they need, following an idea from inception to production. The IMAX Theater, also at the museum has a five-storey-high screen with Surround Sound. It presents nature-related movies on such subjects as volcanoes, Africa and outer space. Aerospace Museum, designed by Frank Gehry, has an F-104 Starfighter jet bolted to its façade. The building features all manner of winged craft, from a Wright Brothers' glider to a Gemini 11 space capsule.

🏛 Fisher Gallery

Bloom Walk. ((213) 740-4561. ○ noon–5pm Tue–Fri; 11am–3pm Sat. ● public hols.

Named after the gallery's benefactor Mrs Walter Harrison Fisher, the collection includes 19th-century French and American landscapes as well as works by the Dutch artist Peter Paul Rubens.

VISITORS' CHECKLIST

Road map inset A. 🚌 DASH Shuttle C from Business District. 🚇 81. Exposition Park (individual sights. University of Southern California ((213) 740-5371. 🎟

🏛 California Afro-American Museum

600 State Drive. ((213) 744-7432. ○ 10am–5pm Tue–Sun. ● 1 Jan, Thanksgiving, 25 Dec.

This museum is a record of Afro-American achievements in the arts, sciences, politics, religion and sports. The permanent art collection includes works by artists such as Martin Pierré, Betye Saar, Noah Purifoy and the 19th-century landscape painter Robert Duncanson. Frequent temporary exhibitions are held in the sculpture court at the entrance to the building.

🏟 Mudd Memorial Hall

Corner of Trousdale Parkway and Exposition Blvd. ○ daily.

The philosophy faculty's hall was modelled after a medieval monastery in Tuscany. Its bell tower is 146 ft (44 m) high and was used in the 1939 film *The Hunchback of Notre Dame*. Statues of great philosophers through the ages are detailed on the exterior, with the Cynic Diogenes placed over the entrance. The Hoose Library of Philosophy has more than 60,000 volumes and is considered to be one of the best in the country.

Italianate façade of the Mudd Memorial Hall

ENTERTAINMENT IN
LOS ANGELES

Hollywood
cinema sign

As the centre of the film industry, Los Angeles has dominated the world stage during much of the 20th century. It is therefore not surprising that the city sees itself as the Entertainment Capital of the World. LA's large and successful artistic community ensures that there is always plenty to do in the city, although only small areas tend to be lively after dark.

LA also has a huge number of cinemas, which range from 1930s movie palaces to state-of-the-art multiplexes. Stage productions are also plentiful and diverse. The city has a well-respected symphony orchestra and opera company, which in the summer give outdoor concerts in venues such as the Hollywood Bowl *(see p107)*. Jazz and blues bars and clubs are centred on Sunset Boulevard.

LA listings
publications

INFORMATION

Various publications can help sift through the city's embarrassment of entertainment riches. The *LA Weekly* – a free paper available at bars, clubs and corner markets across the city – has the most comprehensive entertainment and arts listings. It is aimed at the younger generation and outshines the *Los Angeles View*. The *New Times* is a well-produced magazine and the *Sunday Los Angeles Times* "Calendar" section is another reliable source for information.

The monthly publications include *Los Angeles Magazine*, which lists all the main events in the city and also has reliable restaurant reviews. *Buzz* magazine's recommendations, "Buzz Bets", may appeal to a younger readership. More general information, aimed at tourists, is provided in the monthly *Where Magazine*.

Listings for gay and lesbian readers include *Planet Homo*, *The Edge* and *LA Girl Guide*.

The main branch of the **Los Angeles Convention and Visitors' Bureau** is in Downtown. Staff offer multilingual assistance. Their visitors' guide, *Destination Los Angeles*, gives listings of restaurants, hotels, shops and attractions. There is also a 24-hour events hotline. The city's two other main information centres are the **Hollywood Visitors' Information Center** and the **Beverly Hills Visitors' Bureau**.

BUYING TICKETS

The simplest source of tickets to concerts, plays and sporting events in LA is **Ticketmaster**. You can order the tickets by telephone using a credit card, or visit one of their centres in Music Plus or Tower Records shops, or Robinsons-May department stores. If you want to avoid their service charges, try calling the venues direct. Other agencies include **Tickets LA**, **Telecharge** and **Good Time Tickets**. Theatre productions and times are available by calling **Theater LA**'s information line.

DISCOUNT TICKETS

A good source of discount tickets is **Theater LA**. It supplies information on, and sells, cheap tickets only on the day of performance. **Tickets LA** also offers half-price tickets to some events. Bookings must be made by credit card and tickets can be collected at the venue.

If you are willing to gamble on availability a few hours before the show starts, then you can try telephoning the box office direct. Many venues offer last minute "rush" discounts on unsold seats for performances.

Students who hold a valid ISIC card *(see p590)* may be able to get discounts to some concerts and plays. The best venues to try are those affiliated to Los Angeles's universities, such as UCLA's Geffen Playhouse *(see p164)*.

LACMA *(see pp110–13)*, a venue for free concerts

Hollywood Bowl, one of LA's premier concert venues *(see p107)*

Free Events

MOST OF THE AREAS within Los Angeles have local festivals, particularly in the summer, which feature food, live music, arts and crafts. Contact the **LA Cultural Affairs Department** for details. On Thursday nights in the summer, Santa Monica Pier has concerts featuring a variety of music styles *(see pp74–5)*.

Also in the summer, the LA Philharmonic allows visitors to listen to its midday concert rehearsals at the Hollywood Bowl *(see p107)*.

Some of Los Angeles's museums do not charge entrance fees. They include the California Museum of Science and Industry *(see p161)*, Travel Town in Griffith Park *(see p146)* and the J Paul Getty Museum *(see pp78–81)*. Los Angeles County Museum of Art *(see pp110–13)* hosts concerts of jazz and chamber music on Fridays and Sundays in the museum plaza.

Detail on a LA theatre

Facilities for the Disabled

AS ELSEWHERE in California *(see p590)*, almost all clubs, cinemas and theatres in LA are wheelchair accessible and will provide special seating. Most establishments also have parking and toilets designed to facilitate the needs of people with disabilities.

A brochure published by the **Los Angeles County Commission on Disabilities** lists the services provided by both public- and private-sector agencies. It also includes information on transportation and recreational facilities as well as equipment for sale or hire.

A few local organizations provide services for persons with disabilities, such as the **Westside Center for Independent Living**.

Los Angeles's public transport organization, the Metropolitan Transit Authority *(see pp168–9)* operates a fleet of buses that are equipped with automatic wheelchair lifts. The **Disabled Transit Referral Service** can help arrange local transport for those with special needs.

Art Deco façade of Hollywood's Pantages Theater *(see p108)*

DIRECTORY

USEFUL NUMBERS

Beverly Hills Visitors' Bureau
239 S Beverly Dr,
Beverly Hills, CA 90212.
(*(310) 271-8174.*

Hollywood Visitors' Information Center
Janes House Square,
6541 Hollywood Blvd,
Hollywood, CA 90028.
(*(213) 689-8822.*

LA Cultural Affairs Department
433 S Spring St, 10th Fl,
Los Angeles, CA 90013.
(*(213) 485-2433.*

Los Angeles Convention and Visitors' Bureau
685 S Figueroa St,
Los Angeles, CA 90017.
(*(213) 689-8822.*

TICKET AGENCIES

Good Time Tickets
(*(213) 464-7383.*

Telecharge
(*(800) 762-7666.*

Theater LA
(*(213) 688-2787.*

Ticketmaster
(*(213) 381-2000.*

Tickets LA
(*(213) 660-8587.*

FACILITIES FOR THE DISABLED

Disabled Transit Referral Service
(*(800) 431-7882.*

Los Angeles County Commission on Disabilities
383 Hall of Administration,
500 W Temple St,
Los Angeles,
CA 90012.
(*(213) 974-1053*
or (213) 974-1707.

Westside Center for Independent Living
12901 Venice Blvd,
Los Angeles,
CA 90066.
(*(310) 390-3611.*

Entertainment Venues

As BEFITS A CITY OF ITS SIZE AND REPUTATION, Los Angeles has a vast range of entertainment venues. The Music Center in Downtown Los Angeles *(see p121)* is home to the LA Philharmonic and LA Opera. It also houses two award-winning theatres. Hollywood and West Hollywood are filled with historic cinemas and theatres, and celebrity-owned nightclubs such as the Viper Room *(see p98)*. By day, visitors can join a live television studio audience, or see a game at one of the city's major sporting venues.

Hollywood Galaxy *(see p104)* on Hollywood Boulevard

CINEMAS

MOST VISITORS don't spend a lot of time seeing films in LA, even though all the current releases and countless classics are always being shown. The movie palaces themselves, however, draw the crowds, with Mann's Chinese and El Capitan theatres *(see p106)* on Hollywood Boulevard being the best known. Multiplexes, such as those in **Universal City** and the **Beverly Center**, offer state-of-the-art entertainment. And for a real nostalgia trip, visit **Silent Movie**, which runs classics from the 1920s.

THEATRE

WITH MORE THAN 1,000 professional plays put on in LA each year, there is bound to be something for everyone. Downtown's Music Center *(see p121)* houses two important theatres – the Ahmanson Theatre and the Mark Taper Forum. Pantages *(see p108)* in Hollywood and the **Shubert Theatre** in Century City are the leading venues for touring Broadway musicals. Housed in beautiful Mediterranean-style theatres, the **Pasadena**

Playhouse and the **Geffen Playhouse** both put on new works as well as old favourites. More alternative productions are usually performed at the city's smaller spaces, such as the **Actors' Gang Workshop** or **Theater/Theatre**.

OPERA, DANCE AND CLASSICAL MUSIC

THE LA PHILHARMONIC, which winters at the Dorothy Chandler Pavilion *(see p121)* and summers alfresco at the Hollywood Bowl *(see p107)*, is a first-rate orchestra. The **LA Opera** also performs at the Dorothy Chandler Pavilion between September and June. Chamber groups perform at various venues throughout the city. The **UCLA Center for the Performing Arts** features prominent international artists. Although LA lacks a resident world-class ballet company, all the major companies visit.

ROCK, JAZZ AND BLUES

NAKED AMBITION and unbridled youth fuel the rock clubs that line Sunset Strip *(see pp98–100)*. The venerable

Whiskey a Go Go and **Roxy** compete with relative newcomers such as the **Viper Room** and **Billboard Live**. LA's jazz scene is exemplified by cosy joints such as the **Baked Potato** and **Catalina Bar & Grill**. Dan Ackroyd's **The House of Blues** is just one venue that also serves food *(see p549)*. The biggest names perform at LA's arenas, including the Greek Theater *(see p146)* and **Universal Amphitheatre** *(see p143)*.

CLUBS

WHETHER IT'S 1970s funk-pop at the **Crush Bar**, hip-house at **Catch One** or hipster big beats at **The Garage**, the LA club scene runs all types of dance music. With its large gay population, West Hollywood has a lot of discos. One current favourite is **Axis**. If you want to see celebrities, try **Bar Marmont**. Fashion changes quickly, though, so consult the local listings. The over-21 law is enforced, so make sure you have ID. Comedy clubs include **The Comedy Store** on Sunset Boulevard *(see p99)*.

Club sign on Sunset Boulevard

STUDIO TOURS AND TV SHOWS

MANY OF LA's television and film studios offer behind-the-scenes tours as well as tickets to tapings of popular shows. In the high-tech studios of **CBS-TV**, soap operas such as *The Bold and the Beautiful* and game shows that include *The Price is Right* are taped before live audiences. For

Paramount Studios' famous gates *(see p109)*

tickets, write about six weeks before your trip, specifying the date and show you wish to see. Audience members must speak and understand English.

In Burbank (see pp140–41), **NBC-TV** offers tickets to shows and a tour of the studios. Next door, the **Warner Bros** tour is probably the truest look at modern-day film-making.

Visitors on the Paramount Studios tour (see p109) must be at least ten years old.

OUTDOOR ACTIVITIES

LOS ANGELES'S BEACHES are a great natural resource and offer surfing, swimming and volleyball. Topanga State Park (see p77) and Griffith Park

(see pp146–7) offer miles of hiking trails. Spectator sports include baseball at the Dodger Stadium (see p148), basketball and ice hockey at the Great

Western Forum (see pp158–9), horse racing at the Hollywood Park Racetrack (see p159) and polo at Will Rogers State Historic Park (see p77).

Surfers at Manhattan Beach (see p62)

DIRECTORY

CINEMAS

Cineplex Odeon Beverly Center Cinemas
8522 Beverly Blvd.
Map 6 C2.
📞 (310) 652-7760.

Cineplex Odeon Universal City Cinemas
Universal City, CA 91608.
📞 (818) 508-0588.

Mann's Village Westwood
961 Broxton Ave.
Map 4 A4.
📞 (310) 289-6266.

Pacific Cinerama Dome
6360 W Sunset Blvd.
Map 2 C5.
📞 (213) 466-3401.

Silent Movie
611 N Fairfax Ave.
Map 7 D1.
📞 (213) 653-2389.

THEATRES

Actors' Gang Workshop
6209 Santa Monica Blvd.
Map 8 B1.
📞 (213) 466-1767.

Geffen Playhouse
10886 Le Conte Ave.
Map 4 A4.
📞 (310) 208-5454.

Pasadena Playhouse
39 S El Molino Ave,
Pasadena, CA 91101.
📞 (818) 356-7529.

Shubert Theatre
2020 Avenue of the Stars.
Map 5 D4.
📞 (800) 447-7400.

Theater/Theatre
1713 N Cahuenga Blvd.
Map 2 C4.
📞 (213) 871-0210.

OPERA, DANCE AND CLASSICAL MUSIC

Alex Theater
216 N Brand Blvd,
Glendale, CA 91206.
📞 (818) 243-2539.

Bing Theater
5905 Wilshire Blvd.
Map 7 D4.
📞 (213) 857-6010.

LA Civic Light Opera
📞 (213) 468-1704.

LA Classical Ballet
📞 (310) 427-5206.

LA Opera
135 N Grand Ave.
Map 11 E3.
📞 (213) 972-8001.

UCLA Center for the Performing Arts
405 Hilgard Ave.
Map 4 A4.
📞 (310) 825-2101.

ROCK, JAZZ AND BLUES

Baked Potato
26 E Colorado Blvd,
Pasadena, CA 91105.
📞 (818) 564-1122.

BB Kings' Blues Club
Universal City, CA 91608.
📞 (818) 622-5464.

Billboard Live
9039 W Sunset Blvd.
Map 6 A1.
📞 (310) 274-5800.

Catalina Bar and Grill
1640 N Cahuenga Blvd.
Map 2 C4.
📞 (213) 466-2210.

House of Blues
8430 W Sunset Blvd.
Map 1 A5.
📞 (213) 650-1451.

The Roxy
9009 W Sunset Blvd.
Map 6 A1.
📞 (310) 278-9457.

Universal Amphitheatre
Universal City, CA 91608.
📞 (818) 622-4440.

Viper Room
8852 W Sunset Blvd.
Map 6 B1.
📞 (310) 358-1880.

Whiskey a Go Go
8901 W Sunset Blvd.
Map 6 B1.
📞 (310) 535-0579.

CLUBS

Axis
652 N La Peer Drive.
Map 6 A2.
📞 (310) 659-0471.

Bar Marmont
8171 W Sunset Blvd.
Map 1 B5.
📞 (213) 650-0575.

Catch One
4067 W Pico Blvd,
Los Angeles, CA 90035.
📞 (213) 734-8849.

Crush Bar
1743 N Cahuenga Blvd.
Map 2 C4.
📞 (213) 461-9017.

The Garage
4519 Santa Monica Blvd.
Map 9 F1.
📞 (213) 683-3447.

STUDIO TOURS AND TV SHOWS

CBS-TV
7800 Beverly Blvd.
Map 7 D2.
📞 (213) 852-2458.

NBC-TV
3000 W Alameda Ave,
Burbank,
CA 91523.
📞 (818) 840-3538.
📠 (818) 840-3537.

Warner Bros
4000 Warner Blvd,
Burbank, CA 91522.
📞 (818) 954-1744.

SHOPPING IN LOS ANGELES

WHATEVER MONEY CAN BUY can be found in Los Angeles, from Cartier necklaces to everyday items. While indoor shopping malls are the norm for much of the United States, LA's temperate climate allows for a range of pleasant outdoor alternatives. Melrose Avenue *(see p109)* and Santa Monica's Third Street Promenade *(see p74)* are both young, lively areas, while **LA shopper** up-market Rodeo Drive *(see p90)* is probably the most famous. The best areas for the latest in fashion and home décor are Robertson Boulevard between Melrose Avenue and Burton Way, and Beverly Boulevard at Martel Avenue. Perhaps the most pleasant area to spend your money, however, is Old Pasadena *(see p150)*, which has a range of one-off shops in restored late 19th-century buildings.

Interior of the Westside Pavilion, just south of Westwood Village

SHOPPING CENTRES AND MALLS

LOS ANGELES does have its share of shopping centres, several of which outclass most American malls. The **Beverly Center** has an excellent selection of more than 170 stores. In a sophisticated outdoor setting, the Century City Shopping Center *(see p89)* has more than 120 shops. Nearby, the **Westside Pavilion** has an excellent array of children's shops. A more intimate space, Santa Monica Place *(see p73)* is at the southern end of the Third Street Promenade. In the San Fernando Valley, the **Sherman Oaks Galleria** spawned Frank Zappa's 'Valley Girl' of the 1980s.

DEPARTMENT STORES

EVERY SHOPPING MALL has at least one department store, all of which stock a vast range of goods. The favourites are **Bloomingdales** and **Macy's**.

Where Wilshire Boulevard runs through Beverly Hills' Golden Triangle *(see pp86–7)* is called Department Store Row. Among its four big name retailers are **Barneys New York** and **Saks Fifth Avenue. Nordstrom's** shoe department is legendary, as are its January and June half-price sales.

CLOTHES

FASHION STYLES are casual in LA, but couture clothes are available in Beverly Hills. **Todd Oldham** and **Tyler Trafficante** are two of the hottest women's fashion labels in town. **American Rag** features new and second-hand clothes and shoes for men, women and children. **Shop logo on** **Maxfield, Fred Segal** **Melrose Avenue** and **Ron Ross** are aimed at the well-heeled client who loves exciting and stylish clothes. **Friends** produce dresses and jeans that appeal to girls, while Melrose's **Betsey Johnson** maintains her fun attitude towards women's clothing. **Bernini** and **Mark Michaels** have some of the best fashion for men. For a casual LA look visit **Urban Outfitters** in Santa Monica. And if you have left home without your bikini, try visiting **Canyon Beachwear**.

ART, BOOKS, MUSIC AND ANTIQUES

RESIDENTS OF THIS CITY buy more books than in any city in the country. Some of the favourite independent bookshops are **Book Soup**, **Dutton's** and **Midnight Special Bookstore**. Many large chains, such as **Barnes and Noble** and **Borders**, may also have coffee bars.

Antiques shops are centred around Melrose Place, near Melrose Avenue, while some of the city's leading art galleries are located at Bergamot Station *(see p75)*. Other galleries include **LA Louver**, and **G Ray Hawkins**. There are plenty of record shops located throughout the city. The two shops with the most extensive collections are **Tower Records** and the **Virgin Megastore**, which are both situated on West Sunset Boulevard.

Up-market shops on Rodeo Drive *(see p90)*

SPECIALITY SHOPS

HOLLYWOOD MEMORABILIA is on sale throughout the city. Two of the best shops, however, are **Fantasies Come True** and **Larry Edmund's Cinema Bookshop**. A strong selection of Latin American arts and crafts, popular in Los Angeles, are at **The Folk Tree**. The award for the shop with the most gadgets and toys, aimed at the executive who has everything, goes to Rodeo Drive's Hammacher Schlemmer *(see p90)*.

FOOD AND WINE

CALIFORNIA has been blessed with excellent produce. Both Grand Central Market *(see p120)* and Farmers Market *(see p109)* are overflowing with a wide range of fresh fruit and vegetables. Considered one of the finest reasons to live in LA, **Trader Joe's** sells an array of gourmet foods and wines. The **Whole Foods Market** does the same for its health-conscious customers. The **Wine Merchant**'s cellars in Beverly Hills are superb.

Colourful stalls of produce in Grand Central Market *(see p120)*

DIRECTORY

SHOPPING CENTRES AND MALLS

Beverly Center
8500 Beverly Blvd.
Map 6 C2.
(310) 854-0070.

Sherman Oaks Galleria
15301 Ventura Blvd,
Sherman Oaks, CA 91403.
(818) 783-7100.

Westside Pavilion
10800 W Pico Blvd,
Los Angeles, CA 90064.
(310) 474-6255.

DEPARTMENT STORES

Barneys New York
9570 Wilshire Blvd.
Map 5 F4.
(310) 276-4400.

Bloomingdales
Beverly Center,
8500 Beverly Blvd.
Map 6 C2.
(310) 854-0070.

Macy's
Beverly Center,
8500 Beverly Blvd.
Map 6 C2.
(310) 854-6655.

Nordstrom
Westside Pavilion, 10830
W Pico Blvd, CA 90064.
(310) 470-6155.

Saks Fifth Avenue
9600 Wilshire Blvd.
Map 5 E4.
(310) 275-4211.

CLOTHES

American Rag
150 S La Brea Ave.
Map 7 F2.
(213) 935-3154.

Bernini
Beverly Center,
8500 Beverly Blvd.
Map 6 C2.
(310) 855-1786.

Betsey Johnson
7311 Melrose Ave.
Map 7 F1.
(213) 931-4490.

Canyon Beachwear
Beverly Center,
8500 Beverly Blvd.
Map 6 C2.
(310) 652-7848.

Fred Segal
8118 Melrose Ave.
Map 7 D1.
(213) 651-1935.

Friends
Beverly Center, 8500
Beverly Blvd. Map 6 C2.
(310) 657-6025.

Mark Michaels
4672 Admiralty Way,
Marina del Rey, CA 90292.
(310) 822-1707.

Maxfield
8825 Melrose Ave.
Map 6 B2.
(310) 274-8800.

Ron Ross
12930 Ventura Blvd,
Studio City, CA 91423.
(818) 788-8700.

Todd Oldham
7386 Beverly Blvd.
Map 7 E2.
(213) 936-6045.

Tyler Trafficante
7290 Beverly Blvd.
Map 7 F2.
(213) 624-9299.

Urban Outfitters
1440 Third St Promenade,
Santa Monica,
CA 90401.
(310) 394-1404.

ART, BOOKS, MUSIC AND ANTIQUES

Barnes and Noble
1201 Third St Promenade,
Santa Monica,
CA 90401.
(310) 260-9110.

Book Soup
8818 W Sunset Blvd.
Map 1 A5.
(310) 659-3110.

Borders
1360 Westwood Blvd.
Map 4 A5.
(310) 475-3444.

Dutton's
11975 San Vicente Blvd,
Brentwood, CA 90049.
(310) 476-6263.

G Ray Hawkins
908 Colorado Ave,
Santa Monica,
CA 90401.
(310) 394-5558.

LA Louver
45 N Venice Blvd,
Venice, CA 90291.
(310) 822-4955.

Midnight Special Bookstore
1318 Third St Promenade,
Santa Monica, CA 90401.
(310) 393-2923.

Tower Records
8801 W Sunset Blvd.
Map 1 A5.
(310) 657-7300.

Virgin Megastore
8000 W Sunset Blvd.
Map 1 B5.
(213) 650-8666.

SPECIALITY SHOPS

Fantasies Come True
8012 Melrose Ave.
Map 7 D1.
(213) 655-2636.

The Folk Tree
199 S Fair Oaks Ave,
Pasadena,
CA 91105.
(818) 793-4828.

Larry Edmund's Cinema Bookshop
6644 Hollywood Blvd.
Map 2 B4.
(213) 463-3273.

FOOD AND WINE

Whole Foods Market
239 Crescent Drive.
Map 5 F4.
(310) 274-3360.

Trader Joe's
7304 Santa Monica Blvd.
Map 7 F1.
(213) 851-9772.

The Wine Merchant
9701 S Santa Monica Blvd.
Map 5 E4.
(310) 278-7322.

GETTING AROUND LOS ANGELES

THE SPRAWLING 467 sq miles (1,200 sq km) of Los Angeles may seem daunting to navigate. A network of freeways *(see pp170–71)* provides an accessible, if sometimes crowded, means of travelling in the area. The only time-effective method of touring the city is by car, although the public transport system works well in downtown Los

Angeles and Hollywood. Taxis must usually be ordered by telephone. Taxis run from the airport, but can be expensive. Buses are often crowded and slow. They run on most of the main streets in the city. LA's growing underground system, the Metro, is very useful when exploring the business district. Some neighbourhoods are best seen on foot.

Taxi in Beverly Hills

Driving towards downtown Los Angeles on the freeway

DRIVING

PLANNING IS THE KEY to making driving in Los Angeles less overwhelming. First, refer to the map on pages 170–71 to see which freeway changes or exit you will need. Second, avoid rush hour on the freeways. The peak times are from Monday to Friday, 8am to 9:30am and 4pm to 6:30pm. Some freeways are busy regardless of the hour and it can be less stressful to take one of the city's major streets. When parking, read the posted signs for limitations and carry plenty of 25-cent coins for the parking meters. At night it is safer to valet park.

WALKING

EVEN THOUGH the city is very spread out, some districts are pedestrian-friendly. Third Street Promenade, and the

beach and Main Street in Santa Monica *(see pp72–5)* are all nice areas for walking. Other areas include: the business district in downtown Los Angeles *(see pp118–19)*, Old Pasadena *(see p150)*, Melrose Avenue *(see p109)*, the Golden Triangle in Beverly Hills *(see pp86–7)* and Long Beach's Pine Avenue *(see p128)*. Do not walk at night unless the street is well lit and populated.

CYCLING

THE COASTAL BIKE path that runs for 25 miles (40 km) beside Santa Monica Bay is the best place to cycle. Other popular areas are Griffith Park and the Oceanside Bike Path in Long Beach. Bicycles are not allowed on the freeways. The **LA Department of Transportation** provides detailed route maps. Bicycle rentals are available from **Sea Mist Skate Rentals** at Santa Monica Pier, the pizza stands at Santa Monica Beach and **Alfredo's** in Long Beach.

BUSES AND SUBWAY

GREATER LOS ANGELES is served by the **Metropolitan Transportation Authority (MTA)**. Bus stops display an MTA sign. For sightseeing, the following buses run on main thoroughfares: Wilshire Boulevard to Santa Monica Beach, Nos. 20 and 320; to Westwood and UCLA, No. 21; Santa Monica Boulevard to the beach, No. 4; Sunset Boulevard to Pacific Palisades, No. 2.

The **DASH** shuttle provides convenient travel within small areas, such as Downtown LA and Hollywood, for 25 cents. The **Santa Monica Blue Bus Co.** and **Long Beach Transit** service those communities.

The three major routes of LA's subway system are being extended. The Metro Red Line starts at Union Station and runs to Western Avenue. The Blue Line operates between Downtown Los Angeles and Long Beach. Running from Norwalk to Redondo Beach, the Green Line is useful for the airport.

Cycling through Venice on the coastal bike path

Los Angeles Freeway Route Planner

A CAR IS ESSENTIAL in Los Angeles and is the quickest way of getting around this vast city. All freeways are numbered but most also have names, such as the Golden State Freeway (I-5). Plan your journey before departure as freeway exits are signposted by street name rather than by area. It is advisable not to use the freeways during rush hour (8–9:30am and 4–6:30pm). For more details on getting around LA see pages 168–9.

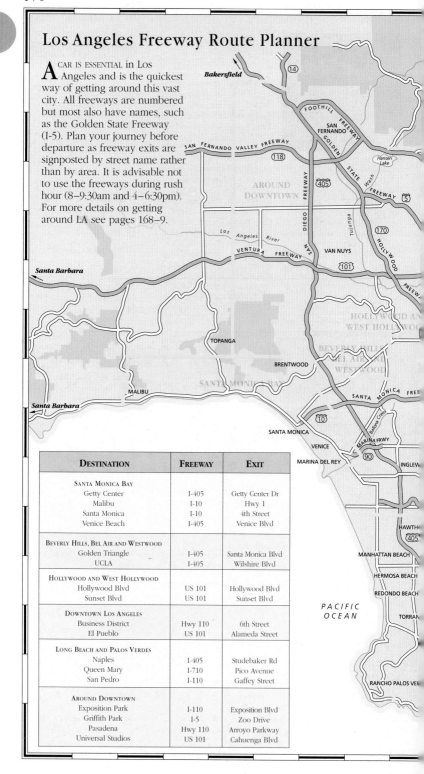

DESTINATION	FREEWAY	EXIT
SANTA MONICA BAY		
Getty Center	I-405	Getty Center Dr
Malibu	I-10	Hwy 1
Santa Monica	I-10	4th Street
Venice Beach	I-405	Venice Blvd
BEVERLY HILLS, BEL AIR AND WESTWOOD		
Golden Triangle	I-405	Santa Monica Blvd
UCLA	I-405	Wilshire Blvd
HOLLYWOOD AND WEST HOLLYWOOD		
Hollywood Blvd	US 101	Hollywood Blvd
Sunset Blvd	US 101	Sunset Blvd
DOWNTOWN LOS ANGELES		
Business District	Hwy 110	6th Street
El Pueblo	US 101	Alameda Street
LONG BEACH AND PALOS VERDES		
Naples	I-405	Studebaker Rd
Queen Mary	I-710	Pico Avenue
San Pedro	I-110	Gaffey Street
AROUND DOWNTOWN		
Exposition Park	I-110	Exposition Blvd
Griffith Park	I-5	Zoo Drive
Pasadena	Hwy 110	Arroyo Parkway
Universal Studios	US 101	Cahuenga Blvd

KEY

Freeway

Other road

River

BURBANK

GLENDALE

134

Los Angeles River

2

PASADENA

ALHAMBRA

GLENDALE FREEWAY

PASADENA FREEWAY

210

210

210

FOOTHILL FREEWAY

ARCADIA

EL MONTE

San Bernardino

DOWNTOWN LOS ANGELES

MONTEREY PARK

10

60

SAN BERNARDINO FREEWAY

PICO RIVERA

605

FREEWAY

Rio Hondo

San Gabriel River

WHITTIER

POMONA FREEWAY

Riverside

110

HARBOR FREEWAY

FREEWAY

LONG BEACH FREEWAY

710

SOUTHGATE

DOWNEY

WATTS

CENTURY

105

FREEWAY

LYNWOOD

COMPTON

91

PARAMOUNT

BELLFLOWER

NORWALK

5

SANTA ANA

BUENA PARK

FULLERTON

ORANGE FREEWAY

GARDENA FREEWAY

ARTESIA FREEWAY

LAKEWOOD

605

91

RIVERSIDE FREEWAY

Riverside

Los Angeles River

Coyote Creek

Dominguez Channel

CARSON

SAN

DIEGO FREEWAY

ANAHEIM

57

ORANGE

SIGNAL HILL

110

LONG BEACH

405

GARDEN GROVE

22

GARDEN GROVE FREEWAY

SANTA ANA

Santa Ana River

San Diego

LONG BEACH AND PALOS VERDES

PEDRO

SAN DIEGO FREEWAY

405

HUNTINGTON BEACH

Laguna Beach

0 kilometres 10

0 miles 10

LOS ANGELES STREET FINDER

THE KEY MAP below shows the areas of LA covered in the *Street Finder*. It includes the city districts of Beverly Hills, Bel Air and Westwood, Hollywood and West Hollywood, and Downtown Los Angeles. All places of interest in these areas are marked on the maps in addition to useful information, such as railway stations, metro stops, bus termini and emergency services. A *Freeway Route Planner*

In-line skater at Venice Beach

can be found on pages 170–71. The map references given with sights described in the LA section of the guide refer to the maps on the following pages. Map references are also given for entertainment venues *(see p165)*, shops *(see p167)*, hotels *(see pp508–13)* and restaurants *(see pp544–50)* in LA. Road map references refer to the map inside the back cover. The symbols used for sights and other features on the *Street Finder* maps are listed in the key below.

KEY TO STREET FINDER

Major sight	Tourist information	Freeway
Place of interest	Hospital with casualty unit	One-way street
Amtrak station	Police station	Pedestrianized street
Metro Red Line station	Post office	**SCALE OF MAPS 1–11**
Metro Blue Line station	Golf course	0 metres 500
Bus terminus	Railway line	0 yards 500

0 kilometres 2

0 miles 2

SOUTHERN CALIFORNIA

Southern California at a Glance

SOUTHERN CALIFORNIA is a region of startling contrasts.
Scorching deserts give way to snow-capped mountains, with views of the coast. It is possible to surf in
the morning, ski in the afternoon and play golf in the
evening. From San Simeon to San Diego, the coast is
lined with resorts, reflecting a shoreline that ranges
from rugged bluffs to golden sands. Attractions along
the way include historic missions, the charming cities
of Santa Barbara and San Diego and the theme parks
of Orange County. Further inland are two of the US's
most startling desert areas: Death Valley National Park
and the Joshua Tree National Park.

Santa Barbara Mission (see
pp212–13) *is the most visited mission in
the state and is the only one in the
chain of missions to have remained in
continuous use since it was founded
in 1786. The church façade is in
Classical style, a theme continued
inside the building.*

SOUTH CENTRAL
CALIFORNIA
(See pp194–215)

LOS ANGELES
(See pp54–183)

Hearst Castle™ (see pp202–
205), *on the south central
coast, was built by publishing
tycoon William R Hearst.
In the 1930s and '40s he
invited Hollywood stars and
royalty here and entertained
them lavishly. The Neptune
Pool is particularly stunning.*

ORANGE COUNTY
(See pp216–33)

*Mission San Juan
Capistrano* (see pp230–31)
*in southern Orange County is
known as the "Jewel of the
Missions". Founded in 1776,
its main buildings have been
beautifully restored and
feature historical exhibits.*

0 kilometres   50

0 miles   50

Death Valley National Park (see pp280–83) *in the Mojave Desert encompasses one of the hottest places on earth and the lowest point in the western hemisphere. Within Death Valley, which is 140 miles (225 km) long, lie dry lake beds, sand dunes and small outposts built around springs. Despite the harsh conditions, the area is rich in flora and fauna. Sights of historical interest in the park include Scotty's Castle.*

THE MOJAVE DESERT
(See pp270–83)

Joshua Tree National Park (see pp268–9) *in the Low Desert is famed for its distinctive trees. Within easy reach of the city of Palm Springs, it offers breathtaking views of the stark desert landscape with its remarkable rock formations.*

THE INLAND EMPIRE AND LOW DESERT
(See pp258–69)

Balboa Park (see pp246–9) *in San Diego was the site of the Panama–Pacific Exposition of 1915. The park is now home to many museums, such as the San Diego Museum of Man, housed in the landmark California Building. The famous San Diego Zoo lies just to the north of Balboa Park.*

SAN DIEGO COUNTY
(See pp234–57)

Surfing and Beach Culture

I F SOUTHERN CALIFORNIANS worship at the altars of youth, health and beauty, then their churches are the beaches. Here, unbelievably beautiful men and women parade their surgically-enhanced bodies beneath the ever-present sun. Sports favoured include skating and volleyball, but the ability to look good on a surf-board is the ultimate cool. Surfing was originally practised by the Hawaiian nobility as a religious ceremony. It **Bust of Duke Kahanamoku** was introduced to California by Hawaiian George Freeth in 1907 *(see p62)* and popularized in the 1920s in Waikiki by Olympic swimmer Duke Kahanamoku. In 1961 the Beach Boys released 'Surfin'' and the sport took off around the world. Today surf culture is part of the mainstream consciousness. The loose-fitting clothes favoured by surfers are reproduced on the catwalk and surfing slang is used by many who have never been near the beach.

The Beach Boys *sang of the joys of surfing despite the fact that none of the group could surf.*

Films such as **Gidget** *(1959),* Ride the Wild Surf *(1964) and* Beach Blanket Bingo *(1965), as well as the documentary* Endless Summer, *helped to establish the cultural allure of surfing. Lengthy beach parties in the style of these films were highly popular during the 1960s.*

WHERE TO LEARN TO SURF

Beginners are advised to start by body surfing without a board. Boogie boarding, with a half-length board, is also far easier to master than surfing. Beaches with waves that break parallel to the beach (a surf break) are the most suitable. The best beaches on which to learn to boogie board include Santa Monica *(see p61)*, Carpinteria *(p199)* and Del Mar *(p239)*. Beginners should avoid famous surfing beaches such as Surfrider *(p60)*, San Clemente *(p220)* and Huntington *(p220)*, as conditions can overwhelm the inexperienced.

Boys with boogie boards weighing up the surf

Lifeguards are stationed on most county and state beaches in California during the summer. Their distinctive grey huts have been made famous throughout the world by the television series Baywatch. *Always follow their instructions on the beach, and ask if you are in doubt about the tidal conditions.*

A **"tube"** is a cylindrical passage formed when a wave breaks and the crest curls over.

SURFING HIGHLIGHTS

One exhilarating surfing experience is to "beat the tube". The surfer rides beneath the crest, regulating his speed and position to stay just ahead of the falling wave. If he goes too fast he comes out of the wave; too slowly and he gets knocked off. The wave loses momentum as it nears the shore. At this point the surfer will shoot out of the tube, remaining upright.

By changing position a surfer can alter the speed and direction in which he or she is travelling. Crouching lowers the centre of gravity and increases stability.

OTHER BEACH ACTIVITIES

Southern California's spectacular beaches are used by a wide variety of sports enthusiasts. Although the beaches are most popular in summer, activities are enjoyed year-round by hardy souls. Sailing is popular, with thousands of yachts of all sizes harboured in a string of marinas along the coast. Windsurfing and kite-flying also take advantage of the prevailing onshore winds. Sea kayakers often explore the rocky coasts of the Channel Islands *(see p214)* and the mainland. Volleyball, once limited to friendly matches, is now a major professional sport with competitions held along the Southern Californian coast each summer.

Modern surfboards are made out of light, man-made materials, such as fibreglass, allowing surfers to reach much higher speeds. Their bright colours make them easy to see in the water.

The first boards came from Hawaii and were called coffin lids because of their distinctive shape. Made out of wood, they were heavy and unwieldy. Early surfboards can be seen at the Lighthouse Surfing Museum in Santa Cruz (see p491).

Friendly volleyball game in Santa Monica

Californian Car Culture

Californian car licence plate

IT IS DIFFICULT TO understand Southern California without considering the influence of the car. The introduction of the freeway system in LA in 1940 *(see p50)* spawned an entirely new culture centred around the automobile. Owning a car became integral to the Californian identity and the open desert road came to symbolize the freedom of the state. Customizing automobiles also made the car an art object. Drive-in movies led to the convenience of drive-in banks and fast-food restaurants. But there was a price to pay: smog, the result of car exhaust and sunlight, has become a fact of life in LA. Today, cars have cleaner exhausts, but LA has to cope with some 8 million cars on its increasingly "gridlocked" streets.

Los Angeles' freeways, *begun in the 1950s, have expanded into a complex network, linking the city with the rest of the state.*

Ford Thunderbird badge

The canvas hood could be lowered for sunny weather or raised in rain.

Chrome concealed the reversing lights.

Chrome waistline strip

BIRTHPLACE OF THE MOTORCYCLE GANG

In the 1950s especially, California was home to rival gangs of "outlaw bikers". The most famous, the Hell's Angels, began with a group of World War II veterans in San Bernardino in 1948. Their notorious reputation was immortalized in the 1953 film *The Wild One* with Marlon Brando. Today, the Hell's Angels have around 1,000 members worldwide, who continue to symbolize defiance of authority.

Marlon Brando

Japanese cars, *such as those imported through Worldport LA (see p62), continue to be hot competition for American-made automobiles.*

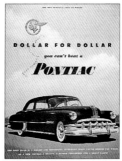

This car advertisement for Pontiac dates from 1950. As automobiles became more of a status symbol, manufacturers competed for customers with increasingly bright adverts.

WHERE TO SEE CALIFORNIAN CAR CULTURE

Californians are very proud of their car culture and history; most towns have a parade or car show featuring vintage, classic and customized automobiles. For information, enquire at the local visitors' centre *(see p589)*. One of the largest automobile shows is held in early April at the LA County Fairgrounds in Pomona. Other meetings include the Muscle Car Show in Bakersfield *(see p215)*, West Coast Kustom Cars in Paso Robles *(see pp200–201)* and the Graffiti USA Festival and Cruise in Modesto. California also hosts several famous motor races, such as the Long Beach Toyota Grand Prix in April *(p32)* and the Savemart 300 Nascar Winston Cup Race in Sonoma *(pp448–9)*. There are several world-class automobile museums in the state, including the Petersen Automotive Museum *(p114)* in Los Angeles and the Behring Auto Museum near San Jose *(pp412–13)*.

Tucker Torpedo, one of the cars on display at the Petersen Automotive Museum in LA

Chrome door quarterlights were turned from inside.

The wraparound windscreen imitated aircraft designs.

PINK CADILLAC

With its glamorous design and convertible roof, the 1959 pink Cadillac suited California's image and climate perfectly. However, the car's two-tonne weight meant that its steering was heavy and it soon gave way to more efficient designs.

Chrome bumpers protected the front of the car.

White sidewall tyres were a popular option because of their smart look.

The Model T Ford (affectionately known as the Tin Lizzie) first appeared in 1908. In 1913, Henry Ford introduced the assembly line and cars could be bought for as little as $500. This photograph of a 1924 beachside traffic jam shows that it took only a few years for Californians to become dependent on the car.

Recreational vehicles (RVs) became popular in the 1960s. Californians could now take to the open road and explore the state's wilderness without leaving any home comforts behind.

Deserts and Water Networks

MUCH OF SOUTHERN CALIFORNIA is desert, and before 1913, migrants to this area depended on wells for their water. The population grew extremely quickly and it soon became necessary to engineer what is now one of the most elaborate water networks on earth. This network has turned parts of what was once inhospitable desert into productive land, and made possible the desert resort of Palm Springs and the huge populations of the Southern Californian cities. However, the South's high rate of water consumption places a great demand on the region's major sources of water: the Colorado River and the Sierra Nevada Mountains.

The Sacramento/San Joaquin River Delta supplies water to the farms of the south. At peak times, pumping causes the river to flow in reverse, bringing salt water from San Francisco Bay.

Owens Lake *(see p479) lies between the Sierra Nevada Mountains and the Mojave Desert, in Owens Valley. The Los Angeles Aqueduct diverted water from Owens River to LA and the 100-sq mile (260-sq km) lake gradually dried up.*

Cuyama River

California Aqueduct

• BAKERSFIELD

SAN LUIS OBISPO

SANTA BARBARA •

SAN GABRIEL MOUNTAI

LOS ANGELES •

The Los Angeles Aqueduct *made the San Fernando Valley fertile (see p140). Land speculators made their fortunes when the aqueduct was completed in 1914.*

WILLIAM MULHOLLAND

As head of the Los Angeles city water department, William Mulholland (1855–1935) *(see p140)* and his colleague Fred Eaton designed an aqueduct and a series of tunnels to lead from Owens Valley to LA. Completed in 1914, it cost more than $24 million. By 1929 the supplies were no longer sufficient and they had to divert water from Mono Basin and the Colorado River, 400 miles (645 km) away.

0 kilometres   75

0 miles   75

KEY

▨	Populated areas
～	Rivers
⚌	Dry rivers
▦	Canals
▩	Aqueducts

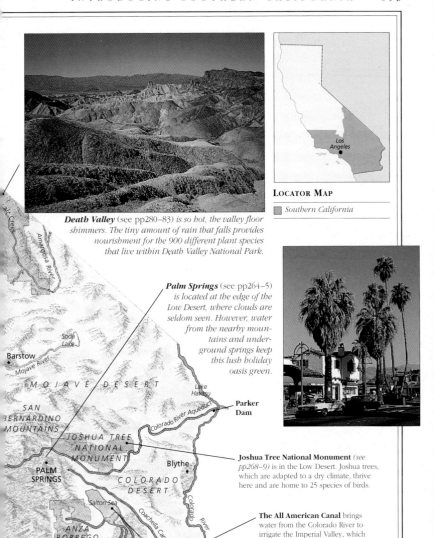

Death Valley (see pp280–83) is so hot, the valley floor shimmers. The tiny amount of rain that falls provides nourishment for the 900 different plant species that live within Death Valley National Park.

LOCATOR MAP

☐ Southern California

Palm Springs (see pp264–5) is located at the edge of the Low Desert, where clouds are seldom seen. However, water from the nearby mountains and underground springs keep this lush holiday oasis green.

Parker Dam

Joshua Tree National Monument (see pp268–9) is in the Low Desert. Joshua trees, which are adapted to a dry climate, thrive here and are home to 25 species of birds.

The All American Canal brings water from the Colorado River to irrigate the Imperial Valley, which provides the US with year-round lettuce, melons, tomatoes and peas.

SOUTHERN CALIFORNIA'S WATER NETWORK

Southern California has two main sources of water: ice-melt from the Sierra Nevada Mountains in the north, brought to LA via the LA Aqueduct, and the Colorado River to the southeast. The Colorado River Aqueduct system carries water 672 miles (1,080 km) from the Parker Dam, via 395 miles (635 km) of pipes. Imperial Valley has a network of canals, making it fertile. The same canals irrigate the desert resort of Palm Springs.

The Salton Sea was formed in 1905 when a break in the Imperial Valley's irrigation system allowed flood waters into the Salton Basin.

SOUTH CENTRAL CALIFORNIA

SOUTH CENTRAL CALIFORNIA *is a land of lonely passes and wooded streams. Broad sandy beaches stretch for miles along the gentle coast with empty, tawny hills as their only backdrop. It is a region of small and friendly towns, scattered farms and vineyards nestled in scenic valleys. Further inland is Los Padres National Forest, where mountain lions roam freely and eagles and condors soar overhead.*

The region's Spanish heritage is highly visible, and no more so than in Santa Barbara. Here the area's most important garrison and the legendary structure that came to be known as "Queen of the Missions" *(see pp212–13)* can be found. The city's red tile Mission Revival-style architecture *(see p27)* has been imitated throughout the State.

Following the break-up of the wealthy missions during the 1830s, the land was divided into a handful of sprawling ranches, then the 1849 Gold Rush brought an influx of Easterners to California. The newcomers subdivided the large estates and set up small farming communities. They touted the land throughout the world as a "semi-tropical paradise", where the first season's crops would pay for the cost of the land.

In the early part of the 20th century the Central Coast was a popular holiday destination, drawing thousands of people each summer to seaside towns such as Pismo and Avila Beach. Further north, at San Simeon, millionaire William Randolph Hearst built his own personal playground, the fabulous private museum now known as Hearst Castle™.

Today, South Central California provides a wealth of activities, from horse-drawn wine-tasting tours in the scenic Santa Ynez valley to relaxation on empty beaches. The more active can try kayaking on the Kern River near Bakersfield. Offshore, the Channel Islands offer a unique view of the area's ecosystems and an opportunity to see the annual passage of the magnificent grey whales. The east of the region is dominated by the Los Padres National Forest, an area of breathtaking beauty with miles of hiking trails and drives through mountain scenery. Here, too, are signs of the Chumash Indians who once lived in thriving communities along the coast. Their enigmatic petroglyphs remain as silent reminders of their presence throughout these hills.

Seasonal produce on display in Morro Bay

◁ **Fishing off the pier at Pismo Beach**

Exploring South Central California

SOUTH CENTRAL CALIFORNIA'S BEACHES and coastal plains
are backed by low rolling hills covered with groves
of oak. Beyond this, the Los Padres National Forest
has hundreds of miles of mountainous hiking trails.
Just north of Santa Barbara, the gentle countryside
around Santa Ynez has proved perfect for growing
vines. Along the coast of San
Luis Obispo County,
the seaside towns of
Morro Bay and Pismo
Beach are known for
their fishing and clamming.
In the northwest, Hearst
Castle is one of California's
most popular tourist attractions.

Mission San Miguel Arcángel's campanario

SIGHTS AT A GLANCE

SEE ALSO
• *Where to Stay* pp514–15
• *Where to Eat* pp551–3

KEY

Freeway
Major road
Minor road
Scenic route
River
Viewpoint

Rugged mountains in the vast Los Padres National Forest

GETTING AROUND

The I-101 and Hwy 1 follow the coast, passing through all the major sights. Amtrak runs a daily service, the Coast Starlight, from Los Angeles to San Francisco, stopping at Santa Barbara and San Luis Obispo. Greyhound buses also stop at these cities. There are roads through the Los Padres National Forest to Bakersfield, but the most common route to that city is the I-5 from Los Angeles. Trips to the Channel Islands National Park leave from Ventura.

Stearns Wharf, the fishing pier at Santa Barbara

California Coastline: South Central

THE SOUTH CENTRAL COAST offers miles of accessible, broad, sandy beaches and some of the best surfing in the state. The water here is cooler than the ocean off the Los Angeles to San Diego coast, but these beaches offer privacy and solitude for swimming, sunbathing and picnicking. The rugged mountain backdrop appears so close you can almost smell the pine and chaparral. Several South Central beaches are within state parks and have hiking and nature trails that climb upwards, offering spectacular views of the unspoiled coast below.

★ **Avila State Beach** ③

This white, sandy beach, near a quiet seaside town, has a wooden fishing pier. It is popular in the summer for surfing and swimming.

MONTEREY

• San Simeon

① 46

SALINAS KING CITY

41

101

Morro Rock

② • San Luis Obispo

227

③ • Pismo Beach

④

1

166

• Santa Maria

101

135

1 **La Purísima Concepción Missio**

Lompoc • 246

1

Point Concepción ⑤

★ **Pismo State Beach** ④

Known primarily for its clams _(see pp206–7)_, the beach's compact sand also makes a perfect surface for volleyball.

0 kilometres   20

0 miles   20

**La Purísima Concepción Mission**, the 11th mission in the chain (see pp42–3), is situated in Lompoc Valley (see p207). La Purísima is the most fully reconstructed of the missions. A visit gives a real insight into the Franciscans' living conditions.

***Morro Rock** is one of South Central California's most endearing landmarks. Used as a navigation point by the first Spanish explorers, it is best seen at sunrise or sunset (see p206).*

LOCATOR MAP

William R Hearst Memorial State Beach ①

Situated below Hearst Castle™ *(see pp202–5)*, this sheltered, crescent-shaped beach is a good spot for a picnic. Boats can be chartered from the pier for deep-sea fishing trips.

Montana de Oro State Park ②

The rocky beach is backed by 8,000 acres (3,250 ha) of park. Hiking trails wind through the hills and, in winter, monarch butterflies can be seen in the eucalyptus trees *(see p209)*.

★ East Beach ⑦

This sandy beach stretches for 1.5 miles (2.5 km) from Stearns Wharf, Santa Barbara's fishing pier. Children will enjoy the playground and paddling pool.

Gaviota State Park ⑤

This 5.5-mile (9-km) beach, in a sheltered cove, has a playground and fishing pier. It adjoins 2,800 acres (1,100 ha) of parkland with hiking trails.

El Capitan State Beach ⑥

El Capitan is a good place for spotting wildlife, both in the rock pools along the beach and in the woods behind. Grey whales pass close to the shore during the winter *(see p580)*.

Carpinteria State Beach ⑧

Backed by the Santa Ynez Mountains, this sheltered beach is one of the safest and most pleasant places to swim in Southern California.

Point Mugu State Park ⑩

At the western end of the Santa Monica Mountains, the park is crisscrossed with hiking trails. Dolphins and Californian sea lions are often seen offshore.

Leo Carrillo State Beach North ⑪

This stretch of Leo Carrillo State Beach *(see p60)*, which extends across the LA County border, is one of the classic spots for surfing in California.

★ San Buenaventura State Beach ⑨

Close to the centre of Ventura *(see p214)*, this broad beach is sheltered by the harbour breakwater, making it a good area for swimming.

KEY

〰	Freeway
▬	Major road
▬	Minor road
〰	River
☆	Viewpoint

Arched colonnade at the Mission San Miguel Arcángel

Mission San Miguel Arcángel ❶

Mission St at 12th St, San Miguel.
Road map B5. **[** (805) 467-3256.
◯ daily. **●** 1 Jan, Easter, Thanksgiving, 25 Dec. **&**

THE 16TH MISSION in the Californian chain *(see pp42–3)* was founded in 1797 by Father Fermín de Lasuén, the successor to Father Junípero Serra *(see p42)*. Nine years later the original church was destroyed by fire and the present building, which is still in use as a parish church, was completed in 1819.

The six rooms in the mission's museum are furnished as they would have been in the early 19th century. The first contains a 16th-century carved wooden statue depicting the mission's patron saint, St Michael the Archangel, vanquishing the devil. The wall decorations in the church were painted by Native Americans in 1822–3, under the direction of Esteban Munras of Monterey.

In addition to growing grain and raising cattle, the padres made their own sacramental wine. Today the surrounding hills shelter over 30 wineries.

Following secularization in 1834, the mission was used as a warehouse and bar. In 1928 it was returned to the padres and restoration was begun. Today it functions as a retreat centre and Franciscan novitiate.

Hearst Castle™ ❷

See pp202–205.

Cambria ❸

Road map B5. **🏠** 5,000. **🚌**
ℹ 767 Main St (805 927-3624).

SITUATED BETWEEN rugged seashore and pine-clad hills, Cambria began as a mercury mining settlement in 1866. Later it became a centre for dairy farming and timber production and today it is a popular location for artists and craftspeople.

The town is divided into two distinct districts: East Village, a charming colony of Arts and Crafts houses *(see p27)*, and West Village, which is more modern. Main Street, which joins the two, is lined with specialist shops, art galleries and restaurants, as well as Lull House, Cambria's oldest residence.

Among the houses on Hillcrest Drive, just north of Main Street, is Nit Wit Ridge. It was built by local contractor Art Beal, who was known as "Captain Nit Wit". This whimsical abode was fashioned over six decades, starting in the 1930s, out of salvaged material, from sea shells to old tyres. To the north of the town, on Moonstone Drive, at the edge

Statue of St Michael the Archangel

of the ocean, is the beautiful Leffingwell Landing, which offers excellent views of the crashing surf and occasionally the sea lions, whales and otters out at sea. At low tide it is also possible to climb down to the rock pools at the bottom of the cliffs. The area is also well-equipped for picnickers.

Paso Robles ❹

Road map B5. **🏠** 21,000. **🚌**
ℹ 1225 Park St (805 238-0506).

PASO ROBLES, or "Pass of the Oaks", was once part of the 26,000-acre (10,500-ha) El Paso de Robles ranch. In 1857, a sulphurous hot spring, long used by Indians for its curative powers, was transformed into a health resort. With the arrival of the Southern Pacific Railway to the area in 1886, the town quickly developed and was incorporated three years later.

Today, Paso Robles is ringed with horse ranches, vineyards, wineries and more than 5,000 acres (2,000 ha) of almond orchards that blossom in early spring. The hot springs have now been capped – they were polluting the Salinas River – but the town still has much to offer. On Vine Street, between 12th and 20th streets, are several restored buildings from the 1890s, including **Call-Booth House Gallery**. Here works by mainly local artists are displayed in a Victorian setting.

Some of Paso Robles' many restaurants are also located in

Nit Wit Ridge in Cambria, made out of junk

Wine festival at the Arciero Winery in Paso Robles

19th-century buildings: Berardi & Sons was once the home of the town's daily newspaper; McLee's Steak House, with its huge stained-glass windows, was formerly a church; and Touch of Paso occupies a former post house on the Overland Stage Company route.

The Paso Robles Inn and Gardens, at 1003 Spring Street, stands on the site of the 1860 Hot Springs Hotel. The latter was replaced in 1891 with a three-storey red-brick hotel designed by Stanford White. This building in turn was burned down in a fire in 1940. Visitors to the town may wander through the current hotel's landscaped gardens.

Two important events on Paso Robles' calendar are the California Mid-State Fair – a large agricultural and livestock fair in early August with a reputation for top entertainment – and the Wine Festival in May, during which visitors can sample wines from more than 20 vineyards in the surrounding area.

ENVIRONS: Situated 17 miles (27 km) northwest of Paso Robles, off County Road G14, **Lake Naciemento** is a local recreational spot. Set in a picturesque valley amid pine and oak trees, the lake offers fishing (bass and catfish are often caught here), camping, water sports and picnicking.

At the junction of Hwy 46 and Hwy 41, 15 miles (24 km) east of Paso Robles, is the stainless steel **James Dean Monument**. Set around a tree of heaven, it is a memorial to the film actor who died here,

aged 24, when he crashed his silver Porsche 550 spider on 30 September 1955. A metal plaque gives details of James Dean's short life.

🏛 **Call-Booth House Gallery**
1314 Vine St. 📞 (805) 238-5473.
🕐 Wed–Sun. ⬤ public hols. 📷

Atascadero ❺

Road map B5. 🚶 25,300.
🚉 San Luis Obispo. 🚌 Dial-A-Ride
(805 466-7433). 🚏 ℹ 6550 El
Camino Real (805 466-2044).

ATASCADERO, which means "muddy place" in Spanish, was founded in 1913 by the publisher Edward G Lewis, who bought the 23,000-acre (9,300-ha) ranch to build his ideal town. Lewis's headquarters were in an attractive Italian Renaissance-style building, constructed in 1914 for almost half a million dollars. Since then it has been used as a boy's school and a veterans' memorial. Today it houses the

City Administration Building. The **Atascadero Historical Society Museum**, situated in the first floor rotunda, houses hundreds of photographs that were taken by Lewis's official photographer. The museum also contains artifacts that belonged to early settlers in the area. The building is set in the pretty Sunken Gardens Park, surrounded by fountains and statuary.

Unfortunately, Lewis went bankrupt before Atascadero was finished. The town continued to grow steadily from the 1950s, however, as more people were attracted by its rural atmosphere. It was incorporated in 1979.

Today's visitors frequent the town's antique shops, smart boutiques and its weekly farmers' market. There is a week-long Colony Days celebration in October, when the town remembers its early history with a parade and other festivities.

Just south of the town, off Hwy 41, Atascadero Park and Lake has pleasant walks and offers fishing, picnic areas and a children's playground. Next door, the 3-acre (1-ha) **Charles Paddock Zoo** houses more than 100 species, including monkeys, meerkats, grizzly bears, a pair of tigers and a jaguar.

🏛 **Atascadero Historical Society Museum**
6500 Palma Ave. 📞 (805) 466-8341.
🕐 Mon–Sat. ⬤ public hols.
Donation.
🐾 **Charles Paddock Zoo**
9100 Morro Rd, Atascadero.
📞 (805) 461-5080. 🕐 daily.
⬤ Thanksgiving, 25 Dec. 📷

Ducks swimming on Atascadero Lake

Hearst Castle™ ❷

Tile detail

Hearst castle™ perches on a hill above the village of San Simeon. The private playground and museum of media tycoon William Randolph Hearst is today one of California's top tourist attractions. Its three guest houses are superb buildings in their own right, but the highlight of the tour is the twin-towered Casa Grande. Designed by the Paris-trained architect Julia Morgan and built in stages from 1922 to 1947, its 115 rooms hold many artworks and epitomize the glamour of the 1930s and 1940s.

Façade
Casa Grande's poured concrete façade is in the Mediterranean Revival style. It is embellished with ancient architectural fragments.

Theater
The walls of Hearst's private cinema are lined with damask. Lamps held by gilded caryatids light the 50 seats.

★ **Billiard Room**
This room features a French early 16th-century millefleurs tapestry.

TIMELINE

1865 George Hearst buys 48,000 acres (19,425 ha) of land near San Simeon	**1921** Casa del Mar completed	*16th-century wooden chest, depicting Christ Meeting St Peter on the lid*	**1958** Hearst Castle™ opens to public
	1924 Casa del Sol completed	**1951** Hearst dies	
1920	**1930**	**1940**	**1950**
1919 WR Hearst inherits family fortune. Plans a house on "Camp Hill"	**1922** Work begins on Casa Grande	**1935** Neptune Pool completed	*Classical Greek amphora dating from 3rd century AD*
		1928 Hearst moves in to Casa Grande	**1947** Hearst has heart attack and leaves San Simeon

★ Gothic Study
When in San Simeon, Hearst ran his empire from the Gothic Study. He kept his books behind grilles.

Celestial Suite
The two Celestial Suite bedrooms are located high up in the north and south towers. They are linked by a spacious sitting room.

★ Assembly Room
A 16th-century French fireplace dominates the Assembly Room. Italian choir stalls line the walls, which are hung with Flemish tapestries.

Main entrance

★ Refectory
Tapestries, choir stalls and colourful banners cover the walls of the massive dining hall. Its long tables are decorated with silver candlesticks and serving dishes.

STAR FEATURES

★ Assembly Room

★ Billiard Room

★ Gothic Study

★ Refectory

Exploring Hearst Castle™

Statue of Victory

Visitors to Hearst Castle™ must take one of four guided tours, all of which start from the Visitors' Center. Tour One is recommended for first-time visitors. It includes the ground floor of Casa Grande, one of the guest houses, both pools and part of the gardens. Other tours cover the upper floors of the main house. During the spring and autumn evening tours of the estate feature actors or "guests" in 1930s costume.

Gold and glass décor of the Roman Pool

Hearst's private cinema. Here, up to 50 guests would watch film premiers. The screen could be removed, revealing a small stage, where famous actors and actresses would sometimes put on plays.

The exquisite heated indoor Roman Pool, entirely covered in mosaics of hammered gold and Venetian glass, was a popular choice for romantic assignations, despite Hearst's disapproval of such activities.

The house was continually being renovated or rebuilt in accordance with Hearst's ever-changing ideas. One supporting wall was moved at great cost to make room for a bowling alley that was never built. With scores of bedrooms and bathrooms, two pools and a cinema, Casa Grande was a gilded playhouse for the many visitors who came here.

Casa Grande: The Big House

La casa grande is built from reinforced concrete to withstand California's earthquakes. However, it has been designed to look like a masonry cathedral in the Mediterranean Revival style.

House guests stayed in one of 22 bedrooms, surrounded by works from the magnate's eclectic art collection. Hearst himself lived in the third-floor Gothic Suite. His bedroom was decorated with a 14th-century Spanish ceiling and a renowned *Madonna and Child* from the School of Duccio di Buoninsegna (c.1255–1318). A sitting room with ocean views linked it to Marion Davies' bedroom.

Across the hall, the Gothic Study housed Hearst's most prized books and manuscripts. It was from this room that he directed his media empire.

The Assembly Room, on the ground floor, was designed around a massive 16th-century French fireplace. It came from the d'Anglure family's Château

des Jours in Burgundy. The high-ceilinged Refectory Room, next door, features a medieval dining table, cathedral seats and flagstones from Siena. Guests at Hearst Castle™ were required to attend their late evening meals here.

The Billiard Room, with its Spanish Gothic ceiling, showcases an early 16th-century millefleurs tapestry of a stag hunt. Adjoining this room is

The Grounds and Neptune Pool

Hearst transformed the barren Californian hillside into a Garden of Eden. Fan palms 15 ft (4.5 m) high, fully-grown Italian cypresses and enormous 200-year-old oaks were hauled up the dirt road at great expense.

Massive loads of topsoil were brought up to create flowerbeds for the 127 acres (51 ha) of gardens. Five greenhouses supplied colourful plants

William Randolph Hearst

The son of a multimillionaire, WR Hearst (1863–1951) was an ebullient personality who made his own fortune in magazine and newspaper publishing. He married Millicent Willson, an entertainer from New York, in 1903. On his mother's death, in 1919, Hearst inherited the San Simeon property. He began to build the castle and grounds as a tribute to his mother. On moving in, he installed his mistress, actress Marion Davies. The couple entertained royally at San Simeon over the next 20 years. When Hearst suffered problems with his heart in 1947, he moved to a house in Beverly Hills, where he died in 1951.

Portrait of WR Hearst, aged 31

throughout the year. To hide a water tank on the adjoining hill, 6,000 Monterey pines were planted in holes blasted out of the rock. An additional 4,000 fruit trees were planted on the estate, providing an abundance of fresh fruit.

Ancient and modern statues were collected to adorn the terraces. Among the finest are four statues of Sekhmet, the Egyptian goddess of war. The oldest works at San Simeon, they date from 1350–1200 BC.

The *pièce de résistance* of the grounds is the 104-ft (32-m) long Neptune Pool. Made in white marble, it is flanked by colonnades and the façade of a reproduction Greek temple. The latter is made from ancient columns and decorated with authentic friezes. The statues around the pool were carved in the 1920s by Charles-George Cassou, a Parisian sculptor.

A great lover of the outdoors, Hearst had a 1-mile (1.6-km) long covered bridlepath built, so that he could ride in all weathers. Two tennis courts were also constructed on top of the indoor Roman Pool.

Hearst had a private zoo on "Camp Hill". The remains of enclosures can still be seen where lions, bears, elephants, pumas and leopards were once kept. Giraffes, ostriches, zebras and even a baby elephant were free to wander the grounds.

JULIA MORGAN

Julia Morgan, the architect of San Simeon, was 47 when she began her 30-year collaboration with Hearst. One of the first women graduates of engineering at the University of California, Berkeley, Morgan was the first woman to receive a certificate in architecture from the Ecole Nationale et Spéciale des Beaux-Arts in Paris. She was a multi-talented architect and artist – she designed almost every aspect of Hearst Castle,

Julia Morgan (1872–1957)

from tiles and windows to swimming pools and fountains – and a rigorous supervisor of the project's many contractors and artisans. Her relationship with Hearst was based on mutual respect, but was often tempestuous. After spending long hours together finalizing a plan, Hearst would often telegraph Morgan with changes.

Tiered façade of Casa del Sol

THE GUEST HOUSES

UNTIL THE MID-1920s, when Casa Grande became ready for occupancy, Hearst lived in the 19-room Casa del Mar, the largest of the three guest houses. He enjoyed his years in the smaller house, but on viewing the completed Casa Grande admitted, "If I had known it would be so big, I would have made the little buildings bigger." The "little buildings", however, are mansions in their own right.

Casa del Sol is built on three levels and has 18 rooms. It features views of the sunset and has a broad terrace with a tall fountain topped with a cast bronze copy of *David* by Donatello. The smallest of the houses, Casa del Monte, faces the hills and has ten rooms.

Neptune Pool, flanked by colonnades and a reproduction Greek temple façade

Fishing boats encircling Morro Rock in Morro Bay

Morro Bay ❻

Road map B5. 🏠 *10,000.* 🚌 *Dial-A-Ride (805 772-2744).* 🚆 ℹ️ *880 Main St (805 772-4467).*

T HIS SEASIDE PORT was founded in 1870 to ship produce from the area's cattle ranching and dairy farming businesses. Today, tourism has become the town's main industry and the waterfront is lined with galleries, shops, an aquarium and seafood restaurants. Whale-watching trips, bay cruises and a commercial fishing fleet also operate from here. A redwood stairway celebrating the town's 100th birthday descends from a stone pelican at clifftop level down to the Embarcadero where a giant chessboard sports redwood pieces up to 33 inches (84 cm) tall. The view from Black Hill Lookout is worth the hike from the car park to the top of the mountain.

The bay's principal feature is Morro Rock, a dome-shaped 576-ft (175-m) high volcanic peak – one of nine in the area. Named "El Moro" by Juan Cabrillo in 1542, who thought it resembled a Moor's turban, it was connected to the mainland by a causeway in 1933. Between 1880 and 1969 it was used as a quarry, and a million tonnes of rock were blasted away to construct breakwaters up and down the coast.

Today, Morro Rock is a wildlife reserve housing nests of peregrine falcons. Cars can be driven to Coleman Park at the rock's base, which is a highly popular fishing spot.

San Luis Obispo ❼

Road map B5. 🏠 *43,000.* ✈️ *San Luis Obispo.* 🚆 🚌 ℹ️ *1041 Chorro St, Suite E (805 541-8000).*

T HIS SMALL CITY, situated in a valley in the Santa Lucia Mountains, developed around the **San Luis Obispo Mission de Tolosa**. The mission was founded on 1 September 1772 by Father Junípero Serra *(see p42)*. Fifth in the chain of 21 missions built by the Franciscan Order, and one of the wealthiest, it is still in use as a parish church. Beside the church, the mission's museum displays Chumash Indian artifacts, such as baskets, vessels and jewellery, the padre's bed and the mission's original altar.

In front of the church is Mission Plaza, a landscaped public square bisected by a tree-lined creek. During the 1860s, bullfights and bear-baiting took place in the park; today it is the site of many of the city's less bloody events.

Just west of the plaza, at 800 Palm Street, is the Ah Louis Store. Founded in 1874 by a Chinese cook and railway labourer *(see pp46–7)*, Ah Louis became the centre of a then thriving Chinatown, and served as a post office, bank and a general store. It is still owned by the Louis family, but it is now a gift shop.

🏛 San Luis Obispo Mission de Tolosa
751 Palm St. 📞 *(805) 781-8220.* ⬜ *daily.* ⬤ *1 Jan, Easter, Thanksgiving, 25 Dec.*

Pismo Beach ❽

Road map B5. 🏠 *8,000.* ✈️ *San Luis Obispo.* 🚆 *San Luis Obispo.* 🚌 ℹ️ *581 Dolliver St (805 773-4382).*

P ISMO BEACH is famous for the Pismo clam. At the turn of the century up to 40,000 clams were harvested per day. In 1911 harvesters were limited to 200 clams per person; now,

Pismo Beach, backed by rolling hills

with a licence, they may pick only ten. A clam festival is held in Pismo Beach every autumn.

The town's beach *(see p198)* stretches south for 8 miles (13 km) to the Santa Maria River. It offers camp sites, boating, fishing and picnic facilities. As the sand is firmly compacted, cars are allowed on to the beach via ramps at Grand Avenue in Grover Beach and Pier Avenue in Oceano.

Extensive sand dunes shelter birdlife, sagebrush, wildflowers, verbena and other seashore plants along with the occasional foxes, rabbits and coyotes. Shell mounds in the dunes, especially near Arroyo Grande Creek, identify sites where Chumash Indians once lived.

During the 1930s and 1940s the dunes were the centre of a cult of artists, nudists and mystics. Film-makers have also been drawn to these sands, which have been compared to the Sahara Desert. One of the many movies made here is *The Sheik* (1921) starring silent screen idol Rudolph Valentino *(see p108).*

Lompoc Valley ●

Road map B5. ✗ *Santa Barbara.* *Lompoc.* *111 S I St, Lompoc (805 736-4567).*

LOMPOC VALLEY is one of the world's major producers of flower-seed. The hills and flower fields surrounding the valley are a blaze of colour between late spring and midsummer. Among the varieties grown are marigolds, sweet peas, asters, lobelia, larkspur,

DUNE ECOLOGY

Coastal dunes are the product of wind and, surprisingly, plants. Just above the high tide line, dry sand is stabilized by sea rocket. Behind it, beach grass and silver lupine trap more sand, creating small hummocks held in place by the plants' roots. Lupine compost mixes with the sand to produce soil, allowing other plants, such as dune buckwheat and hapolappapus, to move in and overcome the lupine itself. Eventually, ice plant, verbena and morning glory take root in the sandy soil. The plants provide food and protection for a broad range of insects and animals, from sand wasps and beetles to Jerusalem crickets and tiny mice. Most beach wildlife depends on the dew that drops from these plants into the sand below. If part of the fragile plant cover is destroyed by sea storms, high winds or people, sand is dispersed further inland and a new dune is formed.

Ice plant growing among the coastal sand dunes

nasturtiums and cornflowers. A map of the flower fields in the area is distributed by the town of Lompoc's Chamber of Commerce. The Civic Center Plaza, between Ocean Avenue and C Street, has a display garden in which all the many flowers are identified.

La Purísima Concepción Mission, 3 miles (5 km) northeast of the town, was the 11th mission to be founded in California. It was declared a State Historic Park during the 1930s. The early 19th-century buildings have now been sympathetically reconstructed and the complex and grounds provide a real insight into the missionary way of life.

Visitors to the mission are able to view the priests' living quarters, furnished with authentic pieces, in the elegant residence building. The simple, narrow church is decorated with colourful stencilwork. In the adjacent workshops, cloth, candles, leather goods and furniture were at one time produced for the mission.

La Purísima's gardens have been faithfully restored. The varieties of fruit, vegetables and herbs that are grown here were all common in the 19th century. Visitors can also view the system that provided the mission with water.

 La Purísima Concepción Mission
2295 Purisima Rd, Lompoc. *(805) 733-3713.* *daily.* *1 Jan, Thanksgiving, 25 Dec.*

La Purísima Concepción Mission in Lompoc Valley

Tour of the Santa Ynez Valley Wineries ⑩

Sᴀɴᴛᴀ ʏɴᴇᴢ ᴠᴀʟʟᴇʏ is one of the newest and most distinctive wine regions in the state. The area is prone to coastal fog, which produces microclimates according to shifts in altitude and distance from the sea. The area also has a longer growing season than Northern California. These unique conditions, coupled with varied soils produce a selection of classic grape varieties.

Local wine

TIPS FOR DRIVERS

Tour length: 30 miles (48 km).
Stopping-off points: Los Olivos Café (see p551) is a pleasant place to stop for lunch. You can buy picnic fare or a packed hamper at the café's deli. The wineries all have picnic areas, where you can enjoy a local wine with your meal.

Fess Parker Winery ⑤
Cabernet Sauvignons, Syrahs and Rieslings are produced at ex-actor Fess Parker's winery. Tastings are available in an attractive building in scenic Foxen Canyon.

Brander Vineyard ⑥
Established in 1975, Brander offers award-winning Sauvignon Blancs and other wines in a French-style building overlooking the vineyards.

Firestone Vineyard ④
The largest producer in the region presents distinctive Rieslings, Chardonnays and Merlots in a large tasting room adjoining the winery.

Carey Cellars ③
A rustic farmhouse provides the tasting room for this vineyard and winery famed for its Cabernet Sauvignon and Merlot vintages.

Gainey Vineyard ①
Distinctive wines are offered for tasting in a Spanish-style building close to Lake Cachuma.

Santa Ynez ②
Among the vineyards and wineries surrounding this town are the Santa Ynez Winery and the Sunstone Vineyards and Winery.

KEY

━━━ Tour route

═══ Other roads

0 kilometres 2

0 miles 2

Mission Santa Inés church façade and campanile

Solvang ⓫

Road map C5. 🚶 5,000. 🚌
ℹ️ 1511-A Mission Drive (805 688-6144).

THIS SCANDINAVIAN-STYLE town was established in 1911 by a group of Danish educators. They paid $360,000 for 9,000 acres (3,650 ha) of mustard and bean fields on which to build a Danish colony and school. The original schoolhouse, a two-storey frame structure on Alisal Road, is no longer standing, having been replaced by the Bit O' Denmark Restaurant. Solvang's Bethnania Lutheran church, built in 1928 to a traditional Danish design, has a model sailing ship hanging from its ceiling. Visitors can tour the town in a horse-drawn tram, the *honen* (hen), and see windmills, chimneys with artificial storks and gas streetlights. Beer gardens serve *aebleskiver* (a type of Danish pastry), especially during the town's Danish Days festival in September *(see p34)*.

Mission Santa Inés ⓬

1760 Mission Drive, Solvang. **Road map** C5. 📞 (805) 688-4815.
⭘ daily. ⬤ Easter, Thanksgiving, 25 Dec. ♿

FOUNDED ON 17 September 1804, Santa Inés was the 19th in the chain of Californian

Statue of the Madonna

missions *(see pp42–3)*. In 1812 an earthquake destroyed the larger part of the church. It was rebuilt with 5-ft (1.5-m) thick walls and re-dedicated five years later. Before secularization in 1834 the mission was prosperous, with a herd of 12,000 cattle; afterwards it fell into disrepair and most of the Native Americans left. In 1843, the mission became the site of the state's first seminary. Restoration work began after World War II, including the campanile (financed by WR Hearst, *see p204*) and the church sanctuary. The mission also has a small museum, with period furnishings, parchment books, the vestments worn by early priests and original murals by Native Americans. There is a landscaped garden.

Chumash Painted Cave State Historic Park ⓭

Painted Cave Road. 📞 (805) 968-3294. 🚌 from Santa Barbara. Parking limited to 2 vehicles.

IN THE Santa Ynez Mountains, 8 miles (13 km) to the northwest of Santa Barbara, are a number of remote and scattered caves with Chumash drawings or pictographs. The most famous example is a 20 by 40 ft (6 by 12 m) cave just off Hwy 154. Inside, an egg-shaped cavity, covered in small ochre scratchings, is protected by a metal screen.

Some caves have primitive drawings that resemble lizards, snakes and scorpions, executed in red, black or white paints. Tribes are known to have traded different pigments with each other. Some experts believe the drawings are symbolic of the Chumash religion; others think they are random, with no significant meaning.

Native American paintings in the Chumash caves

MONARCH BUTTERFLIES

Each year millions of monarch butterflies migrate from the western US and Canada to winter in Southern and Central California and Mexico. Starting their journey in October and November the butterflies cover up to 80 miles (130 km) a day at speeds approaching 30 mph (50 km/h). Along the central coast, they usually settle in eucalyptus groves. After the mating season in January and February, the butterflies attempt the journey back to their summer habitat. In season they can often be seen around Montana de Oro State Park *(see p199)*, Pismo Beach and Ventura.

Monarch butterfly

Street-by-Street: Santa Barbara ⑭

SANTA BARBARA is a Southern Californian rarity: a city with a single architectural style. Following a devastating earthquake in 1925, the centre was rebuilt according to strict rules that dictated Mediterranean-style architecture. The city was founded in 1782 – four years before Santa Barbara Mission *(see pp212–13)* – as a Spanish garrison. During the 19th century Santa Barbara was a quiet pueblo, home to only a few hundred families and a centre for the nearby cattle ranches. Remarkably, about a dozen adobes from that era have survived. Today, Santa Barbara is a quiet administrative centre with a large student population, who lend an informal feel to the city.

Fountain outside the County Courthouse

To Santa Barbara Mission

FIGUEROA STREET

ANACAPA STREET

CARRILLO

★ Museum of Art
This outstanding regional art collection includes Asian art, antiquities, American art, prints, drawings and photography. In the 19th-century French section is Jules Bastien-Lepage's The Ripened Wheat (1884).

★ County Courthouse
The 1929 Spanish Colonial-style court-house is still in use. It is decorated with Tunisian tiles and wrought-iron metalwork. Murals by DS Groesbeck in the Assembly Room depict Californian history (see p38). There are panoramic views from the clock tower.

KEY
‒ ‒ ‒ Suggested route

STAR SIGHTS
★ **County Courthouse**

★ **Museum of Art**

★ **Presidio**

Paseo Nuevo
This colourful outdoor shopping and dining centre complements an older arcade on the opposite side of State Street.

★ Presidio
Santa Barbara's Presidio was built in 1782 by the Spanish. It was the last in a chain of four fortresses erected along the Californian coast.

VISITORS' CHECKLIST

Road map C5. 🏠 *86,000.*
✈ *Santa Barbara Airport, 8 miles (13 km) N of Santa Barbara.*
🚉 *209 State St.* 🚌 *1020 Chapala St.* 🚏 *34 W Carrillo.*
🚋 *Stearns Wharf.* ℹ️ *12 E Carrillo St (805 966-9222).*
📅 *I Madonnari Italian Street Painting Festival (late May); Fiesta (early Aug).* **Museum of Art**
📞 *(805) 963-4364.* ○ *Tue–Sun.*
County Courthouse
📞 *(805) 962-6464.* ○ *Mon–Fri.* 🚻 **Presidio** 📞 *(805) 965-0093.* ○ *daily.* 🚻 🖼 **Santa Barbara Historical Museum**
📞 *(805) 966-1601.* ○ *Tue–Sun.* **Donation.** 🚻 📷

The Cañedo Adobe once housed soldiers and families from the Presidio.

El Cuartel is the Presidio's family living quarters.

Lobero Theatre
This graceful 1924 building stands on the site of the city's original theatre, which was built in 1873 by Jose Lobero, an Italian musician.

To East Beach

0 metres   100

0 yards   100

Historical Museum
The Historical Society's collections are housed in two adobe buildings. Among the many artifacts is a statue of the 4th-century martyr Santa Barbara.

Santa Barbara Mission

LABELLED THE "Queen of the Missions", Santa Barbara is the most visited mission in the state. Founded in 1786 on the feast day of St Barbara, it was the tenth mission built by the Spanish *(see pp42–3)*. After the third adobe church on the site was destroyed by an earth-quake in 1812, the present structure took shape and was completed in 1833. Its twin towers and mix of Roman, Moorish and Spanish styles served as the main inspiration for what came to be known as Mission Style *(see p26)*. The mission was again hit by an earthquake in 1925, damaging the towers and façade of the church. These sections were repaired but, because of a chemical reaction between the alkalies and aggregates in the cement, the entire front had to be rebuilt in 1953, following the original design. Santa Barbara is the only Californian mission to have been in continuous use since it was founded.

Franciscan monk

Central Fountain
Palm trees tower above a central fountain in the Sacred Gardens.

A missionary's bedroom has been furnished as it would have been in the early 1800s.

Entrance

Arcaded Corridor
An open corridor fronts the museum rooms. Originally the living quarters, these now display a rich collection of mission artifacts.

Kitchen
The kitchen has been restored to show the typical cooking facil-ities of the early 1800s. Most of the food eaten was produced on the mission, which had fields and livestock.

STAR FEATURES

★ **Church**

★ **Main Façade**

★ **Sacred Gardens**

★ Sacred Gardens
The beautifully landscaped Sacred Gardens were once a working area for Native Americans to learn Western trades. Workshops and some living quarters were located in the surrounding buildings.

VISITORS' CHECKLIST

2201 Laguna St. ☎ *(805) 682-4713.* 🚌 *22.* ⭕ *9am–5pm daily.* **Donation.** ✝ *7:15am Mon–Fri; 4pm Sat; 7:30am, 9am, 10:30am, noon Sun.* 📷 ♿ 🏪

★ Church
The narrow church has a Neo-Classical interior. Imitation marble columns and detailing have been painted on the walls and doorways. The reredos has a painted canvas backdrop and carved wooden statues.

The side chapel, next to the altar, is dedicated to the Blessed Sacrament.

The width of the nave was determined by the height of the trees used as cross beams.

The cemetery garden contains the graves of some 4,000 Native Americans as well as friars.

★ Main Façade
The church's Classical façade was designed by Padre Antonio Ripoll. Ripoll admired the Roman architect Vitruvius Pollio (working around 27 BC), and drew heavily on his ideas when building the church.

San Buenaventura Mission's church in Ventura

Ventura ⑮

Road map C5. 🏛 *98,000.* 🚍
ℹ️ *89C S California St (805 648-2075).*

ALL THAT REMAINS of the **San Buenaventura Mission**, founded in 1782 and completed in 1809, is a church within a courtyard garden and tiled fountain. A museum at the mission details the buildings of the original complex.

Two mid-19th-century adobe houses survive in the city. The tiny **Ortega Adobe** reveals the harsh living conditions many experienced at that time. In contrast, the Monterey-style *(see p26)* **Olivas Adobe** is a two-storey ranch hacienda, furnished in period, with rose and herb gardens.

Today Ventura is largely an agricultural centre. Ventura Harbor Village has 30 shops, restaurants, a merry-go-round and a community theatre. Harbour and whale-watching cruises, as well as boats to the Channel Islands National Park depart from here.

On a hillside at the northern end of town, the **City Hall** (1913) has a copper-covered dome and marble exterior.

🏛 **San Buenaventura Mission**
211 E Main St. ℹ️ *(805) 643-4318.*
🕐 *daily.* ● *1 Jan, Easter, Thanksgiving, 25 Dec.*
🏛 **Ortega Adobe**
100 W Main St. ℹ️ *(805) 658-4726.*
🕐 *daily.* ● *1 Jan, Easter Sun, Labor Day, Thanksgiving, 25 Dec.*
🏛 **Olivas Adobe**
4200 Olivas Park Drive. ℹ️ *(805) 644-4346.* **Grounds** 🕐 *daily.*
House 🕐 *Sat & Sun.* ● *1 Jan, Easter, Thanksgiving, 25 Dec.*

Channel Islands National Park ⑯

Road map C6. 🚊 *Ventura.* 🚍
Visitors' Center ℹ️ *(805) 658-5700.*
🕐 *daily.* ⛴ *Island Packers, 1867 Spinnaker Drive (805 642-1393).*

THE ISLANDS of Santa Barbara, Anacapa, San Miguel, Santa Cruz and Santa Rosa together make up the Channel Islands National Park, a series of volcanic islands unpopulated by humans. Access to the islands is strictly monitored by park rangers, who issue landing permits from the Visitors' Center. Camping is allowed on all the islands except Santa Cruz, but visitors must make reservations at least two weeks in advance. They must also bring all their own food and water supplies, as there are none available on the five islands.

Depending on the island and the time of year, lucky visitors may spot dolphins, grey whales and California brown pelicans on the passage across the Santa Barbara Channel. Wildlife on the small, picturesque islands is plentiful and includes cormorants, sea lions, elephant seals and gulls.

California brown pelican

Day trips to Anacapa, the nearest island to the mainland, offer an insight into this unique coastal ecosystem. Even more can be learned, however, by taking one of the various guided walks, conducted by park rangers, on San Miguel and Santa Rosa Islands. Visitors must stay on the designated trails and pets are not allowed.

The rock pools on all of the islands are rich in marine life, and the kelp forests surrounding the islands provide shelter for more than 1,000 plant and animal species.

The islands' many sea caves make sea-kayaking a unique and exciting experience. The snorkelling and scuba-diving in this area are also considered to be among the best on the entire Pacific Coast.

Ronald Reagan Presidential Library ⑰

40 Presidential Drive, Simi Valley.
Road map C5. ℹ️ *(800) 410-8354.*
🕐 *10am–5pm daily.* ● *1 Jan, Thanksgiving, 25 Dec.* 🎟 ♿

PRESIDENT REAGAN's papers are all archived in this Mission Revival-style structure, built on a hill. The library also features a permanent exhibition documenting the life of Reagan and his wife, Nancy. There are also temporary exhibitions of gifts, costumes, works of art and other objects related to Reagan and his eight-year tenure at the White House. A full-size replica of the Oval Office is correct in every detail, and a large piece of the Berlin Wall, coloured with its original graffiti, can be seen on the patio against the panoramic backdrop of the nearby Simi Hills and the Santa Susana Mountains.

Reconstruction of the Oval Office at the Reagan Presidential Library

Mission Revival arcade on Main Street, Ojai

Ojai ⓲

Road map C5. 🏛 *7,900.* 🚌 🚆
ℹ️ *150 W Ojai Ave (805 646-8126).*

FOUNDED IN 1874, this town was originally called Nordhoff after the author Charles Nordhoff, who wrote a book promoting California in the 1870s. In 1917 the town was renamed Ojai, a Chumash Indian word for moon, a reference to the crescent-shaped valley in which the town lies.

Ojai's Mission Revival arched arcade was funded by Edward J Libby, a glass-manufacturing millionaire, and was designed in 1917 by Richard Requa. Its tower was modelled on a campanile in Havana, Cuba. The arcade fronts two blocks of shops on the main street.

Another attraction is Barts Corner bookshop at No. 302 West Matilija Street. Here, 25,000 volumes are displayed, many of them outdoors. Late-night readers can browse and then pay for their finds through a slot in the door.

Spiritual groups have been going on retreats in the Ojai Valley since the 1920s. Today several New Age and religious organizations are based here.

Los Padres National Forest ⓳

Road map C5. 🚌 *Santa Barbara.*
Visitors' Center ⏰ *8:30am–4:30pm Mon–Fri.* 📞 *(805) 683- 6711.*

LOS PADRES National Forest covers almost 2 million acres (810,000 ha) of terrain that varies from desert to pine-clad mountains with peaks as high as 9,000 ft (2,700 m). Black bears, foxes, deer and mountain lions are among the animals found here. Birds include golden eagles and giant condors. The latter are North America's largest birds with a wingspan of 9 ft (3 m).

Coastal redwood trees grow on the lower slopes while the higher elevations are thick with firs, bristling with pine cones. Temperatures in the summer can be scorching and there is very little, if any, rain here between May and October.

The forest is criss-crossed by hundreds of miles of hiking trails for experienced hikers, but there are few roads. Hwy 33 and Hwy 150 are two exceptions. Hwy 154 crosses one corner as it runs between Santa Ynez *(see p208)* and Santa Barbara *(see pp210–13)*. On the way, it passes over the spectacular Cold Spring Arch Bridge.

Scattered within Los Padres National Forest are 88 camp sites. Activities available include fishing, horse riding and, on Mount Pinos, skiing.

Bakersfield ⓴

Road map C5. 🏛 *378,000.* 🚌
ℹ️ *1033 Truxtun Ave (805 327-4421).*

BAKERSFIELD WAS NAMED after Colonel Thomas Baker, a settler who planted a field of alfalfa here. The shrub fed the animals of early travellers who rested here before crossing the Tehachapi Mountains, the "border" that divides Northern and Southern California.

Many consider the town to be the final stop on the I-5 from San Francisco before the ascent up Grapevine Canyon to LA. However, it can also be reached from Santa Maria or Ojai along minor roads through the Los Padres National Forest.

Bakersfield's modern history began with the discovery of gold in the 1850s and several oil strikes in the following decades. Many people from Mediterranean countries settled on the fertile land, bringing agriculture to the area.

Today it is among the fastest growing cities in California, but still manages to retain a rural feel and is a recognized centre for country music. There are also fine restaurants, antique shops and the **Kern County Museum**, a 16-acre (6.5-ha) outdoor musuem.

Bisecting Bakersfield, Kern River is renowned for its white-water rafting and kayaking *(see p578)*. Lake Isabella, 40 miles (65 km) east of the city, is a centre for water sports.

🏛 **Kern County Museum**
3801 Chester Ave. 📞 *(805) 861-2132.* ⏰ *daily.* ⬤ *1 Jan, Thanksgiving, 24, 25, 31 Dec.* 📷

Cold Spring Arch Bridge, Los Padres National Forest

ORANGE COUNTY

A CENTURY AGO *Orange County lived up to its name. This dry, sunny land, which stretches from the Santa Ana Mountains to the beautiful Pacific coastline, was indeed scattered with orange orchards and farms. Today, the region is a mass of freeways and suburban housing. Visitors to the county can explore a wide range of museums, sites of historical interest and entertainment complexes.*

In the mid-1950s, the roads leading to the county's theme parks still passed through extensive orange groves. At that time, Disneyland was attracting its first enthusiastic crowds and a local boy called Richard Nixon had become Vice-President of the US. Today, orange groves have given way to urban development and fruit crate labels have become collectors' items. More than two million people live here, enjoying perennial sunshine and a high standard of living.

The coastline of Orange County is lined with wide, sandy beaches and a succession of legendary surfing haunts, marinas and artists' enclaves. In the affluent coastal towns, few visitors can resist the temptation to seek out a clifftop bar and watch the sun set.

Inland lies a variety of cultural sights. Mission San Juan Capistrano, founded in 1776, is a reminder of the days of the Spanish Franciscan settlers. The Bowers Museum of Cultural Art in Santa Ana houses superb examples of the art of indigenous peoples from all around the world. At Yorba Linda, the impressive Richard Nixon Library and Birthplace commemorates the life of the county's most famous son.

Orange County is the entertainment capital of California. For visitors seeking family fun and roller-coaster thrills, there are the homely Knott's Berry Farm, America's oldest theme park, and the fantasy kingdom of Disneyland, which is, as the saying goes, "the most famous people-trap ever built by a mouse".

Reflecting Pool at the Richard Nixon Library and Birthplace

◁ **Log Ride at Knott's Berry Farm theme park**

Exploring Orange County

MUCH OF ORANGE COUNTY'S 798-sq mile (2,050-sq km)
area is covered with sprawling urban communities linked by ever-busy freeways. Anaheim, home of
Disneyland, is its second largest city, after Santa Ana.
The popular Knott's Berry Farm theme park lies a few
miles northwest at Buena Park and together these
cities form the tourist capital of the county. Most of
the coastline is built-up, but its communities have
more variety and character than those around the
theme parks. Inland, open spaces can be found
where the county's eastern region encompasses part of the vast Cleveland National
Forest and the Santa Ana Mountains.

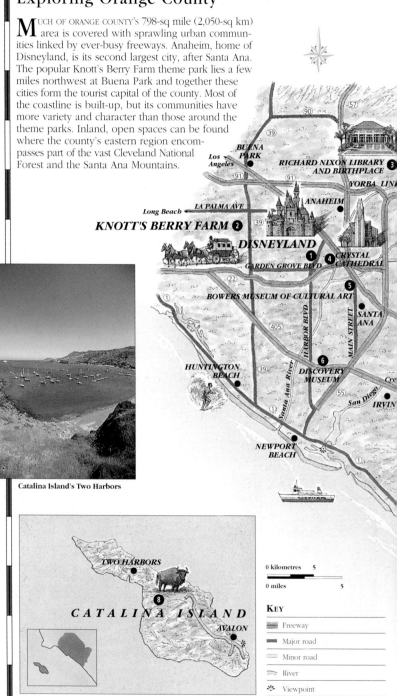

Catalina Island's Two Harbors

BUENA PARK

Los Angeles

RICHARD NIXON LIBRARY
AND BIRTHPLACE ❸

YORBA LIN

Long Beach ←

LA PALMA AVE

ANAHEIM

KNOTT'S BERRY FARM ❷

DISNEYLAND

GARDEN GROVE BLVD ❶ ❹ CRYSTAL CATHEDRAL

BOWERS MUSEUM OF CULTURAL ART ❺

SANTA ANA

HUNTINGTON BEACH

Santa Ana River

HARBOR BLVD

MAIN STREET

DISCOVERY MUSEUM ❻

San Diego

Cre

IRVIN

NEWPORT BEACH

TWO HARBORS

CATALINA ISLAND ❽

AVALON

0 kilometres   5

0 miles   5

KEY

〰	Freeway
▬	Major road
⋯	Minor road
〜	River
✺	Viewpoint

Enormous Crystal Cathedral at Garden Grove, south of Anaheim

SIGHTS AT A GLANCE

Bowers Museum of
Cultural Art ❺
Catalina Island pp232–3 ❽
Crystal Cathedral ❹
Discovery Museum ❻
Disneyland pp222–5 ❶

*Knott's Berry Farm
pp226–7* ❷
*Mission San Juan Capistrano
pp230–31* ❼
Richard Nixon Library and
Birthplace ❸

SEE ALSO

• *Where to Stay* pp516–17

• *Where to Eat* pp553–5

GETTING AROUND

The I-5 is a major north–south artery, which links Los Angeles and San Diego. The more scenic Hwy 1, the Pacific Coastal Highway, unites the county's coastal resorts. A railway line runs south from Los Angeles. Stops on the line include San Juan Capistrano and Anaheim, which are served by Amtrak *(see p600)* and the weekday commuter trains run by Metrolink. Most bus routes are designed to meet the needs of local commuters and are of limited use to the visitor, but shuttle vans and tour buses offer quick connections to the theme parks and to Los Angeles. Ferries to Catalina Island run daily in summer, but travellers should check schedules in winter. Crossings from the mainland to Avalon or Two Harbors take 1–2 hours.

Orange County Coastline

THE BEACHES AND RESORTS that make up Orange County's coast are Southern California at its most classic. The northern shoreline is flat and low-lying. South of the Balboa Peninsula, the coast features scenic cliffs and sheltered coves. Million-dollar homes, luxury marinas, constant sporting activity and a fashionable lifestyle reflect the wealth and vitality of its communities.

The Balboa Pavilion opened in 1905 as a terminus for the Pacific Electric Red Car Line from LA. Stars of the Big Band era, such as Count Basie, played here in the 1930s and 1940s. Today the wooden pavilion is a restaurant and centre for sightseeing cruises around Newport Harbor.

★ **Huntington State Beach** ③

A premier Californian "surf city", Huntington Beach has a surfing museum, international competitions and waters full of surfers whose exploits can be watched from the long pier.

Upper Newport Bay Ecological Reserve is a 750-acre (300-ha) wedge of coastal wetland providing a refuge for wildlife and migratory birds. Facilities in the bay include a cycle path, fishing and guided tours on foot and by kayak.

KEY

	Freeway
	Major road
	Minor road
	River
⁂	Viewpoint

Seal Beach ①

This is a quiet, 1-mile (1.6-km) long beach with level sands and some surfers. The wooden pier is popular with anglers. A walk along its 1,865-ft (570-m) length offers views northwards to the high-rise buildings of Long Beach (see pp128–9).

Bolsa Chica State Beach ②

The name Bolsa Chica means "little pocket" in Spanish. Flat, wilderness sands, oil extractors and the protected wetlands of the 300-acre (120-ha) Bolsa Chica Ecological Reserve give this beach a unique atmosphere.

Newport Beach ④

Famous for its million-dollar homes and lifestyles to match, Newport Beach boasts a 3-mile (5-km) stretch of wide sand and two piers. Fresh fish, caught by the historic Dory fishing fleet, is sold beside Newport Pier at the northern end of the beach.

Aliso Beach ⑦

At the mouth of Aliso Creek lies this small, sandy beach. The 620-ft (190-m) long concrete pier is used by anglers. At the southern end of the beach is a marine life refuge with beds of giant kelp offshore.

Doheny State Beach ⑧

This sandy beach and marine life refuge is close to the mouth of San Juan Creek. The beach attracts a typically Southern Californian mix of swimmers, surfers, bird-watchers, anglers, cyclists and campers.

San Clemente State Beach ⑨

The hillside community of San Clemente has a narrow, sandy beach at its foot. Near the railway station there is a municipal pier. Further south, the 100-acre (40-ha) State Beach has landscaped facilities including picnic areas and a camp site.

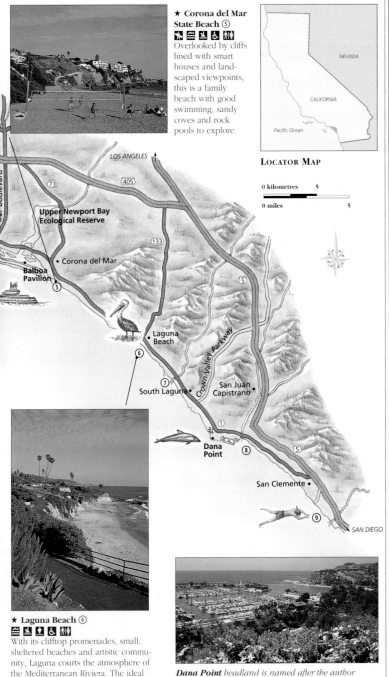

★ **Corona del Mar State Beach** ⑤

Overlooked by cliffs lined with smart houses and land-scaped viewpoints, this is a family beach with good swimming, sandy coves and rock pools to explore.

LOCATOR MAP

NEVADA

CALIFORNIA

Pacific Ocean

0 kilometres   5

0 miles   5

LOS ANGELES

73

405

Upper Newport Bay Ecological Reserve

133

• Corona del Mar

Balboa Pavilion

5

5

Laguna Beach

6

7

South Laguna •

San Juan Capistrano •

Crown Valley Parkway

1

Dana Point

8

5

San Clemente •

9

SAN DIEGO

★ **Laguna Beach** ⑥

With its clifftop promenades, small, sheltered beaches and artistic community, Laguna courts the atmosphere of the Mediterranean Riviera. The ideal venue for a cocktail at sunset, Laguna is famous for its summer arts festival, the Pageant of the Masters *(see p.33)*.

Dana Point *headland is named after the author Richard Dana, whose 1840 book* Two Years Before the Mast *chronicled the early days of California. A replica of the contemporary brig,* Pilgrim, *is moored in the harbour.*

Disneyland® ❶

DISNEY'S "MAGIC KINGDOM" in Anaheim is not only the top tourist attraction in California, it is part of the American Dream. Constantly evolving since its grand opening in 1955, Disneyland's thrilling rides, intricate fantasy worlds and glittering shows and parades have made it the model for theme parks around the globe. Visitors to what is affectionately known as "The Happiest Place on Earth" find a brightly orchestrated land of queues, popcorn and Mickey Mouse that, to generations of Americans, is as familiar as apple pie.

Exploring Disneyland

Spread over 185 acres (75 ha), and linked by monorail to the Disneyland Hotel *(see p516)*, Disneyland is divided into eight theme areas, known as lands. A single admission ticket covers all the rides and shows. These are listed on a daily entertainment schedule, which is available on arrival at the park.

It takes two days to make the best of a visit to Disneyland. Although crowds and queues are part of the experience, it is advisable to visit midweek or during the quieter winter months if possible. Christmas, Thanksgiving, Easter and the months from June to September are peak periods.

It is best to arrive early in the day, as Main Street, USA is usually open half an hour before and after the rest of the park. The park stays open in the evening and it is worth staying late, as this is when the atmosphere is at its most magical.

To make the most of their trip, visitors should decide in advance which Disneyland attractions they most want to experience. It is important to remember that lengthy queues can form during peak times and that many of the rides have height, age and physical condition restrictions.

Transport around the park's perimeter is provided by the Disneyland Railroad. Trains stop at the entrance to the park and in New Orleans Square, Mickey's Toontown and Tomorrowland.

Goofy welcoming Toontown guests

MAIN STREET, USA

THIS SPOTLESSLY CLEAN and colourful street, lined with pastiche turn-of-the-century buildings, welcomes visitors to Disneyland. Culminating in the circular **Central Plaza**, this is the venue for daily parades featuring lavishly decorated floats and cheerfully waving Disney characters.

Main street has a large selection of attractions, shops and food outlets. These include the Blue Ribbon Bakery and the Penny Arcade, where visitors can play on old-style slot machines.

Maps and dining and entertainment schedules, as well as general information about the park, are available from **City Hall** on Main Street. The **Main Street Cinema** screens early Disney silent films. Nearby, the Walt Disney Story recalls the life and times of the park's enigmatic founder.

TOMORROWLAND

VISIONS OF THE FUTURE inspire the attractions here, and sights change regularly to keep one step ahead of real-life technology and retain a sense of fantasy. Space-age travel posters and spoof pre-flight commentaries in the waiting areas for these rides demonstrate how the creators of Disneyland have become masters of queue psychology.

Star Tours

Designed in collaboration with the *Star Wars* genius George Lucas, the use of flight-simulator technology makes this one of the most realistic rides in the park. In the Tomorrowland Spaceport, visitors board a StarSpeeder spaceship. The passengers are taken on a sensational journey through an outer space strewn with starships, comets and asteroids.

Space Mountain

A Disneyland favourite, this attraction provides a high-speed roller-coaster ride, 118 ft (36 m) above ground level. Almost entirely conducted in darkness, the ride is intermittently illuminated by sudden meteoric flashes and celestial showers. The effect is thrilling disorientation. Not suitable for young children.

MICKEY'S TOONTOWN

THE COLOURFUL architecture of cartoons comes to life in Mickey Mouse's home town. Wisely spurning the depravities

Mickey's house in Toontown

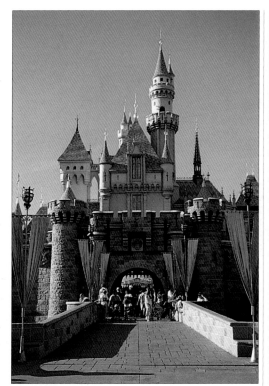

Fairytale façade of Sleeping Beauty Castle in Fantasyland

of Hollywood, all of Disney's
favourite animated characters
are said to reside here. This is
the part of the park where visitors are most likely to find
Mickey Mouse and his friends
strolling around, having their
pictures taken with guests. The
streets of Toontown are full
of surprises – manhole covers
shout back at passers-by who
tread on them.

The most popular celebrity
residence is Mickey's house,
where subtle touches, such as
a book published by Random
Mouse and tins of Maxwell
Mouse coffee, typify Disney's
legendary attention to detail.
Next door, Minnie's pink and
purple house has a dishwasher
full of dancing cups and a
heart-shaped TV set.

**Roger Rabbit's Car Toon
Spin** is Toontown's largest
attraction. It provides a mad-
cap taxi drive through a surreal
cartoon world fraught with
near misses. The ride, with its
spinning cars, is particularly
popular with young children.

FANTASYLAND

D OMINATED BY the pink and
gold towers of **Sleeping
Beauty Castle** and a replica of
the **Matterhorn**, Fantasyland
is a shrine to children's dreams
and adult nostalgia. Nursery
heroes such as Peter Pan,
Dumbo and Snow White pro-
vide the themes for gentle
fairytale rides in vehicles that
range from flying galleons to

canal boats and the Mad
Hatter's giant spinning teacups.
There are almost twice as
many attractions to enjoy here
as in most of the other lands,
and the constant crowds illustrate the enduring appeal of
this part of the park.

Matterhorn Bobsleds
This historic attraction and
major park landmark has been
providing "icy" roller-coaster
rides since 1959. A copy of
the famous peak near Zermatt
in Switzerland, the Matterhorn
Mountain towers 147 ft (45 m)
above Disneyland. Bobsleds
carrying four passengers climb
to the mountain's snow-capped
summit. They then drop into a
steep, high-speed descent,
zooming in and out of the hollow peak, passing glacier caves
and waterfalls as they go. At
the end of the trip, the riders
sitting in the front seats are
splashed as the bobsleds go
careering into a lake.

It's a Small World
This show, created for the 1964
World's Fair, offers a Utopian
vision of global harmony.
Colourful boats transport passengers through the attraction,
which features nearly 300
singing-and-dancing Audio-
Animatronic dolls, all in intricate national costumes.

EATING AND DRINKING

Disneyland has plenty of outlets selling food and
drink. Many of them are fast-food stalls or restaurants,
offering American staples such as hamburgers, French
fries and soft drinks. Each area in the park also has at least
one restaurant offering dishes that will appeal to the more
health-conscious and vegetarians. Long queues can form
at lunchtime so consider eating a little earlier or later.
Reservations for restaurants offering full table service need
to be made at the park reception on the day of your visit.
These include the the park's best restaurant, the Blue
Bayou in New Orleans Square, which serves a selection
of good fish dishes and looks out onto a bayou scene.
No alcoholic drinks are available in the park.

Mark Twain Steamboat navigating on the Rivers of America lake

FRONTIERLAND

THIS AREA IS INSPIRED by the adventurous days of the Wild West. Skirt-lifting song and dance take place on the **Golden Horseshoe Jamboree** stage. Nearby is the **Hunchback of Notre Dame Festival of Fools**. At night Frontierland becomes the venue for the spectacular **Fantasmic!** show.

Mark Twain Steamboat
This area offers visitors a chance to enjoy a relaxing 15-minute cruise aboard this replica paddle-wheel boat, which crosses a lake called Rivers of America. Plastic moose and deer inhabit the lush forests along the shore and on Tom Sawyer Island in the middle of the lake.

Big Mountain Thunder Railroad
Thrill-seekers are served by this ever-popular roller-coaster ride. Open ore trucks set off from the 1880s mining town of Big Thunder without a driver. Seemingly out of control, the runaway train speeds through the cavernous interior of Big Thunder Mountain, only narrowly escaping falling boulders and gushing waterfalls.

CRITTER COUNTRY

BUILT IN A RUSTIC style, based on the rugged American northwest, Critter Country is a 4-acre (1.6-ha) area next to Frontierland. It is home to one of the most popular attractions in Disneyland, Splash Mountain, as well as one of its quieter restaurants, the Hungry Bear.

Splash Mountain
This is a winding, extremely watery ride in hollowed-out logs. Brer Rabbit and Brer Fox are among the furry, singing characters, from the 1946 film *Song of the South*, who inhabit the mountain through which the ride passes. After a rather long rendition of the Disney song *Zip-A-Dee-Doo-Dah*, the ride culminates in a plummet down a steep waterfall. As on the Matterhorn Bobsleds ride, people in the front seats should expect to be splashed.

Mickey Mouse

The Country Bear Playhouse
In this spacious theatre, Audio-Animatronic bears tell corny jokes and perform silly songs in a cheerful musical show.

Teddi Barra's Swingin' Arcade
In keeping with the spirit of Critter Country, this is a frontier-style shooting gallery. Players pay a quarter to take aim at mechanical bears.

SHOPPING

The Disneyland shops, particularly those on Main Street, USA, are often busy at closing time, so it is worth making your purchases early in the day and collecting them later from the Redemption Center. Although many of the goods on sale in the park bear the faces of Disney characters, each land adds its own variations. In Adventureland, you can buy Indiana Jones-style clothing and Native American crafts are on sale in Frontierland. The Disney Gallery in New Orleans Square sells limited-edition lithographs by the Disney cartoonists. The Emporium on Main Street is the largest shop in Disneyland.

NEW ORLEANS SQUARE

THIS CHARMING town square is modelled on the French Quarter in New Orleans, as it was in the city's heyday in the 19th century. The buildings have wrought-iron balconies and house interesting French-style shops. This land is also the site of two of Disneyland's best-known action attractions.

Haunted Mansion

Some of the visitors to this attraction, which promises 999 "ghosts and ghouls", are now so familiar with its introductory commentary that they join in as they descend into its spooky world of mischievous spirits and grave-diggers. The ethereal figures, including a talking woman's head in a crystal ball, are extremely realistic.

Pirates of the Caribbean

Particularly enjoyable at night, this show provides a floating ride through a yo-ho-ho world of ruffians and wenches who have been empowered with the gifts of song, dance and heavy drinking by Audio-Animatronics. This technique, which brings models to life using magnetic tapes to control their sounds and actions, was perfected at Disneyland.

The Disney Gallery

Visitors interested in the art behind the world of Disney should visit this gallery, located above the entrance to Pirates of the Caribbean. Some of the original artwork and designs for Disney's elaborate projects are on display here.

WALT DISNEY

Born in Chicago, Walt Disney (1901–1966) moved to Hollywood at the age of 21. His passion for cartoons and animated adventures coincided with the arrival of sound in films, and his first major success came with *Steamboat Willie* in 1928, a pioneering soundtrack cartoon featuring a lively character called Mickey Mouse. Technological innovation has always been a hallmark of the Disney studios, along with a talent for creating universally appealing characters such as Donald Duck and Pluto. *Snow White* (1937) was the first in a series of full-length animated films that have become fam-

ily favourites. In 1955, Disney's ambition to bring cartoons to life was realized when Disneyland opened. Some of its original attractions still survive, including the Mark Twain Steamboat, Autopia and the Mad Tea Party. New rides, inspired by the latest Disney films and characters, have been steadily added over the years and companion theme parks have opened in Florida, France and Japan.

ADVENTURELAND

THERE IS A JUNGLE atmosphere in Adventureland, which has dark, humid waterways lined with exotic plants. The big attraction in this land is the Indiana Jones™ Adventure. The area around the ride is lined with shops selling adventure clothing and equipment.

Indiana Jones™ Adventure

This is one of Disneyland's newest and most addictive rides. It is inspired by the film trilogy, starting in 1977, made by George Lucas and Steven Spielberg. Passengers set off on a thrilling, jeep-style drive through the ancient Temple of the Forbidden Eye packed with explosive tricks, sudden swerves and lurching drops. Theatrical props and scenery, a realistic soundtrack, sensational film images and the physical excitement of a roller-coaster journey combine to make this the ultimate experience created by Disneyland to date. The combination of special effects is changed every time the Indiana Jones™ Adventure is in action.

Jungle Cruise

This is a safari-style boat ride through a jungle forest that is said to be full of rampant apes and bloodthirsty head-hunters. The journey is narrated by a real-life captain, who tells his captive audience terrible but amusing jokes all the way around the ride's 5 acres (2 ha) of waterways.

Swiss Family Treehouse

This is a full-scale version of the treehouse in the story of the Swiss Family Robinson. Visitors make the climb up the concrete tree themselves, pausing to gaze into its furnished rooms. Once at the top, weary climbers can rest on a bench.

Jungle Cruise boat winding its way along overgrown waterways

Knott's Berry Farm **❷**

**Statues of cowboys on
a Ghost Town bench**

K NOTT'S BERRY FARM is the oldest
theme park in the United States,
its history reaching back to the early
1920s. Once a fruit farm growing
Walter Knott's hybrid boysenberries,
Knott's has grown into a vast entertainment playground. It now offers
more than 165 attractions, ranging
from a gentle flight with Snoopy to
a roller coaster that catapults its victims from 0 to 55 mph
(88 km/h) in five seconds. At the park's heart lie the
rickety wooden buildings of Ghost Town. This area
was originally set up in the 1940s to entertain customers
at Knott's famous "chicken dinner" restaurant, and is
still a firm favourite with visitors of all ages.

Entrance •

KEY

▨   Ghost Town

☐   Knott's Berry Farm

★ School House
*Originally built in
Iowa in 1879, this
one-room school was
bought by Walter
Knott in 1952.*

Bird Cage Theatre
is used to stage old-
time melodramas such
as *The Drunkard*.

★ Western Trails Museum
*This museum is full of
Wild West memorabilia,
ranging from rifles to
an 1853 fire engine
and this statue of
a Native American
woman.*

Gold Panning
is where visitors
can sift through
silt searching
for nuggets
of gold.

Entrance

Wild West Stunt Show
*Live entertainment is one of
Knott's Berry Farm's hall-
marks. Shows featuring
rough-and-tumble cowboy
stunts are staged in this
rustic amphitheatre.*

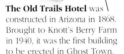

The Old Trails Hotel was
constructed in Arizona in 1868.
Brought to Knott's Berry Farm
in 1940, it was the first building
to be erected in Ghost Town.

★ Calico Railroad
This beautiful steam engine, which dates from 1881, once belonged to the narrow gauge Denver and Rio Grande Railroad. Today it transports visitors around the park, starting from Calico Square.

Calico Saloon has a long wooden bar and a stage where singers perform old songs.

Calico Square is a focal point of Ghost Town. Visitors passing through the square are often invited to join in organized line dancing and square dancing.

Overland Trails Stagecoach
More than 100 years old, this four-horse stagecoach offers visitors a chance to ride around the theme park in nostalgic style.

Calico Mine Ride
Visitors can take a train ride through a replica of the silver mine in Calico (see p275).

Indian Trails Stage
Performances of Native American or Mexican dance and storytelling are held on this circular stage. The park's information centre has show times.

STAR FEATURES

★ **Calico Railroad**

★ **School House**

★ **Western Trails Museum**

House in which Richard Nixon was born

Richard Nixon Library and Birthplace ❸

Road map D6. 18001 Yorba Linda Blvd. 🔾 *(714) 993-3393.* 🚊 *to Fullerton.* ⬜ *10am–5pm Mon–Sat; 11am–5pm Sun.* ⬤ *Thanksgiving, 25 Dec.* 🈳 ♿ ▯

THE LIFE AND achievements of the Republican politician Richard Nixon, president of the United States from 1969 to 1974, are celebrated in this combined museum, memorial and archive. In the immaculately landscaped grounds is the simple wooden house in which the former president was born in 1913. Nearby are a Reflecting Pool and the graves of Nixon and his wife, Pat, marked by matching black granite tombstones.

In the museum, a permanent walk-through exhibit provides a chronological account of Nixon's rise and fall, emphasizing his role as a peacemaker and international statesman. The Foreign Affairs gallery has a reconstruction of a Chinese pavilion housing an exhibit on Nixon's 1972 state visit to China. There is also a replica of St Basil's Cathedral in Moscow, with a display on the former president's trip to the Soviet Union in the same year.

Another interesting gallery is the World Leaders' Room, in which statues of famous politicians, including Mao Tse-tung and Winston Churchill, are surrounded by some of the many gifts that Nixon received while in office, such as a 6th-century BC statue of the goddess Isis from Anwar Sadat of Egypt, a

Sonia Delaunay painting from Georges Pompidou of France and a malachite jewellery box from Leonid Brezhnev of the Soviet Union.

Historic items exhibited in other galleries include a three-billion-year old lump of rock from the moon, a 12-ft (3.5-m) section of the Berlin Wall and dresses worn by the First Lady. Visitors are able to eavesdrop on the infamous "Watergate Tapes", which led to Nixon's resignation. In the Presidential Forum, a touch-screen exhibit using archive footage allows visitors to put questions to the late president. In additional

galleries changing exhibitions are held. These cover popular aspects of US presidential history, such as the visits paid to the White House by pop stars.

Crystal Cathedral ❹

12141 Lewis St, Garden Grove. 🔾 *(714) 971-4000.* 🚌 *45 N.* ⬜ *Mon–Sat.* ♿ ▯ 🈳 *9:30am, 11am, 6:30pm Sun.*

CONSTRUCTED from an elaborate maze of white steel trusses covered with more than 10,000 panes of silvered glass, the Crystal Cathedral is a shimmering monument to the television-led evangelism that enthrals millions of Americans today. The cathedral, which can comfortably hold almost 3,000 worshippers, is the pulpit from which its founder, Dr Robert H Schuller, broadcasts his famous "Hour of Power" service live on Sundays.

Everything about this unique cathedral is large – music is provided by one of the biggest pipe organs in the world and there is a 15-ft (4.6-m) wide colour video screen. A huge glass door opens during the

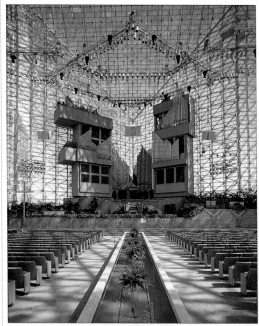

Vast interior of the Crystal Cathedral in Garden Grove

Sunday services, to enable the drive-in congregation outside to listen to the service without leaving their cars. The memorial cemetery has a capacity of 10,000.

Designed in 1980 by Philip Johnson, the star-shaped cathedral is both a spiritual shrine and an architectural wonder. Beside the building is a 236-ft (72-m) steeple, added in 1990 and adorned with polished stainless steel prisms.

The cathedral represents the culmination of a lengthy evangelical crusade that began in 1955 when the indefatigable Dr Schuller started preaching in a nearby drive-in cinema. Today he has many followers in the United States and as far away as Canada and Australia. Worshippers come from afar to attend pageants performed at Christmas and Easter, featuring people dressed as angels flying from the ceiling.

There are free tours of the cathedral and to the adjacent Southern California Community Church, the drive-in church that preceded it. The original drive-in cinema where it all began is still standing nearby.

Bowers Museum of Cultural Art ❺

2002 N Main St, Santa Ana. **Road map** D6. ☎ (714) 567-3600. ☐ to Anaheim. ☐ 45 S. ☐ 10am–4pm Tue–Sun (until 9pm Thu). ● 1 Jan, Thanksgiving, 25 Dec. ⬛ ♿ ✉

THE BOWERS has long been considered to be Orange County's leading art museum. Its serene Mission-style buildings house rich permanent collections and high-profile temporary exhibitions. There is a stylish Californian café (see p554) and a shop packed with ethnic crafts and art books.

The museum was founded in 1932. Its world-class display of African masks, collected by Paul and Ruth Tishman and now on long-term loan from the Disney Corporation, is reason enough for a pilgrimage. Other galleries, with exhibitions of treasures from the precolonial cultures of Southeast Asia, Oceania, Mexico and Native America, reflect the

Entrance arch leading to the Bowers Museum of Cultural Art

Bower Museum's commitment to the art of indigenous peoples. Fascinating examples of their crafts illustrate both the religious beliefs and the daily lives of these peoples.

The upstairs galleries, decorated with 1930s murals and plaster work, cover the mission and rancho periods of Californian and Orange County history (see pp42–3). One block away, a former bank has been converted into the companion **Kidseum**, where children are encouraged to take part in arts-related activities and can try on masks and costumes from all around the world.

Mayan statuette (AD 800– 950), Bowers Museum

⛫ Kidseum

1802 N Main St, Santa Ana. ☎ (714) 480-1520. ☐ 2–5pm Wed–Fri; 10am–4pm Sat & Sun. ⬛ ♿

Discovery Museum of Orange County ❻

3101 W Harvard St, Santa Ana. **Road map** D6. ☎ (714) 540-0404. ☐ to Anaheim. ☐ 45 S. ☐ 1–5pm Wed– Fri; 11am–3pm Sun. ● 1 Jan, Easter Sun, Thanksgiving, 25 Dec. ⬛ ♿ ✉

VICTORIAN TIMES in Orange County are brought to life in this curious three-storey mansion, built in 1898 by a civil engineer, Hiram Clay Kellogg. Fascinated by ships,

Kellogg incorporated several nautical design features into his Santa Ana residence. The oval, cabin-like dining room has an oak and walnut floor, laid in strips to resemble a ship's deck. Some of the drawers in the built-in wooden cabinets can also be opened from the kitchen, on the other side of the wall. Clusters of fruit are painted on the ceiling and the room is overlooked by an elegant circular staircase with a mast-like central pillar.

The mansion now houses an exciting and children-friendly museum, which is also of historic and architectural interest to adults. Young visitors are given the opportunity to dress up in genuine antique clothing and experience life as it was at the turn of the century.

Upstairs, rooms are furnished with antique school desks, dolls' houses and period games. In the master bedroom, now the textile room, a treadle sewing machine and spinning wheel are on display. Downstairs, children are invited to investigate mysterious instruments, including a stereoscope and a hand-crank telephone. Visitors can also explore the old-fashioned kitchen, which is equipped with icebox and butter churn.

Next door stands an 1899 ranch house, carriage barn and water tower. There is also an orchard of orange trees – now a rare sight in the county.

Implements for orange cultivation at the Discovery Museum

Mission San Juan Capistrano ❼

Statue of St John of Capistran

THIS BEAUTIFUL "Jewel of the Missions" was founded in 1776, and its chapel is the only surviving building in California in which the famous Father Junípero Serra *(see p42)* preached. One of the largest and most prosperous in the whole chain, the mission was crowned by a Great Stone Church, completed in 1806. Six years later this was destroyed by an earthquake, leaving a ruined shell set amid a rambling complex of adobe and brick buildings. A restoration programme, ornamental gardens and many historical exhibits now enable visitors to imagine the mission's former glory.

★ Padres' Living Quarters
The fathers of Mission San Juan Capistrano lived in sparsely furnished rooms and slept on hard plank beds. Visitors enjoyed more comfortable accommodation.

The kitchens have corner ovens and displays of utensils.

A domed hut, built from wooden poles, resembles the traditional dwellings of Native American villages at the time of the mission.

Sacred Garden Bells
The original four bells from the Great Stone Church now hang in the wall of a small garden. The larger pair date from 1796.

Junípero Serra
A statue of Father Serra and a Native American boy stands in a corner of the gardens.

STAR FEATURES

★ Courtyard Gardens

★ Padres' Living Quarters

★ Serra's Chapel

★ **Courtyard Gardens**
This courtyard was at the heart of mission life. Surrounded by cloisters, it still has a fountain at its centre and is today graced by mature trees and beautiful gardens.

The Bodega, or warehouse, where tallow, grains, woollens and hides were stored.

Cloisters
Covered walkways with arches frame the mission's central courtyard. With their tiled walls, the cloisters provide a cool, shaded place in which to stroll or sit and contemplate the gardens.

★ **Serra's Chapel**
Built from cherry wood and covered with gold leaf, the 300-year-old altar in the mission's chapel was brought from Barcelona, Spain, in 1906.

Ruins are all that remain of the cruciform Great Stone Church, which is currently undergoing restoration.

SWALLOWS AT THE MISSION

Every spring thousands of migrating swallows return to San Juan Capistrano from South America. Their annual arrival is celebrated with a festival held on 19 March, St Joseph's Day *(see p32).* The birds have been nesting in the tiled roofs and adobe walls of the mission for more than two centuries. They use mud pellets to build enclosed nests, in which four or five eggs are incubated. When the autumn comes, the swallows fly south again.

Migratory swallow at the mission

Catalina Island ⑧

JUST 21 MILES (50 km) from the mainland, Catalina Island is the most accessible of California's Channel Islands. It was named Santa Catalina by the Portuguese explorer Sebastián Vizcaíno when he landed here on the feast day of St Catherine of Alexandria in 1602. Much of the island's mountainous landscape remains unspoilt and it has long been a favourite weekend and holiday destination.

Catalina's main town is the virtually traffic-free port of Avalon. The grandest buildings were constructed by the chewing-gum millionaire William Wrigley, Jr, who bought the island in 1919. Today most of Catalina's 76 sq miles (200 sq km) are owned by the Santa Catalina Island Conservancy, which preserves the island's natural beauty.

Two Harbors
This low-lying isthmus backed by two bays is a popular anchorage for yachts. Facilities include a camp site, diving centre and general store.

West End •

Airport-in-the-Sky and Nature Center

Two Harbors •

Catalina Harbor

El Rancho Escondido
is a ranch on which prize-winning horses are raised. It can be visited on guided tours of the island.

Little Harbor •

El Rancho Escondido

BLACK JACK MOUNTAIN

BIG SPRINGS CANYON

Little Harbor Road

Empire Landing Road

BULLRUSH CANYON

Middle Canyon Trail

Little Harbor
This out-of-the-way spot located on the island's west shore has a sheltered cove with a beach and a scenic harbour. There are also several hiking trails and a good camp site.

Black Jack Mountain, which rises to 2,006 ft (610 m), is the second-highest mountain on Catalina Island and was mined in the 1920s for lead, zinc and silver.

CATALINA WILDLIFE

Over the centuries, Catalina has become a sanctuary for plants and animals that have died out on the mainland. Rare ironwood and mahogany trees and the highly poisonous wild tomato are among eight endemic plants surviving on the island. Distinctive animal subspecies have also evolved, such as the small grey Catalina fox and the beechey ground squirrel. Some animals brought to the island by early settlers have now turned wild, including goats, pigs and deer. Catalina even has a population of bison, ferried over in 1924 for a film shoot and never rounded up.

One of the island's wild bison

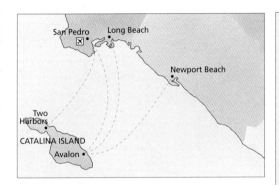

Visitors' Checklist

Road map C6. 🏘 *3,000.*
☒ **Island Express Helicopter
Service** *(310 510-2525) from San
Pedro & Long Beach to Avalon.*
⛴ **Catalina Express** *(310 519-
1212) from San Pedro to Avalon or
Two Harbors & from Long Beach
to Avalon;* **Catalina Cruises** *(800
228-2546) from Long Beach to
Avalon;* **Catalina Flyer** *(714 673-
5245) from Newport Beach to
Avalon.* 🛈 *1 Green Pleasure Pier
(310 510-1520).* 🎭 *Catalina
Arts Festival (late Sep).*

★ Avalon Casino
*Guided tours can be taken of
this 1929 Art Deco jewel, once
a famous venue for big bands
and now lovingly restored.*

Avalon Museum is on
the casino's lower floor.
This historical museum
shows how the island has
been variously used for
ranching, mining, tourism
and as a film location.

Key

═══	Minor road
══	Road in poor condition
▪▪▪	Trail
～～	River
☒	Airport
⛴	Ferry service
🛈	Tourist information
※	Viewpoint

0 kilometres   5

0 miles   2

**Lovers Cove
Marine Reserve**
is visited by glass-
bottomed boats that
reveal the colourful
marine life existing
around Catalina.

★ Avalon Bay
*Around 3,000 people live in Avalon, which
has a pier and souvenir shops. Locals travel
around in golf carts, which visitors can rent.*

Seal Rocks are included on
sightseeing cruises, which visit
this part of the island to admire
colonies of migratory sea lions.

★ Wrigley
Memorial &
Botanical Gardens
*This 38-acre (15-ha)
park honouring
William Wrigley, Jr
has an imposing
memorial and a
collection of plants
endemic to Catalina.*

Star Sights

★ **Avalon Bay**

★ **Avalon Casino**

★ **Wrigley Memorial &
Botanical Gardens**

SAN DIEGO COUNTY

I N SAN DIEGO IN 1769, *the Spanish friar Junípero Serra laid down the first link in the chain of 21 missions that underpins the modern state of California* (see pp42–3). *Blessed with a near perfect climate and a magnificent natural harbour, his settlement has now become the sixth-largest city in America. San Diego County has much to offer visitors, with its Pacific coastline, inland forests and extensive state parks.*

San Diego's character has always been determined by the sea. In the 19th century, gold prospectors, hide dealers and whalers sailed into San Diego Bay. The United States Navy arrived in 1904, starting an enthusiastic courtship that has made San Diego the largest military establishment in the world. Aircraft carriers are a common sight in the bay, but so are cruise ships, fishing boats, yachts and pleasure craft. San Diego is a city of sport and leisure – three times host to the Americas Cup, and home of the Padres baseball team and the Chargers American football team, it offers opportunities for surfing, sailing, golf and water sports.

First-time visitors are always surprised by the sense of space and how much there is to enjoy. Most have heard of San Diego Zoo and the Sea World marine park, but few realize that San Diego is a fast-growing city, with shimmering new skyscrapers soaring beside the waterfront. Culturally, San Diego is rapidly gaining prestige, as the many museums and arts venues of Balboa Park flourish.

North of the city the rugged Pacific Coast is lined with affluent beachside communities and wildlife reserves. Inland lie small towns, surrounded by peaceful countryside and fertile farmland. Deep forests and several state parks make the interior of San Diego County a paradise for hikers and campers escaping the frantic pace of city life. To the east, the region becomes increasingly mountainous, giving way to desert landscapes. And to the south, just a short trolley-ride away from San Diego, is the bustling Mexican border town of Tijuana.

Bazaar del Mundo in San Diego Old Town

◁ **Marina in San Diego Bay, with the skyscrapers of Downtown in the background**

Exploring San Diego County

COVERING MORE than 4,000 sq miles (10,350 sq km), San Diego County has a coastline of rocky cliffs, sandy beaches and wetlands, and a spacious, mountainous hinterland. The Anza-Borrego Desert *(see pp266–7)* forms a natural boundary to the east. San Diego city lies close to the border with Mexico, exploiting a large bay protected by two peninsulas. Stunning beaches and plentiful opportunities for leisure activities are the main attractions along the Pacific shoreline. A drive inland takes the visitor to the tranquillity of the Cleveland National Forest and the wilderness of state parks such as Palomar Mountain and Cuyamaca Rancho.

Cuyamaca Rancho State Park landscape

SEE ALSO

- **Where to Stay** pp517–19
- **Where to Eat** pp555–7

Shelter Island yacht harbour in San Diego Bay

0 kilometres   5

0 miles   5

SIGHTS AT A GLANCE

Chula Vista Nature Center **13**
Cuyamaca Rancho State Park **11**
Julian **10**
La Jolla **5**
Lake Morena Park **12**
Mission Bay **4**
Mission San Diego de Alcalá **2**

Mission San Luis Rey **8**
Palomar Mountain **9**
San Diego pp240–49 **1**
San Diego Wild Animal Park **7**
San Pasqual Battlefield **6**
Sea World **3**
Tijuana **14**

Cabrillo National Monument in San Diego

Surfers at Swami's Beach near Encinitas

KEY

- ▬ Freeway
- ▬ Major road
- ▬ Minor road
- ▬ Scenic route
- ➣ River
- ☀ Viewpoint

GETTING AROUND

The main transport routes run from north to south – the coastal I-5 and Amtrak railway line both provide a fast connection with Los Angeles via the Orange County coast *(see p220)*. The scenic Coaster train route serves stations between San Diego and Oceanside. A car is virtually essential for exploring the county's inland areas. Within San Diego itself, public transport is a viable option for the visitor *(see p256)*. The city has a comprehensive bus network, and the two lines of the efficient San Diego Trolley tram system extend east to El Cajon and south to the Mexican border.

San Diego County Coastline

STRETCHING FROM Orange County to the Mexican border, the coastline of San Diego County has 70 miles (112 km) of lovely sandy beaches, interspersed with cliffs, coves and chic seaside resorts. The beach culture is sophisticated, particularly at Del Mar and Mission Beach, and the sporting activity is frenzied.

Sign at entrance to Swami's Beach

At La Jolla, hanggliders leap from the cliffs and nudists jog along the beach. Peace can be found at Batiquitos Lagoon, Torrey Pines State Reserve and the Chula Vista Nature Center *(see p254),* which are all sanctuaries for coastal wildlife.

SAN CLEMENTE

★ **San Onofre State Beach** ①

Although close to the coastal San Onofre nuclear power plant, and the vast Camp Pendleton military base, this beach is worth visiting to see serious Californian surfers in action.

Swami's ③

This surfing beach is named after the founder of the Self-Realization Fellowship Temple, which overlooks the shore.

Cardiff State Beach ④

On the south side of Encinitas, Cardiff offers swimming, surfing and fine white sand, as well as seafront dining on Restaurant Row at its north end.

Batiquitos Lagoon *lies between South Carlsbad and Leucadia State Beaches. A project is under way to clean up the lagoon and create a wildlife reserve with a nature trail and visitors' centre. The lagoon has a large bird population and a rich variety of saltwater plants.*

The Del Mar Racetrack *was made famous in the 1930s by the singer Bing Crosby and other Hollywood stars. Its annual meetings remain a high point of the social calendar. San Diego's County Fair takes place at the adjacent fairground every June, and the racing season runs from late July to mid-September.*

Torrey Pines State Beach ⑥

This beach is popular for picnics and swimming. Just to the south is the Torrey Pines State Reserve, where several cliff-top hiking trails among the pine trees offer views over the ocean.

Mission Beach ⑨

This is the liveliest beach in San Diego with plenty of opportunity for people-watching, plus the fairground attractions of Belmont Park *(see p251).*

Torrey Pines State Reserve *and Santa Rosa Island (see p214) are the only two places in the world where the Torrey Pine, or Pinus torreyana, survives. A remnant of pre-Ice Age forests, this tree is well-adapted to this area's dry, sandy environment.*

Ocean Beach ⑩

Ocean Beach's T-shaped pier, popular with pelicans, has good views of the coastline.

KEY

▧	Freeway
▬	Major road
▭	Minor road
▱	River
☼	Viewpoint

0 kilometres 5

0 miles 5

Silver Strand Beach ⑫

This long, thin beach is sandwiched between areas of land reserved for naval training. It takes its name from the silvery shells in its sand.

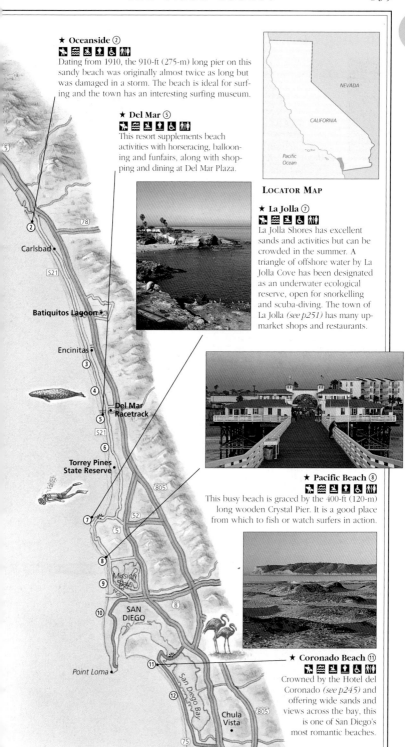

★ **Oceanside** ②

Dating from 1910, the 910-ft (275-m) long pier on this sandy beach was originally almost twice as long but was damaged in a storm. The beach is ideal for surfing and the town has an interesting surfing museum.

★ **Del Mar** ⑤

This resort supplements beach activities with horseracing, ballooning and funfairs, along with shopping and dining at Del Mar Plaza.

LOCATOR MAP

★ **La Jolla** ⑦

La Jolla Shores has excellent sands and activities but can be crowded in the summer. A triangle of offshore water by La Jolla Cove has been designated as an underwater ecological reserve, open for snorkelling and scuba-diving. The town of La Jolla (see p251) has many up-market shops and restaurants.

★ **Pacific Beach** ⑧

This busy beach is graced by the 400-ft (120-m) long wooden Crystal Pier. It is a good place from which to fish or watch surfers in action.

★ **Coronado Beach** ⑪

Crowned by the Hotel del Coronado (see p245) and offering wide sands and views across the bay, this is one of San Diego's most romantic beaches.

Carlsbad •

Batiquitos Lagoon •

Encinitas •

Del Mar Racetrack

Torrey Pines State Reserve •

Mission Bay

SAN DIEGO

Point Loma •

San Diego Bay

Chula Vista •

TIJUANA

San Diego ❶

S HAPED LIKE A HOOK and protected
by the peninsula of Coronado *(see
p245)*, the 22 sq miles (57 sq km) of
San Diego Bay form a natural deep-
water harbour around which the
second largest city in California has
grown. The bay was discovered in
1542 by the Portuguese explorer Juan
Rodríguez Cabrillo. Colonization did
not follow until 1769. In that year, the
founding father of the mission chain,

**Tiles in Santa
Fe Depot**

Shops in Seaport Village

Junípero Serra, arrived in the region as part of a military
expedition to secure Alta California (the part of California
north of the Baja Peninsula) for Spain. Its commanders
built a presidio and mission near the San Diego River,
an area now known as Old Town *(see pp244–5)*.

Exploring Downtown
San Diego

The growth of modern San
Diego began in the 1870s,
when Alonzo Horton, a San
Franciscan businessman, began
to develop the town's waterfront areas. He laid down the
grid of streets of the Gaslamp
Quarter *(see pp242–3)* which,
along with the Horton Plaza
shopping centre, has become
the centrepiece of San Diego's
rejuvenated Downtown district.
Historically, the city's main
street is Broadway, punctuated
at its western end by the **Santa
Fe Depot**. The towers and
brightly tiled interior of this
Spanish Colonial-style railway
station date from 1915. It was
built to impress visitors to the
Panama-Pacific Exposition in
Balboa Park *(see pp246–7)*.
    Since the 1980s, Downtown
San Diego has become the site
of an ongoing architectural
competition. Close to the Santa
Fe Depot, one of the city's
tallest buildings, the **America
Plaza**, is home to the Museum
of Contemporary Art. On the

waterfront, the galleon-
like **San Diego
Convention Center**,
which opened in
1989, overlooks San
Diego Bay.
    The promenades
and piers of the
Embarcadero water-
front pathway pro-
vide an introduction
to San Diego's role
as a major com-
mercial and military
port. At the northern
end are the Maritime
Museum's historic
ships. A short stroll
south is **Broadway
Pier**, where visitors
can join a harbour
excursion. **Seaport
Village**, a shopping
and dining complex,
has views across to
the aircraft carriers
of the **North Island
United States Naval
Air Station**.

🚇 **Horton Plaza**
Broadway, G St, 1st & 4th Aves.
📞 *(619) 239-8180.* ⏰ *daily.*
⬤ *Thanksgiving, 25 Dec.*
This innovatively designed
shopping centre, built in 1985,
has acted as a catalyst in the
regeneration of Downtown San
Diego. The plaza is painted in
a festive array of pastel shades
and built on interlocking levels
lined with 140 shops, department stores and cafés. Visitors
can enjoy some evening shopping, close to the restaurants
of the Gaslamp Quarter.

0 kilometres   1

0 miles   1

**Three of the colourful levels in the
Horton Plaza shopping centre**

SAN DIEGO

🏛 Maritime Museum

Harbor Drive & Ash St. 📞 *(619) 234-9153.* ◯ *daily.* ♿

The lofty masts of the *Star of India*, an 1863 merchantman, dominate this museum of historic vessels. Beside her is the beautiful San Francisco Bay passenger ferry, the *Berkeley*, dating from 1898. The luxurious steam yacht *Medea*, which was built in 1904, is moored alongside.

🏛 Museum of Contemporary Art

1001 Kettner Blvd. 📞 *(619) 234-1001.* ◯ *Tue–Sun.* ● *1 Jan, 25 Dec.* ♿

This two-storey museum, which opened in 1993, is the Downtown counterpart of the museum of the same name in La Jolla *(see p251).* The four galleries display changing exhibitions of new work by living artists, as well as selections from the museum's large permanent collection. There is also a very well-stocked bookshop.

🏛 Villa Montezuma

1925 K St. 📞 *(619) 239-2211.* ◯ *Sat & Sun.* ● *1 Jan, 24 Dec pm, 25 Dec.* ♿

This lavish Victorian mansion was built in 1887 for Jesse Shepard, an author, musician and spiritualist from England. The remarkably well-preserved Queen Anne-style interior gives visitors an insight into life in old San Diego.

Stained glass in Villa Montezuma

🏛 Children's Museum

200 W Island Ave. 📞 *(619) 233-8792.* ◯ *Tue–Sun.* ● *1 Jan, Thanksgiving, 25 Dec.* ♿

A former warehouse has been transformed into a spacious museum devoted to entertaining and educating children. The emphasis is on activity and discovery; facilities include a dressing-up stage, an art zone, virtual reality games and a bus called *The Bookstop.*

KEY

▨	Military zone
✈	Airport
🚉	Railway station
🚎	Trolley station
━	Trolley line
🚌	Coach station
⛴	Ferry terminus
ℹ	Tourist information

Taking part in one of the many activities at the Children's Museum

A Walk through the Gaslamp Quarter

DURING THE BOOM YEARS of the 1880s, the 16 blocks of the San Diego's Gaslamp Quarter became known as the "Stingaree". It was an area notorious for prostitution, gambling and drinking, where naïve customers could easily be "stung" by confidence tricksters. In spite of police clampdowns in the following decades, and the growth of a close-knit Asian community, its streets remained in decline until the 1970s, when moves were made to revive its fortunes and protect its wealth of historic buildings. In 1980, the area was designated a National Historic District. As a result, the Gaslamp Quarter has recently emerged as the new heart of San Diego. It is now renowned as a place to shop, dine and dance. Visitors can also admire the period buildings, ranging from a pie bakery and a hardware store to ornate office blocks and grand Victorian hotels. The district is particularly attractive at night, when it is illuminated by graceful gaslamps that line its pavements.

One of the quarter's gaslamps

VISITORS' CHECKLIST

Broadway & 4th–6th Aves. **Road map** D6. 🚌 1. 🚋 Bayside.
ℹ 410 Island Ave (619 233-4692). 📷 ♿ 🏧 🍴 🛍

Old City Hall
This 1874 Italianate office building once housed the entire city government.

The Lincoln Hotel at No. 536 was built in 1913. Its architecture is influenced by Chinese style.

The Backesto Building office block at No. 614 dates from 1873.

FIFTH AVENUE WEST SIDE ▸▸▸▸▸▸▸▸▸▸▸▸▸▸▸▸▸▸▸▸▸▸▸▸▸▸▸▸▸▸▸▸▸▸▸▸▸▸

★ **Louis Bank of Commerce**
Constructed in 1888, this was the first granite building in the city and housed the Bank of Commerce for just five years. It has also served as an oyster bar and a brothel.

The Marston Building
This retail outlet on the corner of 5th Avenue and F Street dates from 1881. It was built by civic leader George Marston as a department store. The structure was remodelled in 1903 following fire damage.

FIFTH AVENUE EAST SIDE ▸▸▸▸▸▸▸▸▸▸▸▸▸▸▸▸▸▸▸▸▸▸▸▸▸▸▸▸▸▸▸▸▸▸▸▸▸▸

KEY

▶▶▶▶▶ West side walking north

◀◀◀◀◀ East side walking south

Llewelyn Building
Dating from 1877, this structure housed a shoe store until 1906, and then a succession of hotels.

The Gaslamp Quarter at night
In the evening the streets of the Gaslamp Quarter bustle with people eating and drinking in its many restaurants and bars, or simply strolling around.

0 metres	10
0 yards	10

★ Yuma Building
Completed in 1888, this commercial property was one of the first brick buildings in Downtown. In 1915, the Yuma Building housed the first brothel to be closed down during a police raid of the red-light district.

STAR SIGHTS

★ **Louis Bank**

★ **Yuma Building**

Wyatt Earp
Lawman Wyatt Earp ran three gambling halls in the district during the 1880s. In order to distance themselves from the "Stingaree", the area's more respectable businesses moved north of Market Street.

Beyond Downtown

FOUR MILES (6.5 km) north of the present Downtown
lies the area now known as Old Town. Here, visitors
can see San Diego's earliest buildings, many of which
have been restored to their original state, and explore
the fascinating Junípero Serra Museum. To the west of
Old Town, the coast runs south to the end of the Point
Loma Peninsula. From here, visitors have magnificent
views of the Pacific Ocean and the city's waterfront
across the bay. South of Point Loma, Coronado, with
its numerous luxury hotels and popular sandy beaches,
enjoys a privileged location at the end of a low-lying
peninsula thrusting into San Diego Bay.

Victorian house in Heritage Park

Interior of Mason Street School in Old Town

Exploring Old Town

Until the 1870s the city of San
Diego was centred around the
presidio, the site of the original
Spanish military outpost, in an
area now known as Old Town.
Today more than 20 historic
buildings from this period have
been restored or re-created to
form the Old Town San Diego
State Historic Park. At its centre
lies the grassy Plaza where
parades and fiestas once took
place. The **Robinson-Rose
Building** at the western end
of the Plaza now serves as
the park's headquarters and
visitors' centre.

Other buildings of historical
interest include the **Colorado
House** and **Mason Street
School**, which dates from
1866. Mexican themes are
evoked in the vibrant **Bazaar
del Mundo** shopping centre
(see p256) in the north corner
of the Plaza.

Old Town San Diego spreads
far beyond the official limits of
the park. Constructed in 1856,
Whaley House at No. 2482
San Diego Avenue was the first
two-storey brick building in
California and once functioned
as a courthouse.

⏛ Junípero Serra Museum

2727 Presidio Drive. ⟨ (619) 297-
3258. ◯ Tue–Sun. ● Thanksgiving,
25 Dec. ⟨b⟩

Crowning Presidio Park, the
whitewashed Junípero Serra
Museum was built in 1929 in
the Mission Revival style *(see
p27)* and is named after the
founder of California's mission
chain. Overlooking the San
Diego River, the park occupies
the site of the presidio fort
and mission, which were built
by the Spanish in 1769. The
ruins of the presidio are still
being explored by a team of

archaeologists and some of
their finds, from fine china to
cannonballs, can be seen in
the museum. Its displays cover
San Diego's early days and
the city's successive Native
American, Spanish, Mexican
and American residents. Of
particular interest is a didactic
painting *La Madre Santissima
de la Luz*, painted in Mexico by
Luís Mena (c.1760), depicting
Native Americans kneeling
before the Virgin Mary. The
painting is a rare surviving arti-
fact from the time of the first
mission, which moved to San
Diego de Alcalá in 1774 *(see
p250)*. Exhibits upstairs describe the first Spanish expedition to California, daily life in
the presidio and the changing
face of San Diego.

⟨⟩ Heritage Park

2455 Heritage Park Row. ⟨ (619)
565-3600. ◯ daily. ● Thanksgiving, 25 Dec.

On the east side of Old Town,
Heritage Park is a collection of
immaculately restored Victorian
buildings, rescued from various
corners of the city.

Junípero Serra Museum in Old Town San Diego

♦ Casa de Estudillo
4001 Mason St. ((619) 220-5426.
○ daily. ● 1 Jan, Thanksgiving,
25 Dec. **Donation**.
Of the original adobe and
wooden buildings that visitors
can now admire in Old Town
San Diego State Historic Park,
this is one of the oldest and
the most impressive. It was
constructed by the commander
of the presidio, José Mariá de
Estudillo, in 1829. The house
has 13 rooms built around an
internal courtyard and has
been refurnished in the style
of the late Spanish period.

♦ Seeley Stable
Calhoun & Mason Sts. ((619) 220-
5427. ○ daily. ● 1 Jan, Thanksgiving, 25 Dec. **Donation**.
The museum housed in this
reconstructed stable displays
a collection of horse-drawn
carriages and stagecoaches,
as well as some interesting
Wild West memorabilia.

Exploring Point Loma
The 144-acre (58-ha) **Cabrillo
National Monument** park
straddles the southern part of
the Point Loma Peninsula. The
monument was named in honour of Juan Rodríguez Cabrillo
(see p42), the Portuguese
explorer who was the first
European to step ashore in
California in 1542. A statue of
the sailor commands an appropriately panoramic viewpoint
overlooking the ships passing
in and out of San Diego Bay.
  Between late December and
the end of February the nearby
Whale Overlook is a popular
place from which to watch
enormous grey whales under-
taking their annual southward
migration. Visitors can also follow the 2-mile (3-km) Bayside
Trail around the Point, with the
aid of a highly informative
leaflet, and visit rock pools on
its western shore.

⛫ Cabrillo National Monument Visitor Center
1800 Cabrillo Memorial Drive.
((619) 557-5450. ○ daily. ▨ ✇
Close to the Cabrillo National
Monument park entrance, this
excellent visitors' centre has a
small museum. A film recounts
Juan Rodríguez Cabrillo's 800-
mile (1,300-km) voyage along
the Californian coast.

Old Point Loma Lighthouse

♦ Old Point Loma Lighthouse
1800 Cabrillo Memorial Drive.
((619) 557-5450. ○ daily. ▨
♿ ✇
The lighthouse, a short walk
south from the Cabrillo statue,
sent its first beams into the
night in 1855 and operated for
36 years. Although its tower is
usually closed to the public,
the lower rooms re-create the
lighthouse keepers' living
quarters as they were in 1890s.

Exploring Coronado
The city of Coronado, at the
head of a 4,100-acre (1,650-
ha) peninsula in the middle of
San Diego Bay, is moneyed
and self-confident. Businessman Elisha Babcock, Jr bought
the land in 1885 and set out to
develop a world-class resort.
Coronado now boasts San
Diego's most exclusive homes,
boutiques, hotels and restaurants. Its Pacific shore is lined
by a stunning beach *(see
p239)*, which is dominated at
its southern end by the landmark Hotel del Coronado.

⛴ Coronado Ferry
1050 N Harbor Drive. ((619) 234-
4111. ○ daily. ▨
Until the opening of the
spectacular San Diego–
Coronado Bay Bridge in 1969,
the ferry provided the area's
principal link with the mainland, a service that has now
been revived for the benefit
of both tourists and locals.
  The 15-minute trip between
the Broadway Pier on the
Embarcadero and the Ferry
Landing Marketplace is breathtaking at dusk when the setting
sun illuminates the skyscrapers
of Downtown. From the Ferry
Landing, visitors can take a bus
or walk along Orange Avenue
to the Pacific shore.

♦ Hotel del Coronado
1500 Orange Ave, Coronado.
((619) 435-6611; (800) 468-3533.
○ daily. ▨ ♿ ✇
Opened in 1888, the "Del" *(see
p517)* is a lovingly preserved
grand Victorian seaside hotel.
It was built using both architects and labour from the rail-
ways – a heritage that is most
obvious in the domed ceiling
of the Crown Room, which is
built from sugar pine without
a single nail. The list of illustrious guests who have stayed
here reads like a Who's Who
of 20th-century United States
history – presidents from
Franklin D Roosevelt to Bill
Clinton, film stars from Marilyn
Monroe to the *Baywatch*
belles. The hotel has been the
setting for several films, including *Some Like It Hot*, the 1959
classic starring Marilyn Monroe,
Jack Lemmon and Tony Curtis.
"Del" devotees can take a 35-
minute audio tour.

Impressive turrets and gables of the exclusive Hotel del Coronado

Balboa Park and San Diego Zoo

Statue of El Cid in Balboa Park

Named after the Spanish explorer who first set eyes on the Pacific Ocean in 1513, Balboa Park was founded in 1868. Its beauty owes much to the dedicated horticulturalist Kate Sessions who, in 1892, promised to plant trees throughout its 1,200 acres (485 ha) in exchange for renting space for a nursery. In 1915 the park was the venue for the city's Panama-Pacific Exposition *(see p339)*, a world fair celebrating the opening of the Panama Canal. Several of the Spanish Colonial-style pavilions built in that year survive along El Prado (the park's main street), and the animals gathered for the exhibition formed the nucleus from which San Diego Zoo has grown *(see p249)*. Twenty years later the organizers of the California-Pacific International Exposition added more exhibition spaces around Pan-American Plaza. All these buildings now form a rich concentration of museums and performance venues.

Plaza de Panama
This plaza in the centre of the El Prado thorough-fare was at the heart of the Panama-Pacific Exposition.

Skyfari

★ San Diego Museum of Man
This historical museum is housed in the 1915 California Building. Designed in Spanish Colonial style, its façade is decorated with statues representing famous Californians.

Old Globe Theater

El Prado

San Diego Automotive Museum

Aerospace Museum
This A-12 Blackbird, built in 1962, stands beside a museum devoted to the history of flight.

STAR SIGHTS

★ **California Building/San Diego Museum of Man**

★ **San Diego Museum of Art**

★ **San Diego Zoo**

Pan-American Plaza

Spreckels Organ Pavilion

Tour bus

0 metres   100

0 yards   100

Tour bus

San Diego Zoo entrance

Timken Museum

Casa del Prado

San Diego Natural History Museum

★ San Diego Museum of Art
A café and sculpture garden stand next to the principal art museum in the park. Both North American and European works are exhibited.

Reuben H Fleet Space Theater and Science Center

Casa de Balboa

de
ma

VISITORS' CHECKLIST

Park Blvd, Laurel & 6th Sts.
Road map D6. 📞 *(619) 239-
0512.* 🚌 *7.* **Visitors' Center,**
Plaza de Panama 📞 *(619) 239-
0512.* ◗ *9am–4pm daily.* ●
Thanksgiving, 25 Dec, 1 Jan.
Spreckels Organ Pavilion
🎫 *(free concerts Jun–Sep: Mon
at dusk, Sun 2–3pm).* **San Diego
Zoo** 📞 *234-3153.*
◗ *early Sep–Jun: 9am–4pm
daily; Jul–Aug: 9am–5pm daily.*
🎫 🅿 🚻 🍴 📷 🛍 🍽

★ **San Diego Zoo**
*Orang-utans are among
the 4,000 animals that live
in the well-kept enclosures
of this world-famous zoo.*

Botanical Building
*Constructed from thin strips
of redwood, this shaded sanctuary is full of tropical and
subtropical plants.*

Exploring Balboa Park and San Diego Zoo

Topiary elephant at zoo entrance

BALBOA PARK, located at the heart of San Diego, is one of the city's most popular attractions. At the weekend, its pleasant, lush grounds and traffic-free promenades are crowded with strollers, joggers, cyclists and street artists. In between museum tours, visitors can picnic in one of the shady picnic groves or play ball games on the grassy lawns. Just to the north of the museums and recreation grounds of Balboa Park lies San Diego Zoo, where 800 species from all over the world are housed in enclosures designed to resemble as closely as possible their natural habitat.

Sunday afternoon street entertainers in Balboa Park

🏛 San Diego Museum of Man

1350 El Prado. 📞 *(619) 239-2001.*
🕐 *daily.* ⬤ *1 Jan, Thanksgiving, 25 Dec.* 📷

The landmark pavilion of the Panama-Pacific Exposition of 1915 *(see p246)*, also known as the California Building, houses an anthropological museum about the early history of mankind. Exhibits arranged over two floors cover topics such as the cultures of ancient Egypt and the Mayans, and Native American crafts.

🏛 San Diego Museum of Art

1450 El Prado. 📞 *(619) 232-7931.*
🕐 *Tue–Sun.* ⬤ *1 Jan, Thanksgiving, 25 Dec.* 📷

This museum's large, varied art collection is boosted by a programme of special exhibitions. European and American art from 1850 to the 20th century is shown in the first floor galleries, along with exhibits

from southern Asia, Japan and China. The displays on the second floor feature work from 1300 to 1850, including *Coronation of the Virgin* (1508), by Luca Signorelli.

***Portrait of a Gentleman* (1634) by Frans Hals in the Timken Museum**

🏛 Timken Museum of Art

1500 El Prado. 📞 *(619) 239-5548.*
🕐 *Tue–Sun.* ⬤ *1 Jan, 4 Jul, Thanksgiving, 25 Dec.*

Opened in 1965, the Timken exhibits a few exquisite works in an inviting space. On display are works by European masters such as Frans Hals (1581/5–1666), François Boucher (1703–70) and Paul Cézanne (1839–1906). The Timken also has works by 19th-century American artists, including *The Yosemite Fall* (1864) by Albert Bierstadt, and a collection of Russian icons.

🏛 Museum of Photographic Arts

1649 El Prado. 📞 *(619) 238-7559.*
🕐 *daily.* ⬤ *25 Dec.* 📷

This museum is located on the main floor of the ornate Casa de Balboa. It specializes in high-quality travelling exhibitions that demonstrate the art and power of photography. There is also an interesting and well-stocked bookshop.

🏛 Museum of San Diego History

1649 El Prado. 📞 *(619) 232-6203.*
🕐 *Wed–Sun.* ⬤ *1 Jan, Thanksgiving, 24 & 25 Dec.* 📷

As well as a large number of fascinating old photographs and books about the city, the museum has excellent exhibitions about cars, quilts and the quest for a city water supply. "Out of Our Vaults" is an exhibition of new material taken from the museum's research archives, and never before seen by the public.

🏛 Reuben H Fleet Space Theater and Science Center

El Prado, Plaza de Panama & Park Blvd.
📞 *(619) 238-1233.* 🕐 *daily.* 📷 *call ahead for OMNIMAX® show times.*

The big attraction here is the vast dome of the OMNIMAX cinema in the Space Theater, where impressive films about the world around us are projected onto an enormous, tilting screen. Laser and planetarium shows are also staged.

The complex is open in the evenings and has a Science Center with hands-on exhibits that demonstrate the laws of science. There is also a café and a shop selling books and intriguing games and puzzles.

Ornate Colonial-style façade of the San Diego Museum of Art

🏛 San Diego Natural History Museum

Village Place, Park Blvd & El Prado. **[** (619) 232-3821. ⭘ daily. ● 1 Jan, 25 Dec. 🖼 free Tue.

The museum's ground floor displays travelling exhibits on themes such as whales and insects. There is also a Hall of Mineralogy, which is built to resemble a mine. The galleries on the lower level explore Southern California's ecological zones of desert, shore and ocean, highlighting topics such as the mountain lion and off-shore kelp beds.

🏛 San Diego Aerospace Museum

2001 Pan American Plaza. **[** (619) 234-8291. ⭘ daily. ● 1 Jan, Thanksgiving, 25 Dec. 🖼

San Diego has long been a city of pioneering aviation. The *Spirit of St Louis*, in which pilot Charles Lindbergh made the first non-stop solo transatlantic flight in 1927, was built here. A model of the plane takes pride of place among a collection of more than 60 original and full-scale reconstructions of aircraft. Exhibits range from a batwing glider to a Vietnam War helicopter. The Aerospace Hall of Fame pays homage to the heroes and inventors behind flight and space travel.

A 1948 Tucker Torpedo from the Automotive Museum's collection

🏛 San Diego Automotive Museum

2080 Pan American Plaza. **[** (619) 231-2886. ⭘ daily. ● 1 Jan, Thanksgiving, 25 Dec. 🖼

Dream cars and motorcycles from both the United States and Europe shine on in this unashamedly nostalgic museum. Because most of the cars are privately owned, the collection is constantly changing, but gleaming paintwork, aesthetic curves and whitewall tyres are guaranteed.

SAN DIEGO ZOO

San Diego Zoo is one of the best-known zoos in the world, famous both for its conservation programmes and as a highly educational source of family entertainment. With some 4,000 animals dispersed over 100 acres (40 ha), the best introduction is to take the 35-minute narrated bus tour that covers most of the zoo. The aerial Skyfari ride, which offers a trip across the south of the park in gondola cars 180 ft (55 m) up, is also rewarding. After these, visitors can track down their favourites in the animal world by following the paths and moving walkways. There is also a Children's Zoo, and in summer the zoo is open for nocturnal exploration.

FINDING THE ATTRACTIONS

① Flamingo Lagoon
② Reptile House
③ Petting Paddock
④ Bromeliad Garden
⑤ Hummingbird Aviary
⑥ Wegeforth Bowl
⑦ Reptile Mesa
⑧ Tiger River
⑨ Hippo Beach
⑩ Pygmy Chimps
⑪ Scripps Aviary
⑫ Gorilla Tropics
⑬ Bird and Primate Mesa
⑭ Orchid Display
⑮ Sun Bear Forest
⑯ Rain Forest Aviary
⑰ Wings of Australasia
⑱ Horn and Hoof Mesa
⑲ Birds of Paradise
⑳ Hunte Amphitheater
㉑ Dog and Cat Canyon
㉒ African Rock Kopje Exhibit
㉓ Elephant Mesa
㉔ Bear Canyon

Sichuan takin calf resting in San Diego Zoo

Interior of the church at the Mission San Diego de Alcalá

Mission San Diego de Alcalá ❷

10818 San Diego Mission Rd, San Diego. **Road map** D6. ☎ *(619) 283-7319.* 🚌 *20, 13.* ⬜ *daily.* ⬤ *1 Jan, Thanksgiving, 25 Dec.* **Donation.** ✝ *7am & 5:30pm daily.* ♿

Originally sited at what is now the Junípero Serra Museum in Presidio Park (see p244), San Diego's mission was moved to Mission Valley in 1774. The land surrounding the new site was more fertile and had a larger population of potential Native American converts. The name Diego refers to St Didacus, who was born in Alcalá, Spain, in 1400.

The first mission in the Californian chain (see pp42–3) is today engulfed by freeways and urban development, but its harmonious buildings and gardens retain an atmosphere of peace. Early this century, the complex was restored to its appearance of 1813. The church retains some original materials, such as the timbers over its doorways, the floor tiles and the adobe bricks in the baptistry.

In the garden stands the Campanario (bell tower) and a statue representing St Francis. A small museum honours the state's first Christian martyr, Padre Luís Jayme, who was murdered when a gang comprised of 600 Native Americans attacked the newly established mission in 1775.

Statuette at San Diego de Alcalá

Sea World ❸

1750 S Shores Drive. **Road map** D6. ☎ *(619) 226-3901.* 🚌 *9.* ⬜ *daily.* 🅿♿

In this state famous for its theme parks, the great lure of San Diego's Sea World is the chance to get close to the creatures that inhabit our oceans. Steadily expanded since its opening in 1964, this marine park now covers 150 acres (60 ha) of Mission Bay and can provide its visitors with entertainment for a full day.

A good starting point is the five-minute ride up the Skytower, a 320-ft (98-m) column with panoramic views. Another interesting aerial perspective is offered by the 100-ft (30-m) high Bayside Skyride in the park's northwest corner, where gondola cars take passengers in a 0.5-mile (1-km) loop over the waters of Mission Bay.

The stars of Sea World are its performing whales and dolphins. It is advisable to call in advance in order to plan a visit around their shows. One performance reveals the intelligence of dolphins and pilot whales, while another demonstrates the virtuosity of killer whales. Among the many other attractions in the park are pools with sharks, otters and turtles and freshwater aquariums, as well as opportunities to feed killer whales and seals and touch rays and starfish. Close to the Skytower is Shamu's Happy Harbor, an aquatic adventure park for children.

There is also a more serious side to Sea World – its staff are devoted to animal rescue and rehabilitation and take in an average of one sick or abandoned animal per day. The park also runs education and conservation programmes.

Mission Bay ❹

Road map D6. 🚌 *from Downtown San Diego.* **Visitors' Center** ☎ *(619) 276-8200.* ⬜ *daily.*

Mission Bay Park is an area of 4,600 acres (1,850 ha) entirely given over to public recreational use. San Diegans come here to keep fit and relax in the well-tended parkland.

Killer whales performing acrobatic feats for the crowds at Sea World

Sailing on the peaceful waters of Mission Bay

The area was once a marsh, but systematic dredging and landscaping, begun in the 1930s, transformed it. The San Diego River has been corralled into a channel to the south, creating a pleasant world of beaches, water-sports centres and islands. Although the main attraction in Mission Bay is Sea World, visitors can also enjoy kite-flying, volleyball, golf and cycling. Along the 27-mile (43-km) shoreline, swimming, fishing and sailing take place in designated areas.

In the southwest corner of the bay is Mission Beach *(see p238)*, one of the most lively beaches in San Diego County. Lovers of traditional seaside amusements will enjoy the beachfront **Belmont Park**. Its restored wooden Giant Dipper dates from 1925.

Belmont Park
3146 Mission Blvd. *(619) 488-0668.* daily.

La Jolla 5

Road map D6. 32,000. from San Diego. 1055 Wall St, Suite 110 (619 454-1444).

THE ORIGIN of the name La Jolla (which is pronounced "La Hoya") is the subject of an on-going debate – while some people believe it to come from the Spanish *la joya*, meaning "jewel", others claim it was inspired by a Native American word, with the same pronunciation, which means "cave". Located 4 miles (6 km) north of San Diego's Mission Bay, La Jolla is an elegant, up-market coastal resort set amid beautiful cliffs and coves *(see p239)*. Its pretty streets are lined with gourmet chocolatiers, designer clothes shops and top-name jewellers. San Diegans and tourists alike come to enjoy the many art galleries and the chic restaurants promising a "Mediterranean" view.

A companion to the gallery in Downtown San Diego *(see p241)*, La Jolla's **Museum of Contemporary Art** occupies a prime oceanfront location. It displays works from its permanent collection of post-1950 art and houses a bookshop, café and sculpture garden.

The town is also home to the University of California at San Diego and to the famous **Salk Institute for Biological Studies**, founded in 1960 by Dr Jonas Salk, who developed the polio vaccine.

Overlooking Scripps Beach is the Scripps Institution of Oceanography, in which the magnificent **Birch Aquarium at Scripps** is housed. The aquarium provides an insight into the fascinating world of oceanography, through permanent exhibits, interactive displays and even a simulated deep-sea dive. In the adjacent aquarium, visitors can observe sea life from the waters of the north Pacific as well as from the tropics, including a balletic Alaskan giant octopus.

Museum of Contemporary Art
700 Prospect St. *(619) 454-3541.* Tue–Sun. 1 Jan, 25 Dec.
Salk Institute for Biological Studies
10010 N Torrey Pines Rd. *(619) 453-4100.* Mon–Fri. public hols. call ahead.
Birch Aquarium at Scripps
2300 Expedition Way. *(619) 534-3474.* daily. Thanksgiving, 25 Dec.

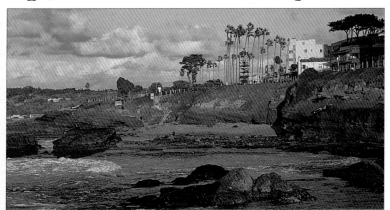
Beautiful rocky shoreline of La Jolla Cove

Memorial plaque at the battlefield site in San Pasqual Valley

San Pasqual Battlefield ❻

Road map D6. 📞 (760) 489-0076. 🔲 Sat & Sun, public hols. ⬤ 1 Jan, Thanksgiving, 25 Dec.

IN 1846, during the war between the United States and Mexico *(see p43)*, the San Pasqual Valley was the scene of a costly victory for the US Army over the rebel Californios (Mexican settlers in California). Handicapped by wet gunpowder, exhaustion and cold, 22 of the 100 soldiers fighting under General Kearny were killed by the Californio lancers and 16 were wounded.

There is a **Visitors' Center**, run by volunteers, in which a film about the battle is shown.

Every December, local history enthusiasts in replica 19th-century military uniforms re-enact the events of the battle.

🏛 **Visitors' Center**
15808 San Pasqual Valley Rd. 📞 (619) 220-5430. 🔲 May–Sep: daily; Oct–Apr: Sat & Sun. ⬤ public hols.

San Diego Wild Animal Park ❼

Road map D6. 📞 (760) 480-0100. 🚂 Escondido. 🔲 daily. 🖼 ♿ 🎥

A RURAL COUNTERPART to San Diego Zoo *(see p249)*, this wildlife park displays an encyclopedic variety of birds and mammals in its 1,800 acres (730 ha) of carefully landscaped grounds. Opened in 1972, the park was conceived as a breeding sanctuary for the world's endangered species and has remained at the forefront of the conservation race. As well as caring for its 3,200 residents, the park exchanges animals with zoological institutions around the world, with the ultimate goal of releasing endangered species back into the wild. Among the scheme's success stories is that of the California condor, a species once close to extinction. Many condors successfully reared in the park have been returned to their natural habitat.

A good way to begin a visit is to take the Wgasa Bush Line Monorail. This 50-minute, five-mile guided ride around the large park passes the principal animal enclosures and provides a useful orientation. Another fascinating journey is along the 2-mile (3-km) Kilimanjaro Safari Walk, offering superb views of re-created African and Asian landscapes.

For many visitors, the big animals, such as elephants, lions and rhinos, are the stars. However, the park's various simulated natural environments, such as the Australian Rainforest and the Hidden Jungle, are also engrossing, and the Petting Kraal is very popular with children. Before visiting the Wild Animal Park, it is worth calling ahead to find out the times of daily events such as the Elephant Show.

Keen photographers and anyone who likes to see wildlife in close-up can book to join a Photo Caravan, which takes small groups on tours inside the park's enclosures in an open-topped truck.

Nairobi Village is a 17-acre (7-ha) area, in which the park's amphitheatres and most of its facilities are to be found. Its many shops sell Africa-related books and souvenirs.

Mission San Luis Rey ❽

Road map D6. 📞 (760) 757-3651. 🚂 from San Diego. 🔲 daily. **Donation**.

ONE OF THE LARGEST and most prosperous estates in the Californian mission chain *(see p42)*, San Luis Rey de Francia

Animals roaming around freely in the San Diego Wild Animal Park

Façade of Mission San Luis Rey

was founded by the Spanish priest Padre Fermín Lasuén in 1798. The mission was named after the canonized 13th-century French king, Louis IX, and owed much of its success to the cooperation of the local Luiseño Indians. More than 3,000 Native Americans lived and worked in Mission San Luis Rey. They kept sheep and cattle and cultivated crops such as grain and fruit.

The majority of the mission's remaining buildings benefited from a long period of restoration in the early 20th century. Visitors are guided first into a **A statue in the church museum** outlining the history of the mission and the surrounding area. Of the vestments and religious artifacts on display, several have only survived because, after the church was secularized in 1833, some of its treasures were hidden by the Christian Native Americans. Their families only returned the artifacts to the mission when it was designated a Franciscan monastery in 1893.

The church at San Luis Rey has a cruciform shape as at San Juan Capistrano (see p231) but was the only one in the chain with a domed wooden ceiling. The wooden pulpit is original and the painted designs are based on surviving stencils. The mission still functions as a church and retreat, and in its grounds are a partly restored laundry area, a large cemetery and California's oldest pepper tree, brought to the state from Peru in 1830.

🏛 Museum
Eastern Cloister. ◯ daily. ● 1 Jan, Thanksgiving, 25 Dec. 🅿 ♿

Palomar Mountain ❾

Road map D6. 🚌 from Julian.

RISING TO 6,200 ft (1,900 m) and thickly forested, Palomar Mountain offers visitors breathtaking views over north San Diego County from the long, winding road that climbs its slopes. The Palomar Mountain State Park encompasses 1,600 acres (645 ha) of the mountain's scenic landscape. It has good hiking trails and also provides facilities for activities, such as camping, hiking and trout fishing.

At the summit of Palomar Mountain is the surreal-looking white dome of the **Palomar Observatory**. Operated by the California Institute of Technology, this internationally renowned observatory first opened in 1948. It houses a computer-controlled Hale telescope with a 200-inch (510-cm) mirror capable of studying areas of the universe that are more than a billion light years away. From 1948 to 1956, the observatory's Oschin telescope was used to photograph the entire night sky. A second survey began in 1983 and is still in progress today. The images it produces will be compared to the earlier ones to reveal the changes that have taken place since the 1950s and thus provide vital data for researchers.

Visitors are not permitted to look through the 540-tonne telescope. However, an exhibition area and photo gallery explain how it functions and reveal the distant worlds it has brought before our eyes.

🏛 Palomar Observatory
35899 Canfield Rd, Palomar Mountain. ● 24 & 25 Dec. 📞 (760) 742-2119.

Dome of the Palomar Observatory at sunset

Julian ⑩

Road map D6. 🏠 2,000. 🚌 from San Diego. ℹ️ 2129 Main St (760 765-1857).

W HEN SAN DIEGANS want to go for a pleasant drive or spend a romantic weekend in the "back country", they often head for the mountain town of Julian. Gold was discovered here in 1870, and the restored 19th-century wooden buildings that line the main street help to re-create the atmosphere of those pioneer days.

Today tourists rather than gold-diggers flock here. In autumn, the "Apple Days" of October attract hundreds of visitors, who come to taste Julian's renowned apple pie and buy rustic souvenirs in the quaint gift shops. The delightfully cluttered **Julian Pioneer Museum** is packed with curiosities and photographs evoking the town's history. Visitors can also venture inside an original gold mine at the **Eagle and High Peak Mines**.

Apple pie shop sign in Julian

For visitors wishing to stay overnight, there is plenty of homely bed-and-breakfast accommodation both in and around the town (see p518).

🏛 **Julian Pioneer Museum**
2811 Washington St. ℂ (760) 765-0027. ☐ Apr–Nov: Tue–Sun; Dec–March: Sat, Sun & public hols. 🎟
🚇 **Eagle and High Peak Mines**
C St. ℂ (760) 765-0036. ☐ daily, but call ahead. ☻ 1 Jan, Easter Sun, Thanksgiving, 25 Dec. 🎟

Cuyamaca Rancho State Park ⑪

Road map D6. 🚌 ℹ️ (760) 765-0755. ☐ daily.

O NLY AN HOUR's drive east of San Diego, Cuyamaca Rancho State Park is a place to get away from it all. Almost half of its 25,000 acres (10,100 ha) are an officially designated wilderness that is home to skunks, bobcats, coyotes, mule deer and mountain lions (also known as cougars).

In addition to horse riding, camping and mountain biking facilities, there are 130 miles (210 km) of hiking trails in the park. The Cuyamaca Peak Trail is an arduous but supremely rewarding ascent by paved fire road. From the summit, hikers can enjoy fine views over the forested hills of northern San Diego County as far as Palomar Mountain (see p253).

Information on other trails and facilities is available from the **Park Headquarters**, located on Highway 79. Also at the Park Headquarters is a **museum** that pays homage to Cuyamaca Rancho's first inhabitants, the Kumeya'ay Indians.

At the northern end of the park lie the forlorn ruins of the Stonewall Gold Mine. Once a 500-strong prospectors' town, it produced more than two million dollars' worth of gold in the 1880s.

ℹ️ **Park Headquarters and Museum**
12551 Hwy 79. ℂ (760) 765-0755. ☐ daily. ☻ public hols.

Shores of Lake Morena

Lake Morena Park ⑫

Road map D6. 🚌 from San Diego. ℂ (619) 478-5473.

T HIS LUSH, oak-shaded park surrounding a large fishing lake forms an oasis in the dry southeastern corner of San Diego County. The park covers 3,250 acres (1,300 ha) of land, ranging from flat terrain to low scrub-covered hills.

The extensive waters of Lake Morena are well-stocked with bass, bluegill, crappie and catfish. For those who come to fish or simply enjoy a peaceful afternoon on the lake, boats are available for hire.

Chula Vista Nature Center ⑬

Road map D6. ℂ (619) 422-2473. 🚌 Chula Vista. ☐ Jun–Aug: daily; Sep–May: Tue–Sun. ☻ 1 Jan, Easter Sun, Thanksgiving & following day, 24, 25 & 31 Dec. 🎟 ♿

T HIS REMARKABLE conservation project beside San Diego Bay was established in 1988 to provide refuge for the wildlife of California's coastal wetlands. A free bus takes visitors to the Nature Center from a car park located by the I-5.

Here visitors can learn about the fragile environment of the 316 acres (130 ha) of protected land. From the Nature Center, several hiking trails lead to the bay shore. Birds that can be seen all year round include herons, ospreys and kestrels. The refuge is also a nesting site for endangered species, such as the California least tern.

Horse riding in the Cuyamaca Rancho State Park

Tijuana

Carved wooden
Mexican bird

FEW VISITORS to San Diego can resist a brief trip south into Baja California. The international border crossing at Tijuana is the busiest in the world and the contrast between the American and Mexican ways of life is marked. The Americans, who come to Tijuana in their thousands every year to enjoy its cheap shopping and exuberant nightlife, often affectionately refer to the city as "TJ".

LOCATOR MAP

— International border

— San Diego Trolley line

▨ Mexico

Exploring Tijuana

The border city of Tijuana is hardly representative of the fabled Mexico of Mayan art and Spanish colonial architecture, but it is interesting as a hybrid frontier town devoted to extracting dollars from its wealthy neighbour.

The city's futuristic **Centro Cultural Tijuana** was built on the banks of the Tijuana River in 1982. This cultural centre has an OMNIMAX cinema, in which films about Mexico are shown on an enormous tilting screen. Changing exhibitions on various Mexican themes are also held here. The open-air **Mexitlán** rooftop exhibition re-creates the country's architectural treasures in miniature.

Most visitors come to shop and party – Tijuana has long been popular with young Americans taking advantage of laws permitting anyone over 18 to drink alcohol.

The best shopping is in the quiet bazaars situated to the sides of the lively Avenida Revolución. Painted pottery, leather boots, silver jewellery

Bottles of liqueur on sale in a street bazaar in Tijuana

and tequila are some favourite buys. Tourists are encouraged to barter with the stallholders.

English-speaking staff at the **Tijuana Tourist Office** can provide maps and free advice on visiting the city.

🏛 **Centro Cultural Tijuana**
Paseo de los Héroes. [(011-52-66) 84-11-46, 84-11-37. ◯ daily. ▨

🏛 **Mexitlán**
Ave Ocampo, Calles 2–3. [(011-52-66) 38-41-33, 38-43-19. ◯ Wed–Sun. ▨

🚹 **Tijuana Tourist Office**
Ave Revolución y Calle. [(011-52-66) 88-05-55. ◯ daily.

TIPS FOR TRAVELLERS

Getting there: As the San Diego Trolley (see p256) runs as far as the international border, the cheapest and simplest way to cross the border into Tijuana is on foot. Take a southbound trolley to San Ysidro and follow the crowds across the pedestrian bridges and walkways that lead to the city. You can also take a bus from San Ysidro across the border to downtown Tijuana, or book an excursion through a San Diego travel agent. Those taking a car or a motorbike will need Mexican vehicle insurance. This is inexpensive and is available at the border.
Visas: Citizens of Australia, Canada and the United Kingdom require passports but not visas to enter Mexico, unless they are planning to remain in the country for longer than six months. When crossing the border, non-American nationals must present a completed Mexican Tourist Card, which may be obtained from the border guards. Citizens of the United States do not require a visa for a stay of less than six months and need only show their driving licence if they are staying for less than 72 hours. Immigration controls for returning to the US are strict so you will need to take your passport or suitable personal identification documents and ensure you meet the necessary US visa requirements. For further information, contact the Mexican consulate in your home country before departure.
Currency: Visitors on a short trip will rarely need to change money as US dollars and major credit cards are widely accepted.

Façade of the Centro Cultural Tijuana

PRACTICAL INFORMATION

SAN DIEGO is an easy city to get to know, with a clean, efficient public transport system and a welcoming attitude towards visitors. The regeneration of the city's heart is evident in the growing number of shops, restaurants and nightspots around Horton Plaza (see p240) and the Gaslamp Quarter (see pp242–3). A variety of public transport penetrates this Downtown area, where there are

Jessop's Clock in Horton Plaza

all the shops and entertainment venues you would expect in a vibrant Californian city. There are also regular connections to Old Town, Balboa Park, Coronado and the Mexican border, while the best way to enjoy the waterfront of the Embarcadero (see p240) is on foot. Tourist information is available from excellent visitors' centres located in Horton Plaza and Balboa Park, as well as in Coronado.

Passengers boarding a San Diego bus

GETTING AROUND

THE TWO LINES of the **San Diego Trolley**, the city's tram system, link Old Town, El Cajon and San Ysidro on the Mexican border with the city centre. Trolleys run every 15 minutes during the day and operate until around 1am. A comprehensive bus network runs throughout the city. The **San Diego–Coronado Bay Ferry** offers a regular service to the Coronado Peninsula (see p245). Maps, timetables and special one- or four-day Day Tripper passes, valid for unlimited travel on any bus, trolley or ferry, can be obtained

from the **Transit Store**. **Old Town Trolley Tours** offer regular guided tours visiting all the principal city sights.

The city's **Amtrak** station is housed in the beautiful Santa Fe Depot in Downtown. **San Diego International Airport** is located 3 miles (5 km) northwest of Downtown. Buses, taxis and hire cars are all available from the airport.

The **Balboa Park Tram** provides free transport around the cultural park (see pp246–7). In the vast Mission Bay aquatic playground (see pp250–1), the **Harbor Hopper** water taxi takes visitors to points of interest around the shoreline.

San Diego is also a cyclist-friendly city, well served with cycle paths and cycle hire shops. There is a gentle route from Mission Beach to La Jolla (see p251), offering fine ocean views. Bikes can be carried on trolleys and buses for a small fee. If you prefer to let someone else do the work, you can hail cycle taxis in Downtown.

It is generally safe to walk around the areas to the north and west of Downtown, even at night. However, the areas to the south of Downtown and, particularly, to the east of the Gaslamp Quarter are best avoided after dark.

Mexican-style shopping in the Bazaar del Mundo

SHOPPING

IF YOU INTEND to visit Tijuana (see p255), avoid doing too much shopping before you go as bargain goods are the main reason for crossing the border. The Bazaar del Mundo in Old Town San Diego (see p244) also has plenty of Mexican crafts and souvenirs.

Horton Plaza is the city's most colourful shopping centre and can meet most tourists' needs, while the Paladion next door sells couture clothing. The oceanfront Seaport Village complex (see p240) is a good place to buy souvenirs and gifts to take home. Further up the coast, Prospect Street in

A San Diego Trolley, offering a fast, frequent service to the Mexican border

Attractive shopping area of Seaport Village, on the waterfront

La Jolla has a selection of elegant stores. Del Mar and Carlsbad also have a good mix of boutiques, antiques shops and art galleries.

There are several factory outlet centres in San Diego County, where outlet stores sell well-known brand-name goods at considerably reduced prices *(see p583)*. The San Diego Factory Outlet Center, located just before the Mexican border crossing in San Ysidro, is one of the largest and best in the region, with more than 30 factory outlet stores. Ask at the information desk in the large car park for a sheet of discount tokens, which allow you to obtain further reductions of up to 15 per cent in many of the shops.

Here, as throughout the state, major credit cards are accepted and the opening hours of most shops are 10am–6pm Monday to Saturday, with some open on Sundays as well. A local sales tax of 8.5 per cent applies to all purchases. This is automatically added to the advertised price of the goods when you pay for them.

ENTERTAINMENT

SAN DIEGO HAS a reputation for its cultural energy and has its own symphony orchestra, opera and repertory theatre companies. Listings of all the current cultural events can be found in the *San Diego Union-Tribune* and a range of complimentary tourist magazines. *The Reader*, available free in cafés, bars and bookshops, is a good weekly source for finding out about poetry readings, live music and the alternative arts. Tickets for all these events can be bought from the **Times Arts Tix** office in Horton Plaza.

The Gaslamp Quarter *(see pp242–3)* is the best area to go to for good restaurants and nightclubs. The nearby Lyceum and Spreckels theatres have regular stage performances. In Balboa Park, the Old Globe Theatre *(see p246)* stages award-winning shows and is one part of a three-stage performing arts complex.

Like most Californians, San Diegans are also avid sports fans – the Chargers football team and the Padres baseball team share a sports stadium in Mission Valley. If, however, you prefer participating in sport to watching it, Mission Bay *(see pp250–1)* offers a wide range of water sports, as well as beach games such as volleyball. San Diego County also benefits from 83 excellent golf courses – ask at hotels or at local visitors' centres for further information.

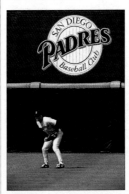

San Diego's famous baseball team, the Padres

THE INLAND EMPIRE AND LOW DESERT

T HE INLAND EMPIRE AND LOW DESERT *landscape is one of the most varied in California. The countryside changes from pine forests, cooled by gentle breezes, to searing desert. The contrast can be startling: passengers taking the Palm Springs Aerial Tramway make the transition between these two ecosystems in 14 minutes.*

The Anza-Borrego Desert State Park was the forbidding entry point to California for tens of thousands of hardy miners and settlers coming overland in the 1850s. Thirty years later communities in the northwest of the region, known as the Inland Empire, were transformed from a small collection of health resorts into the heart of a veritable economic empire based on the navel orange. The thick-skinned seedless Brazilian fruit, which travelled well, came to represent the sweet and healthy promise of California for millions of Americans. Many of the Victorian mansions built by citrus millionaires are still standing in the towns of Redlands and Riverside, but most of the fragrant orange groves have disappeared under tarmac and urban sprawl. Today Riverside is practically a suburb of Los Angeles.

At the heart of this region is Palm Springs, a favourite weekend retreat for Angelenos seeking relaxation and the desert sun. Just under two hours drive from LA, it has luxurious hotels, verdant golf courses, 600 tennis courts and over 10,000 swimming pools.

Lying to the east of Palm Springs is the Joshua Tree National Park. This is a land of hot, dry days, chilly nights, tumbleweed and creosote bushes. The stark and silent beauty of the rocky landscape evokes images of desperados, hardy pioneers in covered wagons, and leather-clad high plains drifters – visions of the Wild West of so many novels and films.

When the desert becomes too hot, travellers can escape to one of the mountain resorts. The Rim of the World Tour is a spectacular drive in the heart of the San Bernardino Mountains.

Western film set in Pioneertown, near Yucca Valley

◁ Joshua tree silhouetted against the barren desert landscape

Exploring the Inland Empire and Low Desert

THE INLAND EMPIRE is a region of vast scenic and climatic contrasts. In the northwest is the San Bernardino National Forest, with its cool mountain air and breathtaking views. Further south lies the sun-baked Coachella Valley, ending in the steamy Salton Sea. Palm Springs, the largest of the desert resorts, is flanked by the stark Joshua Tree National Park and the alpine community of Idyllwild. The forbidding Anza-Borrego Desert State Park, in the southwest of the region, is the gateway to San Diego County.

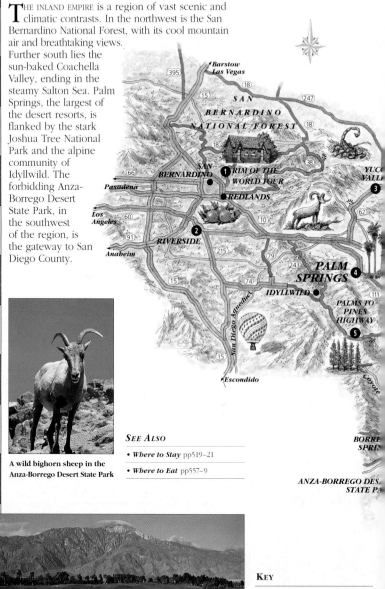

A wild bighorn sheep in the Anza-Borrego Desert State Park

SEE ALSO

• *Where to Stay* pp519–21

• *Where to Eat* pp557–9

View across Desert Dunes golf course, near Palm Springs

KEY

▦	Freeway
▬	Major road
▦	Minor road
▦	Scenic route
➤	River
☀	Viewpoint

SIGHTS AT A GLANCE

Wind turbines in the Coachella Valley

GETTING AROUND

The safest way to explore the desert areas is by car. The I-10 crosses the Inland Empire and Low Desert from east to west. Palm Springs, 107 miles (170 km) southeast of LA and 120 miles (190 km) northeast of San Diego, has a Greyhound coach terminus and airport, and is a good base for exploring the region. Buses regularly go to and from the Amtrak station in nearby Indio.

0 kilometres   20

0 miles   20

Rim of the World Tour ❶

Fʀᴏᴍ ꜱᴀɴ ʙᴇʀɴᴀʀᴅɪɴᴏ this invigorating drive
winds across the forested San Bernardino
Mountains, offering spectacular views of
the desert beyond. The altitude provides for distinct seasons, with warm,
pine-scented air in the summer and
brisk, cool days in the winter, when
the snow-covered mountain trails
Elf at Santa's are perfect for cross-country
Village skiing. The tour passes through
the resorts beside Lake Arrowhead and Big
Bear Lake, both favourite destinations for those
wanting to escape the heat and smog of LA.
In Redlands visitors are offered a sense of the
area's heady Victorian
past, and yet another
pleasure: the sweet
smell of orange groves.

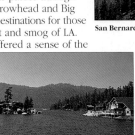

San Bernardino Mountain landscape

Big Bear Lake ③
A popular resort area, Big
Bear Lake offers a range of
sports including fishing, sailing, swimming and, in the
winter, skiing. Its two commercial centres are Big Bear
City, to the east, and Big Bear
Village, to the south.

Heaps Park Arboretum ④
A 1,230-yd (1,130-m) nature
trail winds through this
wooded hillside, planted
with native and other trees.
Species include dogwoods,
Jeffrey pine, ponderosa
pine, black oaks, live
oaks and white fir.

Santa's Village ⑤
Log buildings with
brightly coloured
roofs house Santa
Claus, his elves and
Rudolf the reindeer.
There are pony rides,
a pets' corner and shops.

Lake Arrowhead ⑥
Lake Arrowhead Village, on
the south shore, offers shops,
restaurants and accommodation
in both hotels and log cabins.
Trips up the lake aboard the
Arrowhead Queen also begin
here. The north shore is almost
exclusively residential.

Redlands ①
This town is famous for its
Victorian mansions, built at
the end of the 19th century by
those who made their fortunes
growing navel oranges (*see
p46*). Among the finest are
Kimberly Crest House and
Gardens, the Morey Mansion
and the Edwards Mansion.

Ornate Mission Inn in Riverside

Onyx Summit ②

At 8,443 ft (2,573 m), Onyx Summit is the highest point on the Rim of the World Tour. From a viewpoint near the top there are stunning views across the mountainous San Bernardino National Forest to the desert.

kilometres   10
miles   5

KEY

━━ Tour route
═══ Other roads

Riverside ②

Road map D6. 👥 250,000. 🚌
ℹ️ 3720 Main St (909 684-4636).

SOME OF THE MOST elegant architecture in Southern California is to be found in Riverside. During the late 19th century, the town was the centre of California's citrus industry and by 1905 it had the highest income per capita in the United States. One of the two original orange trees responsible for this great success was planted in 1875 by Eliza and Luther Tihbetts (see p46). It is still thriving in a small park at the intersection of Magnolia and Arlington avenues.

Pot at Hi-Desert Nature Museum

Riverside's **Mission Inn**, built in 1880 as a 12-room adobe house, was expanded early in the 20th century into a 234-room hotel (see p521). Architecturally, the hotel is a mixture of Mission Revival, Moorish and oriental styles, with flying buttresses, spiral staircases and gargoyles. The **Riverside Municipal Museum** features exhibits on the town's history and Native American culture.

Riverside is also known for its two major motor races. The California 500 is held in early September and the Winston Western 500 runs in January.

🏨 **Mission Inn**
3649 Mission Inn Ave. 📞 (909) 784-0300.
🏛️ **Riverside Municipal Museum**
3720 Orange St. 📞 (909) 782-5273. 🕐 daily.

Yucca Valley ③

Road map D5. 👥 44,000. 🚌
ℹ️ 56300 Twenty-nine Palms Hwy, Suite D (760 365-6323).

YUCCA VALLEY is a small town located just north of the Joshua Tree National Park (see pp268–9). On a hillside, the **Desert Christ Park** has 30 statues depicting the life of Jesus, sculpted by Antone Martin in the 1950s. The town's **Hi-Desert Nature Museum** has various exhibits on the region's geology, crafts, flora and fauna.

Pioneertown, 4 miles (6 km) northwest of Yucca Valley, is a hamlet built in 1947 as a Western film set.

🌵 **Desert Christ Park**
End of Mohawk Trail. 📞 (760) 365-6323. 🕐 daily.
🏛️ **Hi-Desert Museum**
57116 Twenty-nine Palms Hwy. 📞 (619) 369-7212. 🕐 Tue–Sun. ● public hols.

Statue of Christ at the Antone Martin Memorial Park

Palm Springs ❶

Popcorn in Ruddy's

THE COACHELLA VALLEY has been inhabited for 10,000 years, but it was only in 1853 that a government survey party came across a grove of palm trees surrounding a mineral pool bubbling up out of the desert sand. The area's first hotel was constructed in 1886, and by the turn of the century the city of Palm Springs was a thriving health spa. In the 1920s and 1930s the area become a fashionable winter resort, colonized by the rich and famous.

Exploring Palm Springs
The postwar building boom *(see p50)* brought rapid hotel and residential development to Palm Springs. Drawn by the city's growing popularity, developers later began opening up the empty desert lands eastwards along the Coachella Valley. From 1967 to 1981, the resort cities of Cathedral City, Rancho Mirage, Palm Desert, Indian Wells and La Quinta shot up between Palm Springs and the date-growing centre of Indio, 22 miles (35 km) away. Desert Hot Springs, a spa just northeast of Palm Springs, also became a popular holiday destination. The extraordinary proliferation of luxury golf courses – there are more than 80 in the region – dates from this period *(see p267)*.

Today Palm Springs remains the largest of the desert cities. Its population doubles each winter, when visitors come to enjoy its healthy, relaxing outdoor lifestyle. First-class accommodation, such as the Marriot and Givenchy hotels, abounds *(see pp521)*. Many celebrities still live here and several companies offer guided tours which point out their houses.

The two main shopping streets in downtown Palm Springs are Palm Canyon and Indian Canyon drives. Each is lined with outdoor restaurants, exclusive boutiques and art galleries. In the city centre, the pedestrianized Desert Fashion Plaza houses two department stores and several smaller luxury shops.

The city's unique sense of desert chic is maintained in discreet ways. Street lights, for example, are secreted within palm leaves and bushes to lend the area a subtle glow.

Old Shredded Wheat advertisement from Ruddy's in Village Green

🐎 Village Green Heritage Center
221 S Palm Canyon Drive. ☎ *(760) 323-8297.* ⬡ *Oct–May: Wed–Sun.* ⬤ *public hols.* 🈁
This quiet enclave, in the heart of Palm Springs' shopping district, contains four historical buildings. Palm Springs' first white resident, John Guthrie McCallum, built the McCallum Adobe in 1884. Originally it stood near the Indian village of Agua Caliente, the site of the natural hot springs that inspired the town's name. The house was moved to its present location during the 1950s.

The Cornelia White House (1893) is built partly out of railway sleepers. It is furnished with antiques dating from Palm Springs' pioneer era.

The heritage of the area's Cahuilla people is related through artifacts and photographs in the Agua Caliente Cultural Museum. There is also a collection of antique baskets that were handcrafted by local Native American weavers.

Also in the Village Green Heritage Center is Ruddy's 1930s General Store Museum. Once the town's only chemist, Ruddy's is an immaculate and well-stocked replica of a Depression-era shop. Authentically packaged goods range from liquorice and shoelaces to flour and patent medicines.

🌊 Oasis Water Resort
1500 Gene Autry Trail. ☎ *(760) 325-7873.* ⬡ *Mar–early Sep: daily; Sep–Oct: Sat & Sun.* ⬤ *public hols.* 🈁
This state-of-the-art water park covers 21 acres (8.5 ha). It boasts 13 waterslides, including an exciting 70-ft (20-m) free-fall slide and a 600-ft (180-m) artificial "river" for riding inflated inner tubes. There are special slides and pools for young children. California's largest wave-action pool creates 4-ft (1.2-m) high artificial waves suitable for surfing and boogie boarding. Surfboards and inner tubes can be rented from the park on either an hourly or a daily basis.

The Oasis Water Resort also includes a hotel, a rock climbing centre, heated spas, a health club and an assortment of fine restaurants.

Children emerging from a Scorpion free-fall slide at the Oasis Water Resort

**Palm Springs Aerial Tramway
ascending to the Mountain Station**

🚡 Palm Springs Aerial Tramway

Tramway Rd. 📞 (760) 325-1391.
🕐 Sep–Jul: daily. 🎟

The Aerial Tramway's two
Swiss-built cars, each holding
80 passengers, are one of
Palm Springs' most popular
attractions. The trams depart
from Valley Station, situated
6 miles (10 km) northwest of
Palm Springs. The 2.5-mile
(4-km) trip at an angle of 50°,
takes 14 minutes and ascends
5,900 ft (1,790 m) over spectacular scenery to the Mountain Station in the Mount San
Jacinto Wilderness State Park.

Passengers travel through
five distinct ecosystems, ranging from desert to alpine forest, which is akin to travelling
from Mexico to Alaska. The
temperature changes dramatically during the journey. The
heat of the valley floor sometimes differs as much as 50° F
(10° C) from the icy temperature at the peak, so make sure
you carry surplus clothing.

At the top there are 54 miles
(85 km) of hiking trails, one
of which leads to Idyllwild
(see p266). A Nordic ski centre
is open in the winter for cross-
country skiing. There are also
a ranger station, camp sites,
picnic areas and 20-minute
mule-pack rides on the slopes.

Observation decks perched
on the edge of the 8,500-ft
(2,600-m) high lookout offer
Olympian views of the Coachella Valley, Palm Springs
and the San Bernadino Mountains to the north. On a very
clear day, it is possible to see
for 50 miles (80 km) to the
Salton Sea (see p267).

Both stations have gift shops,
cocktail lounges and snack
bars. The Mountain Station
also has a cafeteria.

🏛 Palm Springs Desert Museum

101 Museum Drive. 📞 (760) 325-
7186. 🕐 Tue–Sun. ● public hols.
🎟 free first Fri of month.

The Palm Springs Desert
Museum focuses on art, natural
science and the performing
arts. Paintings in the museum's
galleries date from the 19th
century to the present day.
Native American artifacts and
local natural history exhibits
are also on display. A stunning
array of modern sculpture
adorns the patios and gardens.

The adjoining, ultra-modern
Annenberg Theater is a 450-
seat centre for the performing
arts, which features both local
and touring dance, drama and
orchestral companies. The lush
and beautifully tended gardens
are enhanced by fountains and
demonstrate that the desert
need not be a barren place.

Two trails lead out from the
museum and enable visitors
to explore the flora and fauna
of this desert region. The
2-mile (3-km) Museum Trail
climbs 800 ft (244 m) up into
the Mount San Jacinto State
Park. It joins the Lykken Trail
at Desert Riders Overlook
(a viewpoint from which to
look out across Palm Springs
and the Coachella Valley). The

Lykken Trail then continues
for another 4 miles (6 km) to
the mouth of the Tahquitz
Canyon (see p266).

**Sculpture garden in the Palm
Springs Desert Museum**

PALM TREES

Only one palm variety in Palm Springs is native to California,
the desert fan palm (Washingtonia filifera), which crowds
the secluded mountain oases. Unlike other palm varieties,
the dead fronds do not drop off the trunk, but droop down
to form a "skirt" that provides a shelter for wildlife.

Date palms (Phoenix dactylifera) were introduced from
Algeria in 1890 as an experiment. Today, the Coachella Valley
supplies 90 per cent of the dates consumed in the US. A
mature date palm can produce up to 300 lb (135 kg) of dates
a year. An annual ten-day National Date Festival in Indio
features a cornucopia of dried and fresh dates (see p35).

Date palm grove in the Coachella Valley

🏝 Indian Canyons

S Palm Canyon Drive. *(760) 325-5673.* ☐ *daily.* ♿

Approximately 5 miles (8 km) south of Palm Springs are four spectacular natural palm oases, set in stark, rocky gorges and surrounded by barren hills. Clustered along small streams fed by mountain springs, Murray, Tahquitz, Andreas and Palm canyons are located on the land of the Agua Caliente Cahuilla people. Rock art and other traces of the area's early inhabitants can still be seen.

The 15-mile (24-km) long Palm Canyon is the largest of the gorges and contains more wild palms in one place than anywhere else in the world. A trading post near the car park offers refreshments, and from here it is a short but steep walk down to the main trail. Picnic tables have been set out beside a trickling stream in the shade of the 82-ft (25-m) high desert fan palms *(see p265).*

Desert fan palm oasis in the Indian Canyons

🦌 Living Desert Wildlife and Botanical Park

47–900 Portola Ave. **(** *(760) 346-5694.* ☐ *Sep–mid-Jul: daily.* ● *25 Dec.* ♿

The well-designed Living Desert Wildlife and Botanical Park offers a comprehensive view of North America's desert regions. The park covers 1,200 acres (485 ha), but most of its major attractions can be seen in half a day. Broad paths and paved walkways pass through interpretive botanical displays covering North America's 10 desert areas, and describing some of the 130 animal species that inhabit them.

Flowering ocotillo in the Living Desert Wildlife and Botanical Park

Of special interest are golden eagles, mountain lions, a large selection of nocturnal creatures, and the new cheetah exhibit. Roadrunners (desert birds that run rather than fly) roam free in their natural setting. On winter days, walking through the park is a pleasure. A guided tram tour is recommended in hotter weather.

Palms to Pines Highway ❺

Road map D6. **ℹ** *72–990 Hwy 111, Palm Desert (760 346-6111).*

ONE OF THE MOST interesting drives in Southern California begins at the junction of Hwy 111 and Hwy 74 in Palm Desert. As you climb Hwy 74, you gradually leave behind the desert ecosystem with its palms, creosote and desert ironwood trees and move into mountain scenery, made up of pines, juniper and mountain mahogany. The view from Santa Rosa Summit, just under 5,000 ft (1,500 m) high, is spectacular. Continue northwest on Hwy 74 to Mountain Center and the lush meadows of Garner Valley.

At Mountain Center, take Hwy 243 to the picturesque alpine village of Idyllwild, with its many restaurants, lodges and camp sites. The renowned Idyllwild School of Music and the Arts holds regular classical music concerts during the summer. More active visitors can follow one of the many surrounding hiking trails, for which maps are available at the Ranger Station. One 8-mile (13-km) trek leads to the Mountain Station of the Palm Springs Aerial Tramway *(see p265).* This provides the quickest way back to the desert floor. Mule-pack rides are available in the summer, and during the winter months there is cross-country skiing.

Anza-Borrego Desert State Park ❻

Road map D6. 🚃 *Escondido.* **Visitors' Centre (** *(760) 767-4205.* ☐ *Jun–Sep: Sat & Sun; Oct–May: daily.*

STARTING WITH the Gold Rush of 1849 *(see pp44–5),* the Southern Emigrant Trail, the only all-weather land route into California, brought tens of thousands of miners and early settlers through the Anza-Borrego Desert. Today, this former overland gateway is a remote and pristine park,

Picturesque mountain town of Idyllwild

Badlands in the Anza-Borrego Desert State Park

offering visitors a rare insight into a unique and beautiful desert environment.

The desert's well-equipped visitors' centre is in Borrego Springs. This is the only significant town in the otherwise undeveloped park. Nearby, the leisurely 1.5-mile (2.5-km) Palm Canyon Nature Trail leads to an oasis where the endangered bighorn sheep can occasionally be seen.

The Box Canyon Historical Monument is 31 miles (50 km) southwest of the visitors' centre on County Road S2. Here you can view the old road once used by those miners who braved the desert climate on their way to the goldfields, which lay 500 miles (800 km) to the north.

The Anza-Borrego Desert is inhospitable for most of the year. Between March and May, however, following the winter rains, the burning land bursts into life. Cacti and desert flowers such as brittle-bush, desert poppies and dune primroses produce a riot of colour.

The desert's geology is as fascinating as its ecosystem. Over the millennia, a network of earthquake faults lifted and tilted the ground. Winter rains then carved through the shattered landscape, leaving multicoloured "layer-cake" bluffs, steep ravines and jagged canyons such as the famous Borrego and Carizzo Badlands.

Much of the Anza-Borrego State Park, including its well-kept camp sites, is easily accessible via 100 miles (160 km) of surfaced and scenic highways. However, four-wheel drive vehicles are recommended for use on the park's 500 miles (800 km) of unsurfaced roads.

Drivers of standard vehicles should contact the visitors' centre in advance to check on current road conditions.

Salton Sea **7**

Road map E6. 🚗 *Mecca.* 🚌 *Indio.* **Visitors' Centre** ☎ *(760) 393-3052.* ◯ *Nov–Mar: daily; Apr & May: call ahead.*

T HE SALTON SEA was created by accident in 1905 when the Colorado River flooded and flowed into a newly dug irrigation canal leading to the Imperial Valley. It took a team of engineers two years to stem the flow. By then, however, a 35-mile (55-km) inland sea had formed in the Salton Sink, 230 ft (70 m) below sea level.

Despite rising salinity and selenium levels, and algae blooms that turn the water a brownish colour during the summer, there continues to be saltwater game fish in this inland sea, with 10-lb (4.5-kg) orangemouth corvina being caught regularly.

Windsurfing, water-skiing and boating on the Salton Sea are also popular activities. The northeastern shore of the sea has the best spots for swimming, particularly the stretch of water off Mecca Beach.

The sea's adjoining marshlands are a refuge for a wide variety of migrating birds, such as geese, ducks, blue herons and egrets. On the east side of the Salton Sea there are hiking trails and camp sites set within the State Recreation Area. There is also a visitors' centre and a small playground.

DESERT GOLF

Thanks to irrigation with water supplied from underground sources, Palm Springs is now known as the golf capital of the United States. There are more than 80 courses in the region, most of which belong to private clubs or are attached to resorts or hotel complexes. Some courses are rugged, while others are more lush. Among the professional golf events held in the area each year are the Bob Hope Desert Classic in January and the Dinah Shore Tournament at the end of March. A few courses are open to the public, including the Desert Dunes course, noted for adding the desert terrain to its challenging layout. In the summer it is best to tee off early in the morning. November and December offer better value and cooler weather. Most courses are closed in October for reseeding.

Tahquitz Creek Palm Springs Golf Resort

Joshua Tree National Park ❽

THE JOSHUA TREE NATIONAL PARK was established in 1936 to preserve the groves of the unusual, spiny-leaved Joshua tree. The species was named in 1851 by early Mormon travellers, who saw in the twisted branches the upraised arms of the biblical Joshua.

National park sign

This large member of the yucca family is unique to the area and can grow up to 30 ft (9 m) tall, sometimes living for 1,000 years. The 630,800-acre (255,300-ha) park offers uncommon vistas of the stark Californian desert, with its astounding formations of pink and grey rocks and boulders. A climber's paradise, Joshua Tree is also a fascinating area for hikers, who can discover lost mines, palm oases and, in the spring, a wealth of desert flowers. The Visitors' Center provides the latest weather report.

Joshua Trees
Large groves of Joshua trees thrive in the higher, wetter and somewhat cooler desert areas of the park's western half.

Hidden Valley
The gigantic boulders here formed natural corrals, making this a legendary hide-out for cattle rustlers in the days of the Wild West.

Key's View gives a sweeping view of the stunning valley, desert and mountain terrain from its summit.

KEY

▬	Freeway
▬	Major road
▭	Minor road
▭	Unsurfaced road
···	Hiking trail
—	National Park boundary
🚶	Ranger station
🅿	Fee station
🅰	Camp site
🍴	Picnic area
☀	Viewpoint

Lost Horse Mine
A 2-mile (3.2-km) trail leads to this historic gold mine, which was discovered by a cowboy searching for his lost horse. More than $270,000 in gold was extracted during the mine's first decade of operation.

DESERT WILDLIFE

Despite the harshness of the arid desert environment, a variety of animals thrives here. In many cases, they have adapted to cope with lack of water. The kangaroo rat gets both its food and water from seeds alone, while its very large hind feet enable it to travel over the hot sand. Powerful legs, rather than wings, also serve the roadrunner, which gets its moisture from insects and small prey. The jack-rabbit is born with a full coat of muted fur to camouflage it from large predators such as the coyote, bobcat and eagle.

Coyote, wily denizen of the desert

VISITORS' CHECKLIST

Road map D5. 🚌 *Desert Stage Lines from Palm Springs to Twentynine Palms.* 🏛 **Oasis Visitors' Center** *74485 National Park Drive, Twentynine Palms.* 📞 *(760) 367-7511.* ⏰ *8am–4:30pm daily.* ⚫ *25 Dec.*

0 kilometres   10

0 miles   10

The arid wilderness of the Colorado Desert *(see p193)* occupies the park's eastern half. This inhospitable region is difficult to reach.

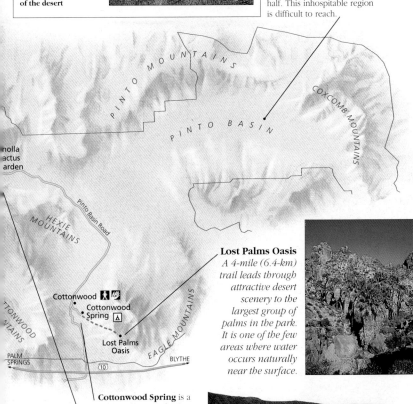

PINTO MOUNTAINS

PINTO BASIN

COXCOMB MOUNTAINS

holla actus arden

HEXIE MOUNTAINS

Pinto Basin Road

Cottonwood 🚶 ⛺

Cottonwood Spring 🏕

Lost Palms Oasis

EAGLE MOUNTAINS

TTONWOOD ↑TAINS

PALM SPRINGS

(10)

BLYTHE

Lost Palms Oasis
A 4-mile (6.4-km) trail leads through attractive desert scenery to the largest group of palms in the park. It is one of the few areas where water occurs naturally near the surface.

Cottonwood Spring is a man-made oasis of palms and cottonwood trees that attracts desert birds. There is a visitors' centre nearby.

Cholla Cactus Garden
A dense concentration of cholla cacti are the focal point of a short nature trail featuring desert flora and fauna. But beware – the cactus's fluffy fingers are really sharp spines.

THE MOJAVE DESERT

THE MOJAVE DESERT *is the state's greatest secret, all too often missed by travellers who zoom through it on the interstate highway. The desert is a harsh environment – Death Valley is one of the hottest places in the United States. But this dry region supports a surprising amount of plant life and for a few weeks each year, when the wild-flowers appear amid the arid rocks, it becomes hauntingly beautiful.*

The Mojave Desert was a year-round overland gateway to California for much of the 19th century. Trappers, traders and early settlers travelled hundreds of miles along the Old Spanish Trail from Santa Fe in New Mexico to Los Angeles. Passing through the towns of Barstow and Tecopa, the journey across the vast desert was both demanding and dangerous.

In the 1870s, gold, silver, borax and various other precious minerals were discovered in the region, attracting large numbers of miners. Instant cities such as Calico sprang up, but when the mines became exhausted, many of the settlements were abandoned. In 1883 commercial mining became more viable when the Santa Fe Railroad was completed. Towns located along the route prospered and the population of the Mojave Desert increased.

In the early 20th century a new breed of desert lovers emerged. Jack Mitchell settled in the empty expanses of the East Mojave Desert in the 1930s and turned the spectacular Mitchell Caverns into a popular tourist destination. Death Valley Scotty was another desert enthusiast. He spent much of his life in a castle built in the 1920s by his friend, Albert Johnson, near the hottest and lowest point in the western hemisphere. Death Valley National Park now attracts thousands of visitors each year, who come to explore the area's wealth of historical landmarks and impressive natural sights.

The main draw of the Mojave Desert region today, however, is Nevada's Las Vegas, a five-hour drive from Los Angeles. This centre of entertainment and gambling is proof that people are still trying to strike it rich in the desert.

Death Valley's Moorish-style Scotty's Castle

◁ **Desert shrubs in Death Valley**

Exploring the Mojave Desert

Most of the mojave desert is at an altitude of over 2,000 ft (600 m). It has cold winters and baking hot summers. Many of the region's rivers and lakes are seasonal and are dry during the summer. The desert is home to an array of plant species and a range of animals, from tortoises to foxes, that have evolved to survive in this climate. Barstow, the largest town in the Mojave region, caters for travellers to and from Las Vegas. The northern Mojave is dominated by the Death Valley National Park. To the east lie the resorts of Lake Havasu.

Premises of a 19th-century ore smelter in Calico Ghost Town

Sights at a Glance

Barstow **3**
Calico Ghost Town **4**
*Death Valley National
Park pp280–83* **9**
Edwards Air Force Base **2**
Kelso Dunes **5**
Lake Havasu **7**
Las Vegas **8**
Mitchell Caverns **6**
Red Rock Canyon State Park **1**

Key

▬	Freeway
▬	Major road
▬	Minor road
▬	Scenic route
▬	River
❋	Viewpoint

See Also

• *Where to Stay* p522

• *Where to Eat* p559

0 kilometres   25

0 miles   25

(Map labels: DEATH VALLEY NATIONAL PARK 9, Mono Lake, LONE PINE, STOVEPIPE WELLS, 136, Owens Lake, 190, OLANCHA, 178, Los Angeles Aqueduct, 395, RIDGECREST, 395, RED ROCK CANYON STATE PARK 1, Bakersfield, 14, MOJAVE, 58, 14, EDWARDS AIR FORCE BASE 2, 395, CALICO GHOST TOWN, 58, BARSTOW 3, Los Angeles, 15, VICTORVILLE, San Bernardino, 18)

Sand dunes north of Furnace Creek in the Death Valley National Park

GETTING AROUND

The I-15 crosses the region. It links San Diego to Las Vegas, which is in the state of Nevada, via San Bernardino. This route follows the northern border of the East Mojave National Preserve; the I-40 skirts the southern border. The main south–north route across the desert is Hwy 127, from which Hwy 190 branches out, crossing the Death Valley National Park from southeast to southwest. In the west, US Hwy 395 leads south to LA. For safety reasons, it is vital that visitors to the desert obey posted signs and do not stray from main roads. Always carry water, a jack and a spare tyre and stay close to your vehicle if you break down. There is no public access to the area's clearly marked military zones *(see p274)*.

Stunning colours of Red Rock Canyon

Red Rock Canyon State Park ❶

Road map D5. 🚌 *from Mojave, Ridgecrest.* **Visitors' Center** 📞 *(805) 942-0662.* ◯ *Feb–May & Oct–Nov: Fri–Sun.*

Alternate layers of white clay, red sandstone, pink volcanic rocks and brown lava are spectacularly combined in Red Rock Canyon. This beautiful state park is situated in the El Paso Mountains, which lie at the southern end of the Sierra Nevada Mountains. Like the High Sierras *(see p468)*, Red Rock Canyon is the product of plate movements that pushed up the bedrock approximately 3 million years ago. The western side of the canyon slopes gently upwards in stark contrast to the high, abrupt cliffs on its eastern side, which have been carved and crenellated by water and wind.

Three major desert ecozones overlap here, providing a wealth of plant and animal life. Eagles, hawks and falcons nest in the cliffs. Coyotes, kit foxes, bobcats and various reptiles, such as the desert iguana, are common. The landscape has been used as the backdrop for countless Westerns, advertisements and science-fiction films, making it oddly familiar to many visitors.

Edwards Air Force Base ❷

Road map D5. 📞 *(805) 258-3446.* 🚌 *from Mojave, Rosamond.* ◯ *Mon–Fri.* ⬤ *public hols.* 🅿️ ♿ 📷 *by appointment only.*

While it is famous around the world as the site of the West Coast space shuttle landings, Edwards Air Force Base has been steeped in the history of America in flight since 1933. The 65 sq mile (168 sq km) flat expanse of Rogers Dry Lake provides an enormous natural runway that is perfect for emergency landings. The area's year-round fine and clear weather adds to its suitability for aircraft testing and the training of test pilots. It was here that the very first jet-propelled aircraft was tested in 1942. Here, too, Captain Chuck Yeager became the first to break the sound barrier on 14 October 1947 in a Bell XS-1

Space shuttle Atlantis landing at Edwards Air Force Base

rocket plane. Fifty pilots still graduate each year from the Test Pilot School.

Edwards is also home to the NASA Dryden Flight Research Center. Free guided tours of the space Aeronautics Center are available by reservation. Tours include a video on the history of aeronautics research and a visit to a hangar housing current aircraft.

Barstow ❸

Road map D5. 🚶 *22,000.* 🚌 ℹ️ *831 Barstow Rd (619 255-8760).*

During the 19th century, this was a small settlement that served farmers as well as emigrants and miners on the Old Spanish Trail *(see p271)*. In 1886 the new Barstow–San Bernardino rail line opened, linking Kansas City with the Pacific Coast. Barstow's original railway station, the Casa del Desierto, has recently been restored.

THE MILITARY IN THE MOJAVE

The United States government has set aside vast areas of the Mojave Desert for military use. All such areas are strictly off-limits to civilians. During World War II, the Desert Training Center covered 17,500 sq miles (45,300 sq km) and was used by General Patton to train his forces. Today, smaller military preserves include the China Lake Weapons Center, northeast of Mojave, which is used for live bombing and artillery testing. North of Barstow, the Fort Irwin National Training Center (NTC), which covers more than 1,000 sq miles (2,600 sq km), is an important US Army installation. The NTC has a population of 12,000, including civilian workers. Its desert terrain was used to prepare troops for the Gulf War in 1990–91, and is one of the main US training areas for tanks and weapons.

T-38 Talon high-altitude jet trainer at Edwards Air Force Base

Restored and reconstructed buildings in Calico Ghost Town

From 1937 to the late 1950s, Barstow was an important town along Route 66, the only surfaced road from Chicago to the West Coast. The town is best known today as being the midway point on the I-15 between Los Angeles and Las Vegas. To the 41 million people who make this journey each year, it is a convenient stopping-off point. But many also come here in search of the precious minerals and gemstones to be found in the surrounding desert.

The **California Desert Information Center**, located in Barstow, has informative indoor displays on the Mojave Desert's flora and fauna. Maps of the area and hotel and restaurant information are also available, and the centre has a good bookshop.

⌂ California Desert Information Center
831 Barstow Rd, Barstow. ☎ *(619) 255-8760*. ○ *daily*. ● *1 Jan, 25 Dec*.

Calico Ghost Town ❹

Road map D5. ☎ *(619) 254-2122*.
🚌 *Barstow*. ○ *daily*. ● *25 Dec*.
🅿 ♿ ✉

CALICO GHOST TOWN, 11 miles (18 km) east of Barstow, is a late-19th-century mining town, which is part-authentic and part-reconstruction. Silver was found in the Calico Mountains on 26 March 1881 and soon hundreds of miners arrived. Some of the veins they struck were so rich that they produced 25 lb (11 kg) of silver per tonne. Two years later, borax was discovered 3 miles (5 km) east of Calico and the town's prosperity seemed assured. During the 1880s, Calico boasted a population of 1,200 – and 22 saloons – but after the price of silver fell

A flint tool from the Early Man Site

and the equally valuable borax gave out, the miners left. By 1907, Calico was a ghost town.

Walter Knott, founder of Knott's Berry Farm *(see p226)*, began the restoration process in the 1950s. Calico's isolation and desert setting reinforce the sense of a rough old mining town. Many of the original buildings remain and visitors can take a ride in a mine train or explore tunnels in Maggie Mine, one of the most famous silver mines on the West Coast. Shows and tours are also held, including mock "shoot-outs" staged on the main street, and walking tours given each day by the town's resident historian.

ENVIRONS: About 10 miles (16 km) west of Calico lies the **Calico Early Man Site**. At this archaeological site, thousands of 100,000-year-old stone tools have been discovered. They were made by North America's earliest-known inhabitants, who once lived in this area on the shores of a great lake. The renowned archaeologist and palaeontologist Dr Louis Leakey was director of the site, consisting of several pits, from 1964 until his death in 1972.

⌂ Calico Early Man Site
Off I-15 & Minneola Rd. ☎ *(619) 256-5102*. ○ *Wed–Sun*. ● *1 Jan, 4 Jul, 25 Dec*. **Donation**.

Casa del Desierto, Barstow's historic railway station

Mesquite mud flats in Death Valley National Park *(see pp280–83)* ▷

Kelso Dunes ➎

Road map E5. 🚌 *Baker.* ⓘ *Mojave National Preserve (760) 733-4040.*

KELSO DUNES tower more than 700 ft (210 m) above the desert floor. Situated in the Mojave National Preserve, the dunes are formed from grains of golden rose quartz that have been blown from the Mojave River basin, 35 miles (56 km) to the west. Known as the "singing" dunes, they occasionally emit buzzing and rumbling sounds. These are thought to be caused by the upper layers of sand sliding down the face of the dune, producing vibrations that are then amplified by the underlying sand.

The desert floor with the Kelso Dunes in the background

Mitchell Caverns ➏

ⓘ *(760) 928-2586.* 🚌 *from Barstow.* 🕐 *Sep–Jun: daily.* 📷 ⓘ *(Sat & Sun in summer only).*

MITCHELL CAVERNS are a spectacular collection of caves along the eastern slope of the Providence Mountains. The caverns were formed 12–

The original London Bridge, now located in Lake Havasu City

15 million years ago, when acidic rainwater began to carve through layers of ancient limestone. Arrowheads and pottery pieces have been found here, left behind by the Chemehuevi people. Until the 1860s, the Native Americans had stored food and held religious ceremonies in the caves for around 500 years. Opened as a tourist attraction in the 1930s, by silver miner Jack Mitchell, the caverns are now owned and run by California State Parks.

Inside, the chambers feature three types of cave formation: flow stones (delicate curtain shapes); drip stones (stalagmites and stalactites); and erratics (ribbons, shields and "staghorn coral"). In one room, the rare combination of a cave shield, flowstone column and coral pipes can be seen. Sturdy walking shoes are recommended for the two-hour tour, which includes El Pakiva (The Sacred Pools), one of the most famous chambers. A nearby 1-mile (1.6-km) trail up Crystal Spring Canyon climbs into the Providence Mountains and offers views of the desert.

Lake Havasu ➐

Road map E5. 🚌 *Las Vegas.* ⓘ *(520) 855-4115.*

LAKE HAVASU is a 46-mile (74-km) long reservoir, which was created in 1938 when the Colorado River was blocked by the Parker Dam *(see p193)*. Lake Havasu City, a resort town on the border between California and Arizona, was developed by the millionaire Robert McCulloch in the 1960s. McCulloch imported the historic London Bridge stone-by-stone to the newly created development. The bridge spans a channel dredged especially for it and overlooks English-style shops and restaurants on a nearby plot of land known as English Village.

The lake itself lies within a National Wildlife Refuge, which is frequented by bird-watchers and anglers. There are many camp sites and marinas which offer houseboats, boats and water-sports equipment for hire. Several short boat tours around the lake are available. A daily three-hour excursion to Topock Gorge, at the northern end of Lake Havasu, offers a more leisurely introduction to this rugged desert setting.

ENVIRONS: Off Hwy 95, 20 miles (32 km) south of Lake Havasu City, lies the Colorado River Indian Reservation. Here, visitors can admire a collection of giant prehistoric figures, carved out of the rocks that form the desert floor. In both human and animal form, it is not known whether the mysterious figures were made for religious or artistic reasons.

Impressive cave formations in Mitchell Caverns

Las Vegas 8

L AS VEGAS LIES in Nevada, just 37 miles (60 km) from the California border. With the construction of the Hoover Dam in the 1930s, it grew into a major city. Gambling was legalized in Nevada in 1931. In 1945 the Flamingo Hotel and Casino were built out of town on what is known as "The Strip". Similar establishments soon sprang up, and Las Vegas became a 24-hour oasis of gambling and entertainment.

One of the city's many neon signs

Las Vegas "Strip" at dusk

Exploring Las Vegas

Today, Las Vegas is changing its image to appeal to families as well as gamblers. The city offers a wide variety of entertainment for all tastes and budgets in some of the most affordable, and largest, hotel and convention complexes in the world. Las Vegas is now a city of nearly one million permanent residents, with its own museums and other cultural institutions. But it is the 30 million tourists that visit Las Vegas each year who continue to fuel the amazing development of

this metropolis. Despite the neon lights, swimming pools and hotels, the blazing sun and cloudless skies serve as a constant reminder that Las Vegas is surrounded by desert.

Hotels in Las Vegas provide more than just food and lodging. They are architectural marvels that offer some of the best sightseeing and entertainment in town. The Treasure Island Hotel and Casino stages mock sea battles between the British Navy and pirates. Next door is the Mirage Hotel and Casino with its massive aquariums, tropical rainforest, white tigers and rumbling "volcano". The Luxor, built on the same scale as the pyramids of Egypt, houses the largest atrium in the world, complete with animatronic camels, Egyptian décor and high-tech laser shows. At night, the Luxor shoots the world's brightest beam of light into the sky from its pinnacle. The nearby MGM Grand offers a theme park called "The Emerald City of Oz", always a firm favourite with children.

🏨 Stratosphere Tower

2000 Las Vegas Blvd S. 【 *(702) 380-7777.*
At 1,149 ft (350 m), Stratosphere Tower is the tallest freestanding observation tower in the United States. At the top there is an incomparable view of Las Vegas (best seen at night), a revolving restaurant and cocktail lounge, three wedding chapels and two thrilling rides. The world's highest roller coaster leaves from 909 ft (275 m) up and runs for 865 ft (265 m) around the outside of the tower.

🏨 Fremont Street Experience

Bordered by Charles & Stewart Sts.
【 *(702) 678-5777.* ⬤ *daily.*
Las Vegas's first gaming licence was issued on Fremont Street in the 1930s. Over the years, this downtown area became known as "Glitter Gulch", because of its profusion of neon signs and lights. Today, five blocks of Fremont Street, stretching from Main Street to Las Vegas Boulevard, have been transformed into the Fremont Street Experience – a pedestrianized covered promenade lined with casinos. A spectacular light and sound show, using more than two million computer-controlled lights, is displayed each night.

ENVIRONS: Lake Mead, which lies 25 miles (40 km) east of Las Vegas, was created by the construction of Hoover Dam, completed in 1931. The lake extends 110 miles (175 km) and has more than 500 miles (800 km) of shoreline. Scuba-diving, boating, water-skiing and fishing facilities are all available. There are daily tours of the 726-ft (220-m) high dam and a visitors' centre with exhibits on the region's natural history. The Valley of Fire State Park, 55 miles (88 km) northeast of Las Vegas, has stunning orange sandstone formations. Petroglyphs and other remains of an ancient Native American civilization can still be seen. Red Rock Canyon (not the same as the park on *page 274*), 15 miles (24 km) west of Las Vegas, has 3,000-ft (900-m) high escarpments, and ridges and trails for all levels of hikers.

Stratosphere Tower

VISITORS' CHECKLIST

Road map E4. 🏙 *986,000.*
✈ *McCarran International Airport, 4 miles (6.5 km) S of Las Vegas.* 🚍 *200 S Main St.*
🚆 *1 Main St.* 🛈 *3150 Paradise Rd (702 733-2323).* **Treasure Island Hotel and Casino** 3300 Las Vegas Blvd. 【 *(702) 894-7111.* **Mirage Hotel and Casino** 3400 Las Vegas Blvd. 【 *(702) 791-7111.* **Luxor Las Vegas Hotel and Casino** 3900 Las Vegas Blvd. 【 *(702) 262-4000.* **MGM Grand Hotel, Casino and Theme Park** 3799 Las Vegas Blvd. 【 *(702) 891-1111.*

Death Valley National Park ❾

THROUGHOUT THE SUMMER MONTHS, the Death Valley National Park has the highest mean temperature of anywhere on the planet. This is a land of wrenching extremes, a sunken trough in the earth's crust that reaches the lowest point in the western hemisphere. The valley is guarded on both sides by ranges of rugged mountains. The range on the western side soars 11,000 ft (3,350 m) to form razor-sharp peaks. While it is always inhospitable, Death Valley is also a place of subtle colours and polished canyons, of burning salt flats and delicate rock formations. It is now one of the most unique and popular tourist destinations in the state of California.

Central Death Valley

Furnace Creek, with its various provisions and accommodation centres, is located in the heart of Death Valley. Many of the most impressive sights in the park are within easy reach of this visitors' complex.

⛏ Salt Creek

Salt Creek supports the hardy pupfish. Endemic to Death Valley, the pupfish can live in water almost four times as salty as the sea and withstand temperatures of up to 111° F (44° C). The fish attract other wildlife, including great blue herons. Wooden walkways allow visitors to explore this unique site without disturbing the fragile habitat.

🏛 Borax Museum

Furnace Creek Ranch. ☎ (760) 786-2345. ◯ daily.
Borax was discovered in Death Valley in 1873, but mining did not begin until the 1880s when crystallized borate compounds

Ruins of the Harmony Borax Works processing plant

were taken to the Harmony Borax Works to be purified. They were then loaded onto wagons and hauled by teams of 20 mules the 165 miles (265 km) to Mojave Station. Each team of mules pulled two wagons carrying up to 10 tonnes of borax each. The wagons carried their heavy mineral loads from 1883 to 1888.

Used for producing glass that is heat-resistant, borax is more commonly used today as an ingredient in washing powder.

The Borax Museum has displays of mining tools and transport machinery used at the 19th-century refinery. On Hwy 190, 1 mile (1.5 km) north of the Death Valley Visitor Center, the eerie ruins of the Harmony Borax Works can still be seen.

🏛 Death Valley Museum and Visitor Center

Rte 190, Furnace Creek. ☎ (760) 786-2331. ◯ daily. ● 1 Jan, 25 Dec, Thanksgiving. 🖼
Interesting exhibits and a slide show every 30 minutes explain the natural and human history of Death Valley. Evening park-ranger programmes and guided walks are available in winter.

Furnace Creek

At Furnace Creek, millennia of winter floods have carved a natural gateway into Death Valley through the hills to the east. The springs here once drew Shoshone Indians each winter. Today, the same abundant springs make Furnace Creek a desert oasis and the de facto centre of Death Valley. Shaded by date-bearing palms are a variety of restaurants and motels. The world's lowest golf course can also be found here, lying at 214 ft (65 m) below sea level. The Furnace Creek Inn *(see p522)*, a four-star hotel built in the 1920s, sits above the valley on a small mesa.

Historic Furnace Creek Inn, set in lush grounds

Salt formations at the Devil's Golf Course

Southern Death Valley

Some of the valley's most breathtaking natural features are to be found in this area south of Furnace Creek.

Golden Canyon

Just over 3 miles (5 km) south of Furnace Creek on Hwy 178, a one-mile (1500-m) hike leads into Golden Canyon. The mustard-coloured walls, after which the canyon was named, are best seen in the afternoon sun. Native Americans used the red clay at the canyon mouth for face paint. These layers of rock were originally horizontal, but geological activity has now tilted them to an angle of 45°.

A paved road once led to the Golden Canyon, but it was washed out by a sudden storm in 1976. The battered state of the few remaining stretches of the road demonstrate the sheer power of fast-flowing water.

Devil's Golf Course

This expanse of salt pinnacles is located 12 miles (19 km) south of Furnace Creek, off Hwy 178. Until approximately 2,000 years ago, successive lakes covered this area. When the last lake evaporated, it left behind alternating layers of salt and gravel deposits, at least 1,000 ft (305 m) deep and covering 200 sq miles (520 sq km). As surface moisture continued to evaporate, ridges and spires of crystallized salt were formed. The ground is now 95 per cent pure salt. Visitors can hear the salt expand and contract in the continual changes of temperature. New crystals (recognized by their whiter hue) are constantly forming.

Badwater

Temperature increases as elevation decreases, so the air at Badwater can reach 120° F (49° C). With the ground temperature 50 per cent higher than the air temperature, it really is possible to fry an egg on the ground here. Rain is very rare, although flash flooding, caused by rain storms, is common. In spite of its inhospitable environment, Badwater is home to several species of insect, and to the endangered Death Valley snail.

Northern Death Valley

This area includes Ubehebe Crater *(see p282)*, where only a few tourists venture, despite the beauty of the landscape. Scotty's Castle, which has more visitors per year than any other sight in the park, is also here.

Scotty's Castle

Hwy 267. (760) 786-2392. **Castle** daily. **Grounds** daily.

Albert Johnson began work on his "Death Valley Ranch" in 1922 after rejecting an original design by Frank Lloyd Wright. Materials were hauled from a railway line 20 miles (32 km) away. When work ended in 1931 the castle covered more than 30,000 sq ft (2,800 sq m). Johnson died in 1948. "Death Valley Scotty" *(see p282)*, who lent his name to Johnson's ranch, was allowed to remain there until his death in 1954.

Western Death Valley

Sand dunes cover 15 sq miles (39 sq km) on this side of the park, not far from the second-largest outpost in Death Valley, Stovepipe Wells *(see p282)*.

Sand Dunes

A walk along the 14 sq miles (36 sq km) of undulating sand dunes, north of Stovepipe Wells, is one of the greatest experiences of Death Valley. Shifting winds blow the sand into the classic crescent dune configuration. Mesquite trees dot the lower dunes. A variety of wildlife feeds on the seeds of these trees, such as kangaroo rats and lizards. Included among the region's other, mainly nocturnal, creatures are the rattlesnake, the chuckwalla lizard and the coyote.

Impressive sand dunes north of Stovepipe Wells

A Tour of Death Valley

THE NATIVE AMERICANS called the valley Tomesha, "the land where the ground is on fire" – an apt name for the site of the highest recorded temperature in the United States: 134° F (57° C) in the shade, in July 1913. Death Valley stretches for some 140 miles (225 km) north to south and was once an insurmountable barrier to miners and emigrants. The valley and surrounding area were declared a National Park *(see pp280–81)* in 1994. Death Valley is now accessible to visitors, who can discover this stark and unique landscape by car and by taking short walks from the main roads to spectacular viewpoints. Yet this remains the Californian desert at its harshest and most awe-inspiring.

Scotty's Castle ⑧
This incongruous Moorish-style castle was commissioned by Albert Johnson at a cost of $2.4 million. However, the public believed it belonged to Walter Scott, an eccentric prospector. The house remained unfinished after Johnson lost his money in the Wall Street Crash of 1929. In 1970 the building was bought by the National Park Service, who now hold hourly guided tours of the interior *(see p281)*.

Ubehebe Crater ⑦
This is one of a dozen volcanic craters in the Mojave area. The Ubehebe Crater is 2,000 years old. It is more than 900 yds (800 m) wide and 500 ft (150 m) deep.

North Hwy
Death Valley Wash
Titus Canyon Rd
Sand Dunes
PANAMINT SPRINGS
190

DEATH VALLEY SCOTTY

Walter Scott, would-be miner, beloved charlatan and sometime performer in Buffalo Bill's Wild West Show, liked to tell visitors to his home that his wealth lay in a secret gold mine. That "mine" was, in fact, his friend Albert Johnson, a Chicago insurance executive, who paid for the castle where Scott lived and received visitors. Built during the 1920s by European craftsmen and local Native American labour, the castle represents a mixture of architectural styles and has a Moorish feel. Scott never owned the land or the building, and Johnson paid all his bills. "He repays me in laughs," said Johnson. Although Scott died in 1954, the edifice is still known as Scotty's Castle.

Stovepipe Wells ⑥
Stovepipe Village, founded in 1926, was the valley's first tourist resort. According to legend, a lumberjack travelling west struck water here and stayed. An old stovepipe, similar to the ones that were then used to form the walls of wells, marks the site.

KEY

▬▬	Tour route
═══	Other roads
ℹ	Tourist information
🏃	Ranger station
⛽	Petrol station

Grandiose Scotty's Castle

Zabriskie Point ②
Made famous by Antonioni's 1960s film of the same name, Zabriskie Point offers views of the multicoloured mud hills of Golden Canyon *(see p281)*. The spot was named after a former general manager of the borax operations in Death Valley *(see p280)*.

Furnace Creek ①
The springs here are one of the few freshwater sources in the desert. They are thought to have saved the lives of hundreds of gold prospectors crossing the desert on their way to the Sierra foothills. The full-service visitors' complex here *(see p280)* is the valley's main population centre.

Dante's View ③
At 5,475 ft (1,650 m), the view takes in the entire valley floor and is best seen in the morning. The name of the viewpoint was inspired by Dante's *Inferno*. In the distance is Telescope Peak in the Panamint Range.

Badwater ④
Badwater *(see p281)* is the lowest point in the western hemisphere. It lies 282 ft (85 m) below sea level and is one of the world's hottest places. The water is not poisonous, but it is unpalatable, filled with sodium chloride and sulphates.

Artist's Palette ⑤
These multicoloured hills of cemented gravels were created by mineral deposits and volcanic ash. The colours are at their most intense in the late afternoon sun.

0 kilometres   10

0 miles   10

SAN FRANCISCO AND THE BAY AREA

San Francisco and the Bay Area at a Glance

SAN FRANCISCO IS A COMPACT CITY and much of the central area can be explored on foot. The many hills give rise to some strenuous climbing, but are useful landmarks for orientation and offer superb views. A rich ethnic mix adds a distinctive character to the city's many neighbourhoods. The smaller cities of Oakland and Berkeley on the East Bay are reached via the Bay Bridge, while to the north, Golden Gate Bridge links the peninsula to the Marin Headlands and the Point Reyes National Seashore. To the south are the colonial city of San Jose and rugged stretches of coastline inhabited by a variety of flora and fauna.

LOCATOR MAP

San Francisco & the Bay Area

Golden Gate Bridge
Over 50 years old, the bridge is as much a part of the landscape as the craggy Marin Headlands and the idyllic bay (see pp370–71).

GOLDEN GATE PARK AND THE PRESIDIO
(see pp354–71)

Palace of Fine Arts
Built for the Panama-Pacific Exposition of 1915, this Neo-Classical monument was fully restored in 1962 (see p341).

BAY AREA
pp394–415

☐ San Francisco

0 kilometres   25

0 miles   25

Coit Tower
The 1933 tower is floodlit at night (see p333).

FISHERMAN'S WHARF
AND NORTH BEACH
(see pp322–33)

CHINATOWN
AND NOB HILL
(see pp314–21)

PACIFIC HEIGHTS
AND THE
CIVIC CENTER
(see pp336–43)

DOWNTOWN
(see pp300–13)

HAIGHT ASHBURY
AND THE MISSION
(see pp344–53)

Chinatown Gateway
This elaborate gate is the entrance to the city's historic Chinatown (see p318).

City Hall
The building is the city's most imposing structure, with a vast rotunda displaying a wealth of architectural detail (see p342).

0 kilometres   2

0 miles   2

Mission Dolores
The oldest building in San Francisco is one of the 21 Franciscan missions in California (see p351).

The Shape of San Francisco

San Francisco road sign

SAN FRANCISCO, with its estimated 43 hills, sits at the tip of a peninsula, surrounded by the Pacific Ocean to the west and San Francisco Bay to the east. To the north, linked by the Golden Gate Bridge, are the rugged Marin Headlands and the protected wildlife area of the Point Reyes Peninsula. The Diablo Coast Range, with the 3,850-ft (1,170-m) Mount Diablo at its heart, forms a mountainous backdrop to the heavily populated cities of Richmond, Oakland and Berkeley in the East Bay, and divides the region from the flat plains of the Central Valley. To the south, the San Bruno Mountains enclose the industrial Silicon Valley and run along the coastline towards Big Sur.

Vallejo
This town, in the north of the bay, is home to Marine World Africa wildlife park and oceanarium, which includes dolphin displays (see p399).

Red and White ferries

Sausalito
This former fishing community, across the Golden Gate Bridge, is lined with Victorian houses looking out towards the bay (see p398).

RICHMOND

RICHMOND BRIDGE

TIBURON

(29)

(37)

(101)

SONOMA MOUNTAINS

MOUNT TAMALPAIS

(1)

POINT REYES NATIONAL SEASHORE

PACIFIC OCEAN

The Marin Headlands
are part of the Golden Gate National Recreation Area. These green hills and quiet beaches offer perfect relaxation away from the city, with hiking, fishing and bird-watching opportunities
(see pp400–401).

Point Reyes Peninsula
The rugged coastline of the peninsula, situated on the San Andreas Fault and only partly attached to the mainland, is abundant with wildlife and is a very productive dairy farming community (see p398).

Downtown
One of the major financial districts in the United States is situated in San Francisco's Downtown area. Its skyline is dominated by the Transamerica Pyramid (see pp300–313).

Livermore
This rural community is home to the world's largest wind farm, making use of the area's strong winds to produce natural energy (see p410).

Berkeley includes the University of California at Berkeley campus, once known for its radicalism *(see pp402–405)*.

The Diablo Coast Range separates the East Bay from the Central Valley. Mount Diablo is at the heart of the range *(see p410)*.

DIABLO COAST RANGE

580

50

880

BAY BRIDGE

SAN MATEO BRIDGE

84

280

1

GOLDEN GATE NATIONAL RECREATION AREA

SAN BRUNO MOUNTAINS

Golden Gate Bridge

San Jose was originally a Spanish colonial city and preserves its history. It is still home to a large Mexican-American population *(see pp412–13)*.

Palo Alto
This town was built up specifically to serve the Stanford University campus, which was created by railroad baron Leland Stanford in 1891 (see p411).

Oakland
This busy city has a multicultural population and many historic landmarks. It is linked to San Francisco by the Bay Bridge (see pp406–409).

Victorian Houses in San Francisco

Italianate window

D ESPITE EARTHQUAKES, fires and the inroads of modern life, thousands of ornate, late-19th century houses still line the streets of San Francisco. In fact, in many neighbourhoods they are by far the most common type of housing. Victorian houses are broadly similar, in that they all have wooden frames, elaborately decorated with mass-produced ornament. Most were constructed on narrow plots to a similar floor plan, but they differ in the features of the façade. Four main styles prevail in the city, although in practice many houses, especially those built in the 1880s and 1890s, combine aspects of two or more styles.

Detail of Queen Anne-style gateway at Chateau Tivoli

GOTHIC REVIVAL (1850–80)

Gothic Revival houses are the easiest to identify, as they always have pointed arches over the windows and, sometimes, over the doors. Other features are pitched gabled roofs, decorated vergeboards (again, with pointed arch motifs) and porches that run the width of the building. The smaller, simpler houses of this type are usually painted white, rather than the vibrant colours often associated with later styles.

No. 1111 Oak Street is one of the city's oldest Gothic Revival buildings. Its front garden is unusually large.

The pitched roof over the main façade often runs lengthways, allowing the use of dormer windows.

A gabled roof with decorated vergeboards is the clearest mark of Gothic Revival.

Gothic porch with cross bracing at No. 1978 Filbert Street

Full-width porches are reached by a central stair.

Balustrades on the porch betray the Deep South origins of the style.

ITALIANATE (1850–85)

Italianate houses were more popular in San Francisco than elsewhere in the US, perhaps because their compact form was suited to the city's high building density. The most distinctive feature of the style is the tall cornice, usually with a decorative bracket, which adds a palatial air even to modest homes. Elaborate decoration around windows and doors is also typical of the style.

No. 1913 Sacramento Street displays a typical formal Italianate façade, modelled on a Renaissance palazzo. The wood boarding is made to look like stone.

Tall cornices, often with decorative brackets, conceal a pitched roof.

Imposing entrance with Italianate porch

Symmetrical windows are capped by decorative arches.

Neo-Classical doorways, sometimes with ornate pedimented porches, are a typical Italianate touch.

STICK (1860–90)

This architectural style, with its ungainly name, is perhaps the most prevalent among Victorian houses in the city. Sometimes also called "Stick–Eastlake" after London furniture designer Charles Eastlake, this style was intended to be more architecturally "honest". Vertical lines are emphasized, both in the wood-frame structure and in ornamentation. Bay windows, false-gabled cornices and square corners are key identifying features.

No. 1715–17 Capp Street is a fine example of the Stick–Eastlake style, with a plain façade enlivened by decorative flourishes.

Gabled roof with Eastlake windows at No. 2931 Pierce Street

Wide bands of trim often form a decorative truss, emphasizing the underlying structure of Stick houses.

Decorative gables filled with "sunburst" motifs are used on porches and window frames.

Adjoining front doors can be protected by a single projecting porch.

QUEEN ANNE (1875–1905)

The name "Queen Anne" does not refer to a historical period; it was coined by the English architect Richard Shaw. Queen Anne houses combine elements from many decorative traditions, but are marked by their towers, turrets and large decorative, panels on wall surfaces. Many of the houses display intricate spindle-work on balustrades, porches and roof trusses *(see pp26–7)*.

Palladian windows were used in gables to give the appearance of an extra floor.

Queen Anne gable filled with ornamental panels at No. 818 Steiner Street

Queen Anne turret topped by a finial at No. 1015 Steiner Street

Round, square and polygonal turrets and towers are typical of Queen Anne-style houses.

Gable pediments hold ornamental windows and decorative panels.

The curved window frame is not itself characteristic of Queen Anne style, but many houses include features borrowed from other styles.

The asymmetrical façade of No. 850 Steiner Street, together with its eclectic ornament, is typical of a Queen Anne house. Such features are often painted in various bright colours.

WHERE TO FIND VICTORIAN HOUSES

1715–1717 Capp St. Map 10 F4.
Chateau Tivoli, 1057 Steiner St. Map 4 D4.
1978 Filbert St. Map 4 D2.
1111 Oak St. Map 9 C1.
2931 Pierce St. Map 4 D3.
1913 Sacramento St. Map 4 E3.
818 Steiner St. Map 4 D5.
850 Steiner St. Map 4 D5.
1015 Steiner St. Map 4 D5.
2527–2531 Washington St. Map 4 D3.
Alamo Square p343.
Clarke's Folly p353.
Haas-Lilienthal House p338.
Liberty Street. Map 10 E3.
Masonic Avenue. Map 3 C4.
Octagon House p341.
Spreckels Mansion p338.

San Francisco's Cable Cars

THE CABLE CAR system was launched in 1873, with its inventor Andrew Hallidie riding in the first car. He was inspired to tackle the problem of transporting people up the city's steep slopes after witnessing a bad accident, when a horse-drawn tram slipped down a hill, dragging the horses with it. His system was a success, and by 1889 cars were running on eight lines. Before the 1906 earthquake *(see pp48–9)*, more than 600 cars were in use. With the advent of the internal combustion engine, cable cars became obsolete, and in 1947 attempts were made to replace them with buses. After a public outcry the present three lines, using 17 miles (25 km) of track, were retained.

Cable car traffic lights

***The Cable Car Barn** garages the cars at night, and is a repair shop, museum and powerhouse for the entire cable car system (see p321).*

***The gripman** has to be strong, with good reflexes. Only a third of candidates pass the training programme.*

Bell

POWEL

Sand box

Grip handle

Centre plate and jaws grip the cable

Emergency brake

Wheel brake

Cable

HOW CABLE CARS WORK

Engines in the central powerhouse wind a looped cable under the city streets, guided by a system of grooved pulleys. When the gripman in the cable car applies the grip handle, the grip reaches through a slot in the street and grabs the cable. This pulls the car along at a steady speed of 9.5 mph (15.5 km/h). To stop, the gripman releases the grip and applies the brake. Great skill is needed at corners where the cable passes over a pulley. The gripman must release the grip to allow the car to coast over the pulley.

Cable car grip mechanism

Grip handle

Destination board

Wooden beams

Grip crotch

Brake lever

Side seating

Cable car floor

Paving stones

Yoke

Hatch House is the name given to a four-storey house that needed to be moved in its entirety in 1913. Herbert Hatch used a system of jacks and hoists to manoeuvre the house across the cable car line without causing any cessation of the service.

A cable car celebration was held in 1984 after a refurbishment of the system lasting two years. Each car was refitted, and all lines were replaced with reinforced tracks. The system should now work safely for 100 years.

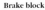

Brake block   Brake shoe

A cable car bell-ringing contest is held at Union Square every July, when conductors ring out their most spirited rhythms. On the street, the bell signals a warning to other traffic.

The original San Francisco cable car, tested by Hallidie on Clay Street on 2 August 1873, is on view in the Cable Car Barn (see p321). The cable car system has remained essentially unchanged since its invention.

Rebuilding the cable cars has to be done with attention to historical detail, as they are designated historic monuments.

ANDREW SMITH HALLIDIE

Andrew Smith was born in London in 1836, and later adopted his uncle's surname. He trained as a mechanic, moved to San Francisco in 1852, and formed a company that made wire rope. In 1873 he tested the first cable car, which soon became profitable and opened the hills of the city to development.

San Francisco's Best: Museums and Galleries

MUSEUMS AND GALLERIES in the city range from the encyclopedic MH de Young and the California Palace of the Legion of Honor, to the contemporary art of the Museum of Modern Art and its neighbour, the Center for the Arts at Yerba Buena. In addition, there are several excellent science museums, including the Exploratorium and the California Academy of Sciences. Other museums celebrate the city's heritage, including its ancestral Native American and Mexican cultures, and the people and events that made the city what it is today.

The Exploratorium *is one of the best science museums in the US. Here visitors experiment with* Sun Painting, *a feast of light and colour.* (See p339.)

California Palace of the Legion of Honor *houses a collection of European art from the Middle Ages to the 19th century, including* Sailboat on the Seine *(c.1874) by Claude Monet.* (See pp364–5.)

Golden Gate Park and the Presidio

Pacific H... and the ... Cente...

MH de Young Museum *has many fascinating artifacts, such as this Mexican female dignitary (AD 600–900). In the same building, the Asian Art Museum houses a world-famous collection of eastern art.* (See pp362–3.)

0 kilometres   2

0 miles   1

California Academy of Sciences *has something of interest for everyone, from alligators to astronomy. The* Fish Roundabout *is a circular aquarium.* (See pp360–61.)

Fort Mason Museums
*house ethnic culture artifacts.
Muto by Mimo Paladino
(1985) is one of the many
exhibits.* (See pp340–41.)

*The Chinese Historical
Society administers one of
the city's smallest museums.
Within is a unique collection
that details the history of
California's Chinese communities and their participation in
the development of the state.
Included among the exhibits is
this magnificent costume
dragon's head.* (See p320.)

*Fisherman's Wharf
and North Beach*

*Chinatown and
Nob Hill*

Downtown

*ight Ashbury
the Mission*

Wells Fargo History Museum
*is a small gallery which illustrates the
colourful history of California, from the early
days of the Gold Rush. This bronze stagecoach
(1984) is by M Casper.* (See p304.)

San Francisco Museum of Modern Art
*is a highly regarded showcase of 20th-
century art. In 1994 the museum moved to
brand new premises, designed by architect
Mario Botta. Back View by Philip Guston
(1977) is in the permanent collection.*
(See pp308–9.)

**San Francisco Main
Library**, *designed in
Beaux-Arts style, contains
a wealth of books and
items tracing significant
events in the city's history.*
(See p343.)

Center for the Arts
*is a new gallery at
Yerba Buena
Gardens which
displays diverse
works of
contemporary art.
These change
regularly, as there is
no permanent
collection here.* (See
pp312–13.)

San Francisco's Murals

SAN FRANCISCO IS PROUD of its reputation as a culturally rich and cosmopolitan city, and these qualities are evident in the bright murals that decorate walls and other public places in several areas of the city. Many were painted in the 1930s, and many more in the 1970s, with some appearing spontaneously while others were specially commissioned. One of the best is the *Carnaval Mural* on 24th Street in the Mission District *(see p352)*; further examples are shown here.

503 Law Office at Dolores and 18th streets

SCENES FROM HISTORY

Some of the best examples of San Francisco's historical mural art can be found inside Coit Tower *(see p333)*, where a series of panels, funded during the Great Depression of the 1930s by President Roosevelt's New Deal programme, is typical of the period. Many local artists participated in creating the work, and themes include the struggles of the working class and the rich resources of California. The city also boasts three murals by Diego Rivera, the Mexican artist who revived fresco painting during the 1930s and 1940s.

Detail from Coit Tower mural illustrating the rich resources of California

The making of a mural depicted by Diego Rivera at San Francisco Art Institute

Architect Frank Lloyd Wright

Emmy Lou Packard, Rivera's assistant on the mural

Otto Diechman, architect

Mussolini, as portrayed by Jack Oakie in *The Great Dictator*

Coit Tower mural showing life during the Great Depression

The 1940 Diego Rivera mural *at City College has a theme of Pan-American unity, and features many important historical figures. The section illustrated here lays emphasis on creative endeavour in the United States, and on the role played by artists in the fight against Fascism.*

Edward G Robinson

Joseph Stalin

Adolf Hitler

Benito Mussolini

Charlie Chaplin in *The Great Dictator*, a film made in 1940 that poked fun at Fascism. Chaplin had two parts, playing both a Jewish barber and Hitler.

MODERN LIFE

Life in the modern metropolis is one of the major themes of mural art in San Francisco, as much now as it was in the 1930s. In the Mission District particularly, every aspect of daily life is illustrated on the walls of banks, schools and restaurants, with lively scenes of the family, community, political activity and people at work and play. The Mission District contains around 200 murals, many painted in the 1970s, when the city government paid disaffected young people to create works of art in public places. The San Francisco Arts Commission continues to foster this art form.

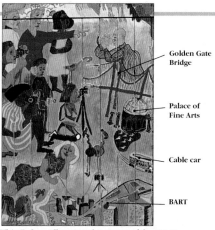

Golden Gate Bridge

Palace of Fine Arts

Cable car

BART

This Balmy Alley mural *is a view of the city as tourists see it. The alley, in the Mission District, is decorated with numerous vivid murals, first painted by local children, artists and community workers in the 1970s. The works are now a major attraction.*

The Learning Wall, Franklin St, depicts education and art

Positively Fourth Street, a weathered mural at Fort Mason

THE MULTICULTURAL CITY

San Francisco's heritage of diversity and tolerance comes alive in the murals that enliven its ethnic neighbourhoods. In Chinatown, Chinese-American artists evoke memories of the "old country". The Mission District is filled with art, some of it politically inspired, that celebrates the struggles and achievements of its Mexican and Latin American population.

Mexican-American dancer

Native American drummer

Caucasian bass player

African-American maracas player

Multicultural San Francisco *is celebrated at Park Branch Library in Haight Ashbury.*

Mural in Washington Street encapsulating life in China

WHERE TO FIND THE MURALS

Balmy Alley, 24th & 25th Sts.
City College of San Francisco 50 Phelan Ave.
Coit Tower *p333*.
Dolores and 18th St. **Map 10 E3**.
Fort Mason *pp340–41*.
Franklin Street. **Map 4 E1**.
Park Branch Library 1833 Page St. **Map 9 B1**.
San Francisco Art Institute *pp330–31*.
Washington Street. **Map 4 E3**.

The 49-Mile Scenic Drive

Official sign

LINKING THE CITY'S most intriguing neighbourhoods, fascinating sights and spectacular views, the 49-Mile Scenic Drive (79 km) provides a splendid overview of San Francisco. Keeping to the well-marked route is easy – just follow the blue-and-white seagull signs. Some of these are hidden by overhanging vegetation, so you need to be alert. Set aside a whole day for this trip; there are plenty of places to stop to take photographs or admire the views.

The Palace of Fine Arts and the Exploratorium 24
The grand Neo-Classical building and its modern science museum stand near the entrance to the Presidio.

Stow Lake 5
There is a waterfall and a Chinese pavilion on the island in this picturesque lake. Boats are for hire.

Sutro Tower 8
This distinctive orange and white tower is visible from all over the city.

Five-tiered pagoda in Japantown

| 0 kilometres | | 2 |
| 0 miles | 1 | |

KEY

—— 49-Mile Scenic Drive

⚹ Viewpoint

Coit Tower ⑳
*Overlooking North Beach, Telegraph Hill is
topped by this tower which has fine murals
and a viewing terrace.*

Marina Green ㉓
*This is an excellent
vantage point from
which to view
or photograph
Golden Gate
Bridge.*

Grace Cathedral ⑱
*This impressive cathedral,
based on Notre Dame in Paris,
dominates the summit of the
city's steepest hill, Nob Hill.*

TIPS FOR MOTORISTS

Starting point: Anywhere. The
circuit is designed to be followed in
an anti-clockwise direction starting
and ending at any point.
When to go: Avoid driving during
rush hours: 7–9am, 4–6:30pm.
Most of the views are as
spectacular by night as by day.
Parking: Use the car parks that are
situated around the Financial
District, the Civic Center, Japantown, Nob Hill, Chinatown, North
Beach and Fisherman's Wharf.
Elsewhere, street parking is usually
easily available.

FINDING THE SIGHTS

① Presidio pp366–7
② Fort Point p368
③ California Palace of the
    Legion of Honor pp364–5
④ Queen Wilhelmina Tulip
    Garden p359
⑤ Stow Lake p358
⑥ Conservatory of Flowers p358
⑦ Haight Street p348
⑧ Sutro Tower p353
⑨ Twin Peaks p353
⑩ Mission Dolores p351
⑪ Ferry Building p306
⑫ Embarcadero Center p304
⑬ Civic Center pp342–3

⑭ St Mary's Cathedral p342
⑮ Japan Center p342
⑯ Union Square p310
⑰ Chinatown Gateway p318
⑱ Grace Cathedral p321
⑲ Cable Car Barn p321
⑳ Coit Tower p333
㉑ San Francisco National
    Maritime Museum p327
㉒ Fort Mason pp340–41
㉓ Marina Green p340
㉔ Palace of Fine Arts and the
    Exploratorium p341

DOWNTOWN SAN FRANCISCO

MONTGOMERY STREET, now right in the heart of the Financial District, was once a street of small shops, where miners came to weigh their gold dust. Wells Fargo built the city's first brick building on the street during the Gold Rush *(see pp44–5)*. Today, old-fashioned banking halls stand in the shadow of modern skyscrapers. Union Square is the city's main shopping district and has a wealth of fine department stores. SoMa (South of Market) has become the city's "artists' quarter", with its old warehouses converted into studios, bars and avant-garde theatres.

Motif on Union Bank

SIGHTS AT A GLANCE

Historic Streets and Buildings
Bank of California ❻
Ferry Building ❿
Jackson Square Historical
    District ❷
Merchant's Exchange ❼
No. 1 Market Street ❿
Old United States
    Mint ㉔
Pacific Coast Stock
    Exchange ❽
Powell Street Cable Car
    Turntable ㉒

Shops
Crocker Galleria ⑰
Gump's ⑱
San Francisco Center ㉓
Union Square Shops ㉑

Modern Architecture
Bank of America ❹
Embarcadero Center ❶
Rincon Center ⑪
Transamerica Pyramid ❺
*Yerba Buena Gardens
    pp312–13* ⑭

Theatres
Theater District ⑳

Hotels
Sheraton Palace Hotel ⑯

Museums and Galleries
Museum of Cartoon Art ⑮
*Museum of Modern Art
    pp308–309* ⑬
Wells Fargo History
    Museum ❸

Parks and Squares
Justin Herman
    Plaza ❾
Union Square ⑲

KEY

▢	Street-by-Street map *See pp302–3*
🚟	Cable car terminus
Ⓑ	BART station
Ⓟ	Parking
⚓	Ferry terminal

GETTING THERE

All streetcar, cable car and BART lines, and most ferries and bus lines, converge at some point on Market Street – the heart of this section. From Market Street, bus lines reach all parts of the district.

0 metres   400

0 yards   400

◁ **A view of downtown San Francisco at night**

Street-by-Street: Financial District

SAN FRANCISCO'S economic engine is fuelled predominantly by the Financial District, one of the chief commercial centres in the US. It reaches from the imposing modern towers and plazas of the Embarcadero Center to staid Montgomery Street, called the "Wall Street of the West". All the principal banks, brokers and law offices are situated within this area. The Jackson Square Historical District, north of Washington Street, was once the heart of the business community.

★ **Embarcadero Center**
The centre houses commercial outlets and offices. A shopping arcade occupies the first three tiers of the towers ❶

La Chiffonière (1978)
by Jean de Buffet,
Justin Herman Plaza

Hotaling Place is a narrow alley known for its many excellent antique shops.

Jackson Square Historical District
This district recalls the Gold Rush era more than any other ❷

The Golden Era Building was built during the Gold Rush and housed the paper *Golden Era*, for which Mark Twain wrote.

Bus stop
(No. 41)

WASHINGTON STREET
BATTERY STREET
SANSOME STREET
MONTGOMERY STREET

★ **Transamerica Pyramid**
This 853-ft (260-m) skyscraper is now the tallest on the city's skyline ❺

Bank of California
The grand banking hall is guarded by fierce stone lions carved by sculptor Arthur Putnam ❻

Merchant's Exchange
Paintings of shipping scenes line the walls ❼

Wells Fargo History Museum
An old stagecoach, evoking the Wild West days, is one of the exhibits in this transport and banking museum ❸

Bank of America
There are fine views from the 52nd floor of this important banking institution ❹

0 metres   100
0 yards   100

California Street, busy with clanging cable cars, sweeps to the top of Nob Hill.

Justin Herman Plaza
On sunny days lunchtime crowds fill the plaza **9**

Hyatt Regency Hotel
(see p526)

Bus stop
(Nos. 2, 9, 42)

FISHERMAN'S WHARF AND NORTH BEACH

CHINATOWN AND NOB HILL

DOWNTOWN

LOCATOR MAP
See Street Finder, maps 5 & 6

DAVIS STREET

SACRAMENTO STREET

FRONT STREET

CALIFORNIA STREET

DRUMM STREET

MARKET STREET

STREET

The Gandhi Monument (1988),
on the east side of the Ferry Building, is by KB Patel.

No. 1 Market Street
The Southern Pacific Railroad Company was once based here **12**

Ferry Building
Before the bridges were built 100,000 people passed through here each day **10**

KEY

– – – Suggested route

Pacific Coast Stock Exchange
This has overtaken the Merchant's Exchange as the focal point of city trade **8**

First Interstate Center towers are linked by glass "sky-bridges".

STAR SIGHTS

★ **Embarcadero Center**

★ **Transamerica Pyramid**

Embarcadero Center ❶

Map 6 D3. 🚌 *1, 32, 42.*
🚋 *J, K, L, M, N.* 🚡 *California St.*
See **Shopping** *p376–79* and **Where to Stay** *p504–37.*

COMPLETED IN 1981 after a decade of construction, San Francisco's largest re-development project stretches from Justin Herman Plaza to Battery Street. Office workers and shoppers use its open spaces to relax in the sun and eat their lunch. Four high-rise towers reach 35 to 45 storeys above the landscaped plazas and elevated walkways.

The Embarcadero Center's most spectacular interior is the foyer of the Hyatt Regency Hotel *(see p525).* Its 17-storey atrium contains an immense sculptured globe by Charles Perry entitled *Eclipse.* Glass lifts glide up and down one wall, carrying visitors up to and from the Equinox, a revolving rooftop restaurant which completes a full circle every 40 minutes.

Lobby of the Hyatt Regency Hotel at the Embarcadero Center

Hotaling Place in Jackson Square

Jackson Square Historical District ❷

Map 5 C3. 🚌 *12, 15, 42, 83.*

RENOVATED IN the early 1950s, this neighbourhood contains many historic brick, cast-iron and granite façades dating from the Gold Rush. From 1850 to 1910 it was known as the Barbary Coast, notorious for its squalor and the crude-ness of its inhabitants. The

old Hippodrome theatre at No. 555 Pacific Street contains bawdy relief sculptures in the recessed front, which recall the risqué shows that were performed there. Today the buildings are used as show-rooms, law offices and fine antique shops; the best can be seen in Jackson Street, Gold Street, Hotaling Place and Montgomery Street.

Wells Fargo History Museum ❸

420 Montgomery St. **Map** 5 C4.
📞 *(415) 396-2619.* 🚌 *1, 12, 15, 42.* 🚡 *California St.* 🕐 *9am–5pm Mon–Fri.* ⬤ *public hols.* ♿

FOUNDED IN 1852, Wells Fargo & Co became the greatest banking and transport company in the West and was influential in the development of the American frontier.

The company moved people and goods from the East to West Coast, and between the mining camps and towns of California. It also transported gold from the West Coast to the East, and delivered mail, placing mailboxes in

convenient locations to enable the messengers to sort letters en route. The Pony Express was another mail venture in which Wells Fargo & Co was to play a major role.

The splendid stagecoaches on display are famous partic-ularly for the legendary stories of their heroic drivers and the bandits who robbed them. The best-known bandit was Black Bart, who left poems at the scene of his crimes. He stalk-ed the many lonely roads from Calaveras County up to the Oregon border from 1875 to 1883, holding up stagecoaches. In one hold-up he mistak-enly left behind one of his handkerchiefs. Its distinctive laundry mark revealed him as min-ing engineer Charles Boles *(see p463).*

Museum visitors can experience how it felt to sit for days in a jostling stage-coach, and listen to the recorded diary of an immigrant called Francis Brocklehurst. Exhibits include Pony Express mail, photo-graphs, bills of exchange, early cheques, gold nug-gets, and the imperial currency of Emperor Norton *(see p47).*

Black Bart, the poet bandit

Bank of America ❹

555 California St. **Map** 5 C4.
📞 (415) 433-7500 (Carnelian Room).
🚌 1, 15. 🚋 California St.

THE RED granite-clad building housing the headquarters of the Bank of America opened in 1972. Its 52 storeys make it the largest skyscraper in San Francisco, and incredible views from the Carnelian Room on the 52nd floor show the fascinating workings of city life. The Bank of America was originally the Bank of Italy, which was founded by AP Giannini in San Jose *(see pp412–13)*. It built up a huge clientele early in the 20th century by catering to immigrants and investing in the booming farmlands and small towns. In the great fire of 1906 *(see pp48–9)* Giannini personally rescued his bank's deposits, carrying them to safety hidden in fruit crates, so there were sufficient funds for the bank to invest in the rebuilding of the city.

Transcendence **by Masayuki Nagari (1972) at the Bank of America**

Transamerica Pyramid ❺

600 Montgomery St. **Map** 5 C3.
🚌 1, 15, 42. ⬛ 8:30am–4:30pm Mon–Fri. ● public hols. ♿

CAPPED WITH a pointed spire on top of its 48 storeys, the pyramid reaches 853 ft (260 m) above sea level. It is the tallest and most widely recognized building in the city, and although San Franciscans disliked it when it opened in 1972, they have since accepted it as part of their city's skyline.

Designed by William Pereira & Associates, the pyramid houses 1,500 office workers on a site that is historically one of the richest in the city. The Montgomery Block, which contained many important offices and was the largest building west of the Mississippi, was built here in 1853. In the basement was the Exchange Saloon, which was frequented by the writer Mark Twain. The Financial District was extended south in the 1860s, and artists and writers took up residence in the Montgomery Block. The Pony Express terminus, marked by a plaque, was at Merchant Street, opposite the pyramid.

The spire is hollow, rising 212 ft (64 m) above the top floor. Lit from inside, it casts a warm, yellow glow at night. Its purpose is purely decorative.

The vertical wings of the building rise from the middle of the ground floor and extend beyond the frame, which tapers inwards. The eastern wing houses 18 lift shafts, and the western wing houses a smoke tower and emergency stairs.

The observation area is situated on the 27th floor, halfway up the building; the northward views of the city are stupendous. Each year more than 50,000 visitors ascend to this level to take in the sights.

Earthquake protection is ensured by white precast quartz aggregate, interlaced with reinforcing rods at four places on each floor, which cover the exterior of the pyramid. Clearance between the panels allows for lateral movement in case of an earthquake.

The shape of the building tapers so that it casts a smaller shadow than a conventional design.

The 3,678 windows take cleaners one month to wash.

The foundations rest on a steel and concrete block, sunk 52 ft (15.5 m) into the ground, and designed to move with earth tremors.

Bank of California 6

400 California St. **Map** 5 C4. (*(415) 765-0400.* 1, 42. *California St.* **Museum of American Money** 10am–4pm Mon–Thu, 10am–5pm Fri. public hols. &

W ILLIAM RALSTON and Darius Mills founded this bank in 1864. Ralston, known as "the man who built San Francisco", invested profitably in the Comstock mines *(see p45)*. He used the bank and his personal fortune to finance many civic projects in San Francisco, including the city's water company, a theatre and the Palace Hotel *(see p526)*. When economic depression struck in the 1870s, Ralston's empire collapsed.

The present colonnaded building was completed in 1908. In the basement, the Museum of American Money displays gold, coins, old banknotes and diagrams of the Comstock mines.

Classical façade of the Bank of California

Merchant's Exchange 7

465 California St. **Map** 5 C4. 3, 4, 15. 9am–8pm Mon–Thu, 9am–6pm Fri. public hols. &

T HE EXCHANGE was designed by Willis Polk in 1903 and fortunately was not badly damaged in the great fire of 1906 *(see pp48–9)*. Inside, fine seascapes by the Irish painter William Coulter line the walls. These depict epic maritime scenes from the age of steam and sail. The building was the focal point of San Francisco's commodities exchange in the early 20th century, when lookouts in the tower relayed news of ships arriving from abroad. Now dwarfed by skyscrapers, the Exchange once dominated the skyline.

Pacific Coast Stock Exchange 8

301 Pine St. **Map** 5 C4. (*(415) 393-4000.* 3, 4, 15, 42. to the public, except by prearranged tour.

A MERICA'S LARGEST stock exchange outside New York was founded in 1882. It now occupies buildings re-modelled in 1930 by Miller and Pflueger from the existing US Treasury. The monumental granite statues that flank the Pine Street entrance were sculpted by Ralph Stackpole in 1930. Activity in the famous trading room is often frantic, especially during the hours of New York's earlier trading day. Visitors may observe the action from the gallery by appointment only.

Justin Herman Plaza 9

Map 6 D3. many buses. J, K, L, M, N. California St.

P OPULAR WITH lunchtime crowds from the nearby Embarcadero Center *(see p304)*, this plaza is best known for its avant-garde Vaillancourt Fountain, built in 1971 by the Canadian artist Armand Vaillancourt. The fountain is modelled from huge concrete blocks, and some people find it ugly, especially when it is allowed to run dry during times of drought. However, you are allowed to climb on and through it, and with its splashing pools and columns of falling water, it is an intriguing public work of art when function-ing as intended.

The area is often rented out to musicians during the lunch hour – the popular rock band U2 performed a lunchtime concert here in 1987, after which they spray-painted the fountain.

The Vaillancourt Fountain in Justin Herman Plaza

Ferry Building 10

Embarcadero at Market St. **Map** 6 E3. many buses. J, K, L, M, N. California St.

C ONSTRUCTED BETWEEN 1896 and 1903, the Ferry Building survived the great fire of 1906 through the inter-cession of fireboats pumping water from the bay. The clock tower is 235 ft (71 m) high, and was inspired by the Moorish bell tower of Seville Cathedral in Spain. In the early 1930s more than 50 million passengers a year passed through the build-ing. Many of these were travellers to and from the transcontinental railroad terminus in Oakland, while others were commuters using the 170 daily ferries between the city and their homes across the bay. With the opening of the Bay Bridge in 1936 *(see pp406–7)*, the Ferry Building ceased to be the city's main point of entry, and began to deteriorate. A few ferries still cross the bay, to Tiburon and Sausa-lito in Marin County *(see p398–9)* and Oakland in the East Bay *(see pp406–7)*.

The clock tower on the Ferry Building

Rincon Annex mural depicting the Spanish discovery of San Francisco

Rincon Center ⓫

Map 6 E4. 14. See ***Shopping*** *pp376–79.*

THIS SHOPPING CENTRE, with its soaring atrium and its 90-ft (27-m) fountain, was added on to the old Rincon Annex Post Office Building in 1989. The Rincon Annex dates from 1940 and is well known for its murals by the Russian-born artist Anton Refregier, showing aspects of the history of San Francisco. Some of the works depict harsh images of important events and people of the city which caused much controversy when first shown.

No. 1 Market Street ⓬

Map 6 D3. *many buses.* *J, K, L, M, N.* *California St.*

THIS ADDRESS encompasses two new office towers as well as the red brick, baroque Southern Pacific Railroad Building, which was built in 1916. The Southern Pacific Railroad was one of the West Coast's most powerful corporations during the last half of the 19th century. It was an offshoot of Central Pacific, the company run by the "Big Four" and which, during the 1860s, constructed the western half of the first transcontinental railroad *(see pp46–7).*

Museum of Modern Art ⓭

See pp308–9.

Yerba Buena Gardens ⓮

See pp312–13.

Cartoon art on a US stamp

Museum of Cartoon Art ⓯

814 Mission St. *(415) 546-9481.* *11am–5pm Wed–Fri; 10am–5pm Sat; 1–5pm Sun.*

FOUNDED IN 1984, this is the only museum of original cartoon art on the West Coast. The 10,000 pieces in the collection date from the 18th century to the present day and include the original artwork for such well-known cartoon characters as Popeye, Charlie Brown, L'il Abner, Little Orphan Annie and Walt Disney's numerous creations. Exhibitions change every four months. The museum also includes a children's area and a CD-ROM gallery.

Sheraton Palace Hotel ⓰

2 New Montgomery St. **Map** 5 C4. *(415) 392-8600.* *7, 8, 9, 21, 31, 66, 71.* *J, K, L, M, N. See **Where to Stay** p526.*

THE ORIGINAL Palace Hotel was opened by William Ralston, one of San Francisco's best-known financiers, in 1875. It was the most luxurious of San Francisco's early hotels, with 7 floors, 700 windows, an inner courtyard and exotic international décor. It was regularly frequented by the rich and famous. Among its patrons were the actress Sarah Bernhardt and writers Oscar Wilde and Rudyard Kipling. The celebrated tenor Enrico Caruso was a guest at the hotel at the time of the earthquake of 1906 when the hotel, like much of the city, caught fire. It was rebuilt shortly after under the direction of the architect George Kelham, and reopened in 1909. The Garden Court dining room can seat nearly 1,000 people and is lit by 20 crystal chandeliers. In 1988 the building was completely refurbished at a cost of $100 million.

The Garden Court at the Sheraton Palace Hotel

San Francisco Museum of Modern Art ⑬

THIS DRAMATIC museum forms the nucleus of San Francisco's reputation as a leading centre of modern art. Created in 1935 with the aim of displaying works by 20th-century artists, it moved into its new quarters in 1995. The focus of Swiss architect Mario Botta's modernist building is the 125-ft (38-m) cylindrical skylight, which channels light down to the first-floor atrium court. More than 17,000 works of art are housed in its 50,000 sq ft (4,600 sq m) of gallery space. The museum offers a dynamic schedule of changing exhibits from around the world.

Zip Light **(1990) by Sigmar Willnauer**

Aerial Gyrations
Charles Sheeler's fascination with American industrial architecture and his experience as a designer influenced this 1953 oil on canvas.

MUSEUM GUIDE

The museum shop, auditorium, café and special events space are on the first floor. On the second floor are works from the permanent collection of paintings, sculptures, architecture and design. Photography and other works on paper are displayed on the third floor, with media arts on the fourth floor. Contemporary works are displayed in fourth and fifth floor exhibition halls, along with temporary exhibits and recent gifts and purchases. The museum's entire collection rotates regularly.

★ Paul Klee Gallery
Nearly Hit *was painted with oil on board in 1928. Klee often used an arrow as a symbol for thought and cosmic forces.*

PM Magazine
Television screens show Dara Birnbaum's innovative 1982 video work.

KEY TO FLOORPLAN

- ☐ Painting and sculpture collection
- ☐ California art
- ☐ Architecture and design
- ☐ Photography and works on paper
- ☐ Media arts
- ☐ Special exhibitions and events
- ☐ Non-exhibition space

125-ft (38-m) tall cylindrical skylight

Auditorium

First floor

Main entrance

Emergency staircase

★ **California Art**
Richard Shaw's sculpted figure Melodius Double Stop *(1980) is a highlight of this collection.*

Fifth floor

Terrace

Third floor

Fourth floor

Untitled 1933
This photograph by Man Ray features the body of a sculpture superimposed on the head of a woman.

★ **The Flower Carrier**
Diego Rivera's powerful irony on the human cost of beauty and luxury was painted in oil and tempura on masonite in 1935.

Atrium

Second floor

Country Dog Gentlemen
Bay Area artist Roy De Forest painted this fantasy of a universe guarded by animals in 1972.

STAR EXHIBITS

★ **The Flower Carrier**

★ **Paul Klee Gallery**

★ **California Art**

Central plaza of the Crocker Galleria

Crocker Galleria ⑰

Between Post, Kearny, Sutter and Montgomery Sts. **Map** 5 C4. 🚌 *2, 3, 4.* 🚋 *J, K, L, M, N. See Shopping pp376–9.*

THE CROCKER GALLERIA was built in 1982. Inspired by Milan's Galleria Vittorio Emmanuelle, the building features a central plaza under an arched atrium. More than 50 shops and restaurants are housed here on three floors, with displays promoting the best of European and American designers.

Gump's ⑱

135 Post St. **Map** 5 C4. 📞 *(415) 982-1616.* 🚌 *2, 3, 4, 30, 38, 45.* 🚋 *J, K, L,M, N.* 🚋 *Powell–Mason, Powell–Hyde.* 🕐 *10am–6pm Mon–Sat (10am–7pm Thu).* 🚻 *See Shopping pp376–9.*

FOUNDED IN 1861 by German immigrants who were once mirror and frame merchants, this indigenous San Franciscan department store has now become a local institution. Many of the city's couples register their wedding present list with the store.

Gump's houses the largest collection of fine china and crystal in the United States, which includes such prestigious designers as Baccarat, Steuben and Lalique.

The store is also celebrated for its oriental treasures, furniture and the rare works of art in the art department. The Asian art is particularly fine, especially the jade collection, which enjoys an international reputation. In 1949 Gump's imported the great bronze Buddha and presented it to the Japanese Tea Garden *(see pp356–7).*

Gump's has a refined atmosphere and is often frequented by the rich and famous. It is renowned for its colourful and extravagant window displays, which change regularly and feature different themes.

Union Square ⑲

Map 5 C5. 🚌 *2, 3, 4, 30, 38, 45.* 🚋 *J, K, L, M, N.* 🚋 *Powell–Mason, Powell–Hyde.*

UNION SQUARE was named after the big, pro-Union rallies held here during the Civil War of 1861–65. The rallies galvanized popular support in San Francisco for the Northern cause, and this was instrumental in bringing California into the war on the side of the Union. The original churches, gentlemen's clubs and a synagogue were eventually overtaken by shops and offices. This green square, lined with palm trees, is now at the heart of the city's shopping district and marks the edge of the Theater District. It is bordered on the west side by the luxurious Westin St Francis Hotel *(see p526).* In the centre there is a bronze statue of the Goddess of Victory. Sculpted by Robert Aitken in 1903, she stands at the top of a 90-ft (27-m) Corinthian column. The monument was erected to commemorate Admiral Dewey's naval victory at Manila Bay during the Spanish–American War of 1898. Union Square also had the world's first multilevel underground car park, which was constructed in 1942.

Theater District ⑳

Map 5 B5. 🚌 *2, 3, 4, 38.* 🚋 *Powell–Mason, Powell–Hyde. See Entertainment pp372–5.*

SEVERAL THEATRES are located near Union Square, all within a six-block area. The two largest are on Geary Boulevard: the Curran Theater, designed in 1922 by Alfred Henry D Jacobs, which imports Broadway shows, and the Geary Theater, with its Edwardian façade, now home to the American Conservatory Theater (ACT). The Theater on the Square mounts avant-garde, off-Broadway shows. The city has a fine reputation for the variety of performances it offers and has always attracted great actors. Isadora Duncan, the innovative 1920s dancer, was born nearby at No. 501 Taylor Street, which is now marked by a plaque.

Union Square Shops ㉑

Map 5 C5. 🚌 *2, 3, 4, 30, 38, 45.* 🚋 *J, K, L, M, N.* 🚋 *Powell–Mason, Powell–Hyde. See Shopping pp376–9.*

MANY OF San Francisco's largest department stores can be found here, including Macy's, Saks Fifth Avenue and

Department stores overlooking Union Square

Rotating a cable car on the Powell Street Turntable

Gump's. The Nieman Marcus store, at the request of San Franciscans, has preserved the 1900 rotunda and skylight from the City of Paris. The latter was the city's most elegant store at the end of the 19th century but was demolished in 1982. As well as the larger stores, the area houses many antiquarian bookshops and smaller boutiques. The Circle Gallery Building, at 140 Maiden Lane, is a contemporary art gallery. Designed by Frank Lloyd Wright in 1947, it was the precursor to his Guggenheim Museum in New York (see p29).

Powell Street Cable Car Turntable ㉒

Hallidie Plaza, Powell St at Market St. **Map** 5 C5. many buses. J, K, M, N. Powell–Mason, Powell–Hyde.

THE POWELL–HYDE and the Powell–Mason cable car lines are the most spectacular routes in San Francisco. They start and end their journeys to Nob Hill, Chinatown and Fisherman's Wharf at the corner of Powell Street and Market Street. Unlike the double-ended cable cars that are found on the California Street line, the Powell Street cable cars were built to move in one direction only – hence the need for a turntable at every terminus.

After the last passengers have disembarked, the car is pushed onto the turntable and rotated manually by the conductor and gripman. The next passengers for the return journey wait for the half-circle to be completed amid an ever-moving procession of street musicians, local shoppers and office workers.

San Francisco Center ㉓

Market St and Powell St. **Map** 5 C5. (415) 495-5656. 5, 7, 8, 9, 14, 21, 71. J, K, L, M, N. Powell–Mason, Powell–Hyde. 9:30am–8pm Mon–Sat, 11am–6pm Sun. See **Shopping** pp376–9.

SHOPPERS ARE CARRIED upward on semi-spiral escalators through this vertical mall, with its nine floors of shops. It is topped by a retractable dome which is opened on fine days. The basement levels provide access to Powell Street Station. Nordstrom, a fashion store, occupies the top four levels. Entrances to Emporium, a department store renowned for its Classical rotunda, are on the lower floors.

Old United States Mint ㉔

Fifth St and Mission St. **Map** 5 C5. (415) 556-6704. 14, 14L, 26, 27. J, K, L, M, N. to the public.

SAN FRANCISCO'S Old Mint produced its last coins in 1937. It was built of granite in the Classical style by AB Mullet between 1869 and 1874, hence its nickname, the "Granite Lady". Its windows were fortified by iron shutters and its basement vaults impregnable. The building was one of the few to survive the 1906 earthquake (see pp48–9). From 1973 to 1994 the building housed a museum, but today it is considered to be seismically unsafe. Closed for an indefinite period, its future is now uncertain.

The impregnable "Granite Lady" Old Mint

Yerba Buena Gardens ⓮

THE CONSTRUCTION of the Moscone Center, San Francisco's largest venue for conventions, heralded the beginning of ambitious plans for Yerba Buena Gardens. New housing, hotels, museums, galleries, shops, restaurants and gardens have followed, rejuvenating a once depressed area. The development is far from complete, but it is already contributing to the city's cultural and economic life.

★ Center for the Arts Galleries
Galleries for the visual arts and a sculpture court feature displays of contemporary art.

Esplanade Gardens
Visitors can wander along the paths or relax on benches.

The Martin Luther King, Jr Memorial has words of peace in several languages.

★ Ansel Adams Center for Photography
Monolith: The Face of Half Dome *is one of many Ansel Adams works in a gallery devoted to the prolific photographer.*

STAR SIGHTS

★ Ansel Adams Center for Photography

★ Center for the Arts Galleries

★ San Francisco Museum of Modern Art

MOSCONE CENTER

Engineer TY Lin found an ingenious way to support the rooftop garden above this huge underground hall without a single interior column. The bases of the eight steel arches are linked, like an archer's bow strings, by cables under the floor. By tightening the cables, the arches exert enormous upward thrust.

Center for the Arts Theatre
Works reflecting the cultural diversity of San Francisco are presented in the 755-seat indoor theatre. There is also an outdoor stage with lawn seating for 3,000.

North entrance to Moscone Center

East Garden

★ **San Francisco Museum of Modern Art**
Orange Sweater (1955) by Elmer Bischoff is among the many modern works of art in this privately funded museum.

South entrance to Moscone Center

Moscone Ballroom is part of San Francisco's extensive convention facilities. It is available for large conferences and symposia.

The children's centre is equipped with facilities that will help to encourage imaginative play.

Ice skating rink

Entrance foyer — **Ballroom** — **Exhibition hall** — **Ground-level rooftop** — **Base of supporting arch**

CHINATOWN AND NOB HILL

THE CHINESE settled in the plaza on Stockton Street during the 1850s; the steep hills had made the area unpopular among wealthier San Franciscans. Today the district recalls the atmosphere of a typical southern Chinese town, although the architecture, customs and public events are distinctly American hybrids on a Cantonese theme. This densely populated neighbourhood has been called the "Gilded Ghetto", because its colourful façades and teeming markets screen a much

Chinese symbol outside the Bank of America

harsher world of sweatshops, cramped living quarters and poor inhabitants.
Nob Hill is San Francisco's most celebrated hilltop, famous for its cable cars, plush hotels and views. In the late 19th century, the "Big Four", who built the first transcontinental railroad, were among its richest tenants, in their large mansions on the hill. In 1906, the earthquake and fire *(see pp48–9)* levelled all but one of these, but today's luxury hotels still recall the opulence of the Victorian era *(see p523)*.

SIGHTS AT A GLANCE

Historic Streets and Buildings
Chinatown Alleys **5**
Chinatown Gateway **1**
Grant Avenue **6**
Nob Hill **10**

Galleries and Museums
Cable Car Barn **11**
Chinese Historical Society **9**
Pacific Heritage Museum **8**

Churches and Temples
Grace Cathedral **12**
Kong Chow Temple **3**
Old St Mary's Church **2**
Tin How Temple **4**

Parks and Squares
Portsmouth Plaza **7**

KEY

Street-by-Street map
See pp316–17

Cable car turntable

P Parking

0 metres   500
0 yards   500

GETTING THERE

Visit on foot if possible. Car drivers can sometimes park in one of the Nob Hill hotel garages, or under Portsmouth Plaza or at St Mary's Square in Chinatown. All cable car lines go to Nob Hill and Chinatown.

◁ **Colourful oriental architecture along Chinatown's streets**

Street-by-Street: Chinatown

GRANT AVENUE is the Chinatown for tourists, with dragon lampposts, up-turned roofs and neighbourhood hardware stores selling everything from kites to cooking utensils. Locals shop on Stockton Street, where boxes of the freshest vegetables, fish and other produce spill over onto crowded pavements. In the alleys in between, look for temples, laundries and family-run restaurants.

A street lamp in Chinatown

★ **Chinatown Alleys**
Authentic sights and sounds of the Orient echo in these busy alleys ❺

Ross Alley

JACKSON STREET

To bus no. 83

WASHINGTON STREET

The Fortune Cookie Factory
welcomes visitors to its tiny premises, to see how the famous San Francisco creation, the fortune cookie, is made (see pp378–9).

Kong Chow Temple
Fine Cantonese wood carvings are a feature of this temple ❸

POWELL STREET

SACRAMENTO STREET

GRANT

Tin How Temple
This was founded in 1852 by Chinese people grateful for their safe arrival in San Francisco ❹

CALIFORNIA STREET

The Bank of Canton was home to Chinatown's telephone exchange until 1946. The operators spoke five Chinese dialects.

STOCKTON STR

Cable Cars run down two sides of Chinatown and are an essential part of the area's bustling atmosphere. Any of the three lines will take you there.

BUSH STR

0 metres   100

0 yards   100

STAR SIGHTS

★ Chinatown Alleys

★ Chinatown Gateway

★ Grant Avenue

Portsmouth Plaza
Laid out in 1839, this was the social centre for the village of Yerba Buena. Today it is a gathering place for players of cards and mahjong ❼

★ Grant Avenue
In the 1830s and early 1840s this was the main thoroughfare of Yerba Buena. It is now the busy commercial centre of Chinatown ❻

FISHERMAN'S WHARF
AND NORTH BEACH

CHINATOWN
AND NOB HILL

PACIFIC HEIGHTS
AND THE CIVIC
CENTER

DOWNTOWN

LOCATOR MAP
See Street Finder, map 5

KEY

– – – Suggested route

The Chinese Cultural Center
contains an art gallery and a small crafts shop. It sponsors a lively programme of lectures and seminars.

Chinese Historical Society
The society's collection of historical artifacts, documents and photographs is exhibited here ❾

Pacific Heritage Museum
Housed in an elegant building below the Bank of Canton, this small museum has fine exhibitions of Asian art, which are regularly changed ❽

KEARNY STREET

CLAY STREET

Old St Mary's Church
The clock tower of this church, built while the city was still in its infancy, bears an arresting inscription ❷

SON.OBSERVE THE TIME
AND FLY FROM EVIL. ECC.IV.23.

PINE STREET

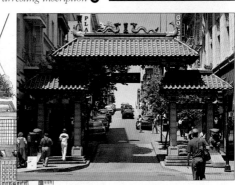

St Mary's Square is a quiet haven in which to rest.

To bus nos.
31, 38

★ Chinatown Gateway
Also known as the "Dragons' Gate", this marks Chinatown's south entrance ❶

Chinatown Gateway ❶

Grant Ave at Bush St. **Map** 5 C4.
🚌 *2, 3, 4, 15, 30, 45.*

THIS ORNATE PORTAL, opened in 1970, was designed by Clayton Lee as an arch over the entrance to Chinatown's main tourist street, Grant Avenue. It was inspired by the ceremonial entrances of traditional Chinese villages. The three-arched gateway is capped with green roof tiles and a host of propitiatory animals, all of glazed ceramic. The gate was erected by an American institution, the Chinatown Cultural Development Committee. The materials were donated by Taiwan (Republic of China).

It is guarded by two stone lions which are suckling their cubs through their claws, in accordance with ancient laws. Once through the gate, visitors can buy antiques, embroidered silks and gems, though prices are aimed at tourists.

Stone lions decorating the Chinatown gateway

Old St Mary's Church ❷

660 California St. **Map** 5 C4.
📞 *(415) 288–3800.* 🚌 *1, 15, 30, 45.* 🚊 *California St.* **Concerts** *12:30pm Tue, Thu.* 🚻

SAN FRANCISCO's first Catholic cathedral, Old St Mary's, was consecrated on Christmas Day 1854 as the seat of the Roman Catholic bishop of the Pacific Coast. Until 1891 it served a largely Irish congregation, when the new St Mary's Cathedral was built on Van Ness Avenue. Because of the unavailability of the right building materials in California, the bricks and iron for the church were imported from the East Coast, while the granite foundation stones came from China. The clock tower of the church bears a large inscription, "Son, observe the time and fly from evil", said to have been directed at the brothels that stood across the street at the time it was built. It was one of the few buildings to remain unharmed by the 1906 earthquake and retains its original foundations and walls. The interior, with stained-glass windows and a balcony, was completed in 1909.

Entrance to Old St Mary's Church below the clock tower and its inscription

Kong Chow Temple ❸

4th floor, 855 Stockton St. **Map** 5 B4.
📞 *(415) 434-2513.* 🚌 *30, 45.* ⭕ *10am– 4pm daily.* **Donation**. ♿

FROM THE TOP FLOOR above the district's post office, the Kong Chow Temple looks out over Chinatown and the Financial District. Although the building itself dates from only 1977, the temple altar and statuary are thought to form the oldest Chinese religious shrine in the United States. One altar was hand-carved in Guangzhou (Canton), and shipped to San Francisco in the 19th century. The main shrine is presided over by a carved wooden statue of Kuan Di, also dating from the 19th century. He is the deity most often found in shrines in Cantonese cities.

Kuan Di is also frequently seen in the city's Chinatown

Carved statue of Kuan Di inside the Kong Chow Temple

district: his highly distinctive face looks down from Taoist shrines in many of the area's restaurants. He is typically depicted holding a large sword in one hand and a book in the other. These are symbols of his unswerving dedication to both the martial and the literary arts.

Tin How Temple **4**

Top floor, 125 Waverly Pl. **Map** 5 C3. 🚌 *1, 15, 30, 45.* 🕐 *10am–5pm daily.* **Donation**.

THIS UNUSUAL temple is dedicated to Tin How (Tien Hau), the Queen of Heaven and protector of seafarers and visitors, and is the oldest operating Chinese temple in the United States. The sanctuary was originally founded in 1852 by a group of Chinese sailors, in gratitude for their safe voyage across the Pacific Ocean from their homeland to San Francisco. The temple is now situated at the top of three steep, wooden flights of stairs, which are considered to place it closer to heaven. The narrow space is filled with the smoke from both incense and burnt paper offerings, and is brightly decorated with hundreds of gold and red lanterns. It is lit by red electric light bulbs and burning wicks floating in oil. Gifts of fruit lie on the carved altar in front of the wooden statue of the temple's namesake deity.

A view along Chinatown's main street, Grant Avenue

The impressive façade of the Tin How Temple on Waverly Place

Chinatown Alleys **5**

Map 5 B3. 🚌 *1, 30, 45.*

CONTAINED WITHIN a busy neighbourhood, the Chinatown Alleys are situated between Grant Avenue and Stockton Street. These four narrow lanes intersect at Washington Street within half a block of each other. Of these, the largest is Waverly Place, known as the "Street of Painted Balconies" for reasons that are apparent to every passer-by. Its other nickname, "15 Cents Street", derives from the cost of a haircut by the Chinese barbers trading here at the turn of the century. Nearby, Sun Yat Sen spent many years in exile at No. 36 Spofford Alley.

The alleys contain many old buildings, as well as traditional shops and restaurants. There are also atmospheric, old-fashioned herbalist shops, displaying elk antlers, sea horses, snake wine and other exotic wares in their windows. Numerous small restaurants, above and below street level, serve cheap and delicious home-cooked food.

Grant Avenue **6**

Map 5 C4. 🚌 *1, 30, 45.* 🚋 *California St.*

GRANT AVENUE is historically important for being the first street of Yerba Buena, the village that preceded San Francisco. A plaque at No. 823 marks the site of the first dwelling, a canvas tent which was erected on 25 June 1835. By 1836 the tent was replaced with a wooden structure, and by 1837 with an adobe house. The street was then named Calle de la Fundacíon, the "Street of the Foundation".

An estimated 25,000 Chinese arrived in San Francisco during the Gold Rush era *(see pp44–5)*. They settled in this area on the undesirable lower east slopes of Nob Hill, which were too steep for horse-drawn carriages. In 1885 the street was renamed Grant Avenue, in memory of Ulysses S Grant, the US president who died that year.

Most of the buildings on Grant Avenue were built after the 1906 earthquake in an Oriental Renaissance style. They now form the main tourist street in Chinatown.

Portsmouth Plaza, at the hub of Chinatown life

Portsmouth Plaza ❼

Map 5 C3. 🚌 *1, 15.*

SAN FRANCISCO'S original town square was laid out in 1839. It was once the social centre for the village of Yerba Buena. On 9 July 1846, just after US rebels in Sonoma had declared California's independence from Mexico *(see pp448–9)*, marines raised the American flag above the plaza, officially seizing the port as part of the United States. Two years later, Sam Brannan announced the discovery of gold in the Sierra Nevada Mountains *(see pp44–5)* here. In the 1850s the area was the hub of this new dynamic city, but in the 1860s the business district shifted to flatlands reclaimed from the bay and the plaza declined in civic importance.

Today Portsmouth Plaza is the social centre of Chinatown. In the morning people practise *t'ai chi*, and from noon to evening gather to play cards.

Pacific Heritage Museum ❽

608 Commercial St. **Map** 5 C3. 📞 *(415) 62-4100.* 🚌 *1, 15.* 🕙 *10am–4pm Mon–Fri, except public hols.* ♿

THE MUSEUM BUILDING is as elegant as the changing collections of Asian arts displayed inside. It is a synthesis of two buildings. The US Sub-Treasury was erected here in 1875–77 by William Appleton Potter, on the site of the city's first mint. Old coin vaults can still be seen in the basement.

In 1984 the 17-storey Bank of Canton headquarters were built above the Treasury, incorporating the old façade and basement. The result is a venue of great refinement.

Chinese Historical Society ❾

650 Commercial St. **Map** 5 C3. 📞 *(415) 391-1188.* 🚌 *1, 15.* 🕙 *Tue & Thu 10am–2pm.* 📷

AMONG THE EXOTIC exhibits in this cluttered basement museum are a ceremonial dragon costume and a "tiger fork". This triton was wielded in one of the battles during the reign of terror known as the Tong Wars. The tongs were rival Chinese clans who fought over the control of gambling and prostitution in the city in the late 19th century. Other objects, documents and photographs illuminate the daily life of Chinese immigrants in San Francisco. There is a yearbook of the neighbourhood written in Chinese, as well as the original Chinatown telephone directory, written by hand.

The contribution of the Chinese to California's development was extensive despite the antagonism and poor treatment they were met with, as the many museum displays make clear. Chinese workers made the perilous voyage to California in their thousands to find gold and escape the economic difficulties of their homeland. Rich merchants used them as cheap labour in the gold mines, and later they were used to build the western half of the transcontinental railroad *(see pp46–7)*. They also constructed dykes in the Sacramento River delta, were great pioneers in the fishing industry and planted the first vines in many of California's early vineyards.

Dragon's head in the Historical Society

Nob Hill ❿

Map 5 B4.

NOB HILL is the highest summit of the city centre, rising 338 ft (103 m) above the bay. Its steep slopes kept prominent citizens away until the opening of the California Street cable car line in 1878. The rich then flocked to build homes here, including the "Big Four" railroad barons *(see pp456–7)*. Its name is thought to come from the Hindi word *nabob*, meaning millionaire. Sadly, all the mansions were burned down in the fire of 1906 *(see pp48–9)*, except the home of James C Flood, now the Pacific Union Club.

Nob Hill still attracts the affluent to its splendid hotels, which benefit from spectacular views of the city.

A panoramic view of the city from a penthouse bar on Nob Hill

Cable Car Barn ⓫

1201 Mason St. **Map** 5 B3. 📞 *(415)*
474-1887. 🚋 *1.* 🚋 *Powell-Mason,*
Powell-Hyde. 🕙 *10am–6pm daily*
(10am–5pm in winter). 🔴 *1 Jan,*
Thanksgiving, 25 Dec. 👵 *mezzanine*
only. **Video show.** 📷

THIS IS BOTH a museum and
the powerhouse of the
cable car system *(see pp292–
3)*. Anchored to the ground
floor are the engines and
wheels that wind the cables
through the system of channels and pulleys beneath the
city's streets. You can observe
them from the mezzanine, then
walk downstairs to see under
the street. The museum also
houses an early cable car and
specimens of the mechanisms
that control the movements of
individual cars. The cable car
system is the last of its kind
in the world. The brick building was constructed in 1909.

**The entrance to the Cable Car
Barn Museum**

Grace Cathedral ⓬

1100 California St. **Map** 5 B4. 📞
(415) 749-6300. 🚋 *1.* 🚋 *California*
St. ⛪ *Choral evensong 5:15pm Thu,*
Sun 3:30pm; Choral Eucharist 7:30am,
8:30am, 11am Sun. 👵 📷 *12:30–*
2pm Sun; 1–3pm Mon–Fri; 11:30am–
1:30pm Sat. 📷

GRACE CATHEDRAL is the main
Episcopalian church in
San Francisco. It was designed
by Lewis P Hobart. Prepara-
tory work began in February
1927 and building started in
September 1928, but the
cathedral was not completed
until 1964. Despite its modern
construction, the building
is inspired by Notre
Dame in Paris, using
traditional materials.
The interior is
replete with marble,
and its leaded win-
dows were design-
ed by Charles
Connick, using the
blue glass of
Chartres as his
inspiration. The
rose window is
made using 1-
inch (2.5-cm)
thick faceted
glass, which is
illuminated

**Cast figure from
the main
entrance**

from inside the building
at night. Other windows
were executed by Henry
Willet and Gabriel Loire.
These include depic-
tions of modern
heroes such as Albert
Einstein and astronaut
John Glenn. Objects in
the cathedral include a
13th-century Catalonian
crucifix and a 16th-
century Brussels
tapestry. The entrance
doors are cast from
moulds of Ghiberti's
"Doors of Paradise",
made for the Bap-
tistry in Florence.

The New Testament Window,
made in 1931 by Charles
Connick, is placed
on the south
side of the
church.

The Rose Window
was made in Chartres by
Gabriel Loire in 1964.

The Carillon Tower
houses 44 bells made
in England in 1938.

**The Chapel of
Grace**, funded by
the Crocker family,
has a 15th-century
French altarpiece.

**The Doors of
Paradise** are decorated
with scenes from the bible
and portraits of Ghiberti
and contemporaries.

Entrances

FISHERMAN'S WHARF
AND NORTH BEACH

ISHERMEN FROM Genoa and Sicily first arrived in the Fisherman's Wharf area in the late 19th century and founded the San Francisco fishing industry. The district has slowly given way to tourism since the 1950s, but brightly painted boats still set out from the harbour on fishing trips early each morning. To the south of

Fisherman's Wharf entrance sign

Fisherman's Wharf lies North Beach, sometimes known as "Little Italy". This lively part of the city has an abundance of delis, bakeries and cafés, from which you can watch the crowds. It is home to many Italian and Chinese families, with a sprinkling of writers and bohemians; Jack Kerouac (*see pp22–3*), among others, found inspiration here.

SIGHTS AT A GLANCE

Museums and Galleries
North Beach Museum **13**
Ripley's Believe It Or Not!
  Museum **5**
San Francisco Art Institute **10**
San Francisco National
  Maritime Museum **8**
USS Pampanito **3**
Wax Museum **4**

Historic Streets and Buildings
Alcatraz Island pp328–9 **1**
Lombard Street **9**
Pier 39 **2**
Vallejo Street Stairway **11**

Shopping Centres
The Cannery **6**
Ghirardelli Square **7**

Restaurants and Bars
Club Fugazi **12**

Parks and Gardens
Levi's Plaza **17**
Telegraph Hill **16**
Washington Square **14**

Churches
Saints Peter and
  Paul Church **15**

KEY

▨	Street-by-Street map *See pp324–5*
🚋	Cable car turntable
⛴	Ferry terminal
P	Parking

0 metres   500
0 yards   500

GETTING THERE

The Powell–Hyde cable car line goes to Ghirardelli Square and Russian Hill. The Powell–Mason line passes through North Beach, to Fisherman's Wharf and Pier 39. Many buses run through the district.

◁ **View of Fisherman's Wharf and Alcatraz Island from the Powell–Hyde cable car**

Street-by-Street: Fisherman's Wharf

ITALIAN SEAFOOD restaurants have now replaced fishing as the primary focus of the Fisherman's Wharf local economy. Both the expensive restaurants and the cheap outdoor crab pots serve San Francisco's celebrated Dungeness crab, in season from November to June. As well as sampling the seafood, visitors also enjoy taking in the many shops, museums and other attractions for which Fisherman's Wharf is noted.

★ **USS Pampanito**
A tour gives an idea of the hardships endured by sailors in this World War II submarine ❸

Fisherman's and Seaman's Chapel

Fisherman's Wharf is now a street lined with seafood restaurants.

Fish Alley is where the morning's catch is landed and prepared.

The Museum of the City of San Francisco is a new museum showcasing exhibits on San Francisco's colourful past.

TAYLOR STREET

JEFFERSON

JONES STREET

LEAVENWORTH STREET

To Powell–Hyde cable car turntable (1 block)

The Cannery
Once a fruit cannery, the building was converted to a mall, housing fine shops, restaurants and a museum ❻

Sea lions basking on
Pier 39's docks delight
tourists, but are a pest
for boat owners. They
arrive here in January.

0 metres   100
0 yards   100

San Francisco Bay

FISHERMAN'S WHARF
AND NORTH BEACH

CHINATOWN
AND NOB HILL

DOWNTOWN

LOCATOR MAP
See Street Finder, map 5

Wax Museum
*Almost 300 life-size
wax figures of past
and present-day
personalities greet
visitors to this
museum* ❹

**Red and White Fleet
and Alcatraz ferry
tickets** (*p383*)

**Blue and Gold
Fleet ferry
tickets** (*p383*)

EMBARCADERO

POWELL STREET

MASON STREET

REET

Bus stop
(No. 32)

Boudin Sourdough Bakery
produces the tangy bread which
is famous in San Francisco.
You can buy it fresh here.

Ripley's
Believe It or Not!®

Ripley's Believe It Or Not! Museum
*This is a selection of the cartoonist's strange
collection of curiosities and odd facts* ❺

★ **Pier 39**
*A collection of restaurants, shops and
amusements, set against a backdrop of
spectacular bay views, is one of the city's
major tourist attractions* ❷

STAR SIGHTS
★ **Pier 39**
★ **USS Pampanito**

KEY

– – – Suggested route

Alcatraz Island ❶

See pp328–9.

Pier 39 ❷

Map 5 B1. 🚌 *32, 25, 42.*
See **Shopping** pp376–9.

Refurbished in 1978 to resemble a quaint wooden fishing village, this 1905 cargo pier now houses many tourist shops and speciality stores spread over two levels.

The pier's street performers and amusements are popular and appealing, particularly to families with children. You can ride on the two-storey carousel, or brave the Turbo Ride, a roller-coaster simulator where a film gives the illusion of speed and danger.

A sensational multimedia show called the San Francisco Experience takes visitors through a whirlwind historical tour of the city, complete with Chinese New Year celebrations and an earthquake.

USS *Pampanito*'s torpedo room

USS Pampanito ❸

Pier 45. **Map** 4 F1. 📞 *(415) 441-8519.* 🚌 *32.* 🕐 *May–Oct: 9am–9pm daily; Nov–Apr: 9am–6pm daily.* ♿ 🎧

This World War II submarine fought in, and survived, several bloody battles in the Pacific, sinking six enemy ships and severely damaging others. Tragically for the allies, two of its fatal targets were carrying British and Australian prisoners of war. The *Pampanito* managed to rescue 73 men, however, and carry them to safety in the United States. A tour of the ship takes visitors from stern to bow and includes visits to the torpedo room, the claustrophobic galley and officers' quarters. In the days when the USS *Pampanito* was in service, it had a crew of ten officers who were in command of 70 enlisted seamen.

Wax Museum ❹

145 Jefferson St. **Map** 5 B1. 📞 *(800) 439-4305.* 🚌 *32.* 🕐 *9am–10:30pm Sun–Thu, 9am–midnight Fri–Sat.* ♿ *limited.*

One of the world's largest and most absorbing collections of life-size wax figures is displayed here. The ancient tomb of Egyptian King Tutankhamun is re-created in one special exhibit, while a tableau of the Last Supper dominates the Hall of Religions. In the Hall of Living Art, portraits such as the Mona Lisa are rendered in wax. A host of fictional characters rubs shoulders with historical luminaries, including 14 US presidents, members of the British Royal Family, Sir Winston Churchill, William Shakespeare, Mozart, Mark Twain, Elvis Presley, Marilyn Monroe and Al Capone.

A gruesome assortment of terrifying ghouls, mythical monsters and infamous murderers occupy the compelling Chamber of Horrors.

Ripley's Believe It Or Not! Museum ❺

175 Jefferson St. **Map** 4 F1. 📞 *(415) 771-6188.* 🚌 *32.* 🕐 *Sep–Jun: 10am–10pm Sun–Thu, 10am–midnight, Fri–Sat; Jul–Aug: 9am–11pm Sun–Thu, 9am–midnight Fri–Sat.* 🎧 ♿

Californian native Robert L Ripley, an illustrator who collected peculiar facts and artifacts, earned fame from syndicating his celebrated US newspaper cartoon strip, "Ripley's Believe It Or Not!". Among the 350 oddities on display are a cable car built of 275,000 matchsticks, a two-headed calf, tombstones with wry epithets, and a life-size replica of a man with two pupils in each eyeball.

The two-storey Venetian Carousel on Pier 39

The Cannery **6**

2801 Leavenworth St. **Map** 4 F1.
19, 30, 32, 42. Powell–Hyde.
Museum 11am–4pm Wed–Sun.
See **Shopping** pp376–9.

Tʜᴇ ɪɴᴛᴇʀɪᴏʀ of this 1909 fruit-canning plant was redeveloped in the 1960s. It now incorporates footbridges, rambling passages and sunny courtyards, with restaurants and shops selling clothing, collector dolls and Native American arts and crafts.

The Cannery also houses the Museum of the City of San Francisco. This museum is new and still depends on exhibits borrowed from other museums to bolster its growing collection of historical artifacts. Among these is the head of the old statue that capped City Hall before its destruction in the 1906 earthquake *(see pp48–9)*. The crown on the head is an interesting example of early electric illumination.

Ghirardelli Square

Ghirardelli Square **7**

900 North Point St. **Map** 4 F1.
19, 30, 32, 42, 47, 49.
Powell–Hyde. See **Shopping** pp376–9.

Tʜɪs ꜰᴏʀᴍᴇʀ chocolate factory and woollen mill is the most attractive of the city's many refurbished sites, with elegant shops and restaurants. The clock tower and roof sign from the original building still remain. The Ghirardelli Chocolate Manufactory on the plaza houses old chocolate-making machinery and sells the confection, but the chocolate bars are now made in San Leandro, across the bay.

Fountain Plaza is a colourful focal point for shoppers, day and evening.

San Francisco National Maritime Museum **8**

900 Beach St. **Map** 4 F1.
(415) 556-8177. **Hyde Street Pier** *556-3002.* *19, 30, 32, 42.* Powell–Hyde. *mid-May–mid-Sep: 10am–6pm daily; mid-Sep–mid-May: 9:30am–5pm daily.* pier only. pier and museum only.
Lectures, maritime demonstrations, activities.

Rᴇsᴇᴍʙʟɪɴɢ a beached ocean liner, this 1939 building first housed the Maritime Museum in 1951. On display is a collection of ship models, vintage nautical instruments, paintings and

Hyde Street Pier

photographs illustrating local nautical history. Moored at the nearby Hyde Street Pier is one of the world's largest collections of old ships.

Among the most spectacular is the *C.A. Thayer*, a three-masted schooner built in 1895. It carried lumber along the North California coast, and later was used as a fishing boat in Alaska. Also at the pier is the 2,320-tonne side-wheel ferry-boat, *Eureka*, built in 1890 to ferry trains between Hyde Street Pier and the counties north of San Francisco Bay. It carried 2,300 passengers and 120 cars, and was the largest passenger ferry of its day.

BALCLUTHA
This ship is the star of Hyde Street Pier. Launched in 1886, she sailed twice a year between Britain and California, trading wheat for coal.

Mainmast

Mizzenmast

Foremast

Quarterdeck

Bowsprit

Alcatraz Island ❶

ALCATRAZ MEANS "pelican" in Spanish and refers to the first inhabitants of this rocky, steep-sided island. Lying 3 miles (5 km) east of the Golden Gate, its location is both strategic and exposed to ocean winds. In 1859, the US army established a fort here that guarded San Francisco Bay until 1907, when it became a military prison. From 1934 to 1963, it served as a maximum-security Federal Penitentiary. In 1969 the island was seized by members of the Native American Movement (see p52) claiming it as their land. They were expelled in 1971, and Alcatraz is now part of the Golden Gate National Recreation Area.

Badge on entrance to cellhouse

★ Cell Block
The cell house contains four cell blocks. No cell has an outside wall or ceiling. The dungeon-like foundation of the prison block shares the original foundation of the old military fortress.

Alcatraz Island from the Ferry
"The Rock" has no natural soil. Earth was shipped from Angel Island to make garden plots for prison guards.

The officers' apartments stood here.

Military parade ground

Barracks buildings

| 0 metres | 75 |
| 0 yards | 75 |

KEY

– – – Suggested route

STAR SIGHTS

★ Cell Block

★ Exercise Yard

The Warden's House was fire damaged during the 1969–71 siege.

Alcatraz Jetty
Prisoners took their first steps ashore here; no other wharf served the steep-sided island. Now visitors alight at this pier.

★ **Exercise Yard**
Meals and a walk around the exercise yard were the highlights of a prisoner's day. The walled yard featured in films made at the prison.

VISITORS' CHECKLIST

Map 6 F1. ☎ *(415) 546-2700.*
🚢 *from Pier 41.* ⏰ *daily from first ferry to last: Mon–Fri: first ferry 9:30am, last ferry 2:45pm; Sat, Sun & public hols: first ferry 9:30am, last ferry 2:15pm.*
⊘ *1 Jan, Thanksgiving, 25 Dec.*
📷 ♿ *in places, but difficult.*
🎫 🎥 *obligatory.*

Metal detectors checked prisoners when they passed to and from the dining hall and exercise yards.

The Military Morgue is tiny and cramped, and is not open to the public.

Water tower

Prison workshops

The Visitors' Center is in the old barracks.

The Military Chapel was built in 1933.

The Post Exchange, dating from the days of Fort Alcatraz, was a military store which also served as the officers' club.

FAMOUS INMATES

Al Capone
The Prohibition gangster, "Scarface" Capone was actually convicted in 1934 for income tax evasion! He spent much of his five-year sentence on Alcatraz in an isolation cell, and left the prison mentally unstable.

Robert Stroud
The original *"Birdman of Alcatraz"* spent the majority of his 17 years on The Rock in solitary confinement.

Carnes, Thompson and Shockley
In May 1946, prisoners led by Clarence Carnes, Marion Thompson and Sam Shockley overpowered guards and captured their guns. The prisoners failed to break out of the cell house, but three inmates and two officers were killed in what became known as the "Battle of Alcatraz". Carnes received

an additional life sentence. Shockley and Thompson were executed at San Quentin prison for their part in the insurrection.

Anglin Brothers
John and Clarence Anglin, together with Frank Morris, chipped through the walls of their cells, and hid the holes with cardboard grates. Leaving dummy heads in their beds, they made a raft to enable their escape and were never caught. Their story was dramatized in the film *Escape from Alcatraz* (1979).

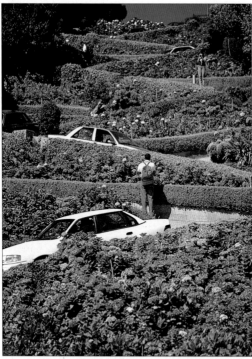

Cars negotiating the steep and crooked section of Lombard Street

Lombard Street ❾

Map 5 A2. 🚌 45. 🚋 Powell–Hyde.

BANKED AT a natural incline of 27°, this hill proved too steep for vehicles to climb. In the 1920s the section of Lombard Street close to the summit of Russian Hill was revamped, and the severity of its gradient was lessened by the addition of eight curves.

Today it is known as "the crookedest street in the world." Cars can travel downhill only at a speed of 5 miles per hour (8 km/h), while pedestrians use steps. There are spectacular views of San Francisco from the summit.

San Francisco Art Institute ❿

800 Chestnut St. **Map** 4 F2. 🇨 (415) 771-7020. 🚌 30. **Diego Rivera Gallery** ◯ 9am–5pm daily. ● public hols. ♿ partial. 🔲 🔲

SAN FRANCISCO'S Art Institute dates from 1871 and once occupied the immense

A 30-Minute Walk through North Beach

SETTLERS ORIGINALLY FROM CHILE, and more recently Italy, have brought their enthusiasm for nightlife to North Beach, earning this quarter its vibrant reputation. Its café-oriented atmosphere has long appealed to bohemians, particularly the 1950s Beat Generation *(see pp22–3)*.

The Beat Neighbourhood

Start the walk from the southwest corner of Broadway and Columbus Avenue at City Lights Bookstore ①. Owned by Beat poet Lawrence Ferlinghetti, City Lights was the first bookshop in the US to sell only paperbacks. The author Jack Kerouac, a friend of Ferlinghetti, coined the word "Beat", later referred to as "Beatnik".

One of the most popular Beat bars was Vesuvio ②, south of City Lights, across Jack Kerouac Alley. Welsh poet Dylan Thomas was a patron here, and it is still a favourite with

Jack Kerouac

poets and artists. From here travel south to Pacific Avenue, cross to the opposite side of Columbus Avenue and walk back towards Broadway, stopping at Tosca ③. The walls of this bar and café display murals of Tuscany, and a jukebox plays selections from Italian opera. A few steps north bring you to Adler Alley. Specs ④, a lively bar filled with memorabilia of the Beat era, is at No. 12. Walking back to Columbus Avenue, turn right into Broadway and at the corner of Kearny Street cross over to Enrico's Sidewalk Café ⑤.

Columbus Café ⑪

The Strip

Enrico's celebrated outdoor café is the best place from which to watch the action on this stretch of Broadway, called The Strip ⑥, noted for its "adult entertainment". At the junction of Broadway and Grant Avenue is the former Condor Club ⑦, where the world's first topless stage show was performed in June 1964.

wooden mansion built for the family of railroad baron Mark Hopkins on Nob Hill *(see p320)*, which burned down in the fire of 1906 *(see pp48–9)*. Its students today are housed in a Spanish Colonial-style building which was constructed in 1926, complete with cloisters, a courtyard fountain and bell tower. A modern extension was added at the rear of the building in 1969. The Diego Rivera Gallery, named after the famous Mexican muralist *(see pp296–7)*, can be found to the left of the main entrance.

The Institute holds temporary exhibitions of works by its young artists.

Diego Rivera's *Making of a Mural* (1931), San Francisco Art Institute

Vallejo Street Stairway ⓫

Mason St and Jones St. **Map** 5 B3. 🚌 *30, 45.* 🚋 *Powell–Mason.*

THE STEEP CLIMB from Little Italy to the summit of Russian Hill reveals some of the best views of Telegraph Hill, North Beach and the bay. The street gives way to steps at Mason Street, which climb up through Ina Coolbrith Park.

Above Taylor Street, there are lanes, with several Victorian houses *(see pp290–291)*. At the crest of the hill is one of the rare parts of the city not destroyed in the earthquake of 1906 *(see pp48–9)*.

Club Fugazi ⓬

678 Green St. **Map** 5 B3. 🅒 *(415) 421-4222.* 🚌 *15, 30, 45.* 🕐 *Wed–Sun. See* **Entertainment** *pp372–5.*

BUILT IN 1912 as a North Beach community hall, the Club Fugazi is the venue for the musical cabaret *Beach*

Blanket Babylon. This is a lively show that has been running for more than two decades and has become an institution among San Franciscans. It is popular with locals and tourists alike, and is famous for its topical and outrageous songs, and for the bizarre hats often worn by the performers.

North Beach Museum ⓭

1435 Stockton St. **Map** 5 B3. 🅒 *(415) 626-7070.* 🚌 *15, 30, 45.* 🕐 *9am–4pm Mon–Thu, 9am–6pm Fri.* 🕐 *public hols.*

THIS SMALL MUSEUM, on the second floor of the Eureka Bank, documents the history of North Beach and Chinatown through exhibitions of old photographs. These celebrate the heritage of the Chilean, Irish, Italian and Chinese immigrants who have arrived in the area since the 19th century. Other photographs illustrate the bohemian community of North Beach.

Upper Grant Avenue
Turn right into Grant Avenue where you will find The Saloon ⑧ with its original 1861 bar. On the corner of Vallejo Street is Caffè Trieste ⑨, the oldest coffee house in San Francisco, and a

genuine Beat rendezvous since 1956. Very much a part of Italian-American culture, it offers live opera on Saturday afternoons. Follow Grant Avenue north past the Lost and Found Saloon ⑩, now a blues club but formerly the Coffee Gallery, another of the Beat haunts. Turn left at Green Street and look for Columbus Café ⑪, whose exterior

Vesuvio, a popular Beat bar ②

walls are decorated with attractive murals. Turning left again at Columbus Avenue, follow this main street of North Beach south past many more Italian coffee houses, to return to your starting point.

TIPS FOR WALKERS

Starting point: *Corner of Broadway and Columbus Avenue.*
Length: *1 mile (1.6 km).*
Getting there: *Muni bus No. 15 runs along Columbus Avenue.*
Stopping-off points: *All the bars and cafés mentioned are worth visiting for a drink and the atmosphere. Children are not usually allowed in bars.*

KEY

••• Walk route

0 metres 200
0 yards 200

The façade of Saints Peter and Paul Church, Washington Square

Washington Square @

Map 5 B2. 🚌 *15, 30, 39, 45.*

Tᴀᴇ sQUARE cONSISTS of a simple expanse of lawn, surrounded by benches and trees, set against the twin towers of Saints Peter and Paul Church. It has an almost Mediterranean atmosphere, appropriate for the "town square" of Little Italy. Near the centre of the square stands a statue of Benjamin Franklin. A time capsule was buried under the statue in 1979 and is scheduled to be reopened in 2079. It is said to contain some Levi's jeans, a bottle of wine and a poem written by Lawrence Ferlinghetti, one of San Francisco's famous beat poets *(see pp22–3).*

Saints Peter and Paul Church @

666 Filbert St. **Map** 5 B2. 📞 *(415) 421-0809.* 🚌 *15, 30, 39, 45.* 🕇 *Italian mass and choir 11:30am Sun; phone for other masses.* 🛦

Sᴛɪʟʟ ᴋɴᴏᴡɴ by many as the Italian Cathedral, this large church is situated at the heart of North Beach, and many Italians find it a welcome haven when they first arrive in San Francisco. It was here that the local baseball hero, Joe Di Maggio, was photographed after his marriage to the actress Marilyn Monroe in 1957, although the actual wedding ceremony was held elsewhere. The building, designed by Charles Fantoni, has an Italianesque façade, with a complex interior

notable for its many columns and ornate altar. There are also statues and mosaics illuminated by stained-glass windows. The concrete and steel structure of the church, with its twin spires rising over the surrounding rooftops, was completed in 1924.

Cecil B De Mille filmed the workers labouring on the foundations of Saints Peter and Paul, and used the scene to show the building of the Temple of Jerusalem in his film *The Ten Commandments,* made in 1923.

The church is sometimes referred to as the Fishermen's Church (many Italians once earned their living by fishing), and there is an annual mass and procession from Columbus Avenue to Fisherman's Wharf to celebrate the Blessing of the Fleet in October. Masses in the church can still be heard in Italian and Cantonese, as well as English.

Telegraph Hill @

Map 5 C2. **Coit Tower** Telegraph Hill Blvd. 📞 *(415) 362-0808.* 🚌 *39.* 🕙 *10am–6pm (7:30pm summer) daily.* 🎟 🛦 *murals only.* 📷

Oʀɪɢɪɴᴀʟʟʏ ᴄᴀʟʟᴇᴅ Alta Loma by the Mexicans, then Goat Hill after the animals that grazed on its slopes, Telegraph Hill was renamed in 1850 after the semaphore installed on its crest. This alerted the city's merchants to the arrival of ships through the Golden Gate. On the eastern side,

Coit Tower mural showing Fisherman's Wharf in the 1930s

Steps at the bottom of Filbert Street leading up to Telegraph Hill

which, until 1914, was regularly dynamited to provide rocks for landfill and paving, the hill falls away abruptly to form steep paths, bordered by leafy gardens.

The western side slopes more gradually into the area known as "Little Italy", around Washington Square, although in recent years the city's Italian population has begun to settle in the Marina District. In the past the hill has been a neighbourhood of immigrants living in wooden cabins, and of struggling artists, who appreciated the panoramic views. These days, however, the quaint pastel clapboard homes are much sought after and this is one of the city's prime residential areas.

Coit Tower was built in 1933 at the top of 284-ft (86-m) high Telegraph Hill, with funds left to the city by Lillie Hitchcock Coit, an eccentric San Franciscan pioneer and philanthropist. The 210-ft (64-m) reinforced concrete tower was designed as a fluted column by the architect Arthur Brown. When floodlit at night, its glow can be seen from most of the eastern half of the city. The encircling view around the North Bay Area from the observation platform (reached by a lift) is quite spectacular.

In the lobby of the tower are absorbing murals *(see pp296–7)*. These were sponsored in 1934 by a government-funded programme designed to keep artists in employment during the Great Depression. Twenty-five

artists worked together on the vivid portrait of life in modern California. Scenes range from the busy streets of the city's Financial District (with a robbery in progress) to factories, dockyards and the Central Valley wheat fields. There are a number of fascinating details – a car crash, a family of immigrants encamped by a river, newspaper headlines, magazine covers and book titles. There is a sense of frustration, satire and whimsy in the pictures. Various political themes also feature. Many of the faces in the paintings are those of the artists and their friends, along with local figures such as Colonel William Brady, the caretaker of Coit Tower. The work's political subject matter caused some public controversy, and delayed its official unveiling.

On the eastern side of Telegraph Hill the streets become steep steps. Descending from Telegraph Hill Boulevard,

Filbert Street is a rambling stairway, constructed of wood, brick and concrete, where rhododendron, fuschia, bougainvillea, fennel and blackberries thrive.

Levi's Plaza ⑰

Map 5 C2. 🚌 42.

THIS SQUARE is where the headquarters of Levi Strauss & Co., the manufacturers of blue jeans, can be found. The square was landscaped by Lawrence Halprin in 1982, with the intention of recalling the company's long history in the state. The plaza is studded with granite rocks and cut by flowing water, thus symbolizing the Sierra Nevada canyon scenery in which the miners who first wore the jeans worked. Telegraph Hill in the background adds a more natural mountainous element.

LEVI STRAUSS AND HIS JEANS

First manufactured in San Francisco in the days of the Gold Rush *(see pp44–5)*, denim jeans have had a great impact on popular culture. One of the leading producers of jeans is Levi Strauss & Co., founded in the city in the 1860s.

The company's story started in 1853, when Levi Strauss left New York to establish a dry goods business with his brother-in-law in San Francisco.

Levi Strauss

In the 1860s, though still primarily a seller of dry goods, he pioneered the use of a durable, brown, canvas-like material to make work-trousers, sold directly to miners. In the 1870s his company began to use metal rivets to strengthen the stress points in the garments, and demand increased. The company then expanded, and early in the 20th century moved to 250 Valencia Street in the Mission District, where it remains today both as a working clothing factory and as a museum.

Two miners sporting their Levis at the Last Chance Mine in 1882

Levi's jeans are now an institution, and are produced, sold and worn all over the world. The company that was first founded by Levi Strauss is still owned and managed by his descendants.

PACIFIC HEIGHTS AND THE CIVIC CENTER

P ACIFIC HEIGHTS is an exclusive neighbourhood, rising 300 ft (90 m) above the city. After cable cars linked it with the city centre in the 1880s, it quickly became a desirable place to live and many fine Victorian houses now line its streets. To the north of Broadway, the streets drop steeply down to the Marina District, with its smart shops, fashionable cafés and two prestigious yacht clubs. To the south of Pacific Heights is the Civic Center, which was built after the earthquake of 1906. It includes some of the best Beaux-Arts architecture in the city, and in 1987 the area was declared an historic site. The Civic Center is perhaps the most elegant city complex in the US.

Fort Mason logo

SIGHTS AT A GLANCE

Historic Streets and Buildings
Alamo Square ⓲
Bill Graham Civic
  Auditorium ⓯
City Hall ⓰
Cow Hollow ➒
Fort Mason ➐
Haas-Lilienthal House ➊
Octagon House ➓
Palace of Fine Arts and
  the Exploratorium ➎
San Francisco Main Library ⓮
Spreckels Mansion ➋
University of San Francisco ⓳

Shopping Areas
Chestnut Street ➑
Fillmore Street ⓫
Hayes Valley ⓱

Modern Architecture
Japan Center ⓬

Churches
St Mary's Cathedral ⓭

Parks and Gardens
Alta Plaza ➍
Lafayette Park ➌
Marina Green ➏

KEY

▨	Street-by-Street map *See pp336–7*
🚇	BART station
🚋	Cable car terminus
P	Parking

GETTING THERE

Muni buses 1 and 12, and the California Street cable car serve the Pacific Heights area. The Civic Center BART/Muni station on Market Street is two blocks east of City Hall. Buses 5, 8, 19 and 42 all travel into the Civic Center.

0 metres	500
0 yards	500

◁ **View from Alamo Square across the Civic Center towards the Financial District**

Street-by-Street: Pacific Heights

THE STEEP blocks between Alta Plaza and Lafayette Park are set in the heart of the exclusive Pacific Heights district. The streets here are quiet and tidy, lined with smart apartment blocks and palatial Victorian houses. Some of these date from the late 19th century, while others were built after the great earthquake and fire of 1906 *(see pp48–9)*. To the north of this area, the streets drop steeply down towards the residential Marina District, which offer outstanding views of San Francisco Bay. Wander through the two large landscaped parks and past the luxurious gardens of the private mansions in between, then visit one of the many fashionable bars, cafés and restaurants along Fillmore Street *(see pp565–6)*.

The Webster Street Row houses have been declared an historic landmark. They were built for a middle-class clientele in 1878 and have since been restored to their original splendour.

Washington Street lies to the east of Alta Plaza. Here the Victorian houses, built in various architectural styles, fill an entire block.

★ **Alta Plaza**
Set aside as a public park in the 1850s, this hilltop green space has a playground, tennis courts and spectacular views of San Francisco ❹

To bus no. 12

WEBSTER STREET

FILLMORE STREET

STEINER STREET

0 metres	100
0 yards	100

KEY

– – – Suggested route

STAR SIGHTS

★ Alta Plaza

★ Spreckels Mansion

Haas-Lilienthal House
Furnished in Victorian style, this mansion is the head-quarters of the Architectural Heritage Foundation ❶

LOCATOR MAP
See Street Finder maps 3, 4

To bus nos. 47, 76

No. 2151 Sacramento Street is an ornate French-style mansion. A plaque commemorates a visit by the author Sir Arthur Conan Doyle in 1923.

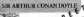

Mansions Hotel
(see p527)

Lafayette Park
This quiet park offers good views of the Victorian houses that surround it ❸

★ Spreckels Mansion
This impressive limestone building, constructed on the lines of a French Baroque palace, has been home to best-selling novelist Danielle Steele since 1990 ❷

No. 2004 Gough Street, one of the more elaborate Victorian houses in Pacific Heights, was built in 1889.

The Haas-Lilienthal House, a Queen Anne mansion from 1886

Haas-Lilienthal House **❶**

2007 Franklin St. **Map** 4 E3.
📞 *(415) 441-3004.* 🚍 *1, 19, 27, 42, 47, 49, 83.* ⏰ *noon–4pm Wed, 11am–5pm Sun.* 🎫 🏠

THIS ATTRACTIVE Queen Anne-style mansion *(see pp290–91)* was built in 1886 for the rich merchant William Haas. Alice Lilienthal, his daughter, lived here until 1972, when it was given to the Foundation for San Francisco's Architectural Heritage. It is the only intact private home of the period in San Francisco that is now open as a museum, and is complete with authentic furniture. A fine example of an upper-middle-class Victorian home, Haas-Lilienthal House has elaborate wooden gables, a circular corner tower and luxurious ornamentation.

A display of photographs in the basement describes the history of the building and reveals that this grandiose house was modest in comparison with some of the mansions destroyed in the great fire of 1906 *(see pp48–9).*

Spreckels Mansion **❷**

2080 Washington St. **Map** 4 E3.
🚍 *1, 47, 49.* ● *to the public.*

DOMINATING the north side of Lafayette Park, this imposing Beaux-Arts mansion is sometimes known as the "Parthenon of the West". It was built in 1912 for the flamboyant Alma de Bretteville Spreckels and her husband Adolph, heir to the sugar baron, Claus Spreckels. The house contains 26 bathrooms, and a large swimming pool in which Alma Spreckels swam daily until the age of 80. Her love of French architecture inspired the design. The architect of Spreckels mansion was George Applegarth, who in 1916 also designed the California Palace of the Legion of Honor in Lincoln Park *(see pp364–5).* The Palace was donated to the city by the Spreckels family in 1924.

Today Spreckels Mansion is privately owned. It occupies a block of Octavia Street, which is paved and landscaped in a similar style to curvy Lombard Street *(see p330).*

Façade of the impressive Spreckels Mansion

Lafayette Park **❸**

Map 4 E3. 🚍 *1, 12.*

ONE OF San Francisco's prettiest hilltop gardens, Lafayette Park is a leafy green haven of pine and eucalyptus trees, although its present tranquillity belies its turbulent history. Along with Alta Plaza and Alamo Square *(see p343),* the land was set aside in 1855 as a city-owned open space. Then squatters and others, including a former City Attorney, laid claim to the land and began to build their houses on it. The largest of these houses continued to stand at the centre of the hilltop park until 1936, the squatter who had built it refusing to move. It was finally demolished after the city authorities agreed to swap it for other land on nearby Gough Street. Steep stairways now lead to the summit of the park and its delightful views.

In the streets surrounding Lafayette Park there are a number of other palatial Victorian buildings. Particularly ornate examples are situated along Broadway, Jackson Street and Pacific Avenue going east-west, and Gough, Octavia and Laguna streets going north-south.

Alta Plaza **❹**

Map 4 D3. 🚍 *1, 3, 12, 22, 24.*

SITUATED IN the centre of Pacific Heights, Alta Plaza is a landscaped urban park, where the San Franciscan elite come to relax. The stone steps rising up from Clay Street on the south side of the park offer good views of Haight Ashbury *(see pp344–53),* the Fillmore district and Twin Peaks *(see p353).* The steps may be familiar to film buffs – Barbra Streisand drove down them in *What's Up Doc?* There are also tennis courts and a playground.

From the north side of the park some splendid Victorian mansions are visible, including Gibbs House, at No. 2622 Jackson Street, built by Willis Polk in 1894. Smith House at No. 2600 Jackson Street was

Relaxing in the peaceful Alta Plaza park

one of the first houses in San Francisco to be supplied with electricity in the 1890s.

Palace of Fine Arts and the Exploratorium ❺

3601 Lyon St. **Map** 3 C2. 🄲 (415) 561 0360. 🚌 22, 28, 30, 41, 43, 45. 🄾 10am–5pm Thu–Tue; 10am–9:30pm Wed. ⬤ Mon (except holidays). 🄼 except 1st Wed of the month. 🄳 **Tactile Dome** 🄲 (415) 561 0362 (reservations).

SOLE SURVIVOR of the many grandiose monuments built as part of the 1915 Panama-Pacific Exposition, the Palace of Fine Arts is a Neo-Classical folly. It was designed by the architect Bernard R Maybeck, who was inspired by the drawings of the Italian architect Piranesi and by the painting *L'Isle des Morts* by Swiss artist, Arnold Böcklin. Originally built of wood and plaster, the Palace eventually began to crumble, until one concerned citizen raised funds for its re-construction in 1959. It was restored to its original splendour between 1962 and 1975 using reinforced concrete.

The central feature is the rotunda, perched on the edge of a landscaped, swan-filled lagoon. Its dome is decorated with allegorical paintings, all depicting the defence of art against materialism. On top of the many Corinthian columns, nymphs with bent heads are symbolic of the "melancholy of life without art".

The Palace's auditorium can hold up to 1,000 spectators and its most important annual event is the May Film Festival, which highlights the work of new directors, particularly those from the Third World.

An elongated industrial shed inside the Palace houses the Exploratorium Museum, one of the most entertaining science museums in the United States. Established in 1969 by the physicist Frank Oppenheimer (whose brother Robert helped to develop the atom bomb), it is filled with more than 650 interactive exhibits, exploring the world of science and the senses. The exhibits, on two floors, are divided into 13 subject areas, each one colour-coded by an overhead sign. These include a room for Electricity, where balls of lightning are produced in a tube, Vision, Colour and Light, where optical illusions are explained, and Motion, featuring the thrilling Momentum Machine. The Tactile Dome offers a sensory journey taken in total darkness.

The gardens form a relaxing and attractive backdrop to this imitation Roman ruin, which is not only a reminder of the Exposition but a firm favourite with San Francisco residents.

The world of science explained in the Exploratorium Museum

PANAMA-PACIFIC EXPOSITION

In 1915 San Francisco celebrated its successful recovery from the 1906 earthquake and fire with a monumental fair. Officially, it was intended to celebrate the opening of the Panama Canal, and was designed to be the most splendid world's fair ever held. Its grand structures were indeed described by one highly enthusiastic visitor as "a miniature Constantinople".

The halls and pavilions of the fair were constructed on land reclaimed from San Francisco Bay, on the site of today's Marina District. They were donated by all the US states and by 25 foreign countries, and lined a concourse 1 mile (1.6 km) long. Many of the buildings were based on such architectural gems as a Turkish mosque and a Buddhist temple from Kyoto. The brilliant Tower of Jewels, at the centre of the concourse, was encrusted with glass beads and lit by spotlights. To the west stood the beautiful Palace of Fine Arts, which visitors reached by gondola across a landscaped lagoon.

Classical rotunda of the Palace of Fine Arts

Marina Green ❻

Map 4 D1. 🚌 22, 28, 30.

A LONG THIN STRIP of lawn running the length of the Marina District, Marina Green is popular with kite-flyers and picnickers, especially on the Fourth of July, when the city's largest firework display can be seen from here. Paths along the waterfront are the city's prime spots for cyclists, joggers and roller-skaters. Golden Gate Promenade leads from the west end of the green to Fort Point, or you can turn east to the Wave Organ at the end of the harbour jetty.

Chestnut Street ❽

Map 4 D1. 🚌 22, 28, 30, 43.

T HE MAIN SHOPPING and nightlife centre of the Marina District, Chestnut Street has a varied mix of cinemas, markets and restaurants, catering more for the local residents than for visitors. The strip stretches just a few blocks from Fillmore Street west to Divisadero Street, after which the neighbourhood becomes residential in character.

Cow Hollow ❾

Map 4 D2. 🚌 22, 41, 45.

C OW HOLLOW is a shopping district along Union Street. It is so called because it was used as grazing land for the city's dairy cows up until the 1860s. It was then taken over for development and turned into a residential neighbourhood. In the 1950s the area became fashionable, and chic boutiques, antique shops and art galleries took over the old neighbourhood shops. Many of these are in restored 19th-century buildings, lending an old-fashioned air to the district, in stark contrast to the sophistication of the merchandise on display.

Union Street itself has more than 300 boutiques, and open-air arts, crafts and food fairs are held regularly in the area.

View from Fillmore Street, overlooking Cow Hollow

Fort Mason ❼

Map 4 E1. ☎ (415) 979-3010. 🚌 22, 28, 30, 42, 43. ♿ partial.

F ORT MASON reflects the military history of San Francisco. The original buildings were private houses, built in the late 1850s, which were confiscated by the US Government when the site was taken over by the US army during the American Civil War (1861–65).

The Fort was an army command post until the 1890s. It later housed refugees whose homes had been destroyed in the 1906 earthquake (see pp48–9). During World War II, it was the embarkation point for around 1.6 million soldiers.

The Fort was converted to peaceful use in 1972 and some of the restored buildings are now open to the public. These include the original barracks, and the old hospital, which serves both as a Visitors' Center and as the headquarters of the Golden Gate National Recreation Area (GGNRA).

Herbst Pavilion

Festival Pavilion

Oceanic Society Expeditions

Museo ItaloAmericano

Magic Theater

Greens Restaurant

Craft and Folk Art Museum

City College of San Francisco Art Campus

African-American Historical and Cultural Society

Entrance

Young Performers Theater

Mexican Museum

Great Meadow

Octagon House ⑩

2645 Gough St. **Map** 4 E2. 🚋 *(415)
441-7512.* 🚌 *41, 42, 45, 47, 49.*
⏰ *noon–3pm on second Sun and
second and fourth Thu of the month,
except Jan.* **Donation.** ∅ ♿ *limited.*

BUILT IN 1861, the Octagon
House, with its eight-sided
cupola, is a well-preserved
example of a house style that
was once popular throughout
the United States. The ground
floor has now been opened
up into one large room, and
this and the first floor house a
small, but engaging, collection
of decorative arts as well as
historic documents of the
Colonial and Federal periods
of the United States. Among
the exhibits are furniture,
paintings, porcelain, silver,
pewter, samplers, playing
cards from the American
Revolution era and signatures
of 54 of the 56 signatories to
the Declaration of Independence. The house now serves
as the headquarters of the
National Society of Colonial
Dames of America.

Octagon House's cupola ensured sunlight in each room

Fillmore Street ⑪

Map 4 D4. 🚌 *1, 2, 3, 4, 22, 24.*

FILLMORE STREET managed to
survive the 1906 earthquake
and fire virtually intact, so
for several years afterwards it
was forced to serve as the
civic heart of the ruined city.
Government departments, as
well as several independent
businesses, were housed in
local shops, homes and even
churches. Today the main
commercial district linking
Pacific Heights and the Civic
Center is located here, from
Jackson Street to the outskirts
of the Japan Center *(see p342)*
around Bush Street. This area
is filled with fine bookshops,
fashionable restaurants and
exclusive boutiques.

---

*International
Youth Hostel*

*Fort Mason
Officers' Club*

Chapel

*Visitors'
Center*

*Golden Gate
National
Recreation Area
headquarters*

*Meta III (1985) by Italo
Scanga at Museo
ItaloAmericano Chapel*

Besides being rich in history
and culture, Fort Mason also
offers some of the city's finest
views, looking across the bay
towards Golden Gate Bridge
(see pp370–71) and Alcatraz
Island *(see pp328–9)*. Starting
from the west gate of the
Fort, Golden Gate Promenade
winds eastwards to Aquatic
Park and then to Fisherman's
Wharf *(see pp324–5)*.

Fort Mason Center

Part of the Fort is now
occupied by one of
San Francisco's major
art complexes. The Fort
Mason Center houses
about 50 cultural organizations, which include art
galleries, museums and
theatres. The Mexican
Museum exhibits contemporary Mexican and
Mexican-American visual
art. Italian and Italian-American artists display
their works at the Museo
ItaloAmericano. The Magic Theater
is an experimental
theatre, while the

Young Performers Theater is
a playhouse for children.
Among the Center's places to
eat is Greens, considered the
best vegetarian restaurant on
the West Coast *(see p565)*.

The Fort Mason Center produces a monthly calendar of
current events.

***Indigo Verdes (1980) by Manuel
Neri at the Mexican Museum***

The pagoda in the Japan Center's Peace Plaza

Japan Center ⓬

Post St & Buchanan St. **Map** 4 E4.
((415) 922-6776. 🚍 *2, 3, 4, 22, 38.* ⭘ *8am–11pm daily.*

THE JAPAN CENTER was built as part of an ambitious 1960s scheme to revitalize the Fillmore District. Many blocks of ageing Victorian houses were demolished and replaced by the Geary Expressway and the large shopping complex of the Japan Center. The neighbourhood has been the heart of the Japanese community for some 75 years. Marking the heart of the complex, and centered upon a five-tiered, 75-ft (22-m) concrete pagoda, is the Peace Plaza. Taiko drummers and others perform here at the annual Cherry Blossom festival each April. To either side of the pagoda are 5 acres (2 ha) of malls lined with Japanese shops, sushi bars, bathhouses and *Shiatsu* massage centres, all modelled on Tokyo's Ginza district. One of the city's best cinemas, the eight-screen AMC Kabuki *(see pp374–5)*, can also be found here. More authentic Japanese shops line the open-air mall across Post Street, flanked by twin steel sculptures by Ruth Asawa.

St Mary's Cathedral ⓭

1111 Gough St. **Map** 4 E4. **(** (415) 567-2020. 🚍 *2, 3, 4, 38.* ⭘ *8:30am–4:30pm Mon–Fri; 9am–3pm Sat–Sun.* ✝ *6:45am, 8am, 10pm Mon–Sat; 7:30am, 9am, 11am, 1pm Sun.* 🚫 *during services.* ♿

SITUATED AT THE summit of Cathedral Hill, St Mary's is one of San Francisco's most prominent architectural landmarks. Designed by Pietro Belluschi and Pier Luigi Nervi, it was completed in 1971.

The four-part arching paraboloid roof stands out like a white-sailed ship on the horizon. The 200-ft (60-m) high concrete structure, which seems to hover effortlessly above the nave, supports the cross-shaped stained-glass ceiling representing the four elements. A canopy of aluminium rods sparkles above the stone altar, from which the priest faces the congregation.

San Francisco Main Library ⓮

100 Larkin St. **Map** 4 F5. **(** (415) 557-4400. 🚍 *5, 8, 19, 21, 26, 42, 47, 49.* 🚇 *J, K, L, M, N.* ⭘ *9am–8pm Tue–Thu, 11am–5pm Fri, 9am–5pm Sat, noon–5pm Sun.* ♿

SAN FRANCISCO'S Main Library was built in 1917. It was designed by George Kelham and with its granite, Beaux-Arts exterior it matches the other buildings in the Civic Center. The statues decorating the façade were inspired by Michelangelo. The interior houses didactic murals. Those in the reference room, painted by artist Frank DuMond for the Panama-Pacific Exposition *(see p339)*, depict pioneer life. The library contains more than a million

books, and is known for its collection of rare and hand-printed editions. The third-floor San Francisco History Room displays objects and documents that detail the early history of the city.

Bill Graham Civic Auditorium ⓯

99 Grove St. **Map** 4 F5. **(** (415) 974-4060. 🚍 *5, 8, 19, 21, 26, 42, 47, 49.* 🚇 *J, K, L, M, N.*

DESIGNED IN Beaux-Arts style by architect John Galen Howard, the city's Civic Auditorium was opened in 1915 and has since become one of San Francisco's major performance venues. It was inaugurated by the French pianist and composer Camille Saint-Saëns. The building was completed along with City Hall, during the architectural renaissance that followed the great earthquake of 1906 *(see pp48–9)*. It was built, together with the adjoining Brooks Exhibit Hall, beneath the Civic Center Plaza. The civic auditorium now serves as the city's main conference centre, and has seating for 7,000 people. In 1964 its name was changed in honour of Bill Graham *(see p349)*, the local rock music impresario of the hippie era.

Staircase of the San Francisco Main Library

The imposing façade of City Hall in San Francisco's Civic Center

City Hall ⓰

400 Van Ness Ave. **Map** 4 F5.
📞 *(415) 554-4000.* 🚌 *5, 8, 19, 21, 26, 42, 47, 49.* 🚇 *J, K, L, M, N.*
🕐 *8am–5pm Mon–Fri.* ♿
📠 *phone (415) 557-4266.*

CITY HALL, completed in 1915, just in time for the Panama-Pacific Exposition *(see p339)*, was designed by the architect Arthur Brown at the height of his career. Its grand baroque dome was modelled on that of St Peter's in the Vatican, Rome, and is higher than the US Capitol in Washington, DC.

The building stands at the heart of the Civic Center complex, and is a magnificent example of the Beaux-Arts style. Allegorical figures evoking the city's Gold Rush past fill the pediment above the main Polk Street entrance, which leads into the marble-floored rotunda, one of the city's finest interior spaces.

Hayes Valley ⓱

Map 4 E5. 🚌 *21, 22.*

SITUATED WEST of City Hall, these few blocks of Hayes Street have become one of San Francisco's trendier shopping districts. After the US 101 highway was damaged in the 1989 Loma Prieta earthquake *(see p489)* the road was demolished. The former

highway had previously divided Hayes Valley from the wealthy power-brokers and theatregoers that frequented the rest of the Civic Center. A small number of adventurous cafés and restaurants, such as Ivy's and Mad Magda's Russian Tea Room, had already established themselves alongside Hayes Street's second-hand furniture and reject shops. Today a new influx of art galleries, interior design shops, trendy cafés and exclusive boutiques has made the area noticeably smarter.

View from Alamo Square towards the Downtown skyscrapers

Alamo Square ⓲

Map 4 D5. 🚌 *21, 22.*

THE MOST photographed row of Victorian houses in the city lines the eastern side of this sloping green square. It is

set 225 ft (68 m) above the Civic Center, offering grand views of City Hall and the Downtown skyscrapers. The square was laid out at the same time as the beautiful squares in Pacific Heights, but it developed later, with speculators building nearly identical houses.

The "Six Sisters" Queen Anne-style houses built in 1895 at 710–20 Steiner Street on the east side of the square appear on numerous postcards of San Francisco. The city has now declared the area to be an historic district.

University of San Francisco ⓳

2130 Fulton St. **Map** 3 B5. 📞 *(415) 666-6886.* 🚌 *5, 31, 33, 38, 43.*
🕐 *8am–5pm Mon–Fri.*

ORIGINALLY FOUNDED in 1855 as St Ignatius College, the University of San Francisco (USF) remains a Jesuit-run institution, though classes are now coeducational and non-denominational. The landmark of the campus is the St Ignatius Church, completed in 1914. Its buff-coloured twin towers are visible from the western half of San Francisco, especially when lit up at night. The campus and the surrounding residential area occupy land that was once San Francisco's main cemetery district, on and around Lone Mountain.

HAIGHT ASHBURY AND THE MISSION

To the north of Twin Peaks – two windswept hills rising 900 ft (274 m) above the city – lies Haight Ashbury. With its rows of Victorian houses (see pp290–91), it is mostly inhabited by the wealthy middle classes, although this is where thousands of hippies lived in the late 1960s (see p349). The Castro District, to the east, is the centre of the city's gay community. Well-known for its hedonism in the 1970s, the area has become far quieter in recent years, although its cafés and shops are still lively. The Mission District, even further east, was first founded by Spanish monks (see pp42–3) and is home to many Latin Americans.

Figure from Mission Dolores

SIGHTS AT A GLANCE

Historic Streets and Buildings
Castro Street **9**
Clarke's Folly **16**
Dolores Street **11**
Haight Ashbury **2**
Lower Haight Neighbourhood **5**
Noe Valley **15**
(Richard) Spreckels Mansion **3**

Churches
Mission Dolores **10**

Landmarks
Sutro Tower **19**

Parks and Gardens
Buena Vista Park **4**
Corona Heights Park **6**
Dolores Park **12**
Golden Gate Park Panhandle **1**
Twin Peaks **17**
Vulcan Street Steps **18**

Museums and Galleries
Carnaval Mural **14**
Mission Cultural Center for the Latino Arts **13**
The NAMES Project **7**

Theatres
Castro Theater **8**

KEY

Street-by-Street map
See pp346–7

BART station

0 metres   750
0 yards   750

GETTING THERE

The Muni N streetcar serves Haight Ashbury, the J streetcar serves the Mission, and all other lines serve the Castro Street station. Bus 33 links all three neighbourhoods.

◁ Street scene in Haight Ashbury

Street-by-Street: Haight Ashbury

Sᴛʀᴇᴛᴄʜɪɴɢ ғʀᴏᴍ Buena Vista Park to the flat expanses of Golden Gate Park, Haight Ashbury was a place to escape to from the city centre in the 1880s. It then developed into a residential area, but between the 1930s and 1960s it changed dramatically from a middle-class suburb to the centre of the "Flower Power" world, with a free clinic to treat hippies without medical insurance. It has now settled into being one of the liveliest and most unconventional places in San Francisco, with an eclectic mix of people, excellent book and music shops, and good cafés.

Haight Ashbury
In the 1960s, hippies met at this crossroads, which gives the area its name ❷

Golden Gate Panhandle
This thin green strip runs west into the heart of Golden Gate Park ❶

Cha Cha Cha is one of the liveliest places to eat in San Francisco, serving Latin American food in a series of small dishes *(see p564)*.

To bus nos. 7, 33

Sᴛᴀʀ Sɪɢʜᴛs

★ Buena Vista Park

★ (Richard) Spreckels Mansion

The Red Victorian Hotel is a relic of the 1960s hippie era. It now caters to a New Age clientele, with health food and rooms with transcendental themes *(see p527).*

No. 1220 Masonic Avenue is one of many ornate Victorian mansions built on the steep hill that runs down from Golden Gate Park Panhandle to Haight Street.

LOCATOR MAP
See Street Finder, map 10

KEY
– – – Suggested route

★ **(Richard) Spreckels Mansion**
This grand home at No.737 Buena Vista Avenue was built in 1897 ❸

★ **Buena Vista Park**
Through its mass of twisting, matted trees, this dramatic park offers magnificent views over the city ❹

0 metres   100
0 yards   100

To bus no. 37

Golden Gate Park Panhandle ❶

Map 9 C1. 🚌 6, 7, 21, 43, 66, 71.

THIS ONE-BLOCK-WIDE and eight-block-long stretch of parkland forms the narrow "Panhandle" to the giant rectangular pan that is Golden Gate Park *(see pp356–9)*. It was the first part of the park to be reclaimed from the sand dunes that rolled across west San Francisco, and its eucalyptus trees are among the oldest and largest in the city.

The Panhandle's winding carriage roads and bridle paths were first laid out in the 1870s, and the upper classes came here to walk and ride. They built large mansions on the outskirts of the park, many of which can still be seen today. In 1906 the Panhandle was used as a refuge for families made homeless by the earthquake *(see pp48–9)*. Today the old roads and paths are frequented regularly by large crowds of joggers and cyclists.

The Panhandle is still remembered for its "Flower Power" heyday of the 1960s. The era's young hippies flocked to the park to listen to the impromptu free concerts held here by the new psychedelic bands from Haight Ashbury. The area is still a popular spot for the city's street musicians and hippie guitarists.

Haight Ashbury ❷

Map 9 C1. 🚌 6, 7, 33, 37, 43, 66, 71. 🚋 N.

TAKING ITS NAME from the junction of two major streets, Haight and Ashbury, this district contains alternative bookshops, large Victorian houses and numerous cafés. Following the reclamation of Golden Gate Park *(see pp356 –9)* and then the opening of a large amusement park called The Chutes, the area was rapidly built up in the 1890s as a middle-class suburb – hence the dozens of elaborate Queen Anne-style houses *(see pp290–91)* lining its streets. The Haight district survived the 1906 earthquake and fire *(see pp48–9)*, and then experienced a brief boom, which was followed by a long period of decline.

After the tram tunnel underneath Buena Vista Park was completed in 1928, the middle classes began their exodus to the suburbs in the Sunset. The area reached its lowest ebb in the years after World War II. The big Victorian houses were divided into apartments and low rents attracted a disparate population. By the 1960s the Haight had become host to a bohemian community that was a hotbed of anarchy. A component of this "hippie scene" was the music of rock bands such as the Grateful Dead, but the area stayed fairly quiet until 1967. Then the "Summer of Love", fuelled by the media, brought some 75,000 young people in search of free love, music and drugs, and the area became the focus of a worldwide youth culture.

Haight retains its radical atmosphere, but now there are problems with crime, drugs and homelessness. However, from the cafés to the second-hand clothing shops, there is still an "only in San Francisco" experience to be found here.

Junction of Haight and Ashbury streets

Late-Victorian mansion built for Richard Spreckels

(Richard) Spreckels Mansion ❸

737 Buena Vista West. **Map** 9 C2. 🚌 6, 7, 37, 43, 66, 71. ⬤ *to the public.*

THIS HOUSE SHOULD not be confused with the grander Spreckels Mansion situated on Washington Street *(see p338)*. It was, however, also built by the millionaire "Sugar King" Claus Spreckels, for one of his many offspring. The elaborate Queen Anne-style house *(see pp290–91)*, built in 1897, is a typical late-Victorian Haight Ashbury home. It was once a guesthouse, whose guests included the acerbic journalist and ghost-story writer Ambrose Bierce, and the adventure writer Jack London, who wrote *White Fang* here in 1906 *(see pp22)*. The house is now in private hands.

Buena Vista Park ❹

Map 9 C1. 🚌 6, 7, 37, 43, 66, 71.

BUENA VISTA PARK rises steeply 570 ft (174 m) above the geographical centre of San Francisco with views over the Bay Area. First landscaped in 1894, it is a pocket of land left to nature. Numerous overgrown and eroded paths wind up from Haight Street to the crest, but there is a paved route from Buena Vista Avenue. It is best to avoid the park at night.

Lower Haight Neighbourhood 5

Map 10 D1. ⬛ 6, 7, 22, 66, 71. 🚇 K, L, M.

View from Corona Heights across the Mission

HALFWAY BETWEEN City Hall and Haight Ashbury, and marking the southern border of the predominantly African-American Fillmore District, the Lower Haight is an area in transition. Unusual art galleries and boutiques, including the Used Rubber USA shop which sells clothes and accessories made entirely of recycled rubber, began to open here in the mid-1980s. These were in addition to the inexpensive cafés, bars and restaurants serving a bohemian clientele already in business in the area. This combination has created one of the most lively districts in San Francisco.

As in nearby Alamo Square *(see p343)*, the Lower Haight has dozens of houses known as "Victorians" *(see pp290 –91)* built from the 1850s to the early 1900s, including picturesque cottages such as the Nightingale House at No. 201 Buchanan Street, built in the 1880s. But the 1950s public housing blocks have discouraged wholesale gentrification. The area is safe during the day but, like Alamo Square, it can seem threatening after dark.

Sign from Cha Cha Cha restaurant on Haight Street *(see p564)*

Corona Heights Park 6

Map 9 D2. ☎ (415) 554-9600. ⬛ 24, 37. **Randall Museum** ◻ 10am–1pm, 2–5pm Tue–Sat. ♿ limited.

CORONA HEIGHTS PARK is a dusty and undeveloped rocky peak. Clinging to its side is an unusual museum for children. The Randall

Museum at No. 199 Museum Way has an extensive menagerie of raccoons, owls, snakes and other animals, many of which the children can handle and stroke. The emphasis of the museum is on participation, with many hands-on exhibits and workshops. Children also enjoy climbing

on the craggy outcrops in the park. Corona Heights was gouged out by brick-making operations in the 19th century. It was never planted with trees, so its red rock peak has an unimpeded panorama over the city. There is a good view of the winding streets of Twin Peaks *(see p353)*.

THE SOUNDS OF 1960s SAN FRANCISCO

During the late 1960s, and most notably during the 1967 "Summer of Love", young people from all over the United States flocked to the Haight Ashbury district. They came not just to "turn on, tune in and drop out", but also to listen to bands such as Janis Joplin's Big Brother and the Holding Company, Jefferson Airplane and the Grateful Dead, all of whom emerged out of a thriving music scene. They established themselves at the city's new music venues.

Premier music venues
The Avalon Ballroom, now the Regency II theatre on Van Ness Avenue, was the first and most significant venue. Run by Chet Helms and the Family Dog collective, the Avalon pioneered the use of colourful psychedelic posters by designers such as Stanley Mouse and Alton Kelly *(see pp424–5)*.

Fillmore Auditorium, facing the Japan Center *(see p342)* and a former church hall, was taken over by impresario

Bill Graham in 1965, after whom the Civic Auditorium *(see p342)* is named. He put unlikely pairs such as Miles Davis and the Grateful Dead on the same bill, and brought in big-name performers from Jimi Hendrix to The Who. The Fillmore Auditorium was damaged in the 1989 earthquake but has recently reopened.

By the time Bill Graham died in 1992 he had become the most successful rock music promoter in the US.

Janis Joplin (1943–70), hard-edged blues singer

The NAMES Project ●

2362A Market St. **Map** 10 D2.
🕻 *863-1966.* 🚌 *8, 24, 35, 37.*
🚋 *F, K, L, M.* ⏰ *noon–7pm Tue–Thu; noon–5pm Fri–Mon.* ♿
📷 *partial.*

THE NAMES PROJECT'S AIDS Memorial Quilt was started in 1987. It is made up of more than 28,000 individual panels, from San Francisco and all over the US. Some panels have been sewn by individuals, but many are the creations of "quilting bees" – friends and relatives who have come together to commemorate a person lost to AIDS. Although all panels are the same size – 3 by 6 ft (90 by 180 cm) – each one is different and reflects the life and personality of the person remembered. Sections of the quilt have been exhibited across the US and abroad.

Although the quilt represents less than 15 per cent of US AIDS deaths, if displayed in its entirety it would cover more than 11 football pitches. There are panels for Arthur Ashe, Rock Hudson and Freddie Mercury.

The NAMES Project is a non-profit-making organization. It operates the Market Street Gallery, where the idea for the quilt was born. Anyone can come here to create their own panels of remembrance.

AIDS memorial panel

AIDS Memorial Quilt on display in Washington, DC in 1992

Historic and ornate Castro Theater

Castro Theater ●

429 Castro St. **Map** 10 D2. 🕻 *621-6120.* 🚌 *8, 24, 33, 35, 37.* 🚋 *F, K, L, M. See* **Entertainment** *pp374–5.*

COMPLETED IN 1922, this brightly lit neon marquee is a Castro Street landmark. It is the most sumptuous and best preserved of San Francisco's neighbourhood film palaces, and one of the first commissions of the architect Timothy Pflueger. With its Arabian Nights interior, complete with a glorious Wurlitzer organ that rises from the floor between the screenings, it is well worth the price of admission. The ceiling of the auditorium is cast in plaster and resembles the interior of a large tent, with imitation swathes of fabric, rope and tassels. The theatre seats 1,500 and shows mainly revival classics. It also hosts the Gay and Lesbian Film Festival, held each June.

Castro Street ●

Map 10 D2. 🚌 *8, 24, 33, 35, 37.* 🚋 *F, K, L, M.*

THE HILLY neighbourhood around Castro Street between Twin Peaks and the Mission District is the heart of San Francisco's high-profile gay and lesbian community. Focused on the intersection of Castro Street and 18th Street, the self-proclaimed "Gayest Four Corners of the World" emerged as a homosexual nexus during the 1970s. Gays of the Flower Power generation moved into this predominantly working-class district and began restoring Victorian houses and setting up businesses such as the bookshop A Different Light, at No. 489 Castro Street. They also opened gay bars such as the Twin Peaks on the corner of Castro Street and 17th Street. Unlike earlier bars, which hid gay people in dark corners out of public view, the Twin Peaks installed large windows. Though the many shops and restaurants attract all kinds of people, the area's openly homosexual identity has made it a place of pilgrimage for gays and lesbians. It symbolizes for this minority group a freedom not often found in cities elsewhere.

The city's first openly gay politician, Harvey Milk, was known as the Mayor of Castro Street before his assassination on 28 November 1978. He and Mayor George Moscone were killed by an ex-policeman, whose lenient sentence caused rioting in the city. Milk is remembered with a plaque outside the Muni stop on Market Street, and a candlelit procession from Castro Street to City Hall every year.

Mission Dolores ⑩

16th St and Dolores St. **Map** 10 F3.
📶 621-8203. 🚌 22. 🚃 J. ◯
9am– 4pm (1 May–31
Oct: 4:30 pm) daily.
● Thanksgiving, 25
Dec. 💵 📷 ♿ 🚻

P RESERVED INTACT
since it was built
in 1791, Mission
Dolores is the oldest
building in the city and
an embodiment of San
Francisco's religious
Spanish colonial roots
(see pp42–3). The mission
was founded by Father
Junípero Serra, and is
formally known as the
Mission of San Francisco
de Asis. The name Dolores

**Figure of saint
in the mission**

reflects its proximity to
Laguna de los Dolores (Lake
of Our Lady of Sorrows), an
ancient insect-plagued swamp.
The building is modest
by mission standards,
but its 4-ft (1.2-m) thick
walls have survived the
years without any
serious decay. Paint-
ings by Native
Americans adorn
the ceiling, which
has been restored.
There is a fine
Baroque altar and
reredos, and a
display of histor-
ical documents in
the small museum.
Most services are
now held in the
basilica, built next

to the mission in 1918. The
cemetery contains graves of
San Franciscan pioneers.
A statue marking the mass
grave of 5,000 Native Americans, most of whom died in
the measles epidemics of 1804
and 1826, was later stolen. All
that now remains is a pedestal,
reading "In Prayerful Memory
of our Faithful Indians".

**The painted and gilded
altarpiece** *was imported from
Mexico in 1780.*

The statue of Father Junípero Serra
is a copy of the work of local
sculptor Arthur Putnam.

The ceramic mural was created by
Guillermo Granizo, a native San
Francisco artist.

**Museum and
display**

The ceiling paintings
are based on original
Ohlone designs using
vegetable dyes.

**Entrance for
the disabled**

**The mission
cemetery** originally
extended across
many streets. The
earliest wooden
grave markers have
disintegrated, but
the Lourdes Grotto
commemorates the
forgotten dead.

**Statue of Our Lady
of Mount Carmel**

**Entrance and
gift shop**

**The mission
façade** has four
columns which
support niches for
three bells,
inscribed with their
names and dates.

Spanish–American War memorial
on Dolores Street

Dolores Street 🄫

Map 10 E2. 🚌 8, 22, 33, 48. 🚃 J.

Lined by lovingly maintained late-Victorian houses (see pp290–91) and an island of palm trees, this street is one of the city's most attractive public spaces. The broad street runs parallel to Mission Street, forming the western border of the Mission District. It starts at Market Street, where a statue honouring soldiers of the Spanish–American War is overwhelmed by the US Mint.

Mission High School, with the white walls and red tile roof typical of Mission-style architecture (see p26), and Mission Dolores (see p351) are both situated on Dolores Street. The street ends in the Noe Valley district.

Dolores Park 🄬

Map 10 E3. 🚌 22, 33. 🚃 J.

Originally the site of San Francisco's main Jewish cemetery, Dolores Park was transformed in 1905 into one of the Mission District's few large open spaces. Bounded by Dolores, Church, 18th and 20th streets, it is situated high on a hill with a good view of the city centre.

Dolores Park is very popular during the day with tennis players, sunbathers and dog walkers, but after dark it is a haven for drug dealers. Above the park to the south and west, the streets rise so steeply that

many turn into pedestrian-only stairways. Some of the city's finest Victorian houses can also be seen here.

Mission Cultural Center for the Latino Arts 🄭

2868 Mission St. **Map** 10 F4. 📞 (415) 821-1155. 🚌 14, 26, 48, 49. 🚃 J. ◷ 10am–4pm Tue–Sat. ♿

This dynamic arts centre is part funded by the city, and caters for the local, predominantly Latino, population. It offers classes and workshops and stages theatrical events and exhibitions. Among these is the festival held in November to celebrate the Day of the Dead (see p34).

Detail from the *Carnaval Mural*

Carnaval Mural 🄮

24th St and South Van Ness Ave. **Map** 10 F4. 🚌 12, 14, 48, 49, 67. 🚃 J.

One of the many brightly painted murals on the walls of the Mission District, the *Carnaval Mural* celebrates the diverse people who come together for the Carnaval festival (see p32). This annual spring event is the highlight of the year.

Guided tours of the other murals, some with political themes, are given by civic organizations. There is also an outdoor gallery with murals in Balmy Alley (see pp296–7).

Noe Valley 🄯

🚌 24, 35, 48. 🚃 J.

Noe Valley is often referred to as "Noewhere Valley" by its residents, who remain determined to keep it off the tourist map. It is a pleasant, comfortable neighbourhood, largely inhabited by young professionals. Its spotless streets and safe atmosphere seem at odds with the surrounding, densely populated Mission District.

The area was named after its original land-grant owner, José Noe, the last *alcalde* (mayor) of Yerba Buena, the Mexican village that eventually grew into San Francisco. The valley was first built up during the 1880s after a cable car line over the steep Castro Street hill was completed. The low rents attracted working-class, largely Irish families. Then, like so many other areas of San Francisco, this once blue-collar district underwent gentrification in the 1970s, raising the value of the properties and resulting in today's engaging mix of boutiques, bars and restaurants. The Noe Valley Ministry, found at No. 1021 Sanchez Street, is a late 1880s Presbyterian church in the "Stick Style" (see pp290–91), the most prevalent architectural style in the city, with its emphasis on vertical lines. The ministry was converted into a community centre in the 1970s.

Victorian façade of the Noe Valley
Ministry on Sanchez Street

Nobby Clarke's Folly

Clarke's Folly ⑯

250 Douglass St. **Map** 10 D3. 🚌 *8, 33, 35, 37, 48.* ⚫ *to the public.*

THIS RESPLENDENT white manor house was at one time set in its own extensive grounds. It was built in 1892 by Alfred Clarke, known locally as Nobby. Clarke had worked for the San Francisco Police Department at the time of the Committee of Vigilance in 1851, when a group of local citizens attempted to control the city's growing lawlessness *(see pp44–5).* The house is said to have cost $100,000 to build, a huge sum in the 1890s.

Although it is now surrounded by other buildings, the house is a fine example of Victorian domestic architecture. The turrets and the gabled roof are typical of the Queen Anne style, while the shingled walls and front porch adopt the elements of Eastlake architecture *(see pp290–91).*

Today the house is divided into private apartments.

Twin Peaks ⑰

Map 9 C4. 🚌 *33, 36, 37.*

THESE TWO HILLS were first known in Spanish as *El Pecho de la Chola,* the "Bosom of the Indian Girl". They lie at the heart of San Francisco, and reach a height of 900 ft (274 m) above sea level. At the top there is an area of parkland with steep, grassy slopes, from which incomparable views of the whole of San Francisco can be enjoyed.

Twin Peaks Boulevard circles both hills near their summits, and there is a parking and viewing point from which to look out over the city. Those who are prepared to climb up the steep path to the very top on foot can leave the crowds behind and get a breathtaking 360-degree view.

Twin Peaks are the only hills in the city left in their original state. The residential districts on the lower slopes have curving streets that wind around the contours of the hills, rather than the grid system that is more common in the rest of San Francisco.

Vulcan Street Steps ⑱

Vulcan St. **Map** 9 C2. 🚌 *37.*

APART FROM a tiny figure of Spock standing on a post-box, there is no connection between the cult television programme *Star Trek* and this block of houses climbing between Ord and Levant Streets. However, the Vulcan Steps do feel light years away from the busy Castro District below. The small, picturesque gardens of the houses spill out and soften the edges of the steps, and a canopy of pines muffles the city sounds. There are grand views of the Mission District and the southern waterfront.

Sutro Tower ⑲

Map 9 B3. 🚌 *36, 37.* ⚫ *to the public.*

MARKING THE SKYLINE like an invading robot, Sutro Tower is 970 ft (295 m) high. It was named after the local philanthropist and landowner Adolph Sutro, and it carries antennae for the signals of most of San Francisco's TV and radio stations. Built in 1973, it is still much used, despite the rise of cable networks. The tower is visible from all over the Bay Area, and sometimes seems to float above the summer fogs that roll in from the sea. On the north side of the tower there are dense eucalyptus groves, first planted in the 1880s by Adolph Sutro.

View of the city and of Twin Peaks Boulevard from the top of Twin Peaks

GOLDEN GATE PARK AND THE PRESIDIO

THE SPECTACULAR Golden Gate Park is one of the world's largest urban parks, created in the 1890s out of sandy wasteland. It houses three museums and a range of sports facilities. Land's End, the city's wildest region and scene of many shipwrecks, is accessible from the park.

To the north of Golden Gate Park, the Presidio, overlooking San Francisco Bay, was established as an outpost of Spain's New World Empire in 1776, and for many years was a military base. In 1993 it became a National Park and visitors can now stroll through its acres of woodland full of wildlife.

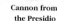

Cannon from the Presidio

SIGHTS AT A GLANCE

Historic Streets and Buildings
Clement Street **12**
Golden Gate Bridge pp370–71 **17**
Presidio Officers' Club **14**

Parks and Gardens
Buffalo Paddock **8**
Conservatory of Flowers **5**
Japanese Tea Garden **3**
Queen Wilhelmina Tulip Garden **9**
Shakespeare Garden **2**
Stow Lake **7**
Strybing Arboretum **6**

Museums and Galleries
California Academy of Sciences pp360–61 **1**
California Palace of the Legion of Honor pp364–5 **10**
Fort Point **16**
MH de Young Memorial Museum pp362–3 **4**
Presidio Museum **15**

Churches and Temples
Holy Virgin Cathedral **11**
Temple Emanu-El **13**

0 kilometres   1

0 miles   0.5

GETTING THERE

For Golden Gate Park, take buses 5, 7, 21, 71 or 73, or the N streetcar. The Presidio is best seen by car, but Muni bus 29 stops at the main sights, bus 43 serves the eastern end, and bus 28 the northern boundary.

KEY

Street-by-Street map
See pp356–7

The Presidio
see pp366–7

P Parking

◁ **Golden Gate Bridge seen from Fort Point**

Street-by-Street: Golden Gate Park

GOLDEN GATE PARK is 3 miles (5 km) long and almost 1 mile (1.6 km) across. It stretches from the Pacific Ocean to the centre of San Francisco, forming an oasis of greenery and calm in which to escape from the bustle of city life. Within the park an amazing number of activities are catered for, both sporting and cultural. The landscaped area around the Music Concourse, with its fountains, plane trees and benches, is the most popular and developed section. Here you can enjoy free Sunday concerts at the Spreckels Temple of Music. A total of three museums stand on either side of the Concourse, and the Japanese and Shakespeare gardens are within walking distance.

Lamp in the Japanese Tea Garden

★ **MH de Young Museum and Asian Art Museum**
These two museums exhibit art from North America, Britain and the Far East. This mahogany chest was made in Philadelphia in 1780 ❹

The Great Buddha reaches almost 11 ft (3 m) in height.

Japanese Tea Garden
This exquisite garden, with its well tended plants and pretty lake, is one of the most attractive parts of the park ❸

KEY

--- Suggested route

0 metres   80
0 yards   80

STAR SIGHTS

★ **California Academy of Sciences**

★ **MH de Young Museum and Asian Art Museum**

Shakespeare Garden /
This tiny garden holds more than 150 species of plants, all mentioned in Shakespeare's poetry or plays ❷

The statue of the *Apple Cider Press*, by sculptor Thomas Shields-Clarke, is one of the few monuments to survive from the California Midwinter Fair of 1894.

LOCATOR MAP
See Street Finder, map 7 & 8

The Music Concourse is the venue for summer concerts.

★ **California Academy of Sciences**
This complex houses a museum, an aquarium and a planetarium, with exhibitions covering many natural sciences ❶

California Academy of Sciences ❶

See pp360–61.

Shakespeare Garden ❷

Music Concourse, Golden Gate Park. **Map** 8 F2. 🚌 44.

Gardeners here have tried to cultivate all the plants mentioned in Shakespeare's works. Relevant quotations are inscribed on plaques set in the wall at the back of the garden. A 19th-century bust of the playwright is kept in a box opened only occasionally; enquire at the Lodge.

Japanese Tea Garden ❸

Music Concourse, Golden Gate Park. **Map** 8 F2. 📞 666-7200. 🚌 44. 🕐 9am–6:30pm or dusk, daily.

Established by the art-dealer George Turner Marsh for the California Midwinter Fair of 1894, this garden was a very popular attraction. A Japanese gardener, Makota Hagiwara, was later contracted to tend it. He and his family maintained and expanded the garden until 1942, when they were interned during World War II. The most spectacular time to visit is when all the cherry trees bloom in April.

A maze of paths winds through the gardens, lined with carefully manicured Japanese trees, shrubs and flowers. There are also ornamental ponds and a wooden pagoda. The steeply arched Moon Bridge forms a circular reflection in the pond below it. The largest bronze Buddha outside Asia, cast in Japan in 1790, is seated at the top of the garden stairs.

MH de Young Memorial Museum and Asian Art Museum ❹

See pp362–3.

Conservatory of Flowers ❺

John F Kennedy Drive, Golden Gate Park. **Map** 9 A1. ☎ 666-7017.
🚌 33, 44. ⬤ to the public. 📷 📷
♿ limited. 🚻

THIS ORNATE glass house, inspired by the one in London's Kew Gardens, is the oldest building in Golden Gate Park. A property developer, James Lick, imported the frame from Ireland, but he died before its erection in 1879. A jungle of ferns, palms and orchids thrived here for more than a century, but a hurricane hit the city in December 1995 and largely destroyed the conservatory. San Franciscans are currently campaigning for its much-needed repair.

Strybing Arboretum ❻

9th Ave at Lincoln Way, Golden Gate Park. **Map** 8 F2. ☎ 661 1316.
🚌 44, 71. ⬤ 8am–4:30pm Mon–Fri; 10am–5pm weekends and public hols. 📷 ♿ ✉ 🚻

ON DISPLAY in the Strybing Arboretum are 7,500 species of plants, trees and shrubs from many different countries. There are Mexican, African, South American and Australian gardens, and one

Garden of Fragrance in the Strybing Arboretum

that is devoted entirely to native Californian plants.

Well worth a visit is the enchanting Moon-Viewing Garden. It exhibits Far Eastern plants in a setting that, unlike that of the Japanese Tea Garden *(see p357)*, is naturalistic rather than formal. Both medicinal and culinary plants are grown in the Garden of Fragrance, which is specifically designed for blind plant-lovers. Here the emphasis is on the senses of taste, touch and smell, and all the plants are identified in Braille.

Another area is planted with indigenous California redwood trees, with a stream winding through them. This re-creates the flora and the atmosphere of a northern Californian coastal forest. There is also a New World Cloud Forest,

with flora from the mountains of Central America. Surprisingly, all these gardens thrive in the Californian fogs.

The Arboretum has a small shop selling seeds and books, and it also houses the Helen Crocker Horticultural Library, which is open to the public. A colourful flower show is held in the summer.

Stow Lake ❼

Stow Lake Drive, Golden Gate Park. **Map** 8 E2. 🚌 28, 29. 🖥 🚤

IN 1895, the President of the Park Commission, WW Stow, ordered the construction of this artificial lake, the largest in the park. It was created encircling Strawberry Hill (named after the wild fruit that once grew here), so that the summit of the hill now forms an island in the lake. It is linked to the mainland by two stone-clad bridges. Stow Lake's circular stream makes an ideal course for rowing laps from the boathouse, although the tranquil atmosphere makes leisurely drifting seem more appropriate. A Chinese pavilion on the island's shore was a gift to San Francisco from its sister city in Taiwan, Taipei. The red and green pavilion arrived in San Francisco by ship in 6,000 pieces, and then reassembled on the island.

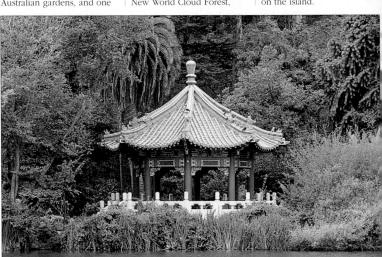

Chinese moon-watching pavilion on Stow Lake

The millionaire railway baron Collis Porter Huntington *(see pp46–7)* donated the money in 1894 to create the reservoir and the waterfall that cascades into Stow Lake. These are known as Huntingdon Falls. Damaged in the 1906 earthquake *(see pp48–9)*, it was restored in the 1980s and is now one of the park's most attractive features.

Buffalo Paddock ●8

John F Kennedy Drive, Golden Gate Park. **Map** 7 C2. 🚌 *5, 29.*

T HE SHAGGY BUFFALO grazing in this specially designed paddock are the largest of all North American land animals. Immediately recognizable by their short horns and humped backs, buffalos are the symbol of the American plains, and are more properly known as the American bison.

This paddock was opened in 1892, with the aim of protecting the species, then on the verge of extinction. The first herd, however, brought in from Wyoming, all died of a tuberculosis epidemic and had to be replaced. In 1902 William Cody, alias the outlaw "Buffalo Bill", traded one of his bulls for one from the Golden Gate Park herd. Both parties thought that they had rid themselves of an aggressive beast, but Cody's newly purchased bull jumped a high fence once it was back at his encampment and escaped. According to one newspaper of the day, the *San Francisco Call*, it took a total of 80 men to recapture it.

Buffalo in the Buffalo Paddock

Queen Wilhelmina Tulip Garden and the Dutch Windmill

Queen Wilhelmina Tulip Garden ●9

Map 7 A2. 🚌 *5, 18.* **Windmill** *closed to the public.* ♿

T HIS GARDEN was named after the Dutch Queen Wilhelmina, and hundreds of tulip bulbs are donated each year by the Dutch Bulb Growers' Association. In the spring months, the area is carpeted with the flowers in full bloom. The Dutch Windmill, near the northwest corner of Golden Gate Park, was built in 1903. Its purpose, along with its companion, the Murphy Windmill, erected in the park's southwest corner in 1905, was to pump water for irrigation from a source underground. The increasing volume of water required – an estimated 5 million gal (230 million litres) per day – soon made the windmills obsolete and they are no longer in use.

JOHN MCLAREN

Although Golden Gate Park was designed by William Hammond Hall, the park's current status owes the most to his successor, John McLaren.

McLaren was born in Scotland in 1846 and studied botany before emigrating to California in the 1870s. He succeeded Hall as administrator in 1887 and devoted the rest of his life to the park.

An expert landscape gardener and botanist, McLaren succeeded in importing exotic plants from all over the world and making them thrive, despite the poor soil and foggy climate. He planted thousands of trees and chose the right shrubs to ensure the park was in full bloom all year round.

John McLaren Lodge, a sandstone villa situated on the park's east side, was built in 1896 as a home for McLaren and his family. As McLaren lay dying in 1943, he requested that the cypress tree outside the lodge be lit with Christmas lights and his request was granted, despite a wartime blackout being in force. The tree is still referred to as "Uncle John's Christmas Tree" and is lit every December in his honour. He is buried in a tomb in the San Francisco City Hall. Golden Gate Park still remains true to his vision – a place in which to escape from city life.

California Academy of Sciences ❶

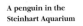

THIS EXPANSIVE MUSEUM was erected in several instalments between 1916 and 1968, yet maintains a unified design around a central courtyard. The original building, located in the city centre, was severely damaged in the 1906 fire. The exhibits in two of the rooms were salvaged,

A penguin in the Steinhart Aquarium

however, becoming the foundation of an exciting new collection. The trademark fountain of the Academy, *Mating Whales*, sculpted by Robert Howard for the 1939 World's Fair on Treasure Island *(see pp50–51)*, spouts at the heart of the courtyard.

Façade of the California Academy of Sciences

MUSEUM GUIDE

The widely varied collections, arranged by subject, are housed in different halls on the first floor around the central courtyard. Several areas are allocated for the display of special exhibitions. The Academy Store, selling books and gifts, has a shop in Cowell Hall and another outside the Auditorium. The Academy library, which contains 70,000 volumes, is on the second floor.

Reptiles and Amphibians

Fish

Wattis Gallery

Far Side of Science Gallery

Discovery Room

Morrison Planetarium
One of the world's most precise star projectors transforms the ceiling here into a night sky.

Auditorium

KEY TO FLOORPLAN

- ☐ African Safari
- ☐ Earth and Space
- ☐ Wallis Hall
- ☐ Life Through Time
- ☐ Steinhart Aquarium
- ☐ Gem and Mineral Hall
- ☐ Wild California
- ☐ Special exhibitions
- ☐ Non-exhibition space

★ SafeQuake
Experience the power and movement of great earth tremors, while learning of their real destructive power.

★ **Steinhart Aquarium**
More than 14,000 specimens of tidepool animals, molluscs, sea mammals, sharks and other fish dwell here in one of the world's largest aquariums.

VISITORS' CHECKLIST

Music Concourse, Golden Gate Park. **Map** 8 F2. ☎ *(415) 221-5100.* ℹ *(415) 750-7145.* 🚌 *5, 44.* ⏰ *10am–5pm daily; end May–early Sep: 9am–6pm daily.* 💺 *free first Wed of month.* ♿ 📷 🖥 🚻

Dolphins and Seals

Fish Roundabout

Gem and Mineral Hall
Among the thousands of minerals on display is this 1,350-lb (612-kg) quartz crystal from Arkansas.

Biodiversity Resource Center

Stairs

Insects

Lift to café

Entrance ♿

Tyrannosaurus Rex Skeleton
This gigantic predator was the most powerful carnivore ever to walk the earth.

African Safari
Realistic models of animals from Africa's jungles and savannahs are displayed here, in life-like dioramas.

STAR EXHIBITS

★ **SafeQuake**

★ **Steinhart Aquarium**

MH de Young Memorial Museum and Asian Art Museum ❹

American tall case clock (c.1890)

EXHIBITS IN THE MH de Young Memorial Museum are changed on a regular basis, as there is only room to display a small part of the huge collection. The museum contains a broad range of American and British art, as well as collections of pre-Columbian-American, African and Oceanic works of art. Within the Asian Art Museum you will find paintings, statuary and applied arts from the Far East, India and Southeast Asia. At its heart is the Avery Brundage jade collection. The main entrance serves both museums.

★ Early American Painting
Indians Hunting Buffalo *was painted by Albert Bierstadt around 1888. It is an example of the many 19th-century works in the MH de Young Museum.*

Caparisoned Horse
Part of the extensive Chinese collection in the Asian Art Museum, this is a Tang dynasty three-colour ceramic horse.

GUIDE TO THE ASIAN ART MUSEUM
The Chinese collections, including the famous jade collection, are arranged in galleries on the first floor. Art from other Asian nations is on the second floor, arranged by country or region.

KEY TO ASIAN ART MUSEUM

- ☐ Chinese exhibits
- ☐ Japanese exhibits
- ☐ Indian exhibits
- ☐ Southeast Asian exhibits
- ☐ Textiles
- ☐ Other exhibits
- ☐ Special exhibitions
- ☐ Non-exhibition space

★ Jade Collection
Standing Female Bear, *from a huge collection, dates from around 206 BC–AD 9.*

Simhavaktra "Dakini"
This Sino-Tibetan dakini (lion-headed sacred guardian) dates from the 19th century.

STAR EXHIBITS

- **★ Early American Painting**
- **★ Jade Collection**

Boatmen on the Missouri
George Caleb Bingham painted these pioneers in 1846.

Mask with Necklace
This wooden mask is from the pre-Columbian-American collection of the de Young Museum. Dated AD 300, it comes from Teotihuacán in Mexico.

GUIDE TO THE MH DE YOUNG MUSEUM
American and Ancient art is arranged round the central Hearst Court in galleries devoted to such topics as folk art or American Impressionists. Galleries to the right of the entrance show the traditional arts of Africa and the Americas.

Entrance to both museums

Pool of Enchantment

Entrance to Asian Art Museum

Portrait of Orleans
Edward Hopper's work conveys a sense of loneliness. This townscape was painted in 1950.

KEY TO DE YOUNG MUSEUM

☐ American exhibits

☐ British exhibits

☐ Textiles

☐ Other exhibits

☐ Temporary exhibitions

☐ Non-exhibition space

California Palace of the Legion of Honor ⓾

INSPIRED BY the Palais de la Légion d'Honneur in Paris, Alma de Bretteville Spreckels built this museum in the 1920s to promote French art in California. Designed by the architect George Applegarth, it contains works of European art from the last eight centuries, with paintings by Monet, Rubens and Rembrandt, and more than 70 statues by Rodin. The Achenbach Foundation, a famous collection of graphic works, occupies part of the gallery.

Old Woman
French artist Georges de la Tour painted this female portrait in about 1618.

The Porcelain Gallery
contains figurines, crockery and other pieces dating from the 18th century.

Florence Gould Theater

Stairs down from first floor

Virgin and Child
This oil-on-panel by the Flemish artist Dieric Bouts dates from the 15th century. It forms part of a series of four panels entitled Life of the Virgin.

STAR FEATURES

★ Green

★ The Thinker

★ Waterlilies

★ **Green** (1968)
Richard Diebenkorn's work of graphic art is painted with the ink wash mediums aquatint and drypoint.

The Tribute Money *(1612)*
The use of primary colours in this oil-on-canvas is typical of the Flemish artist Peter Paul Rubens.

Entrance

The Impresario
In this portrait from around 1877, artist Edgar Degas emphasizes the subject's size by making him appear too large for the frame.

GALLERY GUIDE
The museum's permanent collection of European art is displayed throughout 19 galleries on the first floor. Works are arranged chronologically, from the medieval period, left of the main entrance, through the Renaissance, and on to the 20th century. Temporary exhibitions, graphic art and the porcelain collection are on the lower level.

★ **Waterlilies**
Claude Monet's work from between 1914 and 1917 is one of a series depicting the lily pond in his gardens in Giverny, near Paris.

★ **The Thinker**
The original bronze casting of Rodin's Le Penseur *(1904) is at the centre of the colonnaded Court of Honor. It is one of five moulds of the statue in collections around the world.*

KEY TO FLOORPLAN

☐	Permanent displays
☐	Achenbach Foundation Library
☐	Porcelain gallery
■	Theatre storage
☐	Temporary displays
☐	Non-exhibition space

The Presidio

Presidio Park sign

THE WINDING ROADS and lush green landscaping of the Presidio belie its long military history. This prominent site has played a key role in San Francisco's growth, and it has been occupied longer than any other part of the city. Remnants of its military past, including the well-preserved barracks, artillery emplacements and a museum, can be seen everywhere, and there are many hiking trails, cycle paths and beaches. The coastal path is one of the most popular walks and picnic areas in the city. The striking Golden Gate Bridge crosses the bay from the northwest corner of the Presidio to Marin County.

Fort Point
This impressive brick fortress, now a national historic site, guarded the Golden Gate during the Civil War of 1861–5 16

★ Golden Gate Bridge
Opened in 1937, the bridge has a single span of 4,200 ft (1,280 m) 17

Mountain Lake is a large spring-fed lake and a popular picnicking spot. The original Presidio was established nearby in 1776 to defend the bay area and Mission Dolores *(see p351).*

Crissy Field was reclaimed from marshland for the 1915 Panama-Pacific Exposition *(see p341)*. It was used as an airfield from 1919 to 1936, and is popular today for recreation.

LOCATOR MAP
See Street Finder, map 2 & 3

The Military Cemetery holds the remains of almost 15,000 American soldiers killed during several wars.

Marine Drive is a waterfront roadway, landscaped with palm trees.

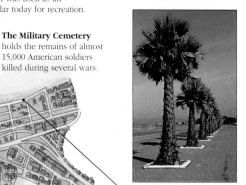

Arguello Gate
This decorative gate with its military symbols marks the entrance to the former army base, now open to the public.

★ **Presidio Museum**
This former hospital contains documents and artifacts relating to California's military history **15**

STAR SIGHTS

★ **Golden Gate Bridge**

★ **Presidio Museum**

0 metres 500
0 yards 500

Holy Virgin Cathedral ⑪

6210 Geary Blvd. **Map** 8 D1. 📞 *221-3255*. 🚌 *2, 29, 38.* 🕐 *8am, 6pm daily, extra services 8am, 9:45am Sun.*

SHINING GOLD onion-shaped domes crown the Russian Orthodox Holy Virgin Cathedral of the Russian Church in Exile, a startling landmark in the suburban Richmond District. Built in the early 1960s, it is generally open to the public only during services. In contrast to those of many other Christian denominations, the services in this cathedral are conducted with the congregation standing, so there are no pews or seats.

The cathedral and the many Russian-owned businesses surrounding it, such as the lively Russian Renaissance restaurant, are situated at the heart of San Francisco's extensive Russian community *(see p31)*. This has flourished since the 1820s, but it reached its highest population influx when a large number of new immigrants arrived after the Russian Revolution of 1917. It has since boomed twice more: in the late 1950s and late 1980s.

Clement Street ⑫

Map 1 C5. 🚌 *2, 28, 29, 44.*

THIS IS THE BUSTLING main thoroughfare of the otherwise sleepy Richmond District. Bookshops and small boutiques flourish here, and the inhabitants of the neighbourhood meet together in a lively mix of bars, fast-food cafés and ethnic restaurants. Most of these are patronized more by locals than by tourists.

Clement Street is surrounded by an area known as New Chinatown, home to more than one-third of the Chinese population of San Francisco. As a result, some of the city's best Chinese restaurants can be found here, and the emphasis in general is on Far Eastern cuisine *(see p564)*.

The area is also known for the diversity of its restaurants, and Danish, Peruvian and French establishments, among others, flourish here. The street stretches from Arguello Boulevard to the north–south cross-streets which are commonly known as "The Avenues". It ends near the California Palace of the Legion of Honor *(see pp364–5)*.

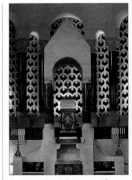

Interior of Temple Emanu-El, showing the Holy Ark

Temple Emanu-El ⑬

Lake St and Arguello Blvd. **Map** 3 A4. 📞 *751-2535.* 🕐 *8:30am–5:30pm Mon–Thu, 8:30am–5pm Fri (8:30am–7:30pm first Fri of month).* 🕐 *5:30pm Fri, 10:30am Sat.* 🚫 *during services.* ♿

AFTER WORLD WAR I hundreds of Jews from Russia and Eastern Europe moved into the Richmond District and built major religious centres. Among these is the Temple Emanu-El, its dome inspired by that of the 6th-century Hagia Sophia in Istanbul.

The temple stands out as a majestic piece of architecture. It was built in 1925 for the longest established congregation of Jews in the city, founded in 1850. The architect was Arthur Brown, who also designed City Hall *(see p342)*. The temple is an architectural hybrid: Mission style *(see pp26–7)*, Byzantine ornamentation and Romanesque arcades. Its interior, which accommodates nearly 2,000 worshippers, is especially fine when sunlight shines through the stained-glass windows.

Presidio Officers' Club ⑭

50 Moraga Ave. **Map** 3 A2. 📞 *(415) 561-2582.* 🚌 *29.* ⚫ *to the public.*

LOOKING OUT across the original parade grounds of the Presidio and the 19th-century wooden barracks, the Officers' Club is built in the Spanish Mission style *(see*

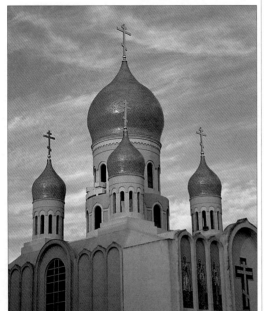

The Russian Orthodox Holy Virgin Cathedral

pp26–7). Although it dates from the 1930s, it was carefully built around the adobe (sun-dried brick) remains of the original 18th-century Spanish fort. There are plans to open the building to the public in the near future; phone ahead to check.

Presidio Museum ⑮

Funston Ave and Lincoln Blvd.
Map 3 B2. ⬛ *(415) 561-4804.*
⭕ *10am–4pm Wed–Sun.* 📷 ♿

THE PRESIDIO MUSEUM is housed in a white wooden building dating from the 1860s, which once served as the Presidio hospital. It contains documents and objects that illustrate the political and military history of California and the West Coast. One section is devoted to the evolution of San Francisco from a small frontier outpost in the 1770s to the major metropolis that it is today. On display are old uniforms, wartime propaganda posters, weapons and tools. On the walls are portraits of prominent Native American statesmen and warriors.

Two cabins stand behind the museum and are representative of the hundreds of temporary shelters set up here following the great earthquake of 1906 *(see pp48–9)*. One tent holds newspaper cuttings reporting the earthquake, the other contains some camp beds and stoves used by the refugees at that time.

Cannon on display outside the Presidio Museum

Golden Gate Bridge, seen from Fort Point

Fort Point ⑯

Marine Drive. **Map** 2 E1.
⬛ *556-1693.* ⭕ *10am–5pm Wed–Sun.* 📷 ♿ *partial.*

COMPLETED BY the US army in 1861, this fort was built partly to protect San Francisco Bay from any impending military attack, and partly to defend ships carrying gold from the Californian mines *(see pp44–5)*. It is the most prominent of the many fortifications constructed along the Pacific coastline, and is a classic example of a pre-Civil War brick and granite fortress. The building soon became obsolete, its 10-ft (3-m) thick brick walls not being strong enough to stand up to powerful modern weaponry. It was closed in 1900, never having come under attack.

The fort's brickwork vaulting is extremely unusual for San Francisco, where the ready availability of good timber was an incentive to build wood-frame constructions. This may have saved the fort from collapse in the 1906 earthquake *(see pp48–9)*. It was nearly demolished in the 1930s to make way for the Golden Gate Bridge, but it survived and is now a good place from which to view the bridge. Restored in the 1970s, the fort now houses a museum displaying military uniforms and arms. Park Rangers dressed in Civil War costume conduct guided tours.

A HISTORY OF THE PRESIDIO

In 1776 José Joaquin Moraga, one of the first Spanish settlers, founded a presidio. His aim in erecting this camp of adobe buildings on the edge of San Francisco Bay was to defend the Mission

The Presidio in the 19th century

Dolores *(see p351)*. Following Mexican independence from Spain, the site remained the northernmost fort of the short-lived republic, until the United States took it over in 1847. The Presidio was used for military purposes until 1990.

From the 1850s to the 1930s, the adobe buildings were replaced, first with wooden barracks, and later with concrete Mission- and Georgian-style cottages for the officers and their families. These buildings remain.

The site covers 1,400 acres (567 ha) and its landscaped forests of eucalyptus and cypress trees are not found on any other army base in the world. The Presidio has now been declared an historic site and is a protected member of the Golden Gate National Recreation Area (GGNRA).

Golden Gate Bridge ⑰

NAMED AFTER THAT PART of San Francisco Bay called "Golden Gate" by John Fremont in 1844, the bridge opened in 1937, connecting the city with Marin County. It took just over four years to build at a cost of $35 million. Breathtaking views are offered from this spectacular, world-famous landmark, which has six lanes for vehicles plus a free pedestrian walkway. It is the world's third largest single-span bridge and, when it was built, it was the world's longest and tallest suspension structure.

Bridge builder wearing protective mask

The twin steel towers rise to a height of 746 ft (227 m) above the sea. The towers are hollow.

Catching the Hot Rivets
Working in gangs of four, one man heated the rivets and threw them to another, who caught them in a bucket. The other two fastened sections of steel with the hot rivets.

The Foundations
The foundations of the twin towers are a remarkable feat of engineering. The south pier, 1,125 ft (343 m) offshore, was sunk 100 ft (30 m) into the sea bed.

Pier base 65-ft (20-m) thick

Fender 155-ft (47-m) high

Reinforcing iron frame

The roadway is 220 ft (67 m) above water 318-ft (97-m) deep.

The Concrete Fender
During construction, the south pier base was protected from the force of the tides by a fender of concrete. Water was pumped out to create a vast watertight locker.

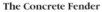

THE GOLDEN GATE BRIDGE
AT SAN FRANCISCO

The Roadway

The original steel-supported concrete roadway was constructed from the towers in both directions, so that weight on the suspension cables was evenly distributed.

The length of the bridge is 1.7 miles (2.7 km), the span is 4,200 ft (1,280 m), and the roadway is 220 ft (67 m) above the sea.

Joseph Strauss

Chicago engineer Joseph Strauss is officially credited as the bridge's designer and he led the opening ceremony in April 1937. He was assisted by Leon Moisseiff and Charles Ellis. Irving F Morrow acted as consulting architect.

View from Vista Point
The best view of both the bridge and the San Francisco skyline is from the Marin County side.

THE BRIDGE IN FIGURES

- Every year more than 40 million vehicles cross the bridge; every day about 120,000 vehicles use it.
- The original coat of paint lasted for 27 years, needing only touch-ups. But since 1965, a crew has been stripping off the old paint and applying a more durable coating.
- The two great 7,650-ft (2,332-m) cables are more than 3 ft (1 m) thick, and contain 80,000 miles (128,744 km) of steel wire, enough to encircle the earth at the equator three times.
- The volume of concrete poured into the piers and anchorages during the bridge's construction would be enough to lay a 5-ft (1.5 m) wide pavement from New York to San Francisco, a distance of more than 2,500 miles (4,000 km).
- The bridge can withstand 100 mph (160 km/h) winds.
- Each pier has to withstand a tidal flow of more than 60 mph (97 km/h), while supporting a 21,500-tonne steel tower.

Painting the bridge

ENTERTAINMENT IN SAN FRANCISCO

S AN FRANCISCO has prided itself on being the cultural capital of the West Coast since the city first began to prosper in the 1850s, and the entertainment on offer is generally of high quality. The performing arts complex of the Civic Center, opposite the City Hall, is the principal venue for classical music, opera and ballet. The latest addition to the city's cultural life is the highly rated Center for the Arts Theater at Yerba Buena Gardens. Many international touring shows can be seen

Beach Blanket Babylon
(see p331)

here. There are numerous repertory cinemas offering filmgoers a wide range of programmes, but theatre, except for some of the "alternative" venues, is not the city's strongest suit. Popular music, in particular jazz and blues, is where San Francisco really excels, and you can hear good bands for the price of a drink, or at the street fairs and music festivals which are held during the summer months. Facilities are also available for a wide variety of sports, from cycling to golf, tennis and sailing.

INFORMATION SOURCES

C OMPLETE LISTINGS of what's on and where are given in the *San Francisco Chronicle* and *Examiner* newspapers. Their combined Sunday edition is most useful. Other good sources are the free weekly newspapers, such as the *San Francisco Weekly* (available in most cafés and bars) or the *San Francisco Bay Guardian*. These give both listings and reviews, especially of live music, films and nightclubs.

Visitors planning further in advance will find the *San Francisco Book* very helpful. This is published twice yearly by the **San Francisco Convention and Visitors' Bureau** and is available free at the **Visitors' Information Center**

at Hallidie Plaza, or costs $2 if sent by post. You can also phone the visitors' bureau's Events Line for recorded information. Numerous free magazines for visitors are available, as well as calendars of events. Among these are *Key This Week San Francisco* and *Where San Francisco*.

BUYING TICKETS

T HE MAIN SOURCE for tickets to concerts, theatre and sporting events is **BASS** (the Bay Area Seating Service). BASS has a virtual monopoly on ticket sales, running an extensive charge-by-phone operation with outlets in the Tower and Wherehouse record shops *(see pp584–5)* all over Northern California.

Shop front of San Francisco ticket agency

There is a "convenience charge" of around $4 per ticket. An alternative to BASS is to buy directly from the box offices, though many of these are open only just before the start of evening performances.

To see productions by the reputable San Francisco Symphony, Ballet and Opera companies, forward planning is essential. All have subscription programmes, which are useful if you are planning to stay in the city for a lengthy period of time.

There are only a few ticket agencies in San Francisco, and they mostly specialize in selling limited seats at marked-up prices. They are all listed in the yellow pages of the telephone directory, found in most public payphones. Ticket touts are invariably found outside sold-out events, offering seats at extortionate prices. If you are willing to bargain (and risk missing the start of the game or the opening act) it is often possible to get a good deal this way.

Front entrance of the War Memorial Opera House

Outdoor chess, popular in Portsmouth Plaza, Chinatown

DISCOUNT TICKETS

DISCOUNT TICKETS for some selected events are available from **TIX Bay Area**, which offers half-price seats from a booth situated on the east side of Union Square *(see p310)*. Tickets are sold from 11am onwards, on the day of the performance only. There are also occasionally some half-price tickets available on Saturdays for events that are taking place on the following Sunday and Monday.

TIX Bay Area is also a full-service BASS outlet, supplying full-price tickets, and will accept all major credit cards for advance sales. It is open on Tuesdays, Wednesdays and Thursdays from 11am to 6pm, and on Fridays and Saturdays from 11am to 7pm.

FREE EVENTS

IN ADDITION to San Francisco's many ticket-only events, a number of free concerts and performances are regularly staged all over the city. Many of these take place during the day and outdoors in the summer, and they can offer a welcome change of pace from the usual standard fare.

The San Francisco Symphony Orchestra *(see pp374–5)* gives a series of late-summer Sunday concerts at Stern Grove, south of the Sunset District. The same venue is also occasionally used for ballets.

Cobb's Comedy Club *(see pp374–5)* hosts the popular San Francisco International Comedy Competition in August and September.

Performers from the San Francisco Opera *(see pp374–5)* can be heard singing some favourite arias in the Financial District as part of the "Brown Bag Operas" series, and in Golden Gate Park in "Opera in the Park" events. In the summer the park is also host to the Shakespeare Festival, Comedy Celebration Day and the San Francisco Mime Troupe. A series of concerts called "Music in the Park" is held on summer Fridays at noon, in the redwood grove behind the Transamerica Pyramid *(see p305)*. At Grace Cathedral *(see p321)* the fine cathedral choir sings choral music at Evensong, at 5:15pm on Thursdays.

FACILITIES FOR THE DISABLED

CALIFORNIA is a national leader in providing facilities for the handicapped. Most theatres and concert halls in San Francisco are therefore fully accessible, and have open areas set aside for wheelchair-users. Some smaller venues may require the use of special entrances, or lifts to reach the upper tiers. Many cinemas offer amplifying headphones. Contact the theatres to be sure of their facilities.

The Presidio Cinema

DIRECTORY

USEFUL ADDRESSES

San Francisco Convention and Visitors' Bureau
Suite 900, 201 3rd St,
((415) 974-6900.

Visitors' Information Center
900 Market St, Hallidie Plaza.
((415) 391-2000.

Events Line (24-hour)
((415) 391-2001 (English).
((415) 391-2003 (French).
((415) 391-2004 (German).
((415) 391-2122 (Spanish).

TICKET AGENCIES

BASS
Charge-by-phone.
((510) 762-2277.

TIX Bay Area
East Side of Union Sq, Stockton St
((415) 433-7827.

---

3 Com Park, home of the San Francisco Giants *(see pp374–5)*

Entertainment Venues

WITH A VARIETY of entertainment options, San Francisco is one of the most enjoyable cities in the world. Whatever your cultural preferences, what you see here is sure to be good. Besides housing the West Coast's best opera and ballet companies, it has a highly regarded symphony orchestra. The city also offers a wide range of jazz and rock music, diverse theatre companies and specialist cinemas. For the sports fan there are also plenty of opportunities to both watch and take part.

FILM AND THEATRE

SAN FRANCISCO has an avid film-going community. The city's best cinema is the **AMC Kabuki**, an eight-screen complex in the Japan Center *(see p342)*, which also hosts the **San Francisco International Film Festival** each May. A main venue for first-run foreign films is the **Opera Plaza**. The **Castro** *(see p350)* shows Hollywood classics and other revivals, with a programme that changes daily.

For theatregoers, major shows are staged at the main Theater District venues *(see p310)*. Other smaller theatres include the **Cable Car Theater** and the **Mason Street Theater**. The most respected company is the **American Conservatory Theater (ACT)**, which performs from October to May.

The Geary Theater *(see p310)*

OPERA, CLASSICAL MUSIC AND DANCE

THE MAIN SEASON of the **San Francisco Opera Association** runs from September to December and tickets can

Louise M Davies Symphony Hall

cost more than $100, but often there is a summer season, with cheaper tickets.

The main venue for opera, classical music and dance is the Civic Center arts complex on Van Ness Avenue. The **Louise M Davies Symphony Hall** is home to the city's symphony orchestra, which performs up to five concerts a week during its winter season.

The **San Francisco Ballet** season of classical and new works runs from February to April. The Center for the Arts *(see pp312–13)* is home to the **LINES Contemporary Ballet**.

ROCK, JAZZ AND BLUES

TWO OF THE BEST rock clubs, **Slim's** and the smaller **Paradise Lounge**, are opposite one another in the SoMa district. Another popular place is the reopened **Fillmore Auditorium**, the legendary birthplace of psychedelic rock during the 1960s *(see p349)*.

There are a number of places to hear live jazz, such as **Jazz at Pearl's**. The entertainment is usually free, if you buy dinner or drinks.

Live blues is played in bars such as **The Saloon** and **Jack's Bar**. The

annual San Francisco Blues Festival *(see p34)* attracts blues bands from all over the United States.

CLUBS

SAN FRANCISCO's largest disco is **DV8**, with its multiple dance floors, flashy décor and mainstream clientele. **Babylon** is smaller and draws an up-market, singles-oriented crowd. Some of the most popular clubs are primarily, though rarely exclusively, gay. These include **Endup** and **Rawhide II**, which has square dancing every night.

Piano bars all have nightly live music which you can enjoy for the price of a drink. One of the best is the beautiful Art Deco-style **Top of the Mark** at the top of the Mark Hopkins InterContinental Hotel *(see p523)*. **Julie's Supper Club** serves up good live jazz and R'n'B along with Cajun food and great cocktails. Some of the best shows of stand-up comedy take place at **Josie's Cabaret and Juice Joint** and **Cobb's Comedy Club**.

SPORTS AND OUTDOOR ACTIVITIES

COM PARK is the home of the **San Francisco 49ers** football team, but tickets for the games are hard to come by and expensive. Other local football teams are fielded by local colleges, the **University of California** *(see p402)* and **Stanford University** *(see p411)*. There are two professional baseball teams that play in the Bay Area, the National League **San Francisco Giants** and the American League **Oakland Athletics**.

There are many opportunities for participating in sports in San Francisco. Golfers have a range of courses to choose from, including the municipal link in **Lincoln Park**. Most of the public swimming pools are situated on the suburban fringes; for details contact the **City of**

Banner for the Jazz Festival *(see p34)*

San Francisco Recreation and Parks Department. To swim in the chilly ocean, head to China Beach, which is the only safe beach in the city.

There are good tennis courts in almost all the public parks in San Francisco, with the largest group in Golden Gate Park (see pp.356–9). The best-quality courts in the city are at the San Francisco Tennis Club, a recreational oasis in the heart of the industrial SoMa district. You will need to telephone well in advance if you want to book a court.

Golden Gate Bridge from Lincoln Park golf course

DIRECTORY

FILM AND THEATRE

AMC Kabuki
Map 4 E4.
931-9800.

American Conservatory Theater (ACT)
Map 5 B5.
(415) 749-2228.

Cable Car Theater
Map 5 B5.
(415) 956-8497.

Castro
Map 10 D2.
(415) 621-6120.

International Film Festival
Map 4 D5.
(415) 929-5000.

Mason Street Theater
Map 5 B5.
(415) 982-5463.

Opera Plaza
Map 4 F5.
(415) 352-0810.

OPERA, CLASSICAL MUSIC AND DANCE

LINES Contemporary Ballet
Yerba Buena Center for the Arts,
700 Howard St.
Map 5 C5.
(415) 978-2787.

Louise M Davies Symphony Hall Box Office
201 Van Ness Ave.
Map 4 F5.
(415) 431-5400.

San Francisco Ballet
455 Franklin St.
Map 4 F4.
(415) 861-5600.

San Francisco Opera Association
301 Van Ness Ave.
Map 4 F5.
(415) 861-4008.

San Francisco Symphony Association
201 Van Ness Ave.
Map 4 F5.
(415) 864-6000.

ROCK, JAZZ AND BLUES

Fillmore Auditorium
1085 Geary at Fillmore St.
Map 4 D4.
(415) 346-6000.

Jack's Bar
1601 Fillmore St.
Map 10 F2.
(415) 567-3227.

Jazz at Pearl's
256 Columbus Ave.
Map 5 C3.
(415) 291-8255.

Paradise Lounge
1501 Folsom St.
Map 10 F1.
(415) 861-6906.

The Saloon
1232 Grant Ave.
Map 5 C3.
(415) 989-7666.

San Francisco Blues Festival
Fort Mason. Map 4 E1.
(415) 826-6837.

Slim's
333 11th St. Map 10 F1.
(415) 522-0333.

CLUBS

Babylon
2260 Van Ness Ave.
Map 4 F3.
(415) 567-1222.

Cobb's Comedy Club
The Cannery at
Beach St. Map 5 A1.
(415) 928-4320.

DV8
540 Howard St.
Map 6 D5.
(415) 957-1730.

Endup
401 6th St.
Map 11 B1.
(415) 487-6277.

Josie's Cabaret and Juice Joint
3583 16th St.
Map 10 E2.
(415) 861-7933.

Julie's Supper Club
1123 Folsom St.
Map 11 A1.
(415) 861-0707.

Rawhide II
280 7th St. Map 11 A1.
(415) 487-6277.

Top of the Mark
Mark Hopkins
Inter-Continental Hotel.
Map 5 B4.
(415) 392-3434.

SPORTS AND OUTDOOR ACTIVITIES

City of San Francisco Recreation and Parks Department
Tennis Information.
(415) 753-7100.

Swimming Information.
(415) 753-7026.

Lincoln Park
(Municipal 18 hole)
Map 1 C5.
(415) 221-9911.

Oakland Athletics
Oakland Coliseum.
(510) 638-0500.

San Francisco 49ers
3 Com Park.
(415) 469-2249.

San Francisco Giants
3 Com Park.
(415) 467-8000.

Stanford University Athletics
Stanford University.
(1 800) 232-8225.

UC Berkeley Intercollegiate Athletics
UC Berkeley.
(1 800) 462-3277.

SHOPPING IN SAN FRANCISCO

SHOPPING in San Francisco is much more than simply making a purchase, it's a whole experience that allows a glimpse into the city's culture. It is the diversity of San Francisco that makes buying anything here an adventure. An enormous range of goods is available, from the practical to the more eccentric, but you can take your time in choosing, as browsers

Clock over entrance to Tiffany's

are generally made to feel welcome, particularly in the many small specialist shops and boutiques of the city. If you want convenience, the numerous shopping centres and department stores are excellent. For those in search of local colour, every neighbourhood shopping district has a charm and personality of its own, with each reflecting a different aspect of the city.

MALLS AND SHOPPING CENTRES

IN CONTRAST to a great many suburban shopping malls, those of San Francisco have character, and one or two of them are of considerable architectural interest. The Embarcadero Center (see p304) has more than 125 shops, in an area covering eight blocks. Ghirardelli Square (see p327) was a well-known chocolate factory from 1893 until early in the 1960s. It is now a mall that is very popular with visitors, and houses more than 70 shops and several restaurants, overlooking San Francisco Bay.

The San Francisco Center (see p311) has nine levels and more than 100 shops. Pier 39 (see p326) is a marketplace on the waterfront, with restaurants, a double-decker Venetian merry-go-round, a marina and many specialist boutiques. In the Cannery (see p327), located at Fisherman's Wharf, you will find a variety of charming small shops. The beautiful

Emporio Armani

Crocker Galleria (see p310) is one of the city's most spectacular malls, with three floors set under a high glass dome built around a central plaza.

The Japan Center (see p342), complete with pagoda, offers exotic foods, goods and art from the East, as well as a Japanese-style hotel and traditional baths. The Rincon Center (see p307), with a 90-ft (27-m) water column at its centre, is an Art Deco haven for shopping and eating.

DEPARTMENT STORES

MOST OF San Francisco's major department stores are in or near Union Square. They are huge emporia that offer their customers an outstanding selection of goods and services.

Macy's department store spans two city blocks. It stocks an enormous range of goods, all beautifully presented and sold by an enthusiastic sales staff. It offers a wide range of extra facilities, including a currency exchange and an interpreting service. The men's department is particularly extensive.

Neiman Marcus is another stylish emporium. Its modern building caused a furore when it was opened in 1982, replacing a popular store built in the 1890s. The huge stained-glass dome in its Rotunda Restaurant was part of the original building, and is well worth going to see.

Nordstrom, known for its fashion and shoes, is often called the "store-in-the-sky" as it is located in the top five floors of the innovative San Francisco Shopping Center.

Selling pictures and prints in Union Square

SHOPPING AROUND UNION SQUARE

SERIOUS SHOPPERS should concentrate on the blocks bordered by Geary, Powell and Post Streets, and on the surrounding blocks between Market and Sutter Streets. Here luxurious shops and inexpensive boutiques sell anything from designer bed linen to pedigree dogs to souvenirs. Exclusive hotels, smart restaurants and colourful flower stalls all add to the fashionable atmosphere.

SHOPS FOR A GOOD CAUSE

SAN FRANCISCANS take great pleasure in shopping for a good cause. The **Planetweavers Treasure Store** is the official UNICEF shop, where crafts and clothes made in developing countries are sold, as well as educational toys from around the world.

Flower stall on Union Square

The charity UNICEF receives 25 per cent of net profits. The **Hospitality House Store** is an art gallery where homeless artists, or artists on low incomes, can sell their work. All the profits that are made at **Under One Roof** benefit the various groups set up to help combat AIDS.

Those who want to protect the environment head for the **Greenpeace Store**, which sells jewellery, prints and a variety of other gifts.

SOUVENIRS

MANY SOUVENIRS, such as T-shirts, keyrings, mugs and Christmas ornaments, are decorated with motifs symbolizing San Francisco at **Only in San Francisco** and the **Bay Company**. Souvenir and novelty caps of every colour, size and shape are available at **Krazy Kaps**, while the shop entrances in Grant Avenue *(see p319)* and Fisherman's Wharf *(see pp324–5)* are lined with baskets filled with inexpensive gifts.

BEST BUYS

GOURMET SHOPPERS should look for seafood, one of the city's specialities. Wine from the Napa Valley *(see pp446–7)* is another good buy. You will find blue jeans at competitive prices, also vintage clothing, ethnic art, books and records.

SHOPPING TOURS

SHOPPERS who want to be guided to the best shops for their own particular needs can go on a specialist tour, organized by companies such as **A Simple Elegance Shopping Tour** or **Shopper Stopper Shopping Tours**. A guide takes you from shop to shop, to find unusual items.

MUSEUMS

MUSEUM SHOPPING offers exquisite gifts to suit all budgets. Among the city's best are the **Academy Store** in the California Academy of Sciences *(see pp360–61)*, the **Museum Shop** at the MH de Young Memorial Museum *(see pp362–3)*, and the **San Francisco MOMA Museum Store** *(see pp308–309)*.

Grant Avenue, Chinatown

San Francisco Specials

ENTREPRENEURIAL SPIRIT in San Francisco is strong and innovative, and the city's sophisticated image is very much deserved. Whether it is a small souvenir, a designer outfit, an antique, or a mouthwatering snack that is required, visitors will never be disappointed amid the shops and markets of San Francisco. The city is also home to many dedicated "foodies", gastronomes whose liking for fine wine and gourmet meals have resulted in unusual and delicious grocery stores. All this creates an environment that makes shopping in San Francisco an exciting experience.

SPECIALIST SHOPS

IF YOU WANT to laugh, go to **Smile–A Gallery with Tongue in Chic**, where humorous art to wear or display is sold, including many objects made by Bay Area artists. **Malm Luggage** has sold luggage, briefcases and leather goods since the Gold Rush days. You can describe the city's attractions on a designer card from **Quantity Postcards**. The city's main toy shop, **FAO Schwartz**, is a three-floor fantasy world for children.

Doorman at Schwartz

CLOTHES

SAN FRANCISCO designer shops include **Diana Slavin** for smart classics, **Joanie Char**'s for sportswear and **Franco Barone** for outerwear. **Levi Strauss & Co**, who have been making jeans since 1853, have factory tours on Wednesdays so that visitors can see how the famous Levis are made *(see p333)*. For discount designer clothes, head to the trendy SoMa district.

Brooks Brothers are well known for their smart men's suits and button-down shirts. Fashionable outdoor clothing for men is available from **Eddie Bauer**.

Small Frys is the locals' favourite for cotton children's clothes, and **Nike Town** is a megastore for training shoes, with televised sporting events to entertain shoppers.

BOOKS, MUSIC, ART AND ANTIQUES

THE LARGEST independent bookshop in the city is **A Clean Well-Lighted Place for Books**, carrying the latest titles, plus classics and works by local authors. Beats once met to talk about the country's emerging 1960s social revolution at the **City Lights Bookstore** *(see pp330–31)*, which stays open late and is a famous San Francisco institution.

A wide selection of music is on offer at various branches of **Tower Records** and **Wherehouse**. More obscure music can usually be found at **Recycled Records**.

Art lovers will find something to their liking in the city's hundreds of galleries. The **John Berggruen Gallery** has the city's largest collection of works by both emerging and more established artists. **Eleonore Austerer Gallery** sells limited edition prints by such modern masters as Picasso, Matisse and Miró. For a local perspective, pay a visit to **Artiques** for the Art Nouveau period and the early Californian artists. Exhibitions at **American Indian Contemporary Arts (AICA)** express the culture and traditions of many Native American people.

Jackson Square is San Francisco's main area for antiques *(see p304).*

Last touches in the Cookie Factory

FOOD AND WINE

FROM ABALONE to zucchini (courgettes), and from fresh Californian produce to imported speciality foods, the gourmet grocers **Bon Appetit** carry a wide variety of items. **Williams-Sonoma** has jams, mustards and much more for gifts or as a special treat. The Italian **Molinari Delicatessen** is famous for its fresh ravioli and tortellini, ready to throw into a saucepan. It is well worth going to Chinatown *(see pp316–17)* for Far Eastern

City Lights Bookstore *(see p330)* on Columbus Avenue

food products. The district's produce stores have the feel of an exotic farmers' market and are open every day. For an authentic atmosphere of Chinatown go to the **Golden Gate Fortune Cookie Company** *(see p316)* where customers can sample the famous San Francisco Chinatown invention. At **Casa Lucas Market** you will find a variety of Spanish and Latin American food specialities. A baguette of fresh sourdough bread from **Boudins Bakery** is a long-standing addiction with locals and a tradition with visitors. Chocoholics are catered for at San Francisco's own **Ghirardelli's**.

San Franciscans are coffee connoisseurs, and there are many specialist houses. **Caffè Trieste** is the city's oldest coffee house and sells a range of custom-roasted and blended coffees and a variety of brewing equipment.

The **Napa Valley Winery Exchange** features selections from the many Californian wineries, including the smaller local producers.

Locally grown fruit and vegetables arrive by the truckload at the regular farmers' markets in the centre of the city. Stalls are erected for the day and the farmers sell their goods directly to the public. The **Heart of the City** is open on Wednesdays and Sundays from 7am to 5pm and **Ferry Plaza Farmers' Market** is held on Saturdays from 9am to 2pm.

Ghirardelli Square, home to San Francisco's famous chocolate

DIRECTORY

SPECIALIST SHOPS

FAO Schwartz
48 Stockton St.
Map 5 C5.
📞 *(415) 394-8700.*

Malm Luggage
222 Grant Ave.
Map 5 C4.
📞 *(415) 392-0417.*

Quantity Postcards
1441 Grant Ave.
Map 5 C2.
📞 *(415) 986-8866.*

Smile–A Gallery with Tongue in Chic
500 Sutter St. **Map** 5 B4.
📞 *(415) 362-3436.*

CLOTHES

Brooks Brothers
201 Post St. **Map** 5 C4.
📞 *(415) 397-4500.*

Diana Slavin
3 Claude Lane.
Map 5 C4.
📞 *(415) 677-9939.*

Eddie Bauer
250 Post St. **Map** 5 C4.
📞 *(415) 986-7600.*

Franco Barone
437 Hayes St. **Map** 4 F5.
📞 *(415) 252-0156.*

Joanie Char
285A Sutter St.
Map 5 C4.
📞 *(415) 399-9867.*

Levi Strauss & Co
250 Valencia St.
Map 10 F1.
📞 *(415) 565-9159.*

Nike Town
278 Post St.
Map 5 C4.

Small Frys
4066 24th St.
Map 10 D4.
📞 *(415) 648-3954.*

BOOKS, MUSIC, ART AND ANTIQUES

American Indian Contemporary Arts
685 Market St. **Map** 5 B5.
📞 *(415) 495-7600.*

Artiques
2167 Union St. **Map** 4 D3.
📞 *(415) 929-6969.*

City Lights Bookstore
261 Columbus Ave.
Map 5 C3.
📞 *(415) 362-8193.*

A Clean Well-Lighted Place for Books
601 Van Ness Avenue.
Map 4 F5.
📞 *(415) 441-6670.*

Eleonore Austerer Gallery
540 Sutter St.
Map 5 B4.
📞 *(415) 986-2244.*

John Berggruen Gallery
228 Grant Ave.
Map 5 C4.
📞 *(415) 781-4629.*

Recycled Records
1377 Haight St.
Map 9 C1.
📞 *(415) 626-4075.*

Tower Records
Columbus Ave & Bay St.
Map 5 A2.
📞 *(415) 885-0500.*
One of several branches.

Wherehouse
3301 Geary Blvd.
Map 3 B5.
📞 *(415) 751-3711.*
One of several branches.

FOOD AND WINE

Bon Appetit
145 Jackson St.
Map 6 D3.
📞 *(415) 982-3112.*

Boudins Bakery
4 Embarcadero Center.
Map 6 D3.
📞 *(415) 362-3330.*

Caffè Trieste
601 Vallejo St. **Map** 5 C3.
📞 *(415) 982-2605.*

Casa Lucas Market
2934 24th St. **Map** 9 C3.
📞 *(415) 826-4334.*

Ferry Plaza Farmers' Market
Base of Market St at the Embarcadero.
Map 6 D3.

Ghirardelli's
Ghirardelli Square.
Map 4 F1.
📞 *(415) 474-3938.*

44 Stockton St.
Map 5 C1.
📞 *(415) 397-3615.*

Golden Gate Fortune Cookie Factory
56 Ross Alley.
Map 5 C3.
📞 *(415) 781-3956.*

Heart of the City Farmers' Market
United Nations Plaza.
Map 10 A1.
📞 *(415) 558-9455.*

Molinari Delicatessen
373 Columbus Ave.
Map 5 C3.
📞 *(415) 421-2337.*

Napa Valley Winery Exchange
415 Taylor St. **Map** 5 B5.
📞 *(415) 771-2887.*

Williams-Sonoma
150 Post St. **Map** 5 C4.
📞 *(415) 362-6904.*

GETTING AROUND
SAN FRANCISCO

AN FRANCISCO occupies a compact area, making it a sightseer's dream. Many of the sights that feature on visitors' itineraries are only a short walk from each other. The public transport system is also easy to use and efficient. Few visitors can resist a cable car ride. Bus routes crisscross town and pass many attractions. Muni Metro streetcars and BART lines serve the suburbs and the outlying neighbourhoods. Taxis are affordable, convenient and recommended for journeys after dark or even during the day through certain areas. Passenger ferries and boat trips run regularly east and north across the bay. If driving in San Francisco see page 603 for details on the city's parking laws.

Do not cross the road   **You may cross the road**

WALKING IN SAN FRANCISCO

THE BEST WAY to explore San Francisco is on foot. The main tourist areas are within 15 to 20 minutes of each other walking at average speed. The hills can be a struggle, but the views over the city and the bay make them worth the strenuous climb.

Most road intersections are marked with a green and white sign bearing the name of the cross street, or names are imprinted in the concrete pavement at street corners.

Vehicles are driven on the right-hand side of the road and are allowed to turn right on a red light if the road is clear, so keep an eye out

Pedestrian crossing

when crossing at traffic lights. Never rely solely on a pedestrian "Walk" signal.

Jaywalking is common, but illegal. Using a crossing when the "Don't Walk" signal is showing can result in a minimum $50 fine.

TAKING A TAXI

TAXIS IN SAN FRANCISCO are licensed and operate 24 hours a day. To catch a cab, wait at a taxi rank, call for a pick-up, or hail a cab when its rooftop sign is illuminated.

There is a flat fee (around $2.00) for the first mile (1.6 km). This increases by about $2 for each additional mile or 35 cents a minute while waiting at an address or in heavy traffic. Pay with notes of $20 or smaller and add a 15 per cent tip onto the fare.

CYCLING

CYCLING IS VERY popular in San Francisco and it is possible to find routes that avoid hills, especially along the waterfront. Bicycles can be hired for around $25 a day or $125 a week. There are cycle lanes in parts of the city, and some buses are equipped to carry bikes strapped to the outside. Details of scenic routes in the area are available from **Start to Finish** and **Wheel Escapes**.

OTHER WAYS TO GET AROUND

PEDICABS and horse-drawn carriages can be found on The Embarcadero, especially near Fisherman's Wharf (see

pp324–5). A fleet of motorized cable cars dashes around the city giving guided tours of all the sights, and passengers can get on or off where they choose. Sightseeing coach tours are offered as either half- or full-day excursions.

Pedicabs, a popular transport

DIRECTORY

TAXI COMPANIES

City Cab
(415) 468-7200.

De Soto Cab
(415) 673-1414.

Veteran's Cab
(415) 552-1300.

Yellow Cab
(415) 626-2345.

CYCLE HIRE

Start to Finish
2530 Lombard St.
Map 3 C2.
(415) 202-9830.

599 2nd St.
Map 11 C1.
(415) 243-8812.

Wheel Escapes
443 Chenery St,
Sausalito,
Marin County.
(415) 586-2377.

Travelling by Bus and Muni Metro Streetcar

SAN FRANCISCO MUNICIPAL RAILWAY, or Muni as it is more commonly called, is the organization that runs the city's public transport system. You can use one interchangeable pass – Muni Passport – to travel on Muni buses, Muni Metro streetcars (electric trams) and the three cable car lines. Buses and streetcars serve most tourist attractions and all neighbourhoods.

FARES AND TICKETS

BUSES AND STREETCARS both cost $1 per ride; for this fare, you can request a free transfer allowing you to change vehicles twice within two hours. There is a supplement for express or limited stop buses. Reduced fares are available for both senior citizens and children aged 5 to 17. Children under 5 travel free.

If you are planning to make a number of trips by Muni, a Muni Passport, valid for 1, 3 or 7 days, allows unlimited travel on the city's buses, streetcars and cable cars. Muni passports are available from the information kiosk at City Hall (see p343), the **Visitors' Information Center** and the Muni kiosk situated at the Powell–Hyde cable car turntable (see p311).

USING BUSES AND STREETCARS

BUSES STOP only at their designated bus stops, placed every two or three blocks. The route number and the destination are printed on the front and side of each bus. Route numbers that are followed by a letter (L, EX, A, B, etc.) are express services.

On boarding, put the exact change or tokens in the fare box, or show your Muni Passport to the driver. To indicate that you want to get off at the next stop, pull the cord that runs along the windows or

A Muni Metro streetcar

Muni Passports

inform the driver. The "Stop Requested" sign above the front window will light up. Bus stops are indicated by signs displaying the Muni logo. Route numbers of buses that stop there are listed below the sign, and route maps and timetables are located on the inside walls of bus shelters. Along Market Street routes alternate between stops at the kerb or at islands in the street.

Muni Metro streetcars and BART trains (see p382) both use the same underground terminals along Market Street. Orange, yellow and white illuminated signs mark their entrances. Once you are inside the terminal, look for the separate "Muni" entrance.

To travel to the west of the city, choose "Outbound"; to travel east, choose "Downtown". Electronic signs indicate which streetcar is about to arrive. Doors open automatically on boarding; push the bar by the door when exiting.

Stops above ground have an orange-and-brown flag or a yellow band around a pole, marked "Muni" or "Car Stop".

SIGHTSEEING BY BUS

POPULAR ROUTES for visitors include 8, 15, 30, 32, 39, 42 and 45. Route 38 runs to the hills above Ocean Beach, and Golden Gate Park (see pp356–9) is on route No. 21. Route 42 is a circuitous route that covers Downtown (see pp300–13), the Civic Center (see pp342–3) and Fisherman's Wharf (see pp324–5). For Chinatown and Nob Hill (see pp314–21) take Route 45; for Haight Ashbury and the Mission District (see pp344–53) take Route 8. The Bay Area (see pp394–415) can be reached within 30 to 45 minutes, depending on traffic.

A Muni "Tours of Discovery" sightseeing brochure is available from the Muni office itself or the city's **Visitors' Information Center**.

Muni bus shelter with payphones

A Muni bus

DIRECTORY

MUNI INFORMATION

Room 238, 949 Presidio Ave.
Map 3 C4. (415) 673-6864.

MUNI PASSPORTS

Visitors' Information Center
Lower level, Hallidie Plaza,
Market & Powell Sts.
Map 5 C5. (415) 554-7111.

Travelling by Cable Car, BART and Ferry

S AN FRANCISCO'S cable cars are world famous (see pp292–3) and every visitor will want to ride one at least once. San Francisco peninsula and the East Bay are linked by BART (Bay Area Rapid Transit), a 71-mile (114-km) light rail system with a high speed, efficient fleet of trains, all wheelchair accessible. Boats and passenger ferries are also a favourite way to see the city's shore-line and get around.

Riding down Hyde Street to the bay

USING THE CABLE CARS

T HE CITY'S CABLE CAR service operates from 6:30am to 12:30am daily. There is a flat fare of approximately $2 for each journey.

Cable cars run along three routes. The name of the line is displayed on the front, back and sides of every cable car. The Powell–Hyde line is the most popular, starting at the Powell and Market turntable (see p311), and ending on Hyde Street, near Aquatic Park. The Powell–Mason line also begins at Powell and Market streets and ends at Bay Street. Sit facing east on the

Powell lines and you will see the best sights as you travel. The California line runs from the base of Market Street, then through part of the Financial District and Chinatown, ending at Van Ness Avenue. Cable cars run at 15-minute intervals.

To catch a cable car, you should be prepared to jump on board quickly. Stops are marked by maroon signs that display the outline of a cable car in white, or by a yellow line painted on the road at right angles to the track.

If you have not already purchased a Muni Passport (see p381), either pay the conductor on board the car or buy a souvenir ticket. These are available at ticket machines or a booth at the terminus, shops along the route, Muni kiosks or at the city Visitor Information Center (see p381). Tickets are collected by the conductor when you board. Fares are for a single journey only.

Commuters like to use cable cars too, so try to avoid travelling during rush hours. Whenever you travel you are more likely to get a seat if you board the car at the end of the line you have chosen.

Cable car ticket machine

Nob Hill, main cable car junction

SIGHTSEEING BY CABLE CAR

T HE CITY'S HILLS present no problem to the cable cars. They tackle precipitous slopes effortlessly, passing sights and areas popular with tourists. The most thrilling descent is the final stretch of the Powell–Hyde line as it dips down from Nob Hill to the bay.

TRAVELLING SAFELY IN A CABLE CAR

I F THERE IS NOT a crowd, you can choose whether to sit or stand inside, sit outside on a bench or stand on a side running board. Wherever you find a place, hold on tight.

Try not to get in the way of the gripman; he needs a lot of room to operate the grip lever. This off-limits area is marked by yellow lines on the floor. Use caution while on board. Passing other cable cars is exciting, but be careful not to lean out too far as they get quite close to one another. Take special care when boarding or alighting. Often cable cars stop at an intersection and you have to get on or off between the car and other vehicles. All passengers must alight at the end of the line.

USEFUL NUMBERS

Cable Car Barn
1201 Mason St. **Map** 5 B3.
📞 (415) 474-1887.

Muni Information
📞 (415) 673-6864. Cable car information, fares, Muni Passports.

Bell ─────   ───── Destination board

POWELL   &   HYDE Sts.

SAN FRANCISCO MUNICIPAL RAILWAY

Side seating | ╲ Running board   Gate |

A San Francisco cable car

MAKING A JOURNEY BY **BART**

The BART logo

BART trains operate daily from early morning until midnight. During rush hours, 7am to 9am and 4pm to 6:30pm, they run at full capacity. The trains are clean and well kept, and the service is efficient.

BART trains stop at five city centre stations, all beneath Market Street – Van Ness, Civic Center, Powell, Montgomery and Embar-cadero – but glide above ground in the majority of outlying areas.

All trains from Daly City stop at city centre stations before heading for the East Bay through a dark, 4-mile (6-km) underwater tunnel.

BART ROUTE MAP

Transfers in the East Bay are possible at only two stations: MacArthur and Oakland City.

To explore the BART system without buying a new ticket for each trip, you can buy an excursion fare.

KEY

— Daly City–Richmond Line

‑‑ Daly City–Concord Line

— Daly City–Fremont Line

⚍ Richmond–Fremont Line

FERRY SERVICES AND BAY TRIPS

RESIDENTS OF THE Bay Area adore their ferries and they are used as much by local com-muters to and from the city as they are by tourists. Although these ferries do not have audio tours to point out and describe the sights, they are less expensive than sightseeing cruises. The Ferry Building (see p306) is the terminal for **Golden Gate Ferries**.

Bay sightseeing cruises from Fisherman's Wharf are oper-ated by **Blue & Gold Fleet** and **Red & White Fleet**. Trips offered include Angel Island, Alcatraz (see pp328–9) and towns that lie on the north shore of the bay (see pp398–9). There are also combined boat and coach tours to Marine World Africa USA and Muir Woods (see p398).

You can dine and dance aboard one of several cruisers that ply the bay's waters.

Sign for bay cruise tickets

Hornblower Dining Yachts offer lunch on Friday, brunch at weekends, and dinner daily on their cruises. Meals are also served at bayside tables that offer diners spec-tacular views of the waterfront. The **Oceanic Society** offers trips with an onboard naturalist around the Farallon Islands, 25 miles (40 km) off San Francisco (see pp396–7). Whale-watching expeditions off the city's west

Red & White Fleet ferry

coast (see p580) are also available. Check with the operators for seasonal details.

DIRECTORY

FERRIES

Golden Gate Ferries
☎ (415) 332-6600.

Red & White Fleet
Pier 41 & 43½.
Map 5 B1.
☎ (415) 546-2700,
or (1 888) 732-3483.
45-minute tour.

BAY TRIPS

Blue & Gold Fleet
Pier 39. **Map** 5 B1.
☎ (415) 705-5444.
75-minute tour.

Hornblower Dining Yachts
Pier 33. **Map** 5 C1.
☎ (415) 394-8900, ext. 7.

Oceanic Society Expeditions
☎ (415) 474-3385.

SAN FRANCISCO STREET FINDER

M AP REFERENCES given with sights, entertainment venues, shops and Practical Information addresses described in the San Francisco section refer to the maps on the following pages. Map references for hotels and restaurants in the city *(see pp523–9 and pp560–68)* also apply to these pages. The

key map below shows the area covered by the Street Finder, including the sightseeing areas and other districts important for restaurants, hotels and entertainment venues. A large-scale map of the city centre appears on pages 5 and 6. The symbols used in the Street Finder maps are listed in the key below.

KEY TO STREET FINDER

Major sight

Places of interest

CalTrain station

BART station

Coach terminus

Streetcar terminus

Bus terminus

Cable car terminus

Ferry terminus

Tourist information

Hospital with casualty unit

Police station

Church

Synagogue

Mosque

Buddhist temple

Hindu temple

Post office

Golf course

Railway line

Freeway

One-way street

<<665 House number (main street)

SCALE OF MAPS 1–4 AND 7–11

| 0 metres | 500 |
| 0 yards | 500 |

SCALE OF MAPS 5 & 6

| 0 metres | 500 |
| 0 yards | 500 |

Golden Gate Park & the Presidio

PACIFIC OCEAN

Land's End

LINCOLN PARK

LINCOLN PARK MUNICIPAL GOLF COURSE

EL CAMINO DEL MAR

LEGION OF HONOR DRIVE

CLEMENT STREET

Municipal
Pier

Hyde Street
Pier

Pier 47

Pier 45

USS Pampanito

Ripley's
Believe It Or Not
Museum

JEFFERSON ST

TAYLOR STREET

The
Cannery

Organ

BEACH STREET

San Francisco
National Maritime
Museum

FISHERMAN'S
WHARF

FORT MASON
(GOLDEN GATE
NATIONAL
RECREATION AREA)

Ghirardelli
Square

NORTH POINT STREET

BERGEN
PL

BRET
HARTE
TERR

1

A GREEN DRIVE

A GREEN

FRANKLIN STREET

MARINA BOULEVARD

FILLMORE STREET

A WAY WAY

WAY DRIVE

JEFFERSON ST

WEBSTER ST

BEACH STREET

BUCHANAN STREET

LAGUNA STREET

McARTHUR AVENUE

GOUGH STREET

OCTAVIA AVENUE

POLK STREET

NORTHPOINT

VAN NESS AVENUE

<<1000

BAY STREET

RUSSIAN
HILL
PARK

San Francisco
Art Institute

5

NORTH POINT STREET

BAY STREET

<<1400

LARKIN STREET

HYDE STREET

LEAVENWORTH

JONES STREET

STREET

GEORGE R MOSCONE
RECREATION CENTER

MAGNOLIA STREET

CHESTNUT STREET

LOMBARD

MONTCLAIR
TERR

SOUTHARD
PL

GREENWICH ST

2

MALLORCA
STREET

BRAZIL
WAY

OLEDO WAY

NUT STREET

MOULTON STREET

LOMBARD STREET

GREENWICH STREET

STREET

FILBERT STREET

ALLEN ST

EASTMAN

STREET

BLACK ST

STREET-
STREET

COW HOLLOW

PIXLEY STREET

BERT STREET

NWICH

AHLERS CT

CHARLTON CT

BUCHANAN STREET

OCTAVIA STREET

LAGUNA STREET

FILBERT STREET

UNION STREET

Octagon
House

Allyne
Park

GREEN STREET

BONITA
ST

GREEN STREET

UNION STREET

MACONDRAY
LN

GREEN STREET

RUSSIAN
HILL

3

UNION STREET

Church of
St Mary the Virgin

WEBSTER STREET

VALLEJO

BROADWAY

<<2400

PACIFIC AVENUE

G

IS

<<2500

BROMLEY
PL

BUCHANAN STREET

LAGUNA STREET

OCTAVIA STREET

VALLEJO STREET

BROADWAY

Spreckels
Mansion

Haas-Lilienthal
House

PACIFIC STREET

JACKSON STREET

FRANKLIN STREET

VAN NESS AVENUE

BROADWAY
TUNNEL

MORRELL
ST

LYNCH ST

AVENUE

STREET

TROY
AL

<<2200

REED ST

LEAVENWORTH

GLOVER ST

PACIFIC

JACKSON STREET

ALTA
PLAZA

CLAY STREET

LAFAYETTE
PARK

WASHINGTON STREET

CLAY STREET

SACRAMENTO STREET

CLAY STREET

<<1500

4

SACRAMENTO STREET

PERINE PL

CALIFORNIA STREET

CALIFORNIA STREET

PINE STREET

SCOTT STREET

PIERCE STREET

WILMOT ST

FILLMORE STREET

MIDDLE ST

STEINER STREET

COTTAGE
ROW

BUSH STREET

PINE STREET

BUCHANAN STREET

LAGUNA STREET

GOUGH STREET

OCTAVIA STREET

AUSTIN

FERN

BUSH STREET

HEMLOCK

SUTTER STREET

FRANKLIN STREET

VAN NESS AVENUE

POLK STREET

LARKIN STREET

F NORRIS
ST

EUREKA
PL

CEDAR ST

<<2900

SGT JOHN
McAULEY PARK

HYDE STREET

STREET

STREET

4

POST STREET

SUTTER STREET

AVERY ST

Japan Center
<<1600

PETER YORK
ST

STARR KING
WAY

GEARY STREET

MYRTLE STREET

OLIVE STREET

WESTERN
ADDITION

GEARY BOULEVARD

WEBSTER STREET

HOLLIS ST

St Mary's
Cathedral

CLEARY CT

ELLIS STREET

WILLOW STREET

EDDY STREET

LARCH ST

TURK STREET

ELM ST

5

ELLIS STREET

BRODERICK STREET

EDDY STREET

WEBSTER STREET

JEFFERSON
SQ

HAYWARD
PLGD

TURK STREET

SEYMOUR ST

GOLDEN GATE AVENUE

JEFFERSON ST

GOLDEN GATE AVENUE

<<3300

McALLISTER STREET

McALLISTER STREET

FULTON STREET

REDWOOD
ST

ELM ST

GATE

VAN NESS AVENUE

Veteran's
Building

War Memorial
Opera House

Louise M Davies
Symphony Hall

City
Hall

CIVIC
CENTER

SF Arts
Commission
Gallery

SF Main
Library

SF New
Public
Library

Bill
Graham
Civic
Auditorium

<<2800

JESSIE

5

ALAMO
SQUARE

HAYES VALLEY

GROVE STREET

BIRCH ST

HAYES STREET

OCTAVIA STREET

LINDEN ST

A   B   C

Pier 45   *USS Pampanito*   Pier 43   Pier 41   Pier 39   Pier 35   Pier 33

Pier 47

1

EMBARCADERO NORTH ST

Ripley's Believe It Or Not Museum   *Wax Museum*   STREET

JEFFERSON   STREET   POWELL STREET   GRANT   KEARNY   MONTGOMERY STREET

The Cannery   BEACH   STREET   STOCKTON   STREET   THE EMBARC

4

FISHERMAN'S   POINT STREET   WHARF   STREET

NORTH   BERGEN PL   BAY   COLUMBUS   VANDEWATER   FRANCISCO   BELLAIR PL   PFEIFFER ST   WINTHROP ST   MONTGOMERY STREET

LARKIN   STREET   BRET HARTE TERR   WATER ST   MASON   AVENUE   STREET   WHITING ST   STREET

RUSSIAN HILL PARK   FRANCISCO   STREET   CHESTNUT   VENARD AL   FIELDING ST   LOMBARD   TELEGRAPH HILL

San Francisco Art Institute   CHESTNUT   JONES   TAYLOR   JANSEN ST   NORTH BEACH PLAYGROUND   GREENWICH   STREET   *Coit Tower*   FILBERT ST

2

CHESTNUT   LEAVENWORTH   STREET   AVENUE   *Saints Peter and Paul Church*   GREENWICH   KEARNY   GENOA PL   VARENNES   CASTLE

LOMBARD   MONTCLAIR TERR   LURMONT TERR   GREENWICH   STREET   VALPARAISO ST   FILBERT   STREET   GRANT   SONOMA   UNION   CALHOUN TR   FILBERT ST   SANSOME

SOUTHARD PLACE   ROACH   ALADDIN TERR   *Washington Square*   BANNAM   GREEN   AVENUE

FILBERT   STREET   BLACK PL   UNION   STREET   *Club Fugazi*   WEBB PL   PARDEE AL

ALLEN ST   HAVENS ST   MACONDRAY LANE   *North Beach Museum*   EATON   STOCKTON   TRACY   FRESNO ST   DUNNES AL   PRESCOTT CT   BROADWAY

UNION ST   WARNER PL   HAMLIN ST   COOLBRITH PARK   CHURCHILL   STREET   STREET   BARTOL ST   HODGES AL   MIDWAY

EASTMAN ST   WHITE ST   WALDO AL   GLOVER ST   *Vallejo Street Stairway*   FALLON PL   POWELL   CORDELIA   PELTON CT   COLUMBUS   OSGOOD CT   BROADWAY

3

RUSSIAN   HILL   BROADWAY   TUNNEL   STREET   SALMON ST   WAYNE   PLEASANT   ROMOLO   AVENUE   GOL

VALLEJO   STREET   BERNARD   JONES   AUBURN   STREET   STONE   *Jackson Square Historical District*

BROADWAY   <<1400   LYNCH   AVENUE   FLORENCE   DORIC   *Transamerica Pyramid*   HOTALING

MODELL PL   LEAVENWORTH   STREET   STREET   CODMAN PL   *Cable Car Barn*   STREET   WETMORE ST   *Chinatown Alleys*   PACIFIC   AVENUE

PACIFIC   JACKSON   STREET   *Tin How Temple*   *Chinese Historical Soc*   *Pacific Mtn*

4

POLK   LARKIN   WASHINGTON   PRIEST ST   REED ST   LEROY PL   *Kong Chow Temple*   STREET   *Old St Mary's Church*   *Wells Fargo History Museum*

NOB   HILL   PLEASANT   HUNTON PARK   *Fairmont Hotel*   SACRAMENTO   CALIFORNIA   ST MARY'S SQUARE   MON

CLAY   TROY AL   STREET   GOLDEN   *Grace Cathedral*   *Pacific-Union Club*   <<895   GROVE   ST GEORGE AL   *Bank of America*

SACRAMENTO   ACORN AL   HELEN   *Mark Hopkins Inter-Continental Hotel*   *Chinatown Gateway*   VINTON CT   KEARNY   CLAUDE   BUSH

CALIFORNIA   <<1500   HYDE   PINE   MULFORD AL   MONROE   STOCKTON TUNNEL   ST   *John Beggruen Gallery*   *Crocker Galleria*

F NORRIS ST   EUREKA PL   HOOKER AL   POWELL   *Gumps*   *Sheraton Hote*

PINE   STREET   BUSH   SUTTER   <<250   CAMPTON PL

4   POLK   STREET   LEAVENWORTH   TAYLOR   HOBART AL   *Saks*   *Westin St Francis Hotel*   STOCKTON STREET   GRANT   AVENUE

FERN   SUTTER   STREET   COSMO PL   STREET   *Neiman Marcus*   <<110   American Indian Contemporary Arts Ga

HEMLOCK   STREET   JONES   SHANNON ST   *UNION SQUARE*   <<323   STREET   *Macy's*

CEDAR   STREET   POST   MEACHAM PL   STREET   STREET   *Macy's*   MARKET

MYRTLE ST   <<900   *SGT JOHN McAULEY PARK*   THEATER   ADA CT   STREET

5   GEARY   STREET   DISTRICT   ANTONIO ST   STEVELOE PL   *Powell St Cable Car Turntable*   4TH

VAN NESS AVENUE   O'FARRELL   STREET   COHEN PL   *SF Visitors Information Center*   *Powell Street Station*   *Cartoon Art Museum*   HOLLAND CT

OLIVE   STREET   ELLIS   STREET   *SF Center*   MINNA ST

WILLOW   EDDY   STREET   <<200   *Old United States Mint*   MINT ST

TURK   STREET   <<96A

A   B   C

1

Alcatraz Island

2

San Francisco Bay

Pier 19

Pier 17

Pier 15

Pier 9

Pier 7

Pier 5

Pier 3

Pier 1

3

THE EMBARCADERO

DAVIS STREET

DRUMM STREET

WASHINGTON STREET

EMBARCADERO PLAZA PARK

JUSTIN HERMAN PLAZA

Embarcadero Center

MARITIME PLAZA

Hyatt Regency Hotel

World Trade Center
Pier 2

Ferry Building

No.1 Market Street

Embarcadero Station

STEUART STREET

SPEAR STREET

Rincon Center

Pier 24

4

MISSION STREET

MAIN STREET

BEALE STREET

FREMONT STREET

1ST STREET

HOWARD STREET

FOLSOM STREET

ELKHART ST

STEWART STREET

Amtrak Terminal Ticket Office

Greyhound Bus Depot

Transbay Terminal

SAN FRANCISCO OAKLAND BAY BRIDGE

Pier 26

Pier 28

5

MINNA STREET

TEHAMA STREET

CLEMENTINA ST

GROTE ST

GUY PLACE

LANSING ST

STERLING ST

ESSEX ST

BRANNAN STREET

BRYANT STREET

RINCON ST

THE EMBARCADERO

Museum of Modern Art

HAWTHORNE STREET

DOW PL

HAMPTON PL

VERONICA PL

HARRISON STREET

STILLMAN ST

DE BOOM ST

Pier 30

Pier 32

Pier 34

Pier 36

Pier 38

A   **1**   B   C

1

SEAL ROCK DRIVE

SHORE VIEW AVE

POINT LOBOS AVENUE

SEAL ROCK DR
ALTA MAR WY

GEARY BOULEVARD   <<7900

GEARY BOULEVA

Seal
Rocks

SUTRO
HEIGHTS
PARK

48TH AVENUE
47TH AVENUE
46TH
45TH
44TH
43RD
42ND AVENUE
41ST AVENUE
40TH AVENUE
39TH
38TH
37TH
36TH
35TH
34TH

ANZA STREET

ANZA   ST

SUTRO HEIGHTS
AVE

LA PLAYA STREET

BALBOA STREET

BALBOA AVENUE

CABRILLO STREET

CABRILLO

CABRILLO
PLAYGROUND

FULTON STREET

GREAT HIGHWAY

<<6900 FULTON STREET

FULTON STREET

SPRECKE

2

Queen
Wilhelmina's
Tulip Garden

N LAKE RD

CHAIN OF LAKES DRIVE

Buffalo Paddock

36TH AVENUE

Spreckels
Lake

JF KENNEDY DRIVE

GOLDEN
GATE PARK
GOLF
COURSE

CHAIN OF LAKES DRIVE WEST

JF KENNEDY DRIVE

GOLDE

Chain
of
Lakes

CHAIN OF LAKES DRIVE EAST

Fly Casting
Pool

Po

Ocean Beach

MIDDLE DRIVE WE

MARTIN LUTHER KING JR DRIVE

MARTIN LUTHER KING JR

3

LINCOLN WAY

GREAT HIGHWAY

<<64700

IRVING STREET

48TH AVENUE
47TH AVENUE
46TH AVENUE
45TH AVENUE
43RD AVENUE
42ND AVENUE
41ST AVENUE
40TH AVENUE
39TH STREET
38TH AVENUE
37TH AVENUE
36TH
35TH AVENUE

JUDAH AVENUE

PINO AL

PACIFIC
OCEAN

KIRKHAM STREET

<<3400

SUNSET

4

LAWTON STREET

MORAGA STREET

BOULEVARD

40TH AVENUE
39TH AVENUE
38TH AVENUE
37TH AVENUE

<<3500

NORIEGA STREET

GREAT HIGHWAY

36TH AVENUE
<<3750

ORTEGA STREET

42ND AVENUE
41ST AVENUE
37TH AVENUE

5

48TH AVENUE
47TH AVENUE
46TH AVENUE
45TH AVENUE
44TH AVENUE
43RD AVENUE
42ND AVENUE

PACHECO STREET

WEST SUNSET
PLAYGROUND

GREAT HIGHWAY

QUINTARA STREET

RIVERA S

A   B   C

THE BAY AREA

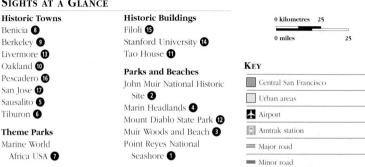

MANY OF THE SETTLEMENTS encircling San Francisco Bay were once summer retreats for the city's residents, but today they are sprawling suburbs or cities in their own right. Two of the most popular destinations in the East Bay are Oakland's museum and harbour, and Berkeley's gardens and famous university. Further south, San Jose has emerged as the region's newest commercial and cultural centre, combining the technology of Silicon Valley with fine museums and preserved architecture of its Spanish Colonial past. Smaller towns such as Tiburon, Pescadero and Sausalito, however, have managed to retain their village atmosphere, despite their closeness to the city. The area also has the advantage of its coastal landscapes: the cliffs of Point Reyes and the Marin Headlands, with their abundance of wildlife, offer perfect afternoon retreats away from the metropolis.

**Detail from
Sather Gate, Berkeley**

SIGHTS AT A GLANCE

Historic Towns
Benicia **8**
Berkeley **9**
Livermore **13**
Oakland **10**
Pescadero **16**
San Jose **17**
Sausalito **5**
Tiburon **6**

Theme Parks
Marine World
    Africa USA **7**

Historic Buildings
Filoli **15**
Stanford University **14**
Tao House **11**

Parks and Beaches
John Muir National Historic
    Site **2**
Marin Headlands **4**
Mount Diablo State Park **12**
Muir Woods and Beach **3**
Point Reyes National
    Seashore **1**

0 kilometres   25
0 miles   25

KEY

▨	Central San Francisco
▢	Urban areas
✈	Airport
🚉	Amtrak station
▬	Major road
▬	Minor road

◁ **Houseboats in the picturesque town of Sausalito**

The Bay Area Coastline

THE COASTLINE AROUND San Francisco varies a great
deal, its rugged cliffs alternating with sandy
beaches. Since the ocean water hovers around 60° F
(15° C) all year round, nobody swims or surfs without
a wet suit, but for sunbathing or aimless beachcombing
strolls, the Bay Area beaches are hard to beat. Much
of the coast is protected by a series of state and federal parks, such as the Point Reyes National Seashore
(see p398), the Marin Headlands section of the Golden
Gate National Recreation Area *(pp400–401)* and the
many state beaches that line the southern coast.

Pacifica *was once the agricultural outpost of
Mission Dolores (see p351). The two-storey
Sanchez Adobe in the town now houses a
museum of 19th-century farming equipment.*

★ **Point Reyes National
Seashore** ①

This protected stretch of land
is noted for its diverse ecosystems and its 360 species
of birds *(see p398)*.

Bolinas ②

Following the Gold Rush
(see pp44–5), Bolinas became
a summer haven for San Franciscans, and some Victorian
buildings still survive. The
town is also a winter home
to monarch butterflies.

Marin Headlands ④

The Marin Headlands benefit
from stunning views of San
Francisco as well as a wilderness rife with diverse birdlife
(see pp400–401).

Treasure Island ⑥

At the centre of the Bay Bridge
(see pp406–407), the island was
the site of the 1939 World's Fair.
A small museum displays memorabilia from the fair. The island
once belonged to the US Navy.

Fort Funston ⑦

The bluff overlooking this
beach, which is also used as
an observation site, is a favourite
launch site for professional and
amateur hang-gliders.

Colma ⑧

This unusual town consists
almost entirely of cemeteries,
containing the graves of former
San Franciscans and Bay Area
residents. Cemeteries are
prohibited within the city of
San Francisco.

Pillar Point Harbour ⑨

This is the only naturally
protected harbour located
between San Francisco and
Santa Cruz. In the late 19th
century it was used as a
whaling station.

★ **Farallon Islands** ⑫

Twenty-seven miles (44 km)
west of Point Bonita, the islands
are the most important nesting
site for sea birds and stopover
point for migratory birds in California. They are also a breeding
ground for elephant seals. There
is no public access.

**Muir Woods National
Monument** *is the last
remaining redwood forest in
the Bay Area. The others were
cut down for timber during the
19th century (see p398).*

SANT.

Tomales Road

①

Point Reyes Station

Petaluma

①

Sir Francis

⑫

***Mount Tamalpais**, reaching a height of 2,604 ft (794 m), is the habitat of various flora and fauna, including the rarely sighted mountain lion. The Mountain Theater is set in a natural bowl overlooking the bay.*

LOCATOR MAP

★ **Muir Beach ③**

Redwood Creek drains down from Mount Tamalpais to the ocean at Muir Beach. It is home to silver salmon and crayfish. South of Muir Beach, Potato Patch Shoal is a low-tide area of turbulence and freak waves.

★ **Point Bonita ⑤**
Point Bonita's lighthouse on this rugged clifftop, was the last manually operated lighthouse in the state, only changing to automation in 1980. The lighthouse is reached via a tunnel carved through solid rock or over a surf-lashed bridge.

★ **Half Moon Bay ⑩**

The oldest town in San Mateo County, the area's soil is ideal for growing artichokes, broccoli and pumpkins. The town holds a pumpkin festival each October in celebration of its prime crop.

★ **Pigeon Point ⑪**

Following numerous shipwrecks in the area, including the *Carrier Pigeon* which gave the area its name, a 115-ft (35-m) lighthouse was erected in 1872. Sea lions can often be spotted offshore.

NEVADA

CALIFORNIA

Pacific Ocean

San Rafael

Woods
nal Monument

③
④
⑤

⑥ BERKELEY

N FRANCISCO
80

35

⑦
⑧

Pacifica

280
101

280

92
35

①
84

⑨
⑩

⑩

SAN JOSE

Pescadero

⑪

MONTEREY

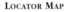

| | 0 kilometres | 10 |
| 0 miles | | 10 |

KEY

Freeway

Major road

Minor road

River

⚡ Viewpoint

Dairy farm at picturesque Point Reyes

Point Reyes National Seashore **❶**

Road map A3. 🚌 *from San Rafael Center (weekends only).* **Bear Valley Visitors' Center** *Bear Valley Rd, main entrance to National Seashore, Point Reyes.* **📞** *(415) 663-1092.* **🕐** *9am–5pm daily.*

THIS TRIANGULAR-SHAPED area of land, only half attached to the San Franciscan coastline, has been gradually drifting north-wards along the Californian coast for more than six million years. Situated due west of the San Andreas Fault, the peninsula moved a full 20 ft (6 m) north of the mainland during the 1906 earthquake *(see pp48–9)*. A displaced fence on the Earthquake Trail near Bear Valley Visitor Center is evidence of this overnight movement. The visitors' centre itself contains interesting displays on local geology and geography and supplies and trail maps for hikers.

A notable feature of this stretch of coastline is its abundance of wildlife, including a herd of tule elk. The area has cattle and dairy ranches, and three small towns: Point Reyes Station, Olema and Inverness.

Drake's Bay is named after the English explorer Sir Francis Drake, who is thought to have anchored here in 1579. He named the land Nova Albion and briefly claimed it for England *(see pp42–3)*.

POINT REYES
NATIONAL SEASHORE
United States Department of the Interior National Park Service
Signpost to Point Reyes

John Muir National Historic Site **❷**

4202 Alhambra Ave, Martinez. **Road map** A3. **📞** *(510) 228-8860.* **🕐** *10am–4:30pm Wed–Sun.* **⬤** *1 Jan, Thanksgiving, 25 Dec.* ♿ *1st floor & grounds only.*

SET AMID the suburban neighbourhood of Martinez, the John Muir National Historic Site preserves the home where the naturalist and writer lived from 1890 until his death in 1914. The 17-room Italianate house is typical of a late Victorian upper-middle-class dwelling, conveying little of Muir's simple tastes and back-to-nature inclinations. Only the library, which Muir called his "scribble den", gives a real sense of the man. The house was once surrounded by 2,600 acres (1,052 ha) of fruit trees, only one of which survives. In season, rangers pick fruit for visitors to sample.

John Muir (1838–1914)

Muir Woods and Beach **❸**

Road map A3. 🚌 *Mill Valley.* **Visitors' Center** *Hwy 1, Mill Valley.* **📞** *(415) 388-2595.* **🕐** *8am–5pm daily.*

NESTLING AT the foot of Mount Tamalpais *(see pp396–7)* is Muir Woods National Monument, one of the few remaining stands of old-growth coastal redwoods. Before the 19th-century lumber industry flourished, these tall trees (the oldest is at least 1,000 years old) once completely covered the coastal area of California. The woods were named in honour of John Muir, the 19th-century naturalist responsible for turning Yosemite into a national park *(see pp472–5)*.

Redwood Creek bubbles out of Muir Woods and makes its way down to the ocean at Muir Beach, a wide expanse of sand popular with beachcombers and picnickers *(see pp396–7)*. Along the road to the beach is the incongruous Pelican Inn, a 16th-century-style English inn which is proud of its traditional English menu, and offers visitors a warm welcome *(see p529)*.

Muir Beach is likely to be crowded at weekends, especially during the summer, but visitors who are prepared to walk for 15 minutes or more along the sand are rewarded with peace and quiet.

Marin Headlands **❹**

See pp400–401.

Sausalito **❺**

Road map inset B. 🏘 *7,300.* 🚗 🚌 🚢 ℹ️ *777 Bridgeway Ave, 4th flr (415 332-0505).*

IN THIS SMALL TOWN that was once a fishing community, Victorian bungalows cling to steep hills rising from San Francisco Bay. Parallel to the waterfront, Bridgeway Avenue serves as a promenade for the weekend crowds that come to patronize the restaurants and shops and enjoy the views.

Harbour scene in Sausalito

"arks". These unique buildings are in fact houseboats from the early 20th century that have been pulled ashore and innovatively refurbished. They now stand in what is called "Ark Row".

Less hectic than nearby Sausalito, Tiburon is a good town for walking. Parks are situated along the waterfront from which you can contemplate the bay. At night, the harbour shines with fairy lights.

Village Fair is an eclectic assembly of trendy shops located in an old warehouse. The **Bay Model** simulates the movement of the bay's tides and currents.

🏠 **Village Fair**
777 Bridgeway Ave. ((415) 332-1902. ⬜ daily. ● public hols.

🏛 **Bay Model**
2100 Bridgeway Ave. ((415) 332-3870. ⬜ Sep–May: Tue–Fri; Jun–Aug: Tue–Sun. ● public hols.

Tiburon ➏

Road map inset B. 🏢 8,200. 🚗 🚌 🚢 🛈 96B Main St (415 435-5633).

THE MAIN STREET of this elegant waterfront town is lined with fashionable shops and restaurants housed in

Marine World Africa USA ➐

Road map inset B. ((707) 643-6722. 🚗 🚌 🚢 🛈 from San Francisco. ⬜ Jun–Aug: 9:30am–6pm Mon–Fri, 9am–6:45pm Sat–Sun; Sep–May: 9:30am–5pm Wed–Sun. ● Thanksgiving, 25 Dec. 🎟 ♿ 📷

THE MOST UNIQUE wildlife park and oceanarium in Northern California, Marine World Africa USA attracts 1.6 million visitors each year. Its lush 160-acre (65-ha) site is located along the I-80 at Hwy 37 on the outskirts of Vallejo.

There is equal emphasis on education and entertainment

Sign for Marine World

in the park, but the primary attractions are the shows featuring marine mammals. Arenas housing large pools showcase killer whales, sea lions and dolphins. In the Shark Experience, visitors walk by way of a transparent tunnel through a tank filled with large sharks and tropical fish swimming overhead.

Land animal attractions include shows featuring Bengal tigers and baboons, an aviary of exotic birds and a collection of brilliantly coloured tropical butterflies.

Benicia ➑

Road map inset B. 🏢 24,400. 🚌 🚢 🚢 🛈 Benicia Chamber of Commerce, 601 1st St (707 745-2120).

SET ON the north side of the Carquinez Straits, the narrow waterway through which the Sacramento and the San Joaquin rivers flow from the Sierra Nevada to San Francisco Bay, Benicia is one of California's most historic small towns.

From February 1853 until February 1854, Benicia served as an early state capital. The purpose-built Greek Revival building which once housed the government has been preserved as a state historic park, complete with many original fixtures and furnishings. Next door to the former capitol, the Fisher-Hanlon House, a former Gold Rush hotel, has also been restored to its original condition as part of **Benicia State Historic Park**.

At the other end of Main Street from the capitol complex is the Benicia waterfront from where ferries shuttled to Port Costa during the 1850s. The former Benicia Arsenal, which stored army weapons from the 1850s to the 1950s, has now been converted into studio space for local artists and craftspeople.

🏛 **Benicia State Historic Park**
1st & G Sts. ((707) 745-3385. ⬜ 10am–5pm daily. ● 1 Jan, Thanksgiving, 25 Dec. 🎟

Attractive main street of Tiburon

A 90-Minute Walk through the Marin Headlands ●

A^T ITS NORTHERN END, the Golden Gate Bridge is anchored in the rolling green hills of the Marin Headlands. This is an unspoilt wild area of windswept ridges, sheltered valleys and deserted beaches, once used as a military defence post and now part of the vast Golden Gate National Recreation Area. From several vantage points there are spectacular views of San Francisco and vast panoramas of the sea and, on autumn days, you can see migrating eagles and ospreys gliding past Hawk Hill.

Schoolchildren on a trip to the Marin Headlands

Rodeo Beach ③

Visitors' Center to Rodeo Beach

Before starting this walk, pause a while at the steepled Visitors' Center ①, which was once the inter-denominational chapel for Fort Cronkhite. It has since been refurbished and is now a museum and information centre, with a natural history bookshop that specializes in books on birds. Here you can discover the history of the Marin Headlands and see a Coast Miwok

Indian shelter. The walk, which will take you around Rodeo Lagoon ②, begins at the gate on the west, ocean side, of the car park. Take the path to the left that leads to the sea. This part of the trail is thick with trees and shrubs, including the poison oak, of which visitors should be aware. The song of birds fills the air and around the edges of the lagoon you will see brown pelicans, snowy egrets and mallards. A 15-minute walk will bring you to the sandy, wind-blown Rodeo Beach ③, and from here you can see Bird Island ④ lying offshore to the south. Fishing boats

Cooper's Hawk

MARIN HEADLANDS STATE PARK (GOLDEN GATE NATIONAL RECREATION AREA)

⑥ MITCHELL ROAD

⑤

R o d L a g ○

White Egret

③ *Rodeo Beach*

Herring Gull

PACIFIC OCEAN

Turkey Vulture

④

Bird Island

MEND

Rodeo Lagoon ②

KEY

••• Walk route

☼ Viewpoint

P Parking

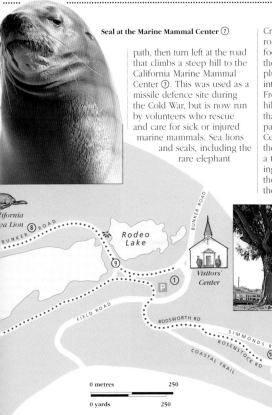

Seal at the Marine Mammal Center ⑦

path, then turn left at the road that climbs a steep hill to the California Marine Mammal Center ⑦. This was used as a missile defence site during the Cold War, but is now run by volunteers who rescue and care for sick or injured marine mammals. Sea lions and seals, including the rare elephant

Cross the bridge, not on the roadway but on the separate footpath at the side. Before the guard rail ends, a path ⑨ plunges down to the right into the dense shrubbery. From here, continue up the hill again, via a series of steps that will return you to the path at the end of the Visitors' Center car park. Walk across the car park and up the hill to a three-storey wooden building, constructed at the turn of the century. This is listed on the National Historic Registry

Visitors' Center ①

and has been officers' headquarters, a hospital and a missile command centre. It is now the Golden Gate Hostel ⑩ for travellers.

The Marin Headlands also offer a wide range of longer, more challenging walks. Wolf Ridge and Bobcat Trail are two popular routes you may like to try.

may be seen bobbing out at sea, but the beach is mostly empty of people, although sometimes you might see groups of children who are likely to be working on coastal ecology programmes. These are run by the Headlands Institute, which is based in the nearby clutch of former army barracks.

Barracks to the California Marine Mammal Center
From the beach, turn inland again as you approach the tip of the lagoon, crossing a wooden footbridge ⑤. Here there are lavatories and barracks ⑥ housing various offices, among them the Headlands District Office, the Raptor Observatory and an energy and resources centre. Walking past the barracks, continue along the

seals, are examined and treated here, in specially designed pens. They are then returned to the sea when they have recovered. You can watch the vets at work and get a close view of the mammals, many of which are orphaned pups. There are also some displays of the marine ecosystem.

Lagoon to the Golden Gate Hostel
Make your way back down the hill and re-turn to the paved road that runs past Rodeo Lagoon ⑧. There is a separate pathway be-side the road for hikers, but you have to climb over a guard rail to get onto it. Just before the road crosses a bridge, there is a large bench where you can view the water birds. There are plenty of birds to be seen in this brackish lagoon with its tall grasses.

Horse Trail

Bike Trail

Sign marking a trail

Berkeley ❾

ERKELEY BEGAN to boom following the earthquake of 1906 (*see pp48–9*), when many San Franciscans fled their ruined city and settled on the east side of the bay. Berkeley did not really find its own voice, however, until the birth of the Free Speech Movement and the student uprisings against the Vietnam War during the 1960s, earning itself the nickname "Beserkeley". Many shops and market stalls still hark back to the hippie era with their psychedelic merchandise, but in recent years Berkeley has begun to raise its profile. Smart restaurants and cafés have emerged, as well as a reputation for fine food – it was here that the popular Californian cuisine was born. Today the city blends idealism and style in unique harmony.

Claremont Resort Hotel

🏛 University of California at Berkeley

((510) 642-6000. **Hearst Museum of Anthropology (** (510) 643-7648. **◯** 10am–4:30pm Wed–Sun (until 9pm Thu). **●** public hols.
Berkeley Art Museum and Pacific Film Archive ((510) 642-0808. **◯** 11am–5pm Wed–Sun (until 9pm Thu). **●** public hols. 🎞 ♿

The reputation of UC Berkeley for counter-cultural movements sometimes eclipses its academic reputation, yet it is one of the largest and most prestigious universities in the world. Founded in 1868, Berkeley numbers nine Nobel laureates among its fellows and staff. The campus (*see pp404–405*) was laid out by the architect Frederick Law Olmsted. Today there are more than 30,000 students and a wide range of museums, cultural amenities and buildings of note to visit. These include the University Art Museum (*see p405*), Sather Tower, also called the Campanile, and the Hearst Museum of Anthropology.

Model of DNA at the Lawrence Hall of Science

🏛 Lawrence Hall of Science

Centennial Drive, UC Berkeley.
((510) 642-5132. **◯** 10am–5pm daily. ♿ 🎞

Science is fun here. Hands-on exhibits tempt visitors to manipulate a hologram, track earthquakes or plot stars in the planetarium. There are also changing exhibitions.

At night, the view of the lights around the northern Bay Area from the Hall's plaza is an extraordinary sight.

🏨 Claremont Resort Spa and Tennis Club

Ashby and Domingo Aves, Oakland.
((510) 843-3000. ♿

The Berkeley hills form a backdrop to this half-timbered, fairytale castle. The enormous Claremont Resort construction began in 1906, and ended in 1915. In the early years the hotel failed to prosper, partly due to a law that forbade the sale of alcohol within a 1-mile (1.6-km) radius of the Berkeley university campus. In 1937 an enterprising student actually measured the distance and discovered that the radius line passed through the *centre* of the building. The Terrace Bar was opened beyond the line, in the same corner of the hotel that it occupies today.

The Bay Area's plushest hotel is a good place to have a drink and enjoy the views.

🌷 University of California Botanical Garden

Centennial Drive, Berkeley. 🎞 (510) 642-3343. **◯** 9am–4:45pm daily. **●** 25 Dec. ♿ limited.

More than 12,000 species from all over the world thrive in the Mediterranean-style climate of Berkeley's Strawberry Canyon. Although primarily used for research, the collections are arranged in thematic gardens linked by paths. Particularly noteworthy are the Asian, African, South American, European and Californian sections. The Chinese medicinal herb garden, the orchid houses, cactus garden and the carnivorous plants are also well worth a visit.

Wellman Hall on the University of California campus

🌿 Tilden Park
🗓 *(510) 843-2137.* **Steam trains**
*run 11am–6pm Sat & Sun, and daily
during summer.* 🚂
Carousel ◻ *10am–5pm Sat &
Sun,11am–5pm daily during summer.*
🌿 **Botanical Garden** *open 8:30am–
5pm daily.* ♿ *limited.*
Though preserved for the most
part in a natural wild condition, Tilden Park offers a
variety of attractions. It is
noted for the enchantingly
landscaped Botanical Garden,
specializing in Californian
plants. Visitors can stroll
from alpine meadows to
desert cactus gardens by
way of a redwood glen,
and there are guided nature
walks. If you have children,
don't miss the carousel, the
miniature farmyard and the
model steam train.

🏛 Judah L Magnes
Museum
2911 Russell St, Berkeley. 🗓 *(510)
549-6950.* ◻ *10am–4pm Sun–Thu.*
⬤ *Jewish and federal hols.*
♿ *arrange in advance.*
Located in a rambling old
mansion, this is California's
largest collection of art and
historical artifacts pertaining
to Jewish culture from ancient
times to the present day.
Among the exhibits are art
treasures from Europe, Turkey

**19th-century Jewish ceremonial
dress, Judah L Magnes Museum**

and India, and graphic works
and paintings by Marc Chagall,
Max Liebermann and others.
There are also mementos of
the experience of Jews during
the Holocaust, such as a
burned Torah scroll rescued
from a German synagogue.
Lectures, video shows and
temporary exhibitions often
enliven the museum's halls.

⛩ Telegraph Avenue
Berkeley's most stimulating
and fascinating street is Telegraph Avenue, which runs

VISITORS' CHECKLIST

Road map inset B. 🏘 *104,900.*
✈ *Oakland, 12 miles (19 km)
SW of Berkeley.* 🚌 🚃 *2160
Shattuck Ave.* ℹ *1834
University Ave (510 549-7040,
800 847-4823).* 🎊 *Fourth of
July Fireworks; Farmers' Market
Grand Opening & Parade (2nd
Sun in Jul); Telegraph Ave Book
Fair (late Jul).*

between Dwight Way and the
University. It has one of
the highest concentra-
tions of bookshops
in the country, and a
plethora of coffee houses
and cheap eateries. The district
was the centre of student protest during the 1960s. It still
swarms with students today
from dawn to dark, along
with street vendors, musicians,
protestors and eccentrics.

🏛 Fourth Street
This gentrified enclave north
of University Avenue is characteristic of Berkeley's fine
craftsmanship and taste. Here
you can buy everything from
stained-glass windows and
furniture, to organically grown
lettuce and designer garden
tools. There is also a handful
of good restaurants *(see p566).*

**BERKELEY CITY
CENTRE**

Claremont Resort Spa and
    Tennis Club ⑥
Judah L Magnes
    Museum ⑤
Lawrence Hall of
    Science ②
Telegraph Avenue ④
University of California
    Botanical Garden ③
University of California
    at Berkeley ①

0 metres   500
0 yards   500

KEY

ℹ Tourist information

A 90-Minute Walk around the University of California Campus in Berkeley

THIS WALK CONCENTRATES on a distinct area of Berkeley, the renowned main campus of the University of California. It allows a stimulating glimpse into the intellectual, cultural and social life of this vibrant university town *(see pp402–403)*.

West Entrance to Sather Tower

From University Avenue ①, cross Oxford Street and then walk along University Drive past the Valley Life Sciences Building ②. Wellman Hall can be seen on the north fork of Strawberry Creek as you follow the road to the right, keeping California Hall ③ on your right. Take a left turn onto Cross Campus Road ④. Wheeler Hall lies to the right and up ahead is the main campus landmark, the 307-ft (94-m) tall Sather Tower ⑤. Built by John Galen Howard in 1914, it was based on the campanile in the Piazza San Marco in Venice.

Before visting the bell tower, go first to the Doe Library ⑥ and then the AF Morrison Memorial Library ⑦ in the north wing. The adjacent Bancroft Library houses the plate supposedly left by Sir Francis Drake in 1579, when he claimed California for England *(see pp42–3)*.

Now return to Sather Tower, which is open 10am–3:30pm Monday to Saturday. Fine views of the bay can be had

from the top. Across the way lies South Hall ⑧, the oldest building on campus.

Hearst Mining Building to the Greek Theater

Continuing north, walk past LeConte Hall then cross over University Drive to the Mining Circle. Here is the Hearst Mining Building ⑨, built by Howard in 1907. Inside are ore samples and pictures of old mining operations. Return to

Students outside Wheeler Hall on Cross Campus Road ④

University Drive, turn left out of East Gate to the Hearst Greek Theater ⑩.

Faculty Club to the Eucalyptus Grove

Follow Gayley Road, which straddles a major earthquake fault, and turn right down the first path past Lewis Hall and

Esplanade near Sather Tower ⑤

KEY	
•••	Walk route
Ⓑ	BART station
Ⓟ	Parking

0 metres 250
0 yards 250

Hildebrand Hall, then left over a footbridge. The path winds between a log house and the Faculty Club ⑪. This rambling, rustic building was partly designed by Bernard Maybeck and dates from 1903. Faculty Glade ⑫ in front of the club is a favourite picnic and resting place with students and visitors alike.

The path now swings to the right, then sharp left. Take a look at Hertz Hall ⑬, then go down the diagonal walk that passes Wurster Hall to Kroeber Hall. Here you can visit the Hearst Museum of Anthropology (see p402).

Included in the museum are artifacts made by Ishi, the last surviving Yahi Indian who was brought by scientists to live on the campus from 1911 until his death in 1916. Cross Bancroft Way to the Caffè Strada ⑭, and then proceed to the University Art Museum ⑮, which includes Picassos and Cézannes among its exhibits (see p402). Continue along Bancroft Way to Telegraph Avenue ⑯, famous for the student riots of the 1960s and '70s (see p403). The entrance to the university opposite Telegraph Avenue opens on to Sproul Plaza ⑰, which is often enlivened by

Within (1969) by A Lieberman at
UCB Art Museum ⑮

street musicians. Step into the lower courtyard with its modern Zellerbach Hall ⑱, then, noting the state-of-the-art Harmon Gym, pass Alumni House and turn right. Cross over the south fork of Strawberry Creek at Bay Tree Bridge, and bear left for the nature area, with some of the world's tallest eucalyptus trees ⑲. The path ends at Oxford Street, near the start of the walk.

HEARST AVENUE

CYCLOTRON ROAD

Hearst Mining Building

GAYLEY RD

⑨

MINING CIRCLE

UNIVERSITY DRIVE

⑩ Hearst Greek Theater

STADIUM RINGWAY

⑤

⑧ ⑫ ⑪

⑬

Sather Gate

PIEDMONT AVENUE

BARROW LANE

P

Sproul Hall

BANCROFT WAY

⑦ ⑭ COLLEGE AVENUE

⑮

BOWDITCH STREET

TELEGRAPH

DURANT AVENUE

TIPS FOR WALKERS

Starting point: *The West Gate at University Avenue and Oxford Street.*
Length: *2.5 miles (4 km).*
Getting there: *San Francisco–Oakland Bay Bridge, Hwy 80 north, University Avenue exit. By BART, Berkeley stop.*
Stopping-off points: *The up-market Caffè Strada, on Bancroft Way, is always crowded with students sipping cappuccinos or eating bagels and cakes. A few steps down the street, in the University Art Museum, is the Café Grace which looks out on to the sculpture garden. You may like to browse in the bookshops on Telegraph Avenue which also have coffee shops, or try one of the food carts that crowd the entrance to Sproul Plaza. Here you could sample a "smoothie" (blended fruit and ice), or a wide selection of Mexican food. In the lower Sproul Plaza of the University, amid a phalanx of bongo drummers, there are several other inexpensive cafés.*

The Hearst Mining Building around the Mining Circle ⑨

Oakland ⓾

AT ONE TIME a small, working-class suburb of San
Francisco, Oakland grew into a city in its own right
when it became the West Coast terminus of the transcontinental railroad. With access to the town, businesses
inevitably boomed and it soon became one of the largest
container ports in the United States. Many of the African
Americans who worked on the railroad then settled
in Oakland, later followed by an Hispanic population,
giving the city a multicultural atmosphere which
continues to this day. Oakland's literary associations,
including Jack London and Gertrude Stein, have also
enhanced the area as a cultural centre.

Façade and gardens of the Mormon Temple

⚜ Mormon Temple
4770 Lincoln Ave. 🅲 (510) 531-
1475. **Visitors' Center** ◯ 6:30am–
8pm Tue–Thu, 6:30am–9pm Fri,
5:30am–1pm Sat. Temple closed to
the public. 🅷
Designed in 1963 and built
on a hilltop, this is Northern
California's only Mormon
temple. Its full name is the
Oakland Temple of the
Church of Jesus Christ of Latter
Day Saints. Floodlit at night,
it can be seen from Oakland
and San Francisco. The central
ziggurat is surrounded by four
shorter terraced towers, all clad
with white granite and capped
by glistening golden pyramids.
   From the temple there are
magnificent views over the
entire Bay Area.

🌊 Lake Merritt
Formed when a saltwater
tidal estuary was dredged,
embanked and partly dam-
med, Lake Merritt and its
surrounding park form an
oasis of rich blue and green
in the urban heart of Oakland.
Designated in 1870 as the first
state game refuge in the US,
the lake still attracts migrating
flocks of birds. Boats can be
hired from two boathouses
on the west and north shores,
and joggers and cyclists can
circle the lake on a 3-mile
(5-km) path. The north shore
at Lakeside Park has flower
gardens, an aviary, and a
Children's Fairyland with pony
rides, puppet shows and
nursery rhyme scenes.

🎡 Jack London Square
Jack London Museum 🅲 (510)
451-8218. ◯ 10:30am–6pm
Tue–Sat, 11:45am–6pm Sun.
Author Jack London (see
p22–3) grew up in Oakland
in the 1880s, and was a frequent visitor to the Oakland
waterfront. Today the area is
a bright promenade of shops,

🌉 Bay Bridge
Treasure Island Museum 🅲 (415)
395-5067. ◯ 10am–3:30pm,Mon–
Fri, 10am–4:30pm Sat–Sun. ● 1
Jan, Easter, Thanksgiving, 25 Dec.
The compound, high-level
San Francisco–Oakland Bay
Bridge was designed by
Charles H Purcell. It has two
distinct structures, joining at
Yerba Buena Island in the
middle of the Bay, and reaches
4.5 miles (7.2 km) from shore
to shore. Its completion in
1936 heralded the end of the
age of ferry boats on San Francisco Bay by linking the pen-
insular city at Rincon Hill to
the Oakland "mainland" with
road and rail. The tracks were
removed in the 1950s, leaving
the bridge for use by more
than 250,000 vehicles a day.
It is five traffic lanes wide and
has two levels. The westbound
traffic into San Francisco uses
the top deck, eastbound to
Oakland the lower.
   The eastern cantilever is
raised on more than 20 piers,
climbing up from the toll plaza
causeway in Oakland to 191 ft
(58 m) above Yerba Buena
Island. In 1989 the bridge was
closed for a month after the
Loma Prieta earthquake (see
p489) when a 50-ft (15-m)
segment became disconnected.

**10 miles (16 km) of cable
holding up the bridge**

2,310 ft (704 m)

The West Bay Crossing section of Bay Bridge

OAKLAND CITY CENTRE

Jack London Square ②
Lake Merritt ④
Oakland Museum of California ③
Old Oakland ①

KEY

🚆	Amtrak
🚌	Tram stop
⛴	Ferry port
ℹ	Tourist information

0 metres   500

0 yards   500

restaurants with outdoor tables and pleasure boats. London's footsteps can be traced to the First and Last Chance Saloon, now sunken with age into the street, and the Yukon cabin occupied by London in 1898. The Jack London Museum has books, photographs and memorabilia.

🏛 **Old Oakland**
Farmers' Market ((510) 452-3276. ⬜ 8am–2pm Fri.
Housewives' Market ((510) 444-4396. ⬜ 9am–6pm Mon–Sat.
Also known as Victorian Row, these two blocks were erected between the 1860s and 1880s, and renovated in the 1980s. Crowds of shoppers come to

the Outdoor Market on Fridays and the Housewives' Market at Clay and 9th streets offers an array of ethnic foods.

At night, try Rattos, at No. 821 Washington Street, an Italian delicatessen famed for its weekend "Pasta Operas", when the management serenades the clientele.

Boring through the island in a tunnel, the roadway emerges at the spectacular West Bay section of the bridge. Two suspension spans join at the central anchorage, which is sunk deeper in the water than that of any other bridge.

Road exits on Yerba Buena Island lead to Treasure Island, where the 1939–40 world's fair was held to celebrate the bridge's completion.

East Bay Crossing

Central anchorage   5-lane double-level roadway   Pylons supporting both road decks

00 ft (122 m)   2,310 ft (704 m)

Oakland Museum of California

CALIFORNIA's only museum exclusively dedicated to documenting the state's art, history and ecology first opened in 1969. The building, handsomely terraced and landscaped with courtyards and gardens, was designed by John Dinkeloo and Kevin Roche, and encompasses three disciplines: the art, social and natural history of California. The natural history dioramas in the Hall of California Ecology are among the most impressive in the United States. The Cowell Hall of California History has one of the largest collections of Californian artifacts in the state, while the Gallery of California Art is renowned for its early oil paintings of Yosemite and San Francisco.

Californian gold miner's banjo

Welcome to California
This display celebrates past and present-day life in California.

Roof and gardens

The Great Hall is used for special exhibitions and functions.

Art Gallery
Modern art includes the painting Spring Nude *(1962) by Nathan Oliveira.*

Level 3

Level 2

10th Street entrance

★ **Dream on Wheels**
A drive-in restaurant sign and jukebox in the 1951 diorama capture the atmosphere of postwar California.

KEY TO THE OAKLAND MUSEUM LEVELS

☐ Art Gallery   ☐ History   ☐ Natural Sciences

California Mud Wagon
Developed for rural life during the mid-19th century, this multipurpose vehicle could be converted easily from a field wagon to a stylish carriage.

Food Chain Diorama
This diorama features a mountain lion and its prey, to show how wildlife competes to survive.

Level 1

MUSEUM GUIDE
Level 1 contains the shop and the Hall of Ecology, where the exhibits show the changes in the state's ecology from west to east. Artifacts in the Cowell Hall on level 2 are arranged chronologically. Level 2 has the cafeteria, level 3 the Art Gallery.

The Great Court has outdoor exhibitions, and is also a popular spot for a picnic.

STAR EXHIBITS

★ **Delta Waters Diorama**

★ **Dream on Wheels**

★ Delta Waters Diorama
This diorama of a Sacramento delta marsh, showing fish, bird and insect life, typifies the high calibre of the Aquatic California Gallery.

Eugene O'Neill's beautiful Tao House, in Danville

Tao House ⑪

Road map inset B. **C** (510) 838-0249. ☐ 10am–noon, 12:30pm–2:30pm Wed–Sun, by reservation only. 🚻 🅿 obligatory.

WHEN THE AMERICAN playwright Eugene O'Neill (1888–1953) won the Nobel Prize for Literature in 1936, he used the stipend to build a home for himself and his wife in the then rural San Ramon Valley at the foot of Mount Diablo. Tao House, a hybrid of Spanish Colonial and oriental styles, was completed in 1937. Over the next six years O'Neill worked in this house on what is now considered his best work, the semi-autobiographical series of tragic plays, including *The Iceman Cometh, A Moon for the Misbegotten* and *Long Day's Journey Into Night*. In 1944, however, O'Neill was struck down with Parkinson's disease. The remote location of the house and the lack of available nursing staff due to the war forced the now disabled O'Neill to abandon his beloved home. He died in a Boston hotel in 1953.

Although the surrounding valleys have now been developed into suburbs of San Francisco, Tao House and its beautiful landscaped grounds have been turned into a National Historic Site, operated by the National Park Service. Both have been preserved in the condition in which the playwright left them.

Mask used in O'Neill's stage plays

Mount Diablo State Park ⑫

Road map inset B. ⌷ 🚂 Walnut Creek. 🚻 Walnut Creek (510 837-2525). **C** (510) 837-6119. ☐ 11am–5pm Wed–Sun.

RISING VOLUMINOUSLY over the inland suburbs, the 3,849-ft (1,173-m) high Mount Diablo dominates the East Bay region. Its summit offers one of the most impressive panoramas in North America. On a fine and clear day it is possible to see for more than 200 miles (320 km) in each direction, stretching from Mount Lassen *(see p437)* and the Cascade Mountains in the north to Mount Hamilton in the south, and from the Sierra Nevada mountains in the east to the Farallon Islands *(see pp396–7)* in the Pacific Ocean to the west.

Almost 20,000 acres (8,000 ha) of land surrounding the summit have now been set aside as a state park, and there is a wide range of hiking trails. A twisting road takes car drivers within 50 ft (15 m) of the summit and is a popular picnic spot. The park's Visitors' Center at the summit offers information on the mountain's fauna and flora, including the numerous wildflowers that cover the mountainside in spring and the abundant oak trees.

Livermore ⑬

Road map inset B. 🚶 67,000. ⌷ 🚂 🚻 2157 First St (510 447 1606).

FOUNDED IN the 1870s as a cattle-ranching and grape-producing community, in more recent years Livermore has grown into an outlying suburb of San Francisco.

Still rural in feel and retaining a few ranches and vineyards, the town is now best known however as the home of the Lawrence Livermore National Laboratory. This state-of-the-art technology research centre is operated by the University of California on behalf of the United States Department of Energy. During the Cold War era the laboratory had primary responsibility for the design of the nation's nuclear weapons arsenal, but in recent years it has diversified into civilian applications.

To the east of Livermore, along the I-580 as it climbs over hilly Altamont Pass, are hundreds of shining high-tech windmills. This is the world's largest wind farm, producing natural, unpolluting energy from the area's constant winds. The windmills are all privately

Windmills producing natural energy at Livermore's wind farm

owned and operated, with no
government funding. They
consist of two main types: the
traditional propeller type, and
the more unusual vertical axis
windmills, which resemble
giant egg-whisks.

Stanford University ⑭

Junipero Serra St. **Road map** inset B.
▐ (415) 723-2560. **Visitors' Centre**
◯ 9am–5pm daily. ● university
hols; call ahead.

Among the most pleasant of
the Bay Area suburbs, the
town of Palo Alto grew up
specifically to serve Stanford
University, one of the United
States' most reputed centres
of higher education.

Founded by the railroad
tycoon Leland Stanford (see
pp46–7) in honour of his son
who died in 1885 at the age
of 16, Stanford University
opened in 1891. The campus
occupies the former Stanford
family farm, covering 8,200
acres (3,320 ha) at the foot of
the coastal mountains – larger
than the entire downtown
district of San Francisco. It
was designed in a mixture of
Romanesque and Mission
styles (see pp26–7) by the
architect Frederick Law
Olmsted, and its
sandstone buildings
and numerous
arcades are
capped by

red-tiled roofs. At the heart of
the university campus is the
Main Quadrangle, where the
Memorial Church is decorated
with a gold-leaf and tile mosaic. Also on the campus is the
Stanford Museum of Art which
holds one of the largest collections of sculptures by
Auguste Rodin, including the
impressive Gates of Hell. The
museum is closed until 1998.

Filoli ⑮

Canada Rd. **Road map** inset B.
▐ (415) 364-2880. ◯ Tue–Sat.
● public hols. ▣ ▤ ▥

One of the most impressive
mansions in Northern
California open to the public,
the Filoli estate was the home
of gold mining millionaire
William Bourn, owner of the
Empire Gold Mine (see p454).
It was designed in Palladian
style by the San Franciscan
architect Willis Polk in 1916.
The red brick exterior resembles a Georgian terrace and
encloses more than 18,000 sq
ft (1,672 sq m) of living space
on two fully furnished floors.

The house is surrounded by
16 acres (6.5 ha) of formal
gardens, landscaped to
provide blooms of varying
colours through the year –
25,000 tulips and daffodils
in spring, roses in
summer and the
brilliant russet of
maple leaves

in the autumn. The estate's
name, Filoli, is an acronym
for the motto "Fight for a just
cause, Love your fellow man,
Live a good life", which commemorates William Bourn's
love for the Irish.

**Picturesque church in the tiny
village of Pescadero**

Pescadero ⑯

Road map inset B. ▨ 360. ▮ 520
Kelley Ave, Half Moon Bay (415 726-
5202).

Only half an hour's drive
from San Francisco to the
north and the Silicon Valley
(see p412) to the south, the
tiny town of Pescadero seems
light years away from the
surrounding modern world.

Pescadero is a sleepy little
farming community, which
produces an abundance of
vegetables such as asparagus,
pumpkins and Brussels
sprouts. It contains little more
than a whitewashed church
(the oldest in the county), a
general store, a post office
and the popular Duarte's
Tavern (see p567) along its
two main streets. Its many
whitewashed buildings are a
tradition that goes back to the
19th century, when a cargo of
white paint was rescued from
a nearby shipwreck.

Eight miles (13 km) south
of town, the Pigeon Point
Lighthouse is well worth a
visit. The lighthouse also operates as a hostel (see pp396–7).

Façade of the Memorial Church at Stanford University

San Jose ⑰

THE ONLY OTHER ORIGINAL Spanish Colonial town in California after Los Angeles *(see pp54–183)*, San Jose was founded in 1777 by Felipe de Neve and has grown to become the state's third-largest city, its population exceeding that of San Francisco. Now the commercial and cultural centre of the South Bay, and civic heart of the Silicon Valley region, San Jose is a bustling and modern city that has only recently taken action to preserve its history. High-rise offices and high-tech factories now stand on what was only farmland in the 1950s, yet the city's fine museums and historic sites offer genuine attractions to the visitor, despite the suburban sprawl.

Statue outside the Egyptian Museum and Planetarium

Exploring San Jose

San Jose's colonial pueblo was situated on what is now Plaza Park, off Market Street. During 1849–50, California's first State Capitol was located in a hotel on the east side of the plaza, roughly on the site of the present Fairmont Hotel *(see p529)*.

Other historic sites along Market Street include the San Jose Museum of Art and the birthplace of Amadeo P Giannini *(see p305)*.

San Jose's main attraction, the Winchester Mystery House *(see pp414–15)*, is located on the town's outskirts.

🏛 Peralta Adobe

175 W St John St. 📞 (408) 993-8182. ◯ Tue–Sun. ● public hols. 📷 ♿ first floor only.

One block to the left of Market Street is San Jose's oldest surviving

building, the Peralta Adobe. Built in 1797 it is the sole remnant of the Spanish pueblo. Up-market bars and cafés now surround the area.

🏛 Mission Santa Clara de Asis

500 El Camino Real. 📞 (408) 554-4023. ◯ daily.

On the campus of the Jesuit University of Santa Clara, 5 miles (8 km) northwest of downtown San Jose, this mission church is a modern replica of the adobe original, first built in 1777 and reconstructed many times thereafter. Relics on display include bells given to the missionaries by the Spanish monarchy. The gardens adjacent to the church are carefully maintained in their original splendour.

Mission Santa Clara detail

🏛 Rosicrucian Egyptian Museum and Planetarium

Naglee & Park Aves. 📞 (408) 947 3636. ◯ daily. ● 1 Jan, Easter Sunday, Thanksgiving, 25 Dec. 📷

This large museum displays the most extensive collection of ancient Egyptian artifacts west of the Mississippi. Housed in a complex of Egyptian- and Moorish-style buildings, each gallery represents a different aspect of Egyptian culture, from mummies, burial tombs and Canopic jars to domestic implements and a variety of children's toys, some of which date back to 1500 BC. There are also replicas of the sarcophagus in which Tutankhamen was discovered in 1922, and of the Rosetta Stone.

The museum is operated by a non-sectarian organization known as the Rosicrucian Order, which is dedicated to spiritual development by combining modern science with the ancient wisdoms.

🏛 Tech Museum of Innovation

145 W San Carlos St. 📞 (408) 279-7150. ◯ Sep–May: Tue–Sun; Jun–Aug: Mon–Sun. ● 1 Jan, Easter, Thanksgiving, 25 Dec. 📷

Located one block south of Plaza Park, in the heart of historic San Jose, this fascinating science museum has its eyes set firmly on the future. The Tech Museum is crowded with hands-on exhibits, which encourage visitors of all ages to discover how various technological inventions work. Its main focus is on understanding the workings of computer hardware and software.

SILICON VALLEY

The world-famous centre of the computer industry, Silicon Valley covers approximately 100 sq miles (260 sq km) from Palo Alto to San Jose. However, the term refers to myriad businesses rather than to a defined geographical location.

The name, based on the material used in the manufacture of semiconductors, was first used in the early 1970s to describe the area's expanding hardware and software industries. The seeds, however, were sown a decade earlier, at Stanford University and the Xerox Palo Alto Research Center, as well as in the garages of computer pioneers William Hewlett, David Packard, and later Steve Jobs and Stephen Wozniak, who invented the personal computer.

Many world-class high-tech firms are now based here, including Intel, Silicon Graphics and Netscape.

Silicon chip circuitry

⬛ San Jose Museum of Art

110 S Market St. **C** *(408) 294-2787.*
⭕ *Tue–Sun.* ⚫ *1 Jan, Thanksgiving,
25 Dec.*

Having constructed a spacious
new wing of galleries in 1991,
this small but daring art museum is now known for some
of the Bay Area's most interesting and popular art exhibitions.

The permanent collection
focuses on well-known contemporary Californian artists
such as Richard Diebenkorn
(1922–93) and Sam Francis
(1923–94). In addition to the
museum's changing shows,
long-term exhibitions drawn
from New York's Whitney
Museum will be on view during the year 2000. These are
a result of a long-term collaboration with the Whitney.

⬛ De Saisset Museum

500 El Camino Real. **C** *(408) 554-
4528.* ⭕ *Tue–Sun.* ⚫ *1 Jan,
Thanksgiving, 25 Dec.* **Donation**.
Next to the Santa Clara Mission, the de Saisset Museum
exhibits artifacts from the 18th-
century mission and other eras
of Californian history, along
with a collection of paintings,
prints and photographs dating
from the Ancient Greeks to
the present day.

**Trolley car at the San Jose
Historical Museum**

⬛ San Jose Historical Museum

1600 Senter Rd. **C** *(408) 287-2290.*
⭕ *daily.* ⚫ *Thanksgiving, 25 Dec.*

One mile (1.5 km) southeast
of downtown San Jose, in
Kelley Park, more than two
dozen historic structures of
San Jose have been reassembled into an outdoor museum.
Highlights include a trolley
car, a petrol station from the
1920s, and 19th-century business premises including a
doctor's office, a hotel and
the original Bank of Italy.

By 2001 the museum aims
to have 75 structures, com-
pleting this lifesize model of
how San Jose used to be.

🎢 Paramount's Great America Amusement Park

2401 Agnew Rd. **C** *(408) 988-1776.*
⭕ *mid-Mar–Jun: Sat & Sun; Jul–
mid-Oct: daily.*
The best amusement park in
Northern California packs a
wide variety of attractions
into its 100-acre (40-ha) site.

The park is divided into
several different areas, each
one designed to evoke various
regions of the United States.
These include Orleans Place,
Yankee Harbor and the Yukon
Territory. Along with high-
speed roller coasters, such as
the Demon and the Tidal
Wave, many rides incorporate
themes from films and television shows produced by
Paramount Studios, including
Top Gun and *Star Trek*. Open-
air pop concerts are often
held on summer evenings in
the large amphitheatre.

SAN JOSE CITY CENTRE

De Saisset Museum ①
Mission Santa Clara de Asis ②
Rosicrucian Egyptian Museum
  and Planetarium ③
San Jose Museum of Art ④
Tech Museum of Innovation ⑤
Winchester Mystery House
  pp414–15 ⑥

KEY
🚆 Amtrak station
🚌 Bus stop
ℹ Tourist information

San Jose: Winchester Mystery House

WINCHESTER MYSTERY HOUSE is a mansion with a remarkable history. Sarah Winchester, heiress of the Winchester Rifle fortune, moved from Connecticut to San Jose in 1884, and bought a small farmhouse. Convinced by a medium that its expansion would exorcise the spirits of those killed by the rifle, she kept builders labouring on the house for 24 hours a day, 7 days a week, for 38 years, until her death in 1922. The result is a bizarre complex of 160 rooms, including stairs that lead nowhere and windows set into floors. The total cost of the construction amounted to $5.5 million. The house has been refurbished with replica 19th-century furniture.

Stone cherub fountain

★ **Main Bedroom**
Sarah Winchester eventually died in her plush bedroom. The flooring is English mitred herring-bone. At night she would play the harmonium situated opposite the elaborately carved bed.

The Greenhouse incorporates 13 glass cupolas.

Tiffany Stained-Glass Window
The full beauty of the multi-coloured Tiffany glass in this window is lost by its situation on an inside wall.

FACTS AND FIGURES

- The house contains 2,000 doors, 10,000 windows, 47 fireplaces and 17 chimneys.
- The number 13 is used superstitiously throughout – 13 bathrooms, 13 windows in a room and 13 lights in the chandeliers.
- When the top of the house collapsed during the 1906 earthquake, building continued outwards rather than upwards.
- Mrs Winchester's height of 4 ft 10 in (147 cm) explains hallways 2 ft (0.6 m) wide and doors only 5 ft (152 cm) high.
- Mrs Winchester selected a new bedroom out of the 40 in the house each night, to confuse the spirits.

★ **Grand Ballroom**
This elaborate organ is one of the main features of the Grand Ballroom. Other features include artglass windows, a panelled ceiling and hand-carved woodwork.

Switchback Stairs
Each of these 44 steps is only 1.5 inches (3.8 cm) high and the entire staircase rises only 9 ft (2.7 m) from start to finish. It is thought they were built in this way to ease Sarah Winchester's arthritis.

VISITORS' CHECKLIST

525 S Winchester Blvd. **Road map** inset B. ☎ (408) 247-2101.
🚌 25, 60, 85. ◯ mid-Feb–mid-Jun: 9am–5pm daily (early May–mid-Jun: until 8pm Fri & Sat); mid-Jun–early Sep: 9am–8pm daily; early Sep–early Oct: 9am–5pm (until 8pm Fri & Sat); early Oct–early Nov: 9am–5pm daily; early Nov–mid-Feb: 9:30am–4pm daily. ⬤ 25 Dec. 📷
♿ gardens only. 🎫 ✓ ▯

Tour entrance

★ Winchester Firearms Museum
Included in this small display are the Winchester Repeating Rifle and the Model 1873, which came to be known as "The Gun that Won the West". Commemorative rifles include the Theodore Roosevelt and the John Wayne.

The Winchester Products Museum contains items, other than rifles, produced by the company, including roller skates, electric irons and lawn mowers.

STAR FEATURES

★ **Grand Ballroom**

★ **Main Bedroom**

★ **Winchester Firearms Museum**

Stairwell to the Ceiling
This stairway leading nowhere is just one of the many unexplained oddities within the house.

NORTHERN
CALIFORNIA

Northern California at a Glance

NORTHERN CALIFORNIA stretches for more than 500 miles (800 km), from the sparsely populated border with Oregon to the high-tech urban civilization that marks the beginning of Southern California. Vast areas of wilderness cover the region, including volcanic landscapes and dense forests, imposing mountain ranges and rugged coastlines, proudly preserved by a series of national parks. Northern California also has a rich history, from the first European settlers in Monterey to the celebrated Gold Rush of 1849. Its natural beauty is enhanced by equally picturesque and significant towns, including the state's capital, Sacramento.

THE NORTH
(see pp426–37)

Redwood National Park (see p434) *is a protected landscape of dense, awe-inspiring redwood forests, including the world's tallest tree, which reaches a height of 368 ft (112 m). The area is perennially popular with anglers, hikers, birdwatchers and campers.*

WINE COUNTRY
(see pp438–49)

Sonoma (see pp448–9) *was the site of the Bear Flag Revolt in 1846, when Americans rebelled against Mexican rule and tried to turn California into a republic. The vineyards of Sonoma County and the Napa Valley* (see pp446–7), *benefiting from good soil and an ideal climate, produce world-class wines.*

Carmel Mission (see pp496–7) *was founded in 1770 by Junípero Serra and became the most important of all the 21 Franciscan missions, serving as the administrative centre for Northern California. Today, restored to its original splendour, it is considered to be the state's most beautiful church.*

0 kilometres 50

0 miles

Lassen Volcanic National Park (see p437) *was formed in 1914, when more than 300 eruptions resulted in a new landscape of mudflows and sulphurous streams heated by molten lava. Mount Lassen, part of the Cascade Mountain Range, is still considered to be active.*

Sacramento (see pp456–9) *has been the state capital since 1854 and the Capitol is one of California's finest buildings. Old Sacramento preserves its historic structures from the 1860s and 1870s, when the town was the western terminus of the transcontinental railroad.*

Yosemite National Park (see pp472–5) *is an unforgettable wilderness of forests, alpine meadows, breathtaking waterfalls and imposing granite rocks. In 1864 it became the first protected park in the US.*

COUNTRY
ND THE
RAL VALLEY
pp450–65)

THE HIGH SIERRAS
(see pp466–81)

NORTH CENTRAL
CALIFORNIA
(see pp482–501)

Columbia State Historic Park (see pp464–5) *was once the second largest town in California and is now the best preserved of the old gold mining centres.*

Wildlife and Wilderness

Aeons ago, most of Northern California was under water, until geological forces pushed up the floor of the Central Valley, causing the Pacific Ocean to recede. Diverse terrains and ecosystems then emerged and Northern California is now a land of peaks, canyons and headlands. Unique flora grows here, such as giant sequoias in the High Sierras *(see pp480–81)* and Monterey cypress trees *(see p495)*. Black bears roam redwood groves and hawks hover above Yosemite Valley *(see pp472–3)*. Legend has it that Bigfoot, America's version of the Yeti, makes his home in these parts. In order to protect this landscape, the environment-friendly Sierra Club began here in 1892, and is still active today.

Prairie Creek State Park has a herd of protected Roosevelt elk, which roam the dunes of Gold Bluff Beach.

Six Rivers National Forest

Kla Nation

Trinity National Forest

Sha Nat Fo Shas

Clair Engle Lake

• Eureka

THE NORTH

Redwood National Park *(see pp432–3) contains the world's tallest redwood tree, reaching 368 ft (112 m). These evergreens soak up the winter's heavy rainfall and are kept moist in summer by fogs which move in from the ocean. Woodpeckers, spotted owls, mule deer, squirrels and banana slugs frequent the groves.*

Sinkyone Wilderness

Eel River

The Sacramento National Wildlife Refuges protect the many birds that stop off on the Pacific Flyway.

Mendocino National Forest

Mendocino

WINE COUNTRY

Lake Sohoma

Sutte Wild

Clear Lake

B

Point Reyes Peninsula *(see pp396–7) is a small "island", almost separated from the mainland by the San Andreas Fault. Its forested ridges, littoral rocks and rock pools are a prime habitat for crustaceans such as the Pacific rock crab.*

Sonom

San Francisco •

San J

The Farallon Islands *(see pp396–7) are an important breeding ground for sea birds, including the puffin, and elephant seals. Visitors are not permitted on the islands.*

Año Nuevo State Reserve *(see p488)* is occupied every winter by hundreds of breeding elephant seals.

KEY

- National Park
- State Park
- National Forest
- Wildlife refuge
- River

The Monterey Peninsula *(see pp494–5) is the winter home of the beautiful migratory monarch butterfly.*

0 kilometres 25

0 miles 25

Tule Lake Wildlife Refuge
(see p437) *is one of the prime bird-watching areas on the West Coast. It is home to a number of bald eagles.*

The Lava Beds Wilderness
is part of the Lava Beds National Monument (see p436) and is inhabited by rattlesnakes and rodents.

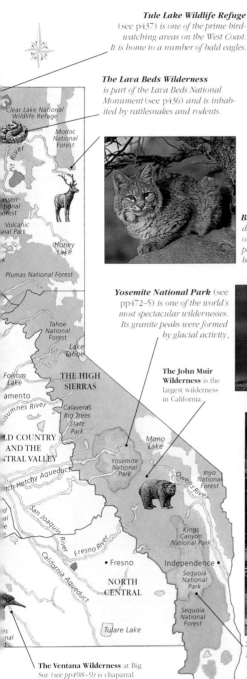

Biscar Wildlife Area, *the desert area of the Great Basin, on the border of Nevada, is populated with bobcats, badgers and antelope.*

Yosemite National Park (see pp472–5) *is one of the world's most spectacular wildernesses. Its granite peaks were formed by glacial activity.*

The John Muir Wilderness is the largest wilderness in California.

Clear Lake National Wildlife Refuge

Modoc National Forest

Pit River

Lassen National Forest

Volcanic National Park

Honey Lake

Plumas National Forest

Tahoe National Forest

Lake Tahoe

Folsom Lake

Sacramento

THE HIGH SIERRAS

Cosumnes River

Calaveras Big Trees State Park

GOLD COUNTRY AND THE CENTRAL VALLEY

Hetch Hetchy Aqueduct

Mono Lake

Yosemite National Park

Inyo National Forest

Owens River

San Joaquin River

Fresno River

Merced River

California Aqueduct

Kings Canyon National Park

• Fresno

NORTH CENTRAL

Independence •

Sequoia National Park

Sequoia National Forest

Tulare Lake

The Ventana Wilderness at Big Sur *(see pp498–9)* is chaparral country. The area is home to 900 plant species, coyotes, jack rabbits and the California quail.

Sequoia and Kings Canyon National Parks (see pp480–81) *together contain over 75 groves of the world's largest living tree, the giant sequoia. The tree is unique to California and Oregon.*

The Wine of Northern California

CALIFORNIA IS THE MOST important wine-growing area in the United States, producing 90 per cent of the nation's wine. More than 327,000 acres (132,000 ha) of the state's land is used for viticulture. Half of the grapes grown here are harvested from the fertile soil of the interior region, particularly the stretch of land bordered by the Sacramento Valley to the north and the San Joaquin Valley to the south. The north coast region accounts for less than a quarter of California's total wine-growing acreage, but many of the country's best Chardonnay, Sauvignon Blanc, Cabernet Sauvignon and Merlot grapes are grown here. The north coast is also home to most of the state's 800 wineries. Chardonnay and Pinot Noir grapes are the mainstays of the central coast region, which extends from the San Francisco Bay Area to Santa Barbara.

LOCATOR MAP

▨ *Northern California
wine region*

Grape harvest at V. Sattui Winery near St Helena in Napa Valley

*Late Harvest Zinfandel
from the Hop Kiln Winery
is a red dessert wine made
from grapes left on the
vine longer than usual to
increase their sweetness.
The winery is housed in
an historic hop kiln barn.*

THE STORY OF ZINFANDEL

The story of Zinfandel is one of the great success stories of California wine. This versatile grape is thought to have been brought to America from Croatia's Dalmatian coast. Zinfandel arrived in California in the 1850s, but only gained widespread popularity relatively recently. The Zinfandel reds, particularly those from the Dry Creek and Russian River valleys, are now in great demand. Some have oaky flavours while others have strong fruity flavours. The rosé White Zinfandel was created by winemakers to use up their surplus red grapes.

*Saintsbury's
Vin Gris is a
Burgundy-style
rosé wine,
which is made
from the juice
of Pinot Noir
grapes.*

KEY

▢ Lake County		▨ Carneros Valley	
▨ Anderson Valley		▨ Santa Cruz Mountains	
▨ Alexander Valley		▨ Livermore Valley	
▨ Dry Creek Valley		▨ Lodi Valley	
▨ Russian River Valley		▢ El Dorado Valley	
▨ Napa Valley		▨ Redwood–Ukiah Valley	
▨ Sonoma Valley		▢ San Joaquin Valley	

KEY FACTS ABOUT CALIFORNIA WINES

Location and Climate
California's latitude, proximity to the ocean and sheltered valleys create a mild climate. Winters tend to be short and mild, while the growing season is long and hot but cooled by summer fogs. Combined with fertile soil, these factors mean that large areas have ideal grape-growing conditions.

Grape Varieties
California's most widely planted grape variety is **Chardonnay**, used to make a dry wine with a balance of fruit, acidity and texture. Other popular whites include **Sauvignon Blanc** (also known as **Fumé Blanc**), **Chenin Blanc, Pinot Blanc, Gewürztraminer** and **Johannisberg Riesling**. California's red wines are typically dry with some tannic astringency and include the rich, full-bodied **Cabernet Sauvignon**, **Merlot**, **Petite Sirah**, **Pinot Noir** and **Zinfandel**.

Good Producers
Chardonnay: Acacia, Byron, Château Montelena, Ferrari-Carano, Kendall-Jackson, Kistler, Kunde Estate, Sonoma-Cutrer *Cabernet Sauvignon:* Beaulieu, Beringer, Grgich Hills, Heitz, The Hess Collection, Jordan, Joseph Phelps, Silver Oak, Robert Mondavi, Stag's Leap, Wente, Whitehall Lane. *Merlot:* Clos du Bois, Duckhorn, Frog's Leap, Silverado, Sterling. *Pinot Noir:* Dehlinger, Etude, Gary Farrell, Saintsbury, Sanford. *Sauvignon Blanc:* Duckhorn, Glen Ellen, Kenwood, Matanzas Creek, J Rochioli. *Zinfandel:* Dry Creek, Lake Sonoma, De Loach, Hop Kiln, Ridge, Rosenblum, Sebastiani.

Good Vintages
(Reds) 1994, 1993, 1992, 1991, 1990, 1987, 1986, 1985, 1984.
(Whites) 1994, 1992, 1991, 1990, 1988, 1987, 1986, 1985.

Yuba City
Yuba River
● NEVADA CITY
Feather River
Butte Creek
Auburn ●
American River
● SACRAMENTO
Cosumnes River
Mokelumne River
Calaveras River
Stanislaus River
● Stockton
● Modesto
Tuolumne River
Merced River
● Merced
mont
Alameda Creek
San Jose
California Aqueduct
San Joaquin River
NTA
UZ
San Benito River
Salinas River

Beaulieu Vineyard's Private Reserve
Cabernet Sauvignon is a medium-bodied red wine with ripe cherry and black-currant aromas. It has been produced since 1936, and was the first wine in the US to be called Private Reserve.

Wente Vineyard's Cabernet Sauvignon *has ample tannins. The Cabernet grape was brought here from France in the 19th century.*

0 kilometres 75
0 miles 75

Fermentation tanks *at Sterling Vineyards are typical of the high-tech methods now used.*

The Bohemian North

PERHAPS BECAUSE the region attracted a wide range of people and enjoyed enormous wealth during the Gold Rush *(see pp44–5)*, Northern California has always tended to be nonconformist and rather hedonistic. This has caused some anguish over the years, as charlatans and crackpots have taken advantage of the region's broad-mindedness, but it has certainly made the area a colourful place. During the late 19th century San Francisco's Barbary Coast was home to casinos, opium dens and brothels *(see p304)*. Utopian communities, organized around humanitarian, religious or dietary principles have been another facet of Northern Californian life. In the 1960s, the area's air of liberality made it a haven for members of the "Make Love, Not War" generation *(see p349)*. It has since attracted everybody from nudists and hot-tub lovers, to religious gurus and the latter-day hippies who helped turn marijuana into a chief crop of Humboldt County.

Spiritual guidance *became popular during the 1850s and 1860s. San Francisco attracted many spiritualist "mediums", who held regular seances. There are still a few spiritualist churches operating in the Bay Area.*

***Sally Stanford**, born in 1903, was a virtual pariah in Sausalito when she took over the Valhalla (now the Chart House), the town's oldest restaurant, in 1950. Local citizens didn't approve of her previous occupation as a San Francisco madam. But Sally's personality eventually won the town over and she served one term as the town's mayor (1976–8). She died in 1982.*

Young and old lived and travelled together in communities.

UTOPIAN COMMUNITIES

From the 1850s to the 1950s, more Utopian communities were founded in Northern California than in any other place in the nation. William Riker's Holy City was established in 1918 in the Santa Cruz Mountains. Riker, a racist and forecaster of apocalypses, called his totalitarian community the "headquarters for the world's perfect government". It eventually died out because the community was celibate.

Fountain Grove was a Utopian outpost north of Santa Rosa, founded in 1875 by New York mystic Thomas Lake Harris. Harris's theory was that God was bisexual and Christ was the Divine Man-Woman. Under attack for alleged sexual and financial abuses, Harris was forced to close his commune in 1892.

William Riker

Bright colours and childlike designs were influenced by the lights and patterns experienced during drug-induced hallucinatory "trips".

Psychedelic Pop Art posters of the 1960s were distinctive for their inflated, crammed typeface, developed by artist Wes Wilson.

Hippies from the 1960s

JIM JONES AND THE PEOPLE'S TEMPLE

The Reverend Jim Jones (1931–78) was a popular cult leader in the Bay Area during the 1970s, preaching an amalgam of racial and religious egalitarianism, political empowerment, doomsday visions and sexual freedom. He was alternately a fundamentalist, supposedly "healing" people through touch, and a modern minister, with his services accompanied by music and dance. But he was also a self-proclaimed messiah. After building up a congregation of some 20,000 at his People's Temple in San Francisco, in 1978 he moved almost 1,000 of them to an isolated agricultural mission in Guyana, South America. After rumours of physical abuse and weapons caches at the colony brought international scrutiny, Jones ordered a mass suicide. Investigators later found hundreds of his followers' corpses in the jungle; they had all drunk a cyanide-laced fruit drink and the despotic reverend had been shot in the head.

Jim Jones

PSYCHEDELIA

The term "psychedelic" originally referred to ideas or approaches that were somehow outrageous, nonconformist or "mind-expanding". But after San Francisco witnessed the opening of the Psychedelic Shop on Haight Street in 1966 *(see p.348)*, the word became associated with the hallucinatory drugs popular among the region's hippie generation.

Psychedelia then turned into a symbol of an entire lifestyle: young hippie communities rejecting conformity and travelling from one gathering to another on brightly painted buses, taking drugs and preaching peace.

The Esalen Institute (see p499) *became famous in the 1960s as the centre of the "human potential movement", a philosophy emphasizing individual responsibility for both the good and bad events in life. Today it is an expensive retreat where former flower children and stressed corporate executives all discuss spiritual insights while reclining in hot springs overlooking the Pacific Ocean.*

THE NORTH

ANGING FROM DESERTED BEACHES *strewn with giant driftwood logs to dense forests at the foot of alpine peaks, the far north of California is the state at its most wild and rugged. The landscape is as diverse as any continent – lush redwood groves, the volcanic Cascade Mountains, the arid plains at the edge of the Great Basin – yet all this is confined within one quarter of the state.*

Native Americans settled in the north of California around 10,000 BC. They co-existed peacefully with each other and with the earth, leaving behind few signs of their existence apart from discarded sea shells along the coast and pictographs on cave walls. When the Europeans arrived in the area in the 19th century, things changed swiftly.

The first to come were fur trappers, in search of beavers, sea otters and other pelts. Soon afterwards gold seekers descended upon the region's rivers, hoping for similar riches to those found in the Sierra Nevada *(see pp44–5)*. Some gold was found, but the real wealth was made at the end of the century when timber companies began to harvest the forests of coastal redwoods. These giant redwood trees *(Sequoia sempervirens)* are the region's defining feature. The finest forests have been protected by state and national parks and exude a palpable sense of history.

Inland, an even more ancient sight confronts visitors to the strange volcanic areas of Mount Lassen and the Lava Beds National Monument. Millions of years worth of geological activity has formed a stunning landscape that is devoid of civilization.

North California is sparsely populated, with only a few small towns, such as Ferndale and Eureka. The prime attractions are natural, and life here, for visitors and residents alike, revolves around the great outdoors.

Lost Creek in Redwood National Park

◁ **Imposing snow-capped peak of Mount Shasta**

Exploring the North

R̲UGGED, WILD AND SPARSELY POPULATED, California's northern extremes have more in common with neighbouring Oregon and Washington than they do with the rest of the state. Dense forests of pines, firs and redwood trees cover more than half the landscape, and two parallel mountain ranges, the Coast Range and, further inland, the Sierra Nevada Mountains, divide the North into three very different sections. Along the coast, Cape Mendocino makes a good base for exploring the often deserted beaches and coastal redwood groves. Inland, the Sacramento Valley provides access to the beautiful snow-capped Mount Shasta and the volcanic spectacles of Lassen Volcanic National Park and the Lava Beds National Monument.

SIGHTS AT A GLANCE

Arcata ❷
Avenue of the Giants ❼
Eureka ❸
Ferndale ❺
Lassen Volcanic
  National Park ❶❺
Lava Beds National
  Monument ❶❹
Mount Shasta ❶❷
Samoa Cookhouse ❹
Scotia ❻
Shasta Dam ❶⓪
Shasta State Historic Park ❶❶
The Lost Coast ❽
Tule Lake National
  Wildlife Refuge ❶❸
Weaverville ❾

Tour
Redwood National
  Park pp432–3 ❶

*Patrick's Point State Park in
Humboldt County*

GETTING AROUND

A car is essential for visiting Northern California. Two north–south routes run parallel up and down the region, but the only comfortable route through the mountains east–west is Hwy 299. Bisecting the North, I-5 runs through the Sacramento Valley, while to the west US Hwy 101 runs through the lush valleys of the Russian and Eel rivers. Public transport is limited to Greyhound buses along the two main highways and a midnight train through the Sacramento Valley to Seattle.

KEY

▬▬ Freeway

▬▬ Major road

▦▦ Minor road

▬▬ Scenic route

〰 River

✲ Viewpoint

SEE ALSO

• *Where to Stay* pp530–31

• *Where to Eat* pp568–9

Impressive peak of Mount Shasta

ord

Klamath Falls ◄

TULE LAKE NATIONAL
WILDLIFE REFUGE ⑬

KLAMATH
NATIONAL
FOREST

Clear
Lake
Reservoir

Goose
Lake

Lakeview

139

395

LAVA BEDS
NATIONAL
MONUMENT ⑭

MODOC

NATIONAL

FOREST

299

MOUNT SHASTA ⑫
✲

89

139
299

ALTURAS

ADIN

Pit River

Sacramento River

299

139

BURNEY
✲

89

DAM

44
89

44

Eagle
Lake

44

395

EDDING

36

LASSEN VOLCANIC
NATIONAL PARK ⑮

139

SUSANVILLE

36

Lake Almanor

Honey
Lake
(dry)

320

BLUFF

32

395

70

PLUMAS

NATIONAL

FOREST

Sacramento River

Chico

QUINCY

70

395

amento

Reno

kilometres 25

miles 25

Redwood National Park ❶

See pp432–3.

Arcata ❷

Road map A2. 🚶 *16,000*. 🚌
🛪 *Arcata/Eureka Airport, 8 miles
(13 km) N of Arcata.* ℹ *62 G St (707
822-3619).*

A RCATA IS a small town and
its life revolves around
Humboldt State University, in
the hills above. Arcata's main
square, with palm trees and
a statue of President McKinley
(1843–1901), is filled with
bookshops and cafés. The
town is a pleasant base for
exploring the redwood region.

The forests east of Arcata are
thought to be the stomping
grounds of Bigfoot, the US
equivalent to Asia's Yeti. No
one has yet proved its existence, but footprints larger
than those of the biggest bear
have been found.

Eureka ❸

Road map A2. 🚶 *27,000*. 🚌
🛪 *Arcata/Eureka Airport, 15 miles
(24 km) N of Eureka.* ℹ *2112
Broadway (707 442-3738).*

E UREKA WAS founded by gold
miners in 1850, who were
so excited by their find that
they proudly named it after

Ornate Carson Mansion in Eureka

REDWOODS AND THE LUMBER INDUSTRY

The tallest tree on earth, the coniferous coastal redwood
(*Sequoia sempervirens*) is unique to northern California and
southern Oregon, although it is also related to the giant
sequoia (*Sequoiadendron gigantea*) of the High Sierras and
the *Metasequoia glyptostrobiodes* species, native to China.
Redwoods can live for 2,000 years and reach 350 ft (107 m),
despite roots that grow up to
200 ft (61 m) horizontally but
only 4–6 ft (1–2 m) deep.

The redwood's fast growth
and resistance to disease
makes it ideal for commercial
use. By the 1920s, logging had
destroyed 90 per cent of the
groves. The Save the Red-
woods League was formed,
buying land now protected
in state parks. However some
groves are still owned by lumber companies, and their
future is a major issue on both
local and national levels.

Stacked redwood lumber

the state's ancient Greek motto
meaning "I have found it". It
has since expanded into the
northern coast's largest industrial centre, with extensive
logging and fishing operations
surrounding the state protected natural harbour.

West of US 101, between E
and M streets along the waterfront, is Eureka's interesting
Old Town. Its restored 19th-
century buildings, many of
them with cast-iron façades,
have now been converted
into fashionable cafés, bars
and restaurants.

Situated at M and
Second streets is
the extravagant
Victorian architec-
ture of Carson Man-
sion (*see pp26–7*).
It was built in 1885
for millionaire lum-
ber baron William
Carson. Its whim-
sical Gothic design
is enhanced by its
redwood construc-
tion typical of the
area, being painted
to resemble the
more expensive
medium of stone.
Carson Mansion is
now a gentlemen's
club and is sadly
closed to the gen-
eral public.

Samoa Cookhouse ❹

1 Cookhouse Rd, Eureka. **Road
map** A2. 📞 *(707) 442-1659*.
⭕ *daily*. ⬤ *25 Dec*. ♿

T HE SAMOA COOKHOUSE was
built in 1900 as a dining
room for workers at the adjacent Louisiana Pacific pulp
mill, one of many lumber mills
standing on the narrow Samoa
Peninsula. It was opened to
the public in the 1960s, when
automation in the mills had
reduced the size of the work-
force and the need for on-site
dining facilities. The restaurant
has retained its rustic décor
and its giant-sized portions of
ham and eggs, fried chicken
and other traditional American
dishes. Old photographs and
antique logging equipment
add to the unique ambience.

Ferndale ❺

Road map A2. 🚶 *1,400*.
🛪 *Arcata/Eureka Airport, 40 miles
(64 km) N of Ferndale* ℹ *PO Box
325, Ferndale (707 786-4477)*.

L OCATED ON a flood plain
near the mouth of the Eel
River, Ferndale is a pastoral
respite from the wilderness of

California's northern coast. The town was founded in 1852 by Danish, Swiss-Italian and Portuguese immigrants who together established a lucrative dairy industry here. Many of Ferndale's Victorian houses have now been converted into inns and restaurants. In 1992, Ferndale was hit by one of the most powerful earthquakes in California's recent history, measuring 7.1 on the Richter scale, though damage was limited. Exhibits of the town's history can be seen in the **Ferndale Museum**.

The town is perhaps best known as the host of the annual Kinetic Sculpture Race, during which contestants ride their self-made vehicles from Arcata to Centerville County Beach, outside Ferndale.

🏛 **Ferndale Museum**
Shaw & 3rd St. ☎ (707) 786-4466.
◯ Feb–Sep: Wed–Sun.

Gingerbread Mansion, one of Ferndale's Victorian houses

Scotia ❻

Road map A2. 🏠 2,500. 🚌
✈ Arcata/Eureka Airport, 40 miles (64 km) N of Scotia. 🛈 715 Wildwood Ave (707 764-3436).

THE TOWN OF SCOTIA was built in 1887 to house the workers from the **Pacific Lumber Company**'s massive redwood mill, which dominates the south end of town. Palco, as the company is better known, was established in 1869 and owns and manages nearly 200,000 acres (80,000 ha) of prime redwood forest along the banks of the Eel River and its tributaries. Incorporating two sawmills, a school, medical clinics and housing for nearly 300 lumber

Palco's redwood visitors' centre in Scotia

employees and their families, Scotia is the only complete lumber community still in existence in California.

Exhibits on the history of Scotia, and on the redwood lumber industry as a whole, are displayed in a small museum in the centre of town, which also dispenses passes for self-guided tours of the lumber mill. Here visitors can see each stage of the milling process: huge logs are debarked by powerful jets of water, sliced by laser-guided saws into lumber, then dried and stacked ready for shipping.

🏭 **Pacific Lumber Company**
125 Main St. ☎ (707) 764-2222.
◯ Mon–Fri. 🎫

Avenue of the Giants ❼

🚌 Garbeville. 🛈 Weott (Mar–Oct: daily; Nov–Feb: Thu–Sun) (707 946-2263).

THE WORLD'S tallest redwood trees and the most extensive primeval redwood groves stand along the banks of the Eel River within the impressive 50,000-acre (20,200-ha) Humboldt Redwoods State Park (see p432). The best overall sense of these redwoods can be had by driving along the 33-mile (53-km) Avenue of the Giants, a winding two-lane highway running parallel to US 101 through the park. For the best experience, however, leave your car in one of the many parking areas provided and walk around the groves, taking in the full immensity and magnificence of the trees.

The tallest individual specimen, the 364-ft (110-m) Dyersville Giant, sadly toppled during a storm in the winter of 1991, but its size is perhaps even more astounding now, lying on its side in Founder's Grove at the north end of the park. Currently the tallest and largest trees stand within the Rockefeller Forest above the west bank of the river.

The visitors' centre, halfway along the Avenue of the Giants on US 101, exhibits displays on the natural history of these mighty forests. It also supplies maps and detailed information on the many hiking and camping facilities available within the park.

Avenue of the Giants, in Humboldt Redwoods State Park

A Tour of Redwood National Park ❶

Redwood National Park protects some of the largest original redwood forests in the world, stretching along the coastline of Northern California. Established by President Johnson in 1968 to promote tourism to the area, the 58,000-acre (23,500-ha) park includes smaller areas which had already been established as state parks. A tour of the area takes one full day, although two days allows time to walk away from the roads and experience the tranquillity of these majestic groves.

Coastal redwood trees

Del Norte Coast Redwood State Park ③
This park became the first protected area in 1926. Part of the old Redwood Highway has been maintained as a hiking trail. In spring, wild flowers cover the hillsides.

Trees of Mystery ④
A major tourist attraction of the area is marked by giant fibreglass statues of the mythical lumberjack Paul Bunyan and his ox, Babe. The two characters were popularized in early 20th-century stories about their journey from Maine to California.

Tall Trees Grove ⑤
The world's tallest tree, a 368-ft (112-m) giant, stands in the aptly named Tall Trees Grove, at the southern end of the park. The park provides a habitat for one of the world's last remaining herds of Roosevelt elk.

Gold Bluffs Beach ⑥
This 11-mile (18-km) beach is rated by many as the most beautiful in Northern California.

Humboldt Lagoons State Park ⑦
Big Lagoon, a freshwater lake stretching for 3 miles (5 km), and two other estuaries form Humboldt Lagoons State Park.

Patrick's Point State Park ⑧
In winter, the headlands are a good place to watch for migrating grey whales. Rock pools abound with smaller marine life.

Fort Dick

Parkway Drive

Klamath

Alder Camp Road

Davison Rd.

Orick

Stone Lagoon

Big Lagoon

0 km   1

0 miles

The Lost Coast, near Crescent City

ediah Smith Redwoods te Park ①

nd among the 9,200 acres '20 ha) of this park are the st awe-inspiring coastal woods. The park was ned after the fur-trapper ediah Smith, the first white n to walk across the US. explored this region in 8 (*see p42*).

scent City ②

s northern town is the site he headquarters and main ormation centre for wood National Park.

Tour route

Other roads

The Lost Coast ⑧

Road map A2. 🚌 *Garberville.* 🛈 *Shelter Cove (707 966-7069).*

COVERING a small section of coastline so craggy and wild that no road could reasonably be built along it, the so-called "Lost Coast" is the largest remaining stretch of undeveloped shoreline in California. Protected by the United States government within the Sinkyone Wilder-ness State Park and the King Range National Conservation Area, the Lost Coast region stretches for more than 40 miles (64 km).

The salmon-fishing port of Shelter Cove, tucked away within a tiny bay, is at the centre of the Lost Coast. Its remote location has kept the village small, but it remains a good base for hikers and wildlife enthusiasts. Sixteen miles (25 km) of hiking trails, inhabited only by fauna such as black bears, deer, mink and bald eagles, run along the clifftops, interspersed with free camp sites. Shelter Cove is only accessible via a wind-ing but well-maintained road.

A good feel for the Lost Coast can be had by taking Hwy 211 west of US 101 and then following the scenic road between Humboldt Redwoods State Park and Ferndale (*see p430*). This beautiful 50-mile (80-km) road runs to the edge of the Pacific Ocean around Cape Mendocino, the westernmost point on the coast of California.

Weaverville ⑨

Road map A2. 🏚 *4,500.* ✈ *Redding Municipal Airport, 40 miles (64 km) E of Weaverville.* 🛈 *317 Main St (916 623-6101).*

THE SMALL rural town of Weaverville, set back in the mountains between the coast and the Central Valley, has changed little in the 150 years since it was founded by gold prospectors.

At the heart of the small commercial district, which boasts the state's oldest drug-store, is the **Jake Jackson Museum**. This small museum has displays tracing both the history of Weaverville and its surrounding gold mining and lumber region. Adjacent to the museum, the Joss House State Historic Site is the oldest and best-preserved Chinese Temple in the country, con-structed in 1874. It serves as a reminder of the many Chinese immigrants who arrived in the US to mine gold and stayed in the state as cheap labour building the Californian rail-ways (*see pp46–7*).

North of Weaverville, the Trinity Alps, part of the Salmon Mountain Range, rise up at the centre of a beautiful mountain wilderness. They are popular with hikers and backpackers in the summer and with cross-country skiers during the winter months.

🏛 **Jake Jackson Museum**
508 Main St. **☎** *(916) 623-5211.* ⚪ *Apr–Nov: daily; Dec–Mar: Tue & Sat only.* **Donation**.

Towering coastal redwood trees in Redwood National Park ▷

Shasta Dam, controlling the North's water supplies

Shasta Dam ⑩

🚃 *Redding.* **Visitors' Center** 📞 *(916) 275-1554.*

IN ORDER TO provide a steady supply of water for agriculture, a cheap source of electricity for manufacturers, prevent flooding in the valley and offer jobs for workers who had been left unemployed by the downturn in local mining industries, the US government funded the Central Valley Project. This was a network of dams, canals and reservoirs, set up during the Depression of the 1930s and centred upon the 602-ft (183-m) high, 3,460-ft (1,055-m) long Shasta Dam. With a spillway three times as high as Niagara Falls, the dam is one of the most impressive civil engineering achievements in the country to this day.

Shasta State Historic Park ⑪

Road map A2. 🚃 *Redding.* **Visitors' Center** 📞 *(916) 243-8194.* ◯ *Wed–Sun.*

DURING THE 1850s, Shasta was one of the largest gold mining camps in the state, and the base of operations for prospectors working along the Sacramento, Trinity, McCloud and Pit rivers. As the Gold Rush faded, however, the town faded too, especially after the railroad was rerouted through the town of Redding, 5 miles (8 km) to the east.

Shasta is now a ghost town, but in the early 1920s the State of California, realizing its historical importance, took over the site and began to restore it. Numerous old brick buildings are preserved in a state of arrested decay, and the old **Shasta Courthouse** has been restored to its original condition. A small visitors' centre has exhibits tracing the history of the town.

One mile (1.5 km) west of Shasta town, the land around Lake Whiskeytown forms the smallest parcel of the three-part Shasta-Whiskeytown-Trinity National Recreation Area, a forest preserve surrounding the three reservoirs. Lake Shasta is the largest of the three. Trinity Lake is also known as Clair Engle Lake, in honour of the local politician who helped make this ambitious reclamation project a reality. All three lakes are popular with fishermen, water-skiers, houseboat owners and other recreational users.

🏛 **Shasta Courthouse and Visitors' Center**
Main St. 📞 *(916) 243-8194.* ◯ *Wed–Sun.*

Mount Shasta ⑫

Road map B1. 🚉 *Dunsmuir.* 🚉 *Siskiyou.* 🚌 *Shasta.* **Visitors' Center** 📞 *(916) 926-4865.* ◯ *May–Oct: Mon–Sat; Nov–Apr: Mon–Fri.*

MOUNT SHASTA reaches a height of 14,162 ft (4,316 m) and is the second-highest of the Cascade Mountains, after Mount Rainier in Washington State. Visible more than 100 miles (160 km) away and usually covered with snow, the summit is a popular destination for mountaineers.

Mount Shasta, towering over the town of Shasta below

Tule Lake National Wildlife Refuges ⑬

Road map B1. 🚌 *Klamath Falls.* **Visitors' Center** 📞 *(916) 667-2231.*

SIX REFUGES on both sides of the California–Oregon border form one of the most popular bird-watching spots in the western United States.

Interior of the preserved Shasta Courthouse

Centring upon Tule Lake and the Lower Klamath River, much of the region has been set aside as wildlife refuges (see pp420–21), popular with bird-watchers. In the autumn the refuges attract hundreds of thousands of wildfowl as they make their migration south, from Canada to the Central Valley and beyond. Tule Lake is also the winter home to as many as 1,000 bald eagles, a comparatively rare species in California.

Lava Beds National Monument ⑭

Road map B1. 🚌 Klamath Falls. **Visitors' Center** ☎ (916) 667-2282. ⬭ daily.

THE LAVA BEDS National Monument spreads over 46,500 acres (18,800 ha) of the Modoc Plateau, the volcanic tableland of northeast California, and preserves an eerie landscape of lava flows and cinder cones. Beneath the lava beds are more than 200 caves and lava tubes – cylindrical tunnels created by exposed lava turning to stone.

The greatest concentration of caves can be visited via the Cave Loop Road, 2 miles (3 km) south of the park's visitors' centre. From here, a short trail leads down into Mushpot Cave, the only one with lights and a paved floor. The name derives from splatters of lava found near the entrance.

Other caves along the road are also named for their main feature: Crystal Cave contains sparkling crystals, while Catacombs Cave requires visitors to crawl through its twisting passages. To visit any of the caves, wear sturdy shoes, carry a torch, and be sure to check first with the visitors' centre.

The park is also notable as the site of the Modoc War of 1872–3, the only major war between the US and the Native Americans in California. After being removed from the area to a reservation in Oregon, a group of Modoc Indians returned under the command of Chief Kientpoos, or "Captain Jack". For six months they evaded the US Cavalry, but

Captain Jack's Stronghold in Lava Beds National Monument

Captain Jack was eventually captured and hanged, and the rest were forced into a reservation in what is now Oklahoma. Captain Jack's Stronghold is along the park's north border.

Lassen Volcanic National Park ⑮

Road map B2. 🚌 Chester, Red Bluff. **Visitors' Center** ☎ (916) 595-4444. ⬭ Jun–Sep: daily; Oct–May: Mon–Fri.

PRIOR TO the eruption of Mount St Helens in Washington in 1980, the 10,457-ft (3,187-m) high Lassen Peak was the last volcano to erupt on the mainland United States. In a series of nearly 300 eruptions between 1914 and 1917, Lassen Peak laid waste to 100,000 acres (40,500 ha) of the surrounding land. The area was set aside as Lassen Volcanic National Park in 1916.

The volcano is the southernmost in the Cascade Mountain range and is still considered to be active. Numerous areas on its flanks show clear signs of the geological processes. Bumpass Hell was

named after an early tour guide, Kendall Bumpass, who lost his leg in one of the boiling mudpots in 1865. This boardwalk trail leads past a series of steaming, sulphurous pools of boiling water, heated by molten rock deep underground. Bumpass Hell is one of the park's most interesting stops, and is located along Hwy 89, 5 miles (8 km) from the Southwest Entrance Station.

In winter, Hwy 89 across the park is closed due to weather conditions. In summer, the road winds through the park, climbing more than 8,500 ft (2,590 m) high, up to Summit Lake. The road continues across to the Devastated Area, a bleak grey landscape of rough volcanic mudflows, ending at Manzanita Lake in the northwest corner of the park. Here the **Loomis Museum** displays a photographic record of Lassen Peak's many eruptions.

The park contains more than 150 miles (240 km) of hiking trails, including a very steep 2.5 mile (4 km) route up the side of Mount Lassen to the ashen grey summit.

🏛 Loomis Museum
Lassen Park Rd, North Entrance. ☎ (916) 595-4444. ⬭ late Jun–mid-Sep: daily. ⬤ 4 Jul.

Sulphur springs in Lassen Volcanic National Park

THE WINE COUNTRY

FAMOUS THROUGHOUT THE WORLD *for its superlative wines, the Wine Country interior has a temperate climate, miles of vine-covered hills and spectacular architecture. To the west lie the dramatic, rocky landscapes of the Sonoma and Mendocino coastlines. Throughout the region, a wide choice of excellent food and, of course, premium wine, is available, making this an ideal place for a relaxing retreat.*

California's wine industry was born in the small, crescent-shaped Sonoma Valley, when, in 1823, Franciscan fathers planted vines to produce sacramental wines. In 1857, the flamboyant Hungarian Count Agoston Haraszthy brought winemaking in California to a new level: using imported European grape varieties, he planted the state's first major vineyard at Sonoma's revered Buena Vista Winery *(see p449)*. Haraszthy made a name not only for himself (he is known as the "father of California wine"), but also for this previously unrecognized wine-producing region.

Over the years, many wine producers have followed in the count's footsteps, most of them favouring the rich, fertile soil of the Napa Valley. Hundreds of wineries now stand side by side along the length of the valley floor. Most of them offer tours of their facilities and wine tastings. Many are also of architectural interest, including such gems as the Mission-style Robert Mondavi Winery and the white Mediterranean-style Sterling Vineyards, which is perched on a volcanic bluff. Nearby, the stunning modern winery of Clos Pegase is distinguished by rows of imposing russet- and earth- coloured columns and towers.

Nestled at the northernmost edge of the Napa Valley is the small town of Calistoga, famous for its restorative mud baths, enormous geysers and hot mineral-water tubs. West of the valley, the Russian River flows into the Pacific Ocean, which is bordered by the Sonoma and Mendocino coastal areas. These wild stretches of shoreline provide perfect opportunities for bird- and whale-watching and beachcombing.

Goat Rock Beach at the mouth of the Russian River

◁ **Mustard plants growing in a Napa Valley vineyard in the spring**

Exploring the Wine Country

T HE SHELTERED VALLEYS of the coastal ranges provide the best conditions for planting vines, particularly within the Russian River, Sonoma and Napa valleys. To the west of these famous wine-producing areas, quaint coastal towns, such as Mendocino, Jenner and Bodega Bay, are surrounded by pristine, secluded beaches and small rock pools. Inland, visitors can explore the ancient redwood groves on foot, horseback or by train. For those who prefer to have a bird's-eye view of the region, trips are available in hot-air balloons that soar gracefully above the vineyards. A short drive away are several immense state historic parks, with dense forests and unique architecture. Nearby, a wide variety of water sports is available at Clear Lake, California's largest freshwater lake, and Lake Berryessa, which is the second-largest artificial lake in the state.

Gerstle Cove, site of a marine reserve at Salt Point

GETTING AROUND

The majority of visitors explore the Wine Country and the scenic areas along the Sonoma and Mendocino coasts by car. From San Francisco, Hwy 1 follows the coast and Hwy 101 runs south–north through the centre of the region and into Humboldt County. Route 20 links Nevada City and the Wine Country, joining Hwy 101 north of Lake Mendocino. Public transport services in the area are very limited, although coach tours from San Francisco are available and train tours of the Napa Valley *(see pp446–7)* and of the northern redwood forests *(see p443)* operate regularly. The closest international airports are in San Francisco and Oakland *(see pp598–9)*.

SEE ALSO

- *Where to Stay* pp531–3
- *Where to Eat* pp569–71

KEY

Freeway
Major road
Minor road
Scenic route
River
Viewpoint

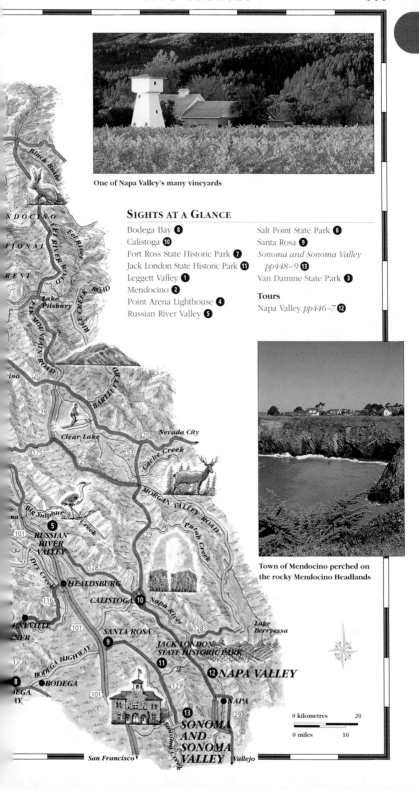

One of Napa Valley's many vineyards

SIGHTS AT A GLANCE

Town of Mendocino perched on
the rocky Mendocino Headlands

Leggett Valley ❶

Road map A2. ⛟ to Leggett.
🛈 70400 Hwy 101 (707 925-6425).

THIS LUSH, GREEN VALLEY, separated from the Pacific Ocean by the King Mountain Range, is famous in California for its majestic giant redwoods. In the 1930s a hole was cut in the trunk of one enormous redwood to allow motorists to drive through the tree.

Hikers come to Leggett Valley and the surrounding area to enjoy the atmospheric redwood forest trails (part of the forest here was used to film scenes for George Lucas's science-fiction epic, *Star Wars*). The local wildlife population includes raccoons and deer, and golden eagles can often be seen soaring above the trees, searching the forest floor for unsuspecting prey.

South Fork Eel River, which is rich in salmon and steelhead trout, attracts many birds, including herons. The river is also popular with anglers and, in summer, swimmers.

Mendocino ❷

Road map A3. 👥 1,100. ⛟ 🛈 332 N Main St, Fort Bragg (707 961-6300; 800 726-2780).

THE SETTLERS who founded this fishing village came to California from New England in 1852. They built their new homes to resemble as closely as possible those they had left behind on the East Coast, with pointed gables and decorative wooden trims. As a result, the Mendocino coastline is often referred to as "California's New England Coast".

Perched on a spectacular rocky promontory high above the Pacific Ocean, Mendocino has retained the picturesque charm of its days as a major fishing and logging centre. Although tourism is now its main industry, the town remains virtually untarnished by commercialism. It is a thriving arts centre and has a large number of resident artists and writers. Visitors can stroll around the many exclusive boutiques, bookshops, art galleries and cafés. Those who prefer the attractions of nature can admire the beauty of the heather-covered bluffs, the migrating grey whales and the stunning ocean vistas.

Giant ferns lining the beautiful Fern Canyon Trail in Van Damme State Park

Van Damme State Park ❸

Road map A3. 📞 (707) 937-5804. 🛈 (707) 937-4016. ⛟ from Point Arena. ◯ May–Sep: daily; Oct–Apr: Sat & Sun. 🅿 ♿

THIS BEAUTIFUL 2,200-acre (890-ha) reserve has some of California's most scenic forest trails, shaded by immense redwoods and giant ferns, and accompanied by meandering creeks. The coastal areas of the park are popular with abalone divers. For visitors who want to enjoy a hike or jog through gorgeous countryside, the lush Fern Canyon Trail is one of the best in the park, which also has several cycle trails.

Visitors also come to Van Damme to contemplate the peculiar Pygmy Forest, an eerie grove of old, stunted trees. Due to a combination of poor soil and bad drainage, these trees grow no taller than about 4 ft (1.2 m). The Pygmy Forest, 3 miles (5 km) north of the park, is accessible on foot or by car.

Point Arena Lighthouse ❹

Road map A3. 📞 (707) 882-2777. ⛟ from Point Arena. **Lighthouse and Museum** ◯ Jan–Nov: daily; Dec: Sat & Sun. 🅿 ♿ museum only. 🎫

ONE MILE (1.5 km) north of the little Point Arena fishing village stands this impressive 115-ft (35-m) lighthouse. Erected in 1870, the original brick building was destroyed in the great earthquake of 1906 *(see p20)*. It was replaced by the present reinforced concrete structure, produced in San Francisco by the Concrete Chimney Company.

A climb up the 145 steps to the top of the lighthouse provides a stunning view of the coastline – the effort is particularly worthwhile on fog-free

Mendocino overlooking the ocean from the bay's rocky headlands

days. Tours of the lighthouse, which are available all year round, give visitors a chance to see its huge original Fresnel lens close-up. Built in France, the lens measures more than 6 ft (1.8 m) in diameter, weighs more than 2 tonnes and floats in a large pool of mercury.

The adjacent fog signal building, which dates from 1869, now houses a museum. Among the exhibits are several compressed-air foghorns and displays on the history of the lighthouse, including some fascinating old photographs.

Point Arena Lighthouse overlooking the Pacific Ocean

Russian River Valley ❺

Road map A3. 🚌 *from Healdsburg.* 🅸 *14034 Armstrong Woods Rd, Guerneville (707 869-9212).*

BISECTED BY the Russian River and its tributaries, the area known as the Russian River Valley is so vast that it contains several smaller valleys, some dominated by hillsides planted with grapevines and apple orchards, others by redwood groves, family farms and sandy river beaches. About 60 wineries, many of which are open for wine tastings, are scattered throughout the valley.

At the hub of the valley is the small town of Healdsburg, where visitors often congregate around the splendid Spanish-style town square, with its shops, cafés and restaurants.

Southwest of Healdsburg lies the tiny, friendly town of Guerneville, a summertime

---

THE SKUNK TRAIN

Since 1885, the Skunk Train has been running from Fort Bragg, a coastal logging town north of Mendocino, into the heart of the redwood groves. Thanks to the odoriferous mix of diesel and gasoline once used to fuel the locomotive, waiting passengers could always smell the train before they could see it, hence its name. Today, locomotive lovers can ride on one of the steam, diesel or electric trains for a half- or full-day tour through the forests.

Skunk Train and its smoke cloud

---

haven for San Francisco Bay Area residents, particularly gay men and women. Every year in September, Guerneville plays host to the very popular Russian River Jazz Festival at Johnson's Beach. Johnson's is also a good place from which to take a canoe or rafting trip down the gentle Russian River, where turtles, river otters and great blue herons are often sighted. Hikers and equestrians flock to Guerneville to visit the 805-acre (330-ha) **Armstrong Redwoods State Reserve**, which is the site of one of the few remaining old-growth redwood forests in California. Among the mighty redwoods in the reserve is a 308-ft (94-m) giant – a 1,400-year-old tree named Colonel Armstrong.

🌿 Armstrong Redwoods State Reserve
17000 Armstrong Woods Rd, Guerneville. 🎫 *(707) 869-2015, 865-2391.* 🕐 *daily.*

Salt Point State Park ❻

Road map A3. 🎫 *(707) 847-3221, 847-3465.* 🚌 *from Santa Rosa.* 🕐 *daily.* 📷 ♿

WITHIN THIS FORESTED 6,000-acre (2,400-ha) seaside park are several rocky coves, frequented by abalone divers and surf fishers. Salt Point also includes Gerstle Cove Marine Reserve, where divers admire protected sea anemones, starfish and various rock fish.

Numerous horse-riding and hiking trails wind through Salt Point's pines, redwoods and flower-filled meadows. In April and May, the most popular park attraction is the route that leads through the 317-acre (130-ha) Kruse Rhododendron State Reserve, where rhododendrons with brilliant pink and purple blooms grow up to 30 ft (9 m) tall.

Gerstle Cove in Salt Point State Park

Cannon on display in front of the Russian Orthodox chapel at Fort Ross

Fort Ross State Historic Park **7**

Road map A3. **☎** *(707) 847-3286.* **🚌** *from Point Arena.* **○** *daily.* **●** *1 Jan, Thanksgiving, 25 Dec.*

ON A WINDSWEPT headland, 12 miles (19 km) north of Jenner, stands the grand Fort Ross State Historic Park. A well-restored Russian trading outpost, the fort was founded in 1812 and was occupied until 1841 (the name "Ross" is a derivative of the Russian word "Rossyia", meaning Russia).

The Russians were the first European visitors to the region, serving as representatives of the Russian-American Company, which had been established in 1799. Although it was the presence of Russian fur hunters in the North Pacific that induced Spain to occupy Alta California in 1769, the Russians never tried to expand their territory in California. After 30 years of peaceful trading, they abandoned the fort.

Built in 1836, the original house of the fort's last manager, Alexander Rotchev, is still intact today and several other buildings have been painstakingly reconstructed within the wooden palisade. The most impressive structure within Fort Ross is the Russian Orthodox chapel, which was constructed from local redwood in 1824.

A small visitors' centre offers picnic facilities and maps and booklets about the fort. Every year, a living history day is held on the last Saturday of July. More than 200 costumed participants re-create life at the outpost in the 1800s.

Bodega Bay **8**

Road map A3. **🏘** *1,200.* **🚌** **🛈** *850 Hwy 1 (707 875 3422).*

IN 1963, THE COASTAL TOWN of Bodega Bay, with its white clapboard houses, appeared in Alfred Hitchcock's classic film, *The Birds*. In the tiny neighbouring town of Bodega, visitors can still see the Potter Schoolhouse, now a private residence, which was featured in the film.

Bodega Head, the small peninsula sheltering Bodega Bay, is one of California's best whale-watching points. Other favourite Bodega Bay pastimes include golfing, bird-watching, digging for clams and deep-sea fishing. In the evening, visitors can watch the fishing fleets unload their day's catch at Tides Wharf dock on Hwy 1.

The northern end of Bodega Bay marks the beginning of the Sonoma Coast State Beach, a 10-mile (16-km) stretch of ten beaches, separated by rocky bluffs. At the northernmost tip of this chain of beaches sits the charming little town of Jenner. Here, the wide Russian River spills into the Pacific Ocean, and hundreds of grey harbour seals bask in the sun and breed on Goat Rock Beach. The most rewarding time to watch the seals is during their "pupping season", which begins in March and lasts until late June.

Santa Rosa **9**

Road map A3. **🏘** *124,900.* **✈** *Sonoma County Airport, 6 miles (10 km) N of Santa Rosa.* **🚌** **🛈** *637 1st St (707 577-8674; 800 404-7673).*

SANTA ROSA, which is one of the fastest-growing cities in California, is best known for its past and present residents, most notably the horticulturist Luther Burbank (1849–1926). Burbank lived here for more than 50 years and became world famous for creating 800 new plant varieties, including fruits, vegetables and ornamental flowers.

Self-guided tours explore the one-acre (0.5-ha) site of the **Luther Burbank Home and Gardens**, which includes a rose garden and an orchard. The Victorian garden features plants often found in domestic gardens in the 1880s.

Robert L Ripley (1893–1949) was also a Santa Rosa hero. An illustrator who collected peculiar artifacts, Ripley created the "Ripley's Believe It or Not!®" cartoon strip *(see p326)*. The **Robert L Ripley Memorial Museum** has unusual displays

A harbour seal on Goat Rock Beach

Fishing boats at North Beach Jetty Marina in Bodega Bay

Spring flowers in bloom at Luther Burbank Home and Gardens

Jack London State Historic Park ⓫

Road map A3. 📞 (707) 938-5216.
🚌 Glen Ellen. **Park and Museum**
⭕ daily. ⬤ 1 Jan, Thanksgiving,
25 Dec. 🏷 ♿ museum only. 🎫

IN THE EARLY 1900s, the world-famous author of *The Call of the Wild, The Sea Wolf* and more than 50 other books *(see p22)* abandoned his hectic lifestyle to live in this tranquil 800-acre (325-ha) expanse of oaks, madrones, California buckeyes and redwoods. London (1876–1916) aptly named this territory the Beauty Ranch and it still contains his stables and vineyards and the cottage where he wrote and where he died. Also here are the eerie ruins of London's dream home, the Wolf House, which was mysteriously destroyed by fire just before its completion. The park is an ideal place for a quiet picnic and a hike.

After London's death, his widow, Charmian Kittredge (1871–1955), built a magnificent home on the ranch, called the House of Happy Walls. The house is now a museum displaying London memorabilia. The author's writing desk and early copies of his work are exhibited, as well as his collection of South Pacific art objects.

about the life of this former Santa Rosa native. A large collection of assorted Ripley memorabilia is also exhibited.

Another internationally acclaimed cartoonist, Charles Schulz, the creator of the "Peanuts" series, is also a resident of Santa Rosa. Admirers of Schulz's cartoon characters can visit **Snoopy's Gallery and Gift Shop**. The shop stocks the widest range of Snoopy products in the world.

🌸 **Luther Burbank Home and Gardens**
204 Santa Rosa Ave. 📞 (707) 524-5445. **Gardens** ⭕ daily.
Home ⭕ Apr–Oct: Wed–Sun. 🎫
🏛 **Robert L Ripley Memorial Museum**
492 Sonoma Ave. 📞 (707) 524-5233.
⭕ Apr–Oct: Wed–Sun. 🏷
🏠 **Snoopy's Gallery and Gift Shop**
1665 Steele Lane. 📞 (707) 546-3385. ⭕ daily. ⬤ Easter Sun.

Calistoga ❿

Road map A3. 👥 4,715. 🚌
ℹ 1458 Lincoln Ave (707 942-6333).

VISITORS HAVE enjoyed taking invigorating mineral or mud baths here since this little spa town was founded in the mid-19th century by the state's first millionaire, Sam Brannan (1819–89). Today, crowds are still drawn to Calistoga by its specialized spa treatments and good Wine Country cuisine. The town also has a range of pleasant accommodation and small boutiques selling everything from hand-made soaps to European home furnishings.

Two miles (3 km) to the north of the town, the **Old Faithful Geyser** spouts jets of boiling mineral water 60 ft (18 m) into the sky approximately once every 40 minutes. To the west lies the **Petrified Forest**. Here hikers can see huge redwoods turned to stone by a volcanic eruption more than three million years ago *(see p446)*.

Many visitors who prefer to hike among living redwoods travel east to the Robert Louis Stevenson State Park, where the author of *Treasure Island* and his wife, Fanny Osbourne, spent their honeymoon in 1880 *(see p22)*. Those who climb the 5 miles (8 km) from the park to the summit of the 4,343-ft (1,325-m) Mount St Helena, the Wine Country's highest peak, are rewarded by a breathtaking view of the vineyards below. To enjoy the bird's-eye view without making the rigorous ascent, it is worth taking a trip in a glider or hot-air balloon. These are available at the gliderport in nearby Calistoga.

🌋 **Old Faithful Geyser**
1299 Tubbs Lane.
📞 (707) 942-6463.
⭕ daily. 🏷
🌲 **Petrified Forest**
4100 Petrified Forest Rd. 📞 (707) 942-6667. ⭕ daily.
⬤ Thanksgiving, 25 Dec. 🏷 ♿ limited.

Old Faithful Geyser spurting hot water into the sky

Napa Valley Tour ⑫

THE SLIVER OF LAND known as Napa Valley is 35 miles (56 km) long and lies at the heart of Northern California's wine industry. More than 250 wineries are scattered across its rolling hillsides and fertile valley floor, some dating from the early 19th century. Most of the wineries hug the scenic Silverado Trail and Hwy 29, two major arteries that run the length of the valley and through the towns of Yountville, Oakville, Rutherford, St Helena and Calistoga (see p445). Many of Napa Valley's popular wineries offer visitors free tours of their facilities, while some charge a small wine-tasting fee.

Statue at Clos Pegase

Clos Pegase ⑥
Renowned architect Michael Graves designed this Post-Modern winery, which is well known for its distinctive art collection and fine wines.

Sterling Vineyards ⑦
An aerial tramway provides access to this large, white, Mediterranean-style winery, which is perched on a hill overlooking the valley and vineyards.

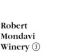

Petrified Forest ⑤
This forest is the home of the largest petrified trees in the world (see p445).

Bale Grist Waterwheel ④
Built in 1846, this waterwheel still grinds grain into meal and flour at weekends.

Robert Mondavi Winery ③
Beautiful sculptures and paintings are on display throughout this huge, Mission-style winery. Guided tours are available year round.

FOOD AND WINE IN THE NAPA VALLEY

In addition to a number of superior wines, the Wine Country is well known for its fresh produce and prestigious chefs. Produce stalls and farmers' markets line the valley roads, selling organic vegetables and fruit and freshly squeezed juices. Restaurants in most small towns serve excellent meals, prepared with the freshest ingredients. Classic Wine Country cuisine includes dishes such as Sonoma leg of lamb with fresh mint pesto, creamy risotto with artichoke hearts and sun-dried tomatoes, wild-mushroom sauté in herb-garlic filo pastry, and Sterling salmon sautéed and served with a Pinot Noir sauce.

Restaurant terrace at Domaine Chandon in Yountville

KEY

▨ Tour route

═ Other roads

❉ Viewpoint

Napa Valley vineyard in the late-afternoon sunlight

Napa Valley Wine Train
Gourmet Wine Country cuisine and fine wines are served on this luxury train *(see p570)* as it makes a three-hour tour of the lush Napa Valley.

Rutherford Hill Winery ⑧
This contemporary winery has caves for ageing wine which are carved half a mile (0.8 km) into the hillsides.

Mumm Napa Valley ⑨
Sparkling wines are made in the classic tradition at this winery partly owned by French champagne producer, GH Mumm.

Yountville ②
Founded in the mid-19th century by pioneer George Clavert Yount, this tiny town is now a popular spot from which to take a hot-air balloon ride over the Wine Country.

Napa ①
Napa's streets are lined with restored buildings housing restaurants, shops and art galleries.

0 kilometres 5

0 miles 2

Sonoma and Sonoma Valley ⑬

Bear flag monument

NESTLING IN THE NARROW, 17-mile (27-km) long Sonoma Valley, cradled by the Mayacama Mountains to the east and by the Sonoma Mountains to the west, are 6,000 acres (2,400 ha) of vineyards. At the foot of the valley lies the tiny town of Sonoma with its 8-acre (3-ha) plaza, a grass-covered town square designed in 1835 by Mexican General Mariano Vallejo (1808–90).

In the early 1840s, American settlers arriving in the area discovered that land ownership was reserved for Mexican citizens. On 14 June 1846, about 30 armed American farmers took General Vallejo and his men prisoner, seized control of Sonoma and declared California an independent republic. The rebels' flag was adorned with a red star and stripe and a crude drawing of a grizzly bear. Although the republic was abolished 25 days later, when the United States annexed California *(see p43)*, the state legislature adopted the Bear Flag design as the official Californian flag in 1911.

Sonoma City Hall at the centre of the historic Sonoma Plaza

Exploring Sonoma

Sonoma's main attractions are its internationally renowned wineries and the attractive area immediately surrounding the Spanish-style **Sonoma Plaza**. The well-shaded plaza is lined with dozens of meticulously preserved historical sites. Many of the adobe buildings around the square house wine shops, charming boutiques and chic restaurants serving excellent Californian and Wine Country cuisine. At the very centre of the town's plaza stands the **Sonoma City Hall**, a stone Mission Revival building *(see p27)* designed in 1908 by the San Francisco architect AC Lutgens. Close to the plaza's northeast corner is the bronze **Bear Flag Monument**, which serves as a memorial to the group of American settlers who rebelled against the ruling Mexican government in 1846.

🏛 Vasquez House

El Paseo. 📞 *(707) 938-0510.*
◯ *Wed–Sun.* 🎟 ✔
This gabled house, built in 1855, belonged to Civil War hero "Fighting Joe" Hooker, who later sold it to settlers Pedro and Catherine Vasquez. The house now serves as the headquarters of the Sonoma League for Historic Preservation. Inside, visitors can see various historical exhibits. Information on Sonoma walking tours is also available here.

🏛 Toscano Hotel

20 E Spain St. 📞 *(707) 938-1519.*
◯ *Fri–Sun.* 🎟 ✔ *obligatory.*
Located on the north side of the plaza, the restored Toscano Hotel is now an historic monument. The two-storey wood-frame building dates from the

SONOMA TOWN CENTRE

Bear Flag Monument ③
City Hall ②
Lachryma Montis ⑨
Mission San Francisco
   Solano de Sonoma ⑤
Sonoma Barracks ⑥
Sonoma Cheese Factory ⑧
Sonoma Plaza ①
Toscano Hotel ⑦
Vasquez House ④

0 metres   250
0 yards   250

KEY

ℹ️ Tourist information

1850s, when it was used as a general store and library. It was converted into an hotel for gold miners in 1886 and now belongs to the state.

🏠 Sonoma Cheese Factory

2 W Spain St. ☎ (707) 996-1931. ⭘ daily. ⬤ 1 Jan, Thanksgiving, 25 Dec.

The famous Sonoma Jack cheese has been produced in the enormous vats in this factory since 1931. Visitors can watch the production process through a large viewing window. The finished mild, white cheese can be purchased in the factory shop.

🏛 Lachryma Montis

W Spain & W 3rd Sts. ☎ (707) 938-9559. ⭘ daily. ⬤ 1 Jan, Thanksgiving, 25 Dec. ♿

Visitors can glimpse the lavish lifestyle of Mexican General Vallejo by exploring Lachryma Montis, his former home. This yellow and white Gothic Revival house was built of redwood in 1852. It features an eclectic array of Vallejo memorabilia, which ranges from the general's silver epaulettes and a cattle brand to his favourite books and photographs.

The name of the house is Latin for "tears of the mountain", a reference to a mineral spring on the property.

Lachryma Montis, once home to Mexican General Mariano Vallejo

🏛 Mission San Francisco Solano de Sonoma

E Spain St. ☎ (707) 938-9560. ⭘ daily. ⬤ 1 Jan, Thanksgiving, 25 Dec. ♿

Named after a Peruvian saint, this beautifully restored old mission (commonly called the Sonoma Mission) was the last of the historic chain of 21

Façade of the Mission San Francisco Solano de Sonoma

Franciscan missions built in California *(see p42)*. Father José Altimira of Spain founded the mission in 1823, at a time when California was under Mexican rule. Today, all that survives of the original building is the corridor of Father Altimira's quarters. The present adobe chapel was built by General Vallejo in 1840, to be used by the town's families and soldiers.

🏛 Sonoma Barracks

E Spain St. ☎ (707) 938-1519. ⭘ daily. ⬤ 1 Jan, Thanksgiving, 25 Dec. ♿

Native American labour was used to build this two-storey adobe structure between 1836 and 1840, when it served as the headquarters for General Vallejo and his troops. After the 1846 Bear Flag Revolt, the barracks became an outpost for the United States Army for about a decade. After being purchased by the state in the late 1950s, the building was restored. It is now a California Historical Landmark.

SONOMA VALLEY WINERIES

The Sonoma Valley has a rare perfect combination of soil, sun and rain for growing superior wine grapes. In 1824, Father José Altimira planted Sonoma's first grapevines, in order to produce sacramental wine for the masses held at the Mission San Francisco Solano de Sonoma. When, in 1834, the ruling Mexican government secularized the mission, General

The arms of the Sebastiani Vineyards

Vallejo replanted grapevines on its land and sold the wine he produced to San Francisco merchants. In 1857, Hungarian Count Agoston Haraszthy *(see p439)* planted the nation's first European varietals at Sonoma's Buena Vista Winery, now the oldest premium winery in the state.

The Sonoma Valley encompasses the Sonoma Valley, Carneros and Sonoma Mountain wine-growing regions. The climate varies slightly in each region, creating different environments suitable for producing particular grape varieties, including Cabernet Sauvignon and Chardonnay. Today, Sonoma is home to more than 35 wineries, which produce a total of 5.4 million cases of wine a year. Some of the valley's most notable wineries are Sebastiani Vineyards, Sonoma's largest premium-variety winery; Glen Ellen Winery; Gundlach-Bundschu Winery; and Château St Jean. Most of Sonoma's wineries offer picnic areas and free wine tastings and tours.

Vineyards in the Sonoma Valley

GOLD COUNTRY
AND THE CENTRAL VALLEY

L OCATED AT THE GEOGRAPHICAL HEART *of California, the Gold Country is also central to the state's allure as the land of overnight success. Long before the gilded world of Hollywood took shape, this was a real life El Dorado, where a thick vein of solid gold, known as the Mother Lode, sat waiting to be discovered.*

The Gold Country is largely rural, despite being the birthplace of modern California, with the Gold Rush of 1849 and the designation of Sacramento as state capital.

Before the miners arrived, this quiet region, located on the far fringes of the Spanish colonial empire, was sparsely populated by members of the Miwok and Maidu peoples. With the discovery of gold flakes in January 1848, however, the region turned into a lawless jamboree, and by 1852 an estimated 200,000 men from all over the world were working in the mines. But by 1860 most of the region had fallen silent again, as the mining boom went bust *(see pp44–5)*.

A few years after the Gold Rush, the region experienced another short-lived boom. The transcontinental rail-road was constructed through the Sierra Nevada Mountains by low-paid labourers, many of whom were Chinese *(see pp46–7)*. In the 20th century, the Central Valley became the heart of the state's thriving agricultural industry, which today exports fruit and vegetables worldwide.

Stretching for more than 100 miles (160 km) north to south, the region's landscape is ideal for leisurely hikes or afternoon picnics. The Gold Country also offers one of California's best scenic drives along Hwy 49. The route climbs up and down rocky ridges between pastoral ranch lands, lined with oak trees and crossed by fast-flowing rivers. Many of the picturesque towns it passes through, such as Sutter Creek, have survived unchanged since the Gold Rush.

Malakoff Diggins State Park, preserving the heyday of the Gold Rush

◁ **California State Capitol in Sacramento**

Exploring the Gold Country

THE GOLD COUNTRY ranges from flat delta flood
plains to the rugged, river-carved foothills of the
Sierra Nevada Mountains. At the heart of the region
is Sacramento, the state capital and
largest Gold Country city,
which has the highest
concentration of sights.
But the real attraction of
this area is in travelling
along its many scenic routes.
The rural landscape is dotted
with small historic towns.
Some are still thriving
communities, while others
are ghostly memorials to their
past. The Central Valley, along
I-5, is scattered with picturesque
farming towns. Larger towns, such
as Nevada City and Sutter Creek,
make excellent bases for a Gold
Country tour, and visitors are welcomed
and well catered for everywhere.

Redding

ORLAND   CHICO

WILLIAMS   YUBA CITY

Stony Creek   Sacramento River   Butte Creek   Feather River   Lake Oro

Tehama Colusa Canal   Yuba R

Cache Creek   Bear

DAVIS   SACRAME

VACAVILLE

FAIRFIELD

Berkeley
Oakland
San Francisco

Suisun Bay

BRANNAN ISLAND

Concord
San Jose

STOCKT

TRACY   Delta M

**Impressive State Capitol building
in Sacramento**

**Parrots Ferry Bridge over the picturesque New Melones Lake
along Hwy 49 in Tuolumne County**

SIGHTS AT A GLANCE

Angels Camp **16**
Chaw'se Indian Grinding
    Rock State Park **11**
Coloma Gold Discovery
    State Park **6**
*Columbia State Historic
    Park pp464–5* **19**
Empire Mine State
    Historic Park **3**

Folsom **7**
Grass Valley **2**
Jackson **12**
Jamestown **20**
Malakoff Diggins State Park **1**
Moaning Cavern **17**
Mokelumne Hill **13**
Murphys **15**
Nevada City **4**

Placerville **8**
*Sacramento
    pp456–9* **5**
San Andreas **14**
Sonora **18**
Stockton **21**
Sutter Creek **9**
Volcano **10**

Replica dwelling in the Chaw'se Indian Grinding Rock State Park

SEE ALSO

- *Where to Stay* pp533–4
- *Where to Eat* pp571–2

GETTING AROUND

A car is all but essential for exploring the Californian Gold Country. Most sights are located along the Gold Rush Highway, Hwy 49. This makes the best and most scenic driving route as it undulates along the foothills through the most interesting Gold Country towns. Public transport is severely limited, with only two long-distance bus services along the two main highways, I-80 and US 50, and a daily train service over the mountains from Sacramento. The area's main domestic airport is also in Sacramento, while the nearest international airport is San Francisco.

KEY

▓▓▓	Freeway
▬▬▬	Major road
▭▭▭	Minor road
▭▭▭	Scenic route
≈≈	River
☼	Viewpoint

0 kilometres   25

0 miles   25

The man-made canyon created by hydraulic mining at Malakoff Diggins

Malakoff Diggins State Park **❶**

Road map B3. ☎ (916) 265-2740.
🚌 from Nevada City. ◯ May-Sep:
daily; Oct-Apr: Sat & Sun. 🏛 ♿ ✉

As THE ORIGINAL gold mining techniques became less rewarding in the late 1850s, miners turned to increasingly powerful and destructive ways of extracting the valuable ore. When the more easily recoverable surface deposits disappeared, the miners began to strip away the soil with powerful jets of pressurized water. Spraying more than 200,000 gal (115,000 litres) of water per hour, the jets washed away entire mountainsides in search of gold. The process was known as hydraulic mining. In 1884 the Californian legislature forbade the dumping of gravel into streams, but huge swathes of land had already been ruined and the rivers had been clogged up with debris (see pp44–5).

One of the largest of these hydraulic mining operations was at Malakoff Diggins, 27 miles (45 km) northeast of Hwy 49, in the mountains above Nevada City. The eroded hillsides created a canyon which now forms an eerily beautiful state park, with several preserved buildings from the 1870s mining town of North Bloomfield.

Grass Valley **❷**

Road map B3. 👥 9,000. 🚗
🛈 248 Mill St (916 273-4667).

Long THE LARGEST and busiest town in the northern Gold Country, Grass Valley served the Empire Mine and other nearby hard rock gold mines.

In the 1870s and 1880s Grass Valley welcomed workers from the tin mines of Cornwall, England, who were affectionately known as "Cousin Jacks". Their expertise enabled the local mines to recover underground ore deposits and so remain in business after the rest of the area had fallen quiet (see pp44–5).

A nugget of gold set inside quartz crystal

Grass Valley is also the location of one of California's best mining museums. The **North Star Mining Museum** is situated in the powerhouse of the former North Star Mine. Surrounding the museum's entrance are the giant Pelton wheels that greatly increased production in the region's underground mines. Displays inside the museum include a stamp mill (a giant pulverizer used to crush ore), a Cornish pump (used to filter out underground water), as well as various artifacts relating to the Cornish background of the local miners.

🏛 North Star Mining Museum
Mill St at McCourtney Rd. ☎ (916) 273-4255. ◯ May–Oct: daily.
Donation.

Empire Mine State Historic Park **❸**

Road map B3. ☎ (916) 273-8522.
🚌 from Nevada City. ◯ daily.
● 1 Jan, Thanksgiving, 25 Dec. 🏛
♿ Grounds & Empire Cottage. ✉

One OF THE LONGEST surviving and most lucrative gold mining operations in the state, the Empire Mine was in business until 1956. It has now been preserved by the state as an historic park. Starting with surface workings in the 1850s, the Empire Mine grew to include 365 miles (585 km) of underground tunnels, from which pure gold estimated at 5.8 million ounces (16.5 million grams) was recovered.

Head frames, which held the mine's lift shafts, and other mining equipment are scattered over the park's 785 acres (318 ha), but for a real sense of how much money was made here you should visit Empire Cottage.

Designed by San Franciscan architect Willis Polk in 1897 for the mine's owner, William Bourn, the granite and red brick exterior resembles an English manor house, while the redwood interior gives an air of casual affluence. The gardens next door to the cottage contain nearly 1,000 rose bushes and a large greenhouse.

Further exhibits on the history of the Empire Mine and on hard rock gold mining are on show in the visitors' centre, along with samples of the precious metal.

Original stamp mill used to crush ore at the Empire Mine

Firehouse Number 1's façade, a
Nevada City landmark

Nevada City ⓸

Road map B3. 🏛 2,855. 🚉 🚌
🛈 132 Main St (916 265-2692).

WITH VICTORIAN HOUSES and
commercial buildings
lining its steep streets, picturesque Nevada City deserves
its reputation as "Queen of
the Northern Mines". Located
at the northern end of the
Mother Lode gold fields,
Nevada City thrived until gold
mining peaked in the 1860s,
then faded into oblivion.
Nearly a century later, the city
was resurrected as a tourist
destination, with galleries,
restaurants and inns re-creating
Gold Rush themes.

Hwy 49 takes visitors arriving in Nevada City to the foot
of Broad Street. Looking up
the street, the large building
on the left is the **National
Hotel**. One of the oldest hotels
in California, it first opened in
the mid-1850s *(see p534)*.

A block east of the hotel is
**Firehouse Number 1 Mus-
eum**, one of the region's most
photographed façades. Dainty
balconies and a white cupola
decorate the exterior, while
inside a small museum displays local Maidu Indian
artifacts, pioneer
relics, including
some relating to the
tragic Donner Party
(see p470), and the
altar from a Gold
Rush Chinese tem-
ple. Antique mining
devices are dis-
played in the park
across the street,
and several plaques

attached to walls throughout
the city commemorate events
from its past.

Back on Broad Street, the
arcaded brick façade marks
the historic **Nevada Theater**,
which has been in use as a
performance venue since
1865. A block to the south is
the **Miner's Foundry**, an old
metalworks where the innovative Pelton wheel was first
developed and produced.
A block to the north is the
Art Deco façade of the city's
County Courthouse, one
of the city's few 20th-century
works of architecture.

🏛 Firehouse Number 1
Museum
214 Main St. 📞 *(916) 265-5468.*
🕐 *daily.* **Donation.**

Nevada Theater, used as a playhouse since 1865

NEVADA CITY CENTRE

County Courthouse ③
Firehouse Number 1 ②
First Methodist
  Church ④
National
  Hotel ①

KEY

🛈 Tourist information

0 metres   100
0 yards   100

Street-by-Street: Old Sacramento 5

Californian
railway logo

COVERING SIX BLOCKS between the
river and the modern city, Old
Sacramento preserves many historic
buildings within a precinct of
shops, restaurants and museums.
Some of the structures protected
here were built to serve the gold
miners of 1849 *(see pp44–5)*, but
most date from the 1860s and 1870s,
when Sacramento confirmed its position as the
link between rural California and the commercial
centres along the coast. The Pony Express and
transcontinental railroad both had their western
terminus here, with paddle-wheel riverboats
providing the connection to San Francisco.
A handful of museums trace the area's historic
importance, and the riverfront location is ideal
for walking and cycling.

Delta King Riverboat
*One of the last Sacramento Delta
riverboats still afloat, this
moored paddle-wheel steamer
is now a hotel and
restaurant.*

The Visitors' Centre is
housed in the former steamboat depot, the embarkation
point for freight bound for
San Francisco in the 1860s.

Old Schoolhouse
*This one-room
building is typical of
a 19th-century Cali-
fornian schoolhouse.*

0 metres   5
0 yards   5

**Theodore Judah
Monument**
*This bas-relief com-
memorates Theodore
Judah, the engineer who
planned the trans-
continental rail-
road (see pp46–7).*

FRONT STREET

L STREET

STAR SIGHTS

★ BF Hastings
Building

★ California State
Railroad Museum

KEY

– – – Suggested route

The Discovery Museum, housed in the city's former municipal buildings, contains memorabilia of Old Sacramento's 19th-century heyday.

★ **California State Railroad Museum**
Immaculately restored locomotives and carriages are part of this extensive collection.

Eagle Theatre
This is a reconstruction of the original theatre, built in 1849 but ruined by a flood in 1850.

Pony Express Monument
This statue commemorates the 1,966-mile (3,163-km) mail run from Sacramento to St Joseph, Missouri.

★ **BF Hastings Building**
For a sense of what the legal system was like in California's early days, visit the restored chambers of the original Supreme Court, above a general store.

The old firehouse, built in 1853, was one of the first buildings to be restored.

Sacramento: California State Capitol

STANDING AT THE CENTRE of a vast, landscaped park, the California State Capitol is Sacramento's primary landmark and one of the state's most handsome buildings. It was designed in 1860 by architect Miner F Butler in grand Renaissance Revival style, with Corinthian porticos and a tall central dome. The building was completed in 1874 after almost 15 years of construction and expenses totalling $2.5 million. The Capitol was expanded in the 1950s, and completely renovated and restored in the 1970s. The Governor of California still operates from his Capitol office, but the building also stands as a shining example of the Golden State's proud past.

Along with the chambers of the state legislature, open to visitors when they are in session, the Capitol serves as a museum of the state's political and cultural history.

VISITORS' CHECKLIST

10th St & Capitol Mall, Capitol Park. **Road map** B3. ☎ (916) 324-0333. 🚆 from Los Angeles & San Francisco. 🚌 30, 31, 32, 61, 62. ◐ 9am–5pm daily. ● 1 Jan, Thanksgiving, 25 Dec. 🖋 📷 ♿ first floor only. ⬛ 🍴 ⬛

★ Capitol Rotunda
The impressive rotunda was restored to its original 19th-century splendour in 1975. The copper ball on top of the dome is plated in gold.

Original 1860 statuary

Entrance

The Historic Offices on the first floor contain a few government offices restored to their turn-of-the-century appearance.

★ State Senate Chamber
The mezzanine gallery is open all year, but it is most interesting when the legislature is in session, making speeches and holding votes on issues of importance.

A portrait of George Washington, the first US president, occupies pride of place on the Chamber wall.

STAR FEATURES

★ Capitol Rotunda

★ State Senate Chamber

🏛 Crocker Art Museum

216 O St. 📞 *(916) 264-5423.*
⏰ *Tue–Sun.* ● *1 Jan, 4 Jul,
Thanksgiving, 25 Dec.* ♿

Founded in 1873, the Crocker
Art Museum is the oldest
public art museum west of
the Mississippi. The collection
includes Victorian painting
and sculpture from Europe
and the United States, but its
real strength is the Californian
art and photography, and the
touring shows that the museum exhibits.

Another prime attraction is
the Italianate Victorian building itself, designed by the
architect Seth Babson. The
gallery includes polychrome
tile floors, elaborately carved
woodwork and a graceful
central staircase. It was built
in 1869 as a home for the
brother of Charles Crocker,
one of the "Big Four" transcontinental railroad barons
(see pp456–7).

Foyer of the Crocker Art Gallery

🏯 Sutter's Fort

2701 L St. 📞 *(916) 324-0539.*
⏰ *daily.* ● *1 Jan, Thanksgiving,
25 Dec.* ♿

Now somewhat marooned
amid the suburban streets of
the modern state capital, in its
heyday, Sutter's Fort was one
of the most important and
populous sites in early Californian history.

Established by John Sutter
in 1839, the fort became the
cultural and economic centre
of Northern California in the
years leading up to the Gold
Rush. Apart from the 21
Spanish missions along the
coast, Sutter's Fort was the
only Anglo-European settlement in California. Throughout the 1840s, new immigrants
following the rugged overland
trails from the United States
stopped here to avail themselves of the fort's blacksmith
shop, grain mill and its many
other facilities.

Reconstructed 19th-century kitchen at Sutter's Fort

The three-storey central building is all that survives of the
original fort. The rest of the
complex has been reconstructed to give a picture of frontier
life. A courtyard, surrounded
by 18-ft (5.5-m) walls, houses
various historical exhibits
along a self-guided audio tour.
These include a prison, a
bakery and a blacksmith's. This
is the one of the few official
sites in California where the
Mexican flag still flies.

🏛 California State Indian Museum

2618 K St. 📞 *(916) 445-4209.*
⏰ *daily.* ● *1 Jan, Thanksgiving,
25 Dec.* ♿

This area of California was
once occupied by the Maidu
people. This small but

fascinating museum, set in
a park adjacent to Sutter's
Fort, explores the different
Native American cultures that
existed in the state before the
16th-century arrival of the
first Europeans *(see pp40–41).*
Displays of handicrafts focus
on the beautiful reed baskets
which held both a practical
and spiritual value to the
Indians, while a series of
dioramas re-create the look
and feel of tribal reservations.
Slide shows, tape recordings
and films document other
aspects of tribal culture, from
language to agricultural skills.

Special programmes, gen-
erally held at weekends, celebrate the survival of ancient
Native American ways of life
into the present day.

JOHN SUTTER

The story of the early Californian entrepreneur John Sutter
is a classic real-life rags to riches to rags adventure. Following
bankruptcy in his native Switzerland, Sutter emigrated to
California in 1839. Only a year after his arrival, he was
granted a 50,000-acre (20,000-ha) tract of land by the
Mexican government which he patriotically named New
Helvetia (New Switzerland). In 1843 Sutter went into debt
once again in order to buy Fort Ross on the northern coast
from its Russian owners *(see p444).* For the next five years
his land and wealth made him virtual
lord and master over most of
Northern California.

However, the discovery of
gold flakes by his employee
James Marshall at his mill in
1848 *(see p454)* spelled the
end of his vast empire.
Thousands of miners swarm-
ed to the region and almost
immediately took over his
land. Sutter spent the rest of
his life in Washington, DC,
hoping for compensation from
the US government, but he
died almost penniless in 1880.

John Sutter (1802–80)

Reconstructed Sutter's Mill, where gold was first discovered

Coloma Gold Discovery State Park **❻**

Road map B3. **☎** (916) 622-3470. **🚌** from Placerville. **◯** daily. **⬤** 1 Jan, Thanksgiving, 25 Dec. **👍** **♿ 🎥**

COVERING SOME 250 acres (101 ha) along the banks of the American River, this peaceful state park protects and interprets the site where gold was first discovered in January 1848. James Marshall spotted shiny flakes in the water channel of a sawmill he and his fellow workmen were building for John Sutter *(see p459)*, and the rest is history.

Within a year, some 10,000 miners had turned Coloma into a thriving city, but with news of even richer deposits elsewhere the boom went bust as quickly as it began, and nowadays there is little sign of this busy era.

A full-scale reproduction of Sutter's Mill stands on the original site, and a statue of James Marshall can be found on a nearby hill to mark the spot where he is buried. The park's visitors' centre includes the small **Gold Country Museum** with Native American artifacts, films and other displays on the discovery of gold, as well as memorabilia relating to James Marshall.

🏛 Gold Country Museum 1273 High St, Auburn. **☎** (916) 889-6500. **◯** Tue–Sun. **⬤** 1 Jan, Thanksgiving, 25 Dec. **🎥**

Folsom **❼**

Road map B3. **👥** 40,000. **🚌 ℹ** 200 Wool St (916 985-2698).

FOLSOM IS NOW a pleasant Sacramento suburb, despite being the site of the state penitentiary made famous by Johnny Cash's 1970s song "Folsom Prison Blues".

It played an important role as the last station on the Pony Express and transcontinental railroad. Folsom is now one of the few remaining trans-continental railroad sites, as documented in the local **Folsom History Museum**. Antique shops line the Wild West-style Sutter Street in the small downtown business district, set amid boxcars and other railroad memorabilia.

At the foot of Riley Street, behind Folsom Dam, there is also a large lake which is a popular summer spot with residents and visitors for boating and fishing.

🏛 Folsom History Museum 823 Sutter St. **☎** (916) 985-2707. **◯** Wed–Sun. **⬤** public hols. **Donation**.

Placerville **❽**

Road map B3. **👥** 9,000. **🚌 ℹ** 542 Main St (916 621-5885).

DURING the Gold Rush, Placerville was a busy supply centre for the sur-rounding mining camps. Still standing on one of the main routes travelling to and from Sacramento, Placerville has retained its importance as a transport centre, although the stagecoaches have long since given way to cars and lorries along US 50.

The downtown business district preserves a handful of historic structures and sites, but the best sense of Placerville's past comes from the **El Dorado County Historical Museum**, set in a permanent fairground site just north of US 50. Among the numerous displays are original coal-fired locomotives, a range of old mining equipment, a replica of a 19th-century general store and other exhibits that relate to local history.

🏛 El Dorado County Historical Museum 104 Placerville Dr. **☎** (916) 621-5865. **◯** Wed–Sun. **⬤** public hols. **Donation**.

Gold Rush general store in Placerville's El Dorado Museum

Sutter Creek **❾**

Road map B3. **👥** 2,000. **🚌 ℹ** 125 Peek St, Jackson (209 223-0350).

NAMED AFTER John Sutter *(see p459)*, Sutter Creek is one of the prettiest Gold Country towns, full of antique shops and whitewashed country inns. It grew up around 1860 to service the Old Eureka Mine, which was owned by Hetty Green, re-putedly the "Richest Woman in the World".

Leland Stanford, one of the "Big Four" railroad barons *(see pp46–7)*, made his fortune in Sutter Creek. He put $5,000 into the town's Lincoln Mine which turned into a multi-million-dollar investment. He used the money to become a railroad magnate and governor of California.

An attractive drive in the region is along Sutter Creek Road to Volcano, past remains of former mining equipment.

Volcano ⑩

Road map B3. 🏛 *150.* 🚌
ℹ *125 Peek St, Jackson (209 223-0350).*

FOR A TASTE of the Gold Rush without the tourist trappings, visit Volcano, a picturesque ghost of a mining town containing a wealth of historic sights.

During the Gold Rush, the town had an unusual reputation for sophistication and culture, creating the state's first library and its first astronomical observatory. The old jail, stagecoach office, brewery and a cannon dating from the American Civil War are among the preserved buildings and artifacts on display around the four-block town. The most attractive Victorian building is the former **St George Hotel**, covered with Virginia creeper.

Springtime visitors to the region should also follow the signs to Daffodil Hill, 3 miles (5 km) north of Volcano, when more than 300,000 naturalized daffodil bulbs come into full bloom on the hillside.

🏨 St George Hotel
16104 Pine Grove, off Volcano Rd.
📞 *(209) 296-4458.* ◯ *mid-Feb–Dec: Wed–Sun.*

Chaw'se Indian Grinding Rock State Historic Park ⑪

Road map B3. 🚌 *from Sacramento.* 🚆 *from Sacramento.* 🚍 *from Jackson.* **Jackson Visitors' Center**
◯ *daily.* 📞 *(209) 296-7488.*

TUCKED AWAY amid the oak trees in the hills above Jackson, this 136-acre (55-ha) park protects one of the largest and most complete Native American sites in the country. The area was once home to the Miwok people and the park is dedicated to their past and future. The aim of this comprehensive museum is to increase understanding of Native American life, centring on the Californian foothill peoples. Exhibits include an array of basketry, dance regalia and ancient tools.

Hundreds of mortar holes form the main focus of the park. Ground into the limestone boulders by generations of Miwoks, they were used to make meal out of acorns. There are also many rock carvings and replica Miwok dwellings, including a ceremonial roundhouse.

St Sava's Serbian Orthodox Church outside Jackson

Jackson ⑫

Road map B3. 🏛 *3,500.* 🚌
ℹ *125 Peek St (209 223-0350).*

LOCATED at the crossroads of two main Gold Rush trails, Jackson was once a bustling gold mining community and has continued to thrive as a commercial centre and lumber mill town since 1850.

The town centre features a number of old Gold Rush buildings, but the most interesting stop is the **Amador County Museum**, located on a hill above the town. Here visitors can view working models of stamp mills *(see p454)* and a variety of other old mining equipment.

North of the town, in a small park off Hwy 49, are the massive tailing wheels from the Kennedy Mine, one of the deepest in the United States. Reaching 58 ft (18 m) in diameter, these wheels were used to dispose of left-over rocks after the gold had been extracted. St Sava's Serbian Orthodox Church, built in 1894 with a delicate white steeple, is also situated within the park. It is a testament to one of the many cultures that have contributed to the history of the Gold Country.

🏛 Amador County Museum
225 Church St, Jackson. 📞 *(209) 223-6386.* ◯ *Wed–Sun.* ◉ *public hols.* **Donation.**

eplica of a Miwok ceremonial roundhouse in Chaw'se State Park

Headstone on "Moke Hill"

Mokelumne Hill ⑬

Road map B3. 🏚 *1,200.*
🛈 *1211 S Main St, Angels Camp*
(209 736-0049).

BYPASSED by Highway 49, Mokelumne Hill is one of the most intriguing old Gold Country towns. A handful of old buildings, including the balconied Hotel Leger and the old Wells Fargo stagecoach station, form a one-block business district. But the sleepy ambience of "Moke Hill", as it is more commonly known, belies the town's unsavoury and violent history.

Although much of the town has fallen into picturesque decay, during the Gold Rush era the hotels and saloons were packed with rowdy miners, whose drunken fights resulted in an average of one killing per week. Many of the victims ended up in the hilltop Protestant Cemetery a short walk to the west of town. Here the multilingual headstones are now all that remain of the international population who came here in search of gold.

San Andreas ⑭

Road map B3. 🏚 *3,200.*
🛈 *1211 S Main St, Angels Camp*
(209 736-0049).

SAN ANDREAS is now a small, bustling city, home to the Calaveras County government. During the Gold Rush era,

however, it was a gritty mining camp, originally built by Mexicans who were later forcibly removed by white Americans after rich deposits of gold were found *(see pp44–5)*. In 1883 the legendary highwayman Black Bart was captured here.

Very little now remains from the Gold Rush days, although San Andreas does house one of the Gold Country's best museums, the **Calaveras County Historical Museum**, in the old courthouse just north of Hwy 49. Along with exhibits tracing gold mining history from 1848 to the 1930s, the collection includes Miwok Indian artifacts and the courtroom where Black Bart was tried and convicted. His prison cell during the trial, situated behind the museum, is now surrounded by a pleasant, if somewhat incongruous, garden of indigenous plants and trees.

🏛 Calaveras County Historical Museum
30 N Main St. 🕽 *(209) 754-6579.*
⬜ *daily.* ⬤ *1 Jan, Thanksgiving, 25 Dec.* 🖼

Murphys ⑮

Road map B3. 🏚 *2,000.*
🛈 *1211 S Main St, Angels Camp*
(209 736-0049).

WITH MATURE sycamores, elms and locust trees lining its quiet streets, Murphys is among the prettiest towns in the southern Gold Country. It offers a quiet break from the frantic tourism of many of

the other Mother Lode towns and sights in the area.

Having played host to such luminaries as Ulysses S Grant, Mark Twain and Will Rogers, the restored Murphys Hotel, built in 1855, is now the town landmark. Across the street, the **Old-Timers' Museum** houses a quirky collection of Gold Rush memorabilia. The outside wall displays a series of humorous plaques detailing the town's history.

🏛 Old-Timers' Museum
450 Main St. 🕽 *(209) 728-1160.*
⬜ *Fri–Sun.* ⬤ *1 Jan, Thanksgiving, 25 Dec.* 🖼

Angels Camp ⑯

Road map B3. 🏚 *3,000.*
🛈 *1211 S Main St (209 736-0049).*

ANGELS CAMP is a former gold mining town that was best known as the real-life location of Mark Twain's classic short story "The Celebrated Jumping Frog of Calaveras County" *(see pp22–3)*. Today the town has grown into a commercial centre for the surrounding area.

A few historic structures, including the Angels Hotel where Twain heard the story of the jumping frog, still line the steep streets of the compact downtown area, which comes alive every May for a popular re-enactment of the frog-jumping competition.

Two huge 19th-century locomotives stand on Hwy 49 in front of the **Angels Camp Museum**, which contains a standard array of old mining

Picturesque main street of the gold mining town, Angels Camp

equipment. There is also a large collection of Indian artifacts and exhibits on Mark Twain and his jumping frog.

🏛 **Angels Camp Museum**
753 S Main St. ☎ *(209) 736-2963.* ☐ *Apr–Nov: daily; Dec–Mar: Wed–Sun.* ● *Thanksgiving, mid–late Dec.* 🅿

Moaning Cavern ⓱

Road map B3. ☎ *(209) 736-2708.* ☐ *daily.* 🅿

ONE OF THE largest of the limestone caverns in the area, Moaning Cavern took its name from the groaning sound emitted by the wind flowing out of the entrance. Unfortunately the sound was destroyed when the cavern was enlarged to improve public access. Guided tours, lasting about an hour, focus on the large main "room", which is approximately 165 ft (50 m) high. Visitors can descend into the caves by way of a spiral staircase or, if they dare, by abseiling down a rope.

A guided tour of Moaning Cavern

Sonora ⓲

Road map B3. 🏠 *5,000.* 🚌 �ℹ *55 W Stockton St (209 533-4420).*

OUTSTRIPPING Columbia *(see pp464–5)* for the seat of county government during the Gold Rush, Sonora is now the Tuolumne County seat and a busy commercial centre and logging town. Its sedate main street shows little sign of the town's once violent reputation during the second half of the 19th century.

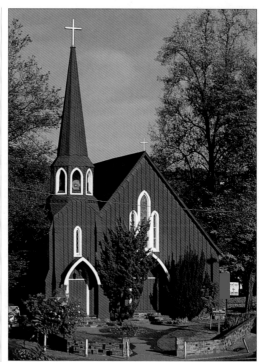
Nineteenth-century St James Episcopal Church in Sonora

Many of its historic buildings have been preserved, including the dainty St James Episcopal Church situated at the top of Washington Street. The town also has a number of interesting Victorian houses.

Sonora's old jail was built in 1857 and renovated after being destroyed by fire in 1866. It is now home to the **Tuolumne County Museum and History Center**. It houses a collection of Gold Rush artifacts including gold nuggets and a number of 19th-century photographs.

🏛 **Tuolumne County Museum and History Center**
158 W Bradford St. ☎ *(209) 532-1317.* ☐ *daily.* ● *1 Jan, 25 Dec.*

BLACK BART

Famous for his politeness to his victims and his habit of leaving doggerel poetry at the scene of his crimes, the highwayman known affectionately as Black Bart has become one of the state's best-loved legends.

After holding up stagecoaches between 1877 and 1883, he was caught when the laundry mark on his handkerchief was traced to San Francisco. Black Bart turned out to be Charles Boles, a mining engineer.

After being tried and convicted in San Andreas, he spent five years in San Quentin prison. He disappeared from public view after his release in 1888.

The highwayman Black Bart

Street-by-Street: Columbia State Historic Park ⑲

Stagecoach schedule sign

AT THE HEIGHT of the Gold Rush, Columbia was one of the largest and most important towns in the Gold Country. Most of California's mining camps were abandoned and quickly disintegrated and disappeared after the gold ran out in the late 1850s. Unusually, Columbia remained active. It was proudly kept intact by its remaining residents until 1945, when the Californian government turned the entire town into a state historic park. A few of the buildings have been reconstructed, but the majority of them have been preserved in their original state.

The Chinese Herb Shop contains traditional medicines brought to the state by Chinese immigrants.

City Hotel

Johnson's Livery Stable
Several old-style wagons are housed here.

Old jail

Museum

★ Wells Fargo Express Office
This stagecoach office was the centre of the town's transport network.

Matelot Gulch Miners Supply
Visitors are sold pans of sand and gravel here so that they can try panning for gold themselves.

Palm Hotel on Main Street, Jamestown

Jamestown ⑳

Road map B3. 🏠 *2,000.* 🚍
ℹ️ *55 W Stockton St, Sonora (209
533-4420).*

JAMESTOWN WAS home to the
largest gold mine in operation until 1993. The mine is still
visible south of the town along
Hwy 49. Some of the historic
town was destroyed by fire in
1966, but Main Street still has
many picturesque buildings.
  **Railtown 1897 State
Historic Park**, north of downtown, preserves the steam
locomotives and historic carriages of the Sierra Railroad.
Rides are offered at weekends

🏛 **Railtown 1897 State
Historic Park**
5th Ave & Reservoir Rd. 📞 *(209)
984-3953.* ⬤ *1 Jan, Thanksgiving,
25 Dec.* **Donation**.

Stockton ㉑

Road map B3. 🏠 *250,000.* 🚍
ℹ️ *46 W Fremont St (209 943-1987).*

STOCKTON IS AN inland port
and a transport terminus
for Central Valley farms. It is
set on the eastern edge of the
delta at the confluence of the
Sacramento, American and
San Joaquin rivers.
  Stockton's history is told at
the Haggin Museum, which
includes everything from
Native American crafts to 19th-
century shopfronts and works
by Renoir. It also traces the
development by a local inventor of the Caterpillar track, later
adapted for use on army tanks.

🏛 **Haggin Museum**
1201 N Pershing Ave. 📞 *(209) 462-
4116.* ⏰ *Tue–Sun.* ⬤ *1 Jan,
Thanksgiving, 25 Dec.* **Donation**.

★ **Columbia Schoolhouse**
*The building was last used
as a school in 1937 but in
1960 it was restored with
the help of funds raised by
Californian schoolchildren.*

metres   100

yards   100

KEY

– – –   Suggested route

STAR SIGHTS

★ **Columbia
  Schoolhouse**

★ **Wells Fargo
  Express Office**

JOAQUIN MURIETA: THE CALIFORNIA BANDIT

Little documentary evidence exists about Joaquin Murieta,
the Gold Country criminal portrayed as everything from a
19th-century Gold Rush Robin Hood to a murderous outlaw.
  His legend can be traced to the writer John Rollins Ridge,
who published a novel called *The Life and Adventures of
Joaquin Murieta, Celebrated
California Bandit* in 1854.
Ridge drew on the criminal
exploits of five outlaws, all
named Joaquin. The Gover-
nor of California offered a
$1,000 reward for the capture
of any of these men. In 1853
a man named Harry Love
delivered the head of one
Joaquin Murieta, which had
been pickled in a glass jar.
Ridge's novel was published
the following year and the
Murieta legend was born.

THE HIGH SIERRAS

ORMING A TOWERING WALL *along the eastern side of central California, the densely forested Sierra Nevada Mountains rise to over 14,000 ft (4,270 m) and include many of the most impressive peaks in the mainland United States. Known as the High Sierras, these rugged mountains make up one of the state's most popular recreation areas, preserved by a series of splendid national parks.*

The most popular High Sierras destination is Yosemite National Park, one of the world's most spectacular natural sights. Waterfalls, ranging from delicate cascades to raging torrents, drop steeply down the granite walls of this alpine valley. Rock-climbers, photographers and sightseers come from all over the globe to experience the park first-hand. South of Yosemite, the Sequoia and Kings Canyon national parks preserve more of the state's high country scenery, including groves of sequoia, the largest living species on earth.

To the north, Lake Tahoe has been a year-round recreational haven for over a century. It offers hiking, camping and water sports on one of the bluest bodies of water in the US. In winter, the region becomes a skier's paradise, with many Olympic-class resorts.

East of the Sierra Nevada's granite spine lies a less-visited but equally compelling region. The ghost town of Bodie is preserved as it was when gold miners abandoned it in 1882. Nearby, Mono Lake is an eerie sight of limestone towers and alkaline water. The eastern slope of the High Sierras merits exploration, including the 14,500-ft (4,420-m) Mount Whitney, the highest peak on the US mainland, and the bristlecone pines of the White Mountains, some of which are more than 4,000 years old.

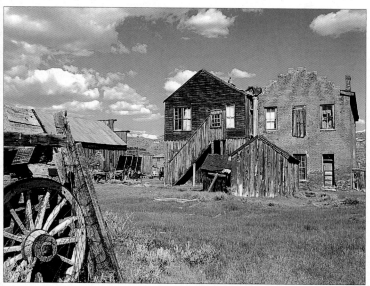

Bodie State Historic Park, a preserved ghost town to the east of the Sierras

◁ Imposing granite peak of Half Dome in Yosemite National Park

Exploring the High Sierras

T̲HE HIGHEST PEAKS, the tallest trees and some of the most impressive natural scenery in the United States are found in California's Sierra Nevada Mountains. This region includes one of the best-known wonders of the world, Yosemite National Park, as well as countless other remarkable examples of nature's prowess. North of Yosemite, the emerald waters of Lake Tahoe are set within an alpine valley at the highest point of the High Sierras, while to the south stand the immense groves of Sequoia and Kings Canyon national parks.

Other than the resorts encircling Lake Tahoe, there are no real towns in the High Sierras. East of the mountains, however, near the shores of the eerily beautiful Mono Lake, the best ghost town in the state, Bodie, is immaculately preserved.

SIGHTS AT A GLANCE

HOW THE SIERRAS WERE MADE

The Sierras were formed 3 million years ago when a giant granite batholith (igneous rock), approximately 6 miles (10 km) deep, lifted up the earth's surface and tilted it from a tectonic "hinge" beneath California's Central Valley. The effects of this uplift are most clearly visible on the steep eastern slopes, typical of mountains on the earth's faults. The western slopes are more gradual, made up of sedimentary, volcanic and metamorphic rock, mixed together over the epochs.

Granite peaks of the High Sierras

Jagged peaks on eastern slopes

Gradual western slopes

Block forced down

Eroded material

Batholith

Block uplifted to form mountain range

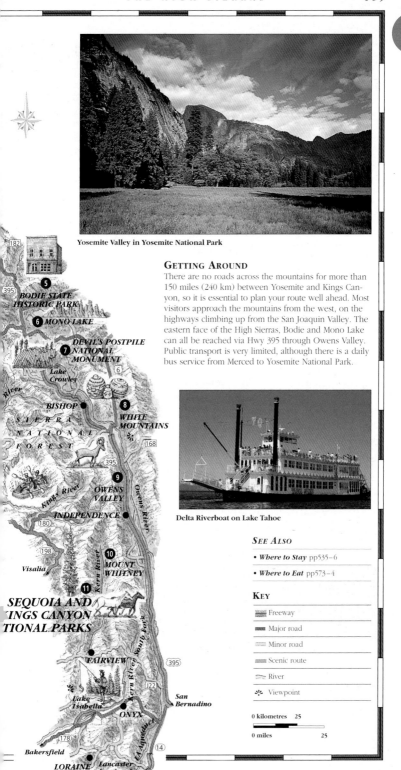

Yosemite Valley in Yosemite National Park

GETTING AROUND

There are no roads across the mountains for more than 150 miles (240 km) between Yosemite and Kings Canyon, so it is essential to plan your route well ahead. Most visitors approach the mountains from the west, on the highways climbing up from the San Joaquin Valley. The eastern face of the High Sierras, Bodie and Mono Lake can all be reached via Hwy 395 through Owens Valley. Public transport is very limited, although there is a daily bus service from Merced to Yosemite National Park.

Delta Riverboat on Lake Tahoe

SEE ALSO

- **Where to Stay** pp535–6
- **Where to Eat** pp573–4

KEY

▦	Freeway
▬	Major road
▭	Minor road
▭	Scenic route
～	River
✳	Viewpoint

0 kilometres 25

0 miles 25

---

5 BODIE STATE HISTORIC PARK

6 MONO LAKE

7 DEVIL'S POSTPILE NATIONAL MONUMENT

Lake Crowley

BISHOP

SIERRA NATIONAL FOREST

8 WHITE MOUNTAINS

Kings River

9 OWENS VALLEY

INDEPENDENCE

Owens River

Visalia

10 MOUNT WHITNEY

Kern River

11 SEQUOIA AND KINGS CANYON NATIONAL PARKS

FAIRVIEW

Lake Isabella

ONYX

San Bernadino

Bakersfield

LORAINE Lancaster Los Angeles

182
395
6
168
395
180
198
395
J22
178
14

Donner Memorial State Park ❶

📞 *(916) 582-7892.* 🚉 *Truckee.*
🚌 *Truckee.*

THIS TRANQUIL 350-acre (140-ha) park, to the south of I-80, marks the site of one of the most tragic episodes of the United States frontier era.

In the winter of 1846–7 a group of 89 California-bound emigrants from Independence, Missouri, were trapped by heavy snowfall. Known as the Donner Party because two of the families shared that surname, the group was one of the many wagon trains bound for the West Coast from the Midwest, along the Oregon Trail. Halfway into their journey, the Donner families, and another family headed by James Reed, decided to leave the established trail and try a short cut recommended by the contemporary adventurer, Lansford Hastings. This turned out, however, to be a far more difficult route, and added three weeks to what in the best of circumstances was already an arduous journey. The Donner

Party finally arrived at the eastern foot of the Sierra Nevada Mountains in October 1846, having lost the majority of their cattle and belongings.

After resting for a week they were caught by an early winter storm east of Truckee. A few members decided to struggle on foot across the snowy mountains to seek help from Sutter's Fort *(see p459)*, but the rest of the party, now trapped by the heavy snow and with insufficient supplies, were forced to resort to cannibalism in order to survive. By the time rescuers were able to reach them in mid-February 1847, 42 of the 89 pioneers had already died.

A statue of this heroic pioneering family, standing atop a 22-ft (6.7-m) pedestal indicating the depth of the snow they encountered, now marks the site. The park's **Emigrant Trail Museum** details the Donner Party's story, as well as describing the natural history of the High Sierras.

🏛 **Emigrant Trail Museum**
12593 Donner Pass Rd. 📞 *(916) 582-7892.* ⬜ *daily.* ⬛ *1 Jan, Thanksgiving, 25 Dec.*

Façade of the 19th-century Old Truckee Jail, now a museum

Truckee ❷

Road map B3. 🏘 *10,000* 🚉 🚌
ℹ *12036 Donner Pass Road (916) 587-2757).*

ONE OF THE HIGHEST and coldest towns in California, Truckee is thought to have got its name when a native Paiute greeted the first white Americans with "Trokay", meaning peace.

Truckee is situated along the main highway (I-80) and rail route across the Sierra Nevada Mountains. Its history as a transport centre goes back to 1863, when it was founded as a changeover point for railway crews along the transcontinental railroad *(see pp46–7)*. The Southern Pacific Depot still serves rail and bus passengers as well as operating as a visitors' centre.

Much of the town's Wild West character and history as a lumber centre survives, especially along Commercial Row in the heart of town, where a line of old brick and wooden buildings faces the railway tracks. Many of these have now been converted into atmospheric shops, restaurants and cafés.

Another evocative survivor of the town's past is the **Old Truckee Jail**, built in 1875. It is now preserved as a small museum depicting the wilder side of life on the frontier.

Situated only 25 miles (40 km) from Lake Tahoe, Truckee is also a popular historical base for winter skiers and summer hikers.

🏛 **Old Truckee Jail**
Jibboom & Spring Sts. 📞 *(916) 582-0893.* ⬜ *May–Sep: Sat & Sun.* ⬛ *public hols.* ♿

SKIING AROUND LAKE TAHOE

The peaks surrounding Lake Tahoe, particularly on the California side, are famous for their ski resorts. The world-class Alpine Meadows and Squaw Valley are where the Winter Olympics were held in 1960. The largest ski area, Heavenly Valley, is above the city of South Lake Tahoe, with many more around the lake and at Donner Pass, west of Truckee, along I-80. There are also cross-country ski areas with groomed trails. The Lake Tahoe area receives upwards of 10 ft (3 m) of snow each winter, and is the state's major centre for winter recreation from November to March.

Skiing at Lake Tahoe's Alpine Meadows resort

A Tour of Lake Tahoe ❸

THE MOST BEAUTIFUL body of water in California, Lake Tahoe is 1,645 ft (501 m) at its deepest point and is surrounded by forested peaks. The area began to develop as a tourist resort after the construction of the first road in 1915 made it more accessible. Casinos opening on the Nevada border in the 1930s and the Winter Olympics in 1960 further increased its popularity.

View of Lake Tahoe from Heavenly Valley

Ponderosa Ranch ④
Near the northeast shore of the lake, this summer-only amusement park is based on the cult 1960s Wild West TV show, *Bonanza.*

Cave Rock and Cave Rock Tunnel ⑤
Lake Tahoe's east shore is so rugged that part of the highway is tunnelled through solid granite.

DL Bliss State Park and Ehrman Mansion ③
A popular picnic area surrounds Ehrman Mansion, built in 1903 and now a visitors' centre.

Stateline ⑥
Situated on the border of California and the more liberal state of Nevada, Stateline is the main gambling town of the Lake Tahoe region.

South Lake Tahoe ①
The largest town in the area, South Lake Tahoe caters for visitors to Nevada's casinos.

Emerald Bay State Park and Vikingsholm ②
The beautiful inlet of Emerald Bay is the most photographed part of the lake. Vikingsholm, built as a summerhouse in the 1920s, is an incongruous reproduction of an old Nordic castle.

TIPS FOR TRAVELLERS

Tour length: 65 miles (105 km).
Getting there: I-80 and US 50 are open all year round. Amtrak trains operate to Truckee. Greyhound buses and limited flights from San Francisco and Oakland serve South Lake Tahoe.
When to go: Peak tourist seasons are July, August and winter, when the ski resorts are open. Spring and autumn are less crowded, but some facilities may be closed.
Where to stay and eat: For the best information contact Lake Tahoe Visitors' Authority.
Tourist information: Lake Tahoe Visitors' Authority, South Lake Tahoe. ☎ (800) 288-2463.

0 kilometres 10

0 miles 10

KEY

━━━ Tour route

═══ Other roads

☆ Viewpoint

Yosemite National Park ❹

A WILDERNESS of evergreen forests, high meadows and sheer walls of granite, much of Yosemite National Park is accessible only to experienced hikers or horse riders. The spectacular Yosemite Valley, a good base from which to explore the park, is easily reached by car and there are a further 200 miles (320 km) of paved roads providing access to more remote areas. Soaring cliffs, plunging waterfalls, gigantic trees, rugged canyons, mountains and valleys all combine to lend Yosemite its incomparable beauty.

Yosemite Museum
The history of the Miwok and Paiute people is displayed here, along with works by Yosemite artists.

Valley
Visitor Center

To Upper
Yosemite Falls

Yosemite Creek

Yosemite
Village

Yosemite Falls Trail

Lower Yosemite Falls
Yosemite Creek drops 2,425 ft (740 m), to form the highest waterfall in the US (see p474).

Sunnyside

Northside Drive

Yosemite
Lodge

Lower River

Merced River

Southside Drive

Sentinel Creek

Four-Mile Trail

Stair
Fa

SENTINEL ROCK
▲
7,038 ft (2,145 m)

Sentinel
Falls

Ahwahnee Hotel
Rustic architecture, elegant décor and beautiful views make this hotel one of the most renowned in the country (see p475).

Yosemite Chapel *(1879)*
This tiny wooden church is all that is left of Yosemite's 19th-century Old Village.

Sentinel Dome can be reached on foot from the valley floor. The trail continues to Glacier Point.

Mirror Meadow
As park rangers no longer interfere with nature by dredging the lake, the water at the foot of Half Dome is now silting up and forming a meadow (see p475).

Visitors' Checklist

Road map C3. *PO Box 577, Yosemite.* *(900) 454-9673.* *(209) 372-0200.* *from Merced.* *Yosemite Valley.* *from Merced.* *daily.*

Key

- Major road
- Minor road
- Paths and trails
- Shuttle bus
- Cycle route
- Rivers
- Parking
- Petrol station
- Camping
- Picnic area
- Tourist information
- Viewpoint

Half Dome
A formidable trail climbs to the top of this cliff which juts above the valley floor (see p474).

Vernal Falls
The Merced River pours into its canyon over the 317-ft (97-m) lip of these falls.

Merced River
This beautiful river can be appreciated along both the Mist Trail and the Panorama Trail. Anglers enjoy fishing for brown trout in its waters.

Exploring Yosemite National Park

SOME OF THE WORLD'S most beautiful mountain terrain is protected within the 1,170 sq miles (3,030 sq km) of Yosemite National Park. Hundreds of thousands of visitors descend upon the park each year to admire its breathtaking views, formed by millions of years of glacial activity. Each season offers a different experience, from the swelling waterfalls of spring to the rustic colours of autumn. The summer months are the most crowded, but during the snowbound winter months several roads are inaccessible. Bus tours and well-maintained cycle paths, hiking trails and motor routes are all aimed at leading visitors from one awe-inspiring panoramic scene to another.

Upper Yosemite Falls, swollen with ice-melt in the spring

🎋 Half Dome

Eastern end of Yosemite Valley.
🔲 *daily.*

Standing nearly 1 mile (1.6 km) above the valley floor, the silhouette of Half Dome has become a symbol of Yosemite. Its curved back rises to a wave-like lip, before dropping vertically to the valley below.

Geologists believe that Half Dome is now three-quarters of its original size, rather than a true half. It is thought that as recently as 15,000 years ago, glacial ice floes moved through the valley from the Sierra crest, scything off rock and depositing it downstream.

The 8,840-ft (2,695 m) summit of Half Dome offers an unsurpassed view of the valley. Follow the 9-mile (14-km) trail from Happy Isles trailhead to reach the peak.

🎋 Yosemite Falls

North Yosemite Valley. 🔲 *daily.*
Yosemite Falls are the highest waterfalls in North America and tumble from a height of 2,425 ft (740 m) in two great leaps, Upper Yosemite and Lower Yosemite Falls. One of the most recognizable features of the park, the cascades are visible all over the valley.

The top of Upper Yosemite Falls, by far the longer and more elegant of the pair, can be reached via a strenuous 7-mile (11-km) round-trip trail. The Lower Falls are easier to visit, via a short trail that starts next to Yosemite Lodge and frames an unforgettable view of both falls.

As with all the park's waterfalls, Yosemite Falls are at their peak in May and June, when the winter snows melt and fill the creek to capacity. Conversely, by September the falls often dry up and disappear altogether, their presence marked only by a dark stain on the granite wall.

🎋 Vernal and Nevada Falls

Eastern end of Yosemite Valley.
🔲 *daily.*
A popular half-day hike in Yosemite National Park is the Mist Trail, which visits these two waterfalls.

The first falls visited on this 7-mile (11-km) round-trip are Vernal Falls, which plunge 320 ft (95 m) and spread their spray across the trail. The trail then continues for 2 miles (3 km) to the top of Nevada Falls, which drops an impressive 595 ft (180 m). At the top of Nevada Falls the Mist Trail joins the John Muir Trail, which runs around the back of Half Dome all the way south to the summit of Mount Whitney (see p479).

Distinctive shape of Half Dome

Glacier Point
Glacier Point Rd. ⬤ *daily.*

The great Yosemite panorama can be experienced from Glacier Point, which rests on a rocky ledge 3,215 ft (980 m) above the valley floor. Most of the waterfalls and other features of Yosemite Valley are visible from here, but the dominant feature is Half Dome. The panorama also includes much of the surrounding landscape, a beautiful area of alpine peaks and meadows.

Glacier Point can be reached only during the summer. The road is blocked by snow during winter at Badger Pass, which was developed in 1935 as California's first commercial ski resort. An alternative route is the Four-Mile Trail, which begins at the western side of the valley. Summer bus services also allow hikers to ride up to Glacier Point then hike down to the valley.

Mariposa Grove
Visitors' Center Hwy 41, South Entrance. ⬤ *mid-May–Oct: daily.*

At the southern end of Yosemite, this beautiful grove was one of the main reasons the park was established. More than 500 giant sequoia trees can be seen here, some of which are more than 3,000 years old, 250 ft (75 m) tall and more than 30 ft (9 m) in diameter at their base. A series of hiking trails winds through

Tunnel View, looking across Yosemite Valley

the grove, and open-air trams make a 5-mile (8-km) circuit along roads constructed during the early years of Yosemite tourism.

Tunnel View
Visitors' Center Hwy 41 overlooking Yosemite Valley. ⬤ *daily.*

One of the most photographed views of Yosemite can be had from this lookout on Hwy 41 at the western end of the valley. Despite the name, which is taken from the highway tunnel that leads to Glacier Point Road, the view is incredible, with El Capitán on the left, Bridalveil Falls on the right and Half Dome at the centre.

El Capitán
Northwestern end of Yosemite Valley. ⬤ *daily.*

Standing guard at the western entrance to Yosemite Valley, the granite wall of El Capitán rises more than 4,500 ft (1,370 m) from the valley floor. The world's largest exposed rock, El Capitán is a magnet to rock-climbers, who spend days on its sheer face to reach the top. Less adventurous visitors congregate in the meadow below, watching the rock-climbers through binoculars.

Named by US soldiers, who in 1851 were the first white Americans to visit the valley, El Capitán is the Spanish phrase for "captain".

Tuolumne Meadows
Hwy 120, Tioga Rd. ⬤ *Jun–Sep: daily.*

In summer, when the snows have melted and the wildflowers are in full bloom, the best place to experience the striking beauty of the Yosemite landscape are these sub-alpine meadows along the Tuolumne River. Located 55 miles (88 km) from Yosemite valley via Tioga Pass Road, Tuolumne Meadows are also a base for hikers setting off to explore the area's many granite peaks and trails.

Black-tailed deer roaming Yosemite's meadows

Ahwahnee Hotel
Yosemite Valley. 📞 *(209) 252-4848.* ⬤ *daily. See* **Where to Stay** *p536.*

A building that comes close to matching Yosemite's natural beauty, the Ahwahnee Hotel was built in 1927 at a cost of $1.5 million.

It was designed by Gilbert Stanley Underwood, who used giant granite boulders and massive wood timbers to create a rustic elegance that is in tune with its surroundings. The interior of the Ahwahnee Hotel also emulates the natural setting, decorated in a Native American style. A few Native American arts and crafts are on display in the public areas. The hotel is also noted for its high-quality restaurant *(see p574).*

Giant sequoia trees in Mariposa Grove

Sierra Nevada Mountains, near Lone Pine ▷

Ghostly wooden buildings in Bodie State Historic Park

Bodie State Historic Park ❺

Road map C3. 🚶 10. 🚌 from Bridgeport. ℹ️ End of Hwy 270 (760 647-6445).

HIGH UP IN the foothills of the eastern Sierra Nevada Mountains, Bodie is the largest ghost town in California.

Now protected as a state historic park, Bodie was, during the second half of the 19th century, a bustling gold mining town, with a population that topped 8,000 in 1880. Named after the gold prospector Waterman S Bodey, who first discovered placer deposits (surface gold) here in 1859, Bodie boomed with the discovery of hard rock ore in the mid-1870s. Soon many different mines had been established in the area, but it all came to an end when the gold ran out in 1882. Later, a series of fires destroyed much of the town. Only the Standard Mine remained in business, but it closed in 1942 because of a wartime ban on mining.

The state acquired the entire town in 1962, and has maintained the 170 buildings in a condition of "arrested decay". The result is an evocative experience of empty streets lined by deserted wooden buildings. The Miners' Union Hall has been converted into a visitors' centre and museum, with artifacts from Bodie's early days.

Mono Lake ❻

Road map C3. 📞 (760) 647-3044. 🚌 Merced. 🚉 Merced.

ONE OF THE strangest looking places in the United States, and possibly one of the oldest lakes in the world, Mono Lake is a 60-sq mile (155-sq km) body of alkaline water at the eastern foot of the Sierra Nevada Mountains, set between two volcanic islands. The lake has no natural outlet, but evaporation in the summer heat combined with water diversion to LA has caused it to shrink to one-fifth of its original size. The result is extremely brackish water, three times saltier than sea water. It has also exposed a number of contorted tufa spires. These were formed when calcium from underground springs came into contact with carbonates in the lake water, forming limestone. The tufa formations once sat under water, but the evaporation has left them arrayed along the lakeside.

In recent years, Mono Lake has also been the subject of a heated political and environmental debate, part of an ongoing battle over water rights. The City of Los Angeles purchased a large amount of land in the eastern Sierras and Owens Valley in 1905, and began diverting the streams and rivers through a system of aqueducts to LA in 1941. This has accelerated the lake's shrinkage and put local wildlife, particularly the state's large seagull population which breeds on the lake's islands, in danger *(see pp192–3)*. In 1994 the California State Government ruled that LA must preserve the lake and its surrounding ecosystem at 6,392 ft (1,950 m) above sea level.

Tufa spires rising out of Mono Lake

Devil's Postpile National Monument ❼

Road map C4. **℡** *(760) 934-2289.* **⊞** *shuttle from Mammoth Mountain Inn.* ☐ *Jul–Sep: daily.* 🖼️ ♿ ✔️

ON THE WEST of the Sierra Nevada crest, but most easily accessible from the eastern resort of Mammoth Lakes, Devil's Postpile National Monument protects one of the most impressive geological formations in the state.

A wall of basalt columns, in varying geometrical shapes, predominantly pentagons and hexagons, cover a 545 sq yard (652 sq m) area. More than 60 ft (18 m) tall, they rise 7,560 ft (2,320 m) above sea level. The columns were formed around 100,000 years ago, when molten lava cooled and fractured. Set at the heart of an 800-acre (320-ha) park, they resemble a tiled floor from above. The monument is covered in snow most of the year and is only accessible in summer via a shuttle bus.

Rainbow Falls, 2 miles (3 km) from the Postpile, are named after the refraction of sunlight in their spray.

White Mountains ❽

ℹ️ *798 N Main St, Bishop (760 873-2500).*

RISING ALONG the eastern side of Owens Valley, the White Mountains, at 12,000 ft (3,660 m), are almost as high but far drier than the 13,000-ft (3,960-m) parallel range of Sierra Nevada Mountains. Lack of water has kept the peaks rugged and largely free of vegetation, but the few trees that do survive here, the bristlecone pines *(Pinus aristata)*, are among the oldest living things on earth.

These gnarled pine trees seem to thrive on the adverse conditions, which batter them into strange, contorted shapes. The species is only found on the lower slopes of the White Mountains and on a few of the mountains in neighbouring Nevada. Extremely slow

Bristlecone pines on the slopes of the White Mountains

growing, they seldom reach more than 50 ft (15 m) in height, despite living for more than 4,000 years – 1,000 years longer than the oldest sequoia tree *(see pp480–81).*

Owens Valley ❾

🚆 *Lone Pine.* **ℹ️** *126 S Main St, Lone Pine (760 876-4444).*

OWENS VALLEY has more in common with Nevada than with the rest of California. Sparsely populated but ruggedly beautiful, the valley is wedged between the White Mountains and the Sierra Nevada Mountains.

Once covered with farms and ranches, the land here was bought secretly in 1905 by agents working for the City of Los Angeles. Los Angeles needed to secure a water supply and the aqueducts still drain the valley, destroying local agriculture.

In 1942 a detention camp was established at Manzanar for 10,000 Japanese-Americans, who were deemed a threat to national security and imprisoned for the duration of World War II. Exhibits on this and other aspects of Owens Valley can be seen at the **Eastern California Museum**, in the town of Independence.

🏛️ Eastern California Museum
155 Grant St, Independence. **℡** *(760) 878-0364.* ☐ *Wed–Mon.* ⬤ *1 Jan, Easter, Thanksgiving, 25 Dec.* **Donation.**

Mount Whitney ❿

℡ *(760) 876-6200.* **🚆** *Merced.* **🚌** *Lone Pine.*

THE HIGHEST PEAK on the US mainland, Mount Whitney rises to a height of 14,496 ft (4,420 m), forming a sheer wall above the town of Lone Pine. A steep 11-mile (18-km) trail leads from Whitney Portal Road to the summit, offering a panorama over the High Sierras. A permit is required to hike the trail. The first ascent of the mountain, named in honour of the geologist Josiah Whitney, was in 1873.

Mount Whitney borders Sequoia National Park *(see pp480–81),* and the surrounding alpine meadows are ideal for backpacking in summer.

Owens Valley, backed by the White Mountains

Sequoia and Kings Canyon National Parks ⓫

SEQUOIA NATIONAL PARK

Sequoia National Park signpost

THESE TWIN national parks preserve lush forests, granite peaks and glacier-carved canyons. Breathtaking scenery complements a habitat rich with wildlife. The parks embrace 34 separate groves of the giant sequoia tree, the earth's largest living species. America's deepest canyon, the south fork of the Kings River, cuts a depth of 8,200 ft (2,500 m) through Kings Canyon. Along the eastern boundary of Sequoia is Mount Whitney (see p479), the highest summit on the mainland US.

Roads serve the western side of the parks; the rest is accessible only to hikers or with hired pack-trains of horses or mules. Winter visitors can ski cross-country over both marked and unmarked trails.

Road "tunnel" formed by a felled giant sequoia in Sequoia National Park

Wilsonia •

(180)

Cedar Brook

Redwood Mountain Grove

North Fork Kaweah River

Redwood Creek

BIG BAI
▲
8,209 ft (2,

SEQUC
NATIO
PAR

Yucca C

M465

General Grant Tree
The third-largest sequoia is known as the "Nation's Christmas Tree".

KEY

▬▬	Major road
▬▬	Minor road
- - -	Paths and trails
──	National Park boundary
∼∼	River
▶	Skiing
Ⓐ	Camping
🏕	Picnic area
ℹ	Tourist information
☆	Viewpoint

Big Stumps
The sequoia's unyielding nature makes it uneconomical for timber, as these tall stumps, left by loggers in the 1880s, prove.

Moro Rock
A staircase carved into the rock takes visitors to the top of this granite monolith and affords a 360° view of the High Sierras and the Central Valley.

General Sherman's Tree
The world's largest living thing is 275 ft (84 m) tall, with a trunk measuring 36 ft (11 m) around its base. The tree still grows 0.4 inches (1 cm) every ten years.

Tharp's Log, a hollowed-out sequoia, was home to Hale Tharp, a 19th-century farmer who was introduced to the area by Native Americans.

Crescent Meadow
An array of sequoias border this area, which is more of a marsh than a meadow and too wet at its heart for the trees to survive.

...al Cavern, one of ...w caves open to visitors, ...d with stalagmites and stalactites.

Giant Forest contains one of the largest groves of living sequoias in the world.

0 kilometres   2

0 miles   2

NORTH CENTRAL CALIFORNIA

WITH A RUGGED SHORELINE *rising from the Pacific Ocean and dense forests covering coastal mountains, North Central California marks the visual transition between the north and south of the state. The landscape here leaves visitors spoilt for choice, with golden beaches, splendid wilderness and inland valleys which include some of the world's most productive agricultural regions.*

The natural beauty of the area, combined with a wealth of cultural history, makes this one of the state's most engaging regions. Native Americans lived along the coast and in the inland valleys for centuries prior to the arrival of Europeans in the 17th century. More than a century later the first European settlement was established at Monterey on 3 June 1770, marking the beginning of today's California. Monterey remained the capital of Upper California until the United States took formal control in 1848. The city still retains a unique character, with its many historic buildings now protected and restored.

North Central California has also inspired some of the state's significant literature, from the poetry of Robinson Jeffers to the novels of Nobel prize-winner John Steinbeck. Many of the world's best photographers, including Ansel Adams and Edward Weston, have lived and worked here.

For all its culture and history, the region also abounds in recreational activities. Visitors can enjoy the historic amusement park at Santa Cruz, play golf on the world-famous courses at Pebble Beach, or simply walk around the many nature reserves, including the state's most beautiful stretch of coastline, Big Sur.

Writer John Steinbeck's house in Salinas

◁ Bixby Creek Bridge on Coastal Hwy 1 at Big Sur

Exploring North Central California

Monterey, the Spanish colonial capital of
California, is at the heart of North Central California, and the best base from which to explore the
region. The wealthy resorts of Pacific Grove and
Carmel stand on a rugged peninsula just south of the
town. Further south is the wildest length of coastline
in the state, Big Sur, where otters and whales can be
spotted offshore. To the north is Santa Cruz, a lively
beach town, backed by densely forested mountains.
Inland, the Salinas and San Joaquin valleys give a
taste of California's productive agricultural areas.

Pfeiffer Burns State Park at Big Sur

San Francisco

1 BIG BASIN REDWOODS STATE PARK

2 ANO NUEVO
STATE RESERVE

3 ROARING
CAMP &
BIG TREES
NARROW
GAUGE
RAILWAY

4 SANTA CRUZ

San Francisco
San Jose

152

San Luis Reservoir

LOS BANO

152

156

5 SAN JUAN BAUTISTA

25

156

9 SALINAS

Delta

5

J1

PACIFIC GROVE

6

MONTEREY

7 CARMEL MISSION

Salinas River

101

San Benito River

J1

SOLEDAD

10 PINNACLES NATIONAL MONUMENT

8 BIG SUR

101

25

KING CITY

198

G14

San Antonio River

San Antonio Reservoir

Salinas River

1

101

San L Obisp

Looking out across Big Sur along Hwy 1

GETTING AROUND

Hwy 1, which runs along the coast south from Monterey to Big
Sur, is one of the world's most beautiful drives, and a must on any
tour of California. A car, or a bicycle and strong legs, is the best
way to get around, although there is a skeletal network of buses
centring upon Monterey. Inland from the coast, Hwy 101 and I-5
run north–south through the predominantly agricultural region, but
there are very few roads between the coast and inland valleys.

SIGHTS AT A GLANCE

Elephant seals at the Año Nuevo State Reserve

KEY

▬▬▬	Freeway
▬▬▬	Major road
▬▬▬	Minor road
▬▬▬	Scenic route
▬▬▬	River
☼	Viewpoint

Yosemite

●*OAKHURST*

(49)

(41)

Stockton
Modesto

Madera Canal

(99)

(145)

●*MADERA*

(41)

(145)

San Joaquín River

(180)

●*OOTA*

11 *FRESNO*

(180)

(168)

(245)

California Aqueduct

(145)

Kings River

Friant-Kern Canal

(99)

(41)

(198)

LEMORE ●

12
HANFORD

VISALIA

(198)

●*ALINGA*

(5)

(41)

Tulare
Lake
Bed

CORCORAN

(99)

Elk Bayou

(65)

(137)

(190)

PORTERVILLE ●

(190)

(33)

J22

J22

(99)

(5)

(65)

J22

(190)

Bakersfield
↓*Los Angeles*

0 kilometres   20

0 miles   20

The North Central Coastline

THE BEACHES of North Central California are varied, from long, thin stretches to tiny coves at the foot of coastal bluffs. In summer, sun-worshippers and volleyball players congregate on the sands, and while the water is generally too cold for swimming, surfers don wet suits to brave the chilly waves. With almost no commercial developments along this stretch of coastline, these beaches are also ideal for leisurely walks, searching for driftwood or seashells. You may also catch a glimpse of the area's abundant wildlife, which ranges from shore birds and tidepool-dwellers to elephant seals and migrating grey whales.

SAN FRANCISCO
PACIFICA

Boulder Creek

Sco
Val

Wilder Ranch State Park

Moss Landing is a colourful harbour and the home port for most of Monterey Bay's commercial fishing boats. It has many good seafood restaurants along its wharves.

0 kilometres   5

0 miles   5

★ **Santa Cruz Beach** ③
With free volleyball courts and barbecue pits backed by the popular Boardwalk Amusement Park *(see p490)*, this broad golden strand is the area's most popular beach.

Waddell Creek Beach ①
This long golden strand of beach is part of the Big Basin Redwoods State Park *(see p488)* and is a favourite spot for picnickers, anglers and windsurfers.

Lighthouse Field State Beach ②
This rugged 36 acres (14 ha) of shoreline is well suited to surfing or simply admiring the sculpted 40-ft (12-m) sandstone headlands. It is also a good place to spot sea otters, brown pelicans and the occasional whale offshore.

Capitola Beach ④
A wooden railway trestle bridges the small creek that meets the ocean at this sandy beach. Next to the beach is Capitola Wharf, lined with restaurants, shops and viewing decks. The Capitola Bluffs are an important palaeontological site, and the prehistoric shells can be seen at low tide.

Marina State Beach ⑤
Backed by sand dunes, this beach was once a part of a Marine Corps base and is now part of a university campus.

KEY

	Freeway
	Major road
	Minor road
	River
❊	Viewpoint

Wilder Ranch State Park, at the northern edge of Santa Cruz, is an historic coastal dairy farm. Complete with ranch house and barns dating from the 1890s, it has been preserved as a state park.

LOCATOR MAP

Elkhorn Slough, halfway along Monterey Bay, is one of the prime bird-watching areas along the North Central coastline.

★ **Asilomar State Beach** ⑦

This broad, rocky beach is an ideal place for watching migrating grey whales as they pass offshore every winter on their way south.

★ **Lovers' Point** ⑥

Originally called Lovers of Jesus Point, the headlands form a natural amphitheatre which was used for religious revivals in the 1880s. It is one of the few sandy beaches on the northern Monterey Peninsula.

★ **Carmel City Beach** ⑧

Bright white sand and brilliant blue water are the distinguishing characteristics of this long beach, which sits at the foot of central Carmel's popular shopping and restaurant district *(see p494)*.

Elephant seals ashore at Año Nuevo State Reserve

Big Basin Redwoods State Park ❶

🏌 Santa Cruz, Boulder Creek Golf Course. **Visitors' Center** 📞 (408) 338-8860.

IN 1900 A GROUP of environmentalists formed the Sempervirens Club with the aim of preventing the logging of redwoods. This resulted in Big Basin Redwoods State Park, California's first state park, established in 1902. It covers 16,000 acres (6,475 ha) and protects the southernmost groves of the coastal redwood tree (see p430), and forests of Douglas fir and other conifers. It is also home to wildlife such as black-tailed deer and the mountain lion.

Trails lead through redwood groves to the park's many waterfalls, including the popular Berry Creek Falls. There are also more than 100 miles (160 km) of other routes, including the Skyline-to-Sea Trail, which drops down to the Pacific Ocean at Waddell Creek (see pp486–7).

Exhibits detailing the park's history are on display inside the visitors' centre.

Año Nuevo State Reserve ❷

Road map B4. 🚌 Santa Cruz, Waddell Creek. ℹ️ (415) 879-2025; 879-0227. ⬜ daily.

THE AÑO NUEVO State Reserve, 60 miles, (96 km) north of Monterey, has as its main point of interest the breeding grounds of the Northern elephant seal, one of the world's most fascinating creatures. A short stretch of sandy beach and a small offshore island are populated each winter by hundreds of these giant mammals, which arrive here from all over the Pacific Ocean to mate and give birth.

Elephant seals were hunted almost to extinction in the 19th century because of their valuable oil-bearing blubber. A few survivors found refuge off the coast of Mexico and made their way back to California in the 1950s. The first pups were born at Año Nuevo in 1975. There are now some 120,000 elephant seals off the coast of California.

The seals are named after the dangling proboscis of the male, which can reach 20 ft (6 m) in length and weigh upwards of 2 tonnes. Ungainly on land, elephant seals can perform incredible feats in the sea – remaining under water for up to 20 minutes at a time and diving more than 4,000 ft (1,220 m) beneath the surface. Each December, the male seals arrive here and begin the battle for dominance, engaging in violent fights. Only a handful of the most powerful males are able to mate, but one male can father pups with as many as 50 different females in one season. After spending most of the year at sea, the females arrive in January to give birth to young conceived the previous winter. Mating follows soon after, although conception is delayed for up to four months while the female recovers from giving birth.

The name Año Nuevo ("New Year") was given to the island by explorer Sebastián Vizcaíno, who sailed past the area on 1 January 1603 (see pp42–3). The park is open all year, but during the winter when the elephant seals are present, visitors are only allowed on guided tours. Tickets are available through the California State Parks reservation service, DestiNet (see p576).

Roaring Camp and Big Trees Narrow Gauge Railroad ❸

📞 (408) 335-4400. 🚌 Santa Cruz. ⬜ Jan–Mar: Sat & Sun. ⬤ public hols. 🅿️ ♿ 📷 noon, 1:30pm, 3pm.
Santa Cruz Big Trees Railroad
📞 (408) 335-4400. ⬜ call ahead for times. 🅿️ ♿ 📷

HIGH UP in the Santa Cruz Mountains, near the town of Felton, a pair of historic logging railways have been kept in operation as the focus

Roaring Camp and Big Trees Railroad

Façade of Mission San Juan Bautista

of a family-orientated theme park devoted to the late 19th-century and early 20th-century lumber industry. Between December and March, a narrow gauge train departs on a weekend 6-mile (10-km) round trip through the adjacent forests of Henry Cowell Redwoods State Park. From April to November, the traditional gauge Big Trees, Santa Cruz and Pacific Railroad, sets off from Roaring Camp on an hour-long trip through the mountains and down to Santa Cruz. There is a three-hour stopover, during which passengers can enjoy the beach and Boardwalk Amusement Park before the return journey *(see pp490–91)*. The trip can also be taken as a round-trip from Santa Cruz.

Santa Cruz ❹

See pp490–91.

San Juan Bautista ❺

Road map B4. 👥 *1,650.* 🚌 *from Hollister.* ℹ️ *402 3rd St (408 623-2454).*

F OR A QUICK INSIGHT into California's multi-faceted history, there is no better place than San Juan Bautista. This small town has retained its rural character, despite being a mere 30 miles (48 km) from the heart of the high-tech Silicon Valley *(see p412).*

The main attraction of the town is Mission San Juan Bautista, which stands to the west of the central plaza. The largest of the missions built during Spanish colonial rule, it is also the only one to have aisles along the nave. Alfred Hitchcock used the mission's façade for the final scenes of his film *Vertigo.* The adjacent monastery has

ORIGINAL ROUTE
EL CAMINO REAL

El Camino Real sign

been converted into a museum of mission history, displaying mission artifacts and photographs of the town at various stages of development.

On the north side of the church there is a cemetery, next to which a faint trail marks the historic route of El Camino Real. This 650-mile (1,050-km) path linked the 21 Californian missions, all within a day's journey of their nearest mission *(see pp42–3)*. By coincidence, this trail also follows the San Andreas Fault, the underlying source of all California's earthquakes *(see pp20–21)*. A small seismograph on the edge of the town's plaza monitors tectonic activity along the fault line.

The east and south sides of the plaza are lined by three historic buildings, all of which have been preserved as part of San Juan Bautista State Historic Park. The Plaza Hotel incorporates part of the original barracks built in 1813. The town's stables now house antique carriages and stagecoaches, and Castro House was owned by Patrick Breen, a survivor of the tragic Donner Party *(see p470).*

THE LOMA PRIETA EARTHQUAKE

The powerful tremor that rocked San Francisco on 17 October 1989 had its epicentre beneath Loma Prieta, a hill between Santa Cruz and San Juan Bautista. Although the international media concentrated on the extensive damage caused in and around San Francisco, the worst damage occurred in Santa Cruz and the surrounding communities, where a number of homes and commercial buildings were destroyed. Approximately 40 businesses were forced to relocate to tent-like temporary buildings occupying three full blocks. The downtown district of Santa Cruz was a vast building site until the end of 1994. The majority of the damaged structures have now been repaired or replaced but empty lots still remain where buildings once stood.

Destruction caused by the Loma Prieta earthquake

Santa Cruz ❹

Perched at the northern tip of Monterey Bay, Santa Cruz is a composite of small-town California, with an agricultural rather than suburban feel. Its surrounding farmland forms a broad shelf between the bay and the densely forested Santa Cruz Mountains that rise to the east. These mountains separate Santa Cruz from the urban Silicon Valley (see p412) and, along with the scenic coastline, provide residents and visitors with an easy access to nature. The city's past is preserved in a replica 18th-century mission and in the excellent local history museum. The large University of California campus in the town, attracting students and professors from all over the world, also gives Santa Cruz a cosmopolitan and erudite character.

Reconstructed façade of Santa Cruz Mission

Exploring Santa Cruz

The downtown area, which centres on Pacific Avenue, is 875 yards (800 m) inland. Much of this area was badly damaged by the Loma Prieta earthquake (see p489), but the city has recovered swiftly, with many good bookshops, art galleries and cafés lining the streets. The historic core of the city, including the remains of the 1791 Mission Santa Cruz, is on a hill to the northeast of the town.

The highlight of Santa Cruz is the waterfront, including the Boardwalk Amusement Park, and scenic Cliff Drive which runs along the coast.

Detail of the Giant Dipper

🎢 Santa Cruz Beach Boardwalk

400 Beach St. [(408) 423-5590. ◯ call ahead for opening times.
The last surviving old-style amusement park on the West Coast, the Santa Cruz Beach Boardwalk offers a variety of attractions and games lined up along the beachfront. Visitors can wander freely, deciding which of the many exciting rides to try.

The main attraction is the Giant Dipper roller coaster, built in 1924 by Arthur Looff and now a National Historic Landmark. The car travels along the 1-mile (1.6-km) wooden track at 55 mph (88 km/h). The carousel nearby features horses and chariots hand-carved by Looff's father, craftsman Charles Looff, in 1911. The ride is accompanied by a 100-year-old pipe organ. The park also has 27 more modern rides and an Art Deco dance hall.

🔒 Mission Santa Cruz

Emmet & High Sts. [(408) 426-5686. ◯ daily. **Donation**.
On top of a hill overlooking the town, Mission Santa Cruz was founded on 25 September 1791 by Father Lasuén, as the 12th Franciscan mission in California. The buildings were completed three years later. The mission was never a great success, however, due to earthquakes, poor weather and its isolated location, which have eliminated any remains of the original structure. A park outlines the site, and a 1931 replica of the mission has been constructed. This houses a small museum which contains 18th-century relics and displays on mission history.

🏛 Museum of Art and History at the McPherson Center

705 Front St. [(408) 454-0697. ◯ Tue–Sun. ● 1 Jan, Thanksgiving, 25 Dec. 🎟
One positive development to arise out of the rubble of the 1989 Loma Prieta earthquake was this 20,000 sq ft (1,858 sq m) cultural centre, which opened in 1993 to house the local art and history galleries. The Art Gallery shows works primarily by North Central artists depicting the local landscape. The History Gallery includes a series of displays tracing the development of Santa Cruz County, from the pre-colonial and mission eras through to the present day.

Also in the History Gallery are colourful and organized exhibits detailing the region's agricultural and industrial heritage, with photographs of late 19th-century and early 20th-century farms and logging operations. The museum also incorporates the adjacent Octagon Gallery which was completed in 1882 as the County Hall of Records.

Giant Dipper roller coaster in the Boardwalk Amusement Park

Eroded archway at the Natural Bridges State Beach

VISITORS' CHECKLIST

Road map B4. 🏠 238,900.
✈ San Jose International
Airport. ✖ Monterey Peninsula
Airport. 🚌 920 Pacific Ave.
ℹ 701 Front St (408 425-1234).
🎪 Santa Cruz Fungus Fair (Jan);
Clam Chowder Cook-Off (Feb).

🏖 Natural Bridges State Beach

2531 W Cliff Dr. 📞 (408) 423-4609.
🕐 daily. 🅿 **Visitors' Center** end of
W Cliff Drive. 🕐 daily.
Natural Bridges State Beach
takes its name from the picturesque archways which
were carved into the cliffs by
the ocean waves. Two of the
three original arches collapsed,
but one still remains, through
which waves roll into a small
sandy cove. The park also
preserves a eucalyptus grove
and a nature trail, showing all
the stages in the life cycle of
the beautiful monarch butterfly
(see p209).

🏛 Santa Cruz Surfing Museum

Lighthouse Point, W Cliff Drive
📞 (408) 429-3429. 🕐 Wed–Mon.
⬤ 1 Jan, Thanksgiving, 25 Dec.
Donation.
In a lighthouse overlooking
the region's main surfing area,
this museum has artifacts from
every era of Santa Cruz surfing.
The sport was brought to the
state from Hawaii to promote
tourism. It evolved into a truly
Californian pursuit with the
music of the Beach Boys in the
1960s *(see pp52–3)*. The surfboards range from the redwood planks of the 1930s to
today's high-tech laminates.

🏖 Mystery Spot

465 Mystery Spot Rd. 📞 (408) 423-
8897. 🕐 daily. 🅿
Two miles (3 km) east of
downtown Santa Cruz, a redwood grove has been drawing
visitors for decades because
of the strange events that occur
here. Balls roll uphill, parallel
lines converge, and the laws of
physics seem to be suspended.
Part tourist trap, part genuine
oddity, the Mystery Spot has
to be seen to be believed.

SANTA CRUZ CITY CENTRE

Mission Santa Cruz ⑤
Museum of Art and History at the
McPherson Center ④
Natural Bridges State Beach ①
Santa Cruz Beach Boardwalk ③
Santa Cruz Surfing Museum ②

KEY

🚌 Bus stop
ℹ Tourist information

Street-by-Street: Monterey ⑥

THE PORTUGUESE EXPLORER, Sebastián
Vizcaíno, landed here in 1602 and
named the bay after his patron, the Count
of Monterrey. But it was not until the
Spanish captain Gaspar de Portolá (1717–
1784) and Father Serra *(see pp42–3)* landed
here in 1770 and established a church and
presidio that the garrison grew into a pueblo.
Monterey served as the capital of California
until 1848. After the Gold Rush *(see pp44–5)*
the city lost its status to San Francisco and
settled into the role of a hard-working
fishing port, market town and military base.

Today, visitors come to tour the historic
sites, dine on seafood at Fisherman's Wharf
and attend the annual jazz festival.

California's First Theater
*Built in 1847 as a boarding
house, it became a theatre in
1848. Victorian melodramas
are still performed here
every night.*

★ Colton Hall
*The California State Constitution was
first signed here in 1849. The hall now
houses a museum commemorating
the event.*

Larkin House
*Thomas Larkin, an East Coast mer-
chant, built this house in 1832. The
architecture has become representative of Monterey style (see pp26–7).*

**The Sherman
Quarters** were
General Sherman's
military base from
1847–1849.

**The Cooper-Molera
Complex** combines a garden,
a carriage display and personal mementos of three
generations of the Cooper
family, who built the house
between 1827 and 1900.

STAR SIGHTS
★ Colton Hall
★ Fisherman's Wharf

0 metres 100

0 yards 100

KEY

– – – Suggested route

VISITORS' CHECKLIST

Road map B4. 🏘 *32,000.*
✈ *Monterey Peninsula Airport.*
🚌 *Tyler, Pearl & Munras Sts,*
(408) 899-2555. ℹ *401 Camino*
el Estero (408 648-5350).
🎫 *Monterey Blues Festival (Jul);*
Monterey Jazz Festival (Sep);
Laguna Seca Races (May–Oct).

★ **Fisherman's Wharf**
Once the centre of the fishing and whaling
industries, the area is now known for its
shops, seafood restaurants and markets.

Custom House
This old government
building is preserved
as it was in the
1830s and '40s.

Old Whaling Station
Mementos of the Monterey whaling
industry are displayed in the house.
The paving outside the building
was made using whale bones.

Stevenson House
Robert Louis Stevenson lived here in
1879. The house is now a museum.

The Royal Presidio Chapel,
built in 1794, is the town's
oldest surviving building.

Exploring Monterey Peninsula

WRITERS AND ARTISTS have long extolled the spectacular coastline of the Monterey Peninsula. Its granite rocks have been cut into rugged coves and jutting points by the ocean. Forests of Monterey cypress and pine trees, wintering grounds of the monarch butterfly, cover the inland area. Otters and sea lions swim in the kelp forests beyond the shore. The peninsula is home to three main towns: Monterey, the capital of Spanish California (*see pp492–3*); the former religious retreat, Pacific Grove; and the picturesque village of Carmel-by-the-Sea.

Marine bird at the Monterey Bay Aquarium

➤ Monterey Bay Aquarium
886 Cannery Row. 🅲 *(408) 648-4888.* ⬤ *daily.* ⬤ *25 Dec.* 🖼
Monterey Bay Aquarium is the largest aquarium in the US. More than 570 species and 350,000 specimens portray the rich marine environment of Monterey Bay. Among the exhibits are an enclosed kelp forest, a rock pool and a display of live jellyfish. Visitors are allowed to touch the specimens, including sea stars and bat rays, relatives of sting rays.

A pool connected to the open bay attracts sea otters. The Outer Bay Wing has a 1 million-gal (4.5 million-litre) tank, in which the conditions of the ocean are re-created. It contains yellowfin tuna, ocean sunfish, green sea turtles and barracuda, most of them oblivious to onlookers. Exhibits due to open in 2001, will complete the picture with the mysterious luminous fish from the deepest levels of the ocean.

♿ Cannery Row
David Ave & Coastguard Pier. 🅲 *(408) 649-6695.* ⬤ *daily.*
This six-block harbour-front street, celebrated by John Steinbeck in his ribald novels

Cannery Row and *Sweet Thursday (see p501)*, was once the site of more than 20 fish-packing plants which processed sardines from Monterey Bay. The canneries thrived from the early 20th century, reaching their greatest volume of production in the early 1940s. In 1945 the sardines suddenly disappeared, perhaps as a result of overfishing, and most of the canneries were abandoned, later to be demolished or burned down. The buildings that remain today house an eclectic collection of shops and restaurants. One notable historic building that remains, at No. 800, is the old laboratory of "Doc" Ricketts, noted marine biologist, beer drinker and best friend of Steinbeck. The building is now a private club.

Street sign in Cannery Row

♿ Pacific Grove
Forest & Central Aves. 🅲 *(408) 373-3304.* ⬤ *daily.* ⬤ *1 Jan, Thanksgiving, 25 Dec.*
This sedate town was founded in 1889 as a religious retreat, where alcohol, dancing and even the Sunday newspaper were banned. Today it is best known for its wooden houses, many now converted into inns, its beautiful coastal parks and the monarch butterflies that arrive between October and April *(see p209).* The annual return of the insects, which are protected by city ordinance, occasions a lively parade.

The Point Pinos Lighthouse was built in 1852 and is now the oldest operating lighthouse in California.

♿ Carmel-by-the-Sea
San Carlos, 5th & 6th Sts. 🅲 *(408) 624-1711.* ⬤ *Mon–Sat.* ⬤ *1 Jan, Thanksgiving, 25 Dec.*
The varied array of homes in this picturesque village border the steep hillsides down to the ocean. City ordinances restricting streetlamps, post deliveries and pavements gives the town its quaint atmosphere.

Art galleries and shops abound along Ocean Avenue and the town also sponsors an annual playwriting contest, a Bach Festival and many art exhibitions.

♿ Carmel River State Beach
Carmelo & Scenic Rds. 🅲 *(408) 624-4909.* ⬤ *7am–sunset, daily.*
This 106-acre (43-ha) state park straddles the mouth of the Carmel River, containing a lagoon and wetland nature preserve for a bountiful population of native and migratory birds. Fishing is permitted on the beach, but swimming is discouraged because of dangerous currents and cold temperatures. The beach is a favourite picnicking spot of Carmel residents.

Point Pinos Lighthouse at Pacific Grove

The 17-Mile Drive

SIGHTSEERS MAY TOUR the Monterey Peninsula via a toll road, the 17-Mile Drive. The road offers spectacular views of the best the area has to offer, including crashing surf, coastal flora and enchanting forests. The extraordinary beauty of the region has also attracted many wealthy people to build magnificent estates and mansions in the area. Most celebrated of all its attractions are the country clubs and championship golf courses.

Spanish Bay ①
The shore within this cove at the southern edge of Pacific Grove is a popular picnicking area.

Spyglass Hill ⑥
This golf course was named after a location in Robert Louis Stevenson's *Treasure Island*. Stevenson often described the local scenery in his novels.

Huckleberry Hill ②
This hill in the Del Monte forest is popular in the summer with fruit pickers.

TIPS FOR DRIVERS

Duration of journey: 3 hours.
Entrance: There is a toll charge for each car. Cycling is free.
Getting there: There are four toll gates: 17-Mile Drive, San Antonio Ave, Hwy 1 and SFB Morse Drive. The tour is marked by red and yellow lines.
When to go: Summer can be crowded and foggy. In any season, traffic is lighter during the week.
Where to stay and eat: Carmel, Monterey and Pacific Grove have a wide selection of hotels and restaurants (see pp504–75).
Visitor Information: Monterey Peninsula Chamber of Commerce, 380 Alvarado St, Monterey.
☎ (408) 649-1770.

Lone Cypress ⑤
On a rock overlooking the ocean, this is perhaps the most photographed tree in the world.

Tor House ④
This striking rock house was built by the poet Robinson Jeffers between 1919 and 1957.

Carmel Mission ③
At one time this beautiful mission was the administrative centre for Northern California (*see pp496–7*).

KEY

▬▬▬	Tour route
═══	Other roads
▢	Golf courses

0 metres   500
0 yards   500

Carmel Mission ⑦

Decorative wall plaque

FOUNDED IN 1770 by Father Junípero Serra (1713–84) and built of adobe brick by Native American labourers, Carmel Mission served as the administrative centre for all the Northern Californian missions. Father Serra resided here until his death, and is now buried at the foot of the altar. The mission was secularized and abandoned in 1834, quickly falling into disrepair. Restoration work began in 1924, carefully following the plans of the original mission, and replanting the gardens. The reconstructed living quarters detail 18th-century mission life. The mission still functions as a Catholic church.

The sarcophagus depicts Father Serra recumbent in death, surrounded by three mourning padres. It is among the finest of its type in the United States.

Kitchen
This restored room shows the kitchen as it was in missionary days, including the oven brought from Mexico. A section of the original adobe wall can be seen.

Dining room

Bell tower

Statue of Junípero Serra
Set within the beautiful front courtyard, a statue of Serra faces the mission church he founded.

★ **Serra's Cell**
Father Serra's simple way of life is evident in this sparse, restored cell. The wooden bed, chair, desk and candlestick were the only pieces of furniture he possessed. He died here in 1784.

Façade and front courtyard of Carmel Mission

VISITORS' CHECKLIST

3080 Rio Rd, Carmel. **Road map** B4. *(408) 624-3600.* 9:30am–4:30pm Mon–Sat; 10:30am–4:30pm Sun. Thanksgiving, 25 Dec. Sun: 7am, 8am, 9:30am, 11am, 12:30pm, 5:30pm.

Father Serra's burial place under the altar is marked with a plaque.

The Chapel Window is the only place where the original paintwork can still be seen.

The cemetery contains the graves of 18th-century missionaries.

Museum
Situated in the old living quarters of the mission, the museum contains several relics belonging to Father Serra.

STAR FEATURES

★ Main Altar

★ Serra's Cell

★ **Main Altar**
The Gothic arch of Carmel's altar, with its ornate decoration, is the only one of its kind among all the 21 Franciscan missions in California.

Big Sur 🔞

I N THE LATE 18TH CENTURY, Spanish colonists at Carmel named this stretch of land *El Pais Grande del Sur*, the "big country to the south", and the coastline of Big Sur has been attracting hyperbole ever since. The novelist Robert Louis Stevenson called it "the greatest meeting of land and sea in the world", and the 100 miles (160 km) of breathtaking mountains, cliffs and rocky coves still leave visitors grasping for adjectives.

The scenic Hwy 1 was constructed across this rugged landscape during the 1930s, but otherwise Big Sur has been preserved in its natural state. There are no large towns and very few signs of civilization in the area. Most of the shoreline is protected in a series of state parks, which offer dense forests, broad rivers and crashing surf, all easily accessible within a short walk of the road.

Crashing surf and rocky cliffs, typical of the Big Sur coastline

Point Lobos State Reserve
This is the habitat of the Monterey cypress, the only tree to survive the region's mixture of fog and salt spray. Its branches are shaped by the sea winds.

GARRAPATTA
STATE PARK
①

Little Sur

Coast Ridge

Big Sur ●

Point Sur Lighthouse sits atop a volcanic cone. It was manned until 1974 but is now automated.

Nepenthe is a pretty resort hidden from the road by oak trees. It has long been frequented by Hollywood movie stars.

Bixby Creek Bridge
This photogenic arched bridge was built in 1932. For many years it was the world's largest single-arch span, at 260 ft (79 m) tall and 700 ft (213 m) long. Hwy 1 was named the state's first scenic highway here in 1966.

KEY

═══	Minor road
═══	Scenic route
▪▪▪	Hiking trails
───	National park boundaries
〰	Rivers and lakes
Ⓐ	Camping
☀	Viewpoint

Andrew Molera State Park
Opened in 1972, this park includes 10 miles (16 km) of hiking trails and 2.5 miles (4 km) of quiet sandy beach.

Julia Pfeiffer Burns State Park
*A tunnel under Hwy 1, accessible only on foot, leads to the
100-ft (30-m) high bluff from which the McWay Creek
waterfall spills into the Pacific Ocean.*

VISITORS' CHECKLIST

Road map B4. 🏃 1,500.
🚌 Nepenthe Park. ℹ (408)
667-2100.

The Esalen Institute was
set up in the 1960s to hold
New Age seminars. Its hot
springs were first frequented
by Native Americans, and
still attract visitors *(see p425)*.

Ventana Wilderness
*Part of the Los Padres
National Forest, many of
the steep ridges of this
beautiful wilderness are
accessible only to experienced hikers. Camp sites
cover the lower reaches.*

VENTANA
WILDERNESS

Tassajara Creek

LOS PADRES

NATIONAL FOREST

Big Creek

Lucia •

Nacimiento Fergusson Rd

Jade Cove
*This beautiful cove can only
be reached by way of a
steep path down the cliff
face. The removal of
jade is prohibited above
the high tide level.*

Plaskett •

Los Burros Rd

Antonio River

Lake San
Antonio

San Simeon Point is
a natural harbour which
was used by William
Randolph Hearst to
ship in materials for
his estate, Hearst Castle,
on the inland hilltop
(see pp202–205).

Plaskett Creek

Nacimiento River

Alder Creek

Lake Nacimiento

0 kilometres   10

0 miles   10

San Simeon •

Nobel prize-winning author, John Steinbeck (1902–68)

Salinas **9**

Road map B4. 122,000.
119 E Alisal St (408 424-7611).

SITUATED AT THE north end of the predominantly agricultural Salinas Valley, which stretches for more than 50 miles (80 km) between San Francisco and San Luis Obispo, Salinas is the region's primary agricultural centre. Vegetable-packing plants and canneries line the major highways and railway tracks. The region is often referred to as the "salad bowl of the nation", its prime produce being lettuce, as well as tomatoes and garlic.

The town is perhaps best known, however, as the birthplace of the Nobel prize-winning author John Steinbeck, who set many of his natural-istic stories here and in the surrounding area. A selection of books, manuscripts, photographs and personal memorabilia relating to the author is on permanent display in a special room of the **John Steinbeck Library**. The library also supplies information on Steinbeck-related

places to visit in the area and on the Steinbeck Festival, held in Salinas every August.

Hat in Three Stages of Landing, a large-scale, bright yellow steel sculpture of three cowboy hats by the acclaimed Pop artist Claes Oldenberg, was erected in the town in the 1970s. It stands, appropriately, in front of the entrance to the California State Rodeo. Each Fourth of July one of the largest rodeos in the world is held here, bringing riders and their livestock from all over the United States, as well as various other entertainments.

John Steinbeck Library
350 Lincoln Ave. (408) 758-7311.
Mon–Sat. public hols.

Pinnacles National Monument **10**

Road map B4. (408) 389-4485.
King City & Soledad. daily.
some trails.

HIGH IN THE HILLS above the Salinas Valley, 12 miles (20 km) east of the town of Soledad on US-101, the Pinnacles National Monument preserves 16,000 acres (6,500 ha) of a unique volcanic landscape. A solid ridge of lava flows, eroded over millions of years into oddly contorted crags and spires, runs through the centre of the park, in places forming cliffs more than 500 ft (150 m) tall. There are no roads across the park, but there are many carefully-maintained hiking trails.

One of the most popular and accessible spots in the park is the Balconies formation, reached by a 1.5-mile

(2.5 km) leisurely trail. Here beautiful red and gold cliffs rise high above the ground, attracting rock-climbers, photographers and bird-watchers. At the base of the cliffs, huge boulders caught between the narrow canyons have formed a series of dark talus caves. These were reputedly used in the past as hide-outs by highwaymen and other outlaws.

The park is best visited in spring, when the temperature is cool and the wildflowers are in bloom. Mountain lions, coyotes and eagles can occasionally also be sighted.

Volcanic crags of the Pinnacles National Monument

Fresno **11**

Road map C4. 402,500.
Fresno Air Terminal.
2331 Fresno St (209 495-4800).

FRESNO IS LOCATED at approximately the geographical centre of the state and is its eighth largest city. A busy commercial centre, Fresno is often referred to as the "Raisin Capital of the World" because of its abundant production of

Vegetable pickers and packers in the Salinas Valley

the dried fruit. Its central position also makes it a convenient base from which to make excursions to the eastern mountain recreational areas of the High Sierras, including the stunning Kings Canyon, Sequoia and Yosemite National Parks *(see pp466–81)*.

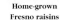

Home-grown Fresno raisins

ENVIRONS: In Kearney Park, 7 miles (11 km) west of downtown Fresno, is **Kearney Mansion**. This elaborate French Renaissance-style house was erected in 1903 by Theodore Kearney, an agriculturalist who helped establish California's raisin industry. The house is now a museum, furnished as it was when first completed.

🏛 **Kearney Mansion**
Kearney Blvd, Hwy 99. [(209) 441-0862. ◯ Fri–Sun. 🖼

Colonel Allen Allensworth, resident of Hanford

Hanford ⑫

Road map C4. 🏚 *37,000*. 🚊 🚌
ℹ *200 Santa Fe Ave, Suite D (209 582-5024)*.

Oⁿᴱ ᴼᶠ ᴹᴬⁿʸ medium-sized farming communities in the area, Hanford is significant because of its diverse, multi-ethnic heritage. The China Alley neighbourhood was once inhabited by one of the largest Chinese communities in California, many of whom worked on the construction of the transcontinental railroad *(see pp46–7)*. Located east of the town centre, it

surrounds the historic **Taoist Temple**, built in 1893. The temple operated as a hostel for Chinese immigrants and a Chinese school as well as a religious shrine. Downtown Hanford, around Courthouse Square, has a beautiful antique carousel and a number of elegant buildings dating from the late 19th century, now converted into shops and restaurants.

🏯 **Taoist Temple**
China Alley. [(209) 582-0483.
◯ *by appointment only*. 🖼

JOHN STEINBECK

One of California's most successful 20th-century writers, John Steinbeck (1902–68) was born in Salinas to an established family of farmers and ranchers. When he dropped out of Stanford University *(see p411)*, Steinbeck moved to the Monterey Peninsula in the late 1920s to write fiction. After several attempts he eventually gained a measure of success with the publication of the novella *Tortilla Flat* in 1935. Steinbeck then began a series of short stories and novels, the majority of them focusing on the people and places he knew well in the Salinas Valley and Monterey area. These included some of his greatest work: *Of Mice and Men* (1937), *Cannery Row* (1945) and *East of Eden* (1952).

His best-known work is *The Grapes of Wrath* (1939). The novel fictionalizes the mass westward migration that took place during the Depression of the 1930s, by documenting the struggles of the Joad family as they fled the dust bowl of Oklahoma for the greener pastures of California. It was an immediate bestseller and earned Steinbeck a Pulitzer Prize, although many Californians took its unhappy ending as an insult to their state, and even as Communist propaganda. Steinbeck reacted to this antipathy in 1943 by going to North Africa to become a war correspondent. On his return to the United States in 1945 he settled in Long Island, New York. In 1962, he was awarded the Nobel Prize for Literature. Steinbeck is the only American author to have received both the Pulitzer Prize and the Nobel Prize.

He died in New York City on 20 December 1968, but is buried in his home town, in the Garden of Memories at No. 768 Abbott Street.

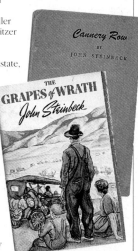

First editions of Steinbeck's most famous works, *Cannery Row* and *The Grapes of Wrath*

ENVIRONS: The **Colonel Allensworth State Historic Park** is 30 miles (50 km) south of Hanford. Colonel Allen Allensworth believed his fellow African-Americans could combat racism by building their own future, and established a unique farming community in 1908 with a group of African-American families. Memorabilia of this independent community are now on display in the old farmhouses.

🏛 **Colonel Allensworth State Historic Park**
Off Hwy 99 on County Rd J22, Earlimart. [(805) 849-3433.
◯ *daily*. 🖼

TRAVELLERS'
NEEDS

WHERE TO STAY

FRAMED BY RUGGED coastal mountains, lush wooded hills, sophisticated urban centres and a long stretch of coastline, California is one of the premier holiday destinations in the world. Whether rustic lodges or five-star resorts suit your budget, there is a wealth of options for travellers to the state.

Top hotels can range from film-star luxury to high-tech business centres. Budget accommodation is widespread, from roadside motels to atmospheric inns which offer an insight into the state's history. All accommodation, however, is likely to

Doorman

offer double beds, *en suite* bathrooms and comfortable surroundings. A range of camping facilities is also available for those interested in the great outdoors.

Free magazines containing discount coupons for all sorts of accommodation are available from street distribution bins at freeway rest stops and at car hire centres. Many hotels also offer discounts on telephone bookings during the off season and it is worth booking ahead to negotiate the rate. The listings on pages 508–37 give full descriptions of quality accommodation to suit all budgets throughout the state.

HOTEL CLASSIFICATIONS

THE CALIFORNIA tourist industry is recognized for its quality lodgings. A guideline of value to travellers is the diamond rating system of the California State Automobile Association. Every lodging, from the most expensive four-diamond hotel to the budget one-diamond motel, is rated for service, cleanliness and the range of facilities on offer.

Another guideline is *Relais et Châteaux*, a 40-year-old French organization that rates top holiday destinations worldwide. Only 26 properties in the United States have been invited to join the organization in total and seven of these are located in California.

HOTELS

IN CALIFORNIA, hotels come in every shape and size. There are the historic showplaces such as the Sheraton Palace

in San Francisco *(see p526),* the Biltmore in Los Angeles *(see p509)* and the Ahwahnee in Yosemite National Park *(see p536).* These were originally built to impress East Coast bankers and prove that the West Coast was worth their investment. There are also the trendy, visually stunning urban getaways such as the Triton Hotel in San Francisco *(see p523)* and the Mondrian in West Hollywood *(see p513).* There are hotels with fashion shops, with corporate conference centres, chandelier ballrooms or landscaped gardens. There are also small hotels, called "boutique hotels", that have fewer than 100 rooms and the intimate ambience of a bed-and-breakfast.

No matter the size, you can always count on every hotel having a spacious foyer, a restaurant or café, a pool or exercise room and a range of services such as laundry, ironing and in-room video movies.

Lounge bar in the exclusive Beverly Wilshire Hotel *(see p508)*

If the hotel does not have its own exercise facility on-site, there is often an arrangement with a nearby health club which hotel guests can use for a fee of $8–$12 per day. Non-smoking rooms are always available – many hotels have now set aside entire floors for non-smokers only.

Rates for hotels range from an inexpensive $75 per night to a moderate $175. Rooms at up-market, well-located hotels can range from $175–$275. There are some luxury hotels in California, however, be it in Beverly Hills, Big Sur or Napa Valley, that charge $185 for the smallest room off season, and in peak season can be as much as $500 a night.

Hotels are also subject to city and state taxes, which range from 11 per cent in San

Biltmore Hotel in Los Angeles

Francisco to 14 per cent in Los Angeles. Not included in room rates are additional charges for parking and heavy surcharges for outgoing telephone calls.

CORPORATE HOTELS

THESE CATER TO business travellers by offering weekly and monthly rates. There are also a number of all-suite hotels, with living rooms, in-room computers and fax connections. Some even have on-site computer centres, providing ample work space for business travellers. Check the hotel listings on pages 508–37 to see where these services are available.

CHAIN HOTELS

YOU CAN COUNT on good service, moderate prices and comfortable (if somewhat bland) surroundings at a chain hotel. The popular chains in California include the **Westin**, **Hilton**, **Sheraton**, **Marriott**, **Ramada**, **Hyatt** and **Holiday Inn**. Some of these chains operate more than one hotel in each city and designate one location as the flagship facility. These tend to offer their best rooms at higher prices. Call the hotel's free number to ask about the range of rates and availability.

Chateau Marmont on Sunset Boulevard *(see p513)*

TIPPING

THE HOTEL PORTER will often carry your bags to your room on arrival and load up your car on departing. A tip of $1–$2 per bag is fair for this service. If the hotel has valet parking, a tip of 15–20 per cent of the parking charge should be given to the driver only when you leave. Room service also requires a 15–20 per cent tip. A $2–$5 tip for maid service, especially after a long stay, is acceptable.

RESORTS

WHETHER A RESORT has less than 100 rooms or close to 300, the cottages, villas and grounds are always arranged to encourage privacy. Resorts have all the services of a hotel, but are spread over larger grounds.

The key to a quality resort is the range of indoor and outdoor facilities that are on offer, be it horse riding, tennis courts, golf courses, Olympic-size swimming pools, yoga instruction, full-service health spa or a four-star restaurant. A holiday at a resort is a destination in itself – the natural setting and range of on-site activities will more than hold your attention. Stays in resorts are expensive but for both relaxation and sports they are worth every penny.

You may want to choose a resort based on location – wine country, oceanside, mountain hideaway or urban retreat. California has many such hidden treasures and some of the best are listed on pages 508–37.

Sign over small chain hotel

San Diego Marriott Hotel, on San Diego Bay

Historic Mendocino Hotel *(see p532)*

MOTELS

INEXPENSIVE ROADSIDE motels sprang up in California in the 1950s, as a product of an increasingly car-orientated lifestyle. Motels offer minimal facilities – double, queen or king-size beds, television, telephone, tea and coffee and bathroom facilities. There is always ample parking for cars and many motels also have outdoor swimming pools – a necessity for travellers in California's summertime heat. Some have kitchen facilities and most offer non-smoking rooms. Check with the motel to see if they allow pets.

There are a number of popular motel chains throughout the state that have a reputation for clean rooms and good service at inexpensive prices. These include **Best Western**, **Quality Inn**, **Motel 6** and **Travelodge**. Rates range from $30–$65 a night.

HISTORIC INNS

RICH IN regional history, these inns are often all that remain of late 19th-century buildings in many of California's small towns. As well as reflecting local history, some inns also have their own story to tell, having been, perhaps, a hunting and fishing lodge, a stern-wheeler riverboat, a Victorian mansion, or a hideaway for Hollywood movie stars in earlier times. Whatever their heritage, they all share a unique architecture and ambience. Many such inns, built during the era of railway expansion in the West,

have achieved protected status, and cannot be demolished or architecturally altered.

Similar to bed-and-breakfast hotels in atmosphere, historic inns are larger, with 20–100 rooms. Most serve complimentary continental breakfast and afternoon snacks of cake or biscuits. For more information, contact **California Historic Country Inns**.

Smaller lodgings, many also with a claim to historical significance, may comprise small, individual cabins with kitchen facilities for a self-catering holiday. Very rarely do these inns have on-site restaurants, cafés or room service. The majority of them allow you to bring along pets, many have outdoor swimming pools and larger ones may also have tennis courts. Check in advance whether smoking is allowed in the cabins – some inns in California now pride themselves on providing guests with a completely smoke-free environment.

BED-AND-BREAKFAST ACCOMMODATION

MOST BED-AND-BREAKFASTS in California were originally private homes built many years ago and retain the charm of a bygone era. In addition to breakfast, afternoon snacks or evening drinks may also be available. Prices range from $60–$175 a night. Ask whether the room has its own bathroom. There is often a two-night minimum stay, especially in peak season.

Libraries, living rooms, landscaped gardens and swimming pools are common features of bed-and-breakfasts. The manager is often the owner and can provide details of local history and sights. See pages 508–37 for a range of bed-and-breakfasts or contact **Bed-and-Breakfast California**.

Casa Laguna Bed-and-Breakfast in Laguna Beach *(see p517)*

SELF-CATERING

WHILE MANY small inns and lodges may offer kitchen facilities, there is nothing like staying in a private home to gain a real flavour of a specific city or town. There are

Deetjen's Big Sur Inn *(see p536)*

Big Bear Log Cabin, near Lake Arrowhead

two ways you can arrange this type of accommodation. The first is to rent an apartment or house from a real estate agency. Every city and town in the state has at least one, if not several, estate agencies that specialize in holiday rental property. These agencies will quote rental rates by the night, week, month or even longer. Prices per week can range anywhere between $300–$3,000, depending on location and size of the rented property. You will have to pay a cleaning deposit which is refundable when you leave. For the widest choice of properties, it is best to make reservations at least one month in advance. Contact any town's Chamber of Commerce for details of agencies.

Another option is to arrange a house exchange with a Californian resident. **Intervac US** is part of a worldwide home exchange network and publishes quarterly directories of people willing to exchange their homes for yours during the holidays. Fees to obtain or be listed in this directory range from $65–$85 per year. The network does not match people up; arrangements are made by the individuals.

YOUTH HOSTELS

THIS IS THE least expensive accommodation option in California. Hostels offer clean, modern facilities, often in picturesque locations (including lighthouses, on national parkland and mountain hideaways). They offer dormitory-style,

single-sex sleeping arrangements, although some do have one or two private rooms available only to married couples. Most hostels also provide kitchen facilities.

Despite the name, youth hostels in the United States are not only for the young. There are also a number of Elder Hostels, catering for senior citizens who opt for budget travel. Contact **American Youth Hostels** for a full list of accommodations.

CAMPING AND CARAVANS

CARAVANS and tent campers are always welcome in California's national and state park system (*see p576*). There is also a large network of privately run camp sites with a range of facilities for caravanning vehicles, such as electricity hook-up, water supply, disposal stations, picnic areas and grocery shops.

Camping in Yosemite National Park *(see pp472–5)*

(*see p576*)

DIRECTORY

CHAIN HOTELS

Hilton
((800) 445-8667.

Holiday Inn
((800) 465-4329.

Hyatt
((800) 233-1234.

ITT Sheraton
((800) 325-3535.

Marriott
((800) 228-9290.

Ramada
((800) 272-6232.

Westin
((800) 228-3000.

CHAIN MOTELS

Best Western
((800) 528-1234.

Motel 6
((800) 466-8356.

Quality Inn
((800) 228-5151.

Travelodge
((800) 578-7878.

HISTORIC INNS

California Historic Country Inns
313 W Carmel Valley Rd,
PO Box 568,
Carmel Valley, CA 93924.
((408) 659-1415.

BED-AND-BREAKFAST

Bed-and-Breakfast California
PO Box 420009,
San Francisco.
((415) 479-1913.

SELF-CATERING

Intervac US
PO Box 590504,
San Francisco,
CA 94159.
((415) 435-3497.

YOUTH HOSTELS

American Youth Hostels
312 Mason St,
San Francisco,
CA 94102.
((415) 788-5604.

Choosing a Hotel

THE HOTELS in this guide have been selected across a wide price range for their excellent facilities and locations. Many also have a recommended restaurant. The chart lists the hotels by region, starting with Los Angeles; the colour-coded thumb tabs indicate the regions covered on each page. For restaurant listings, see pp544–75.

	NUMBER OF ROOMS	RESTAURANT	CHILDREN'S FACILITIES	GARDEN/TERRACE	SWIMMING POOL
LOS ANGELES					
AIRPORT: *Los Angeles Airport Hilton and Towers* $$ 5711 W Century Blvd, CA 90045. **Road map** inset A. ▐ (310) 410-4000; (800) 445-8667. FAX (310) 410-6250. Located next to the airport, this huge hotel caters mostly for business travellers. Excellent facilities. 🚌 24 📺 ⅖ 🅿 🍴 🏊	1100	●	▨	●	▨
AIRPORT: *Sheraton Los Angeles Airport Hotel* $$ 6101 W Century Blvd, CA 90045. **Road map** inset A. ▐ (310) 642-1111; (800) 445-7999. FAX (310) 645-1414. This corporate chain hotel offers inexpensive week-end packages. Free airport shuttle every five minutes. 🚌 24 📺 ⅖ 🅿 🍴 🏊	610	●	▨		▨
AIRPORT: *Wyndham Hotel at Los Angeles Airport* $$ 6225 West Century Blvd, CA 90045. ▐ (310) 670-9000; (800) 327-8321. FAX (310) 670-7852. A luxury business hotel next to the airport with comfortable, soundproof rooms. Service is excellent. 🚌 📺 ⅖ 🅿 🍴 🏊	591	●	▨		
BEL AIR: *Summit Hotel Bel-Air* $$$ 11461 Sunset Blvd, CA 90049. **Road map** inset A. ▐ (310) 476-6571; (800) 468-3541. FAX (310) 471-6310. This resort-style hotel with spacious rooms is set in landscaped grounds; it offers tennis and a spa. 🚌 📺 ⅖ 🅿 🍴 🏊	162	●	▨	▨	▨
BEL AIR: *Hotel Bel-Air* $$$$$ 701 Stone Canyon Rd, CA 90077. **Map** 4 A2. ▐ (310) 472-1211; (800) 648-4097. FAX (310) 476-5890. Some rooms have open fires at this glamorous resort-style hotel (*see p91*) with villas set in lush gardens. 🚌 24 📺 ⅖ 🅿 🏊	92	●	▨	▨	▨
BEVERLY HILLS: *Beverly Carlton* $$ 9400 W Olympic Blvd, CA 90212. **Map** 5 F4. ▐ (310) 277-5221; (800) 535-4715. FAX (310) 277-4928. This friendly 1940s Art Deco hotel near Rodeo Drive (*see p90*) is pleasantly furnished with large beds; double rooms have separate sitting areas. There is a fully kosher restaurant. 🚌 📺 ⅖ 🅿 🏊	88	●	▨	▨	▨
BEVERLY HILLS: *Summit Hotel Rodeo Drive* $$$ 360 N Rodeo Drive, CA 90210. **Map** 5 F3. ▐ (310) 273-0300; (800) 468-3541. FAX (310) 859-8730. This hotel is prettily furnished, light and sunny. Guests can also use the amenities at the Summit Hotel Bel-Air. 🚌 📺 ⅖ 🅿 🏊	86	●	▨		▨
BEVERLY HILLS: *Beverly Hilton* $$$$ 9876 Wilshire Blvd, CA 90210. **Map** 5 E4. ▐ (310) 274-7777; (800) 445-8667. FAX (310) 285-1313. This large corporate hotel has spacious rooms with views of LA. Many rooms have private patios. 🚌 24 📺 ⅖ 🅿 🍴 🏊	581	●	▨	●	▨
BEVERLY HILLS: *Beverly Hills Hotel and Bungalows* $$$$$ 9641 Sunset Blvd, CA 90210. ▐ (310) 276-2251; (800) 283-8885. FAX (310) 281-2905. At this luxury complex set in tropical gardens (*see p91*), some rooms have a kitchen and private terrace. 🚌 24 📺 ⅖ 🅿 🏊	194	●	▨	●	▨
BEVERLY HILLS: *Peninsula Beverly Hills* $$$$$ 9882 Little Santa Monica Blvd, CA 90212. **Map** 5 E4. ▐ (310) 551-2888; (800) 462-7899. FAX (310) 788-2319. Celebrities come to be pampered at this luxurious five-star hotel with rooms, suites and villas. 🚌 24 📺 ⅖ 🅿 🏊	196	●	▨	●	▨
BEVERLY HILLS: *Regent Beverly Wilshire* $$$$$ 9500 Wilshire Blvd, CA 90212. **Map** 5 F4. ▐ (310) 275-5200; (800) 545-4000. FAX (310) 274-2851. The palatial splendour of this famous hotel opposite Rodeo Drive attracts many celebrities (*see p87*). The rooms – and baths – are enormous, and there are full spa facilities. 🚌 24 📺 ⅖ 🅿 🏊	278	●	▨	●	▨
CENTURY CITY: *Century Plaza Hotel and Tower* $$$$$ 2025 Ave of the Stars, CA 90067. **Map** 5 D5. ▐ (310) 277-2000; (800) 228-3000. FAX (310) 5513355. The service is friendly at this large, elegant hotel. Rooms in both of the buildings have panoramic views of the city. 🚌 📺 ⅖ 🅿 🏊	1032	●	▨	●	▨

Price categories for a standard double room per night, inclusive of service charges and any additional taxes, such as local sales tax: ⑤ under \$100 ⑤⑤ \$100–\$150 ⑤⑤⑤ \$150–\$200 ⑤⑤⑤⑤ \$200–\$250 ⑤⑤⑤⑤⑤ over \$250	**RESTAURANT** Hotel restaurant or dining room usually open to non-residents unless otherwise stated. **CHILDREN'S FACILITIES** Indicates child cots and/or a baby-sitting service available. A few hotels also provide children's portions and high chairs in the restaurant. **GARDEN/TERRACE** Hotels with a garden, courtyard or terrace, often providing tables for eating outside. **SWIMMING POOL** Hotel with indoor or outdoor swimming pool.	NUMBER OF ROOMS	RESTAURANT	CHILDREN'S FACILITIES	GARDEN/TERRACE	SWIMMING POOL

CENTURY CITY: *Park Hyatt* ⑤⑤⑤⑤⑤
2151 Ave of the Stars, CA 90067. **Map 5 E5.** ((310) 277-2777. FAX (310) 785-9240. A business hotel with good facilities and city views. Limousines can be provided for shopping or theatre visits. 🚗 24 TV & P 🍴 🏊

| | | 367 | ● | ● | ● | ● |

DOWNTOWN: *Best Western Dragon Gate Inn* ⑤
818 N Hill St, CA 90012. **Map 11 F2.** ((213) 617-3077; (800) 282-9999. FAX (213) 680-3753. This comfortable, basic hotel in Chinatown attracts business travellers during the week and families at weekends. 🚗 TV & P 🏊

| | | 50 | ● | | | |

DOWNTOWN: *The Inn at 657* ⑤
657 W 23rd St, CA 90007. **Road map** inset A. ((213) 741-2200; (800) 347-7512. These one- and two-bedroom suites have kitchens and private entrances that open onto garden or balcony areas. All are non-smoking, and the price includes full breakfast and local telephone calls. 🚗 TV P

| | | 6 | | | ● | |

DOWNTOWN: *Wilshire Royale Hotel* ⑤
2619 Wilshire Blvd, CA 90057. **Map 10 A3.** ((213) 387-5311; (800) 421-8072. FAX (213) 380-8174. This beautiful Art Deco hotel is ten minutes from Downtown. The 65 suites have kitchen facilities. 🚗 TV & P 🏊

| | | 200 | ● | ● | ● | ● |

DOWNTOWN: *Best Western, The Mayfair* ⑤⑤
1256 W 7th St, CA 90017. **Map 10 C4.** ((213) 484-9789; (800) 821-8682. FAX (213) 484-2769. This smart, friendly hotel has rooms, suites and services well suited to the business traveller. 🚗 24 TV & P 🏊

| | | 295 | ● | | ● | |

DOWNTOWN: *Figueroa Hotel* ⑤⑤
939 S Figueroa St, CA 90015. **Map 10 C5.** ((213) 627-8971; (800) 421-9092. FAX (213) 689-0305. This friendly hotel near the convention centre was originally a YWCA. Rooms vary in size and are decorated in Spanish Colonial style. The exquisite garden has fruit trees and cacti. 🚗 TV & P 🏊

| | | 285 | ● | | ● | ● |

DOWNTOWN: *Holiday Inn LA Downtown* ⑤⑤
750 S Garland Ave, CA 90017. **Map 10 B4.** ((213) 628-5242; (800) 628-5240. FAX (213) 628-1201. Half the rooms have king-size beds at this chain hotel one block west of the Financial District. 🚗 TV & P 🏊

| | | 205 | ● | | | ● |

DOWNTOWN: *Los Angeles Athletic Club* ⑤⑤
431 W 7th St, CA 90014. **Map 11 D5.** ((213) 625-2211; (800) 421-8777. FAX (213) 689-1194. Built as a club in 1904, this hotel has luxurious Victorian-style rooms and racquetball courts. 🚗 TV & P 🍴 🏊

| | | 72 | ● | ● | | ● |

DOWNTOWN: *Miyako Inn and Spa* ⑤⑤
328 E 1st St, CA 90012. **Map 11 F4.** ((213) 617-2000; (800) 228-6596. FAX (213) 617-2700. This hotel in Little Tokyo has a karaoke lounge and separate spa facilities for men and women. The spacious rooms are furnished in traditional American style. Children under 12 stay free. 🚗 24 TV & P 🏊

| | | 174 | ● | | | |

DOWNTOWN: *Sheraton Grande* ⑤⑤⑤
333 S Figueroa St, CA 90071. **Map 11 D4.** ((213) 617-1133; (800) 325-3535. FAX (213) 613-0291. Complimentary butler service and limousine service to Downtown sights are offered at this luxury hotel. 🚗 24 TV & P 🍴 🏊

| | | 469 | ● | ● | ● | ● |

DOWNTOWN: *Biltmore* ⑤⑤⑤⑤
506 S Grand Ave, CA 90071. **Map 11 D4.** ((213) 624-1011; (800) 245-8673. FAX (213) 612-1545. The palatial splendour of the foyer extends to the large comfortable rooms and suites at this luxury hotel *(see p118)*. There is a spa and complimentary continental breakfast. 🚗 24 TV & P 🍴 🏊

| | | 690 | ● | ● | ● | ● |

DOWNTOWN: *Hyatt Regency* ⑤⑤⑤⑤
711 S Hope St, CA 90017. **Map 11 D4.** ((213) 683-1234; (800) 233-1234. FAX (213) 629-3230. Floor-to-ceiling windows give good views from the comfortable rooms of this four-star hotel in the Broadway Plaza. 🚗 TV & P 🍴 🏊

| | | 485 | ● | ● | ● | ● |

For key to symbols see back flap

Price categories for a standard double room per night, inclusive of service charges and any additional taxes, such as local sales tax:

⑤ under $100
⑤⑤ $100–$150
⑤⑤⑤ $150–$200
⑤⑤⑤⑤ $200–$250
⑤⑤⑤⑤⑤ over $250

RESTAURANT
Hotel restaurant or dining room usually open to non-residents unless otherwise stated.

CHILDREN'S FACILITIES
Indicates child cots and/or a baby-sitting service available. A few hotels also provide children's portions and high chairs in the restaurant.

GARDEN/TERRACE
Hotels with a garden, courtyard or terrace, often providing tables for eating outside.

SWIMMING POOL
Hotel with indoor or outdoor swimming pool.

	NUMBER OF ROOMS	RESTAURANT	CHILDREN'S FACILITIES	GARDEN/TERRACE	SWIMMING POOL
DOWNTOWN: *New Otani Hotel and Garden* ⑤⑤⑤⑤ 120 S Los Angeles St, CA 90012. **Map 11 E4.** ☎ *(213) 629-1200; (800) 273-2294.* FAX *(213) 622-0980.* Some rooms are furnished in traditional Japanese style at this de luxe hotel; there is a sauna and health spa.	424	●	●		
DOWNTOWN: *Westin Bonaventure Hotel and Suites* ⑤⑤⑤⑤ 404 S Figueroa St, CA 90071. **Map 10 C5.** ☎ *(213) 624-1000; (800) 228-3000.* FAX *(213) 612-4797.* Rooms are large and comfortable at this immense hotel, made up of five glass towers built around a central atrium *(see p118).* It has all the facilities of a luxury hotel	1368	●		●	●
DOWNTOWN: *Wyndham Checkers Hotel* ⑤⑤⑤⑤ 535 Grand Ave, CA 90071. **Map 11 4D.** ☎ *(213) 624-0000; (800) 996-3426.* FAX *(213) 626-9906.* With four-star ratings, this hotel is extremely luxurious – there are even thermometers in the marble baths. It has a spa and also offers free limousine service around Downtown.	173	●		●	●
GLENDALE: *Chariot Inn Motel* ⑤ 1118 E Colorado St, CA 91205. **Road map** inset A. ☎ *(818) 507-9600; (800) 458-4080.* FAX *(818) 507-9774.* The large rooms have queen- or king-size beds; some have whirlpool baths. Continental breakfast is included.	30			●	●
HOLLYWOOD: *Best Western Hollywood Plaza* ⑤ 2011 N Highland Ave, CA 90068. **Map 2 B4.** ☎ *(213) 851-1800; (800) 232-4353.* FAX *(213) 851-1836.* This chain hotel, two blocks from Hollywood Boulevard, has comfortable rooms with refrigerators.	82	●		●	●
HOLLYWOOD: *Clarion Hollywood Roosevelt* ⑤ 7000 Hollywood Blvd, CA 90028. **Map 2 B4.** ☎ *(213) 466-7000; (800) 950-7667.* FAX *(213) 462-8056.* A beautiful old brick hotel recently restored to its original splendour. Often used for glamourous celebrity parties.	321	●	●		●
HOLLYWOOD: *Hollywood Orchid Suites* ⑤ 1753 Orchid Ave, CA 90028. **Map 2 B4.** ☎ *(213) 874-9678; (800) 537-3052.* FAX *(213) 874-9931.* This small hotel is a converted apartment building so the rooms are very spacious and some have kitchens.	40			●	●
HOLLYWOOD: *Norja Bed-and-Breakfast Inn* ⑤ 1139 S Tremaine Ave, CA 90019. **Map 8 A5.** ☎ *(213) 933-3652.* Built in 1929, this romantic bed-and-breakfast inn is situated in a quiet residential street. The rooms are all very comfortable and decorated with fresh flowers. The inn is convenient for all the local sights. �& *limited.*	5		●	●	
HOLLYWOOD: *Ramada Inn* ⑤ 1160 N Vermont, CA 90029. **Road map** inset A. ☎ *(213) 660-1788; (800) 272-6232.* FAX *(213) 660-8069.* This well-run chain hotel near Universal Studios has suites and rooms, free continental breakfast and a Jacuzzi.	98		●		●
HOLLYWOOD: *Beverly Garland's Holiday Inn* ⑤⑤ 4222 Vineland Ave, CA 91602. **Road map** inset A. ☎ *(818) 980-8000; (800) 238-3759.* FAX *(818) 766-0112.* This hotel offers comfortable rooms with private balconies or patios, a spa, tennis courts and laundry.	255	●		●	●
INGLEWOOD: *Los Angeles Adventura* ⑤ 4200 W Century Blvd, CA 90304. **Road map** inset A. ☎ *(310) 419-0999; (800) 852-0011.* FAX *(310) 412-9100.* This friendly hotel, close to the airport, has large, comfortable rooms and offers free breakfast, afternoon tea, airport shuttle and tours to Venice Beach, shops, casinos and golf courses.	150	●	●		●
LONG BEACH: *Inn of Long Beach* ⑤ 185 Atlantic Ave, CA 90802. **Road map** inset A. ☎ *(310) 435-3791; (800) 230-7500.* FAX *(310) 436-7510.* This pleasant motel with comfortable rooms offers a spa and free continental breakfast.	46		●		●

LONG BEACH: *Super 8 Motel* $ 49
4201 E Pacific Hwy, CA 90804. **Road map** inset A. 【 *(310) 597-7701; (800) 800-8000.*
FAX *(310) 494-7373.* This reliable budget motel has king-size beds. The half-suites have kitchens. Rates include breakfast. 🛏 📺 ♿ 🅿 🍴 📧

LONG BEACH: *Best Western Golden Sails* $$ 172
6285 E Pacific Coast Hwy, CA 90803. **Road map** inset A. 【 *(310) 596-1631; (800)*
762-5333. **FAX** *(310) 594-0623.* This hotel overlooking the marina features whirlpool baths and free golf. Rates include breakfast and dinner. 🛏 📺 🅿 🍴 📧

LONG BEACH: *Lord Mayor's Inn* $$ 5
435 Cedar Ave, CA 90802. **Road map** inset A. 【 *(310) 436-0324.* Set in a restored Edwardian house, this bed-and-breakfast inn is near downtown Long Beach. The pretty rooms are all furnished with antiques. 🛏 🅿 📧

LONG BEACH: *Renaissance Long Beach Hotel* $$ 374
111 E Ocean Blvd, CA 90802. **Road map** inset A. 【 *(310) 437-5900; (800) 468-3571;*
(800) 228-9898. **FAX** *(310) 499-2509.* Some of the spacious rooms have ocean views at this luxury hotel in the business district. 🛏 📺 ♿ 🅿 🍴 📧

LONG BEACH: *Hotel Queen Mary* $$$ 365
1126 Queen's Hwy, CA 90802. **Road map** inset A. 【 *(310) 435-3511; (800) 437-*
7934. **FAX** *(310) 437-4531.* The famous ocean liner's first-class staterooms have been updated and restored *(see p133).* Breakfast is included. 🛏 📺 ♿ 🅿 📧

LONG BEACH: *Hyatt Regency* $$$$ 520
200 S Pine Ave, CA 90802. **Road map** inset A. 【 *(310) 491-1234; (800) 233-*
1234. **FAX** *(310) 983-1491.* The rooms in this corporate hotel *(see p129)* have views of Long Beach harbour.Weekend discounts available. 🛏 📺 ♿ 🅿 📧

MALIBU: *Casa Malibu Inn on the Beach* $$ 21
22752 Pacific Coast Highway, CA 90265. **Road map** inset A. 【 *(310) 456-2219; (800)*
831-0858. **FAX** *(310) 456-5418.* This hotel is built on its own private beach. Some rooms have balconies, fireplaces, VCRs and kitchens. 🛏 📺 🅿 📧

MALIBU: *Malibu Beach Inn* $$$ 47
22878 Pacific Coast Hwy, CA 90265. **Road map** inset A. 【 *(310) 456-6444; (800)*
462-5428. **FAX** *(310) 456-1499.* All rooms have a balcony overlooking the beach at this stylish luxury hotel with Mexican tiled floors. 🛏 24 📺 ♿ 🅿 📧

MARINA DEL REY: *Mansion Inn* $$ 43
327 Washington Blvd, CA 90291. **Road map** inset A. 【 *(310) 821-2557; (800) 828-*
0688. **FAX** *(310) 827-0289.* This hotel near the beach, on the border of Venice, has country-style rooms and free continental breakfast. 🛏 📺 ♿ 🅿 📧

MARINA DEL REY: *Marina del Rey Hotel* $$ 158
13534 Bali Way, CA 90292. **Road map** inset A. 【 *(310) 301-1000; (800) 882-4000.*
FAX *(310) 301-8167.* Most of the rooms and a gazebo at this resort-style hotel overlook the marina. Free airport shuttles are provided. 🛏 📺 ♿ 🅿 📧

MONROVIA: *Holiday Inn* $ 174
924 W Huntington Drive, CA 91016. **Road map** inset A. 【 *(818) 357-1900;*
(800) 465-4329. **FAX** *(818) 359-1386.* Close to shops and sights, this hotel has spacious rooms and free morning coffee and muffins. 🛏 📺 ♿ 🅿 📧

NAPLES: *Seal Beach Inn* $$$ 20
212 5th St, CA 90740. **Road map** inset A. 【 *(310) 493-2416; (800) 443-3292.*
FAX *(310) 799-0483.* All rooms at this luxurious inn, one block from the beach, are furnished with antiques. Breakfast is included. 🛏 📺 ♿ 🅿 📧

PASADENA: *Comfort Inn Eagle Rock* $ 58
2300 W Colorado Blvd, CA 90041. **Road map** inset A. 【 *(213) 256-1199; (800) 221-*
2222. **FAX** *(213) 255-7768.* This basic inn near the Rose Bowl *(see p148)* offers continental breakfast, a Jacuzzi and a discount for senior citizens. 🛏 📺 🅿 📧

PASADENA: *White Horse Estate* $ 6
2170 Los Lomas Rd, Duarte, CA 91010. **Road map** inset A. 【 *(818) 358-0798; (800) 653-*
8086. **FAX** *(818) 793-6409.* This lovely, antique-filled house just east of Pasadena offers full breakfast and a fireplace in every room. 🛏 📺 ♿ 🅿 📧

PASADENA: *Artist's Inn* $$ 5
1038 Magnolia St, CA 91030. **Road map** inset A. 【 *(818) 799-5668.* **FAX** *(818) 799-*
5678. Each room in this bed-and-breakfast inn is furnished with a specific artist in mind. The colourful Van Gogh Room is the most exciting. 🛏 📺 ♿ 🅿 📧

Price categories for a standard double room per night, inclusive of service charges and any additional taxes, such as local sales tax:
- $ under $100
- $$ $100–$150
- $$$ $150–$200
- $$$$ $200–$250
- $$$$$ over $250

RESTAURANT
Hotel restaurant or dining room usually open to non-residents unless otherwise stated.

CHILDREN'S FACILITIES
Indicates child cots and/or a baby-sitting service available. A few hotels also provide children's portions and high chairs in the restaurant.

GARDEN/TERRACE
Hotels with a garden, courtyard or terrace, often providing tables for eating outside.

SWIMMING POOL
Hotel with indoor or outdoor swimming pool.

	Price	Number of Rooms	Restaurant	Children's Facilities	Garden/Terrace	Swimming Pool
PASADENA: *Pasadena Hotel* 76 Fair Oaks Ave, CA 91103. **Road map** inset A. **(** (818) 568-8172; (800) 653-8886. **FAX** (818) 793-6409. All the rooms have VCRs but the bathrooms are shared at this bed-and-breakfast inn in Old Pasadena (*see pp150–1*). The service is of a high standard and the owners are very welcoming. TV	$$	12	●			
PASADENA: *The Bissell House Bed and Breakfast* 201 Orange Grove Ave, CA 91030. **Road map** inset A. **(** (818) 441-3535. **FAX** (818) 441-3671. Built in 1887 on the famous "Millionaires' Row", the rooms have Victorian décor and claw-foot baths. TV P	$$$	4			●	
PASADENA: *Ritz Carlton Huntingdon Hotel* 1401 S Oak Knoll Ave, CA 91106. **Road map** inset A. **(** (818) 568-3900; (800) 241-3333. **FAX** (818) 568-3700. Dating from 1907, this luxury hotel, set in a residential area, has elegant rooms. A wooden bridge between the two wings overlooks the Japanese gardens in the courtyard. 24 TV P	$$$$	383	●	●	●	●
SANTA MONICA: *Belle Bleu Inn By The Sea* 1670 Ocean Ave, CA 90401. **Road map** inset A. **(** (310) 393-2363. **FAX** (310) 393-1063. This small bed-and-breakfast hotel on the beach has lovely ocean views from some rooms. All rooms are non-smoking. TV P	$	20			●	
SANTA MONICA: *Best Western Gateway Hotel* 1920 Santa Monica Blvd, CA 90404. **Road map** inset A. **(** (310) 829-9100; (800) 528-1234. **FAX** (310) 829-9211. This downtown hotel is excellent value, with spacious rooms, free airport shuttle and sun terraces. TV P	$	122	●			
SANTA MONICA: *Hotel Carmel by the Sea* 201 Broadway, CA 90401. **Road map** inset A. **(** (310) 451-2469; (800) 445-8695. **FAX** (310) 393-4180. This 1920s hotel near the beach has spacious rooms and suites with ocean views. Children under 17 stay free. TV P	$	110				
SANTA MONICA: *Doubletree Guest Suites* 1707 4th St, CA 90401. **Road map** inset A. **(** (310) 395-3332; (800) 424-2900. **FAX** (310) 452-7399. The large two-room suites at this luxury hotel near the beach have fabulous views. There is also a games room. TV P	$$	253	●	●	●	●
SANTA MONICA: *Radisson Huntley Hotel* 1111 2nd St, CA 90403. **Road map** inset A. **(** (310) 394-5454; (800) 333-3333. **FAX** (310) 458-9776. Just one block from the beach, this hotel has spacious rooms, good views and facilities for business travellers. TV P	$$	213	●	●		
SANTA MONICA: *Holiday Inn Bay View Plaza* 530 W Pico Blvd, CA 90405. **Road map** inset A. **(** (310) 399-9344; (800) 465-4329. **FAX** (310) 399-2504. Five minutes from the beach, this hotel has comfortable rooms, most with balconies. It offers a free airport shuttle, two Jacuzzis and tours to local sights and Tijuana (*see p255*). TV P	$$$	309	●	●	●	●
SANTA MONICA: *Miramar Sheraton Hotel* 101 Wilshire Blvd, CA 90401. **Road map** inset A. **(** (310) 576-7777; (800) 325-3535. **FAX** (310) 458-7912. This glamorous hotel built on the cliffs overlooking the ocean has a health centre and many other amenities. Betty Grable was discovered here – singing in the lounge. 24 TV P	$$$	302	●	●	●	●
SANTA MONICA: *The Georgian* 1415 Ocean Ave, CA 90401. **Road map** inset A. **(** (310) 395-9945; (800) 538-8147. **FAX** (310) 451-3374. This four-diamond hotel with large rooms and suites, on the beach by Palisades Park, has been here since 1931. TV P	$$$	84	●	●	●	
SANTA MONICA: *Loews Santa Monica Beach Hotel* 1700 Ocean Ave, CA 90401. **Road map** inset A. **(** (310) 458-6700. **FAX** (310) 458-6761. An elegant four-star hotel on the beach, within walking distance of Santa Monica pier. The ocean views are wonderful. 24 TV P	$$$$$	343	●	●		●

SANTA MONICA: *The Shutters* $$$$$ 198
1 Pico Blvd, CA 90405. **Road map** inset A. 【 *(310) 458-0030; (800) 334-9000.*
FAX *(310) 458-4589.* Luxury and glamour abound at this four-star hotel on the beach. Rooms are spacious and many have balconies.

UNIVERSAL CITY: *Hilton Universal* $$$ 420
555 Universal Terrace Parkway, CA 91608. **Road map** inset A. 【 *(818) 506-2500; (800) 445-8667.* **FAX** *(818) 509-2058.* A high-rise hotel overlooking Universal Studios. Rooms are spacious. Book ahead in summer.

UNIVERSAL CITY: *Sheraton Universal* $$$$ 440
333 University Terrace Parkway, CA 91608. **Road map** inset A. 【 *(818) 980-1212; (800) 325-3535.* **FAX** *(818) 985-4980.* Free shuttles run to Universal Studios and City Walk from this busy, recently refurbished corporate hotel.

VAN NUYS: *Travelodge* $ 74
6909 Sepulveda Blvd, CA 91405. **Road map** inset A. 【 *(818) 787-5400; (800) 578-7878.* **FAX** *(818) 782-0239.* Children under 12 stay free at this two-diamond motel in the San Fernando Valley with large rooms and breakfast.

VENICE BEACH: *The Cadillac* $ 41
8 Dudley Ave, CA 90291. **Road map** inset A. 【 *(310) 399-8876.* **FAX** *(310) 399-4536.* This gorgeous Art Deco hotel attracts a young, smart crowd. It is right on the beach, with a sauna, pool tables and sun terrace.

VENICE BEACH: *The Venice Beach House* $$ 9
15 30th Ave, CA 90291. **Road map** inset A. 【 *(310) 823-1966.* **FAX** *(310) 823-1842.* This is a delightful bed-and-breakfast inn a short walk from the beach. The guest rooms are beautifully furnished with antiques.

WEST HOLLYWOOD: *Best Western Sunset Plaza Hotel* $$$ 89
8400 Sunset Blvd, CA 90069. **Map** 6 C1. 【 *(213) 654-0750; (800) 528-1234.* **FAX** *(213) 650-6146.* Ideally located on busy Sunset Boulevard, this elegant chain hotel has pleasant rooms and a secluded pool area.

WEST HOLLYWOOD: *Hyatt Hotel* $$$ 262
8401 Sunset Blvd, CA 90069. **Map** 6 C1. 【 *(213) 656-1234.* **FAX** *(213) 650-7024.* This chain hotel, with a rooftop pool, is close to the House of Blues night-club *(see p459)*. The rooms are modern and clean.

WEST HOLLYWOOD: *Chateau Marmont* $$$$ 62
8221 Sunset Blvd, CA 90046. **Map** 1 B5. 【 *(213) 656-1010; (800) 242-8328.* **FAX** *(213) 655-5311.* Decorated in 1940s style *(see p100)*, the Chateau's rooms, suites and cottages are a haven for celebrities.

WEST HOLLYWOOD: *Mondrian Hotel* $$$$ 224
8440 Sunset Blvd, CA 90069. **Map** 6 C1. 【 *(213) 650-8999; (800) 525-8029.* **FAX** *(213) 650-5215.* Part of a small chain, this elegant hotel *(see p99)* is popular with musicians. Rooms have city views.

WEST HOLLYWOOD: *Argyle Hotel* $$$$$ 64
8358 Sunset Blvd, CA 90069. **Map** 6 C1. 【 *(213) 654-7100; (800) 225-2637.* **FAX** *(213) 654-1004.* Originally built as apartments for film stars *(see p99)*, the rooms here are Italian Art Deco in style.

WESTWOOD: *Hilgard House Hotel* $ 47
927 Hilgard Ave, CA 90024. **Map** 4 A4. 【 *(310) 208-3945; (800) 826-3934.* **FAX** *(310) 208-1972.* This busy hotel, close to UCLA, is decorated in old European style and offers breakfast and special business rates.

WESTWOOD: *Hotel del Capri* $$ 81
10587 Wilshire Blvd, CA 90024. **Map** 4 B4. 【 *(310) 474-3511; (800) 444-6835.* **FAX** *(310) 470-9999.* A basic, modern hotel within walking distance of the UCLA campus and restaurants. Some rooms have kitchen facilities.

WESTWOOD: *Doubletree Hotel Westwood* $$$ 295
10740 Wilshire Blvd, CA 90024. **Map** 4 B4. 【 *(310) 475-8711; (800) 472-8556.* **FAX** *(310) 475-5220.* The rooms in this hotel have Jacuzzis and Victorian-style decor. Facilities include a games room for children.

WESTWOOD: *Westwood Marquis Hotel and Gardens* $$$$ 258
930 Hilgard Ave, CA 90024. **Map** 4 A4. 【 *(310) 208-8765; (800) 323-7500.* **FAX** *(310) 824-0355.* Rooms in this four-star hotel have every amenity. A buffet breakfast is included.

Price categories for a standard double room per night, inclusive of service charges and any additional taxes, such as local sales tax: ⑤ under $100 ⑤⑤ $100–$150 ⑤⑤⑤ $150–$200 ⑤⑤⑤⑤ $200–$250 ⑤⑤⑤⑤⑤ over $250	**RESTAURANT** Hotel restaurant or dining room usually open to non-residents unless otherwise stated. **CHILDREN'S FACILITIES** Indicates child cots and/or a baby-sitting service available. A few hotels also provide children's portions and high chairs in the restaurant. **GARDEN/TERRACE** Hotels with a garden, courtyard or terrace, often providing tables for eating outside. **SWIMMING POOL** Hotel with indoor or outdoor swimming pool.	**NUMBER OF ROOMS**	**RESTAURANT**	**CHILDREN'S FACILITIES**	**GARDEN/TERRACE**	**SWIMMING POOL**

SOUTH CENTRAL CALIFORNIA

BAKERSFIELD: *Courtyard by Marriott* ⑤ 3601 Marriott Drive, CA 93308. **Road map** C5. ℂ *(805) 324-6660; (800) 321-2211.* **FAX** *(805) 324-1185.* The service is excellent at this modern chain hotel, which is well suited to business travellers.	146	●	▦	●	▦
CAMBRIA: *Best Western Fireside Inn* ⑤ 6700 Moonstone Beach Drive, CA 93428. **Road map** B5. ℂ *(805) 927-8661; (800) 528-1234.* **FAX** *(805) 927-8584.* This basic waterfront hotel has large rooms, large beds, gas fires and continental breakfast.	46		▦		▦
CAMBRIA: *Burton Drive Inn (Silvia's)* ⑤⑤ 4022 Burton Drive, CA 93428. **Road map** B5. ℂ *(805) 927-5125.* Run by a friendly English couple, this modern inn with large suites is in a bustling downtown street. Breakfast is served in your room.	8			●	
CAMBRIA: *Blue Whale Inn* ⑤⑤⑤ 6736 Moonstone Beach Drive, CA 93428. **Road map** B5. ℂ *(805) 927-4647.* **FAX** *(805) 927-4647.* Built on a bluff overlooking the sea, every room in this top-rated bed-and-breakfast inn has an ocean view. You can observe seals and grey whales through a telescope.	6			●	
MONTECITO: *Montecito Inn* ⑤⑤⑤⑤ 1295 Coast Village Rd, CA 93108. **Road map** C5. ℂ *(805) 969-7854; (800) 843-2017.* **FAX** *(805) 969-0623.* This Mediterranean-style hotel near the beach was built in 1928 by film star Charlie Chaplin.	60	●	▦		▦
MONTECITO: *San Ysidro Ranch* ⑤⑤⑤⑤⑤ 900 San Ysidro Lane, CA 93108. **Road map** C5. ℂ *(805) 969-5046; (800) 368-6788.* **FAX** *(805) 565-1995.* Luxury cottages, each with a wood stove or fireplace, lie hidden from view in this stunning mountain resort. This is the perfect place to get away from it all.	42	●	▦	●	▦
MORRO BAY: *Blue Sail Inn* ⑤ 851 Market Ave, CA 93442. **Road map** B5. ℂ *(805) 772-2766; (800) 336-0707.* **FAX** *(805) 772-8406.* Even the best rooms with fireplaces are a bargain here. There is an observation deck for viewing ships at sea.	48		▦	●	
MORRO BAY: *Embarcadero Inn* ⑤ 456 Embarcadero, CA 93442. **Road map** B5. ℂ *(805) 772-2700; (800) 292-7625.* **FAX** *(805) 772-2700.* All rooms face the bay in this modern hotel; most have balconies and fireplaces. Continental breakfast is included.	32		▦		
MORRO BAY: *Inn at Morro Bay* ⑤⑤ 60 State Park Rd, CA 93442. **Road map** B5. ℂ *(805) 772-5651; (800) 321-9566.* **FAX** *(805) 772-4779.* Built beside the bay, this hotel has de luxe country-style rooms with fireplaces and balconies.	96	●	▦		▦
PASO ROBLES: *Paso Robles Inn* ⑤⑤ 1103 Spring St, CA 93446. **Road Map** B5. ℂ *(805) 238-2660.* **FAX** *(805) 238-4707.* This small, basic hotel, which has recently been refurbished, is ideally located halfway between Los Angeles and San Franscisco.	106	●		●	▦
SAN LUIS OBISPO: *Lamplighter Inn* ⑤ 1604 Monterey St, CA 93401. **Road map** B5. ℂ *(805) 547-7777; (800) 547-7787.* **FAX** *(805) 547-7787.* Accommodation in this motel includes a cottage that sleeps several and family suites, some with full kitchens.	40				▦
SAN LUIS OBISPO: *Garden Street Inn* ⑤⑤ 1212 Garden St, CA 93401. **Road map** B5. ℂ *(805) 545-9802.* Built in 1860, this restored Victorian house is furnished with original antiques. Some rooms have claw-foot baths or fireplaces and Jacuzzis.	13			●	

SAN LUIS OBISPO: *The Madonna Inn* $$$ 109
100 Madonna Rd, CA 93405. **Road map** B5. (*(805) 543-3000; (800) 543-9666.*
FAX *(805) 543-1800.* All the rooms have themes – for example, the Caveman Room is made entirely out of rock. Book in advance. 🛏 TV 🚫 P 🍽

SANTA BARBARA: *Inn at the Harbor* $ 43
433 W Montecito St, CA 93101. **Road map** C5. (*(805) 963-7851; (800) 626-1986.*
FAX *(805) 962-9428.* Just two blocks from the beach, rooms in this rustic-style hotel are set around a lovely tropical-style courtyard. 🛏 TV 🚫 P 🍽

SANTA BARBARA: *The Schooner Inn* $ 96
533 State St, CA 93101. **Road map** C5. (*(805) 965-4572.* **FAX** *(805) 962-2412.*
The original cage elevator is still the centrepiece of this hotel, built in 1926, five blocks from the beach. Breakfast is included. TV 🚫 P 🍽

SANTA BARBARA: *Glenborough Inn* $$ 11
1327 Bath St, CA 93101. **Road map** C5. (*(805) 966-0589; (800) 962-0589.*
FAX *(805) 564-8610.* This very romantic bed-and-breakfast inn is in three Victorian houses near Downtown. It has a hot tub. P 🍽

SANTA BARBARA: *El Encanto Hotel and Garden Villas* $$$ 84
1900 Lasuen Rd, CA 93103. **Road map** C5. (*(805) 687-5000; (800) 346-7039.*
FAX *(805) 687-3903.* This grand old hotel in the hills has stunning ocean views. The rooms are in bungalows and cottages. 🛏 TV 🚫 P 🍽

SANTA BARBARA: *Olive House* $$$ 6
1604 Olive St, CA 93101. **Road map** C5. (*(805) 962-4902; (800) 786-6422.*
FAX *(805) 899-2754.* In a quiet area, this beautifully restored 1904 house has rooms with lovely views; some have terraces and hot tubs. 🛏 P 🍽

SANTA BARBARA: *Tiffany Inn* $$$ 7
1323 De La Vina St, CA 93101. **Road map** C5. (*(805) 963-2283; (800) 999-5672.* **FAX** *(805) 962-0994.* Dating from 1898, this beautifully restored house has antiques and pretty views. Breakfast is included. 🛏 P 🍽

SANTA BARBARA: *Upham Hotel* $$$ 50
1404 De La Vina, CA 93101. **Road map** C5. (*(805) 962-0058; (800) 727-0876.*
FAX *(805) 963-2825.* This downtown landmark was built in 1871. The rooms have Victorian décor and there is a good restaurant *(see p552).* 🛏 TV P 🍽

SANTA BARBARA: *Four Seasons Biltmore* $$$$$ 234
1260 Channel Drive, CA 93108. **Road map** C5. (*(805) 969-2261; (800) 332-3442.* **FAX** *(805) 969-4682.* A luxury resort since the 1920s, the rooms, suites and cottages are set in coastal gardens. 🛏 24 TV 🚫 P 🍽 🍴

SANTA PAULA: *Fern Oaks Inn* $$ 4
1025 Ojai Rd, CA 93060. **Road map** C5. (*(805) 525-7747.* This stunning 1920s Mission Revival-style inn is set in idyllic landscaped gardens. The Casablanca Room has its own private sun porch. 🛏 P 🍽

SIMI VALLEY: *Simi Valley Travelodge* $ 96
2550 Erringer Rd, CA 93065. **Road map** C5. (*(805) 584-6006; (800) 433-6030.*
FAX *(805) 527-5629.* All rooms in this bargain hotel have cable TV and VCRs. There is also a sauna. Children under 17 stay free. 🛏 TV 🚫 P 🍽

SIMI VALLEY: *Clarion Hotel* $$$ 120
1775 Madera Rd, CA 93065. **Road map** C5. (*(805) 584-6300.* **FAX** *(805) 527-7969.* The emphasis is on personal attention at this friendly hotel, which offers continental breakfast, special rates and discounts. 🛏 TV 🚫 P 🍽

SOLVANG: *Royal Copenhagen Motel* $ 48
1579 Mission Drive, CA 93463. **Road map** C5. (*(805) 688-5561; (800) 624-6604.*
FAX *(805) 688-7029.* Rooms in this motel resemble those in traditional Danish houses and overlook Solvang's Danish-style village square. 🛏 TV 🚫 P 🍽

SOLVANG: *Storybook Inn* $$ 9
409 1st St, CA 93463. **Road map** C5. (*(805) 688-1703; (800) 786-7925.*
FAX *(805) 688-0953.* Rooms at this pretty bed-and-breakfast inn are named after Hans Christian Andersen stories. Breakfast is included. 🛏 🚫 P 🍽

SOLVANG: *Petersen Village Inn* $$$ 40
1576 Mission Drive, CA 93463. **Road map** C5. (*(805) 688-3121; (800) 321-8985.*
FAX *(805) 688-5732.* Canopied beds and antique furnishings add charm to this family-owned inn. A perfect place for a romantic getaway. 🛏 TV 🚫 P 🍽

	NUMBER OF ROOMS	RESTAURANT	CHILDREN'S FACILITIES	GARDEN/TERRACE	SWIMMING POOL

Price categories for a standard double room per night, inclusive of service charges and any additional taxes, such as local sales tax:
$ under $100
$$ $100–$150
$$$ $150–$200
$$$$ $200–$250
$$$$$ over $250

RESTAURANT
Hotel restaurant or dining room usually open to non-residents unless otherwise stated.

CHILDREN'S FACILITIES
Indicates child cots and/or a baby-sitting service available. A few hotels also provide children's portions and high chairs in the restaurant.

GARDEN/TERRACE
Hotels with a garden, courtyard or terrace, often providing tables for eating outside.

SWIMMING POOL
Hotel with indoor or outdoor swimming pool.

ORANGE COUNTY

		NUMBER OF ROOMS	RESTAURANT	CHILDREN'S FACILITIES	GARDEN/TERRACE	SWIMMING POOL
ANAHEIM: *Castle Inn and Suites* 1734 S Harbour Blvd, CA 92802. **Road map** D6. ((714) 774-8111; (800) 227-8530. FAX (714) 956-4736. The bizarre castle-style exterior belies the comfortable but ordinary rooms. It is just opposite Disneyland *(see pp222–5)*. 🛏 TV 🚹 P 🅿	$	200		■	●	■
ANAHEIM: *Crystal Suites Hotel* 1752 S Clementine St, CA 92802. **Road map** D6. ((714) 535-7773; (800) 992-0823. FAX (714) 776-9073. Benefits here include breakfast, a free shuttle and early entry to Disneyland. Children under three stay free. 🛏 TV 🚹 P 🅿	$	130		■	●	■
ANAHEIM: *Anaheim Marriott Hotel* 700 W Convention Way, CA 92802. **Road map** D6. ((714) 750-8000; (800) 228-9290. FAX (714) 750-9100. This high-rise, child-friendly hotel near Disneyland has a video arcade, sauna and laundry facilities. 🛏 TV 🚹 P 🅿	$$$	1033	●	■	●	■
ANAHEIM: *Disneyland Hotel* 1150 W Cerritos, CA 92802. **Road Map** D6. ((714) 956-6582. FAX (714) 778-6600. This large hotel with guest rooms or cottages is linked to Disneyland by monorail. The emphasis is on entertainment, with lots to see and do within the hotel, including six restaurants. 🛏 TV 🚹 P 🅿	$$$$	1136	●	■	●	■
AVALON: *Hotel Metropole* Metropole Market Place, Crescent Ave, Catalina Island, CA 90704. **Road map** C6. ((310) 510-1884; (800) 541-8528. FAX (310) 510-2534. This Mediterranean-style hotel on the beach offers spacious rooms and breakfast. 🛏 24 TV 🚹 🅿	$$$	48		■	●	
AVALON: *Hotel Vista Del Mar* 417 Crescent Ave, Catalina Island, CA 90704. **Road map** C6. ((310) 510-1452; (800) 601-3836. FAX (310) 510-2917. Rooms have fridges and fireplaces at this luxury hotel overlooking the bay. Breakfast is included. 🛏 TV 🅿	$$$	15		■	●	
COSTA MESA: *Sandpiper Motel* 1967 Newport Blvd, CA 92627. **Road map** D6. ((714) 645-9137; (800) 648-9137. FAX (714) 650-1702. This super-value motel, close to Disneyland, has large, comfortable rooms, continental breakfast and weekly rates. 🛏 TV 🚹 P 🅿	$	44				
COSTA MESA: *Wyndham Garden Hotel* 3350 Ave of the Arts, CA 92626. **Road map** D6. ((714) 751-5100; (800) 996-3426. FAX (714) 751-0129. This comfortable hotel is close to beaches, jogging trails, Disneyland and Orange County Airport. 🛏 TV 🚹 P 🅿	$	203	●	■	●	■
COSTA MESA: *Residence Inn* 881 W Baker St, CA 92626. **Road map** D6. ((714) 241-8800; (800) 331-3131. FAX (714) 546-4308. Suites here have private entrances, a balcony or patio and a kitchen. Continental breakfast is included. 🛏 TV 🚹 P 🅿	$$	144		■	●	■
COSTA MESA: *Country Side Inn and Suites* 325 Bristol St, CA 92626. **Road map** D6. ((714) 549-0300; (800) 322-9992. FAX (714) 662-0828. Rooms in this European-style hotel have antiques and four-poster beds. Disneyland is nearby. 🛏 TV 🚹 P 🅿	$$$	300	●	■	●	■
DANA POINT: *Blue Lantern Inn* 34343 Street of the Blue Lantern, CA 92629. **Road map** D6. ((714) 661-1304; (800) 950-1236. FAX (714) 496-1483. This romantic Victorian bed-and-breakfast inn is perched on a cliff overlooking the harbour. Rooms have fireplaces and Jacuzzis; some have terraces. Ask about package deals. 🛏 TV 🚹 P 🅿	$$$	29		■	●	
DANA POINT: *Ritz-Carlton Laguna Niguel* 1 Ritz-Carlton Drive, CA 92629. **Road map** D6. ((714) 240-2000; (800) 241-3333. FAX (714) 240-0829. A path leads to the ocean from this large luxury hotel. Rooms are tasteful and have coastal views. 🛏 24 TV 🚹 P 🅿	$$$$	393	●	■	●	■

HUNTINGTON BEACH: *Quality Inn* $$
800 Pacific Coast Hwy, CA 92648. **Road map** D6. **C** *(714) 536-7500; (800) 228-5151.* **FAX** *(714) 536-6846.* This plain hotel near the beach offers fabulous sunset views, oceanfront suites, a rooftop spa and breakfast. 📺 & 🅿 🗐
50

HUNTINGTON BEACH: *The Waterfront Hilton Beach Resort* $$$$
21100 Pacific Coast Hwy, CA 92648. **Road map** D6. **C** *(714) 960-7873; (800) 822-7873.* **FAX** *(714) 960-3791.* The spacious rooms at this four-diamond resort, opposite the beach, have balconies with ocean views. 🛏 📺 & 🅿 🗐
290

LAGUNA BEACH: *Casa Laguna Inn* $$
2510 S Coast Hwy, CA 92651. **Road map** D6. **C** *(714) 494-2996; (800) 233-0449.* **FAX** *(714) 494-5309.* Situated on the oceanfront, this is a Mission-style bed-and-breakfast inn. Rooms have private patios – there is even an aviary. 🛏 📺 🅿 🗐
20

LAGUNA BEACH: *Hotel Laguna* $$
425 S Coast Hwy, CA 92651. **Road map** D6. **C** *(714) 494-1151; (800) 524-2927.* **FAX** *(714) 497-2163.* The town's oldest hotel, right on the beach, has smaller-than-average rooms but excellent service and great views. 🛏 📺 & 🅿 🗐
65

LAGUNA BEACH: *Surf and Sand Hotel* $$$$$
1555 S Coast Hwy, CA 92651. **Road map** D6. **C** *(714) 497-4477; (800) 524-8621.* **FAX** *(714) 494-2897.* The de luxe rooms, suites and penthouses at this luxury hotel on the beach have whirlpool baths, balconies and ocean views. There is also a superb restaurant. 🛏 📺 & 🅿 🗐
150

NEWPORT BEACH: *The Sutton Place Hotel* $$$
4500 MacArthur Blvd, CA 92660. **Road map** D6. **C** *(714) 476-2001; (800) 243-4141.* **FAX** *(714) 476-0153.* The emphasis is on luxury at this four-star hotel. Some rooms have balconies and ocean views. 🛏 24 📺 & 🅿 🗐
435

NEWPORT BEACH: *Four Seasons Hotel* $$$$$
690 Newport Beach Center Drive, CA 92660. **Road map** D6. **C** *(714) 759-0808; (800) 332-3442.* **FAX** *(714) 760-8073; 759-0568.* You'll be treated like royalty at this luxurious five-diamond hotel. Some rooms have terraces and ocean views. There are tennis courts and golf courses nearby. 🛏 24 📺 & 🅿 🗐
285

SUNSET BEACH: *Harbor Inn* $
16912 Pacific Coast Hwy, 90742. **Road map** D6. **C** *(310) 592-4770; (800) 546-4770.* **FAX** *(310) 592-3547.* This bed-and-breakfast inn near the beach has extra-large rooms and discounts for longer stays. 🛏 📺 & 🅿 🗐
25

TWO HARBORS: *Banning House Lodge* $
Two Harbors, Catalina Island, CA 90704. **Road map** C6. **C** *(310) 510-2800.* **FAX** *(310) 510-0244.* This intimate inn was built in 1910 as a hunting lodge. Rooms have antiques and wood floors; larger modern rooms in the out-buildings have big picture windows. Breakfast is included. 🛏 & 🗐
11

SAN DIEGO COUNTY

CARLSBAD: *Best Western Beach Terrace Inn* $$
2775 Ocean St, CA 92008. **Road map** D6. **C** *(760) 729-5951; (800) 433-5415.* **FAX** *(760) 729-1078.* Rooms here have kitchens, private terraces and balconies overlooking the ocean. The beach is just minutes away. 🛏 📺 🗐
49

CARLSBAD: *Pelican Cove Inn* $$
320 Walnut Ave, CA 92008. **Road map** D6. **C** *(760) 434-5995.* This delightful New England-style bed-and-breakfast inn is near the beach. The rooms have antiques, fireplaces and private entrances. 🛏 📺 & 🅿 🗐
8

CORONADO: *Loews Coronado Bay Resort* $$$
4000 Coronado Bay Rd, CA 92118. **Road map** D6. **C** *(619) 424-4000; (800) 815-6397.* **FAX** *(619) 424-4400.* Rooms have bay views at this four-star resort set on a peninsula. There are tennis courts and a marina. 🛏 24 📺 & 🅿 🗐
440

CORONADO: *Hotel del Coronado* $$$$$
1500 Orange Ave, CA 92118. **Road map** D6. **C** *(619) 435-6611; (800) 468-3533.* **FAX** *(619) 522-8238.* This grand Victorian hotel *(see p245)* on the beach has been updated with modern annexes and a spa. 🛏 24 📺 & 🅿 🗐
700

CORONADO: *Le Meridien* $$$$$
2000 2nd St, CA 92118. **Road map** D6. **C** *(619) 435-3000; (800) 285-4660.* **FAX** *(619) 435-3032.* This luxury four-star hotel, built on the edge of the beach, has modern rooms and spa facilities. 🛏 24 📺 & 🅿 🗐
300

For key to symbols see back flap

Price categories for a standard double room per night, inclusive of service charges and any additional taxes, such as local sales tax:

$ under $100
$$ $100–$150
$$$ $150–$200
$$$$ $200–$250
$$$$$ over $250

RESTAURANT
Hotel restaurant or dining room usually open to non-residents unless otherwise stated.

CHILDREN'S FACILITIES
Indicates child cots and/or a baby-sitting service available. A few hotels also provide children's portions and high chairs in the restaurant.

GARDEN/TERRACE
Hotels with a garden, courtyard or terrace, often providing tables for eating outside.

SWIMMING POOL
Hotel with indoor or outdoor swimming pool.

	Price	NUMBER OF ROOMS	RESTAURANT	CHILDREN'S FACILITIES	GARDEN/TERRACE	SWIMMING POOL
DEL MAR: *Del Mar Hilton* 15575 Jimmy Durante Blvd, CA 92014. **Road map** D6. 📞 (619) 792-5200; (800) 445-8667. **FAX** (619) 792-9538. Guests can play tennis, golf or relax in the Jacuzzi at this Tudor-style hotel near the racetrack. 🛏 📺 ♿ 🅿 🌐	$	245	●			●
DEL MAR: *Clarion Carriage House Del Mar Inn* 720 Camino Del Mar, CA 92014. **Road map** D6. 📞 (619) 755-9765; (800) 451-4515. **FAX** (619) 792-8196. A quiet hotel situated on bluffs overlooking the ocean. It has pretty rooms and English-style gardens. 🛏 📺 ♿ 🅿 🌐	$$	80		●	●	●
DEL MAR: *L'Auberge Del Mar Resort and Spa* 1540 Camino Del Mar, CA 92014. **Road map** D6. 📞 (619) 259-1515; (800) 553-1336. **FAX** (619) 755-4940. Set on the beach, this New England-style hotel has elegant décor and sunset views, tennis and a spa. 🛏 📺 ♿ 🅿 🍴 🌐	$$$	120	●	●	●	●
ENCINITAS: *Radisson Inn* 85 Encinitas Blvd, CA 92024. **Road map** D6. 📞 (760) 942-7455; (800) 333-3333. **FAX** (760) 632-9481. Rooms at this small hotel have balconies with either ocean or city views. Complimentary continental breakfast. 🛏 📺 ♿ 🅿 🌐	$$	89	●	●		●
JULIAN: *Julian Hotel* 2032 Main St, CA 92036. **Road map** D6. 📞 (760) 765-0201; (800) 734-5854. This historic Victorian inn is the oldest operating hotel in California. Most rooms have open fires. Full breakfast and afternoon tea are included. 🌐	$$	18			●	
LA JOLLA: *Embassy Suites Hotel* 4550 La Jolla Village Drive, CA 92122. **Road map** D6. 📞 (619) 453-0400; (800) 362-2779. **FAX** (619) 453-4226. This modern hotel with two-room suites is perfect for families. It offers breakfast and a games room. 🛏 📺 ♿ 🅿 🌐	$$	335	●	●		●
LA JOLLA: *Marriot and La Jolla* 4240 La Jolla Village Drive, CA 92037. **Road map** D6. 📞 (619) 587-1414; (800) 228-9290. **FAX** (619) 546-8518. This high-rise hotel is 2 miles (3.2 km) from the beaches and near many downtown attractions. 🛏 📺 ♿ 🅿 🌐	$$	360	●	●	●	●
LA JOLLA: *La Jolla Beach and Tennis Club* 2000 Spindrift Drive, CA 92037. **Road map** D6. 📞 (619) 454-7126; (800) 624-2582. **FAX** (619) 456-3805. This small Mediterranean-style resort hotel has retained its 1920s charm. Some rooms have balconies. It has a private beach, tennis courts, a golf course and croquet lawn. 🛏 📺 ♿ 🅿 🍴 🌐	$$$	90	●	●	●	●
LA JOLLA: *La Valencia Hotel* 1132 Prospect St, CA 92037. **Road map** D6. 📞 (619) 454-0771; (800) 451-0772. **FAX** (619) 456-3921. This Spanish-style luxury hotel is located near the beach and the many local art galleries. The rooms are sumptuous and there is a wonderful hotel terrace. 🛏 24 📺 ♿ 🅿 🍴 🌐	$$$	100	●	●	●	●
LA JOLLA: *The Bed and Breakfast Inn at La Jolla* 7753 Draper Avenue, CA 92037. **Road map** D6. 📞 (619) 456-2066; (800) 582-2466. **FAX** (619) 456-1510. The building, designed in 1913 by Irving Gill, has been named an Historic Site. Some of the elegantly furnished rooms have ocean views and two-person baths. 🛏 ♿ 🅿 🌐	$$$	16			●	
RANCHO SANTA FE: *Rancho Valencia Resort* Box 9126, 5921 Valencia Circle, CA 92067. **Road map** D6. 📞 (619) 756-1123; (800) 548-3664. **FAX** (619) 756-0165. This glamorous resort hotel is set in parkland, close to the beach and the racetrack. It has four golf courses, tennis courts, hiking trails, mountain bikes and spa facilities. 🛏 24 📺 ♿ 🅿 🌐	$$$$$	43	●	●	●	●
SAN DIEGO: *Beach Cottages* 4255 Ocean Blvd, CA 92109. **Road map** D6. 📞 (619) 483-7440. **FAX** (619) 273-9365. This family hotel on the beach offers cottages, suites, apartments and rooms. Most of the rustic-style rooms have kitchens. 🛏 📺 ♿ 🅿 🌐	$	78		●	●	

SAN DIEGO: *Beach Haven Inn* $ 23
4740 Mission Blvd, CA 92109. **Road map** D6. ☎ (619) 272-3812; (800) 831-6323.
FAX (619) 272-3532. This modern inn near the beach and Sea World *(see p250)* has family suites with kitchenettes and cable TV. ♨ TV 㒵 P ⌨

SAN DIEGO: *Blom House* $ 4
1372 Minden Drive, CA 92111. **Road map** D6. ☎ (619) 467-0890; (800) 797-2566.
FAX (619) 467-0890. This friendly bed-and-breakfast inn has cosy rooms and a hot tub on the wooden terrace overlooking the city. ♨ TV P ⌨

SAN DIEGO: *Hotel Circle Inn and Suites* $ 200
2201 Hotel Circle South, CA 92108. **Road map** D6. ☎ (619) 291-2711; (800) 621-1341. FAX (619) 542-1227. This family-style motel, near all the sights, has a spa and sun terrace. Some of the suites have kitchens. ♨ TV 㒵 P ⌨

SAN DIEGO: *Travelodge* $ 307
3350 Kemper St, Old Town, CA 92110. **Road map** D6. ☎ (619) 223-3395; (800) 219-6824. FAX (619) 224-9248. Features at this chain hotel include a sun terrace and sports bar. Rooms are large; some have balconies. ♨ TV 㒵 P ⎚ ⌨

SAN DIEGO: *Wyndham Garden Hotel* $ 180
5975 Lusk Blvd, CA 92121. **Road map** D6. ☎ (619) 558-1818; (800) 996-3426.
FAX (619) 558-0421. North of Downtown, this hotel is perfect for the business traveller on a budget. Buffet breakfast is included. ♨ TV 㒵 P ⎚ ⌨

SAN DIEGO: *Heritage Park Bed and Breakfast Inn* $$ 10
2470 Heritage Park Row, Old Town, CA 92110. **Road map** D6. ☎ (619) 299-6832; (800) 995-2470. FAX (619) 299-9465. Rooms in these two Victorian houses are furnished in period style. Classic films are shown in the parlour. ♨ 㒵 P ⌨

SAN DIEGO: *San Diego Mission Valley Hilton* $$ 350
901 Camino Del Rio South, CA 92108. **Road map** D6. ☎ (619) 543-9000; (800) 733-2332. FAX (619) 296-9561. This modern 13-storey hotel is close to Downtown. Rooms are comfortable and well equipped. ♨ TV 㒵 P ⎚ ⌨

SAN DIEGO: *Hyatt Regency* $$$ 875
1 Market Place, CA 92101. **Road map** D6. ☎ (619) 232-1234; (800) 233-1234.
FAX (619) 233-6464. Views of the city and ocean are fabulous from the top of this modern hotel (the city's tallest building). ♨ 24 TV 㒵 P ⎚ ⌨

SAN DIEGO: *The Rancho Bernardo Inn* $$$ 287
17550 Bernardo Oaks Drive, CA 92128. **Road map** D6. ☎ (619) 487-1611; (800) 542-6096. FAX (619) 675-8501. This four-star hacienda-style hotel offers golf, tennis, spa or meal package deals and seven outdoor Jacuzzis. Dine at the award-winning El Bizocho *(see p556)* restaurant. ♨ TV 㒵 P ⌨

SAN DIEGO: *US Grant Hotel* $$$ 280
326 Broadway, CA 92101. **Road map** D6. ☎ (619) 232-3121; (800) 237-5029.
FAX (619) 232-3626. This four-diamond hotel downtown was built by a former US president, Ulysses Grant, in 1910 in honour of his father. It is furnished with reproduction antiques. ♨ 24 TV 㒵 P ⎚ ⌨

SAN DIEGO: *Marriott Hotel* $$$$ 1354
333 W Harbor Drive, CA 92101. **Road map** D6. ☎ (619) 234-1500; (800) 228-9290.
FAX (619) 234-8678. A 25-storey luxury hotel next to San Diego Bay with exceptional outdoor landscaping and facilities. ♨ 24 TV 㒵 P ⎚ ⌨

TIJUANA: *Grand Hotel Tijuana* $ 423
4500 Blvd Agua Caliente, C.P. 22420. **Road map** D6. ☎ (011-52-66) 81-70-00. FAX (011-52-66) 81-70-16. This is a large hotel complex with twin towers. Facilities include tennis courts and Jacuzzis. ♨ 24 TV 㒵 P ⎚ ⌨

THE INLAND EMPIRE AND LOW DESERT

BIG BEAR LAKE: *Grey Squirrel Resort* $ 17
39372 Big Bear Blvd (PO Box 1711), CA 92315. **Road map** D5. ☎ (909) 866-4335. FAX (909) 866-6271. Charming one- to three-bedroom cottages with open fires dot the mountain landscape at this year-round lake resort. ♨ TV P ⌨

BIG BEAR LAKE: *Hillcrest Lodge* $ 12
40241 Big Bear Blvd (PO Box 3945), CA 92315. **Road map** D5. ☎ (909) 866-7330; (800) 843-4449. FAX (909) 866-1171. Mountain ski slopes surround these motel rooms, cabins and suites near Big Bear village *(see pp264–5)*. Rooms with Jacuzzis and open fires are available. ♨ TV 㒵 P ⌨

<table>
<tr><td colspan="2">

Price categories for a standard double room per night, inclusive of service charges and any additional taxes, such as local sales tax:

$ under $100
$$ $100–$150
$$$ $150–$200
$$$$ $200–$250
$$$$$ over $250

</td><td>

RESTAURANT
Hotel restaurant or dining room usually open to non-residents unless otherwise stated.

CHILDREN'S FACILITIES
Indicates child cots and/or a baby-sitting service available. A few hotels also provide children's portions and high chairs in the restaurant.

GARDEN/TERRACE
Hotels with a garden, courtyard or terrace, often providing tables for eating outside.

SWIMMING POOL
Hotel with indoor or outdoor swimming pool.

</td></tr>
</table>

	NUMBER OF ROOMS	RESTAURANT	CHILDREN'S FACILITIES	GARDEN/TERRACE	SWIMMING POOL
BIG BEAR LAKE: *Apples Bed & Breakfast* $$$ 42430 Moonridge Rd, CA 92315. **Road map** D5. ☎ *(909) 866-0903.* FAX *(909) 866-6524.* The rustic, Victorian-style rooms are named after varieties of apples at this luxury inn, surrounded by pine trees. 🏠 📺 ♿ 🅿 🍽	12	●	■		■
BIG BEAR LAKE: *Windy Point Inn* $$$ 39015 N Shore Drive (PO Box 375), Fawnskin, CA 92333. **Road map** D5. ☎ *(909) 866-2746.* FAX *(909) 866-1593.* This intimate, contemporary inn has award-winning architecture and spectacular views of the ski slopes. Rooms have open fires. Midweek discounts are available. 🏠 📺 🅿 🍽	3			●	
BORREGO SPRINGS: *Palms at Indian Head* $ 2220 Hoberg Rd, CA 92004. **Road map** D6. ☎ *(760) 767-7788; (800) 519-2624.* FAX *(760) 767-9717.* A former playground hideaway for the Hollywood elite, this hotel lies at the foot of Indian Head Mountain, near hiking trails. 🏠 📺 🅿 🍽	10	●		●	■
BORREGO SPRINGS: *La Casa Del Zorro* $$$ 3845 Yaqui Pass Rd (PO Box 127), CA 92004. **Road map** D6. ☎ *(760) 767-5323; (800) 824-1884.* FAX *(760) 767-4782.* A romantic, well-appointed oasis in the Anza-Borrego Desert State Park *(see p266)*. The lodgings range from large rooms to four-bedroom cottages, most with open fires. 🏠 📺 ♿ 🅿 🍽	77	●	■	●	■
DESERT HOT SPRINGS: *Two Bunch Palms* $$$ 67425 Two Bunch Palms Trail, CA 92240. **Road map** D6. ☎ *(760) 329-8791; (800) 472-4334.* FAX *(760) 329-1317.* Al Capone had a famous hideout here among the palms, mineral pools and secluded bungalows of this glamorous resort. No-one under 18 is allowed. It is closed in August. 🏠 📺 🅿 🍽	45	●		●	■
IDYLLWILD: *Fern Valley Inn* $ 25240 Fern Valley Rd (PO Box 116), CA 92549-0116. **Road map** D6. ☎ *(909) 659-2205.* FAX *(909) 659-2630.* Rooms in this charming Idyllwild getaway, set in expansive grounds, have hand-sewn quilts and antiques. 🏠 📺 ♿ 🅿 🍽	11			●	■
IDYLLWILD: *Idyllwild Inn* $ 54300 Village Center Drive (PO Box 515), CA 92549. **Road map** D6. ☎ *(909) 659-2552.* Service is first rate at Idyllwild's oldest and largest inn, dating from 1904. There are miles of nearby hiking trails. 🏠 📺 ♿ 🅿 🍽	28		■	●	
IDYLLWILD: *Creekstone Inn* $$ 54950 Pine Crest Ave (PO Box 1897), CA 92549. **Road map** D6. ☎ *(909) 659-3342; (800) 409-2127.* Formerly a general store, this landmark bed-and-breakfast inn has pleasant, rustic-style rooms. 🏠 ♿ 🅿 🍽	9			●	
INDIAN WELLS: *Indian Wells Resort Hotel* $$$ 76–661 Hwy 111, CA 92210. **Road map** D6. ☎ *(760) 345-6466; (800) 248-3220.* FAX *(760) 772-5083.* Set at the base of the Santa Rosa Mountains, by the 11th tee of a golf course, rooms here have spectacular views and oriental touches; the two-room suites have large sunken baths. 🏠 📺 ♿ 🅿 🍽	152	●	■		■
INDIAN WELLS: *Hyatt Grand Champions Resort* $$$$ 44600 Indian Wells Lane, CA 92210. **Road map** D6. ☎ *(760) 341-1000.* FAX *(760) 568-2236.* This luxurious resort is a golfer's paradise, with the use of two world-famous championship golf courses. 🏠 📺 ♿ 🅿 🍽	336	●	■	●	■
INDIO: *Best Western Indio Date Tree Hotel* $ 81909 Indio Blvd, CA 92201. **Road map** D6. ☎ *(760) 347-3421; (800) 292-5599.* FAX *(760) 347-3421.* Popcorn is free at this hotel set in landscaped grounds with cacti and palms. Rates include continental breakfast. 🏠 📺 ♿ 🅿 🍽	120		■	●	■
LAKE ARROWHEAD: *Eagle's Landing Bed & Breakfast* $$ 27406 Cedarwood & Blue Jay 92317, Lake Arrowhead, CA 92352. **Road map** D5. ☎ *(909) 336-2642; (800) 835-5085.* These hospitable lodgings have stained glass, high ceilings, enormous windows and sweeping views. 🏠 📺 🅿 🍽	4			●	

PALM DESERT: *Shadow Mountain Resort and Racquet Club* $$$ 167
45–750 San Luis Rey, CA 92260. **Road map** D6. (760) 346-6123; (800) 472-3713.
FAX (760) 346-6518. This friendly hotel also has condominiums and villas.
Amenities include Jacuzzis, saunas and tennis courts.

PALM DESERT: *Marriott Desert Springs Resort and Spa* $$$$ 844
74855 Country Club Drive, CA 92260. **Road map** D6. (760) 341-2211; (800)
331-3112. FAX (760) 341-1739. Rooms have fabulous mountain views at this
enormous hotel, with two golf courses, tennis and a spa.

PALM SPRINGS: *Desert Lodge* $ 51
1177 S Palm Canyon Drive, CA 92264. **Road map** D6. (760) 325-1356; (800)
385-6343. FAX (760) 325-7124. This great bargain hotel has stunning mountain
views, a Jacuzzi, films and home-baked continental breakfast.

PALM SPRINGS: *Palm Springs Super 8 Lodge* $ 65
1900 N Palm Canyon Drive, CA 92262. **Road map** D6. (760) 322-3757; (800)
800-8000. FAX (760) 323-5290. This quiet hotel near Downtown is a good
choice for budget travellers. Breakfast is included.

PALM SPRINGS: *Spa Hotel and Casino* $$ 230
100 N Indian Canyon Drive, CA 92262. **Road map** D6. (760) 325-1461; (800)
854-1279. FAX (760) 325-3344. A natural hot mineral spring and 24-hour
casino are the highlights of this downtown hotel.

PALM SPRINGS: *Terra Cotta Inn* $$ 17
2388 E Raquet Club Rd, CA 92262. **Road map** D6. (760) 327-1504; (800) 786-
6938. FAX (760) 322-4169. This clothing-optional hotel has tropical décor, a
Jacuzzi, spa treatments, video library and free breakfast.

PALM SPRINGS: *Desert Shadows Inn* $$$ 74
1533 Chaparral Rd, CA 92262. **Road map** D6. (760) 325-6410; (800) 292-
9298. FAX (760) 327-7500. This luxury nudist resort has tennis courts and
Jacuzzis. Some rooms have balconies and patios.

PALM SPRINGS: *Hyatt Regency* $$$ 192
285 N Palm Canyon Drive, CA 92262. **Road map** D6. (760) 322-9000; (800)
233-1234. FAX (760) 322-6009. This luxury downtown hotel can arrange
golf and free tennis for guests at a nearby resort.

PALM SPRINGS: *Villa Royale* $$$ 33
1620 Indian Trail, CA 92264. **Road map** D6. (760) 327-2314. FAX (760) 322-3794.
This perfect romantic getaway does not welcome children. Each room is
decorated in the style of a different European country.

PALM SPRINGS: *Givenchy Hotel and Spa* $$$$$ 98
4200 E Palm Canyon Drive, CA 92264. **Road map** D6. (760) 770-5000; (800)
276-5000. FAX (760) 324-7280. This hotel is the epitome of understated elegance. It has a golf course, tennis courts and a spa.

PALM SPRINGS: *The Palm Springs Hilton Resort* $$$$ 260
400 E Tahquitz Canyon Way, CA 92262. **Road map** D6. (760) 320-6868; (800)
522-6900. FAX (760) 320-2126. Near Downtown, this hotel's sports facilities
include tennis courts and access to local golf courses.

RANCHO MIRAGE: *Ritz Carlton Rancho Mirage* $$$ 239
68900 Frank Sinatra Drive, CA 92270. **Road map** D6. (760) 321-8282; (800)
241-3333. FAX (760) 321-6928. This modern resort-style hotel is on a plateau
in the mountains. Rooms are large.

RANCHO MIRAGE: *Rancho Las Palmas Marriott Resort* $$$$ 450
41000 Bob Hope Drive, CA 92270. **Road map** D6. (760) 568-2727; (800) 458-
8786. FAX (760) 568-5845. This luxury resort is situated on three nine-hole
golf courses. Tennis and spa facilities are also available.

RIVERSIDE: *Historic Mission Inn* $$$ 233
3649 Mission Inn Ave, CA 92501. **Road map** D6. (909) 784-0300. FAX (909)
683-1342. Craftsmen built this elegant hotel in a variety of styles in 1888
(*see p264*). Some rooms have original furniture.

TWENTYNINE PALMS: *Tower Homestead Bed and Breakfast* $ 2
SE corner of Amboy Rd & Mojave Drive, CA 92277. **Road map** D5. (760) 367-
7936. This 100-year-old house, near Joshua Tree National Park (*see pp268–9*),
was moved here from Pasadena. The huge rooms have open fires.

For key to symbols see back flap

....

<table>
<tr><td colspan="2">

Price categories for a standard double room per night, inclusive of service charges and any additional taxes, such as local sales tax:
$ under $100
$$ $100–$150
$$$ $150–$200
$$$$ $200–$250
$$$$$ over $250

</td><td colspan="5">

RESTAURANT
Hotel restaurant or dining room usually open to non-residents unless otherwise stated.

CHILDREN'S FACILITIES
Indicates child cots and/or a baby-sitting service available. A few hotels also provide children's portions and high chairs in the restaurant.

GARDEN/TERRACE
Hotels with a garden, courtyard or terrace, often providing tables for eating outside.

SWIMMING POOL
Hotel with indoor or outdoor swimming pool.

</td></tr>
</table>

		NUMBER OF ROOMS	RESTAURANT	CHILDREN'S FACILITIES	GARDEN/TERRACE	SWIMMING POOL
	THE MOJAVE DESERT					
BARSTOW: *Best Western Desert Villa Motel* 1984 E Main St, CA 92311. **Road map** D5. ☎ *(760) 256-1781.* ⟨FAX⟩ *(760) 256-9265.* The 18 mini-suites (9 of which have an in-room whirlpool bath) make a perfect place for an extended stay in the desert. 🛏 📺 ♿ P 🍽	$	95	●	▦		▦
BARSTOW: *El Rancho Motor Court* 112 E Main St, CA 92311. **Road map** D5. ☎ *(760) 256-2401.* ⟨FAX⟩ *(760) 256-7421.* Built in 1947 entirely out of railway sleepers, this newly refurbished motel is a "must stop" on California's historic Route 66. Elaborate murals depict the famed highway and its surrounding desert life. 🛏 📺 P 🍽	$	100			●	
BARSTOW: *Holiday Inn* 1511 E Main St, CA 92311. **Road map** D5. ☎ *(760) 256-5673.* ⟨FAX⟩ *(760) 256-5917.* The rooms in this clean but basic chain hotel have queen-sized beds and some have whirlpool baths. Free morning newspapers. 🛏 📺 ♿ P 🍽	$	148	●	▦		▦
DEATH VALLEY: *Amargosa Hotel and Opera House* Death Valley Junction, CA 92328. **Road map** D4. ☎ *(760) 852-4441.* ⟨FAX⟩ *(760) 852-4138.* This 1920s hotel in an old mining town was refurbished by former ballerina Marta Becket, who performs cabaret shows in the small theatre. Rooms are air-conditioned; food and drinks are sold. 🛏 P 🍽	$	14		▦		
DEATH VALLEY: *Delight's Hot Spa* Tecopa Hot Springs Rd, Tecopa, CA 92389. **Road map** D4. ☎ *(619) 852-4343.* These clean cabins with kitchenettes retain the atmosphere of the 1940s. Healing mineral waters are found in four hot tubs. ♿ P	$	9				▦
DEATH VALLEY: *Shoshone Inn* Junction of SR127 & SR178, Shoshone, CA 92384. **Road map** D4. ☎ *(760) 852-4335.* ⟨FAX⟩ *(760) 852-4250.* This simple 1950s brick motel is on the border of Death Valley Park *(see pp280–3)*, with caves nearby. 🛏 📺 ♿ P 🍽	$	16	●		●	▦
DEATH VALLEY: *Stove Pipe Wells Village* Stove Pipe Wells, CA 92328. **Road map** D4. ☎ *(760) 786-2387.* ⟨FAX⟩ *(760) 786-2389.* No televisions or telephones make this rustic all-year resort near the Death Valley Sand Dunes *(see p281)* a perfect desert escape. 🛏 ♿ P 🍽	$	83	●	▦	●	▦
DEATH VALLEY: *Furnace Creek Ranch* 1 Main St (PO Box 1), CA 92328. **Road map** D4. ☎ *(760) 786-2345.* ⟨FAX⟩ *(760) 786-2514.* Children will enjoy the horse riding at this Californian ranch with stunning scenery and many de luxe features. 🛏 📺 P 🍽	$$	251	●	▦	●	▦
DEATH VALLEY: *Furnace Creek Inn* 1 Main St, CA 92328. **Road map** D4. ☎ *(760) 786-2345.* ⟨FAX⟩ *(760) 786-2514.* This marvellous, historic resort is one of the most stylish places in the desert, with spring-fed pools, tennis and golf. 🛏 24 📺 ♿ P 🍽	$$$$	68	●	▦	●	▦
EAST MOJAVE: *Hotel Nipton* 107355 Nipton Rd (HCL Box #357), CA 92364. **Road map** E5. ☎ *(760) 856-2335.* ⟨FAX⟩ *(760) 856-2352.* This rustic turn-of-the-century hotel is in Nipton, a historic gold-mining town with a population of 40. ♿ P 🍽	$	4			●	
LAKE HAVASU: *Hidden Palms Allsuite Inn* 2100 Swanson Ave, AZ 86403. **Road map** E5. ☎ *(520) 855-7144; (800) 254-5611.* ⟨FAX⟩ *(520) 855-2620.* The one-bedroom suites can accommodate four adults at this quiet inn, close to Lake Havasu *(see p278).* 🛏 📺 ♿ P 🍽	$	22		▦	●	▦
LAKE HAVASU: *London Bridge Resort* 1477 Queens Bay, AZ 86403. **Road map** E5. ☎ *(520) 855-0888.* ⟨FAX⟩ *(520) 855-2414.* Enjoy fine views of London Bridge *(see p278)* from this resort, with live music in the lounge and boats and jet skis for hire. 🛏 📺 ♿ P 🍽	$$	150		▦	●	▦

SAN FRANCISCO

CHINATOWN AND NOB HILL: *Hotel Astoria* 510 Bush St, CA 94108. **Map** 5 C4. ☎ *(415) 434-8889; (800) 666-6696.* **FAX** *(415) 434-8919.* Conveniently situated between Chinatown and Union Square, this modest hotel has reasonably priced single rooms. 🚪 TV 🗨	$	80		▦		
CHINATOWN AND NOB HILL: *Hotel Triton* 342 Grant Ave, CA 94108. **Map** 5 C4. ☎ *(415) 394-0500; (800) 433-6611.* **FAX** *(415) 394-0555.* Small but stylish, this hotel has a cheerful atmosphere and is opposite Chinatown in the heart of the art gallery district. 🚪 TV 🗨	$$	140	●	▦		
CHINATOWN AND NOB HILL: *Holiday Inn, Chinatown* 750 Kearny St, CA 94108. **Map** 5 C3. ☎ *(415) 433-6600; (800) 465-4329.* **FAX** *(415) 765-7891.* This chain hotel has a good location near Portsmouth Plaza, close to cable car lines. Children under 19 stay free. 🚪 TV & P 🗨	$$$	563	●	▦		▦
CHINATOWN AND NOB HILL: *Huntington Hotel* 1075 California St, CA 94108. **Map** 5 B4. ☎ *(415) 474-5400; (800) 652-1539.* **FAX** *(415) 474-6227.* Built in 1922 as luxury apartments atop Nob Hill, the spacious rooms and suites have magnificent views. 🚪 TV & limited. P 🗨	$$$	140	●	▦		
CHINATOWN AND NOB HILL: *Mark Hopkins Inter-Continental* 999 California St, CA 94108. **Map** 5 B4. ☎ *(415) 392-3434; (800) 327-0200.* **FAX** *(415) 421-3302.* This landmark Nob Hill hotel is known for its striking Art Deco rooftop bar and its spectacular views. 🚪 TV & P 🗨	$$$	391	●	▦		
CHINATOWN AND NOB HILL: *Fairmont Hotel* 950 Mason St, CA 94108. **Map** 5 B4. ☎ *(415) 772-5000; (800) 527-4727.* **FAX** *(415) 837-0587.* Famous for its gorgeous foyer, this is the grandest hotel on Nob Hill. The panoramic views are unbeatable. 🚪 24 TV & P 🗨	$$$$	596	●	▦		
CHINATOWN AND NOB HILL: *The Ritz-Carlton, San Francisco* 600 Stockton St, CA 94108. **Map** 5 C4. ☎ *(415) 296-7465; (800) 241-3333.* **FAX** *(415) 291-0288.* Superb comfort and service are the hallmarks of this historic Beaux-Arts hotel near the top of Nob Hill. 🚪 24 TV & P 🎬 🗨	$$$$	336	●	▦		▦
CHINATOWN AND NOB HILL: *Stouffer Renaissance Stanford Court* 905 California St, CA 94108. **Map** 5 B4. ☎ *(415) 989-3500; (800) 622-0957.* **FAX** *(415) 391-0513.* This luxurious Nob Hill retreat caters for busy executives, with opulent rooms and limousine service. 🚪 24 TV & P 🗨	$$$$$	392	●	▦		
CIVIC CENTER: *Pension San Francisco* 1668 Market St, CA 94102. **Map** 10 F1. ☎ *(415) 864-1271.* **FAX** *(415) 861-8116.* This charming, small budget hotel is on a quiet stretch of Market Street, near public transport and close to restaurants and nightlife venues. 🗨	$	36				
CIVIC CENTER: *Alamo Square Inn* 719 Scott St, CA 94117. **Map** 4 D5. ☎ *(415) 922-2055; (800) 345-9888.* **FAX** *(415) 931-1304.* These two beautifully restored historic buildings overlook the square. Breakfast is included; no smoking allowed. 🚪 TV P 🗨	$$	15		▦		
CIVIC CENTER: *Best Western Carriage Inn* 140 7th St, CA 94103. **Map** 11 A1. ☎ *(415) 552-8600; (800) 444-5817.* **FAX** *(415) 626-3974.* There are spacious rooms, some with fireplaces, but the neighbourhood is rather dull. Continental breakfast and transport from train and bus stations and to Union Square are free. 🚪 24 TV & limited. P 🗨	$$	48		▦		
CIVIC CENTER: *Chateau Tivoli* 1057 Steiner St, CA 94115. **Map** 11 A1. ☎ *(415) 776-5462; (800) 228-1647.* **FAX** *(415) 776-0505.* Guests are given a taste of 19th-century San Francisco in this friendly Victorian house furnished with authentic antiques. 🗨	$$	8		▦		
CIVIC CENTER: *Phoenix Inn* 601 Eddy St, CA 94109. **Map** 4 F4. ☎ *(415) 776-1380; (800) 248-9466.* **FAX** *(415) 885-3109.* This classic 1950s motel has been called the "hippest hotel in town". The on-site Miss Pearl's Jam House *(see p561)* makes it a lively spot. Rooms open on to the courtyard or have balconies. 🚪 TV & P 🗨	$$	44	●	▦		▦
CIVIC CENTER: *Archbishop's Mansion Inn* 1000 Fulton St, CA 94117. **Map** 4 D5. ☎ *(415) 563-7872; (800) 543-5820.* **FAX** *(415) 885-3193.* Inside this imposing 1904 building is an elaborate open staircase. The luxurious rooms are designed around operatic themes and many have fireplaces with carved mantelpieces. 🚪 TV 🗨	$$$	15		▦		

						NUMBER OF ROOMS	RESTAURANT	CHILDREN'S FACILITIES	GARDEN/TERRACE	SWIMMING POOL

Price categories for a standard double room per night, inclusive of service charges and any additional taxes, such as local sales tax:
⑤ under $100
⑤⑤ $100–$150
⑤⑤⑤ $150–$200
⑤⑤⑤⑤ $200–$250
⑤⑤⑤⑤⑤ over $250

RESTAURANT
Hotel restaurant or dining room usually open to non-residents unless otherwise stated.

CHILDREN'S FACILITIES
Indicates child cots and/or a baby-sitting service available. A few hotels also provide children's portions and high chairs in the restaurant.

GARDEN/TERRACE
Hotels with a garden, courtyard or terrace, often providing tables for eating outside.

SWIMMING POOL
Hotel with indoor or outdoor swimming pool.

Entry	Price	Rooms	Rest.	Child.	Garden	Pool
DOWNTOWN: *Adelaide Inn* 5 Isadora Duncan Place (off Taylor St), CA 94102. **Map** 5 B5. **(** *(415) 441-2261.* **FAX** *(415) 441-0161.* This inn has simple rooms with shared bathrooms, in the tradition of a European *pension*, and a quiet location. TV 🖨	⑤	18				
DOWNTOWN: *Aida Hotel* 1087 Market St, CA 94103. **Map** 5 B5. **(** *(415) 863-4141; (800) 863-2432.* **FAX** *(415) 863-5151.* This hotel provides very basic accommodation in a bustlng part of Downtown San Francisco. The décor is rather outdated but the rooms are clean and comfortable. TV 🖨	⑤	162				
DOWNTOWN: *Golden Gate Hotel* 775 Bush St, CA 94108. **Map** 5 B4. **(** *(415) 392-3702; (800) 835-1118.* **FAX** *(415) 392-6202.* Small and charming family-run hotel on Nob Hill, near Union Square. European-style rooms are furnished with antiques. TV P 🖨	(⑤)	23				
DOWNTOWN: *Sheehan Hotel* 620 Sutter St, CA 94102. **Map** 5 B4. **(** *(415) 775-6500; (800) 848-1529.* **FAX** *(415) 775-3271.* This former YWCA has the city's largest indoor pool. Rooms are plain, with fluorescent lighting, but the staff are friendly. 🔲 TV 🗍 P 🖨	⑤	68		▦		▦
DOWNTOWN: *Andrews Hotel* 624 Post St, CA 94109. **Map** 5 B5. **(** *(415) 563-6877; (800) 926-3739.* **FAX** *(415) 928-6919.* Rates include continental breakfast at this small, family-owned hotel near Union Square. Rooms are comfortable. 🔲 TV 🖨	⑤⑤	48	●			
DOWNTOWN: *Hotel Bedford* 761 Post St, CA 94109. **Map** 5 B5. **(** *(415) 673-6040; (800) 227-5642.* **FAX** *(415) 563-6739.* This 17-storey hotel near Union Square has spectacular city views. The plain rooms have mini-bars and VCRs. 🔲 TV 🗍 limited. 🖨	⑤⑤	144	●	▦		
DOWNTOWN: *Chancellor Hotel* 433 Powell St, CA 94102. **Map** 5 B4. **(** *(415) 362-2004; (800) 428-4748.* **FAX** *(415) 395-9476.* This small hotel in the theatre district dates from 1911 and has Edwardian-style beds, baths and shower fittings. 🔲 TV P 🖨	⑤⑤	137	●			
DOWNTOWN: *Hotel Rex* 562 Sutter St, CA 94102. **Map** 5 B4. **(** *(415) 433-4434; (800) 433-4434.* **FAX** *(415) 433-3695.* Recently refurbished, with European style and décor, this hotel has comfortable, quiet rooms and helpful staff. 🔲 TV 🗍 limited. 🖨	⑤⑤	94	●	▦	●	▦
DOWNTOWN: *The Maxwell Hotel* 386 Geary St, CA 94102. **Map** 5 B5. **(** *(415) 986-2000; (888) 734-6299.* **FAX** *(415) 397-2447.* Situated at the heart of the city's Theater District *(see p310)*, this older property is spacious and sunny and has good views. 🔲 TV 🗍 🖨	⑤⑤	152	●	▦		
DOWNTOWN: *Monticello Inn* 127 Ellis St, CA 94102. **Map** 5 B5. **(** *(415) 392-8800; (800) 669-7777.* **FAX** *(415) 398-2650.* Named after the home of Thomas Jefferson, this intimate hotel has recently been renovated and furnished with colonial-style replica antiques. Complimentary wine in the evening. 🔲 TV 🗍 P 🖨	⑤⑤	90	●	▦		
DOWNTOWN: *The Savoy Hotel* 580 Geary St, CA 94102. **Map** 5 B5. **(** *(415) 441-2700; (800) 227-4223.* **FAX** *(415) 441-2700.* Elegance, helpful service and feather beds with goosedown pillows in all the rooms are the hallmarks of this moderately priced hotel. Continental breakfast and afternoon tea are included. 🔲 TV 🖨	⑤⑤	83	●	▦		
DOWNTOWN: *York Hotel* 940 Sutter St, CA 94109. **Map** 5 A4. **(** *(415) 885-6800; (800) 808-9675.* **FAX** *(415) 885-2115.* There are comfortable, quiet rooms, particularly at the back of the hotel, and a highly rated small cabaret show in the bar. The staircase was featured in Alfred Hitchcock's film, *Vertigo*. 🔲 TV 🗍 limited. 🖨	⑤⑤	96		▦		

DOWNTOWN: *ANA Hotel* $$$ 667
50 3rd St, CA 94103. **Map** 5 C5. ((415) 974-6400; (800) ANA-HOTELS.
FAX (415) 543-8268. Views from the floor-to-ceiling windows of this luxurious
hotel are breathtaking. It has good weekend discounts.

DOWNTOWN: *Harbor Court Hotel* $$$ 131
165 Steuart St, CA 94105. **Map** 6 E4. ((415) 882-1300; (800) 346-0555.
FAX (415) 882-1313. This is the only hotel in the city situated right on the
waterfront. Rooms are small, but some have good views.

DOWNTOWN: *Holiday Inn, Union Square* $$$ 401
480 Sutter St, CA 94108. **Map** 5 B4. ((415) 398-8900; (888) 218-0808.
FAX (415) 989-8823. On the Powell Street cable car line, this hotel boasts
magnificent views of Nob Hill and Golden Gate Bridge.

DOWNTOWN: *Hotel Griffon* $$$ 62
155 Steuart St, CA 94105. **Map** 6 E4. ((415) 495-2100; (800) 321-2201.
FAX (415) 495-3522. Some of the rooms in this elegant hotel have views of
the Golden Gate Bridge. Popular with business travellers.

DOWNTOWN: *Kensington Park Hotel* $$$ 86
450 Post St, CA 94102. **Map** 5 B5. ((415) 788-6400; (800) 553-1900. **FAX** (415)
885-3268. Close to Union Square, this Spanish-Revival hotel has a beautiful
lobby, spacious rooms and continental breakfast. *limited.*

DOWNTOWN: *San Francisco Marriott* $$$ 1500
55 4th St, CA 94103. **Map** 5 C5. ((415) 896-1600; (800) 228-9290. **FAX** (415)
896-6176. This futuristic-style, 39-storey tower hotel is popular with
convention groups. Children under 18 stay free.

DOWNTOWN: *Sir Francis Drake Hotel* $$$ 417
450 Powell St, CA 94102. **Map** 5 B4. ((415) 392-7755; (800) 227-5480.
FAX (415) 395-8559. Now restored to its Art Deco splendour, this Union Square
hotel is famous for its Beefeater doormen and rooftop bar.

DOWNTOWN: *White Swan Inn* $$$ 26
845 Bush St, CA 94108. **Map** 5 B4. ((415) 775-1755; (800) 999-9570. **FAX** (415)
775-5717. Rooms in this small, country-style hotel are bright with floral
prints and artificial open fires. English breakfast is included.

DOWNTOWN: *Grand Hyatt San Francisco* $$$$ 693
345 Stockton St, CA 94108. **Map** 5 C4. ((415) 398-1234; (800) 233-1234.
FAX (415) 392-2536. Rooms in this 36-storey tower on Union Square have
good views. There is a rooftop cocktail bar.

DOWNTOWN: *Hotel Nikko* $$$$ 522
222 Mason St, CA 94102. **Map** 5 B5. ((415) 394-1111; (800) NIKKO-US. **FAX** (415)
394-1159. This ultra-modern hotel caters for business travellers, especially
Japanese, with top-notch services and facilities.

DOWNTOWN: *Parc Fifty Five* $$$$ 1008
55 Cyril Magnin Street, CA 94102. **Map** 5 C5. ((415) 392-8000; (800) 650-7272.
FAX (415) 421-5993. This huge hotel is not very stylish for the price, but the
special weekend offers make it worth considering

DOWNTOWN: *Prescott Hotel* $$$$ 166
545 Post St, CA 94102. **Map** 5 B5. ((415) 563-0303; (800) 283-7322. **FAX** (415)
563-6831. Business travellers predominate at this luxurious hotel, which is
decorated like a gentlemen's club with dark wood walls.

DOWNTOWN: *San Francisco Hilton* $$$$ 1900
333 O'Farrell St, CA 94102. **Map** 5 B5. ((415) 771-1400; (800) 445-8667.
FAX (415) 771-6807. The city's largest hotel has excellent views from its 46-
torey tower. It has good service and numerous facilities.

DOWNTOWN: *Westin St Francis* $$$$ 1200
35 Powell St, CA 94102. **Map** 5 B4. ((415) 397-7000; (800) 228-3000.
FAX (415) 774-0124. The triple towers of this landmark hotel have defined
Union Square's skyline since 1904.

DOWNTOWN: *Campton Place Hotel* $$$$$ 117
340 Stockton St, CA 94108. **Map** 5 C4. ((415) 781-5555; (800) 235-4300.
FAX (415) 955-5536. This small, elegant hotel off Union Square offers plush
rooms, good service and sumptuous public areas.

Price categories for a standard double room per night, inclusive of service charges and any additional taxes, such as local sales tax:
- $ under $100
- $$ $100–$150
- $$$ $150–$200
- $$$$ $200–$250
- $$$$$ over $250

RESTAURANT
Hotel restaurant or dining room usually open to non-residents unless otherwise stated.

CHILDREN'S FACILITIES
Indicates child cots and/or a baby-sitting service available. A few hotels also provide children's portions and high chairs in the restaurant.

GARDEN/TERRACE
Hotels with a garden, courtyard or terrace, often providing tables for eating outside.

SWIMMING POOL
Hotel with indoor or outdoor swimming pool.

	NUMBER OF ROOMS	RESTAURANT	CHILDREN'S FACILITIES	GARDEN/TERRACE	SWIMMING POOL
DOWNTOWN: *Four Seasons Clift Hotel* $$$$$ 495 Geary St, CA 94102. **Map** 5 B5. (415) 775-4700; (800) 652-5438. **FAX** (415) 441-4621. Well-appointed rooms, an old-fashioned ambience and gracious service characterize this fine hotel.	329	●			
DOWNTOWN: *Hyatt Regency San Francisco* $$$$$ 5 Embarcadero Center, CA 94111. **Map** 6 D3. (415) 788-1234; (800) 233-1234. **FAX** (415) 398-2567. Built around a 15-storey atrium lobby, this hotel is part of the prestigious Hyatt chain. It has recently been renovated and its rooms upgraded.	803	●	■		
DOWNTOWN: *Mandarin Oriental* $$$$$ 222 Sansome St, CA 94104. **Map** 5 C4. (415) 885-0999; (800) 622-0404. **FAX** (415) 433-0289. This luxury hotel at the top of the 48-storey First Interstate Center has magnificent views.	158	●	■		
DOWNTOWN: *Pan Pacific* $$$$$ 500 Post St, CA 94102. **Map** 5 B5. (415) 771-8600; (800) 533-6465. **FAX** (415) 398-0267. The public areas are glamorous, the bedrooms elegant at this modern hotel with a 17-storey atrium.	331	●	■		
DOWNTOWN: *Park Hyatt San Francisco* $$$$$ 333 Battery St, CA 94111. **Map** 6 D3. (415) 392-1234; (800) 233-1234. **FAX** (415) 421-2433. Located next to the Embarcadero Center (see p304), this is the most luxurious Hyatt in San Francisco. The hotel offers weekend rates that provide particularly good value.	360	●	■		
DOWNTOWN: *Sheraton Palace Hotel* $$$$$ 2 New Montgomery St, CA 94105. **Map** 5 C4. (415) 392-8600; (800) 325-3535. **FAX** (415) 543-0671. At the turn of the century the Palace was one of the world's most famous hotels and a favourite of visiting VIPs. Today its focal point is the glamorous Garden Court.	550	●	■	●	■
FISHERMAN'S WHARF: *San Remo Hotel* $ 2237 Mason St, CA 94133. **Map** 5 B2. (415) 776-8688; (800) 352-REMO. **FAX** (415) 776-2811. The area's only budget hotel is known for its friendly atmosphere. It has shared bathrooms, except for the Honeymoon Suite.	62				
FISHERMAN'S WHARF: *Hyatt at Fisherman's Wharf* $$$ 555 North Point, CA 94133. **Map** 5 A1. (415) 563-1234; (800) 233-1234. **FAX** (415) 749-6122. More family-orientated than the city's other Hyatts, it has good service and family discounts on a second room.	313	●	■		■
FISHERMAN'S WHARF: *Hyde Park Suites* $$$ 2655 Hyde St, CA 94109. **Map** 5 A2. (415) 771-0200; (800) 227-3608. **FAX** (415) 346-8058. The self-catering suites available at this pleasant hotel have kitchen and dining facilities and are spacious enough to accommodate four people in comfort. limited.	24		■		
FISHERMAN'S WHARF: *Sheraton at Fisherman's Wharf* $$$ 2500 Mason St, CA 94133. **Map** 5 B1. (415) 362-5500; (800) 325-3535. **FAX** (415) 956-5275. This family-orientated, tourist hotel is also popular with business people and has easy access to many attractions.	525	●	■		■
FISHERMAN'S WHARF: *Tuscan Inn* $$$ 425 North Point St, CA 94133. **Map** 5 B1. (415) 561-1100; (800) 648-4626. **FAX** (415) 561-1199. Children under 18 stay free at this spacious, stylish hotel with large rooms and local limousine service.	221	●	■		
HAIGHT ASHBURY: *Beck's Motor Lodge* $ 2222 Market St, CA 94114. **Map** 10 E1. (415) 621-8212; (800) 227-4360. **FAX** (415) 241-0435. Handy for the Castro and Mission districts, this standard 1960s motel has a quiet location and low out-of-season rates.	57				

HAIGHT ASHBURY: *Red Victorian Bed and Breakfast* $$ 18
1665 Haight St, CA 94117. **Map** 9 B1. ☎ (415) 864-1978; (800) 435-1967. **FAX** (415) 863-3293. This unique hotel offers New Age accommodation in themed rooms such as the Flower Child Suite; no radios, TVs or smoking.

HAIGHT ASHBURY: *Stanyan Park Hotel* $$ 36
750 Stanyan St, CA 94117. **Map** 9 B2. ☎ (415) 751-1000. **FAX** (415) 668-5454. This comfortable hotel overlooking Golden Gate Park has antique furnishings and fireplaces. Breakfast is included. limited.

HAIGHT ASHBURY: *Victorian Inn on the Park* $$ 12
301 Lyon St, CA 94117. **Map** 9 C1. ☎ (415) 931-1830; (800) 435-1967. **FAX** (415) 931-1830. Housed in a mansion opposite Golden Gate Park, this stylish bed-and-breakfast hotel has Arts and Crafts reproduction furniture.

NORTH BEACH: *Washington Square Inn* $$ 15
1660 Stockton St, CA 94133. **Map** 5 B2. ☎ (415) 981-4220; (800) 388-0220. **FAX** (415) 397-7242. Smoking is not allowed at this bed-and-breakfast hotel facing Washington Square Park. Children under five stay free. P

PACIFIC HEIGHTS: *Art Center Bed & Breakfast* $ 5
1902 Filbert St, CA 94123. **Map** 4 E2. ☎ (415) 567-1526. This small, pretty New Orleans-style house is one of the Marina's oldest buildings and dates from 1857. One-, two- and three-room suites are available.

PACIFIC HEIGHTS: *Holiday Lodge* $ 77
1901 Van Ness Ave, CA 94109. **Map** 4 F3. ☎ (415) 776-4469; (800) 367-8504. **FAX** (415) 474-7046. The standard motel rooms, in an attractive ranch-style building, are rather noisy, but handy for public transport. P

PACIFIC HEIGHTS: *Marina Inn* $ 40
3110 Octavia St, CA 94123. **Map** 4 E2. ☎ (415) 928-1000; (800) 346-6118. **FAX** (415) 928-5909. The hotel has a good location, near Fort Mason and Union Street, but the traffic noise can be intrusive. limited.

PACIFIC HEIGHTS: *Motel Capri* $ 46
2015 Greenwich St, CA 94123. **Map** 4 D2. ☎ (415) 346-4667. **FAX** (415) 346-3256. This family-owned motel in a quiet residential street at the centre of the Marina district is good for budget travellers. P

PACIFIC HEIGHTS: *Pacific Heights Inn* $ 40
1555 Union St, CA 94123. **Map** 4 E2. ☎ (415) 776-3310; (800) 523-1801. **FAX** (415) 776-8176. This pleasant 1960s-era motel is in a quiet street near public transport and serves continental breakfast. limited. P

PACIFIC HEIGHTS: *Bed and Breakfast Inn* $$ 11
4 Charlton Court, CA 94123. **Map** 4 E3. ☎ (415) 921-9784. In a quiet cul-de-sac off Union Street, the city's oldest bed-and-breakfast hotel was once a Victorian farmhouse. Guests can use the library. limited. P

PACIFIC HEIGHTS: *Holiday Inn, Golden Gateway* $$ 498
1500 Van Ness Ave, CA 94109. **Map** 4 F4. ☎ (415) 441-4000; (800) HOLIDAY. **FAX** (415) 776-7155. Popular with groups, this 26-storey modern tower is within easy access of the rest of the city. limited. P

PACIFIC HEIGHTS: *Miyako Hotel* $$ 218
1625 Post St, CA 94115. **Map** 4 E4. ☎ (415) 922-3200; (800) 533-4567. **FAX** (415) 921-0417. Some rooms have steam baths or tatami mats in this stylish hotel in the Japan Center. Children under 12 stay free. P

PACIFIC HEIGHTS: *Majestic Hotel* $$$ 57
1500 Sutter St, CA 94109. **Map** 4 E3. ☎ (415) 441-1100; (800) 869-8966. **FAX** (415) 673-7331. Most rooms in this ornate hotel have canopied beds, open fires and antiques. It is in a quiet area. limited. P

PACIFIC HEIGHTS: *Mansions Hotel* $$$ 21
2220 Sacramento St, CA 94115. **Map** 4 E3. ☎ (415) 929-9444; (800) 826-9398. **FAX** (415) 567-9391. Dating from the 1880s, this quirky bed-and-breakfast hotel has dance-hall memorabilia and weekend entertainment. P

PACIFIC HEIGHTS: *Sherman House* $$$$$ 14
2160 Green St, CA 94123. **Map** 4 D3. ☎ (415) 563-3600; (800) 424-5777. **FAX** (415) 563-1882. Publicity-shy stars favour this quiet, luxuriously appointed small hotel. Rooms have woodburning fireplaces and antiques.

For key to symbols see back flap

			NUMBER OF ROOMS	RESTAURANT	CHILDREN'S FACILITIES	GARDEN/TERRACE	SWIMMING POOL

Price categories for a standard double room per night, inclusive of service charges and any additional taxes, such as local sales tax:
$ under $100
$$ $100–$150
$$$ $150–$200
$$$$ $200–$250
$$$$$ over $250

RESTAURANT
Hotel restaurant or dining room usually open to non-residents unless otherwise stated.
CHILDREN'S FACILITIES
Indicates child cots and/or a baby-sitting service available. A few hotels also provide children's portions and high chairs in the restaurant.
GARDEN/TERRACE
Hotels with a garden, courtyard or terrace, often providing tables for eating outside.
SWIMMING POOL
Hotel with indoor or outdoor swimming pool.

THE BAY AREA

Entry	Rooms	Restaurant	Children's	Garden/Terrace	Pool
BENICIA: *Captain Walsh House* $$ 235 E L St, CA 94510. **Road map** inset B. **[** (707) 747-5653. **FAX** (707) 747-6265. This Gothic-style bed-and-breakfast inn near the ocean was named one of the top three by the US in *Better Homes & Gardens* magazine. 🛏 📺 ⚫ P ⚫	5			●	
BENICIA: *Union Hotel* $$ 401 1st St, CA 94510. **Road map** inset B. **[** (707) 746-0100. **FAX** (707) 746-6458. Some rooms here have views of the docks, while others enjoy a quiet garden setting. All are decorated with antiques. 🛏 📺 P ⚫	22	●		●	
BERKELEY: *Bancroft Hotel* $ 2680 Bancroft Way, CA 94704. **Road map** inset B. **[** (510) 549-1000; (800) 549-1002. **FAX** (510) 549-1070. This elegant 1920s Arts and Crafts hotel opposite the university was formerly a private women's club. Some of the spacious rooms have balconies with views of the hills and the bay. 🛏 📺 P ⚫	22		■	●	
BERKELEY: *Gramma's Rose Garden Inn* $$ 2740 Telegraph Ave, CA 94705. **Road map** inset B. **[** (510) 549-2145. **FAX** (510) 549-1085. Some rooms in this gorgeous Victorian mansion have fireplaces and balconies. Cooked breakfast is included. 🛏 📺 ⚫ P ⚫	40	●	●	●	
BERKELEY: *Hotel Durant* $$ 2600 Durant Ave, CA 94704. **Road map** inset B. **[** (510) 845-8981; (800) 238-7268. **FAX** (510) 486-8336. This central hotel is large without being impersonal. Some of the spacious rooms have bay views. 🛏 📺 ⚫ P ⚫	140	●	■		
BERKELEY: *Claremont Resort, Spa and Tennis Club* $$$ Ashby & Domingo Aves, Oakland, CA 94623. **Road Map** inset B. **[** (510) 843-3000; (800) 843-7924. **FAX** (510) 549-8582. With its Spanish Revival bell tower, this beautiful building at the foot of the Berkeley Hills is the area's grandest old hotel *(see p402)* and has wonderful views. 🛏 📺 ⚫P ⚫	239	●	■	●	■
BOLINAS: *Smiley's Schooner Saloon and Hotel* $ 41 Wharf Rd, CA 94924. **Road map** inset B. **[** (415) 868-1311. **FAX** (415) 868-0502. Straight out of a Hollywood Western, this hotel is directly above the bar. It is friendly and comfortable but noisy in the evenings. 🛏 P ⚫	5			●	
HALF MOON BAY: *Zaballa House* $$ 324 Main St, CA 94019. **Road map** inset B. **[** (415) 726-9123. Quaint, country-style accommodation is provided in a converted farmhouse, surrounded by lush gardens. Full breakfast is included. 🛏 P ⚫	9			●	
HALF MOON BAY: *Mill Rose Inn* $$$ 615 Mill St, CA 94019. **Road map** inset B. **[** (415) 726-8750; (800) 900-7673. **FAX** (415) 726-3031. Rooms at this bed-and-breakfast inn have VCRs and fireplaces. It has midweek rates, but no children under 10. 🛏 📺 P ⚫	6			●	
INVERNESS: *Manka's Inverness Lodge* $$ Corner of Argyle & Callendar, CA 94937. **Road map** A3. **[** (415) 669-1034. **FAX** (415) 669-1598. The cabins and rooms of this romantic, rustic retreat feature balconies, fireplaces and views of Tomales Bay. 🛏 📺 P ⚫	11	●	■	●	
LAFAYETTE: *Lafayette Park Hotel* $$$ 3287 Mount Diablo Blvd, CA 94549. **Road map** inset B. **[** (510) 283-3700; (800) 368-2468. **FAX** (510) 284-1621. Just east of Berkeley, this hotel has an award-winning bar and restaurant, a whirlpool and sauna. 🛏 📺 ⚫ P ⚫	139	●	■	●	■
MENLO PARK: *Mermaid Inn* $ 727 El Camino Real, CA 94025. **Road map** inset B. **[** (415) 323-9481; (800) 237-4622. **FAX** (415) 323-0662. This plain, modern family-owned hotel is near Palo Alto and convenient for Stanford University. 🛏 📺 ⚫ P ⚫	39		■	●	

MENLO PARK: *Stanford Park Hotel* $$$$ 162
100 El Camino Real, CA 94025. **Road map** inset B. [(415) 322-1234.
FAX (415) 322-0975. Many of these elegantly appointed rooms near Stanford
University have fireplaces and separate sitting areas.

MILL VALLEY: *Travelodge* $ 55
707 Redwood Hwy, CA 94941. **Road map** inset B. [(415) 383-0340; (800) 578-
7878. FAX (415) 383-0312. Just west of Tiburon, this motel is close to Muir
Woods and the city. Some rooms have Jacuzzis.

MOSS BEACH: *Seal Cove Inn* $$$ 10
221 Cypress Ave, CA 94038. **Road map** inset B. [(415) 728-7325; (800) 995-
9987. FAX (415) 728-4116. Set on a hill overlooking the ocean, this charming
inn has open fires in the rooms and a free video library.

MUIR BEACH: *The Pelican Inn* $$$ 7
10 Pacifica Way, CA 94965. **Road map** inset B. [(415) 383-6000. FAX (415) 383-
3424. Roaring fires, British beers and gorgeous rooms, some with four-
poster beds, are all within walking distance of Muir Woods.

OAKLAND: *Waterfront Plaza Hotel* $$$ 144
10 Washington St, CA 94607. **Road map** inset B. [(510) 836-3800. FAX (510)
832-5695. Many rooms have fireplaces and views across the bay at this
well-appointed hotel at the edge of Jack London Square.

PRINCETON-BY-THE-SEA: *Pillar Point Inn* $$$ 11
380 Capistrano Rd, CA 94018. **Road map** inset B. [(415) 728-7377. FAX (415)
728-8345. All the rooms at this romantic inn have ocean views, fireplaces,
feather mattresses and VCRs; business services available.

SAN JOSE: *Hotel De Anza* $$ 101
233 West Santa Clara St, CA 95113. **Road map** inset B. [(408) 286-1000; (800)
843-3700. FAX (408) 286-0500. The emphasis is on personal attention at this
luxurious Art Deco hotel near the convention centre.

SAN JOSE: *Fairmont Hotel San Jose* $$$ 541
Fairmont Plaza, 170 S Market St, CA 95113. **Road map** inset B. [(408)
998-1900; (800) 527-4727. FAX (408) 287-1648. This rather impersonal luxury
hotel has excellent business and leisure facilities.

SAN JOSE: *San Jose Hilton and Towers Hotel* $$$ 355
300 Almaden Blvd, CA 95110. **Road map** inset B. [(408) 287-2100; (800) 445-
8667. FAX (408) 947-4489. This chain hotel is well equipped for the business
traveller. Each floor has its own concierge.

SAN RAFAEL: *Panama Hotel* $ 15
4 Bayview, CA 94901. **Road map** inset B. [(415) 457-3993. FAX (415) 457-6240.
Each room at this hotel has its own distinct character, eclectically
furnished with antique and second-hand furniture.

SAN RAFAEL: *Embassy Suites Hotel and Conference Center* $$ 228
101 McInnis Parkway, CA 94903. **Road map** inset B. [(415) 499-9222; (800)
362-2779. FAX (415) 499-9268. This large chain hotel has basic rooms, a
business centre and 24-hour access to leisure facilities.

SAUSALITO: *Hotel Alta Mira* $$ 30
125 Bulkley Ave (PO Box 706), CA 94966. **Road map** inset B. [(415) 332-1350.
FAX (415) 331-3862. Set on a hill with exceptional views of the bay, rooms
here are comfortably furnished and the staff are welcoming.

SAUSALITO: *Casa Madrona Hotel* $$$ 32
801 Bridgeway, CA 94965. **Road map** inset B. [(415) 332-0502. FAX (415) 332-
2537. Climbing up the hillside from the waterfront, this lovely hotel has
distinctive rooms in an old house and adjacent cottages.

SAUSALITO: *The Inn Above Tide* $$$ 30
30 El Portal, CA 94965. **Road map** inset B. [(415) 332-9535; (800) 893-8433.
FAX (415) 332-6714. Rooms at this relaxing harbour-front hotel have open
fires and balconies over the bay; some have Jacuzzis.

WALNUT CREEK: *Marriott Hotel* $$ 337
2355 N Main St, CA 94596. **Road map** inset B. [(510) 934-2000.
FAX (510) 934-6374. This well-appointed hotel has a variety of
conference facilities catering to business travellers.

Price categories for a standard double room per night, inclusive of service charges and any additional taxes, such as local sales tax:
$ under $100
$$ $100–$150
$$$ $150–$200
$$$$ $200–$250
$$$$$ over $250

RESTAURANT
Hotel restaurant or dining room usually open to non-residents unless otherwise stated.
CHILDREN'S FACILITIES
Indicates child cots and/or a baby-sitting service available. A few hotels also provide children's portions and high chairs in the restaurant.
GARDEN/TERRACE
Hotels with a garden, courtyard or terrace, often providing tables for eating outside.
SWIMMING POOL
Hotel with indoor or outdoor swimming pool.

THE NORTH

ARCATA: *Fairwinds Motel* $
1674 G St, CA 95521. **Road map** A2. ((707) 822-4824. This small, family-owned hotel, close to Arcata's Humboldt University, provides reasonably priced but basic accommodation. 🛏 TV & limited. P 🅿
Number of Rooms: 27. *Children's Facilities.*

ARCATA: *Hotel Arcata* $$
708 9th St, CA 95521. **Road map** A2. ((707) 826-0217. FAX (707) 826-1737. This fully modernized hotel on the central square has a wide range of rooms, some of which have separate sitting areas. 🛏 TV 🅿
Number of Rooms: 32. *Restaurant. Children's Facilities.*

CRESCENT CITY: *Curley Redwood Lodge* $
701 S Redwood Hwy, CA 95531. **Road map** A1. ((707) 464-2137. FAX (707) 464-1655. Located just across the water from the harbour area, this rustic-style motel was constructed from a single redwood tree. 🛏 TV P 🅿
Number of Rooms: 36. *Children's Facilities.*

DUNSMUIR: *Caboose Motel* $
100 Railroad Park Rd, CA 96025. **Road map** B2. ((916) 235-4440. FAX (916) 235-4470. The unusual rooms housed in renovated railway guard's vans have a pleasant setting with stunning views of the nearby peaks. 🛏 TV P 🅿
Number of Rooms: 27. *Restaurant. Children's Facilities. Garden/Terrace. Swimming Pool.*

EUREKA: *Best Western Thunderbird Inn* $
232 W 5th St, CA 95501. **Road map** A2. ((707) 443-2234; (800) 521-6996. FAX (707) 443-3489. Stunning redwood forests and beaches lie just a 15-minute drive away from this rather basic chain motel. 🛏 TV & P 🅿
Number of Rooms: 115. *Restaurant. Children's Facilities. Swimming Pool.*

EUREKA: *Carson House Inn* $
1209 4th St, CA 95501. **Road map** A2. ((707) 443-1601. FAX (707) 444-8365. Along with a prime location at the heart of Eureka's Old Town, this hotel offers spacious rooms and suites, plus a sauna. 🛏 TV P 🅿
Number of Rooms: 60. *Restaurant. Children's Facilities. Swimming Pool.*

EUREKA: *Eureka Inn* $$
518 7th St, CA 95501. **Road map** A2. ((707) 442-6441. FAX (707) 442-0637. Tudor-style architecture gives this large historic hotel an old-fashioned atmosphere. Top-quality facilities include a sauna and business services, as well as a good restaurant, the Rib Room *(see p569)*. 🛏 TV P 🅿
Number of Rooms: 105. *Restaurant. Children's Facilities. Swimming Pool.*

EUREKA: *Hotel Carter* $$$
301 L St, CA 95501. **Road map** A2. ((707) 444-8062; (800) 404-1390. FAX (707) 444-8067. The rooms in this Victorian hotel in Old Town Eureka have contemporary furnishings. Close to forests and beaches. 🛏 TV & P 🅿
Number of Rooms: 24. *Restaurant. Garden/Terrace.*

FERNDALE: *Gingerbread Mansion* $$
400 Berding St, CA 95536. **Road map** A2. ((707) 786-4000; (800) 952-4136. Surrounded by delightful gardens, this ornate inn dates from 1899. Rooms are luxuriously appointed, and a de luxe breakfast is included. 🛏 P 🅿
Number of Rooms: 9. *Children's Facilities. Garden/Terrace.*

GARBERVILLE: *Humboldt House Inn* $
701 Redwood Drive, CA 95542. **Road map** A2. ((707) 923-2771. FAX (707) 923-4259. The most comfortable motel in redwood country has large rooms, most with balconies. Continental breakfast is included. 🛏 TV P 🅿
Number of Rooms: 76. *Children's Facilities. Garden/Terrace. Swimming Pool.*

GARBERVILLE: *Benbow Inn* $$$
445 Lake Benbow Drive, CA 95542. **Road map** A2. ((707) 923-2124; (800) 355-3301. FAX (707) 923-2897. Built in 1924, this landmark inn looks like an English country house amid the redwood groves. It has an opulent restaurant and sunny terrace; it is closed from January to March. 🛏 TV P 🅿
Number of Rooms: 55. *Restaurant. Children's Facilities. Garden/Terrace. Swimming Pool.*

McCLOUD: *McCloud Guest House* $$
606 W Colombero Drive, CA 96057. **Road map** B1. ((916) 964-3160. A lumber baron built this old mansion; rooms have window seats looking out over the forest. Guests can also use the antique billiards table. 🛏 TV P 🅿
Number of Rooms: 5. *Restaurant. Garden/Terrace.*

MOUNT LASSEN: *Mineral Lodge* $ 20
PO Box 160 Mineral, CA 96063. **Road map** B2. ((916) 595-4422. Popular
with hunters and hikers, this rustic lodge offers motel-style rooms, plus
a tavern and general store. It is on the southern fringes of Lassen
Volcanic National Park (*see p437*). 🖪 TV P 🖉

MOUNT SHASTA: *Mount Shasta Ranch Bed and Breakfast* $ 8
1008 W A Barr Rd, CA 96067. **Road map** A3. ((916) 926-3870. This rustic retreat
has amazing views of Mount Shasta (*see p436*). Half the rooms are in the
spacious main house, the others are in the smaller carriage house and
share bathrooms. A big country breakfast is included. TV P 🖉

MOUNT SHASTA: *Mountain Air Lodge* $ 38
1121 S Mount Shasta Blvd, CA 96067. **Road map** A2. ((916) 926-3411; (800)
727-3704. This simple lodge-style hotel is in a wonderful mountain setting.
Ski slopes and water-sports facilities are just a short drive away. TV P 🖉

MOUNT SHASTA: *Strawberry Valley Inn* $ 15
1142 S Mount Shasta Blvd, CA 96067. **Road map** A2. ((916) 926-2052.
Popular with skiers, reservations are recommended at this quiet inn with
views of Mount Shasta. Each room has a different theme. 🖪 TV & P 🖉

MOUNT SHASTA: *Tree House Inn* $ 95
111 Morgan Way, CA 96067. **Road map** A2. ((916) 926-3101. FAX (916) 926-
3542. Furniture and fixtures made of redwood add to the cosy ambience
of this modern motel. Some rooms have mountain views. 🖪 TV P 🖉

SCOTIA: *Scotia Inn* $$ 11
100 Main Street, CA 95565. **Road map** A2. ((707) 764-5684. FAX (707) 764-1707.
Built for workers at Scotia's massive lumber mill (*see p431*), this beautiful
inn is a showcase of redwood craftsmanship. The renovated rooms feature
such period furnishings as canopy beds and claw-foot baths. 🖪 TV P 🖉

WEAVERVILLE: *Motel Trinity* $ 25
1112 Main St, CA 96093. **Road map** A2. ((916) 623-2129. FAX (916) 623-6007.
Accommodation in this small motel ranges from single rooms to two-
bedroom suites with kitchenettes. Some rooms have Jacuzzis. 🖪 TV 🖉

WEAVERVILLE: *Victorian Inn* $ 61
1709 Main St, CA 96093. **Road map** A2. ((916) 623-4432.
Located at the edge of a historic mountain town (*see p433*), this medium-
sized motel offers spacious modern rooms. 🖪 TV P 🖉

WEAVERVILLE: *Weaverville Hotel* $ 8
201 Main St, CA 96093. **Road map** A2. ((916) 623-3121. For a true taste of
old Weaverville, stay the night at this bargain-priced, old-fashioned hotel,
which occupies the upper floors of a historic building. 🖪 TV P 🖉

WINE COUNTRY

BODEGA BAY: *Bodega Coast Inn* $$$ 45
521 Hwy 1 (PO Box 55), CA 94923. **Road map** A3. ((707) 875-2217; (800) 346-
6999. FAX (707) 875-2964. This modern hotel, a stone's throw from the beach,
has a spa, spectacular views and fireplaces in some rooms. 🖪 TV & P 🖉

BOYES HOT SPRINGS: *Sonoma Mission Inn & Spa* $$$ 168
18140 Sonoma Hwy 12, CA 95476. **Road map** A3. ((707) 938-9000; (800) 862-
4945. FAX (707) 935-1205. Established in the mid-19th century, this inn has
luxurious rooms, many with fireplaces, and tennis courts. 🖪 TV & P 🖉

CALISTOGA: *Calistoga Spa Hot Springs Resort Motel* $ 57
1006 Washington St, CA 94515. **Road map** A3. ((707) 942-6269. This
friendly motel with mineral soaking pools and spa facilities (including
mud baths and massages) is perfect for families. 🖪 TV & P 🖬 🖉

CALISTOGA: *Comfort Inn* $$ 55
1865 Lincoln Ave, CA 94515. **Road map** A3. ((707) 942-9400; (800) 228-5150.
FAX (707) 942-5262. This pleasant hotel has a mineral water pool, as well
as a whirlpool, steam room and sauna. 🖪 TV & P 🖉

GEYSERVILLE: *Campbell Ranch Inn* $$ 5
1475 Canyon Rd, CA 95441. **Road map** A3. ((707) 857-3476; (800) 959-3878.
FAX (707) 857-3239. Most rooms have balconies and fireplaces. Tennis courts,
a hot tub, bicycles and home-made desserts are also on offer. 🖪 TV P 🖉

For key to symbols see back flap

	NUMBER OF ROOMS	RESTAURANT	CHILDREN'S FACILITIES	GARDEN/TERRACE	SWIMMING POOL
GUALALA: *Whale Watch Inn* $$$ 5100 Hwy 1, CA 95445. **Road map** A3. (*(707) 884-3667.* FAX *(707) 884-4815.* Perched on a bluff above the ocean, this hotel has spectacular views from every room. All rooms have fireplaces and balconies, some have whirlpool baths, and none have phones or TVs. Breakfast is included. 🛏 🕭 P 🖉	18			●	
HEALDSBURG: *Dry Creek Inn* $ 198 Dry Creek Rd, CA 95448. **Road map** A3. (*(707) 433-0300; (800) 222-5784.* FAX *(707) 433-1129.* Part of the Best Western chain, this hotel has spacious rooms, a spa and is convenient for the local wineries. 🛏 TV 🕭 P 🖼 🖉	103		■	●	■
HEALDSBURG: *Camellia Inn* $$ 211 North St, CA 95448. **Road map** A3. (*(707) 433-8182; (800) 727-8182.* FAX *(707) 433-8130.* This lovely, Italianate Victorian bed-and-breakfast inn has some rooms with open fires and whirlpool baths. 🛏 🕭 P 🖉	9		■	●	■
HEALDSBURG: *Madrona Manor* $$$ 1001 Westside Rd, CA 95448. **Road map** A3. (*(707) 433-4231; (800) 258-4003.* FAX *(707) 433-0703.* This Victorian mansion is surrounded by vineyards and wineries. Some rooms have fireplaces and claw-foot baths or Jacuzzis, as well as private terraces or balconies. 🛏 🕭 P 🖉	21	●	■	●	■
MENDOCINO: *Mendocino Hotel* $$ 45080 Main St (PO Box 587), CA 95460. **Road map** A3. (*(707) 937-0511; (800) 548-0513.* FAX *(707) 937-0513.* This friendly Victorian hotel overlooking the dramatic coastline also has detached garden rooms. 🛏 🕭 P 🖉	51	●		●	
MENDOCINO: *MacCallum House* $$$ 45020 Albion St (PO Box 206), CA 95460. **Road map** A3. (*(707) 937-0289; (800) 609-0492.* Not all rooms have private baths at this 19th-century inn. Ask for one of the annexes, many of which also have fireplaces. 🛏 🕭 P 🖉	21	●	■	●	
NAPA: *The Chateau Hotel* $ 4195 Solano Ave, CA 94558. **Road map** B3. (*(707) 253-9300; (800) 253-6272.* FAX *(707) 253-0906.* This European-style hotel is geared towards business travellers, with comfortable rooms and a spa. 🛏 TV 🕭 P 🖉	115		■		■
NAPA: *The Elm House* $$$ 800 California Blvd, CA 94559. **Road map** B3. (*(707) 255-1831; (800) 788-4356.* FAX *(707) 255-8609.* Some rooms in this cosy bed-and-breakfast inn have fireplaces. Book early for summer visits. Close to wineries. 🛏 TV P 🖉	16		■	●	
NAPA: *Silverado Country Club Resort* $$$$ 1600 Atlas Peak Rd, CA 94558. **Road map** B3. (*(707) 257-0200; (800) 532-0500.* FAX *(707) 257-5400.* Luxurious guest bungalows surround an old mansion set in 1,200 acres (485 ha). Fabulous recreational facilities. 🛏 TV 🕭 P 🖼 🖉	300	●	■	●	■
RUTHERFORD: *Rancho Caymus* $$$ 1140 Rutherford Rd (PO Box 78), CA 94573. **Road map** A3. (*(707) 963-1777; (800) 845-1777.* FAX *(707) 963-5387.* This hacienda-style hotel, with beehive fireplaces and Mexican-tiled bathrooms, is built around a pretty courtyard. Some rooms have private balconies and Jacuzzis. 🛏 TV 🕭 P 🖉	26		■	●	
RUTHERFORD: *Auberge du Soleil* $$$$$ 180 Rutherford Hill Rd, CA 94573. **Road map** A3. (*(707) 963-1211; (800) 348-5406.* FAX *(707) 963-8764.* The stylish cottages of this country inn and spa resort have fireplaces, bars and exquisite views of the Napa Valley *(see pp446–7).* There is also a notable sculpture garden. 🛏 TV 🕭 P 🖉	50	●	■	●	■
ST HELENA: *White Sulphur Springs Resort and Spa* $ 3100 White Sulphur Springs Rd, CA 94574. **Road map** A3. (*(707) 963-8588.* FAX *(707) 963-2890.* This rustic retreat has tiny log cabins and excellent spa facilities, including hot sulphur springs. 🛏 🕭 P 🖉	37	●	■	●	■

St Helena: *Inn At Southbridge* $$$$ — 21
1020 Main St, CA 94574. **Road map** A3. **C** *(707) 967-9400; (800) 520-6800.*
FAX *(707) 967-9486.* This modern haven offers a welcome escape from
Wine Country chintz. All rooms have vaulted ceilings, fireplaces and
French doors opening on to balconies. 🛏 📺 🕭 🅿 🖋

St Helena: *Meadowood Resort Hotel* $$$$$ — 99
900 Meadowood Lane, CA 94574. **Road map** A3. **C** *(707) 963-3646; (800)
458-8080.* **FAX** *(707) 963-3532.* Some of the lodges have stone fireplaces,
balconies and terraces at this romantic retreat with golf courses, tennis
courts, spa facilities and croquet lawns *(see p571).* 🛏 📺 🕭 🅿 🖋

Santa Rosa: *Hotel La Rose* $$ — 49
308 Wilson St, CA 95401. **Road map** A3. **C** *(707) 579-3200; (800) 527-6738.*
FAX *(707) 579-3247.* Country-style décor and friendly service give this hotel in
Railroad Square the ambience of a bed-and-breakfast inn. 🛏 📺 🕭 🅿 🖋

Sonoma: *Sonoma Valley Inn* $ — 75
550 2nd St, CA 95476. **Road map** A3. **C** *(707) 938-9200; (800) 334-5784.* **FAX** *(707)
938-0935.* This Mission-style hotel Downtown has rooms with balconies
over a courtyard, fireplaces and continental breakfast. 🛏 📺 🕭 🅿 🖋

Sonoma: *Victorian Garden Inn* $$ — 5
316 E Napa St, CA 95476. **Road map** A3. **C** *(707) 996 5339.* **FAX** *(707) 996 1689.*
This peaceful Greek Revival farmhouse offers the perfect antidote to a
hectic tour of the region's wineries. Breakfast is included. 🛏 🕭 🅿 🖋

Yountville: *Napa Valley Lodge* $$ — 55
2230 Madison St, CA 94599. **Road map** B3. **C** *(707) 944-2468; (800) 368-2468.*
FAX *(707) 944-9362.* Creature comforts at this hotel include a whirlpool
and sauna. Some rooms have fireplaces and balconies. 🛏 📺 🕭 🅿 🖋

Yountville: *Vintage Inn* $$$$ — 80
6541 Washington St, CA 94599. **Road map** B3. **C** *(707) 944-1112.* **FAX** *(707)
944-1617.* The service is excellent at this hotel set in stunning gardens.
Bicycles and golfing facilities are available nearby. 🛏 📺 🕭 🅿 🍽 🖋

GOLD COUNTRY AND THE CENTRAL VALLEY

Amador City: *Imperial Hotel* $ — 7
14202 Hwy 49, CA 95601. **Road map** B3. **C** *(209) 267-9172; (800) 242-5594.*
FAX *(209) 267-9249.* This lovely 19th-century building near Sutter Creek has
been thoughtfully modernized. Breakfast is included. 🛏 🅿 🖋

Auburn: *Best Western Golden Key* $ — 68
13450 Lincoln Way, CA 95603. **Road map** B3. **C** *(916) 885-8611; (800) 528-1234.*
FAX *(916) 888-0319.* Located a few miles northeast of Sacramento, this basic
hotel provides continental breakfast. Pets are allowed. 🛏 📺 🕭 🅿 🖋

Grass Valley: *Best Western Gold Country* $$ — 84
11972 Sutton Way, CA 95945. **Road map** B3. **C** *(916) 273-1393; (800) 247-6590.*
FAX *(916) 273-4229.* Complimentary continental breakfast is offered at this
basic hotel, which is surrounded by pines. 🛏 📺 🕭 🅿 🖋

Grass Valley: *Holbrooke Hotel and Restaurant* $$ — 27
212 West Main St, CA 95945. **Road map** B3. **C** *(916) 273-1353; (800) 933-7077.*
FAX *(916) 273-0434.* Rooms in this downtown hotel – a California Historic
Landmark – are named after famous guests. 🛏 📺 🕭 🅿 🖋

Murphys: *Murphys Historic Hotel and Lodge* $ — 35
457 Main St, CA 95247. **Road map** B3. **C** *(209) 728-3444; (800) 532-7684.* **FAX** *(209)
728-1590.* With bullet holes in the doorway and a fabulous Western bar, this
historic monument epitomizes California's Wild West. Modern rooms in a
separate wing have TV and private baths. 🛏 🕭 🅿 🖋

Nevada City: *Emma Nevada House* $$ — 6
528 E Broad St, CA 95959. **Road map** B3. **C** *(916) 265-4415; (800) 916-3662.*
FAX *(916) 265-4416.* This lovely Victorian bed-and-breakfast inn provides a
perfect place to unwind. Some of the rooms have Jacuzzis. 🛏 🅿 🖋

Nevada City: *The Parsonage Bed and Breakfast* $$ — 6
427 Broad St, CA 95959. **Road map** B3. **C** *(916) 265-9478.* **FAX** *(916) 265-8147.*
This family-run Victorian inn, furnished with antiques, is a peaceful and
romantic haven. A huge cooked breakfast is included. 🛏 🔳 🅿 🖋

Price categories for a standard double room per night, inclusive of service charges and any additional taxes, such as local sales tax:

⑤ under $100
⑤⑤ $100–$150
⑤⑤⑤ $150–$200
⑤⑤⑤⑤ $200–$250
⑤⑤⑤⑤⑤ over $250

RESTAURANT
Hotel restaurant or dining room usually open to non-residents unless otherwise stated.

CHILDREN'S FACILITIES
Indicates child cots and/or a baby-sitting service available. A few hotels also provide children's portions and high chairs in the restaurant.

GARDEN/TERRACE
Hotels with a garden, courtyard or terrace, often providing tables for eating outside.

SWIMMING POOL
Hotel with indoor or outdoor swimming pool.

	NUMBER OF ROOMS	RESTAURANT	CHILDREN'S FACILITIES	GARDEN/TERRACE	SWIMMING POOL
NEVADA CITY: *National Hotel* ⑤ 211 Broad St, CA 95959. **Road map** B3. ((916) 265-4551. FAX (916) 265-2445. This historic building surrounded by pine trees has been a hotel since 1855. All the rooms have Victorian furnishings. 📶 TV ⛿ P 🌿	42	●	■	●	■
NEVADA CITY: *Grandmere's Inn* ⑤⑤⑤ 449 Broad St, CA 95959. **Road map** B3. ((916) 265-4660. FAX (916) 265-6569. The finest hotel in town, this Colonial-style house is surrounded by terraced gardens. Breakfast includes freshly baked pastries and fruit. 📶 ⛿ P 🌿	7		■	●	
SACRAMENTO: *River Boat Delta King Hotel* ⑤⑤ 1000 Front St, CA 95814. **Road map** B3. ((916) 444-5464. FAX (916) 444-5314. This steam paddle boat *(see pp456–7)* has been restored to its original 1930s splendour and is furnished with antiques. It has large rooms and a de luxe continental breakfast is provided. 📶 TV ⛿ P 🍽 🌿	44	●		●	
SACRAMENTO: *Amber House* ⑤⑤⑤ 1315 22nd St, CA 95816. **Road map** B3. ((916) 444-8085; (800) 755-6526. FAX (916) 552-6529. Thoughtful touches characterize this very special bed-and-breakfast inn. Some rooms have two-person Jacuzzis. 📶 TV P 🌿	9			●	
SACRAMENTO: *Sheraton Hotel* ⑤⑤⑤⑤ 1211 Point East Drive, Rancho Cordova, CA 95742. **Road map** B3. ((916) 638-1100; (800) 325-3535. FAX (916) 635-8356. This sophisticated modern hotel is perfect for the business traveller as well as the tourist. 📶 TV ⛿ P 🌿	265	●	■	●	■
SACRAMENTO: *Sterling Hotel* ⑤⑤⑤⑤ 1300 H St, CA 95814. **Road map** B3. ((916) 448-1300; (800) 365-7660. FAX (916) 448-8066. This luxurious hotel in a restored Victorian mansion is partly furnished with period, Art Deco and oriental pieces. Rooms have Italian marble Jacuzzis and continental breakfast is included. 📶 TV ⛿ P 🍽 🌿	17	●	■	●	
SOMERSET: *Fitzpatrick Winery and Lodge* ⑤ 7740 Fairplay Rd, CA 95684. **Road map** B3. ((916) 620-3248; (800) 245-9166. FAX (916) 620-6838. Set in a vineyard in the Sierra foothills, this bed-and-breakfast inn has spectacular views. Some rooms have balconies and there is an outdoor hot tub and evening wine tasting. 📶 ⛿ P 🌿	5			●	
SONORA: *Serenity* ⑤⑤ 15305 Bear Cub Drive, CA 95370. **Road map** B3. ((209) 533-1441; (800) 426-1441. FAX (209) 533-1441. Built like a 19th-century farmhouse in extensive grounds, this inn has private sitting areas, fireplaces and breakfast. 📶 P 🌿	4			●	
SONORA: *Sonora Inn & Café* ⑤⑤ 160 South Washington St, CA 95370. **Road map** B3. ((209) 532-7468; (800) 580-4667. FAX (209) 536-1303. Housed in an 1890s Spanish-style building in old downtown Sonora; there is a motel annexe at the back. 📶 TV ⛿ P 🌿	64	●	■	●	■
SUTTER CREEK: *Sutter Creek Inn* ⑤ 75 Main St, CA 95685. **Road map** B3. ((209) 267-5606. FAX (209) 267-9287. This English-style country inn has swinging beds which hang by chains from the ceiling. Some rooms have fireplaces and private patios. 📶 P 🌿	18			●	
SUTTER CREEK: *Foxes* ⑤⑤ 77 Main St (PO Box 159), CA 95685. **Road map** B3. ((209) 267-5882. FAX (209) 267-0712. This friendly bed-and-breakfast inn has comfortable, antique-furnished rooms and a honeymoon suite. 📶 P 🌿	7			●	
SUTTER CREEK: *Gold Quartz Inn* ⑤⑤ 15 Bryson Drive, CA 95685. **Road map** B3. ((209) 267-9155; (800) 752-8738. FAX (209) 267-9170. This pretty bed-and-breakfast inn has a romantic ambience. The back rooms overlook the rose garden, and some rooms have private porches. No children under ten allowed. 📶 TV ⛿ P 🌿	24			●	

THE HIGH SIERRAS

BISHOP: *Best Western Bishop Holiday Spa Lodge* $
025 N Main St, CA 93514. **Road map** C4. **C** *(760) 873-3543; (800) 576-3543.* **FAX** *(760) 72-4777.* Popular with outdoor recreation enthusiasts, this motel offers good value or money, with fridges, microwave and an indoor whirlpool. 🛏 📺 P 🅿

80

BISHOP: *Creekside Inn* $
25 N Main St, CA 93514. **Road map** C4. **C** *(760) 872-3044; (800) 273-3550.* **FAX** *(760) 72-1300.* This modern motel is set in spacious, attractively landscaped gardens long a natural creek. Some rooms have kitchen facilities. 🛏 📺 P 🅿

89

EL PORTAL: *Cedar Lodge* $
966 State Hwy 140, CA 95318. **Road map** C3. **C** *(209) 379-2612; (800) 321-5261.* **X** *(209) 379-2712.* At the western entrance to Yosemite National Park *(see p472–5)*, rooms range from standard to large suites. 🛏 📺 ♿ P 🅿

206

FISH CAMP: *Narrow Gauge Inn* $$
8571 State Hwy 41, CA 93623. **Road map** C4. **C** *(209) 683-7720.* **FAX** *(209) 683-139.* This small, romantic inn offers old-fashioned hospitality and has an xcellent restaurant *(see p573)*. It is closed during the winter. 🛏 P 🅿

26

FISH CAMP: *Tenaya Lodge* $$$
122 State Hwy 41, CA 93623. **Road map** C4. **C** *(209) 683-6555; (800) 635-5807.* **X** *(209) 683-8684.* Managed by the Marriott chain, this hotel has the best facil-es around Yosemite, including a sauna and steam room. 🛏 📺 P 🍴 🅿

242

JUNE LAKE: *Boulder Lodge* $
ne Lake (PO Box 68), CA 93529. **Road map** C3. **C** *(760) 648-7533.* **FAX** *(760) 8-7330.* Surrounded by lakeside grounds, this peaceful, relaxing lodge fers standard rooms and de luxe two-bedroom cottages. 🛏 📺 P 🅿

60

KINGS CANYON NATIONAL PARK: *Sequoia Lodge* $$
) Box 858, Grant Grove, CA 93633. **Road map** C4. **C** *(209) 565-3388.* **FAX** *(209) 5-3223.* Set amid groves of giant sequoias, this family-orientated lodge is en all year and offers standard rooms with bathrooms and rustic cabins thout bathrooms. Boat hire is available on the adjacent lake. P 🅿

52

KIRKWOOD: *Kirkwood Resort* $$
kwood (PO Box 1), CA 95646. **Road map** C3. **C** *(209) 258-7000.* **FAX** *(209) 258-00.* Located 30 miles (48 km) south of Lake Tahoe *(see pp470–71)*, this llic resort offers year-round recreation, from horse riding to cross-country ing. Most of the suites have kitchens and fireplaces. 🛏 📺 P 🅿

120

LEE VINING: *Lake View Lodge* $
Box 345, CA 93541. **Road map** C3. **C** *(760) 647-6543.* **FAX** *(760) 647-6325.* Set the western shore of Mono Lake *(see p479)*, this motel makes an excel-t base for exploring the area. Some rooms have kitchens. 🛏 📺 P 🅿

46

LONE PINE: *Frontier Motel* $
8 S Main St, CA 93545. **Road map** C4. **C** *(760) 876-5571.* **FAX** *(760) 876-5357.* ular with fishermen and hikers, this motel offers continental breakfast l large rooms, many with whirlpool baths. 🛏 📺 P 🅿

73

MAMMOTH LAKES: *Austria Hof Lodge* $
Canyon Blvd, CA 93546. **Road map** C4. **C** *(760) 934-2764.* **FAX** *(760) 934-1880.* hort walk from the ski slopes of Mammoth Mountain, this charming el is especially popular on winter weekends. 🛏 📺 P 🅿

22

MAMMOTH LAKES: *Shilo Inn* $$
3 Main St, CA 93546. **Road map** C4. **C** *(760) 934-4500.* **FAX** *(760) 934-7594.* ests are accommodated in large suites, with private bars and sitting s. Facilities include a sauna. 🛏 📺 P 🍴 🅿

71

SOUTH LAKE TAHOE: *Lake Tahoe Inn* $$
) Lake Tahoe Blvd, CA 96150. **Road map** C3. **C** *(916) 541-2010.* **FAX** *(916) -1428.* There are pleasant, spacious grounds and some two-bedroom s for families in addition to the standard motel rooms. 🛏 📺 P 🅿

400

SOUTH LAKE TAHOE: *Timber Cove Inn* $$
I Lake Tahoe Blvd, CA 96150. **Road map** C3. **C** *(916) 541-6722.* **FAX** *(916) 7959.* Built on the shores of Lake Tahoe, this motel has its own beach. rooms here, most of which have lovely views, are much more fortable than those in many of the nearby motels. 🛏 📺 P 🅿

262

				Price categories for a standard double room per night, inclusive of service charges and any additional taxes, such as local sales tax: $ under $100 $$ $100–$150 $$$ $150–$200 $$$$ $200–$250 $$$$$ over $250	RESTAURANT Hotel restaurant or dining room usually open to non-residents unless otherwise stated. CHILDREN'S FACILITIES Indicates child cots and/or a baby-sitting service available. A few hotels also provide children's portions and high chairs in the restaurant. GARDEN/TERRACE Hotels with a garden, courtyard or terrace, often providing tables for eating outside. SWIMMING POOL Hotel with indoor or outdoor swimming pool.	NUMBER OF ROOMS	RESTAURANT	CHILDREN'S FACILITIES	GARDEN/TERRACE	SWIMMING POOL

	NUMBER OF ROOMS	RESTAURANT	CHILDREN'S FACILITIES	GARDEN/TERRACE	SWIMMING POOL
SQUAW VALLEY: *Resort at Squaw Creek* $$$$ 400 Squaw Creek Rd, CA 96146. **Road map** B3. 📞 *(916) 583-6300; (800) 327-3353.* FAX *(916) 581-6632.* This luxurious resort lies at the foot of Squaw Mountain. It is popular with skiers in winter and golfers in summer. 🛏 📺 ♿ 🅿 🍴 🌿	402	●	▨		●
TAHOE CITY: *Chaney House* $$ 4725 West Lake Blvd (PO Box 7852), CA 96145. **Road map** B3. 📞 *(916) 525-7333.* FAX *(916) 525-4413.* Set in pine woods and surrounded by gardens, the house has its own private beach and pier and a huge fireplace. 🛏 🅿 🌿	4			●	
TAHOE CITY: *Tahoe City Travel Lodge* $$ 455 North Lake Blvd, CA 96145. **Road map** B3. 📞 *(916) 583-3766.* FAX *(916) 583-8045.* Services at this basic motel include free cable TV, dry sauna, outdoor Jacuzzi and discounts at nearby restaurants. 🛏 📺 🅿 🌿	47		▨		●
TRUCKEE: *Donner Lake Village Resort* $$ Suite 101, 15695 Donner Pass Rd, CA 96161. **Road map** B3. 📞 *(916) 587-6081; (800) 621-6664.* FAX *(916) 587-8782.* With its own beach and marina, this resort offers year-round recreation. It has some two-bedroom suites. 🛏 📺 🅿 🌿	64		▨		●
YOSEMITE NATIONAL PARK: *Wawona Hotel* $$ State Hwy 41, CA 95389. **Road map** C3. 📞 *(209) 252-4848.* FAX *(209) 456-0542.* This characterful old hotel, dating back to the 1870s, is a cherished High Sierras landmark. Accommodation includes a handful of rustic cottages and there is golf, horse riding and tennis. 🛏 🅿 🌿	104	●	▨	●	●
YOSEMITE NATIONAL PARK: *Yosemite Lodge* $$ Yosemite Valley, CA 95389. **Road map** C3. 📞 *(209) 252-4848.* FAX *(209) 456-0542.* Near Yosemite Falls *(see p474),* you'll find the best selection of lodgings in the valley, with modern motel rooms and several rustic cabins. 🅿 🌿	495	●	▨	●	●
YOSEMITE NATIONAL PARK: *Ahwahnee Hotel* $$$$ Yosemite Valley, CA 95389. **Road map** C3. 📞 *(209) 252-4848.* FAX *(209) 456-0542.* With its unique mix of sophistication and rusticity, this is Yosemite's most stylish hotel *(see p475).* Built in 1927, it features grand public areas and a fine restaurant *(see p574).* Bicycles and horses can be hired. 🛏 🅿 🌿	123	●	▨	●	●

NORTH CENTRAL CALIFORNIA

	NUMBER OF ROOMS	RESTAURANT	CHILDREN'S FACILITIES	GARDEN/TERRACE	SWIMMING POOL
APTOS: *Best Western Seacliff Inn* $ 7500 Old Dominion Court, CA 95003. **Road map** B4. 📞 *(408) 688-7300; (800) 367-2003.* FAX *(408) 685-3603.* This basic hotel is very close to the beach. The rooms are large and some have whirlpool baths. 🛏 📺 ♿ 🅿 🌿	140	●	▨		
APTOS: *Rio Sands Motel* $$ 116 Aptos Beach Drive, CA 95003. **Road map** B4. 📞 *(408) 688-3207; (800) 826-2077* FAX *(408) 688-6107.* All rooms have patios or balconies overlooking landscaped gardens. Some rooms have kitchen facilities. 🛏 📺 ♿ 🅿 🌿	50				●
BIG SUR: *Big Sur River Inn* $$ Hwy 1, Pheneger Creek, CA 93920. **Road map** B4. 📞 *(408) 667-2700; (800) 548-3610.* FAX *(408) 667-2743.* The rooms at this rustic inn are basic and comfortable. The restaurant has live music at the weekend. 🛏 ♿ 🅿 🌿	19	●	▨	●	
BIG SUR: *Deetjen's Big Sur Inn* $$ Castro Canyon, CA 93920. **Road map** B4. 📞 *(408) 667-2377.* This delightful hotel, in a rustic building with a good restaurant, has a loyal clientele. Children are only allowed in the two-room cottages. 🛏 ♿ 🅿 🌿	20	●		●	
BIG SUR: *The Ventana Inn* $$$$ Hwy 1, CA 93920. **Road map** B4. 📞 *(408) 624-4812; 667-2331; (800) 628-6500.* FAX *(408) 667-2419.* Surrounded by forest, most rooms have fireplaces and some have ocean views. There are saunas and a library. 🛏 📺 ♿ 🅿 🌿	62	●			●

BIG SUR: *Post Ranch Inn* $$$$$ | 30
PO Box 219, Hwy 1, CA 93920. **Road map** B4. (*(408) 667-2200; (800) 527-2200.*
FAX *(408) 667-2824.* Buildings at this extraordinary resort with spa facilities
include tree houses and earth shelters built into the hillside.

CARMEL: *Robles Del Rio Lodge* $$ | 33
200 Punta Del Monte, Carmel Valley, CA 93924. **Road map** B4. (*(408) 659-2264;
(800) 833-0843.* FAX *(408) 659-5157.* Breakfast, a hot tub, tennis and views of
the Carmel Valley are among the lodge's many attractions.

CARMEL: *Crystal Terrace Inn* $$$ | 16
24815 Carpenter St, CA 93921. **Road map** B4. (*(408) 624-6400; (800) 600-4488.*
FAX *(408) 624-5111.* This quiet, romantic hotel near the town centre is geared
towards couples. Some rooms have fireplaces and bars.

CARMEL: *Cypress Inn* $$$ | 34
Lincoln & 7th Ave, CA 93921. **Road map** B4. (*(408) 624-3871; (800) 443-7443.*
FAX *(408) 624-8216.* Owned by the actress Doris Day, this inn encourages
pets, even in the public areas. Some rooms have Jacuzzis.

CARMEL: *La Playa Hotel* $$$ | 75
Camino Real & 8th Ave, CA 93921. **Road map** B4. (*(408) 624-6476; (800) 582-
8900.* FAX *(408) 624-7966.* This Spanish-style hotel also has five cottages with
open fires and kitchenettes and is excellent for families.

CARMEL: *Pine Inn* $$$ | 47
Ocean Ave & Lincoln, CA 93921. **Road map** B4. (*(408) 624-3851; (800) 228-3851.*
FAX *(408) 624-3030.* Carmel's oldest hotel, dating from 1889, has cosy rooms
and a magnificent red lobby furnished with antiques.

CARMEL: *Carmel Valley Ranch* $$$$ | 100
1 Old Ranch Rd, CA 93923. **Road map** B4. (*(408) 625-9500; (800) 422-7635.*
FAX *(408) 624-2858.* Some rooms have open fires and Jacuzzis at this
luxurious modern hotel and golf club.

CARMEL: *Quail Lodge* $$$$ | 100
8205 Valley Greens Drive, CA 93923. **Road map** B4. (*(408) 624-1581; (800)
538-9516.* FAX *(408) 624-3726.* This complex is the height of luxury, with a
golf course, hiking trails and even a pet-sitting service.

CARMEL: *Highlands Inn and Restaurant* $$$$$ | 142
Pacific Coast Hwy 1, CA 93923. **Road map** B4. (*(408) 624-3801; (800) 682-4811.*
FAX *(408) 626-1574.* This rustic hotel, set in woodland on a bluff overlooking
the coast, has pretty views. Some rooms have Jacuzzis.

MONTEREY: *Casa Munras Garden Hotel* $$ | 152
700 Munras Ave, CA 93940. **Road map** B4. (*(408) 375-2411; (800) 222-2446.*
FAX *(408) 375-1365.* Within walking distance of all the sights, this hotel has
a loyal clientele. The comfortable rooms have fireplaces.

MONTEREY: *Monterey Plaza Hotel* $$ | 285
400 Cannery Row, CA 93940. **Road map** B4. (*(408) 646-1700; (800) 334-3999.*
FAX *(408) 646-5937.* Some rooms have balconies with views over Monterey
Bay. The hotel is near all the town sights.

MONTEREY: *Old Monterey Inn* $$$$ | 10
500 Martin St, CA 93940. **Road map** B4. (*(408) 375-8284; (800) 350-2344.*
FAX *(408) 375-6730.* Guests are pampered at this Tudor-style manor set in English-
style gardens. Rooms have fireplaces and Jacuzzis. Adults only.

PACIFIC GROVE: *The Martine Inn* $$$ | 20
255 Ocean View Blvd, CA 93950. **Road map** B4. (*(408) 373-3388; (800) 852-
5588.* FAX *(408) 373-3896.* This Mediterranean-style inn has an 1890s billiard
table and old MGs on display. Some rooms have open fires.

SANTA CRUZ: *Sunset Inn* $ | 28
2424 Mission St, CA 95060. **Road map** B4. (*(408) 423-3471.* Rooms are
large at this basic hotel. Some have kitchens, but the ones overlooking
the busy street can be noisy. Pets are allowed.

SANTA CRUZ: *Babbling Brook Inn* $$ | 12
1025 Laurel St, CA 95060. **Road map** B4. (*(408) 427-2437; (800) 866-1131.*
FAX *(408) 427-2457.* Rooms have fireplaces, Jacuzzis or balconies at this
perfect romantic retreat. Breakfast is included.

For key to symbols see back flap

WHERE TO EAT

OF ALL THE STATES IN THE US, California has perhaps the widest variety of places to eat. "Californian cuisine" – light food prepared in a range of international styles using locally grown ingredients – was pioneered by chefs such as Jeremiah Towers, Wolfgang Puck and Alice Waters and is now internationally recognized. There is an ample number of Italian and French restaurants, but many other international cuisines are also available.

Californian diner sign

In every town you can eat Japanese sushi, Thai noodles, Chinese dim sum, Mexican burritos, Middle Eastern falafel or Indian tandoori. While ethnic cooking reflects the state's many cultures, there is also no shortage of that classic all-American meal: hamburger, French fries and cola. The restaurants listed on pages 544–75 have been selected for their variety, service and good value. Some typical meals served in California are shown on pages 540–41.

CALIFORNIAN EATING PATTERNS

SOME SAY AMERICANS make the best breakfast in the world and this is evident in California. From diners to top restaurants, the breakfast menu is vast. Omelettes with fries and toast, pancakes or waffles topped with fruit and syrup, and eggs, bacon or sausage served with toast or a muffin are popular options. Less filling choices are coffee with a bagel or pastry, or cereal topped with raisins or bananas. Breakfast is served from 6:30am to 11am. Brunch extends the breakfast menu with grilled meats. It is always available on Sundays, and at selected restaurants on Saturdays, from 9am to 2pm.

Californian lunch is light – soup and salad or a sandwich. Dinner is the main meal of the day for Americans. Many restaurants make dinner a special occasion by setting out candles and tablecloths, and presenting the chef's specialities as creatively as possible. Dinner is served from 5:30pm to 10:30pm.

PRICES AND TIPPING

EATING OUT in California is very reasonable. A snack in a café should cost no more than $5 per person. A main meal in a diner will set you back up to $15. A three-course meal in a good restaurant, excluding wine, will cost $25–$30, but gourmet meals can begin at $40. Fixed-price menus are rare, but lunch menus are much cheaper and are generally very similar to the dinner menu.

Tipping should be based on service: if satisfactory, leave 15 per cent; if superlative,

Planet Hollywood (see p546)

leave 20 per cent. Make sure the tip is calculated on the net cost of the meal and does not include the tax. Restaurant tax in California is 8.5 per cent.

FAST FOOD

A UBIQUITOUS FEATURE of the Californian landscape, fast-food outlets are rarely more than five minutes away. They offer filling, inexpensive food, which stretches the travel budget for families. Chain-owned diners include Starbucks, Denny's, Sizzlers and Marie Callendar. While the seating areas are large and the selections on the menu are extensive, the food is prepared in bulk and may therefore be a little bland.

HEALTHY EATING

A NUMBER OF restaurants in California now follow the American Heart Association's guidelines for reducing cholesterol and dietary fat. A red heart beside a dish denotes an AHA-approved "Healthy Heart" meal, low in calories and cholesterol. If a restaurant does not offer such meals, you can ask your waiter to omit certain ingredients where appropriate.

Vegetarian cuisine is not a strong feature in Californian restaurants, but they all offer salads and many of them will make up meat-free meals for customers if requested.

Rex Restaurant in the Oviatt Building, LA (see p545)

COFFEE HOUSES, TEA HOUSES AND CAFÉS

COFFEE HOUSES exist all over California. At "internet" coffee houses, patrons plug into computers as they eat and drink. Other coffee houses are attached to bookshops, where customers can drink and read. Coffee houses do not offer a full menu, but specialize in drinks (coffees, sodas, juices and wine) and cakes.

Tea houses are also popular, particularly in LA, for their elegant and subdued atmosphere.

Cafés usually only have one or two tables for outside dining, but the atmosphere inside is usually informal and long stays are encouraged.

Ratto's Italian delicatessen in Oakland

PICNICS AND TAKEAWAYS

DELICATESSENS and supermarkets with deli counters stock cold meats, cheeses, pickles and salads. They will also make up fresh sandwiches to your personal order to take away and enjoy in one of the parks or open areas that abound in California.

You can also order takeaways from any restaurant, although the prices for this are the same as eating in the restaurant itself.

MICROBREWERY BARS

IN THE WORLD of beer, micro breweries are big news. In every city there is a healthy number of on-site brewmasters with bars serving a selection of national and international

El Paseo Restaurant, Santa Barbara *(see p552)*

beers, but also brewing their own specials, such as Anchor Steam in San Francisco and Karl Straus Amber Lager in San Diego *(see pp542–3)*. If a beer proves successful locally, they can then go on to earn national and sometimes international recognition.

A variety of snack foods is also served at microbrewery bars to soak up the beer.

SMOKING

CALIFORNIA is an anti-smoking state and the Californian State Legislature has banned smoking in all restaurants. Cigarettes are now only permitted in the bar area and occasionally in the gardens of some restaurants, but cigar smoking is rarely allowed. In addition, further state legislation is planned to ban cigarette smoking in all parts of restaurants, including the bar.

Elegant and leisurely Craviotto's Café in Santa Barbara

WHEELCHAIR ACCESS

ALL NEW RESTAURANTS in California, and old restaurants undergoing renovation, must make their site accessible to wheelchair users. This means that there should be no steps into the restaurant or to the tables, and that there should be wide bathroom doors.

CHILDREN'S FACILITIES

MOST RESTAURANTS are children-friendly and offer a children's menu and high chairs or booster seats. However, in the quieter, upmarket restaurants, parents are expected to keep children seated at the table and take noisy or upset children outside until they calm down.

DRESS CODES

WITH CALIFORNIA'S leisurely lifestyle, many gourmet restaurants do not require men to wear jackets and ties or women to wear dresses, although jeans, shorts, trainers and vests are definitely not allowed.

BOOKING AHEAD

IT IS ALWAYS best to make a reservation in advance to avoid disappointment. City restaurants, in particular, are often very busy, and established or fashionable venues are sometimes booked up more than a month in advance. If you make a reservation that you later cannot keep, ring the restaurant and cancel.

What to Eat in California

FOOD IN CALIFORNIA reflects the ethnic diversity of the state's population – Chinese and Italian dishes are popular and there is a strong emphasis on Mexican-style cuisine. Due to similarities in climate, Californian cooking is also very much influenced by Mediterranean cuisine. Traditional Provençal or Italian recipes are given a Californian twist, often with the addition of an exciting new ingredient, resulting in exotic, colourful salads and innovative pasta dishes. California is rich in natural resources. Fresh, seasonal fruit and vegetables, grown year-round in the many fertile valleys, are a hallmark of Californian cuisine. The long coastline means that there is also an abundance of seafood, as well as freshwater fish from the state's rivers and lakes.

Flavoured olive oil

Waffles
Topped with fruit and whipped cream, waffles are often part of a full breakfast in California.

Bagels

Focaccia

Sourdough bread

Bread
Distinctive breads are used for sandwiches or served with soup or salads.

Deli Sandwiches
In most delicatessens, customers choose from various fillings to create substantial sandwiches.

Guacamole (avocado and garlic dip)

Taco (filled and folded tortilla)

Salsa (chunky tomato, onion and chilli sauce)

Arroz (rice), flavoured with tomato

Burritos (steamed and rolled tortilla, with various fillings)

Nachos (crisp fried corn chips, often with a spicy flavour)

Frijoles (black or pinto beans)

Burger and Fries
American burgers are usually made of beef and served with cheese, relish and onion rings.

MEXICAN FOOD
Spicy Mexican food, which is available all over the state, always includes a salsa, rice and beans and steamed, fried or baked flour or corn tortillas (thin pancakes).

Dim Sum
A Chinese speciality, these little dumplings are stuffed with fish, meat or vegetables.

Ahi Tuna
Wafer-thin slices of Ahi tuna are served rare with a pepper sauce. Vegetables add colour.

Spaghetti Vongole
This Italian dish of pasta and steamed clams is on offer at many oceanfront restaurants.

Lobster and Vegetables
Lobster is one of the many seafood delicacies popular along the region's coastline.

Californian Pizza
Californian pizzas have imaginative toppings, such as grilled vegetables, meat or fish.

Courgettes

Red pepper

Grilled polenta

Aubergine

Grilled Vegetables Mediterranean Style
Vegetables are marinated in olive oil, garlic and herbs, and then grilled until they are soft and tender. They are often served with grilled polenta (solid maize porridge).

Salad in Tortilla
This Californian-style salad is beautifully presented in a crisp tortilla shell.

Fruit Dessert
Fresh fruit is often served as a dessert, sometimes with a passion fruit or other sauce.

Dates

Cherries

Peaches

Cantaloupe melon

Strawberries   Apricots

Pineapple

CALIFORNIAN FRUIT
Limes

Figs

Much of the fruit available in California is grown in the state's sunny, fertile valleys and makes a refreshing breakfast, dessert or snack.

Kumquats

What to Drink in California

Beer label

CALIFORNIANS ARE devoted to the consumption of beverages, partly because they tend to do so much outdoor exercise in the heat and partly as a social activity. Soft drinks, or "sodas", play the largest role in the state's beverage culture, although alcohol is also important. Many restaurants tempt weekend customers with champagne brunches. Beer can be enjoyed on the beach or while watching a game of baseball. Wine, particularly local California wine (see pp422–3), is popular with dinner.

Sign in the Napa Valley wine-producing region in Northern California

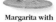

Tequila bottle **Colourful Sunset Strip** **Strawberry Daiquiri** **Margarita with slice of lime**

COCKTAILS

SIPPING COCKTAILS beside the ocean at sunset is part of the popular image of the "Californian dream". The margarita cocktail still ranks as the firm favourite throughout the state. Served in ever-wider glasses, margaritas are a blend of tequila, lime juice and an orange-flavoured liqueur, with the rim of the glass dipped in salt.

The Sunset Strip, named after the infamous section of Sunset Boulevard (see pp98–103), consists of equal parts of gin, rum, triple sec, vodka, pineapple juice and lemonade. Another cocktail popular in the state is the pina colada. This is a blend of fresh pineapple, cream of coconut and equal parts of papaya juice, lime mix, orange juice and pineapple juice. A shot of rum is added and the finished drink is served over ice in tall, elegant glasses.

SOFT DRINKS

CALIFORNIANS ARE generally very health-conscious and they consume a lot of fruit juice. Staff at juice stalls in shopping centres or on the street will squeeze juice from almost any kind of fruit, or a mixture of fruit and vegetables, while you wait. Also available on the street, as well as in most hotel lobbies, are machines supplying soft drinks and free cold water and crushed ice. Most fast-food outlets offer a range of soft drinks in three sizes, although the same products can usually be purchased more cheaply from supermarkets.

Iced cola

The most popular non-alcoholic drink in the state remains the all-American cola. However, health awareness has led to a growth in the consumption of diet and caffeine-free versions of colas and other carbonated soft drinks.

Sports-loving Californians often carry flexible thermos flasks filled with drinks chilled overnight in the refrigerator.

Freshly squeezed strawberry juice

TEA AND COFFEE

PEOPLE IN CALIFORNIA consume large quantities of "designer" coffee. Café latte, café au lait, cappuccino, frappuccino (iced coffee) and flavoured brews, such as almond and mocha, are on hand at coffee houses and street stalls. Tea is also becoming increasingly popular and imported teas come in every imaginable flavour.

Cappuccino **Café latte**

Frappuccino **Lemon tea**

WINE

VINES THRIVE IN the mild climate of Northern California, where cooling fogs help the grapes to reach perfection. The main red wine varieties grown in the region are Cabernet Sauvignon, Pinot Noir, Merlot and Zinfandel *(see pp422–3)*. White wines are also classified by grape variety, with Chardonnay by far the most popular of recent years. Grown throughout the West Coast region, this prestige grape produces wines varying in character from dry, light, lemon and vanilla-scented to the more headstrong and oaky.

California has acquired an international reputation for excellent champagne-style wines at the right price, reflected in the fact that the finest French producers have huge investments in the state. Moët & Chandon and Mumm, among others, have set up wineries in the Napa Valley and elsewhere.

Wine is much cheaper in supermarkets or liquor stores than in restaurants. State law allows customers to take their own bottles into restaurants, where the corkage fee is generally $5–10.

Sparkling Cuvée Napa by Mumm

Rosé or blush wine

Napa Chardonnay

Cabernet Sauvignon

WATER

A VARIETY OF mineral waters is produced in the state, the best of which comes from the spa town of Calistoga in the Napa Valley *(see p445)*. Many mineral waters are flavoured with fresh fruit and most are carbonated. Most public places, including office buildings, have water dispensers. Californian tap water is fresh, clean and safe to drink.

Calistoga mineral water

ALCOHOLIC DRINKS

Alcohol cannot be purchased or consumed in California by anyone under the age of 21. It is not uncommon for shops and bars to refuse service or admittance to anyone not carrying documents proving that they are at least 21 years old. Licensing hours, however, are relaxed; those old enough to drink legally can buy or consume alcohol from 6am until 2am, seven days a week.

Busy bar in Santa Barbara

BEER

BEERS OF EVERY variety – foreign, American, even home-made – have become highly desirable. The recent resurgence in small breweries across the United States can be credited to the success of San Francisco's Anchor Brewery, whose Steam Beer, Liberty Ale and other products show that American beer need not be bland and tasteless. Other excellent local brews to look out for include Mendocino County's rich Boont Amber and Red Tail Ale.

Copying the self-brewing concept that began in Canada, many Californians are now opening do-it-yourself breweries. Experts are on hand to assist with malting, boiling, carbonating, hopping, fermenting and bottling. A personal-label brew takes two to six weeks to ferment. Microbrewery beers, brewed on the premises of a bar *(see p539)*, are also extremely popular.

Anchor Steam Beer

Red Tail Ale

Liberty Ale

Choosing a Restaurant

THE RESTAURANTS in this guide have been selected across a wide range of price categories for their exceptional food, good value and interesting location. They are listed here by region, starting with Los Angeles. The thumb tabs on the pages use the same colour-coding as the corresponding regional chapter in the main section of the guide.

	OUTDOOR EATING	VEGETARIAN SPECIALITIES	BAR AREA/COCKTAIL BAR	FIXED-PRICE MENU	CHILDREN'S FACILITIES

LOS ANGELES

	OUTDOOR EATING	VEGETARIAN SPECIALITIES	BAR AREA/COCKTAIL BAR	FIXED-PRICE MENU	CHILDREN'S FACILITIES
BEL AIR: *Bel-Air Hotel Restaurant* $$$$$ 701 Stone Canyon Rd, CA 90077. **Map** 4 A2. (*(310) 472-1211*. At this award-winning restaurant, you can dine in the elegant dining room, the library-like lounge or on the lovely terrace which overlooks gardens and a lake with swans. The cuisine is Californian-French. 🅿 🍴 *D.* 🎵 📶 💬 ✉	▦	●	▦		▦
BEVERLY HILLS: *Factor's Deli* $ 9420 W Pico Blvd, CA 90035. **Map** 5 F5. (*(310) 278-9175*. The portions are enormous at this genuine Jewish deli, so you may want to split a sandwich between two. The service is brisk but friendly. ● *Sun.* 🅿 ✉		●			▦
BEVERLY HILLS: *Koo Koo Roo* $ 262 S Beverly Drive, CA 90212. **Map** 5 F4. (*(310) 274-3121*. This restaurant chain sells healthy fast food all over LA – delicious turkey sandwiches, flame-grilled skinless chicken, salads and home-made breads. 🅿 ✉		●			
BEVERLY HILLS: *Nate 'n' Al's Deli* $ 414 N Beverly Drive, CA 90210. **Map** 5 F3. (*(310) 274-0101*. Everyone comes here for fabulous sandwiches, deli items and dinners (roast turkey or chicken with mashed potatoes and gravy). Breakfast is served all day. 🅿 ✉		●			▦
BEVERLY HILLS: *Barney Greengrass* $$ Barney's New York, 9570 Wilshire Blvd, CA 90210. **Map** 5 F4. (*(310) 777-5877*. This is one of the hippest places to eat lunch, with a wonderful view and delicious up-market deli fare. It's also great for tea and desserts. 🅿 ✉	▦	●	▦		▦
BEVERLY HILLS: *Benihana of Tokyo* $$ 38 N La Cienega Blvd, CA 90211. **Map** 6 C4. (*(310) 659-1511*. A chef prepares the food at your table – vegetables, chicken, seafood and beef – at this Japanese steakhouse. The spectacle is fun and the food is good. It gets very busy so book ahead. ● *Sat & Sun L.* 🅿 ✉			▦		
BEVERLY HILLS: *Café Rodeo* $$ 360 N Rodeo Drive, CA 90210. **Map** 5 F3. (*(310) 273-0300*. This busy restaurant has a good choice of dishes for breakfast, lunch and dinner. It has seating on the pavement for good people-watching. 🅿 ✉	▦	●	▦		
BEVERLY HILLS: *Jackson's Farm* $$$ 439 N Beverly Drive, CA 90210. **Map** 5 F3. (*(310) 273-5578*. This open and airy restaurant is excellent for salads, cheese platters, sandwiches and pastas, with a wonderful selection of breads and desserts. 🅿 ✉	▦	●			
BEVERLY HILLS: *Lawry's Prime Rib* $$$ 100 N La Cienega Blvd, CA 90211. **Map** 6 C4. (*(310) 652-2827*. This is the place to go in LA for prime rib. Enormous, succulent portions of beef are carved at the table and served with Yorkshire pudding. ● *L.* 🅿 ✉		●	▦		▦
BEVERLY HILLS: *McCormick & Schmick's The Fish House* $$$ 206 N Rodeo Drive,CA 90210. **Map** 5 F3. (*(310) 859-0434*. This excellent restaurant serves up to 30 varieties of fresh fish, including a huge selection of oysters. The large menu also offers pastas, meat and poultry. 🅿 ✉	▦	●	▦		
BEVERLY HILLS: *Piazza Rodeo* $$$ 208 Rodeo Drive, CA 90210. **Map** 5 F3. (*(310) 275-2428*. The fabulous pasta dishes are recommended at this busy Italian restaurant. For lighter fare, there is also a good selection of antipasti, salads and sandwiches. 🅿 ✉	▦	●	▦		▦
BEVERLY HILLS: *Kate Mantilini* $$$$ 9109 Wilshire Blvd, CA 90210. **Map** 5 F4. (*(310) 278-3699*. Californian cuisine is on offer at this spacious, airy restaurant. Sample the fabulous white chilli (made with chicken and white beans). 🅿 📶 ✉		●	▦		▦

Price categories for a three-course meal for one, including a half bottle of house wine, sales tax and service:
$ under $25
$$ $25–$35
$$$ $35–$50
$$$$ $50–$70
$$$$$ over $70

OUTDOOR EATING
Some tables on a patio or terrace.

VEGETARIAN SPECIALITIES
One menu always includes a selection of vegetarian dishes.

BAR AREA/COCKTAIL BAR
There is a bar area or cocktail bar within the restaurant.

FIXED-PRICE MENU
A good-value fixed-price menu on offer at lunch, dinner or both, usually with three courses.

CHILDREN'S FACILITIES
Small portions and/or highchairs available on request.

		OUTDOOR EATING	VEGETARIAN SPECIALITIES	BAR AREA/COCKTAIL BAR	FIXED-PRICE MENU	CHILDREN'S FACILITIES
BEVERLY HILLS: *Matsuhisa*	$$$$		●	▦	●	▦
129 N La Cienega Blvd, CA 90211. **Map** 6 C4. ☎ *(310) 659-9639.* This outstanding Japanese seafood restaurant serves exotic dishes, such as hot sea urchin or green-lipped mussels. Reservations are recommended. ☑						
BEVERLY HILLS: *Dining Room, Regent Beverly Wilshire Hotel*	$$$$$		●	▦	●	▦
9500 Wilshire Blvd, CA 90212. **Map** 5 F3. ☎ *(310) 275-5200.* This extremely elegant hotel supper club *(see p508)* attracts a smart older crowd with its European old world ambience. The paella is extraordinary. ☝ 🍴 🎵 ☑						
BEVERLY HILLS: *Mr Chow*	$$$$$		●	▦	●	▦
344 N Camden Dr, CA 90210. **Map** 5 F3. ☎ *(310) 278-9911.* Celebrities come to this stylish restaurant for delicious Peking-style cuisine. Favourites include drunken fish and gamblers' duck. ● *Sat & Sun L.* ☝ 🍴 🎵 ♟ ☑						
BEVERLY HILLS: *Spago*	$$$$$		●			
1114 Horn Ave, CA 90069. **Map** 6 C1. ☎ *(310) 652-4025.* Celebrity chef Wolfgang Puck's first restaurant *(see p98)* is now one of the most famous in the US. From the contemporary décor to the magnificent Californian cuisine, it is an experience not to be missed. ● *Sun.* ☝ ♟ ☑						
CENTURY CITY: *Dive L.A.*	$		●	▦	●	▦
10250 Santa Monica Blvd, CA 90067. **Map** 5 D4. ☎ *(310) 788-3483.* Children love this restaurant, which serves gourmet sandwiches, pizzas and "dive fries" with dipping sauces. It is decorated like a submarine inside and out, with portholes for windows and a simulated diving sequence hourly. ☝ ☑						
CENTURY CITY: *La Cachette*	$$$$		●			
10506 Santa Monica Blvd, CA 90025. **Map** 4 C5. ☎ *(310) 470-4992.* This very chic restaurant, one of LA's best, serves French-Mediterranean cuisine. The spacious surroundings are light and airy. ☝ ♟ ☑						
DOWNTOWN: *Bernard's*	$		●	▦	●	▦
Biltmore Hotel, 506 S Grand Ave, CA 90071. **Map** 11 D4. ☎ *(213) 612-1580.* This elegant restaurant features fixed-price and *à la carte* menus and special wine dinners and lunches. They have a good selection of fish dishes as well as steak and lamb specialities. ● *Sun, Mon D, Sat L.* ☝ 🍴 ♟ ☑						
DOWNTOWN: *Patinette at Moca*	$	▦	●			▦
250 S Grand Ave, CA 90012. **Map** 11 E3. ☎ *(213) 626-1178.* This café-style restaurant in the courtyard of the Museum of Contemporary Art *(see p121)* serves great salads and sandwiches. ● *Mon, Tue & Wed D, Fri & Sat D.* ☝ 🎵 ☑						
DOWNTOWN: *Checkers*	$$$		●	▦		▦
535 S Grand Ave, CA 90071. **Map** 11 D4. ☎ *(213) 624-0000.* Furnished with marble and antiques, this intimate hotel restaurant *(see p510)* has an award-winning menu featuring eclectic Californian cuisine. ☝ ☑						
DOWNTOWN: *Water Grill*	$$$		●	▦		
544 S Grand Ave, CA 90017. **Map** 11 D4. ☎ *(213) 891-0900.* This restaurant has an oyster bar and serves delicious seafood, from crab cakes to Santa Barbara prawns. They also have a live lobster and crab tank. ☝ ☑						
DOWNTOWN: *Sonora Café*	$$$$	▦	●	▦		▦
180 S La Brea, CA 90036. **Map** 7 F3. ☎ *(213) 857-1800.* Wonderful Mexican-influenced southwestern staples are on offer at this candlelit restaurant. Favourites include fabulous *quesadillas* (Mexican stuffed pasties) filled with goat's cheese, brie and smoked bacon. ● *Sat & Sun L.* ☝ ☑						
DOWNTOWN: *Rex Il Ristorante*	$$$$$		●	▦	●	
617 S Olive St, CA 90014. **Map** 11 D4. ☎ *(213) 627-2300.* The contemporary Italian cuisine packs in the customers at this beautiful Art Deco restaurant in the Oviatt Hotel. ● *Sun, Mon–Wed L, Sat L.* 🍴 🎵 ♟ ☑						

Price categories for a three-course meal for one, including a half bottle of house wine, sales tax and service:
$ under $25
$$ $25–$35
$$$ $35–$50
$$$$ $50–$70
$$$$$ over $70

OUTDOOR EATING
Some tables on a patio or terrace.
VEGETARIAN SPECIALITIES
One menu always includes a selection of vegetarian dishes.
BAR AREA/COCKTAIL BAR
There is a bar area or cocktail bar within the restaurant.
FIXED-PRICE MENU
A good-value fixed-price menu on offer at lunch, dinner or both, usually with three courses.
CHILDREN'S FACILITIES
Small portions and/or highchairs available on request.

	OUTDOOR EATING	VEGETARIAN SPECIALITIES	BAR AREA/COCKTAIL BAR	FIXED-PRICE MENU	CHILDREN'S FACILITIES

GLENDALE: *Kix* $
343 N Central Ave, CA 91203. **Road map** inset A. ((818) 956-7800. This roomy, light and casual restaurant serves delicious Californian cuisine. There is a good selection of pastas, salads and fresh fish. ● Sun, Mon, Sat L. 🔊 ♀ 🖼
Outdoor Eating ■ · Vegetarian ● · Bar Area ■

HOLLYWOOD: *Canter's Deli* $
419 N Fairfax Ave, CA 90036. **Map** 7 D2. ((213) 651-2030. The hip crowd ends up at this wonderful 24-hour deli between 2am and 4am for the huge, delicious sandwiches and diner-style meals. 🔊 🖼
Vegetarian ● · Bar Area ■ · Children's ■

HOLLYWOOD: *Cha Cha Cha* $
656 N Virgil Ave, CA 90004. **Map** 9 F1. ((213) 664-7723. Paella and jerk chicken are especially good at this contemporary Caribbean restaurant. The spicy sauces can be served on the side. 🔊 🎵 🖼
Vegetarian ● · Bar Area ■ · Children's ■

HOLLYWOOD: *Kokomo Café* $
Farmer's Market, 6333 W 3rd St, CA 90036. **Map** 7 D3. ((213) 933-0773. This café is a great place to eat breakfast and lunch and as a result is often packed with hungry customers. Try the applewood-smoked chicken breast sandwiches or the delicious turkey burgers. ● D. 🔊 🖼
Outdoor Eating ■ · Vegetarian ● · Children's ■

HOLLYWOOD: *Mario's Peruvian* $
5786 Melrose Ave, CA 90038. **Map** 8 B1. ((213) 466-4181. This uninspired-looking venue serves wonderful Peruvian dishes including a delicious fish stew and fish marinated in lemon juice (served cold). Arrive early as it gets busy. Alcohol is not served but you can bring your own. 🔊 🖼
Vegetarian ● · Children's ■

HOLLYWOOD: *Planet Hollywood* $
9560 Wilshire Blvd, CA 90212. **Map** 5 F4. ((310) 275-7828. Owned by a group of film stars, this theme restaurant has displays of film memorabilia. The food consists of hamburgers, pizzas and salads. 🔊 🖼
Vegetarian ● · Bar Area ■ · Children's ■

HOLLYWOOD: *Souplantation* $
Beverly Center, 8491 W 3rd St, CA 90048. **Map** 6 C3. ((213) 655-0381. This all-you-can-eat restaurant chain is a real bargain. Serve yourself from the buffet bars with a huge selection of soups, salads, baked goods, fruit and yogurt. Children under five eat for only 49 cents. 🔊 🖼
Outdoor Eating ■ · Vegetarian ● · Children's ■

HOLLYWOOD: *The Gumbo Pot* $
Farmer's Market, 6333 W 3rd St, CA 90036. **Map** 7 D3. ((213) 933-0358. Try gumbo stew and enormous Po'Boys (foot-long sandwiches) at this cajun fast-food bar, with occasional live cajun bands. ● D. 🔊 🎵 🖼
Outdoor Eating ■ · Vegetarian ●

HOLLYWOOD: *Hollywood Canteen* $$
1006 N Seward St, CA 90038. **Map** 2 C5. ((213) 465-0961. American cuisine with Italian influences is served at this lovely 1940s-style restaurant. New York steaks and marinated salmon are good. ● Sun, Mon–Sat L. 🔊 🎵 🖼
Outdoor Eating ■ · Vegetarian ● · Bar Area ■

HOLLYWOOD: *Katsu* $$
1972 Hillhurst Ave, CA 90027. **Road map** inset A. ((213) 665-1891. The salmon tempura at this minimalist Japanese restaurant is wonderful, as is the sushi and sashimi (raw fish) or the steamed lobster salad. Order the bento box to taste a little bit of everything. ● Sun, Mon–Sat L. 🔊 🖼
Vegetarian ●

HOLLYWOOD: *The Clay Pit* $$
3465 W 6th St, CA 90020. **Map** 9 E4. ((213) 382-6300. The neighbourhood is not very smart but the food is worth the detour at this excellent northern Indian restaurant. The lunch buffet is a real bargain. 🔊 🖼
Outdoor Eating ■ · Vegetarian ● · Fixed-Price ● · Children's ■

HOLLYWOOD: *Ca'brea* $$$
346 S La Brea Ave, CA 90036. **Map** 7 F3. ((213) 938-2863. The surroundings are stylish and the atmosphere is warm at this busy restaurant serving hearty northern Italian cuisine, including a tasty lentil soup. ● Sun. 🔊 🖼
Vegetarian ● · Bar Area ■

HOLLYWOOD: *Mandalay* $$$
611 N La Brea Ave, CA 90036. **Map** 7 F3. **(** (213) 933-0717. This hip French-
Vietnamese restaurant has an eclectic menu which includes sushi, dumplings
and traditional Vietnamese dishes such as spicy beef salad. ● *L.* ⌷ ⦿ ♫ ⊘

HOLLYWOOD: *Campanile* $$$$
624 S La Brea Ave, CA 90036. **Map** 7 F4. **(** (213) 938 1447. The cuisine is
Californian-Mediterranean at this stylish restaurant. Smoking is allowed
at the bar where there are 70 grappas on offer. ● *Sun D.* ⌷ ♟ ⊘

LONG BEACH: *Shenandoah Café* $
4722 E 2nd St, CA 90803. **Road map** inset A. **(** (310) 434-3469. Home-made
apple fritters and hickory-smoked ribs are favourites at this quaint
café serving Southern-style food. It can get busy. ● *Sat & Sun L.* ⌷ ⊘

LONG BEACH: *M Bar & Grill* $$
213A Pine Ave at Broadway St, CA 90802. **Road map** inset A. **(** (310) 435-2525.
A fusionof Mediterranean and Latin flavours highlights the cuisine at this trendy
café with rotating art exhibits and good live bands. ● *Sat & Sun L.* ⌷ ♫ ⊘

LONG BEACH: *Parker's Lighthouse* $$
435 Shoreline Drive, CA 90802. **Road map** inset A. **(** (310) 432-6500. A nautical
atmosphere prevails in this converted lighthouse serving excellent seafood.
The mesquite-grilled fresh fish and harbour views are memorable. ⌷ ⊘

LONG BEACH: *Sir Winston's Restaurant* $$$
Queen Mary Seaport, 1126 Queen's Hwy, CA 90801. **Road map** inset A. **(** (310)
435-3511. Majestic dark-wood décor sets the tone for romantic formal dining
aboard the Queen Mary. The cuisine is continental. ● *L.* ⦿ ♟ ♫ ⊘

MALIBU: *Gladstone's 4 Fish* $$
17300 Pacific Coast Hwy, CA 90272. **Road map** inset A. **(** (310) 454-3474. This
oceanside seafood restaurant is great fun for families. Portions are huge,
but you can take home the leftovers in an aluminium foil sculpture. ⌷ ⊘

MALIBU: *Bambu* $$$
3835 Cross Creek Rd, CA 90265. **Road map** inset A. **(** (310) 456-5464.
The varied Pacific Rim-Californian cuisine includes a sushi bar during
the week. The Sunday brunch is wonderful. ● *Mon L.* ⌷ ♫ ♟ ⊘

MALIBU: *Saddle Peak Lodge* $$$$
419 Cold Canyon Road, CA 91302. **Road map** inset A. **(** (818) 222-3888.
A smart crowd frequents this restaurant hidden away in the Santa Monica
Mountains. It is the best place in LA for game. ● *Mon, Tue.* ⌷ ♟ ⊘

MARINA DEL REY: *Alejo's* $
4002 Lincoln Blvd, CA 90292. **Road map** inset A. **(** (310) 822-0095. Bring your
own alcohol to this fabulous restaurant serving good cheap Italian food at
formica-top tables. There are always queues to get in. ● *Sat & Sun L.* ⊘

MARINA DEL REY: *Killer Shrimp* $
523 Washington St, CA 90292. **Road map** inset A. **(** (310) 578-2293.
Nothing except shrimp in divine sauces is on offer at this stylish
chain restaurant, and it never fails to attract customers in droves. ⊘

MARINA DEL REY: *The Cheesecake Factory* $
4142 Via Marina, CA 90292. **Road map** inset A. **(** (310) 306-3344. People queue
to get into this local chain restaurant. The menu ranges from Asian to French
to Italian – and features more than 30 varieties of cheesecake! ⌷ ⊘

PASADENA: *Yujean Kang's* $
67 N Raymond Ave, CA 91103. **Road map** inset A. **(** (818) 585-0855. Presentation
is everything at this very elegant Chinese restaurant which is always busy. Try
the "lobster with strange flavours". Lunch is good value. ● *Tue.* ⌷ ⊘

PASADENA: *Gordon Biersch Brewery* $$
41 Hugus Alley, CA 91103. **Road map** inset A. **(** (818) 449-0052. A mostly
young singles crowd frequents this up-market chain restaurant with its own
brewery. The beer is really good, as are the burgers, pasta and fish. ⌷ ⊘

PASADENA: *Parkway Grill* $$$
510 S Arroyo Pkwy, CA 91105. **Road map** inset A. **(** (818) 795-1001. This
restaurant serving Californian cuisine is one of the region's best. The dining
room is like a garden, with trees and flowers. ● *Sat L.* ⌷ ♟ ♫ ⊘

For key to symbols see back flap

<table>
<tr><th></th><th>Outdoor Eating</th><th>Vegetarian Specialities</th><th>Bar Area/Cocktail Bar</th><th>Fixed-Price Menu</th><th>Children's Facilities</th></tr>
</table>

Price categories for a three-course meal for one, including a half bottle of house wine, sales tax and service:
$ under $25
$$ $25–$35
$$$ $35–$50
$$$$ $50–$70
$$$$$ over $70

Outdoor Eating
Some tables on a patio or terrace.
Vegetarian Specialities
One menu always includes a selection of vegetarian dishes.
Bar Area/Cocktail Bar
There is a bar area or cocktail bar within the restaurant.
Fixed-Price Menu
A good-value fixed-price menu on offer at lunch, dinner or both, usually with three courses.
Children's Facilities
Small portions and/or highchairs available on request.

Pasadena: *Shiro* $$$
1505 Mission St, CA 91030. **Road map** inset A. (818) 799-4774. Voted the top restaurant in LA in 1996 by the Zagat's survey, this very popular restaurant serves excellent French-Japanese cuisine. Mon, Tue–Sun L.

San Pedro: *22nd Street Landing* $$$
141 W 22nd St, CA 90731. **Road map** inset A. (310) 548-4400. This large sea-food restaurant on San Pedro harbour has nautical-style décor and is always busy and bustling. Try the seafood cassoulet baked in filo pastry.

Santa Monica: *Broadway Bar & Grill* $
1460 Third Street Promenade, CA 90401. **Road map** inset A. (310) 393-4211. Business is brisk at this stylish bar and grill serving continental food, notably grilled fish and steaks, with an extensive wine list.

Santa Monica: *Schatzi on Main* $
3110 Main St, CA 90405. **Road map** inset A. (310) 399-4800. Hollywood star Arnold Schwarzenegger owns this pleasant restaurant serving Austrian specialities and healthy Californian cuisine. There is a Sunday champagne brunch.

Santa Monica: *Café Delfini* $$$
147 W Channel Rd, CA 90402. **Road map** inset A. (310) 459-8823. This intimate and romantic restaurant serves delicious Italian dishes, including hand-made gnocchi (only on Thursdays). Reservations are advised. L.

Santa Monica: *Drago* $$$
2628 Wilshire Blvd, CA 90403. **Road map** inset A. (310) 828-1585. Wonderful Sicilian dishes are served in this lovely, sleek restaurant. Try the risotto with pheasant and morel mushroom ragout. Sat & Sun L.

Santa Monica: *Ocean Avenue Seafood* $$$
1401 Ocean Ave, CA 90401. **Road map** inset A. (310) 394-5669. This very busy restaurant has an oyster bar and a relaxed atmosphere. Go there for the flakiest, tenderest Chilean sea bass marinaded in saki sauce.

Santa Monica: *Buffalo Club* $$$$
1520 Olympic Blvd, CA 90404. **Road map** inset A. (310) 450-8600. Consistently voted among the top ten restaurants in LA, the food here is delicious – American cuisine at its most imaginative. The shrimp and lobster dumplings with spicy black bean sauce are fabulous. Sun & Mon, Tue–Sat L.

Santa Monica: *Chinois on Main* $$$$$
2709 Main St, CA 90405. **Road map** inset A. (310) 392-9025. Wolfgang Puck's establishment is another of LA's top ten, presenting a mixture of Chinese, Japanese and Californian cuisine. Dishes such as the sizzling sea scallops with potato strings are truly special. Sat–Tue L.

Santa Monica: *Michael's* $$$$$
1147 3rd St, CA 90403. **Road map** inset A. (310) 451-0843. People dress up to go to this award-winning restaurant serving American cuisine in 1930s surroundings, with original works by notable painters. Special dishes include salmon with caviar and chives. Sun & Mon, Sat L.

Santa Monica: *Valentino* $$$$$
3115 Pico Blvd, CA 90405. **Road map** inset A. (310) 829-4313. Voted the best Italian cuisine in LA, this northern Italian restaurant also has one of the city's best wine lists. Everything is made on the premises, from the bread and pasta to the desserts and sorbets. Sun, Mon–Thu L, Sat L.

Studio City: *Asenebo* $$$
11941 Ventura Blvd, CA 91604. **Road map** inset A. (818) 760-3348. This famously good Japanese restaurant in a mini mall serves delicious sashimi food, authentic Japanese dishes and a variety of flavoured sakes. L.

STUDIO CITY: *Il Mito* $$$
11801 Ventura Blvd, CA 91604. **Road map** inset A. ((818) 762-1818. This northern Italian Art Deco restaurant is very busy, noisy and hip – and famous for its risottos, veal T-bone steak and Caesar salad. ● *Sun, Sat L.* 🔥 💡 🌿

STUDIO CITY: *Pinot Bistro* $$$
12969 Ventura Blvd, CA 91604. **Road map** inset A. ((818) 990-0500. This French bistro is a little bit of Paris in LA. The cosy room provides the perfect setting for the wonderful cuisine. ● *Sat & Sun L.* 🔥 💡 🎵 🌿

UNIVERSAL CITY: *BB King's Blues Club* $$$
1000 Universal Center Drive, CA 91608. **Road map** inset A. ((818) 622-5480. There is a gospel brunch on Sundays, at this Southern restaurant serving fried chicken with biscuits and gravy and cajun catfish. ● *L.* 🔥 🎵 🌿

VENICE: *Café 50s Diner* $
838 Lincoln Blvd, CA 90291. **Road map** inset A. ((310) 399 1955. This tiny 50s café serves typical diner food – sandwiches, salads, hamburgers and milkshakes – and "blue plate special" dinners, such as pot roast, in the evenings. 🔥 🌿

VENICE: *Jody Maroni's Sausage Kingdom* $
2011 Ocean Front Walk, CA 90291. **Road map** inset A. ((310) 306-1995. A sausage sandwich on an onion roll with onions and peppers is a favourite at this casual walk-up sausage stand on the boardwalk (no seating). 🔥

VENICE: *The Rose Café & Market* $
220 Rose Ave, CA 90291. **Road map** inset A. ((310) 399-0711. This casual café at the corner with Main Street serves tasty standards such as burgers and chicken. The Chinese chicken salad is very good. ● *Sun D.* 🔥 🎵 🌿

VENICE: *Hal's* $$$
1349 Abbot Kinney Blvd, CA 90291. **Road map** inset A. ((310) 396-3105. This friendly, busy, hip bistro serves classic American food and pastas in light, airy surroundings with contemporary art on the walls. 🎵 🌿

WEST HOLLYWOOD: *Book Soup Bistro* $
8800 Sunset Blvd, CA 90069. **Map** 6 B1. ((310) 657-1072. This hip neighbourhood café is a great place to have brunch after visiting the bookshop next door. Cuisine is bistro fare – pastas, salads, burgers and sandwiches. 🔥 🌿

WEST HOLLYWOOD: *Jones Hollywood* $
7205 Santa Monica Blvd, CA 90046. **Map** 2 A5. ((213) 850-1726. Try the New York steaks, seared and grilled in the woodburning pizza oven, at this busy restaurant serving Californian-Italian fare. ● *Sat & Sun L.* 🔥 🌿

WEST HOLLYWOOD: *Marix* $
1108 N Flores St, CA 90069. **Road map** inset A. ((213) 656-8800. Fabulous Mexican food is served in this noisy, laid-back restaurant which is popular with the gay crowd. It also has a huge selection of Margaritas. 🔥 🌿

WEST HOLLYWOOD: *The Rainbow Bar and Grill* $
9015 Sunset Blvd, CA 90069. **Map** 6 A1. ((310) 278-4232. This high-energy hang-out for the entertainment industry *(see p98)* features continental cuisine with Italian flair. It is also a nightclub in the evenings. ● *Sat & Sun.* 🔥 💡 🌿

WEST HOLLYWOOD: *The Source* $
8301 Sunset Blvd, CA 90069. **Map** 6 C1. ((213) 656-6388. Professional athletes and other health-conscious celebrities frequent this trendy café *(see p99)* serving fresh fruits, vegetables, pastas, sandwiches and blended juice specialities. 🔥 🌿

WEST HOLLYWOOD: *Talesai* $$
9043 Sunset Blvd, CA 90069. **Map** 6 A1. ((310) 275-9724. This Thai restaurant is friendly and the food is delicious. The steamed duck, deep fried and served with a ginger soybean sauce, is spectacular. ● *Sun, Sat L.* 🔥 🌿

WEST HOLLYWOOD: *Eclipse* $$$
8800 Melrose Ave, CA 90069. **Map** 6 B2. ((310) 724-5959. The Californian-Mediterranean-style cuisine at this very hip restaurant includes lamb and fresh fish roasted in fruitwood-burning ovens. ● *Sun, Mon–Sat L.* 🔥 💡 🌿

WEST HOLLYWOOD: *House of Blues* $$$
8430 Sunset Blvd, CA 90069. **Map** 6 C1. ((213) 650-2964. Housed in a large Southern-style tin shack *(see p99)*, this trendy restaurant turns out fabulous soul food dishes such as chicken and sausage gumbo. 🔥 🎵 🌿

		OUTDOOR EATING	VEGETARIAN SPECIALITIES	BAR AREA/COCKTAIL BAR	FIXED-PRICE MENU	CHILDREN'S FACILITIES

Price categories for a three-course meal for one, including a half bottle of house wine, sales tax and service:
$ under $25
$$ $25–$35
$$$ $35–$50
$$$$ $50–$70
$$$$$ over $70

OUTDOOR EATING
Some tables on a patio or terrace.
VEGETARIAN SPECIALITIES
One menu always includes a selection of vegetarian dishes.
BAR AREA/COCKTAIL BAR
There is a bar area or cocktail bar within the restaurant.
FIXED-PRICE MENU
A good-value fixed-price menu on offer at lunch, dinner or both, usually with three courses.
CHILDREN'S FACILITIES
Small portions and/or highchairs available on request.

WEST HOLLYWOOD: *Le Dome* $$$
8720 Sunset Blvd, CA 90069. **Map** 6 C1. (310) 659-6919. Portions are huge at this popular restaurant serving continental cuisine. The *filet mignon* with three-peppercorn sauce is excellent. ● *Sun.*
‑ Outdoor Eating ●, Vegetarian Specialities, Bar Area ●

WEST HOLLYWOOD: *Pane e Vino* $$$
8265 Beverly Blvd, CA 90048. **Map** 6 C1. (213) 651-4600. This busy Italian restaurant serves pasta, risottos and fish. The walls are decorated with a heavenly fresco. Get there early if you want a seat outside. ● *Sun L.*
‑ Outdoor ●, Veg ●, Bar ●, Fixed ●, Children ●

WEST HOLLYWOOD: *Cicada* $$$$
478 Melrose Ave, CA 90069. **Map** 6 C2. (213) 655-5559. The Italian country look of this busy restaurant is reflected in its cuisine. It offers a great selection of pasta, salads, specials and risottos made to order. ● *Sun.*
‑ Veg ●, Bar ●

WEST HOLLYWOOD: *Citrus* $$$$
6703 Melrose Ave, CA 90038. **Map** 8 A1. (213) 857-0034. This award-winning restaurant dishes up French-Californian cuisine on its covered patio. It gets busy so make sure you book ahead. ● *Sun.*
‑ Outdoor ●, Veg ●, Bar ●, Fixed ●

WEST HOLLYWOOD: *Georgia* $$$$
7250 Melrose Ave, CA 90046. **Map** 7 F2. (213) 933-8420. The food is superb at this stylish, up-market soul food restaurant, with dishes such as Georgia meatloaf and Southern fried chicken with collard greens. Corn bread, candied yams and fried green tomatoes are served on the side.
‑ Outdoor ●, Veg ●, Bar ●

WEST HOLLYWOOD: *Le Chardonnay* $$$$
8284 Melrose Ave, CA 90046. **Map** 6 C1. (213) 655-8880. Mirrors and carved rosewood provide an elegant and romantic setting for the fine French cuisine. The crab cakes are really good. They also serve venison, rabbit and ostrich. ● *Sun, Mon, Sat L.*
‑ Veg ●, Fixed ●

WEST HOLLYWOOD: *Fenix at the Argyle* $$$$$
Argyle Hotel, 8358 Sunset Blvd, CA 90069. **Map** 6 C1. (213) 848-6677. The French-Californian cuisine at this hotel restaurant *(see p99)* is served in elegantly stark surroundings. Book a week ahead. ● *Sun, Mon–Sat L.*
‑ Veg ●, Bar ●, Fixed ●

WEST HOLLYWOOD: *L'Orangerie* $$$$$
903 N La Cienega Blvd, CA 90069. **Map** 6 C1. (310) 652-9770. This five-diamond French restaurant is extremely elegant and always busy. The stunning specials include fillet of John Dory with roasted figs. ● *Mon.*
‑ Outdoor ●, Veg ●, Bar ●, Fixed ●

WEST HOLLYWOOD: *Patina* $$$$$
5955 Melrose Ave, CA 90038. **Map** 8 B2. (213) 467-1108. This truly fabulous restaurant serving French-Californian cuisine is considered by many to be one of the best eating establishments in Los Angeles. Try the delicious peppered tuna with Chinese vegetables.
‑ Veg ●, Bar ●

WESTWOOD/WEST LA: *John O'Groats* $
10516 W Pico Blvd, CA 90064. **Road map** inset A. (310) 204-0692. For years, this place was only open for breakfast and lunch. Now a good selection of classic American dinner dishes have been added to the menu. The John O'Groats is very popular with families. ● *Sun–Wed D.*
‑ Veg ●

WESTWOOD/WEST LA: *Bombay Café* $$
12113 Santa Monica Blvd, CA 90025. **Road map** inset A. (310) 820-2070. One of the best Indian restaurants in LA, this place serves home-cooked dishes from the owner's native city. It gets very busy. ● *Sat & Sun L.*
‑ Veg ●, Children ●

WESTWOOD: *La Buschetta* $$$
1621 Westwood Blvd, CA 90024. **Road map** inset A. (310) 477-1052. This friendly, award-winning restaurant serves Italian cuisine featuring home-made pasta and regional dishes from all over Italy. ● *Sun.*
‑ Veg ●

SOUTH CENTRAL

BAKERSFIELD: *Wool Growers* $
620 E 19th St, CA 93305. **Road map** C5. (*(805) 327-9584.* This restaurant serves French Basque cuisine as well as American standards. Everything comes with salad and French fries. Perfect for children. ● *Sun.* ⅃ ⬚

CAMBRIA: *The Brambles* $$
4005 Burton Drive, CA 93428. **Road map** B5. (*(805) 927-4716.* This lovely restaurant near Hearst Castle *(see pp202–5)* serves international dishes as well as steaks. The menu is cheaper from 4–6pm. ● *Mon–Sat L.* ⅃ ⬚

GOLETA: *The Good Earth Restaurant and Bakery* $
5955 Calle Real, CA 93117. **Road map** B5. (*(805) 683-6101.* The emphasis is on healthy food at this restaurant, 9 miles (14 km) outside Santa Barbara, including a wonderful vegetarian lasagne. Families are welcome. Eat indoors or outside among the apple trees on the brick patio. ⅃ ⬚

LOS OLIVOS: *Los Olivos Café* $
2879 Grand Ave, CA 93441. **Road map** C5. (*(805) 688-7265.* This charming Mediterranean-style bistro serves pizzas, pastas and salads along with good local wine. They also make up picnic baskets for wine tours. ⅃ ⅂ ⬚

MONTECITO: *Montecito Café* $$
1295 Coast Village Rd, CA 93108. **Road map** B5. (*(805) 969-3392.* This restaurant, housed in a hotel originally owned by Charlie Chaplin, serves good American food, such as grilled *filet mignon* with forest mushroom sauce. It gets busy so you may wait for a table. ⅃ ⅂ ⬚

MONTECITO: *Ristorante Piatti* $$
516 San Ysidro Rd, CA 93108. **Road map** B5. (*(805) 969-7520.* This popular Italian restaurant serves a selection of seafood, meat dishes, pasta and pizza. ⅃ ⬚

MONTECITO: *Stonehouse* $$$$
San Ysidro Ranch, 900 San Ysidro Lane, CA 93108. **Road map** B5. (*(805) 969-4100.* There are mountain views from the terrace of this restaurant. Diners enjoy southwestern American cuisine, such as crispy Pacific oysters with spinach. Three fixed-price menus are available. ⅃ ⅂ ⬚

MORRO BAY: *Hoppe's at 901* $$$
901 Embarcadero, CA 93442. **Road map** B5. (*(805) 772-9012.* Overlooking the ocean, this restaurant serves French-Californian cuisine. Dishes include lobster ravioli with peanut sauce. ● *Mon–Thu L, Tue D.* ⅃ ⅂ ⬚

OJAI: *Wheeler Hot Springs Spa and Restaurant* $$$
16825 Maricopa Hwy, CA 93024. **Road map** C5. (*(805) 646-8131.* This spa resort is worth a detour from Santa Barbara. Enjoy a massage or hot tub before a delicious modern continental meal. ● *Mon–Wed.* ⅃ ♫ ⬚

PISMO BEACH: *Spyglass Inn Restaurant* $
2703 Spyglass Drive, CA 93449. **Road map** B5. (*(805) 773-1222.* Every table in this clifftop restaurant has spectacular ocean views. Steak and seafood, particularly crab and lobster, are specialities. ⅃ ⅂ ♫ ⬚

SAN LUIS OBISPO: *Tio Alberto's* $
1131 Broad St, CA 93401. **Road map** B5. (*(805) 546-9646.* The speciality is *carne asada* (grilled beef) at this old-style Mexican restaurant, which is popular with the locals and open until 4am. No alcohol is served or allowed. ⅃ ⬚

SAN LUIS OBISPO: *Buono Tavola* $$
1037 Monterey St, CA 93401. **Road map** C5. (*(805) 545-8000.* This tiny but stylish restaurant serves northern Italian cuisine. The bread, dressings, pasta and desserts are all made on the premises. ● *Sat & Sun L.* ⅃ ⬚

SAN LUIS OBISPO: *Café Roma* $$
1819 Osos St, CA 93401. **Road map** B5. (*(805) 541-6800.* The Tuscan décor of this Italian restaurant reflects its cuisine. There is a selection of pastas, pizzas and flavoured olive oils. ● *Oct–Apr: Mon; Sat & Sun L.* ⅃ ⅂ ⬚

SANTA BARBARA: *Be Bop Burgers* $
111 State St, CA 93101. **Road map** C5. (*(805) 966-1956.* This 1950s-style diner has a classic car indoors, karaoke and a DJ at weekends. It serves burgers, sandwiches, milkshakes and ice-cream sundaes. No alcohol. ⅃ ⬚

For key to symbols see back flap

Price categories for a three-course meal for one, including a half bottle of house wine, sales tax and service:
$ under $25
$$ $25–$35
$$$ $35–$50
$$$$ $50–$70
$$$$$ over $70

OUTDOOR EATING
Some tables on a patio or terrace.
VEGETARIAN SPECIALITIES
One menu always includes a selection of vegetarian dishes.
BAR AREA/COCKTAIL BAR
There is a bar area or cocktail bar within the restaurant.
FIXED-PRICE MENU
A good-value fixed-price menu on offer at lunch, dinner or both, usually with three courses.
CHILDREN'S FACILITIES
Small portions and/or highchairs available on request.

	OUTDOOR EATING	VEGETARIAN SPECIALITIES	BAR AREA/COCKTAIL BAR	FIXED-PRICE MENU	CHILDREN'S FACILITIES

SANTA BARBARA: *La Super-Rica Taco* $
622 N Milpas St, CA 93103. **Road map** C5. ((805) 963-4940. Cookery writer Julia Child recommends this wonderful Mexican *taqueria*. Specials vary daily and include *tamales* and *enchiladas* as well as vegetarian dishes. &

SANTA BARBARA: *Piranha* $
714 State St, CA 93101. **Road map** C5. ((805) 965-2980. It can get very busy at this lively restaurant. The style is modern but cosy. Delicious treats include grilled salmon with shiso leaf and pesto sauce, peppercorn-coated Ahi tuna, as well as fabulous sushi. ● *Mon, Tue–Sun L.* & 🗎

SANTA BARBARA: *Something's Fishy* $
502 State St, CA 93101. **Road map** C5. ((805) 966-6607. The crowd is mixed at this lively Japanese restaurant. Sit at the all-you-can-eat sushi bar or have a Benihana-style dinner cooked and served at your table. & 🗎

SANTA BARBARA: *El Paseo* $$
10 El Paseo, CA 93101. **Road map** C5. ((805) 962-6050. This historic hacienda offers a taste of the real Mexico, with pork, fish and shrimp dishes and 90 kinds of tequila. Drinks are served in hand-made glassware. & 🎜 🗎

SANTA BARBARA: *The Harbor Restaurant & Longboards Grill* $$
210 Stearns Wharf, CA 93101. **Road map** C5. ((805) 963-3311. Built on a pier, every seat has an ocean view. Longboards serves fish and chips, pizzas and buffalo wings and has a huge patio. The Harbor is more up-market, specializing in fresh fish, seafood and prime rib. & 🗎

SANTA BARBARA: *Louie's at the Upham* $$
1404 de la Vina St, CA 93101. **Road map** C5. ((805) 963-7003. Set in the oldest hotel in town *(see p515)*, this restaurant is very romantic. The food is Californian-continental, featuring fish and pasta. ● *Sat & Sun L.* & 🗎

SANTA BARBARA: *The Patio at the Four Seasons Biltmore Hotel* $$
1260 Channel Drive, CA 93108. **Road map** C5. ((805) 969-2261. This elegant hotel restaurant *(see p515)* serves Californian-style cuisine in a dining room with ocean views. The evening buffet is a great bargain. & 🍷 🗎

SANTA BARBARA: *Cold Spring Tavern* $$$
5995 Stagecoach Rd, CA 93105. **Road map** C5. ((805) 967-0066. This small restaurant is housed in an old stagecoach stop. The Old West décor reflects the rustic Californian food, with an emphasis on game. & 🎜 🗎

SANTA BARBARA: *Downey's* $$$
1305 State St, CA93101. **Road map** C5. ((805) 966-5006. The regional American cuisine here has won the Distinguished Restaurants of North America award. Their dessert of fresh raspberries with white chocolate mousse in puff pastry deserves world fame. ● *Mon, Tue–Sun L.* & 🍷 🗎

SANTA BARBARA: *La Marina, Four Seasons Biltmore Hotel* $$$
1260 Channel Drive, CA 93108. **Road map** C5. ((805) 969-2261. The ocean views from this hotel restaurant *(see p515)* are breathtaking. From the *à la carte* menu, try the caramelized sea scallops and griddled plantain cake with mango and papaya chutney. ● *L.* & 🎜 🍷 🗎

SANTA BARBARA: *Paradise Café* $$$
702 Anacapa St, Ca 93101. **Road map** C5. ((805) 962-4416. All meals come with either soup, salad or vegetables at this "scene" café, which gets very busy. The chocolate mousse pie with espresso topping is famous. & 🗎

SANTA BARBARA: *The Wine Cask* $$$
813 Anacapa St, CA 93101. **Road map** C5. ((805) 966-9463. Mediterranean cuisine is on offer here, and one of the best wine lists in the US. Eat inside under the decoratively painted ceiling or in the courtyard. ● *L.* & 🍷 🗎

SANTA BARBARA: *Citronelle*   ⑤⑤⑤⑤⑤
901 E Cabrillo Blvd, CA 93103. **Road map** C5. 【 *(805) 963-0111.* Good French-
Californian cuisine is served here against fine views of the ocean. A
classical guitarist plays on Sundays, Mondays and Tuesdays. 🅱 🎵 🍷 📧

SHELL BEACH: *McLintok's*   ⑤⑤
750 Mattie Rd, Shell Beach, CA 93449. **Road map** B5. 【 *(805) 773-1892.* Come
here for a great American barbecque in upbeat, Western-style surroundings.
Steaks and chicken are grilled over an oak fire. ⬤ *Mon–Sat L.* 🅱 🎵 📧

SHELL BEACH: *Sea Cliffs Restaurant*   ⑤⑤
2757 Shell Beach Rd, CA 93449. **Road map** B5. 【 *(805) 773-3555.* Sunday
brunch is exceptional at this relaxed resort restaurant with gorgeous
ocean views. The cuisine is Mediterranean. Book ahead. 🅱 🎵 🅱

ORANGE COUNTY

ANAHEIM: *Goofy's Kitchen*   ⑤
Disneyland Hotel, 1150 W Cerritos, CA 92803. **Road map** D6. 【 *(714) 778-
6600.* Children love this buffet hotel restaurant *(see p516)*, where they can
eat simple food with favourite Disney characters. ⬤ *Sep–May: Mon–Fri L.* 🅱 📧

ANAHEIM: *Mandarin Gourmet*   ⑤
1500 Adams Ave, CA 92626. **Road map** D6. 【 *(714) 540-1937.* This Chinese
restaurant has a comprehensive menu, and standards such as chicken
chow mein are delicious. The service is friendly, even when busy. 🅱

ANAHEIM: *Mr Stox*   ⑤⑤⑤⑤
1105 E Katella Ave, CA 92805. **Road map** D6. 【 *(714) 634-2994.* This
smart restaurant serves an eclectic continental-style cuisine. Salads, fish,
pasta and meat dishes are imaginatively presented. The *crème brûlée*
is one of the best in Orange County. ⬤ *Sat & Sun L.* 🅱 🎵 🍷 📧

AVALON: *Ristorante Villa Portofino*   ⑤
Hotel Villa Portofino, Avalon, Catalina Island, CA 90704. **Road map** D6. 【 *(310)
510-0508.* The Italian dishes are home-made at this elegant restaurant with
lovely views. ⬤ *Jan–mid-Feb: daily; mid-Feb–Dec: Mon & Tue, Wed–Sun L.* 🅱 🍷 📧

CORONA DEL MAR: *Oyster's*   ⑤⑤⑤
2515 E Coast Hwy, CA 92625. **Road map** D6. 【 *(714) 675-7411.* This local
nightspot is popular for its live jazz and its delicious food, so book ahead.
The tempura Ahi tuna appetizer is spectacular. ⬤ *L.* 🅱 🎵 🍷 📧

CORONA DEL MAR: *The Five Crowns*   ⑤⑤⑤
3801 E Coast Hwy, CA 92965. **Road map** D6. 【 *(714) 760-0331.* This English
pub-style restaurant has brocade furnishings, antiques and a continental
menu. The wine list features over 800 selections. ⬤ *Mon–Sat L.* 🅱 🍷 📧

COSTA MESA: *Wolfgang Puck Café*   ⑤⑤⑤
South Coast Plaza, 3333 Bristol Ave, CA 92626. **Road map** D6. 【 *(714) 546-9653.*
Celebrity chef Wolfgang Puck's café is a cheaper version of his smarter
restaurants. Great pizzas, salads and pasta dishes are on offer. 🅱 📧

COSTA MESA: *Armani Café*   ⑤⑤⑤⑤⑤
South Coast Plaza, 3333 Bristol St, CA 92626. **Road map** D6. 【 *(714) 754-0300.*
Armani-clad waiters dish up Italian sandwiches, pizzas, salads and pasta
dishes in trendy surroundings next door to the Armani boutique. The
Portelli alla Piacentina pasta is a recipe from Armani's grandmother. 🅱 📧

FULLERTON: *The Cellar*   ⑤⑤⑤⑤
305 N Harbor Blvd, CA 92632. **Road map** D6. 【 *(714) 525-5682.* This fine
French restaurant has a wine list with over 1,200 selections. Early diners
can order the cheaper fixed-price menu. ⬤ *Sun, Tue–Sat L.* 🍷 📧

GARDEN GROVE: *Belisle's*   ⑤
12001 Harbor Blvd, CA92840. **Road map** D6. 【 *(714) 750-6560.* This all-
American restaurant is open until late and is popular with locals. Meatloaf, sandwiches and desserts are served in enormous portions. 🅱 📧

IRVINE: *Chevy's*   ⑤
4700 Barranca Parkway, CA92714. **Road map** D6. 【 *(714) 559-5808.* The
food at Chevy's chain of Mexican restaurants is reliably good. The *burritos*
are freshly made on the premises and the sizzling meat and vegetable
fajitas are fabulous. Swill them down with a cranberry margarita. 🅱 📧

For key to symbols see back flap

TRAVELLERS' NEEDS

554

Price categories for a three-course meal for one, including a half bottle of house wine, sales tax and service:
$ under $25
$$ $25–$35
$$$ $35–$50
$$$$ $50–$70
$$$$$ over $70

OUTDOOR EATING Some tables on a patio or terrace.
VEGETARIAN SPECIALITIES One menu always includes a selection of vegetarian dishes.
BAR AREA/COCKTAIL BAR There is a bar area or cocktail bar within the restaurant.
FIXED-PRICE MENU A good-value fixed-price menu on offer at lunch, dinner or both, usually with three courses.
CHILDREN'S FACILITIES Small portions and/or highchairs available on request.

	OUTDOOR EATING	VEGETARIAN SPECIALITIES	BAR AREA/COCKTAIL BAR	FIXED-PRICE MENU	CHILDREN'S FACILITIES

IRVINE: *Il Fornaio* $$$
18051 Von Karman Ave, CA 92715. **Road map** D6. ((714) 261-1444. Part of a chain, this Italian restaurant serves a good selection of pizzas and pasta dishes. Fresh-baked Italian breads are available to take away.

IRVINE: *The Chanteclair* $$$$
18912 MacArthur Blvd, CA 92714. **Road map** D6. ((714) 752-8001. French cuisine is served at this lovely, antique-filled restaurant. The salmon with raspberry butter sauce is outstanding. ● *Sun, Sat L.*

LAGUNA BEACH: *Café Zinc* $
350 Ocean Ave, CA 92651. **Road map** D6. ((714) 494-6302. Locals come here for breakfast or just for coffee. The soups and sandwiches are very good, as are the desserts. It's great for a cheap lunch. ● *D.*

LAGUNA BEACH: *Las Brisas* $$
361 Cliff Drive, CA 92652. **Road map** D6. ((714) 497-5434. This Mexican restaurant is always crowded because of its stunning clifftop view. The menu features fresh seafood, beef and salads. This is an ideal place to go for margaritas at sunset or a champagne brunch on Sundays.

LAGUNA BEACH: *Splashes* $$$
Surf and Sand Hotel, 1555 South Coast Hwy, CA 92651. **Road map** D6. ((714) 497-4477. The Mediterranean-style cuisine and the stunning view of the ocean, with waves crashing nearby, are superb at this hotel restaurant *(see p517)*. Go at sunset to really appreciate it.

LAGUNA NIGUEL: *The Lounge at the Ritz Carlton Hotel* $$$$
Ritz Carlton Hotel, 1 Ritz Carlton Drive, CA 92629. **Road map** D6. ((714) 240-2000. One of three hotel restaurants, the Lounge has a splendid view of the ocean. It serves appetizers, pasta, club sandwiches and seafood, as well as traditional English high tea.

NEWPORT BEACH: *John Dominis* $$$$
2901 W Coast Hwy, CA 92663. **Road map** D6. ((714) 650-5112. This popular continental-style seafood restaurant has harbour views and live Hawaiian music on Sundays. ● *Mon–Sat L.*

NEWPORT BEACH: *The Ritz* $$$$
880 Newport Center Drive, CA 92660. **Road map** D6. ((714) 720-1800. The continental-style cuisine has won several food and wine awards. On Sundays there is a cheaper fixed-price dinner menu. ● *Sat & Sun L.*

ORANGE: *The Hobbit* $$$$$
2932 Chapman Ave, CA 92669. **Road map** D6. ((714) 997-1972. The fixed-price, seven-course dinner here starts with champagne and hors d'oeuvres while you choose from the famous wine cellar. The continental menu changes daily. Book months ahead. ● *Mon, Tue–Sun L.*

SANTA ANA: *Topaz* $$$
Bowers Museum, 2002 N Main St, CA 92706. **Road map** D6. ((714) 835-2002. This museum restaurant *(see p229)* serves sandwiches, salads and a children's menu at $1 per plate. ● *Sun & Mon, Tue D.*

SUNSET BEACH: *Harbor House Café* $
16341 Pacific Coast Hwy (Anderson St), CA90742. **Road map** D6. ((310) 592-5404. This 24-hour diner on the beach serves enormous plates of classic American food. Breakfast here will set you up for the day.

TUSTIN: *Zov's Bistro* $$
17440 E 17th St, CA92680. **Road map** D6. ((714) 838-8855. This popular bistro serves delicious Mediterranean dishes such as lamb burger on a ciabatta bun with yogurt mint dressing. ● *Sun, Mon–Tue L.*

Two Harbors: *Doug's Harbor Reef Restaurant* $$
Two Harbors, Catalina Island, CA 90704. **Road map** C6. *(310) 510-2800.*
Boats dock here for the fresh fish, baby back ribs and chicken. There is
weekend dancing at the outdoor bar. ● *Jun–Nov: L; Dec–May: daily.*

Yorba Linda: *El Torito* $
22699 Oakcrest Circle, CA 92887. **Road map** D6. *(714) 921-2335.* Generous
portions of authentic Mexican cuisine are served at this quality chain
restaurant. It also offers Sunday brunch and happy-hour specials.

San Diego County

Coronado: *The Brigantine* $$
1333 Orange Ave, CA 92118. **Road map** D6. *(619) 435-4166.*
Specializing in steak and seafood, this restaurant has wonderful views of
San Diego Bay. The marinated swordfish is excellent. ● *Sat & Sun.*

Coronado: *Poehe's* $$$
1201 1st St, Old Ferry Landing Plaza. **Road map** D6. *(619) 437-4474.*
There are lovely views of Downtown San Diego from this restaurant,
which serves creative Polynesian cuisine. The setting is very Hawaiian,
with waterfalls and tropical plants everywhere you look.

Coronado: *Prince of Wales Grill* $$$$
1500 Orange Ave, CA 92118. **Road map** D6. *(619) 522-8818.* Set in the
elegant Hotel del Coronado *(see p245),* this Art Deco restaurant retains
its 1930s décor. The cuisine is classic American. ● *L.*

Del Mar: *The Dining Room at L'Auberge* $$
1540 Camino Del Mar, CA 92105. **Road map** D6. *(619) 259-1515.* American
standards and pasta dishes are served in this resort restaurant *(see p518).*
As a treat, eat outside on the patio overlooking the waterfall garden.

Encinitas: *Potato Shack Café* $
120 W I Street, CA 92024. **Road map** D6. *(619) 436-1282.* A popular breakfast
spot with locals, the filling omelettes and old-style biscuits and gravy are
also served for lunch until 2pm. ● *D.*

La Jolla: *Alfonso's of La Jolla* $
1251 Prospect St, CA 90237. **Road map** D6. *(619) 454-2232.* This family-
friendly restaurant serves imaginative Mexican food as well as authentic
standards. The bar, open until 2am, can be very lively. ● *Sun D.*

La Jolla: *The French Pastry Shop Café and Restaurant* $$
5550 La Jolla Blvd, CA 92037. **Road map** D6. *(619) 454-9094.* This San
Diego favourite has been operating for 15 years. It serves fresh bread,
pastries, *crêpes* (savoury and sweet) and pasta. ● *Mon D, Sat.*

La Jolla: *George's at the Cove* $$$
1250 Prospect St, CA 92037. **Road map** D6. *(619) 454-4244.* This restaurant
serves fresh seafood in light sauces, as well as lamb, steak and chicken
dishes. The chocolate soufflé is a fitting end to the evening.

La Jolla: *Marine Room* $$$$$
2000 Spindrift Drive, CA 92037. **Road map** D6. *(619) 459-7222.* At
this elegant beach restaurant, Californian cuisine is given a French
twist – dishes include *filet mignon* with wild mushroom sauce. The
cheesecake with bittersweet chocolate shavings is superb.

La Jolla: *Top O' The Cove* $$$$$
1216 Prospect St, CA 92037. **Road map** D6. *(619) 454-7779.*
Fabulous coastal views, celebrity customers and delicious food
guarantee the success of this famous restaurant. The cuisine is contemporary French with a Pacific Rim influence. Dress up.

Pacific Beach: *Nick's At The Beach* $
809 Thomas St, CA 92109. **Road map** D6. *(619) 270-1730.* This beach café
serves American standards such as meatloaf and crab cakes from its seasonal menu. Don't leave without trying the blueberry *crème brûlée.*

San Diego: *Fifth and Hawthorn* $
5th Ave & Hawthorn St, CA 92101. **Road map** D6. *(619) 544-0940.* This small,
cosy restaurant, popular with locals, has a fine selection of seafood as
well as classic dishes such as *filet mignon.*

For key to symbols see back flap

Price categories for a three-course meal for one, including a half bottle of house wine, sales tax and service:
$ under $25
$$ $25–$35
$$$ $35–$50
$$$$ $50–$70
$$$$$ over $70

OUTDOOR EATING
Some tables on a patio or terrace.
VEGETARIAN SPECIALITIES
One menu always includes a selection of vegetarian dishes.
BAR AREA/COCKTAIL BAR
There is a bar area or cocktail bar within the restaurant.
FIXED-PRICE MENU
A good-value fixed-price menu on offer at lunch, dinner or both, usually with three courses.
CHILDREN'S FACILITIES
Small portions and/or highchairs available on request.

	Price	Outdoor Eating	Vegetarian Specialities	Bar Area/Cocktail Bar	Fixed-Price Menu	Children's Facilities
SAN DIEGO: *Hob Nob Hill* 2271 1st Ave, CA 92101. **Road map** D6. ((619) 239-8176. This 1940s diner is the place to go for breakfast – buttermilk pancakes, pecan waffles and coffee cake are served up in authentic surroundings. ● *Sat.* & ✉	$		●		●	■
SAN DIEGO: *Mandarin China* 4110 W Point Loma Blvd, CA 92110. **Road map** D6. ((619) 222-6688. Known for its *dim sum*, this restaurant serves Mandarin, Szechuan and Cantonese cuisine. Book in advance or eat a takeaway overlooking the ocean. & ✉	$		●		●	■
SAN DIEGO: *Bali Hu'i* 2230 Shelter Island Drive, CA 92106. **Road map** D6. ((619) 222-1181. Set on a man-made island, this round Polynesian restaurant offers diners stunning views of San Diego Bay. The food is Cantonese-Polynesian, featuring such specials as "Chicken of the Gods" in sesame sauce. ● *Sat L.* ♫ ✉	$$	■	●			■
SAN DIEGO: *Buffalo Joe's* 600 5th Ave, CA 92101. **Road map** D6. ((619) 236-1616. This American restaurant serves mostly barbecued ribs, as well as ostrich, alligator, buffalo and chicken specials. The portions are enormous. & ♫ ✉	$$		●	■		■
SAN DIEGO: *Café Pacifica* 2414 San Diego Ave, Old Town, CA 92110. **Road map** D6. ((619) 291-6666. Twinkling tree lights enhance the atmosphere at this romantic seafood restaurant. There is also a pre-theatre menu. ● *Sat & Sun L.* & ♙ ✉	$$	■	●	■	●	■
SAN DIEGO: *Harbor House* 831 W Harbor Drive, CA 92101. **Road map** D6. ((619) 232-1141. Located on the boardwalk with a beautiful view of the ocean, this restaurant serves seafood with contemporary California flare. There is an oyster bar. & ♙ ✉	$$	■	●	■		■
SAN DIEGO: *Karl Strauss' Old Columbia Brewery and Grill* 1157 Columbia St, CA 92101. **Road map** D6. ((619) 234-2739. This bar and restaurant serves American food and home-brewed beers, with no additives or preservatives. It can be very busy at weekends. & ✉	$$		●	■		■
SAN DIEGO: *Anthony's Star of the Sea Room* 1360 N Harbor Drive, CA 92101. **Road map** D6. ((619) 232-7408. The ocean views at this seafood restaurant are almost as good as the food. Rolled sole stuffed with lobster, crab and shrimp is particularly good. For dessert try banana flambé or French wedding cake. ● *L.* & ♟ ♙ ✉	$$$		●	■	●	■
SAN DIEGO: *Bayou Bar and Grill* 329 Market St, CA 92101. **Road map** D6. ((619) 696-8747. The seafood at this Cajun-Creole restaurant is flown in fresh from Louisiana every day. Try the delicious Mardi Gras pasta (with crayfish, shrimp, sherry, creole spices and cream sauce). The atmosphere is always festive. & ✉	$$$	■		■		
SAN DIEGO: *El Bizcocho* 17550 Bernardo Oaks Drive, CA 92128. **Road map** D6. ((619) 487-1611. This elegant French-Californian restaurant, set in the Rancho Bernardo Inn *(see p519)*, has views of the golf course and mountains. Try the roast Long Island duck or the Colorado rack of lamb. & ♟ ♫ ♙ ✉	$$$		●	■		■
SAN DIEGO: *Fio's* 801 5th Ave, CA 92101. **Road map** D6. ((619) 234-3467. This modern Italian restaurant serves a selection of pasta and pizzas. Candlelit tables and live piano music add to the atmosphere. ● *Sat & Sun L.* & ♫ ♙ ✉	$$$		●	■		■
SAN DIEGO: *Grant Grill* 326 Broadway, CA 92101. **Road map** D6. ((619) 239-6806. This continental-style restaurant is most famous for its seafood, but also serves prime rib and rack of lamb. Live jazz is played in the lounge. & ♫ ♙ ✉	$$$	■	●	■		■

SAN DIEGO: *Dobson's* $$$$
956 Broadway Circle, CA 92101. **Road map** D6. ((619) 231-6771. This award-winning restaurant is famous for its mussel bisque with puff pastry top. A divine *crème brûlée* is always on the menu. ● Sun, Sat L. 🔇 🥾

SAN DIEGO: *Old Trieste* $$$$
2335 Morana Blvd, CA 92110. **Road map** D6. ((619) 276-1841. Hearty Italian cuisine is the order of the day at this candlelit restaurant. The walnut cake has been a speciality for years. ● Sun & Mon, Sat L. 🔇 🍷 🥾

SAN DIEGO: *Wine Seller & Brasserie* $$$$
9550 Waples St, #115, CA 92121. **Road map** D6. ((619) 450-9557. This small brasserie serves French-influenced Californian cuisine. On Saturday they have special tasting lunches – three tastings of wine with three courses. Book well in advance. ● Sun L, Mon, Tue–Fri L. 🔇 🍷 🥾

SAN DIEGO: *Humphrey's* $$$$$
2241 Shelter Island Drive, CA 92106. **Road map** D6. ((619) 224-3577. Named after Humphrey Bogart and decorated in the style of his film *Casablanca*, this seafood restaurant serves lobster fresh from the tank. 🔇 🎵 🍷 🥾

SAN DIEGO: *Marius at Le Meridien* $$$$$
2000 2nd St, CA 92118. **Road map** D6. ((619) 435-3000. Dress up to go to what some consider to be the best restaurant in San Diego. The cuisine is Provençale-style. ● Sun & Mon, Tue–Sat L. 🎵 🍷 🥾

SAN DIEGO: *Mister A's* $$$$$
2250 5th Ave, Ca 92103. **Road map** D6. ((619) 239-1377. This restaurant, on the 12th floor of the Financial Center, has fabulous views of downtown. The continental-style cuisine includes such dishes as mock turtle soup, baked oysters and a selection of pasta. ● Sat L. 🔇 🎵 🍷 🥾

THE INLAND EMPIRE AND LOW DESERT

BIG BEAR LAKE: *Madlon's* $$
829 W Big Bear Blvd, Big Bear City, CA 92314. **Road map** D5. ((909) 585-3762. This English cottage-style restaurant is a favourite with locals. The varied menu has something for everyone; service is excellent. 🔇 🍷 🥾

BORREGO SPRINGS: *Borrego Springs Country Club* $
1112 Tilting "T" Drive, CA 92004. **Road map** D6. ((760) 767-3057. Classic American cuisine is served in an ornate, yet informal, setting. Sunday brunch and happy hour (4–6pm) at the bar are both very popular. 🔇 🥾

BORREGO SPRINGS: *Pablito's of the Desert* $
390 Palm Canyon Drive, CA 92004. **Road map** D6. ((760) 767-5753. Excellent Mexican cuisine is served in an Old West setting in this resort restaurant. Reservations are recommended for dinner. ● Mon–Thu D. 🔇 🎵 🥾

IDYLLWILD: *Jan's Red Kettle* $
54220 North Circle Drive, CA 92549. **Road map** D6. ((909) 659-4063. Open for breakfast and lunch, many Idyllwild residents start their day here. The food is excellent, plentiful and well priced. ● D. 🔇 🥾

IDYLLWILD: *Gastrognome* $$
54381 Ridgeview Drive, CA 92549. **Road map** D6. ((909) 659-5055. Set against a mountain backdrop, this restaurant features American cuisine in a French-country setting. Try the deep-fried sage leaves. 🔇 🍷 🥾

LA QUINTA: *La Quinta Cliffhouse* $$$
78250 Hwy 111 (Washington St), CA 92253. **Road map** D6. ((760) 360-5991. Perched on top of a mountain, it is worth eating here for the views alone. The menu is also impressive with a daily fresh-fish special. 🔇 🥾

LA QUINTA: *Cunard's* $$$$
78045 Calle Cadiz, CA 92253. **Road map** D6. ((760) 564-4443. This restaurant has mountain views, a cosy cocktail bar and a good menu. Try home-made gnocchi with wild mushrooms. 🍷 🥾

PALM DESERT: *Tuscany Ristorante* $$
Marriott's Desert Springs Resort and Spa, Country Club Drive, CA 92260. **Road map** D6. ((760) 341-1839. This Italian-style hotel restaurant *(see p521)* serves excellent pasta dishes and specials such as veal. The twilight dinner specials (5:30–6:30pm) are a real bargain. ● L. 🔇 🍷 🥾

		OUTDOOR EATING Some tables on a patio or terrace. VEGETARIAN SPECIALITIES One menu always includes a selection of vegetarian dishes. BAR AREA/COCKTAIL BAR There is a bar area or cocktail bar within the restaurant. FIXED-PRICE MENU A good-value fixed-price menu on offer at lunch, dinner or both, usually with three courses. CHILDREN'S FACILITIES Small portions and/or highchairs available on request.	OUTDOOR EATING	VEGETARIAN SPECIALITIES	BAR AREA/COCKTAIL BAR	FIXED-PRICE MENU	CHILDREN'S FACILITIES

Price categories for a three-course meal for one, including a half bottle of house wine, sales tax and service:
Ⓢ under $25
ⓈⓈ $25–$35
ⓈⓈⓈ $35–$50
ⓈⓈⓈⓈ $50–$70
ⓈⓈⓈⓈⓈ over $70

PALM DESERT: *Cuistot* ⓈⓈⓈⓈⓈ
73111 El Paseo, CA 92260. **Road map** D6. (*(760) 340-1000.* This elegant French-Californian restaurant offers three or four fish specials every night. The exotic floating islands dessert is delicious. ● *Sun L, Mon.* & ♥ 🖰

PALM SPRINGS: *Cactus Corral* Ⓢ
67501 Hwy 111, Cathedral City, CA 92234. **Road map** D6. (*(760) 321-8558.* Great barbecues and live country-and-western music await you at this American country-style restaurant and club. ● *Mon, Tue.* & 🎵 🖰

PALM SPRINGS: *John Henry's Café* Ⓢ
1785 E Tahquitz Canyon Way, CA 92262. **Road map** D6. (*(760) 327-7667.* It is as difficult to get into this wonderful restaurant as it is to find it. Enormous portions of meat, fish and pasta are always on offer and the specials change daily. Book well in advance. ● *Sun, Mon–Sat L.* & 🖰

PALM SPRINGS: *Louise's Pantry* Ⓢ
124 S Palm Canyon Drive, CA 92262. **Road map** D6. (*(760) 325-5124.* Located next door to the Plaza Theater, this 1940s-style diner serves such American standards as corn bread, pies, roast leg of lamb with gravy and a delicious home-made meatloaf with mashed potatoes. 🖰

PALM SPRINGS: *Lyon's English Grille* Ⓢ
233 E Palm Canyon Drive, CA 92264. **Road map** D6. (*(760) 327-1551.* Lyon's has an extensive British menu, featuring steak-and-kidney pie and beef Wellington. All meals come with salad or vegetables. ● *L.* & 🎵 🖰

PALM SPRINGS: *Billy Reeds* ⓈⓈ
1800 N Palm Canyon Drive, CA 92262. **Road map** D6. (*(760) 325-1946.* This restaurant gets very busy, particularly at weekends when there is live jazz. The food is pure American and breakfasts are very good. & 🎵 🖰

PALM SPRINGS: *Europa* ⓈⓈ
1620 Indian Trail, CA 92264. **Road map** D6. (*(760) 327-2314.* One of the prettiest restaurants in Palm Springs, this is part of the Villa Royale Inn *(see p521).* The cuisine is northern Italian. ● *Mon, Tue–Sun L.* & ♥ 🖰

PALM SPRINGS: *Flower Drum* ⓈⓈ
424 S Indian Canyon Drive, CA 92262. **Road map** D6. (*(760) 323-3020.* Five chefs serve five regional styles of Chinese cooking. There is a stream running through the centre of the restaurant filled with fish and, from Wednesday to Saturday, there are Chinese classical dancers. ● *L.* & 🖰

PALM SPRINGS: *Le Vallauris* ⓈⓈ
385 W Tahquitz Canyon Way, CA 92262. **Road map** D6. (*(760) 325-5059.* Classic French cuisine is served in this ornately decorated restaurant. Cocktails can be enjoyed on the shaded patio. & ♥ 🖰

PALM SPRINGS: *Lord Fletcher Inn* ⓈⓈ
70385 Hwy 111 (Country Club Drive), CA 92270. **Road map** D6. (*(760) 328-1161.* The food here is British-American, such as prime rib steak with Yorkshire pudding. The atmosphere, however, is British, with Toby jugs and royal portraits. ● *Jul & Aug: daily; Sep–Jun: Sun & Mon, Tue–Sat L.* & 🖰

PALM SPRINGS: *Riccio's* ⓈⓈ
2155 N Palm Canyon Drive, CA 92262. **Road map** D6. (*(760) 325-2369.* This smart restaurant serves traditional Italian cuisine. The wine list features Italian reds, dessert wines and ports. ● *Sat & Sun L.* & 🎵 ♥ 🖰

PALM SPRINGS: *Cedar Creek Inn* ⓈⓈⓈ
1555 S Palm Canyon Drive, CA 92264. **Road map** D6. (*(760) 325-7300.* Superb salads and sandwiches are served all day and main courses are served from 4:30pm. Service is friendly and efficient. & 🎵 🖰

RANCHO MIRAGE: *Ritz-Carlton Rancho Mirage Hotel* $$$$
68900 Frank Sinatra Drive, CA 92270. **Road map** D6. (*(760) 321-8282.*
The dining room at this elegant hotel *(see p521)* serves French cuisine.
A jazz band provides ambience. ● *Mon, Tue, Wed–Sun L.* ⓑ ⓣ ⓙ ⓟ ⓔ

REDLANDS: *Joe Greensleeves* $$$
220 North Orange St, CA 92373. **Road map** D6. (*(909) 792-6969.* Game
dishes (venison, wild boar, rabbit) are the speciality of this restaurant.
Seafood and Canadian salmon are also on offer. ● *Mon.* ⓑ ⓟ ⓔ

RIVERSIDE: *Mario's Place* $$$
1725 Spruce St, CA 92507. **Road map** D6. (*(909) 684-7755.* Chef Leone
Palagi seamlessly fuses French and Italian cuisine with pasta, meat and
fish dishes. There is live music several nights a week. ● *Sun.* ⓑ ⓙ ⓟ ⓔ

THE MOJAVE DESERT

BAKER: *The Mad Greek's Diner* $
Hwy 127 & I-15 intersection, CA 92309. **Road map** D5. (*(760) 733-4354.* This
restaurant is a corner of Greece set in the tiny town of Baker. Specialities
are *gyros* (sliced roast lamb), *shish kebab* (meat cooked on skewers) and
tabbouleh (a bulgur wheat salad). American food is also available. ⓑ ⓔ

BARSTOW: *Cactus Club* $
1511 E Main St, CA 92311. **Road map** D5. (*(760) 256-8806.* American food
is on offer at this café set in a large Holiday Inn. After a hearty meal,
the popular Calico Ghost Town *(see p275)* is just minutes away. ⓑ ⓔ

BARSTOW: *Idle Spurs Steak House* $$
690 Hwy 58, CA 92311. **Road map** D5. (*(760) 256-8888.* This is a Western-
style steakhouse where the meat is thickly sliced and the atmosphere
is friendly. The prime rib is tender and delicious. ● *Sat & Sun L.* ⓑ ⓟ ⓔ

DEATH VALLEY: *Wrangler Steakhouse* $$
Furnace Creek Ranch, CA 92328. **Road map** D4. (*(760) 786-2345 (ext. 250).*
This classic steak house offers steaks, chops, chicken and seafood in a
southwestern setting. There is also a well-stocked salad bar. ⓑ ⓔ

DEATH VALLEY: *Timo's* $$$
Furnace Creek Inn, CA 92328. **Road map** D4. (*(760) 786-2345 (ext. 253).*
There are wonderful mountain views to be had from this popular Italian
café set in the Furnace Creek Inn *(see p522).* ● *Mon.* ⓑ ⓙ ⓟ ⓔ

LAKE HAVASU: *Krystal's Fine Dining* $$
560 El Camino Way, AZ 86403. **Road map** E5. (*(520) 453-2999.* This family-
friendly, unpretentious restaurant offers steak, seafood and chicken
dishes. There is also a large selection of desserts and cheesecakes. ⓑ ⓔ

LAKE HAVASU: *London Arms Pub and Restaurant* $$
422 English Village, AZ 86403. **Road map** E5. (*(520) 855-8782.* Fish and
chips are the house speciality at this English restaurant. Desserts such
as bread pudding and English trifle complete the atmosphere. English
beers are on tap and there is a happy hour from 4–6pm daily. ⓑ ⓔ

LAKE HAVASU: *Shugrue's Restaurant* $$
1425 McCulloch Blvd, AZ 86403. **Road map** E5. (*(520) 453-1400.* This
family restaurant, with a view of London Bridge *(see p278)*, serves
seafood and steaks. The library setting is quiet and relaxing, and the
bakery on the premises makes desserts and dinner loaves. ⓑ ⓟ ⓔ

LAS VEGAS: *Battista's Hole in the Wall* $
4041 Audrie Lane, NV 89109 **Road map** E4. (*(702) 732-1424.* A strolling
accordion player sets the scene at this old-fashioned Italian spot. The
price includes all the wine you can drink. Book ahead. ⓑ ⓙ ⓔ

LAS VEGAS: *Stratosphere Tower Revolving Restaurant* $$$
Stratosphere Tower Hotel, 2000 South Las Vegas Blvd, NV 89104. **Road
map** E4. (*(702) 380-7777.* Dress up for the adults-only formal dining
room. The continental cuisine features meats and seafood. ⓑ ⓟ ⓔ

LAS VEGAS: *Andre's* $$$$
401 S 6th St, NV 89101. **Road map** E4. (*(702) 385-5016.*
This up-market French restaurant is set in an old house, decorated with
tapestries and lace. Typical dishes include Châteaubriand. ● *L.* ⓑ ⓟ ⓔ

Price categories for a three-course meal for one, including a half bottle of house wine, sales tax and service:
Ⓢ under $25
ⓈⓈ $25–$35
ⓈⓈⓈ $35–$50
ⓈⓈⓈⓈ $50–$70
ⓈⓈⓈⓈⓈ over $70

OUTDOOR EATING
Some tables on a patio or terrace.
VEGETARIAN SPECIALITIES
One menu always includes a selection of vegetarian dishes.
BAR AREA/COCKTAIL BAR
There is a bar area or cocktail bar within the restaurant.
FIXED-PRICE MENU
A good-value fixed-price menu on offer at lunch, dinner or both, usually with three courses.
CHILDREN'S FACILITIES
Small portions and/or highchairs available on request.

SAN FRANCISCO

CHINATOWN AND NOB HILL: *Cordon Bleu* Ⓢ
1574 California St., CA 94109. **Map** 5 A4. ☎ *(415) 673-5637.* This tiny hole-in-the-wall restaurant serves good Vietnamese food at low prices. The menu is short, but includes a wonderful "five-spice" roast chicken. ● *Sun L, Mon.*

CHINATOWN AND NOB HILL: *Kan's* Ⓢ
708 Grant Ave, CA 94108. **Map** 5 C4. ☎ *(415) 982-2388.*
This traditional Chinese restaurant, located in the heart of Chinatown, is famous for its Peking duck and honey walnut prawns. 🍽 🎵 🗔

CHINATOWN AND NOB HILL: *Pot Sticker* Ⓢ
150 Waverly Pl, CA 94109. **Map** 5 C4. ☎ *(415) 397-9985.* This popular northern Chinese restaurant is located in one of Chinatown's more attractive side streets. It is best known for its dumplings and its budget menus. ♿ 🗔

CHINATOWN AND NOB HILL: *Swan Oyster Depot* Ⓢ
1517 Polk St, CA 94109. **Map** 4 F3. ☎ *(415) 673-1101.* If you crave fresh oysters and a glass of Anchor Steam beer, go to Swan, the oldest oyster bar in the city. The friendly bar staff will advise on the best varieties. ● *Sun.* ♿

CHINATOWN AND NOB HILL: *Yamato* Ⓢ
717 California St, CA 94108. **Map** 5 C4. ☎ *(415) 397-3456.* High-quality Japanese-style cuisine is available at this restaurant and sushi bar. The furnishings were made in Japan and shipped to America. ● *Sun L, Mon, Sat L.* 🗔

CHINATOWN AND NOB HILL: *Empress of China* ⓈⓈ
838 Grant Ave, CA 94108. **Map** 5 C3. ☎ *(415) 434-1345.* This is a good place to come for authentic Chinese food in the centre of Chinatown. The Peking duck is excellent. Call ahead to reserve – it can be busy. ♿ 🗔

CHINATOWN AND NOB HILL: *Fornou's Oven* ⓈⓈⓈ
905 California St, Stanford Court Hotel, CA 94108. **Map** 5 C3. ☎ *(415) 989-3500.* The name comes from the large Portuguese tile oven in the centre of this Mediterranean-style restaurant. The rack of lamb is wonderful. ♿ 🍽 🗔

CHINATOWN AND NOB HILL: *Big Four Restaurant* ⓈⓈⓈⓈ
1075 California St, CA 94108. **Map** 5 B4. ☎ *(415) 771-1140.* Next to the foyer of the Huntington Hotel *(see p523)*, the formal setting includes memorabilia relating to the "Big Four" railroad barons *(see pp46–7)*. The food is excellent, if not very adventurous. ♿ *limited.* 🍽 🎵 🗔

CHINATOWN AND NOB HILL: *Tommy Toy's* ⓈⓈⓈⓈ
655 Montgomery St, CA 94111. **Map** 5 C3. ☎ *(415) 397-4888.* Tapestries and antique mirrors adorn San Francisco's only four-star Chinese restaurant, where diners eat by lamplight. French nouvelle cuisine is fused with traditional Chinese cooking. ● *Sat & Sun L.* ♿ 🍽 🗔

CHINATOWN AND NOB HILL: *Masa's* ⓈⓈⓈⓈⓈ
648 Bush St, CA 94108. **Map** 5 B4. ☎ *(415) 989-7154.* Masa's serves nouvelle cuisine to an exceptionally high standard. The wines are also world-class, and the desserts excellent. ● *Sun, Mon.* ♿ 🍽 🍷 🗔

CHINATOWN AND NOB HILL: *The Dining Room* ⓈⓈⓈⓈⓈ
600 Stockton St, CA 94108. **Map** 5 C4. ☎ *(415) 296-7465.* Located in the Ritz Carlton Hotel *(see p523)* the excellent Californian cuisine here is prepared with a French flourish. ● *Sun, Mon–Sat L.* ♿ 🍽 🍷 🎵 🗔

CIVIC CENTER: *Mifune* Ⓢ
Japan Center, 1737 Post St, CA 94115. **Map** 4 E4. ☎ *(415) 922-0337.* Mifune is a long-standing favourite for noodle soup. The Japanese noodles are made daily on the premises, with a choice of more than 20 toppings. ♿ *limited.* 🗔

	OUTDOOR EATING	VEGETARIAN SPECIALITIES	BAR AREA/COCKTAIL BAR	FIXED-PRICE MENU	CHILDREN'S FACILITIES
Cordon Bleu					
Kan's		●	●	●	
Pot Sticker		●		●	●
Swan Oyster Depot			●		
Yamato		●	●	●	●
Empress of China		●	●		
Fornou's Oven			●		●
Big Four Restaurant		●	●		●
Tommy Toy's		●			●
Masa's			●		
The Dining Room		●	●	●	●
Mifune		●			

CIVIC CENTER: *Sanppo* $
Japan Center, 1702 Post St, CA 94115. **Map** 4 E4. 【 *(415) 346-3486*. A range of
traditional dishes is served in this popular restaurant. The atmosphere
is welcoming and the food is inexpensive and reliable. ● *Sun L, Mon.*

CIVIC CENTER: *Ivy's* $$
398 Hayes St, CA 94102. **Map** 4 F5. 【 *(415) 626-3930*. For good food in a
typically Californian setting, Ivy's is hard to beat. The simple menu
includes fresh meats, pastas, salads and desserts. ● *Sun D.* 🔌 🖥

CIVIC CENTER: *Maharani* $$
1122 Post St, CA 94112. **Map** 5 A5. 【 *(415) 775-1988*. This is perhaps the best
Indian restaurant in the city. Settle down on the cushions in the Fantasy
Room, and enjoy the succulent tandooris and curries. ● *L.* 🔌 🖥

CIVIC CENTER: *Miss Pearl's Jam House* $$
601 Eddy St, CA 94109. **Map** 5 A5. 【 *(415) 775-5267*. This is a piece of
Jamaica in the middle of San Francisco, with colourful décor, reggae music,
copious cocktails and traditional Creole dishes. ● *Mon, Tue.* 🔌 🎵 🖥

CIVIC CENTER: *Stars Café* $$
500 Van Ness Ave, CA 94102. **Map** 4 F5. 【 *(415) 861-4344*. This bright café
is a spin-off of Stars, also owned by chef Jeremiah Tower. The Californian-
style dishes include crab cakes and hand-made pasta pillows. 🔌 🖥

CIVIC CENTER: *Elka* $$$
Japan Center, 1611 Post St, CA 94115. **Map** 4 E4. 【 *(415) 922-7788*.
The distinctive union of Japanese and European cuisine includes
dishes such as coriander-encrusted tuna and lobster gnocchi. 🔌 🖥

CIVIC CENTER: *Hayes Street Grill* $$$
320 Hayes St, CA 94102. **Map** 4 F5. 【 *(415) 863-5545*. This is an unpreten-
tious place serving the freshest of fish, grilled, steamed or sautéed. The
restaurant is popular with politicians and operagoers. ● *Sat & Sun L.* 🔌 🖥

CIVIC CENTER: *Stars* $$$
555 Golden Gate Ave, CA 94102. **Map** 4 F5. 【 *(415) 861-7827*. This bustling
restaurant claims to have the longest bar in San Francisco. The food is
American bistro-style with fabulous desserts. ● *Sat & Sun L.* 🔌 🍷 🎵 🖥

CIVIC CENTER: *Zuni Café* $$$
1658 Market St, CA 94102. **Map** 10 F1. 【 *(415) 552-2522*. Some of the city's
freshest seafood is available here, with as many as ten different kinds
of oysters. The smokey pizzas are also good. ● *Mon.* 🔌 *limited.* 🎵 🖥

CIVIC CENTER: *Acquerello* $$$$
1722 Sacramento St, CA 94109. **Map** 5 A4. 【 *(415) 567-5432*. The beautiful
décor matches the sophisticated menu, which includes grilled tuna
in a piquant Sicilian olive and pepper sauce. ● *Sun, Mon.* 🍷 🖥

CIVIC CENTER: *Postrio* $$$$
545 Post St, CA 94102. **Map** 5 B5. 【 *(415) 776-7825*. A mix of Mediterranean and Californian-Asian dishes are on the menu of Wolfgang
Puck's restaurant. Pizzas and drinks are available at the bar. 🔌 🖥

DOWNTOWN: *Café Bastille* $
22 Belden Place (north of Bush St between Kearny St and Montgomery St), CA 94104.
Map 5 C4. 【 *(415) 986-5673*. This small café offers traditional bistro food
and a range of beer and wine. At night there is live jazz. ● *Sun.* 🔌 🎵 🖥

DOWNTOWN: *Delancey Street Restaurant* $
600 Embarcadero, CA 94107. **Map** 6 E5. 【 *(415) 512-5179*. Delancey Street Restaurant serves a variety of American dishes as well as more eclectic ethnic
fare. From the patio the Bay Bridge looms high overhead. ● *Mon.* 🔌 🖥

DOWNTOWN: *House of Nan King* $
919 Kearny St, CA 94133. **Map** 5 C3. 【 *(415) 421-1429*. Many consider this
the best cheap Chinese restaurant in the country. There is an extensive,
Shanghai menu of braised meats and vegetable dishes. ● *Sun L.*

DOWNTOWN: *Café La Presse* $$
459 Bush St, CA 94108. **Map** 5 C4. 【 *(415) 249-0900*. All the ingredients of
classic French cooking are to be found in this good-value restaurant.
The bar is popular with locals. 🔌 🖥

Price categories for a three-course meal for one, including a half bottle of house wine, sales tax and service:
$ under $25
$$ $25–$35
$$$ $35–$50
$$$$ $50–$70
$$$$$ over $70

OUTDOOR EATING
Some tables on a patio or terrace.
VEGETARIAN SPECIALITIES
One menu always includes a selection of vegetarian dishes.
BAR AREA/COCKTAIL BAR
There is a bar area or cocktail bar within the restaurant.
FIXED-PRICE MENU
A good-value fixed-price menu on offer at lunch, dinner or both, usually with three courses.
CHILDREN'S FACILITIES
Small portions and/or highchairs available on request.

	Price	OUTDOOR EATING	VEGETARIAN SPECIALITIES	BAR AREA/COCKTAIL BAR	FIXED-PRICE MENU	CHILDREN'S FACILITIES
DOWNTOWN: City of Paris	$$		●			●
DOWNTOWN: Harbor Village Restaurant	$$		●			●
DOWNTOWN: John's Grill	$$		●			●
DOWNTOWN: MacArthur Park	$$		●			●
DOWNTOWN: Nanbantei of Tokyo	$$		●			●
DOWNTOWN: Sam's Grill and Seafood Restaurant	$$		●	●		
DOWNTOWN: Splendido	$$		●	●		●
DOWNTOWN: Yank Sing	$$		●			
DOWNTOWN: Carnelian Room	$$$		●	●		
DOWNTOWN: Il Fornaio	$$$	●	●			●
DOWNTOWN: Kuleto's	$$$		●	●		
DOWNTOWN: Kyo-ya	$$$		●			●

DOWNTOWN: *City of Paris* $$
101 Shannon Alley, CA 94114. **Map** 5 B5. (415) 441-4442. The City of Paris is a modest bistro. Reasonable prices and good food, including excellent fried potatoes, make it a popular lunch spot. ● Mon L.

DOWNTOWN: *Harbor Village Restaurant* $$
4 Embarcadero Center, lobby level, CA 94111. **Map** 6 D3. (415) 781-8833. Traditional Cantonese fare and innovative contemporary dishes are served here, to a largely expatriate Chinese clientele.

DOWNTOWN: *John's Grill* $$
63 Ellis St, CA 94102. **Map** 5 C5. (415) 986-0069. Crime writer Dashiell Hammett made this restaurant famous when he used it as a setting in *The Maltese Falcon* in 1930. It still serves old-fashioned American fare. The walls are covered with Hammett memorabilia. ● Sun L. limited.

DOWNTOWN: *MacArthur Park* $$
607 Front St, CA 94111. **Map** 6 D3. (415) 398-5700. Grilled meats are the speciality here, especially the delicious oak-smoked baby back ribs, grilled fish and steaks. The atmosphere is comfortable and casual. ● Sun L.

DOWNTOWN: *Nanbantei of Tokyo* $$
156 Cyril St, CA 94102. **Map** 5 B5. (415) 421-2101. "Nan-ban" is the name the Japanese gave to Dutch traders in the 17th century, and the food here combines the Dutch taste for charcoal-grilled meats and vegetables with Japanese delicacy and visual presentation. ● L.

DOWNTOWN: *Sam's Grill and Seafood Restaurant* $$
374 Bush St, CA 94104. **Map** 5 C4. (415) 421-0594. One of San Francisco's oldest and best seafood restaurants. The famously grumpy waiters deal efficiently with the crowds at lunchtime. ● Sat & Sun. limited.

DOWNTOWN: *Splendido* $$
4 Embarcadero Center, CA 94111. **Map** 6 D3. (415) 986-3222. Splendido is a huge restaurant with a good view of San Francisco Bay. It serves a range of Mediterranean-based foods including *tapas* (starters) and pizzas.

DOWNTOWN: *Yank Sing* $$
427 Battery, CA 94111. **Map** 6 D3. (415) 781-1111. There are more than 100 different varieties of *dim sum* (see p540) here, which are chosen from passing trolleys. Prices are only around $3 to $4 a plate. ● D.

DOWNTOWN: *Carnelian Room* $$$
Bank of America, 555 California St, CA 94104. **Map** 6 D3. (415) 433-7500. Fine Californian cuisine can be enjoyed on the 52nd floor, while looking out on a panoramic view of the city. ● Mon–Sat L.

DOWNTOWN: *Il Fornaio* $$$
1265 Battery St, CA 94111. **Map** 5 C2. (415) 986-0100. Il Fornaio is a stylish but unpretentious trattoria, best known for its home-baked breads and pizzas. The menu also offers well-prepared pasta and grilled meats, and a spicy dish of sausage and polenta. Desserts are excellent.

DOWNTOWN: *Kuleto's* $$$
221 Powell St, CA 94109. **Map** 5 B5. (415) 397-7720. Although it is always crowded, it is worth the wait to eat here. Theatregoers often fill up on pre-show starters at the bar, which are as good as the main meals. limited.

DOWNTOWN: *Kyo-ya* $$$
2 New Montgomery St, CA 94105. **Map** 5 C4. (415) 392-8600. The luxurious Kyo-ya, in the Sheraton Palace Hotel (see p526) has a number of traditional Japanese dishes that are rarely seen on American menus, as well as sushi and other more familiar meals. ● Sun, Sat L.

DOWNTOWN: *Palio D'Asti* $$$
640 Sacramento St, CA 94111. **Map** 5 C4. ((415) 395-9800. This restaurant caters for business people and is popular at lunchtimes. The menu features antipasti, pizzas and pastas of high quality. ● *Sun, Sat L.* & €

DOWNTOWN: *Perry's Sports Bar and Grill* $$$
185 Sutter St, CA 94111. **Map** 5 C4. ((415) 989-6895. Perry's is a popular after-work stop for office workers. There is an attractive bar, and live music is played on weekday nights. ● *Sun L.* & *limited.* €

DOWNTOWN: *St Francis Grill* $$$
335 Powell St, CA 94102. **Map** 5 B4. ((415) 774-0233. The St Francis Grill in the Westin St Francis Hotel *(see p526)* has an elegant, peaceful wood-panelled dining room and excellent food. ● *L.* & €

DOWNTOWN: *Tadich Grill* $$$
240 California St, CA 94111. **Map** 6 D4. ((415) 391-1849. Tadich Grill opened during the Gold Rush *(see pp44–5)* and is the longest-established restaurant in California, serving superb seafood. ● *Sun.* & €

DOWNTOWN: *Aqua* $$$$
252 California St, CA 94111. **Map** 5 D4. ((415) 956-9662. Fish-lovers will enjoy this sophisticated seafood restaurant. Try the Dungeness crab, followed by smoked swordfish wrapped in prosciutto. ● *Sun, Sat L.* & €

DOWNTOWN: *Bix* $$$$
56 Gold St, CA 94133. **Map** 5 C3. ((415) 433-6300. This beautiful restaurant re-creates a 1920s supper club, with a sophisticated, almost decadent atmosphere. The food is contemporary American. ● *Sat & Sun L.* & €

DOWNTOWN: *Boulevard* $$$$
1 Mission St, CA 94105. **Map** 6 E4. ((415) 543-6084. Traditional dishes such as roast meats and mashed potatoes are enlivened by chef Nancy Oakes with unusual sauces and a theatrical presentation. ● *Sat & Sun L.* & €

DOWNTOWN: *Silks* $$$$
222 Sansome St, CA 94104. **Map** 5 C4. ((415) 986-2020. Californian-Asian cuisine is the speciality at Silks, in the Mandarin Oriental Hotel *(see p525)*. Try the spiced jumbo prawns, grilled on a skewer. Book ahead. & €

DOWNTOWN: *Campton Place* $$$$$
340 Stockton St, CA 94108. **Map** 5 C4. ((415) 955-5555. Set in the Campton Place Hotel *(see p525)*, many consider this the best restaurant in the city. The food is notable for its sophisticated preparation. & €

DOWNTOWN: *Cypress Club* $$$$$
500 Jackson St, CA 94133. **Map** 5 C3. ((415) 296-8555. There is no more attractive combination of good food, great style and indefinably San Franciscan "buzz" than in this popular Jackson Square haunt. ● *L.* & €

DOWNTOWN: *Essex Supper Club* $$$$$
847 Montgomery St, CA 94133. **Map** 5 C3. ((415) 397-5969. Californian cuisine with a French flavour is served in this charming restaurant. The plush interior was shown in Alfred Hitchcock's film *Vertigo.* ● *Sun.* & €

DOWNTOWN: *Fleur de Lys* $$$$$
777 Sutter St, CA 94109. **Map** 5 B4. ((415) 673-7779. This is one of the city's most expensive and highly regarded restaurants. The food is excellent, with a wide range of carefully presented dishes. ● *Sun, Mon–Sat L.* & *limited.* €

FISHERMAN'S WHARF: *Pompei's Grotto* $
340 Jefferson St, CA 94133. **Map** 5 A1. ((415) 776-9265. The locals flock to this Italian-style seafood restaurant, which has operated here since the 1940s. Specialities include wonderful fresh Dungeness crab. & €

FISHERMAN'S WHARF: *Fog City Diner* $$
1300 Battery St, CA 94111. **Map** 5 C2. ((415) 982-2000. A range of burgers, ribs, chops and chicken dishes is on offer here. Situated near the waterfront, with a good bar, it is often crowded but well worth a visit. & €

FISHERMAN'S WHARF: *Scoma's* $$
Pier 47, Fisherman's Wharf, CA 94133. **Map** 5 A1. ((415) 771-4383. Fresh fish is delivered daily straight to this seafood restaurant located on the pier. The shellfish sauté, with four types of shellfish, is delicious. & €

<table>
<tr><td colspan="2">

Price categories for a three-course meal for one, including a half bottle of house wine, sales tax and service:
$ under $25
$$ $25–$35
$$$ $35–$50
$$$$ $50–$70
$$$$$ over $70

</td><td>

OUTDOOR EATING
Some tables on a patio or terrace.
VEGETARIAN SPECIALITIES
One menu always includes a selection of vegetarian dishes.
BAR AREA/COCKTAIL BAR
There is a bar area or cocktail bar within the restaurant.
FIXED-PRICE MENU
A good-value fixed-price menu on offer at lunch, dinner or both, usually with three courses.
CHILDREN'S FACILITIES
Small portions and/or highchairs available on request.

</td></tr>
</table>

	OUTDOOR EATING	VEGETARIAN SPECIALITIES	BAR AREA/COCKTAIL BAR	FIXED-PRICE MENU	CHILDREN'S FACILITIES
FISHERMAN'S WHARF: *Asabella's* $$$ 2766 Taylor St, CA 94133. **Map** 5 A1. ((415) 771-6775. This elegant Italian restaurant has lovely views of the ocean. It serves exquisite seafood, such as "pirate salad", containing lobster, crab and shrimps.		●	■		■
FISHERMAN'S WHARF: *Alioto's* $$$$ 8 Fisherman's Wharf, CA 94133. **Map** 5 A1. ((415) 673-0183. Fresh seafood has been served here by the Alioto family since 1930. Fine views of Golden Gate Bridge.		●	■		■
FISHERMAN'S WHARF: *Greens* $$$$ Building A, Fort Mason Center, CA 94123. **Map** 4 E1. ((415) 771-6222. This is the most highly regarded vegetarian restaurant on the West Coast. It is famous for its fixed-price Saturday dinners. There is a simpler mid-week menu, which includes unusual vegetable stews. ● *Sun D, Mon L.*		●		●	■
GOLDEN GATE PARK AND THE PRESIDIO: *PJ's Oysterbed* $ 737 Irving St, CA 94122. **Map** 8 F3. ((415) 566-7775. It is worth a short detour to visit this seafood specialist, a block south of Golden Gate Park. Choose from the range of char-grilled fish and other dishes.					
GOLDEN GATE PARK AND THE PRESIDIO: *Pacific Café* $$ 7000 Geary Blvd, CA 94121. **Map** 7 C1. ((415) 387-7091. Seafood has been served here for many years and the café is the best value in San Francisco. There is free wine while you wait for a table. ● *L.* limited.					■
GOLDEN GATE PARK AND THE PRESIDIO: *Straits Café* $$ 3300 Geary Blvd, CA 94118. **Map** 3 B5. ((415) 668-1783. A mouthwatering array of Cantonese, Indonesian and Indian cuisine is on offer here. Try *kway paita* – a pastry filled with a shrimp and vegetable mixture.		●			
GOLDEN GATE PARK AND THE PRESIDIO: *Ya Ya* $$ 1220 9th Ave, CA 94122. **Map** 8 F3. ((415) 566-6966. Ya Ya has become one of the most exciting and popular restaurants in San Francisco. Its blend of Middle Eastern and Mediterranean dishes includes grilled meats served with citrus-rich sauces on a bed of rice or bulgar wheat. ● *Mon.*		●			
HAIGHT ASHBURY: *Cha Cha Cha* $ 1801 Haight St, CA 94133. **Map** 9 B1. ((415) 386-5758. You will have to wait for a table at this very popular *tapas* bar. The menu changes daily, and mixes Caribbean, Cajun and Mexican influences. Cha Cha Cha is notable for its crazy décor and its individualistic Haight Street clientele.			■		
HAIGHT ASHBURY: *Indian Oven* $ 233 Fillmore St, CA 94117. **Map** 10 E1. ((415) 626-1628. Traditional Indian cuisine has been updated with Californian panache here. The vegetarian dishes are impressive and vary according to the seasons.		●			
NORTH BEACH: *Brandy Ho's* $ 450 Broadway, CA 94133. **Map** 5 C3. ((415) 362-6268. The Hunan food here is very good, although the modern décor is rather brash. The smoked meats are delicious, but not for the faint-hearted. limited.		●			
NORTH BEACH: *Capp's Corner* $ 1600 Powell St, CA 94133. **Map** 5 B2. ((415) 989-2589. This good-value North Beach institution is popular with families. It offers a wide range of Italian-American dishes from a set menu. ● *Sat & Sun L.* limited.		●		●	■
NORTH BEACH: *Il Pollaio* $ 555 Columbus Ave, CA 94133. **Map** 5 B2. ((415) 362-7727. This friendly, family-run restaurant specializes in chicken that is marinated then grilled to perfection. Complementing the poultry are fresh salads, good soups and inexpensive Italian table wines. ● *Sun.*					■

NORTH BEACH: *Little Joe's* $
523 Broadway, CA 94133. **Map** 5 C3. (415) 433-4343. Little Joe's is one of the best cheap Italian eating places in San Francisco. It is very lively, and the food is good. The garlic squid is particularly popular. limited.

NORTH BEACH: *Caffè Macaroni* $$
59 Columbus Ave, CA 94111. **Map** 5 C3. (415) 956-9737. The food at Caffè Macaroni is always reliable, with very good daily special menus and reasonable prices. The portions are extremely generous. Sat & Sun L.

NORTH BEACH: *Helmand* $$
430 Broadway, CA 94133. **Map** 5 C3. (415) 362-0641. Afghan food is served in this small restaurant. Main dishes come with vegetables, rice or sautéed barley and lentils. The prices are good value. Sat & Sun L

NORTH BEACH: *Julius' Castle* $$
1541 Montgomery St, CA 94133. **Map** 5 B2. (415) 362-3042. Italian and French cuisine is served in a romantic setting with views of Telegraph Hill. L

NORTH BEACH: *Little City Antipasti Bar* $$
673 Union St, CA 94133. **Map** 5 B2. (415) 434-2900. Little City serves Californian versions of Mediterranean *tapas* in a stylish, often crowded room. Order a series of small starters rather than a main dish.

NORTH BEACH: *Stinking Rose: A Garlic Restaurant* $$
325 Columbus Ave, CA 94133. **Map** 5 C3. (415) 781-7673. This busy North Beach restaurant serves every dish strongly flavoured with garlic. The décor is rustic, with terracotta walls and marble tables. limited.

NORTH BEACH: *Café Jacqueline* $$$
1454 Grant Ave, CA 94133. **Map** 5 C2. (415) 981-5565. This romantic French café features airy soufflés with a choice of different ingredients such as garlic or prosciutto. Each soufflé serves two. Mon, Tue, Wed–Sun L.

NORTH BEACH: *Moose's* $$$
1652 Stockton St, CA 94133. **Map** 5 B2. (415) 989-7800. This large, noisy North Beach restaurant is frequented by politicians and media people. The food is reliably good and the setting is sunny. Mon.

PACIFIC HEIGHTS: *Baja Cantina* $
3154 Fillmore St, CA 94123. **Map** 4 D2. (415) 885-2252. This lively, inexpensive restaurant serves traditional Mexican specialities in large portions. Meals are complemented with pitchers of ice-cold margaritas.

PACIFIC HEIGHTS: *Golden Turtle* $
2211 Van Ness Ave, CA 94109. **Map** 4 F3. (415) 441-4419. A selection of traditional Vietnamese dishes is available here, including three types of crab. The atmosphere is casual. Mon, Tue–Sun L.

PACIFIC HEIGHTS: *North India Restaurant* $
3131 Webster St off Lombard St, CA 94123. **Map** 4 D2. (415) 931-1556. This outstanding restaurant serves home-style North Indian cuisine, including tandoori and seafood dishes. Excellent value. Sat & Sun L.

PACIFIC HEIGHTS: *Scott's Seafood Grill* $
2400 Lombard St, CA 94123. **Map** 4 D2. (415) 563-8988. The fish is wonderfully fresh at this cheerful seafood restaurant housed in a Victorian building. Changing exhibitions of local artists' work are held here.

PACIFIC HEIGHTS: *Balboa Café* $$
3199 Fillmore St, CA 94123. **Map** 4 D2. (415) 921-3944. This café serves excellent all-American food at good prices. It is housed in a white timber-framed shed that looks like a dive in a 1940s gangster film.

PACIFIC HEIGHTS: *Café Marimba* $$
2317 Chestnut St, CA 94123. **Map** 3 C2. (415) 776-1506. The brightly painted café in the Marina district makes a perfect backdrop for the innovative southern Mexican specialities served here. Mon.

PACIFIC HEIGHTS: *Elite Café* $$$
2049 Fillmore St, CA 94115. **Map** 4 D4. (415) 346-8668. This busy, moderately priced restaurant has long been a neighbourhood favourite. The bar is lively, and the seating consists of old wooden booths. Mon–Sat L.

For key to symbols see back flap

Price categories for a three-course meal for one, including a half bottle of house wine, sales tax and service:		OUTDOOR EATING Some tables on a patio or terrace.	
$	under $25	VEGETARIAN SPECIALITIES One menu always includes a selection of vegetarian dishes.	
$$	$25–$35	BAR AREA/COCKTAIL BAR There is a bar area or cocktail bar within the restaurant.	
$$$	$35–$50	FIXED-PRICE MENU A good-value fixed-price menu on offer at lunch, dinner or both, usually with three courses.	
$$$$	$50–$70	CHILDREN'S FACILITIES Small portions and/or highchairs available on request.	
$$$$$	over $70		

Restaurant	Price	OUTDOOR EATING	VEGETARIAN SPECIALITIES	BAR AREA/COCKTAIL BAR	FIXED-PRICE MENU	CHILDREN'S FACILITIES
PACIFIC HEIGHTS: *Prego* 2000 Union St, CA 94123. **Map 4 D2.** ☎ *(415) 563-3305.* A wide range of well-prepared food is on offer here, and is presented with flair. The appetizing antipasti dishes are some of the best in town. 🕭 *limited.* 🗺	$$$		●			■
PACIFIC HEIGHTS: *Harris'* 2100 Van Ness Ave, CA 94109. **Map 4 F3.** ☎ *(415) 673-1888.* This award-winning restaurant specializes in steaks and prime ribs. The décor is old San Francisco-style, with booths and wooden floors. 🕭 🍷 🎵 🗺	$$$$		●	■		■
THE MISSION DISTRICT: *El Nuevo Frutilandia* 3077 24th St, CA 94110. **Map 10 F4.** ☎ *(415) 648-2958.* The authentic Cuban and Puerto Rican specialities here are complemented by a casual Caribbean atmosphere. Tropical fruitshakes are on the menu. ● *Mon.* 🗺	$		●			■
THE MISSION DISTRICT: *Mission Villa Restaurant* 2391 Mission St, CA 94110. **Map 10 F3.** ☎ *(415) 826-0454.* This historic Mexican restaurant opened in 1906 and is decorated with antiques. All the traditional Mexican dishes are served with rice and beans. 🕭	$		●		●	■
THE MISSION DISTRICT: *The Original Cuba Restaurant* 2886 16th St, CA 94110. **Map 10 F2.** ☎ *(415) 255-0946.* Diners from all over the city come here for traditional Cuban food, although the location is a little on the rough side. The three-course set lunches are excellent value, but the gourmet dinners are the real attraction. ● *Thu.* 🕭	$$		●		●	
THE MISSION DISTRICT: *Ti Couz* 3108 16th St, CA 94110. **Map 10 F2.** ☎ *(415) 252-7373.* Savoury *crêpes* filled with meats, vegetables or cheese and sweet *crêpes* topped with chocolate and other sauces are specialities. It is cheap and always crowded. 🕭 🗺	$		●			■

THE BAY AREA

Restaurant	Price	OUTDOOR EATING	VEGETARIAN SPECIALITIES	BAR AREA/COCKTAIL BAR	FIXED-PRICE MENU	CHILDREN'S FACILITIES
BERKELEY: *Bette's Ocean View Diner* 1807 4th St, CA 94710. **Road map inset B.** ☎ *(510) 644-3230.* Located at the centre of Berkeley's popular shopping district, this 1940s-style diner has great American food. Be prepared to wait for a table. ● *D.* 🗺	$		●			■
BERKELEY: *Plearn Thai* 2050 University Ave, CA 94704. **Road map inset B.** ☎ *(510) 841-2148.* There are so many Thai restaurants in the East Bay that they must be really good to succeed. People queue up here for delicious, cheap food. 🕭 🗺	$		●			■
BERKELEY: *Cambodiana's* 2156 University Ave, CA 94704. **Road map inset B.** ☎ *(510) 843-4630.* This restaurant is well worth a visit for its superb French-Cambodian cooking, with delights such as quail in lemon-and-ginger sauce. ● *Sat & Sun L.* 🕭 🗺	$$		●			■
BERKELEY: *Ginger Island* 1820 4th St, CA 94710. **Road map inset B.** ☎ *(510) 644-0444.* This busy, noisy restaurant in the trendy Fourth Street section of Berkeley serves good Asian-influenced American food in sunny surroundings. 🕭 🗺	$$	■	●	■		■
BERKELEY: *Chez Panisse Restaurant* 1517 Shattuck Ave, CA 94709. **Road map inset B.** ☎ *(510) 548-5525.* Founder chef Alice Waters is credited with having invented Californian cuisine here. One of the country's top restaurants, it is expensive but upstairs is a café with a cheaper menu. ● *Sun.* 🕭 🍷 🗺	$$$$		●	■	●	
BOLINAS: *Bolinas Bakery and Café* 20 Wharf Rd, CA 94924. **Road map inset B.** ☎ *(415) 868-0211.* This is basic hippie fare. Sample the microbrewed beers and wine, home-made quiches, pizzas, soups and probably the best cheesecake in the world. 🕭 🗺	$	■	●			

BOLINAS: *The Shop* $
46 Wharf Rd, CA 94294. **Road map** inset B. (415) 868-9984. This tiny restaurant serves basics, from pasta to great fish and chips, and is friendly, slightly disorganized and busy. ● *Mon, Tue D.*

BURLINGAME: *Kuleto's Trattoria* $$$
1095 Rollins Rd, CA 94010. **Road map** inset B. (415) 342-4922. Centred around an open kitchen with a woodburning pizza oven, this lively restaurant serves fine Italian food in a family atmosphere. ● *Sat L.*

HALF MOON BAY: *San Benito House* $$
356 Main St, CA 94019. **Road map** inset B. (415) 726-3425. This lovely restaurant serves Mediterranean food in a tiny dining room. The deli is open every day from 11am–3pm. ● *Mon–Wed, Thu–Sat L.*

LAFAYETTE: *Tourelle* $$$
3565 Mount Diablo Blvd, CA 94549. **Road map** Inset B. (510) 284-3565. The rustic décor of this restaurant reflects its Mediterranean cuisine: fresh seafood, oven-roast meats and a choice of pasta.

LARKSPUR: *Lark Creek Inn* $$$$
234 Magnolia Ave, CA 94939. **Road map** inset B. (415) 924-7766. This well-known restaurant serves chef-owner Bradley Ogden's award-winning American country-style cuisine. ● *Sun D, Sat L.*

MILL VALLEY: *Samurai* $
425 Miller Ave, CA 94941. **Road map** inset B. (415) 381-3680. Fried tempura, succulent seafood and absolutely fresh sushi rule at this crowded Mill Valley Japanese restaurant. ● *Sun, Mon–Sat L.*

MILL VALLEY: *Buckeye Roadhouse* $$
15 Shoreline Hwy, CA 94941. **Road map** inset B. (415) 331-2600. This roadside restaurant may look like part of a steakhouse chain but, once inside, expect a roaring fire and good, simple American cooking.

MILL VALLEY: *Piazza d'Angelo* $$
22 Miller Ave, CA 94941. **Road map** inset B. (415) 388-2000. The simple Italian cuisine served in a spacious dining room attracts a mixed crowd, from young Marin County teenagers to film directors and rock stars.

MILL VALLEY: *Frantoio* $$$
152 Shoreline Hwy, CA 94941. **Road map** inset B. (415) 289-5777. Named after the on-site olive press, this restaurant makes its own extra-virgin olive oil – a main ingredient in its Mediterranean cuisine.

OAKLAND: *Rockridge Café* $
5492 College Ave, CA 94618. **Road map** inset B. (510) 653-1567. For a hearty breakfast or a fine hamburger, look no further than this popular neighbourhood haunt, which is styled like a 1940s diner.

OAKLAND: *Milano* $$
3425 Grand Ave, CA 94610. **Road map** inset B. (510) 763-0300. This stylish restaurant has a loyal following of regulars who come here to enjoy huge helpings of Northern Italian cuisine. ● *Sat & Sun L.*

OAKLAND: *Bay Wolf* $$$
3853 Piedmont Ave, CA 94611. **Road map** inset B. (510) 655-6004. The menu at this elegant establishment changes every two weeks. The American-Mediterranean cuisine is deservedly acclaimed. ● *Sat & Sun L.*

ORINDA: *Siam Orchid Thai* $
23-H Orinda Way, CA 94563. **Road map** inset B. (510) 253-1975. In a small village 4 miles (6 km) east of Berkeley, this pleasant restaurant offers Thai staples at bargain prices. The staff are very friendly. ● *Sat & Sun L.*

PALO ALTO: *Gordon Biersch* $$$
640 Emerson St, CA 94301. **Road map** inset B. (415) 323-7723. The Gordon Biersch brewery restaurant is characterized by good Californian cuisine, stylish décor and a choice of beers brewed on the premises.

PESCADERO: *Duarte's Tavern* $$
202 Stage Rd, CA 94060. **Road map** inset B. (415) 879-0464. In business for over a century, and still run by the same family, this landmark restaurant serves hearty seafood and great home-made pies.

Price categories for a three-course meal for one, including a half bottle of house wine, sales tax and service: **$** under $25 **$$** $25–$35 **$$$** $35–$50 **$$$$** $50–$70 **$$$$$** over $70	**OUTDOOR EATING** Some tables on a patio or terrace. **VEGETARIAN SPECIALITIES** One menu always includes a selection of vegetarian dishes. **BAR AREA/COCKTAIL BAR** There is a bar area or cocktail bar within the restaurant. **FIXED-PRICE MENU** A good-value fixed-price menu on offer at lunch, dinner or both, usually with three courses. **CHILDREN'S FACILITIES** Small portions and/or highchairs available on request.	OUTDOOR EATING	VEGETARIAN SPECIALITIES	BAR AREA/COCKTAIL BAR	FIXED-PRICE MENU	CHILDREN'S FACILITIES
POINT REYES STATION: *Station House Café* **$$** 11180 Main St, CA 94956. **Road map** C4. *(415) 663-1515.* This modest restaurant is a casual gourmet treat. When in season, you should not miss the barbecued oysters. 🥗			●	■	●	■
SAN JOSE: *Tied House Café and Brewery* **$$** 65 N San Pedro St, CA 95112. **Road map** C4. *(408) 295-2739.* Best known for its beers, which are made on the premises, this lively, airy restaurant features especially good seafood dishes. ● *Sun L.* 🥗			●			■
SAN JOSE: *Emile's* **$$$$** 545 South 2nd St, CA 95112. **Road map** C4. *(408) 289-1960.* This restaurant is famous for its classic continental cuisine, award-winning wine list and elegant surroundings. ● *Sun & Mon, Tue–Thu L, Sat L.* ⚐ ♀ 🥗			●		●	
SAUSALITO: *Gate 5* **$$$** 305 Harbor Drive, CA 94965. **Road map** C4. *(415) 331-5355.* The open fire, wonderful atmosphere and innovative menu make this casual Sausalito restaurant one of the best in the Bay Area. ⚐ 🥗	■	●	■		
TIBURON: *Guaymas* **$$** 5 Main St, CA 94920. **Road map** C4. *(415) 435-6300.* This restaurant serves authentic Mexican regional cooking. Its views of San Francisco can be enjoyed from the terrace on a sunny day or a clear night. ⚐ 🥗	■	●	■		
TIBURON: *Sam's Anchor Café* **$$** 27 Main St, CA 94920. **Road map** C4. *(415) 435-4527.* Thanks to its location on the docks of San Francisco Bay, this casual restaurant and cocktail bar draws a lively crowd, especially on summer weekends. 🥗	■	●	■		
WALNUT CREEK: *Spiedini* **$$** 101 Ygnacio Valley Blvd, CA 94596. **Road map** C4. *(510) 939-2100.* Located near John Muir National Historic Site *(see p398)*, this fashionable Northern Italian restaurant serves meat and poultry spit-roasted over a wood fire, home-made pasta, pizzas and charcoal-grilled fish. ● *Sat & Sun L.* ⚐ 🥗	■	●	■		
THE NORTH						
ARCATA: *Crosswinds Vegan Restaurant* **$** 860 10th St. **Road map** C4. *(707) 826-2133.* On Saturday and Sunday, diners enjoy a free glass of champagne at this homely restaurant. Food is American-style, adapted for the vegan diet. ● *Mon, Tue–Sun D.* ⚐ ♫ *(Sun).* 🥗			●		●	■
ARCATA: *TJ's Classic Café* **$** 1057 H St, CA 95521. **Road map** C4. *(707) 822-4650.* Typical American breakfasts and lunches are on offer in this rustic restaurant. They specialize in skillet dishes, served still sizzling in the hot pan at your table. ● *D.* ⚐			●		●	■
CRESCENT CITY: *Ship Ashore* **$** 12370 Hwy 101 North, CA 95531. **Road map** C4. *(707) 487-3141.* Housed alongside a permanently dry-docked ship, this popular family restaurant serves up generous portions of fresh seafood. 🥗			■			■
EUREKA: *Samoa Cookhouse* **$** 59 Coohouse Lane, CA 95501. **Road map** C4. *(707) 442-1659.* For a taste of the North Coast woods as they used to be, nothing beats this century-old dining hall, which still serves mountains of good food *(see p430)*. ⚐ 🥗					●	■
EUREKA: *Rib Room* **$$** 518 7th St, CA 95501. **Road map** C4. *(707) 442-6441.* This de luxe restaurant is housed in the landmark Eureka Inn *(see p530)*. Attentive service from tuxedo-clad waiters, silver plates and cutlery and excellent food all make this a memorable experience. ● *L.* ♀ ♫ 🥗			■			

EUREKA: *Hotel Carter Restaurant* $($\$$)($\$$)($\$$)
301 L St, CA 95501. **Road map** C4. **[** *(707) 444-8062.* This stylish haunt
serves adventurous, well-prepared dishes, such as pork tenderloin
with home-made apple chutney. ● *L.* 🍷 🎵 🌿

GARBERVILLE: *Woodrose Café* $($\$$)
911 Redwood Drive, CA 95442. **Road map** C4. **[** *(707) 923-3191.* Located
in the heart of redwood country, this friendly café serves healthy
food such as tofu burgers and vegetable soups. ● *Sat & Sun, Mon–Fri D.*

LEWISTON: *Hitching Post Café* $($\$$)
Turnpike & Deadwood Rds, CA 96052. **Road map** C4. **[** *(916) 778-3486.* This
classic American coffee shop serves huge portions of home-style
food. The roast chicken is excellent, as are the fresh pies. 🌿

MOUNT SHASTA: *Lily's* $($\$$)($\$$)
1013 S Mount Shasta Blvd, CA 96067. **Road map** C4. **[** *(916) 926-3372.* A little
bit of everything is on the menu at this very popular restaurant, from
eggs Benedict and breakfast burritos to classic meat, poultry, seafood
and pasta dinners. Reservations are recommended. 🌿

MOUNT SHASTA: *Michael's* $($\$$)($\$$)
313 N Mount Shasta Blvd, CA 96067. **Road map** C4. **[** *(916) 926-5288.*
Delicious sandwiches, light lunches and Italian dinners have made this
a favourite restaurant in the Mount Shasta area for many years. ● *Sun.* 🌿

ORICK: *Rolf's Park Café* $($\$$)($\$$)
Hwy 101 at Davidson Rd, CA 95555. **Road map** C4. **[** *(707) 488-3841.* With
portions to match the scale of the mighty redwood trees, this German-run
café serves hearty breakfasts and a range of Bavarian specialities. 🌿

REDDING: *Jack's Grill* $($\$$)($\$$)
1743 California St, CA 96002. **Road map** C4. **[** *(916) 241-9705.* Jack's is a
truly old-fashioned roadhouse – a bar that serves great food – which has
specialized in hearty beef dinners since the 1930s. ● *Sun, Mon–Sat L.* 🌿

REDDING: *Nello's Place* $($\$$)($\$$)
3055 Bechelli Lane, CA 96002. **Road map** C4. **[** *(916) 223-1636.* This
romantic and old-fashioned supper club (female diners are all given a
fresh flower) serves traditional Italian meals. There is an excellent
range of Italian and Californian wines. ● *Sun & Mon, Tue–Sat L.* 🍷 🌿

REDWAY: *Mateel Café* $($\$$)
3342 Redwood Drive, CA 95560. **Road map** C4. **[** *(707) 923-2030.* Doubling
as a regional cultural centre, this café has salads and pizzas for lunch
and a range of international dishes for dinner. ● *Sun, Mon D.* 🎵

SUSANVILLE: *St Francis Café* $($\$$)($\$$)
830 Main St, CA 96130. **Road map** C4. **[** *(916) 257-4820.* Every Friday
and Saturday night, this lively restaurant draws a crowd from miles
around to enjoy the prime rib and Basque soups. ● *Sun L.* 🌿

TRINIDAD: *Larrupin' Café* $($\$$)($\$$)
1658 Patrick's Point Drive, CA 95570. **Road map** C4. **[** *(707) 677-0230.* This
little restaurant, 20 miles (32 km) north of Arcata, overlooks Humboldt
Bay and serves fresh seafood. ● *Mon & Tue, Wed–Sun L.*

WEAVERVILLE: *La Grange Café* $($\$$)($\$$)
315 N Main St, CA 96093. **Road map** C4. **[** *(916) 623-5325.* Adventurous,
Californian health food is on offer here at moderate prices, including
organic salads and a wide range of vegetarian dishes. ● *Sun.* 🌿

WINE COUNTRY

BOONVILLE: *Boonville Hotel* $($\$$)($\$$)($\$$)
Hwy 128 by Lambert Lane, CA 95415. **Road map** C4. **[** *(707) 895-2210.*
Food aficionados flock to sample chef John Schmidt's Californian
cuisine with Mexican and Italian influences. ● *Tue, Wed–Mon L.* ♿ 🌿

CALISTOGA: *All Seasons Café* $($\$$)($\$$)
1400 Lincoln Ave, CA 94515. **Road map** C4. **[** *(707) 942-9111.* The menu in
this popular restaurant changes regularly and is designed to accompany
the award-winning wine list. A wine shop and tasting area is situated at
the back of the restaurant. ● *Thu.* ♿ 🍷 🌿

Price categories for a three-course meal for one, including a half bottle of house wine, sales tax and service:
Ⓢ under $25
ⓈⓈ $25–$35
ⓈⓈⓈ $35–$50
ⓈⓈⓈⓈ $50–$70
ⓈⓈⓈⓈⓈ over $70

OUTDOOR EATING
Some tables on a patio or terrace.
VEGETARIAN SPECIALITIES
One menu always includes a selection of vegetarian dishes.
BAR AREA/COCKTAIL BAR
There is a bar area or cocktail bar within the restaurant.
FIXED-PRICE MENU
A good-value fixed-price menu on offer at lunch, dinner or both, usually with three courses.
CHILDREN'S FACILITIES
Small portions and/or highchairs available on request.

	Price	OUTDOOR EATING	VEGETARIAN SPECIALITIES	BAR AREA/COCKTAIL BAR	FIXED-PRICE MENU	CHILDREN'S FACILITIES
CALISTOGA: *Catahoula and Wappo Bar and Bistro* 1457 Lincoln Ave, CA 94515. **Road map** C4. [(707) 942-2275. American cuisine inspired by the deep South is on offer at this contemporary restaurant. Delicious pan-fried catfish is one of the specialities. ● *Tue.* & ♟ 🖫	ⓈⓈⓈ		●	●		
FORESTVILLE: *Russian River Vineyards Restaurant* 5700 Gravenstein Hwy North, CA 95436. **Road map** C4. [(707) 887-1562. Located in the Russian River Valley in 23 acres (9 ha) of organically farmed grapes, this idyllic restaurant serves old Greek family recipes mixed with continental cuisine. ● *Mon & Tue.* & ♫ ♟ 🖫	ⓈⓈⓈ	●	●			●
NAPA: *Downtown Joe's Restaurant and Brewery* 902 Main St, CA 94558. **Road map** C4. [(707) 258-2337. This busy microbrewery is great for American breakfasts, burgers, salads and pizzas. They have live bands in the bar in the evenings. & ♫ 🖫	Ⓢ	●	●	●		
NAPA: *La Boucane* 1778 2nd St, CA 94559. **Road map** C4. [(707) 253-1177. Classic French cuisine is served in a beautifully restored Victorian dining room. All main dishes are accompanied by soup or salad. The wine list is the produce of some of California's top vineyards. ● *Jan; L.* ♟ 🖫	ⓈⓈⓈ		●	●		
NAPA: *Napa Valley Wine Train* 1275 McKinstry St, CA 94559. **Road map** C4. [(707) 253-2111. Gourmet Californian cuisine is served on this luxury diesel train *(see p447)*, as you enjoy the views of the beautiful Wine Country. ● *Mon & Tue D.* & 🖫	ⓈⓈⓈⓈ		●	●	●	●
OAKVILLE: *Stars, Oakville Café* 7848 St Helena Hwy, CA 94562. **Road map** C4. [(707) 944-8905. A satellite restaurant of the celebrity chef Jeremiah Towers' group, the décor is rather plain but the food is famously good. ● *Tue & Wed.* & 🖫	ⓈⓈⓈ	●	●	●		●
RUTHERFORD: *Auberge du Soleil* 180 Rutherford Hill Rd, CA 94573. **Road map** C4. [(707) 963-1211. Fireplaces and high beamed ceilings lend a rustic stylishness to this dining room. The views from the terrace are the best in the Napa Valley. & ♟ 🖫	ⓈⓈⓈ	●	●	●		●
ST HELENA: *Trilogy* 1234 Main St, CA 94574. **Road map** C4. [(707) 963-5507. Owned and run by a husband-and-wife team, this small restaurant serves light French dishes prepared and presented with Californian flair. The Trilogy is renowned for its large selection of good Zinfandel wines. ● *Mon–Sat L.* & ♟ 🖫	ⓈⓈ	●			●	
ST HELENA: *Brava Terrace* 3010 N St Helena Hwy, North St, CA 95470. **Road map** C4. [(707) 963-9300. This stylish restaurant attracts a mixed crowd who come here to enjoy French- and Italian-influenced Californian cuisine. Don't leave without buying a bottle of their lemon-infused olive oil. ● *Nov–Apr: Wed.* & 🖫	ⓈⓈⓈ		●	●		●
ST HELENA: *Showley's* 1327 Railroad Ave, CA 94574. **Road map** C4. [(707) 963-1200. This restaurant provides excellent Provençale cuisine with Italian influences. On Friday evenings, there is live jazz. ● *Mon L.* & ♫ ♟ 🖫	ⓈⓈⓈ	●	●	●		●
ST HELENA: *Tra Vigne* 1050 Charter Oak, CA 94574. **Road map** C4. [(707) 963-4444. This popular Italian restaurant has its own bakery, where bread and pasta are made outdoors in the vine-covered courtyard. & ♟ 🖫	ⓈⓈⓈ	●	●	●	●	●
ST HELENA: *Wine Spectator Greystone Restaurant* 2555 St Helena Hwy, CA 94574. **Road map** C4. [(707) 967-1010. Part of the Culinary Institute of America, the chefs here are culinary students. The cuisine is Mediterranean-influenced. ● *public hols, Tue.* & ♟ 🖫	ⓈⓈⓈ	●	●	●		●

St Helena: *Meadowood Restaurant* $$$$
900 Meadowood Lane, CA 94574. **Road map** C4. (707) 963-3646.
Exquisite Provençale cuisine, beautiful presentation and exceptional
service are the key features of this elegant restaurant, which is part
of the Meadowood Resort Hotel *(see p533).* ● *Mon–Sat L.*

Santa Rosa: *Lisa Hemenway's* $$$
Village Court Mall, Farmer's Lane, CA 95401. **Road map** C4. (707) 526-5111.
A regular visitor to Thailand, chef-owner Lisa Hemenway serves Far
Eastern-inspired Californian cuisine in her tiny restaurant.

Santa Rosa: *Mixx-An American Bistro* $$$
135 Fourth St, CA 95401. **Road map** C4. (707) 573-1344. This 1940s-style
restaurant has matching background jazz music. It is known for the
nicest ambience in Santa Rosa. ● *Sat & Sun L.*

Sonoma: *Ristorante Piatti* $$
405 1st St West, CA 94576. **Road map** C4. (707) 996-2351. This bustling Italian
bistro is part of a small Californian chain. The risotto of the day is always
delicious, as are the signature pizzas, pasta dishes and chicken.

Yountville: *The Diner* $
6476 Washington St, CA 94599. **Road map** C4. (707) 944-2626. The
menu at this well-established diner mixes American- and Mexican-
influenced dishes. Don't leave without trying the home-made fresh
seafood sausage, served with polenta and wilted greens. ● *Mon.*

Yountville: *Mustards Grill* $$$
7399 St Helena Hwy, CA 94558. **Road map** C4. (707) 944-2424. The
emphasis is on Californian cuisine at this popular roadside restaurant. The wine list is extensive. Book well in advance.

Yountville: *Napa Valley Grill* $$$
6795 Washington St, Hwy 29 at Madison, CA 94599. **Road map** C4. (707)
944-8686. The chef at this popular roadside restaurant, Bob Hurley, serves
delicious Wine Country cuisine, using fresh local ingredients.

Yountville: *Domaine Chandon* $$$$
1 California Drive, CA 94599. **Road map** C4. (707) 944-2892. Set in one of
the Napa Valley's most famous wineries, this elegant French restaurant has
views of the surrounding vineyards. ● *Oct–Apr: L.* (Mon pm).

Yountville: *The French Laundry* $$$$
6640 Washington St, CA 94599. **Road map** C4. (707) 944-2380. You have
to book in advance to ensure a place at this excellent restaurant. It serves
American cuisine, with an impressive selection of half bottles of rare
wines. The fixed-price menus are bargains. ● *Sun L, Mon, Tue L.*

GOLD COUNTRY AND THE CENTRAL VALLEY

Amador City: *Imperial Hotel and Restaurant* $$$
14202 Hwy 49, CA 95601. **Road map** C4. (209) 267-9172. French windows
overlook the flower-filled patio at this hotel restaurant *(see p533).* All
dishes on the menu can be ordered as a light meal. ● *L.*

Chico: *Sierra Nevada Brewing Company Restaurant and Tap Room* $$
1075 E 20th St, CA 95928. **Road map** C4. (916) 345-2739. The beer
brewed on the premises is one of the most popular in California.
The food is good standard pub fare. ● *Sun D, Mon, Fri & Sat L.*

Grass Valley: *Scheidel's Old European Restaurant* $
10100 Alta Sierra Drive, CA 95949. **Road map** C4. (916) 273-5553. An old-
fashioned German-style restaurant, serving traditional Bavarian cuisine.
The atmosphere is pleasantly informal. ● *Mon & Tue, Wed–Sun L.*

Grass Valley: *Holbrooke Hotel and Restaurant* $$$
212 West Main St, CA 95945. **Road map** C4. (916) 273-1353. This
spacious hotel restaurant *(see p533)* fills up at weekends. Live music
can be heard from the oldest saloon bar in California next door.

Jamestown: *Bella Union* $$$
18242 Main St, CA 95327. **Road map** C4. (209) 984-2421. Housed in an
historic building, dishes here include alligator fried in breadcrumbs,
and stuffed pheasant served with couscous. ● *Mon, Tue L.*

For key to symbols see back flap

	OUTDOOR EATING	VEGETARIAN SPECIALITIES	BAR AREA/COCKTAIL BAR	FIXED-PRICE MENU	CHILDREN'S FACILITIES

Price categories for a three-course meal for one, including a half bottle of house wine, sales tax and service:
$ under $25
$$ $25–$35
$$$ $35–$50
$$$$ $50–$70
$$$$$ over $70

OUTDOOR EATING
Some tables on a patio or terrace.
VEGETARIAN SPECIALITIES
One menu always includes a selection of vegetarian dishes.
BAR AREA/COCKTAIL BAR
There is a bar area or cocktail bar within the restaurant.
FIXED-PRICE MENU
A good-value fixed-price menu on offer at lunch, dinner or both, usually with three courses.
CHILDREN'S FACILITIES
Small portions and/or highchairs available on request.

Restaurant	Price	OUTDOOR EATING	VEGETARIAN SPECIALITIES	BAR AREA/COCKTAIL BAR	FIXED-PRICE MENU	CHILDREN'S FACILITIES
NEVADA CITY: *Potager* 110 York St, CA 95959. **Road map** C4. **(** *(916) 265-5697*. Classic French-style cuisine is served at this very romantic restaurant. The proprietor grows most of the fresh vegetables used in his own garden. ● *Sun & Mon, Tue–Sat L.*	$		●			
NEVADA CITY: *Country Rose Café* 300 Commercial St, CA 95959. **Road map** C4. **(** *(916) 265-6248*. This busy bistro-style café, housed in an 1860s brick building, specializes in French country cuisine such as sautéed chicken breast. A classical guitarist often plays at weekends. Reservations are recommended.	$$	▥	●	▥		▥
SACRAMENTO: *Aldo's* 2914 Passatiempo Lane, CA 95814. **Road map** C4. **(** *(916) 452-8382*. A variety of French and Californian cuisine, with a delicious dessert menu, is available at this popular, good-value restaurant.	$		●	▥		
SACRAMENTO: *El Taquito* 6223 Franklin Blvd, CA 95824. **Road map** C4. **(** *(916) 392-5290*. Steak *fajitas* served with rice, beans, fried potatoes, salad and tortillas is a popular choice at this little Mexican restaurant. ● *Mon D.*	$	▥	●	▥		▥
SACRAMENTO: *Fat City Bar & Grill* 1001 Front St, CA 95814. **Road map** C4. **(** *(916) 446-6768*. Situated in a 19th-century building in the heart of Old Sacramento *(see pp456–7)*, the restaurant serves substantial American fare. Ideal for children.	$		●	▥		▥
SACRAMENTO: *Capitol Grill* 2730 N St, CA 95816. **Road map** C4. **(** *(916) 736-0744*. Old political memorabilia covers the walls of this Sacramento restaurant. The varied menu features contemporary American cuisine. Book ahead.	$$		●	▥		▥
SACRAMENTO: *Paragary's* 1401 28th St, CA 95618. **Road map** C4. **(** *(916) 457-5737*. The décor here is New York bistro-style. Italian specialities include a wide range of pizzas and rosemary noodles with seared chicken, cheddar and garlic. The restaurant is popular with locals, particularly families with children.	$$		●	▥		▥
SACRAMENTO: *Pilot House Restaurant* 1000 Front St, CA 95814. **Road map** C4. **(** *(916) 441-4440*. Housed in a refurbished 1930s steam paddle boat *(see p534)*, this hotel restaurant has river views and serves American standards such as prime rib or grilled salmon. The Sunday champagne buffet brunch is extremely popular.	$$	▥	●	▥		▥
SACRAMENTO: *The Firehouse* 1112 2nd St, CA 95814. **Road map** C4. **(** *(916) 442-4772*. The original fire pole still stands in this converted fire station, built in the 1850s. Dishes include glazed duck and *filet mignon*. ● *Sun, Mon D, Sat L.*	$$	▥	●	▥	●	▥
SACRAMENTO: *Sterling Hotel* 1300 H St, CA 95814. **Road map** C4. **(** *(916) 442-0451*. This intimate hotel restaurant *(see p534)* serves French-Californian cuisine with good vegetarian choices such as Anaheim chilli pepper stuffed with three cheeses. Meat eaters are equally well catered for. Book in advance.	$$$	▥	●	▥		
SONORA: *Wilma's Café* 275 S Washington St, CA 95370. **Road map** C4. **(** *(209) 532-9957*. This cheerful diner serves classic American cuisine such as steaks, burgers, barbecued ribs and home-made fruit pies in substantial portions.	$		●			▥
SONORA: *Banny's Café* 83 S Stewart St, Suite 100, CA 95370. **Road map** C4. **(** *(209) 533-4709*. An eclectic mixture of Californian, Italian, Mediterranean and Thai cuisine is served from the seasonal menu at this pleasant café. ● *Sun.*	$$		●	▥		▥

THE HIGH SIERRAS

BIG PINE: *Rossi's* Ⓢ
100 N Main St, CA 93513. **Road map** C4. 【 *(760) 938-2254.* This large, family-run restaurant serves a variety of Italian-American dinners. The walls are covered with photographs tracing the history of the Owens Valley. 🍷 🥗

BISHOP: *Firehouse Grill* Ⓢ
2206 N Sierra Hwy, CA 93514. **Road map** C4. 【 *(760) 873-4888.* Continental-style grilled fare is available at this restaurant. The décor is elegant and old-fashioned. Popular with tourists and business people. ♿ 🍷 🥗

BISHOP: *Whiskey Creek* ⓈⓈ
524 N Main St, CA 93514. **Road map** C4. 【 *(760) 873-7174.* An extensive menu of traditional American meat and fish dishes is available at this spacious, rustic restaurant. The soups and salads are delicious. 🥗

FISH CAMP: *Narrow Gauge Inn* ⓈⓈⓈ
48571 State Hwy 41, CA 93623. **Road map** C4. 【 *(209) 683-7720.* Part of the Narrow Gauge Inn hotel *(see p535)*, this small restaurant serves some of the best food in the High Sierras. The setting is romantic, with oil lamps on the tables and a large fireplace. ⬤ *Nov–Apr: L.* 🥗

MAMMOTH LAKES: *Anything Goes* Ⓢ
645 Old Mammoth Rd, CA 93546. **Road map** C4. 【 *(760) 934-2424.* Before a day's skiing, have a delicious breakfast of fresh scones and pastries. Evening meals range from Italian to Southeast Asian fare. ⬤ *Tue D, Wed.*

MAMMOTH LAKES: *Whiskey Creek Restaurant* ⓈⓈ
Minaret & Old Main Sts, CA 93541. **Road map** C4. 【 *(760) 934-2555.* Barbecued ribs, prime rib steaks and seafood are among the specialities at this attractive American restaurant. ⬤ *L; Mon.* ♿ 🍷 🥗

MAMMOTH LAKES: *Restaurant at Convict Lake* ⓈⓈⓈ
Convict Lake, CA 93546. **Road map** C4. 【 *(760) 934-3803.* The ambience is rustic at this comfortable High Sierras lodge. Dinners feature local trout, plus well-prepared beef, lamb and seafood dishes. ⬤ *L.* 🥗

NORTH LAKE TAHOE: *Bridgetender Tavern and Grill* Ⓢ
50 Westlake Blvd, CA 96145. **Road map** C4. 【 *(916) 583-3342.* This water-front tavern is next to Fanny Bridge, a popular spot for watching fish. The Bridgetender is known for its exceptional hamburgers. ♿ 🥗

NORTH LAKE TAHOE: *Soule Domain* ⓈⓈⓈ
9983 Cove St, King's Beach, CA 96143. **Road map** C4. 【 *(916) 546-7529.* This rustic log cabin restaurant is casual but elegant. The Californian cuisine includes dishes such as *filet mignon* with burgundy butter sauce, shiitake mushrooms, Gorgonzola and brandy. ⬤ *Mon–Sun L.* ♿ 🥗

SOUTH LAKE TAHOE: *Carlos Murphy's* Ⓢ
3678 Lake Tahoe Blvd, CA 95731. **Road map** C4. 【 *(916) 542-1741.* Huge portions of traditional Mexican-American food and inexpensive cocktails are the main attractions of this popular, casual restaurant. 🥗

SOUTH LAKE TAHOE: *Evans American Gourmet Café* ⓈⓈⓈ
536 Emerald Bay Rd, CA 95731. **Road map** C4. 【 *(916) 542-1990.* Tahoe's best Californian cuisine is on offer at this stylish, semi-formal restaurant. Come here to enjoy the great desserts and award-winning wine list. The café is very small, so book in advance. ⬤ *Sun, Mon–Sat L.* ♿ 🍴 🍷 🥗

STATELINE: *Sage Room* ⓈⓈⓈ
Hwy 50, CA 89449. **Road map** C4. 【 *(702) 588-2411.* Housed in the venerable Harvey's casino resort, this gourmet restaurant boasts Tahoe's finest beef dishes, as well as wild boar and venison. ⬤ *L.* 🥗

TAHOE CITY: *Grazis* ⓈⓈ
700 N Lake Blvd, CA 96145. **Road map** C4. 【 *(916) 583-0233.* An extensive choice of pizzas is available at this Italian restaurant. Ask to sit on the porch or on the lovely wooden terrace overlooking Lake Tahoe. ♿ 🥗

TAHOE CITY: *Tahoe House* ⓈⓈ
625 W Lake Blvd, CA 96145. **Road map** C4. 【 *(916) 583-1377.* Dinner consists of Swiss specialities, such as *ramschnitzel* (veal escalope). The European-style bakery, open all day, produces bread, cakes and sandwiches. 🍷 🥗

For key to symbols see back flap

	OUTDOOR EATING	VEGETARIAN SPECIALITIES	BAR AREA/COCKTAIL BAR	FIXED-PRICE MENU	CHILDREN'S FACILITIES

Price categories for a three-course meal for one, including a half bottle of house wine, sales tax and service:
- $ under $25
- $$ $25–$35
- $$$ $35–$50
- $$$$ $50–$70
- $$$$$ over $70

OUTDOOR EATING
Some tables on a patio or terrace.
VEGETARIAN SPECIALITIES
One menu always includes a selection of vegetarian dishes.
BAR AREA/COCKTAIL BAR
There is a bar area or cocktail bar within the restaurant.
FIXED-PRICE MENU
A good-value fixed-price menu on offer at lunch, dinner or both, usually with three courses.
CHILDREN'S FACILITIES
Small portions and/or highchairs available on request.

TAHOE CITY: *Christy Hill* $$$ 115 Grove St, CA 96145. **Road map** C4. (*(916) 583-8551.* Stylish surroundings set the stage for a stylish feast from a daily-changing menu of the freshest ingredients available. ● *Mon, Tue–Sun L.* 🍴 🅿		●			
TAHOE VISTA: *Le Petit Pier* $ 7252 N Lake Blvd, CA 96148. **Road map** C4. (*(916) 546-4464.* French-style cuisine is served at this romantic restaurant beside Lake Tahoe. Maine lobster and tenderloin of lamb are among the dishes on offer. ● *Tue.* ♿ 🅿		●	▨	●	
TRUCKEE: *The Left Bank* $$ 10096 Donner Pass Rd, CA 95734. **Road map** C4. (*(916) 587-4694.* In the heart of Truckee lies this elegant little French restaurant. Rustic décor matches innovative French provincial cuisine. ● *Tue, Wed–Mon L.* 🅿					▨
YOSEMITE NATIONAL PARK: *Wawona Dining Room* $$ State Hwy 41, CA 95389. **Road map** C4. (*(209) 252-4848.* American cuisine is served in the comfortable dining room of a 19th-century hotel *(see p536)*. Although the food is unremarkable, the ambience is relaxing. ● *Nov–Mar.* 🅿		●	▨		
YOSEMITE NATIONAL PARK: *Ahwahnee Dining Room* $$$$ Yosemite Valley, CA 95389. **Road map** C4. (*(209) 252-4848.* The soaring ceiling of this beautiful hotel dining room *(see p536)* makes up for rather bland food. Steaks and other simple dishes are a safe bet. ♿ 🍴 🍴 🅿			▨		▨

NORTH CENTRAL CALIFORNIA

APTOS: *Chez Renée* $$ 9051 Soquel Drive, CA 95003. **Road map** C4. (*(408) 688-5566.* This restaurant, nestled in a redwood grove, has won awards for its Californian cuisine with French and Italian influences. Fixed-price dinner menus are available on Sundays. ● *Sun L, Mon & Tue.* ♿ 🍴 🅿	▨	●	▨	●	
BIG SUR: *Deetjen's* $$$ Castro Canyon, CA 93920. **Road map** C4. (*(408) 667-2378.* This hotel restaurant *(see p536)* is set in rustic surroundings. It is famous for its breakfasts and its French-Californian dinner menu. ● *L.* ♿ 🅿	▨	●	▨		▨
BIG SUR: *Nepenthe* $$$ Hwy 1, CA 93920. **Road map** C4. (*(408) 667-2345.* Originally a honeymoon retreat for Orson Welles and Rita Hayworth, on a clear day this restaurant has a view of a 35-mile (56-km) stretch of coastline. The emphasis is on basic American cuisine; desserts and breads are home-made. ♿ 🅿	▨	●	▨	▨	▨
BIG SUR: *Sierra Mar* $$$$$ Hwy 1, CA 93920. **Road map** C4. (*(408) 667-2800.* Part of the Post Ranch Inn *(see p537)*, the restaurant is stylish and has fabulous ocean views. The cuisine is exquisite and everything is available *à la carte.* ♿ 🍴 🅿		●	▨	●	▨
CARMEL: *Ridge Restaurant* $$$ 200 Punta del Monte, Carmel Valley, CA 93924. **Road map** C4. (*(408) 659-0170.* Part of the Robles del Rio Lodge hotel *(see p537)*, excellent French-Californian cuisine is served in a lovely dining room with a fireplace. ♿ 🅿		●	▨		▨
CARMEL: *The French Poodle* $$$ Junipero & 5th Ave, CA 93921. **Road map** C4. (*(408) 624-8643.* This intimate restaurant was selected as one of the best French restaurants in the US by the International Restaurant Rating Bureau. ● *Sun, Mon–Sat L.* ♿ 🍴 🅿		●			
CARMEL: *The Terrace Grill, La Playa Hotel* $$$ 8th Ave/Camino Real, CA 93920. **Road map** C4. (*(408) 624-6476.* Californian cuisine is served in the dining room of this hotel *(see p537)*, overlooking beautiful gardens and the ocean. The early-bird menu is a bargain. ♿ 🅿	▨	●	▨	●	▨

CARMEL: *Hog's Breath Inn* $$$$
San Carlos/5th, CA 93921. **Road map** C4. (*(408) 625-1044.* This Clint Eastwood-owned restaurant serves cowboy fare (prime rib, steaks and hamburgers) in pub-like surroundings. ● *Fri & Sat L.* & ✎

CARMEL: *Anton and Michel* $$$$
Mission & 7th St, CA 93921. **Road map** C4. (*(408) 624-2406.* This elegant Carmel restaurant serves international cuisine. Famous dishes include the Châteaubriand and rack of lamb. ♟ ♟ ✎

CARMEL: *Covey, Quail Lodge* $$$$$
8205 Valley Greens Drive, Carmel Valley, CA 93923. **Road map** C4. (*(408) 624-1581.* This hotel restaurant *(see p537)* has won several awards for its Californian cuisine and wine. A pianist plays nightly. ● *L.* & ♫ ♟ ✎

CASTROVILLE: *The Franco Restaurant* $
10639 Merrit St, CA 95012. **Road map** C4. (*(408) 633-2090.* Housed in a 1930s Art Deco building, Franco's serves diner food, including enormous hamburgers, amid Marilyn Monroe memorabilia. & ✎

HANFORD: *Imperial Dynasty* $$
2 China Alley, CA 93230. **Road map** C4. (*(209) 582-0196.* This family-owned restaurant serves continental and American staples, including prime rib, seafood and steak, in oriental surroundings. ● *Mon, Tue–Sun L.* ✎

MONTEREY: *Thai Hut* $
580 Broadway, CA 93955. **Road map** C4. (*(408) 899-1191.* Diners come here to enjoy delicious Thai food. On Mondays, Wednesdays and Fridays a very reasonable all-you-can-eat lunch buffet is offered. ● *Sun L.* & ✎

MONTEREY: *Tarpy's Roadhouse* $$
2999 Monterey-Salinas Hwy, CA 93940. **Road map** C4. (*(408) 647-1444.* Basic American food, from cheeseburgers and T-bone steaks to game and fresh seafood, is served in an old ranch house. & ♟ ✎

MONTEREY: *Domenica's on the Wharf* $$$
50 Fisherman's Wharf, CA 93940. **Road map** C4. (*(408) 372-3655.* Enjoy fine dining in relaxed surroundings overlooking the wharf. The menu features seafood and mesquite barbecues. There is also an oyster bar. & ♟ ✎

MONTEREY: *Fresh Cream* $$$
99 Pacific St, Suite 100C, Heritage Harbor, CA 93940. **Road map** C4. (*(408) 375-9798.* This award-winning restaurant, with its harbour views, offers some of the best French food in Northern California. ● *L.* & ♟ ✎

PACIFIC GROVE: *Fandango* $$$
223 17th St, CA 93950. **Road map** C4. (*(408) 372-3456.* The menu here is varied, featuring Mediterranean food from pasta to lobster. One room is warmed by an open mesquite grill. & ♟ ✎

SANTA CRUZ: *Santa Cruz Brewing Company and Restaurant* $
516 Front St, CA 95060. **Road map** C4. (*(408) 429-8838.* Warm and casual, with lots of wooden décor, this hamburger/grill "pub" attracts a mixed crowd who are mostly here for the home-made beer. & ♫ ✎

SANTA CRUZ: *The Crêpe Place* $
1134 Soquel Ave, CA 95062. **Road map** C4. (*(408) 429-6994.* The décor at this restaurant is as eclectic as its menu. Choose from a wide selection of *crêpes* or invent your own. ● *Fri & Sat D.* & ♫ ✎

SANTA CRUZ: *Whole Earth Restaurant* $
Redwood Building, University of California, CA 95064. **Road map** C4. (*(408) 426-8255.* The décor at this campus restaurant is rustic and the food ranges from Mexican to Asian and European. ● *university holidays, Sat & Sun D.* & ♫

SANTA CRUZ: *Gabriella's* $$$
910 Cedar St, CA 95060. **Road map** C4. (*(408) 457-1677.* This popular restaurant serves Italian cuisine with an emphasis on organic vegetables, seafood and pasta. The wine list features mostly local wines. ♟ ✎

SEASIDE: *El Migueleño* $
1066 Broadway, CA 93955. **Road map** C4. (*(408) 899-2199.* This Salvadoran restaurant serves Mexican and Salvadoran food. The house special is *Playa Azul,* a dish composed of seven different kinds of seafood. ✎

For key to symbols see back flap

SPECIALIST HOLIDAYS AND ACTIVITIES IN CALIFORNIA

CALIFORNIA is practically synonymous with the great outdoors. The state has protected its landscape so that future generations can visit places of beauty. The deserts, redwood forests, alpine meadows, granite mountains, lakes and white beaches all welcome visitors. California

Whitewater rafting on the Merced River *(see p578)*

has a culture rich with physical activity, and wilderness is never far from any city. Golfers are well catered for around the Monterey Peninsula *(see p495)* and winter skiers flock to Lake Tahoe *(see p471)*. For details of main events in the sporting calendar, see pages 32–5.

Tahquitz Golf Course, Palm Springs

SPECIALIST HOLIDAYS

DETAILS OF special interest holidays are available from the **California Office of Tourism**. One of the most popular of these are tours of California's missions along El Camino Real *(see pp42–3)*.

Writers who make California their home often give readings at local writers' workshops. The best of these are the **Santa Barbara Writers' Conference** and the **Squaw Valley Community of Writers**.

Keen artists can take advantage of the state's various craft centres. Nationally renowned artists hold painting courses at the **North Coast Art Center** in Crescent City and at the **Mendocino Arts Center**.

Institutes such as **Great Chefs** at the Robert Mondavi Winery *(see p447)* and **Tante Marie's Cooking School** provide accommodation, cookery classes, shopping tours, visits to the Wine Country and fine meals during week-long intensive courses in the summer.

CAMPING

CALIFORNIA has always valued its wilderness: Yosemite Valley *(see pp472–5)* and the Mariposa Grove of giant redwoods were protected parkland as early as 1864. Today there are more than 250 places classified as either state parks, wilderness areas, historic sites or recreation areas.

At every site, there are hiking trails and car parks. Many also provide bathrooms and camp sites. All state and federal parks allow day-use visitors, charging only a small parking fee. For camping overnight, reserve a site with **Destinet**, **Mistix** or **Yosemite Reservations**. Most camp sites accept reservations eight weeks in advance.

Camping trips into the state's desert are organized by **Desert Survivors**. They include environmental information.

HIKING

DAY HIKES and longer trips in the country are popular with both residents and visitors. There are more than 1 million miles (1.6 million km) of trails in California, the longest being the Pacific Crest Trail. The 2,640-mile (4,245-km) route stretches from Canada to Mexico. One of its highlights is the 200-mile (320-km) John Muir Trail, from Yosemite's high country to Mount Whitney *(see pp472–9)*. The **Sierra Club** organizes guided outings and provides detailed maps.

Hiking along the John Muir Trail at Mount Whitney

HORSE RIDING

EQUESTRIANS will find a wide variety of riding trails in California, across all types of landscape – conifer mountains, lush meadows, chaparral hills and dry valleys. Many state and national parks allow horses and pack mules on their trails.

Traditional cowboy life can still be found at privately owned ranches, such as **Spanish Springs Ranch** in Ravendale. These are working ranches, and guests can ride with the ranch hands and herd animals, or simply ride for pleasure on their extensive network of trails. **El Alisal Guest Ranch and Resort** holds annual roundups and cattle drives.

Horse riding in Ventura County

MOUNTAIN BIKING

MANY STATE PARKS allow cyclists on their hiking trails. One spectacular trail for cyclists begins at High Camp in Squaw Valley, Lake Tahoe *(see p471)*. A 2,000-ft (610-m) ascent via an aerial tram is followed by a heart-stopping downhill ride to Shirley Lake. Contact the **Bicycle Trails Council** to find out where mountain bikes are welcome.

Outfitters such as **Back-roads** also lead groups of cyclists on tours of the state's abundant rolling countryside, often with stops for leisurely gourmet lunches. Transport vans accompany the cyclists, carrying heavy equipment and camping gear for week-long trips. Popular destinations

Mountain biking in Marin County

include the Napa Valley *(see pp446–7)* and the country lanes of Sonoma, Monterey and Santa Barbara Counties.

BEACHES

BEACHES along California's 900-mile (1,450-km) coast-line vary considerably. Some have rough waves and rocky beaches, ideal for rock pool exploration and quiet reflection. Others sport the white sand, arching waves and warm water that attract the surfers of Californian legend.

Whether you want to surf yourself or simply watch the golden boys of summer, the best beaches include the Leo Carrillo State Beach in Orange County *(see pp220–21)*, Windansea Beach in La Jolla *(see pp238–9)* and Corona del Mar in Newport Beach *(see pp220–21)*. The **Club Ed Surf and Windsurf School** offers a 7-day surfing camp for beginners to the sport, between April and October.

Many spots along the coast are good diving areas, including Scripps Shoreline Underwater Preserve in La Jolla *(see p239)*, the coves of Laguna Beach *(see p221)* and Monterey Bay *(see p495)*. Equipment can be hired from the **Aquarius Dive Shop**. The **Underwater Schools of America** in Oceanside also offers diving lessons for beginners.

Natural Bridges State Park in Santa Cruz *(see pp490–91)*, and Pfeiffer State Beach in Big Sur *(see pp498–9)* are good sites for rock pool exploration, where the ocean has eroded the rock in unusual formations. Torrey Pines State Beach *(see p238)* offers forests and dramatic white-capped swells. Pismo Beach is famous for its sand dunes, surfing and clam digging *(see p198)*.

Southern California's water is warm enough for swimming from April to November. In the sea north of San Francisco a wet suit should be worn at all times of the year.

Golden beaches of La Jolla cove

WHITEWATER RAFTING AND KAYAKING

WHITEWATER RAFTING is like a thrilling roller coaster ride combined with stunning scenic views. Specialist outfitters such as **Mariah Wilderness Expeditions**, **Outdoor Unlimited** and **Whitewater Voyages** provide rafts, paddles and life jackets. They take groups of six to eight people, accompanied by a guide, down a tributary of one of California's major rivers. Trips may last one day only or include an overnight stay.

The rafting season lasts from April to September. Trips are graded by their level of difficulty: Classes I and II are relatively safe, with a few exciting twists and turns. Beginners wanting a safe but slightly more exciting ride should book a trip on a Class III river. Only experienced rafters should go on a Class IV or higher trip.

Most organizations that offer river rafting also provide kayak and canoe trips. For further information, contact **Friends of the River** or the **American River Touring Association**.

Water-skiing in San Diego

WATER SPORTS

THE LAKES and beaches in California offer a variety of activities. Houseboats are available to rent for a slow cruise through the maze of inlets in the Sacramento Delta. Speedboats are available at Lake Tahoe *(see p471)*, Lake Shasta *(see p436)* and the man-made lakes that are part of the state recreation system.

One of the newest sports is parasailing. With water skis and a parachute, participants are harnessed to a speedboat and launched into the air for an exhilarating ride. It's a safe sport, but life jackets should be worn. Contact **Parasailing Catalina** for details.

BIRD-WATCHING

CALIFORNIA's coastline and rivers are feeding grounds for migrating birds. In autumn, ducks, geese and other shorebirds leave Canada to winter in South America, stopping in California along the way. The Point Reyes National Seashore *(see pp396–7)* supports at least 45 per cent of US bird species. More than 425 species have been sighted here.

Just south of San Diego, the **Tijuana Slough National Estuarine Research Reserve** hosts 400 species, best seen in spring and autumn.

Bird-watching in La Jolla *(see p251)*

FISHING

CALIFORNIA is an angler's paradise. From the end of April through to the middle of November, anglers head to the rivers and streams of the Sierra Nevada Mountains for trout fishing. Bass fishing in California's multitude of lakes and reservoirs is plentiful throughout the year. During the autumn and winter months, shoals of salmon and steelhead make their way up river, with especially good fishing in the Klamath, American, Eel and Sacramento rivers. Sturgeon and striped bass can also readily be caught in the Sacramento River Delta.

Almost every coastal city in the state offers charter boats for deep-sea ocean fishing. In Northern California, the summer months are particularly good for halibut and ocean salmon, but throughout the Pacific, from autumn to early spring, 40–50-lb (18–23-kg) hauls of cod and rock fish are not unusual. In the warmer waters off Southern California, blue fin, yellow fin and

Rafting at Yosemite National Park *(see pp472–5)*

Fishing on Lake Molena in San Diego

skipjack tuna, as well as barracuda are particularly plentiful during the summer. To hire a charter boat for fishing contact **Helgren's Sportfishing Trips**, **Hot Pursuit Sport Fishing** or **Dolphin Charters**.

To find out which fish are in season, contact the **State Department of Fish and Game**. Fly fishing, another popular Californian sport, is available at the **Mammoth Adventure Connection** in the eastern Sierras.

ROCK CLIMBING AND CAVING

ROCK CLIMBING combines the dexterity of gymnastics with the grace of dance, as individuals scale vertical rock walls using only their hands and high-friction shoes.

Rock climbing at Joshua Tree National Park

The sport can be practised all year round in rock-climbing gyms in major cities. Other places to learn how to rock climb or simply to watch others in action are the Joshua Tree National Park *(see pp268–9)*, the alpine village of Idyllwild, near Palm Springs *(see p266)* and Squaw Valley in Lake Tahoe *(see p471)*. Contact the **American Mountain Guides Association** for information on all regional rock-climbing lessons and instructors.

Spelunkers (cave explorers) should head for the Pinnacles National Monument *(see p501)*, or Lassen Volcanic National Park *(see p437)* where volcanoes have created unusual caves and rock formations.

HANG-GLIDING

IF YOU'VE EVER wanted to ride the thermal air currents at speeds of 25–50 mph (40–80 km/h), this is the sport for you. You will be harnessed into a hang-glider consisting of a plastic-covered metal frame and a triangular control bar with a hammock-like harness. The take-off is usually from a cliff edge – a daunting prospect for some! For beginners, flights can be made in tandem with a qualified pilot, equipped with a safety parachute.

The main hang-gliding areas, for both participants and spectators, are

Fort Funston off the Bay Area coastline *(see pp396–7)*, **Torrey Pines Glider Port** in San Diego, or Vista Point in Palm Desert *(see p264)*. If you want to learn the sport, **SF Air Time** will recommend instructors. They also sell and hire out gliding equipment.

GARDENS

THE WARM, SUNNY climate of California has inspired numerous skilled and amateur gardeners to experiment with horticulture. The result is a rich variety of arboretums, botanical gardens, city parks and private estates all over the state that are now open to the public.

Huntington Library Art Collections and Botanical Gardens are Henry Huntington's idealistic monument to art and culture. Work began on the gardens in 1904. They cover three-quarters of the 200-acre (80-ha) estate, and are among the finest of their kind in California *(see pp154–7)*.

The **Descanso Gardens** offer 4 acres (1.6 ha) of roses, an impressive 30-acre (12-ha) grove of live oaks and a protected forest of camellia trees. William Bourn's landscaped grounds and elegant estate of Filoli in the Bay Area town of Woodside *(see p411)* and **Villa Montalvo Arboretum** in Saratoga are both carefully tended so that their flowers are in bloom all year round. Weekend jazz concerts are held at the latter during the summer months, which only add to the opulent and cultured environment.

Hot air ballooning over California's landscape

HOT AIR BALLOONING

H OT AIR BALLOONING is a popular excursion in the Napa Valley *(see pp446–7)*, Monterey *(see pp494–5)* and Temecula County. The rides are taken at sunrise or sunset when there is the least wind, and are quiet and gentle, offering incomparable panoramic views of the countryside. Outfitters such as **Adventures Aloft** and **Napa Valley Balloons** provide private and group outings which are then followed by a picnic.

WHALE-WATCHING

F ROM DECEMBER through to April, grey whales journey 7,000 miles (11,260 km) along the Californian coast, having left Alaska's Bering Strait for the warmer climate of Mexico's Baja Peninsula. Ocean cruises offer views of these impressive mammals. Humpback, killer whales, pilot and blue whales also frequent the coast between San Francisco and Monterey in late summer. Charter operators such as **Shearwater Journeys** provide a glimpse of the grey whales, as well as the dolphins and porpoises that accompany them on their trips. For more information, contact **Oceanic Society Expeditions**.

HOT SPRINGS

A LONG SOAK in a hot spring (a bubbling tributary of an underground river, heated by the earth) is said to be very good for one's health. Calistoga in Northern California *(see p445)* has numerous spas, offering everything from heated pools with mineral water to mud baths, steam baths and massages. Contact the **Calistoga Chamber of Commerce** for a full list of area resorts.

ISLAND HOPPING

F IVE VOLCANIC ISLANDS off the coast of Southern California comprise the Channel Islands National Park *(see p214)*. This stark nature reserve is ideal for hiking, viewing wildlife and exploring rock pools. It is also an excellent spot to see whales and dolphins, as well as many species of shore birds. Ferries depart from Ventura and Santa Barbara harbours. Reserve a trip with **Island Packers**.

The Wrigley Memorial Garden on Santa Catalina Island is accessible by ferry from San Pedro, Long Beach, Redondo Beach and Balboa. It is more developed than the Channel Islands National Park, with shops, restaurants and accommodation. Developed as a summer resort in the 1920s by chewing gum magnate William Wrigley, Jr, the island offers trails for cycling, hiking and opportunities for diving and snorkelling *(see pp232–3)*.

Further north, **Angel Island**, off San Francisco Bay, is a 740-acre (300-ha) marine sanctuary, reached by ferry from Fisherman's Wharf. Extensive hiking trails, picnic areas and camp sites are on offer to visitors. Grey whales and a wide range of shore birds can be observed.

Two Harbors at Ismus Cove on Catalina Island

DIRECTORY

SPECIALIST HOLIDAYS

California Office of Tourism
PO Box 9278,
Van Nuys, CA 91409.
☎ (800) 862-2543.

Great Chefs
PO Box 106,
Oakville, CA 94562.
☎ (707) 944-2866.

Mendocino Arts Center
PO Box 765,
Mendocino, CA 95460.
☎ (707) 937-5818.

North Coast Art Center
299 I St,
Crescent City, CA 95531.
☎ (707) 464-4137.

Santa Barbara Writers' Conference
PO Box 304,
Carpinteria, CA 93014.
☎ (805) 684-2250.

Squaw Valley Community of Writers
PO Box 2352,
Olympic Valley,
CA 96146.
☎ (916) 583-5200.

Tante Marie's Cooking School
271 Francisco St,
San Francisco,
CA 94133.
☎ (415) 788-6699.

CAMPING

Desert Survivors
PO Box 20991,
Oakland, CA 94620-0991.
☎ (510) 769-1706.

Destinet
9450 Carroll Park Drive,
San Diego, CA 92121.
☎ (800) 444-7275.

Mistix
PO Box 85705,
San Diego,
CA 92138-5705.
☎ (619) 452-0150.

Yosemite Reservations
☎ (209) 252-4848.

HIKING

Sierra Club
730 Polk St,
San Francisco,
CA 94109.
☎ (415) 977-5500.

HORSE RIDING

El Alisal Guest Ranch and Resort
1054 Alisal Rd,
Solvang, CA 93463.
☎ (805) 688-6411.

Spanish Springs Ranch
PO Box 270,
Ravendale, CA 96123.
☎ (800) 560-1900.

MOUNTAIN BIKING

Backroads
801 Cedar St,
Berkeley, CA 94710.
☎ (510) 527-1555.

Bicycle Trails Council
PO Box 494,
Fairfax, CA 94978.
☎ (415) 456-7512.

BEACHES

Aquarius Dive Shop
32 Cannery Row,
Monterey, CA 93940.
☎ (408) 375-6605.

Club Ed Surf and Windsurf School
5 Isabel Drive,
Santa Cruz,
CA 95060.
☎ (408) 459-9283.

Underwater Schools of America
1707 Oceanside Blvd,
Oceanside, CA 92054.
☎ (619) 722-7826.

WHITEWATER RAFTING AND KAYAKING

American River Touring Association
2400 Casa Loma Rd,
Groveland, CA 95321.
☎ (209) 962-7873.

Outdoor Unlimited
Box 0234A,
San Francisco, CA 94117.
☎ (415) 476-2078.

Whitewater Voyages
PO Box 20400,
El Sobrante, CA 94820.
☎ (510) 222-5994.

WATER SPORTS

Parasailing Catalina
PO Box 2275,
Avalon, CA 90704.
☎ (310) 510-1777.

BIRD-WATCHING

Tijuana Slough National Estuarine Research Reserve
301 Caspian Way,
Imperial Beach, CA 91932.
☎ (619) 575-3613.

FISHING

Dolphin Charters
Noyo Harbor,
Fort Bragg, CA 95437.
☎ (707) 964-7441.

Hot Pursuit Sport Fishing
Fisherman's Wharf,
San Francisco, CA 94133.
☎ (415) 965-3474.

Mammoth Adventure Connection
PO Box 353,
Mammoth Lakes,
CA 93546.
☎ (619) 934-0606.

State Department of Fish and Game
1416 9th St, 12th Floor,
Sacramento, CA 95814.
☎ (916) 653-7664.

ROCK CLIMBING AND CAVING

American Mountain Guides Association
PO Box 2128, Estes Park,
Colorado 80517.
☎ (970) 586-0571.

HANG-GLIDING

SF Air Time
3620 Wawona St,
San Francisco, CA 94116.
☎ (415) 759-1177.

Torrey Pines Glider Port
2800 Torrey Pines Scenic Drive, La Jolla,
CA 92037.
☎ (619) 452-6914.

GARDENS

Descanso Gardens
1418 Descanso Drive,
La Canada-Flintridge,
CA 91011.
☎ (818) 952-4400.

Villa Montalvo Arboretum
15400 Montalvo Rd,
Saratoga, CA 95071.
☎ (408) 741-3421.

HOT AIR BALLOONING

Adventures Aloft
6525 Washington St,
Yountville, CA 94599.
☎ (707) 944-4408.

Napa Valley Balloons
6975 Washington St,
Yountville, CA 94599.
☎ (707) 253-2224.

WHALE-WATCHING

Oceanic Society Expeditions
Fort Mason Center,
San Francisco, CA 94123.
☎ (415) 441-1106.

Shearwater Journeys
PO Box 190,
Hollister, CA 95024.
☎ (408) 637-8527.

HOT SPRINGS

Calistoga Chamber of Commerce
1458 Lincoln Ave, No. 9,
Calistoga, CA 94515.
☎ (707) 942-6333.

ISLAND HOPPING

Angel Island Red & White Fleet
☎ (415) 546-2896.

Island Packers
1867 Spinnaker Drive,
Ventura, CA 93001.
☎ (805) 642-1393.

SHOPPING IN CALIFORNIA

CALIFORNIA is a manufacturing giant and a major player in the global economy. It is the largest producer of children's clothing in the US, and is equally famous for its sportswear and swimwear. Produce from the San Joaquin Valley, including fruit, nuts and vegetables, feeds the nation. Aside from the shopping districts of LA *(see pp166–7)* and San Francisco *(see*

Antique Dealers' Association sign

pp376–9), the state's smaller towns and countryside offer a wide range of merchandise and local produce. Roadside food stalls, wineries, antique shops and crafts by local artisans are some of the attractions of California's backroads. Prices tend to be cheaper than in the cities, and in some venues, such as flea markets, you will be expected to barter and negotiate.

Window-shopping along Ocean Avenue, Carmel *(see p494)*

SHOPPING HOURS

SINCE THE LOCAL population tends to view shopping as a recreational activity, most major stores in California open for business seven days a week. Typical business hours are 10am–6pm, Monday to Saturday, and noon–5pm on Sundays. In smaller communities, shops may be closed on Sunday or Monday. Opening hours for these stores are sometimes 11am–7pm.

HOW TO PAY

MOST STORES accept credit cards, including Master-Card, American Express and Visa, and traveller's cheques. Paying by traveller's cheques requires some form of identification, such as a passport or driver's licence. Few shops will accept cheques drawn on foreign banks. Cash is the best way to pay for any small purchases *(see pp594–5)*.

VAT AND TAX-FREE SHOPPING

SALES TAX (VAT) ranges from 7.25 to 8.5 per cent. All items except groceries and prescription drugs are taxed. Tax is not included in the advertised price, but is added separately at the cash till.

RIGHTS AND REFUNDS

MERCHANTS are not required by law to give a cash refund or credit for returned goods, although most do so. All stores will refund the cost of a defective item, if it is not marked "flawed" or "sold as is". Inspect the item before you buy it and keep all receipts. If an item is faulty, go back to the shop with the receipt and original packaging. Many stores will refund your money up to 30 days after purchase.

SHIPPING PACKAGES

FOR A CHARGE, most stores ship goods worldwide, or send your items home via Federal Express or US Express Mail Service *(see pp596–7)*. You will be asked to fill out a form giving a short description of the goods and stating their monetary value. Keep receipts of the transaction in case the items should get lost in transit.

WHERE TO SHOP

A NUMBER OF COASTAL towns noted for their locally owned shops can be found along Hwy 1 or US 101. These include Santa Barbara *(see pp210–11)*, Big Sur *(see pp498–9)*, Carmel *(see p494)*, Santa Cruz *(see pp490–91)* and Sausalito *(see pp398–9)*.

On Hwy 99 and other roads that cross the San Joaquin Valley, many farms sell locally grown fruit and vegetables. Palm Springs *(see pp264–5)* is known for its fashion shops. Antique dealers are plentiful in the Sierra foothills, such as Sutter Creek *(see p460)*.

FASHION

CALIFORNIA is known for its casual clothing – the dress-down Friday business look was invented here. However, the East Coast also looks to California for the very best of cutting-edge fashion.

Seventy per cent of all swimwear designed in the US is designed here, by names such as

San Franciscan original, The Gap

Catalina and **California Wave**. Sixty-five per cent of the country's younger female fashion is also produced here.

Children's wear is a speciality of the state. **Sara's Prints**, **Back to Back Kidswear** and **Traci Lynn** are the best.

Other local heroes include designer Nicholas Graham of **Joe Boxer Inc**, who turned men's boxer shorts into art statements, and **Jessica McClintock Inc**, known for her ballgowns and bridal wear. **The Gap**, now an international retail giant, originated in San Francisco in 1969 and was the first store to mass-market denim jeans.

FLEA MARKETS

FLEA MARKETS (also called swap meets) are held at weekends, usually on Sundays. Vendors set up booths within a vast car park, football stadium, or even in the grounds of one of the famous missions. Just about everything imaginable is for sale. It is often possible to find a one-of-a-kind treasure at a good price, but don't accept the quoted price – bargaining is *de rigueur*. Be sure to bring cash with you as most vendors will not accept credit cards or traveller's cheques.

Notable flea markets include the **Berkeley Flea Market**, the **San Jose Flea Market**, the **Rose Bowl Flea Market** in Pasadena and **San Juan Bautista Peddlars Fair**. Flea markets may charge a nominal entrance fee of 75 cents or $1.

Cover of a vintage Hollywood magazine from the 1950s

POP CULTURE ANTIQUES

MEMORABILIA stores are a Californian speciality. Berkeley's **For Amusement Only** sells a variety of pinball machines and jukeboxes. **Hello Central** sells antique telephones, from early models to the 1940s black rotary dial telephones. **Hillcrest Vintage Paper Collectables** and **Sarah Stocking Fine Vintage Posters** specialize in old movie

posters. A range of Hollywood memorabilia is easily found in LA *(see pp166–7)*. Other stores, such as **Camperos Collectables** in Sutter Creek, also sell such items.

OUTLET CENTRES

ONE OF THE STATE'S most popular retail trends is factory outlet malls. These sell off-season or surplus goods, such as clothing and household items, directly to consumers at prices lower than those in department stores.

Outlet centres usually have around 20 shops, but the **Factory Stores of America at Nut Tree** has more than 100 stores. Other popular centres include the **American Tin Cannery Factory Outlets** in Monterey, **Napa Factory Stores**, **Desert Hills Factory Stores**, **Palm Springs Square**, **Pismo Beach Outlet Center**, and the **San Diego Factory Outlet Center.** For outlet centre tours contact **Shopper Stopper Shopping Tours**.

SIZE CHART

For Australian sizes follow the British and American conversions.

Children's clothing

American	2–3	4–5	6–6x	7–8	10	12	14	16 (size)
British	2–3	4–5	6–7	8–9	10–11	12	14	14+ (years)
Continental	2–3	4–5	6–7	8–9	10–11	12	14	14+ (years)

Children's shoes

American	7½	8½	9½	10½	11½	12½	13½	1½	2½
British	7	8	9	10	11	12	13	1	2
Continental	24	25½	27	28	29	30	32	33	34

Women's dresses, coats and skirts

American	4	6	8	10	12	14	16	18
British	6	8	10	12	14	16	18	20
Continental	38	40	42	44	46	48	50	52

Women's blouses and sweaters

American	6	8	10	12	14	16	18
British	30	32	34	36	38	40	42
Continental	40	42	44	46	48	50	52

Women's shoes

American	5	6	7	8	9	10	11
British	3	4	5	6	7	8	9
Continental	36	37	38	39	40	41	44

Men's suits

American	34	36	38	40	42	44	46	48
British	34	36	38	40	42	44	46	48
Continental	44	46	48	50	52	54	56	58

Men's shirts

American	14	15	15½	16	16½	17	17½	18
British	14	15	15½	16	16½	17	17½	18
Continental	36	38	39	41	42	43	44	45

Men's shoes

American	7	7½	8	8½	9½	10½	11	11½
British	6	7	7½	8	9	10	11	12
Continental	39	40	41	42	43	44	45	46

Browsers at an open-air flea market in Sausalito

Antiques shops in Temecula, near Palm Springs

BOOKS, MUSIC AND CRAFTS

BOOKSHOPS, whether part of a large chain or independent, are a feature of even the smallest Californian town.

The best selection of music is generally only available in major cities, in chains such as **Tower Records**, **Virgin Megastore** and **Wherehouse**. If a town has a university, head towards the student district where new and used record stores thrive.

Native American and Mexican arts and crafts are available throughout California. Contact the **American Indian Contemporary Arts Center** and the Mexican Museum *(see p255)* for more information.

ANTIQUES

CALIFORNIA'S small towns are awash with traditional antiques such as fine gold and silver jewellery, Native American Indian artifacts, textiles, antique clothing, Bakelite jewellery and period furniture dating back to the 18th and 19th centuries.

The West Coast is the port of entry to the US for many Pacific Rim countries and, as a result, many antique porcelain sculptures from Japan and China and period Asian furniture are available. Twentieth-century collectables include Arts and Crafts and Art Deco furniture, clothing, posters, prewar tin toys, blown glass and pottery.

Antiques dealers often rent space together in one large mall, barn or warehouse building that is open to the public. The largest antiques mall is **Antique Plaza**, just east of Sacramento. Almost 300 dealers trade here. There is also a café serving coffee and sandwiches.

FOOD

MANY OF CALIFORNIA'S farms, particularly in Sonoma or Fresno counties, sell their produce to visitors on self-guided farm trails. In Sonoma, contact the **Sonoma County Farm Trails** or the **Sonoma Valley Chamber of Commerce**. The Fresno County Blossom Trail is a 62-mile (100-km) trail passing through groves, orchards and vineyards. It begins at **Simonian Farms**, which sells local fruits, honey and mustards. Contact the **Fresno County Farm Bureau** for information.

California has a number of unique food shops scattered around the state. In Napa's Anderson Valley, the **Apple Farm** is a year-round fruit

Fresh local produce at a farmers' market

stand selling locally grown apples and pears. Also in Napa, the **Jimtown Store** sells local jams, honey, olives, mustards, vinegars and salad dressings. On Hwy 152, east of Gilroy, **Casa de Fruta**, which began as a simple cherry stand in the 1940s, has grown into a vast complex with a fruit stand, coffee shop (Casa de Coffee), restaurant (Casa de Burger) and gift shop (Casa de Gift).

Harris Ranch, almost midway between LA and San Francisco on I-5, is a vast complex set amid a working cattle ranch. The Spanish-style hacienda has a gift shop featuring Harris Ranch produce and fresh meat, as well as a restaurant, coffee shop and overnight lodging.

Italian Marketplace at the Viansa Winery

WINERIES

IN ADDITION TO the fine wine of Napa and Sonoma counties, wineries are known for the shops located inside their tasting rooms. A range of merchandise related to wine is for sale. For a list of California's wineries, contact the **Wine Institute of San Francisco**.

The Italian Marketplace at the **Viansa Winery** sells Italian cheeses and breads, cookbooks and kitchenware. The **Sebastiani Vineyards** sell a variety of wine-related souvenirs. The gift shop in the **Sterling Vineyards** offer silk scarves, silver jewellery and regional history books.

The **Hakusan Sake Garden** serves *sake* in a picturesque Japanese garden and sells it in their on-site shop.

DIRECTORY

FASHION

Back to Back Kidswear
8669 Hayden Place,
Culver City,
CA 90232.
[(310) 842-6690.

California Wave
1247 E 58th Place,
Los Angeles, CA 90001.
[(213) 233-0077.

Catalina
6040 Bandini Blvd,
City of Commerce,
CA 90040.
[(213) 726-1262.

The Gap
1 Harrison St,
San Francisco,
CA 94105.
[(415) 952-4400.

Jessica McClintock Inc
1400 16th St,
San Francisco, CA 94103.
[(415) 495-3030.

Joe Boxer Inc
1265 Folsom St,
San Francisco, CA 94103.
[(415) 882-9406.

Sara's Prints
3018 Alvarado St,
San Leandro, CA 94577.
[(510) 352-6060.

Traci Lynn
655 E 30th St,
Los Angeles, CA 90011.
[(213) 235-2181.

FLEA MARKETS

Berkeley Flea Market
1837 Ashby Ave,
Berkeley, CA 94703.
[(510) 644-0744.

Pasadena's Rose Bowl
1001 Rose Bowl Drive,
Pasadena, CA 91103.
[(818) 577-3100.

San Jose Flea Market
1590 Berryessa Road,
San Jose,
CA 95133.
[(408) 453-1110.

San Juan Bautista Peddlars Fair
Mission San Juan Bautista
San Juan Bautista, CA 95023.
[(408) 623-2454.

POP CULTURE ANTIQUES

Camperos Collectables
PO Box 1629,
Sutter Creek, CA 95685.
[(209) 245-3725.

For Amusement Only
1010 Grayson St,
Berkeley, CA 94710.
[(510) 548-2300.

Hello Central
2463 Ladera Court,
San Luis Obispo,
CA 93401.
[(805) 541-9123.

Hillcrest Vintage Paper Collectables
3412 W MacArthur Blvd,
Unit G, Santa Ana,
CA 92704.
[(714) 751-4030.

Sarah Stocking Fine Vintage Posters
3032 Claremont Ave,
Berkeley, CA 94705.
[(510) 658-6609.

OUTLET CENTRES

American Tin Cannery Factory Outlets
125 Ocean View Blvd,
Monterey, CA 93942.
[(408) 372-1442.

Desert Hills Factory Stores
48400 Seminole Rd,
Cabazon, CA 92230.
[(909) 849-5018.

Factory Stores of America at Nut Tree
321–322 Nut Tree Rd,
Vacaville, CA 95687.
[(707) 447-5755.

Napa Factory Stores
629 Factory Stores Drive,
Napa, CA 94558.
[(707) 226-9876.

Palm Springs Square
Palm Springs,
CA 92173.
[(619) 320-7444.

Pismo Beach Outlet Center
Pismo Beach,
CA 93449.
[(805) 773-4661

San Diego Factory Outlet Center
4498 Camino de la Plaza,
San Ysidro,
CA 92173.
[(619) 690-2999.

Shopper Stopper Shopping Tours
PO Box 535,
Sebastopol,
CA 95473.
[(707) 829-1597.

BOOKS, MUSIC AND CRAFTS

American Indian Contemporary Arts Center
685 Market Street,
San Francisco,
CA 94105.
[(415) 495-7600.

Tower Records
2500 Del Monte St,
Sacramento,
CA 95691.
[(916) 373-2500.

Virgin Megastore
8912 Burton Way,
Beverly Hills,
CA 90211.
[(310) 724-5967.

Wherehouse
19701 Hamilton Ave,
Torrance, CA 90502.
[(800) 776-8290.

ANTIQUES

Antique Plaza
11395 Folsom Blvd,
Rancho Cordova,
CA 95742.
[(916) 852-8517.

FOOD

Apple Farm
18501 Greenwood Rd,
Philo, CA 95466.
[(707) 895-2333.

Casa de Fruta
10031 Pacheco Pass Hwy,
Hollister, CA 95023.
[(408) 637-0051.

Fresno County Farm Bureau
1274 West Hedges,
Fresno, CA 93728.
[(209) 237-0263.

Harris Ranch
24505 West Dorris Ave,
Coalinga, CA 93210.
[(209) 935-0717.

Jimtown Store
6706 Hwy 128,
Healdsburg,
CA 95448.
[(707) 433-1212.

Simonian Farm
2629 S Clovis Ave,
Fresno, CA 93725.
[(209) 237-2294.

Sonoma County Farm Trails
PO Box 6032,
Santa Rosa, CA 95406.
[(707) 996-2154.

Sonoma Valley Chamber of Commerce
645 Broadway,
Sonoma, CA 95476.
[(707) 996-1033.

WINERIES

Hakusan Sake Garden
1 Executive Way,
Napa, CA 94558.
[(707) 258-6160.

Sebastiani Vineyards
389 Fourth St East,
Sonoma, CA 95476.
[(707) 938-5532.

Sterling Vineyards
1111 Dunaweal Loane,
Calistoga, CA 94515.
[(707) 942-3300.

Viansa Winery
25200 Arnold Drive,
Sonoma, CA 95476.
[(707) 935-4700.

Wine Institute of San Francisco
425 Market St,
Suite 1000,
San Francisco, CA 94105.
[(415) 512-0151.

SURVIVAL
GUIDE

PRACTICAL INFORMATION

CALIFORNIA IS A VIBRANT and diverse holiday destination. The spirit of the state can be felt in the busy cities of San Francisco, LA and San Diego as much as in the quiet wilderness of the Sierra Nevada Mountains; and all over the state the needs of visitors are generally attended to. Even so, it is advisable to plan ahead, especially outside the main cities. Most places have visitors' centres providing local information for the

UNITED STATES POSTAL SERVICE®
United States Postal Service logo

surrounding areas. The Survival Guide that follows contains valuable information that will help in every aspect of a visit. Personal Security and Health *(pp592–3)* outlines a number of recommended precautions. Banking and Currency *(pp594–5)* answers the essential financial questions faced by visitors. There are also sections on how to use the Californian telephone system and the US postal service *(pp596–7)*.

Skiing on the slopes of Alpine Meadows in Lake Tahoe *(see p470)*

WHEN TO GO

HIGH SEASON, from mid-April to September, sees a rush of visitors to the state's major tourist destinations. The winter months are also very popular with visitors, either for the warm climate of the south or the ski slopes of Lake Tahoe. During the quieter off-season it is sometimes possible to visit many of the tourist attractions at lower admission prices and without the usual crowds.

ADMISSION CHARGES

MAJOR MUSEUMS, theme parks, art galleries and other tourist attractions generally charge an admission fee. Entry fees range from $5 to $8, with discounts for the disabled *(see p590)*, students, senior citizens and children. Smaller tourist attractions are

either free or request a small donation. At most larger institutions entrance is free on one day a month (telephone for details). Free guided tours, demonstrations and lectures are frequently on offer.

OPENING HOURS

MOST BUSINESSES are open on weekdays from 9am to 5pm and do not close for lunch. Many are also open on Sundays. In addition, some grocer shops, chemists and petrol stations in the larger towns and cities are open 24 hours a day.

Most museums are closed on Mondays and/or Tuesdays and on major public holidays, but occasionally stay open until early evening.

Many Californians eat early in the evenings, and restaurants often have their last sitting at about 10pm. Most bars are open until 2am, particularly on Fridays and Saturdays.

TOURIST INFORMATION

ADVANCE INFORMATION can be obtained from the **California Division of Tourism** or the nearest US Consulate. Maps, guides, event listings and discount passes for public transport and tourist attractions are available at local Visitors' and Convention Bureaux. These offices are usually open from Monday to Friday, 9am to 5:30pm.

This guide provides the address and telephone number of the tourist information office in each town or city.

SIGHTSEEING TIPS

TO AVOID the crowds, visit the region's major sights in the morning and leave the more unstructured visits and tours until after lunch. Visit a group of sights in the same vicinity on the same day to save time and transport costs. Sights are more crowded at

Spanish colonial façade of the San Diego Museum of Art *(see p247)*

weekends than on weekdays. Rush hours are Monday to Friday, 7am to 9am and 4pm to 6:30pm, when transport and city streets are full to capacity.

VISAS

VISITORS HOLDING an EU passport and planning to stay less than 90 days do not require a visa. However, it is necessary to fill out a visa waiver form provided at the airport check-in desk or on the aeroplane. Visitors from all other parts of the world need a valid passport and a non-immigrant visitor's visa. This can be obtained from a US Embassy or Consulate.

TAX AND TIPPING

THE CALIFORNIA State Government levies a 7.25 per cent general sales and use tax. In major cities, a further 1–1.25 per cent tax is added on to all bought items except items for out-of-state delivery and food for preparation *(see p582).*

Visitor Information Center in Hallidie Plaza, San Francisco

There are no sales tax charges against hotel rooms, but a 12–14 per cent transient occupancy tax is generally incurred.

In restaurants, it is normal to tip 15–20 per cent of the total bill. Allow for a tip of 15 per cent for taxi drivers, bar staff and hairdressers. Porters at hotels and airports expect $1–1.50 per bag. It is also usual to leave hotel chambermaids $1–2 for each day of your stay.

SMOKING

IT IS ILLEGAL to smoke in any public building, except in bars and the bar area of some restaurants. By law, hotels must keep 35 per cent of their rooms and 75 per cent of the foyer as non-smoking. Ask about smoking policies when booking hotels and restaurants. In some areas smoking is banned anywhere in public.

TOURIST INFORMATION

STATEWIDE

California Division of Tourism
801 K St, Suite 1800,
Sacramento,
CA 58814.
☎ *(916) 322-2881.*
FAX *(916) 322-3402.*

SAN FRANCISCO

San Francisco
Lower Level of Hallidie Plaza,
Powell and Market sts.
☎ *(415) 391-2000,*
(415) 974-6900.

THE NORTH

Redding
777 Auditorium Drive.
☎ *(916) 225-4100,*
(800) 874-7562.

Eureka
2112 Broadway.
☎ *(707) 442-3738,*
(800) 346-3482.

WINE COUNTRY

Mendocino County
239 S Main St,
Willits.
☎ *(707) 459-7910.*

Napa Valley
1310 Napa Town Center.
☎ *(707) 226-7459.*

GOLD COUNTRY

Sacramento
1421 K St.
☎ *(916) 264-7777.*

Tuolumne County
55 W Stockton St,
PO Box 4020, Sonora.
☎ *(209) 533-4420,*
(800) 446-1333.

HIGH SIERRAS

Tahoe North
950 N Lake Blvd, Suite 3,
Tahoe City.
☎ *(916) 583-3494,*
(800) 824-6348.

Bishop
690 N Main St.
☎ *(619) 873-8405.*

NORTH CENTRAL

Fresno City and County
808 M St.
☎ *(209) 233-0836.*

Monterey County
380 Alvarado St.
☎ *(408) 649-1770.*

LOS ANGELES

Downtown Los Angeles
685 S Figueroa St.
☎ *(213) 689-8822.*

Hollywood
6541 Hollywood Blvd.
☎ *(213) 689-8822.*

SOUTH CENTRAL

Santa Barbara
510 State St, Suite 1.
☎ *(805) 966-9222,*
(800) 927-4688.

San Luis Obispo County
1041 Chorro St.
☎ *(805) 541-8000,*
(800) 634-1414.

ORANGE COUNTY

Anaheim/Orange County
800 W Katella Ave.
☎ *(714) 999-8999.*

SAN DIEGO

San Diego
11 Horton Plaza.
☎ *(619) 236-1212.*

Escondido
720 N Broadway.
☎ *(760) 745-2125.*

PALM SPRINGS

Riverside
3443 Orange St.
☎ *(909) 787-7950.*

Palm Springs
69 Hwy 111, Suite 201,
Rancho Mirage.
☎ *(760) 770-9000.*

MOJAVE DESERT

Death Valley
118 Hwy 127,
Shoshone.
☎ *(619) 852-4524.*

Selection of newspapers available in California

Street distribution bin for newspapers

town's visitors' centre. These should give all the up-to-date information on local entertainment and festivals, and details of popular bars and restaurants. In the major cities there is a variety of listings sources, including the *Bay Guardian* in San Francisco, *LA Weekly* and *Los Angeles Reader* and the *San Diego Reader*.

NEWSPAPERS, TELEVISION AND RADIO

IT IS POSSIBLE to buy the *New York Times* and the *Wall Street Journal* throughout most of California and the *Los Angeles Times* is read all over the state. There is a selection of local daily papers available, many of which can be purchased from street distribution bins or in bookshops.

Television in California is similar to that all over the US. Much of it is supplied by cable or satellite systems. Most hotel rooms have a television, and bars frequently have screens showing sport. There is a wide selection of national, and a few local, channels, most of them showing sitcoms, magazine programmes, children's cartoons and chat shows. There are also Mexican and Asian foreign language channels and news and music channels. Most newspapers cover programme times, and hotel rooms often supply local television schedules.

Similarly, there are numerous commercial radio stations. They cover many subject matters, languages and music styles. Listings of stations can be found in the local newspapers mentioned above.

ENTERTAINMENT LISTINGS

MOST SIZEABLE communities have free newspapers that can be found in street distribution bins or at the

DISABLED TRAVELLERS

CALIFORNIAN LAW requires that every public building is accessible to travellers with disabilities. Disabled people also receive privileges such as free parking and admission reductions to many national and state parks. It is advisable to notify sights and hotels in advance, so that they can prepare for special needs. The Society for the Advancement of Travel for the Handicapped (SATH) uses a blue H sign to symbolize special facilities in restaurants, hotels and tourist sights. For information contact the **Disability Rights, Education and Defense Fund**. Travel for the disabled can be arranged by the **California Relay Service**.

Parking bay for the disabled

GAY AND LESBIAN TRAVELLERS

CALIFORNIA'S large gay community is mainly focused in the major cities, particularly in the Castro District of San Francisco *(see p350)*, Hillcrest in San Diego and the West Hollywood area of LA *(see pp96–115)*. Free newspapers and magazines that contain gay listings include *The Edge* in Los Angeles, *Frontier* which covers the whole of Southern California, or the many magazines in San Francisco, such as *Gay Times*. Listings of gay events in San Francisco and the Bay Area can also be obtained from the **Out and About** telephone newsletter. The **Gay Switchboard** is a referral service in the Bay Area that provides both crisis support and listings.

STUDENT TRAVELLERS

THERE ARE FEW reductions for students in California. The ISIC (International Student Identity Card) is rarely accepted, and it is advisable for the young to carry a passport for entry into bars, as the under 21 ban is strictly enforced. The **Student Travel Association** has two offices in the Bay Area and three in LA. There are many youth hostels in the state. For handbooks, listings and advance information contact **Hosteling International-American Youth Hostels**.

Hitchhiking should be avoided. Check noticeboards at hostels or universities for safe car-sharing opportunities.

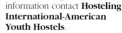

International Student ID Card

CONSULATES

MOST COUNTRIES have consulates in both San Francisco and Los Angeles. They are usually open from 9am to 5pm, Monday to Friday. Although not expressly concerned with visitors' problems, it is very important to contact them in times of emergency. The consulate will not lend money, but they can help with lost passports and give advice on legal matters in emergencies. The address of the nearest office in each city can be found in the local telephone directory.

ELECTRICAL APPLIANCES

IN THE UNITED STATES all electrical current flows at a standard 110–120 volts AC (alternating current). To operate 220-volt appliances requires a voltage converter and an adapter plug with two flat parallel prongs to fit US outlets. The same applies to battery pack rechargers. Many hotels have hair dryers mounted on the bathroom wall and special plugs for electric shavers that carry 110- or 220-volt current.

Standard plug

CONVERSION CHART

Bear in mind that 1 US pint (0.5 litre) is a smaller measure than 1 UK pint (0.6 litre).

US Standard to Metric
1 inch = 2.54 centimetres
1 foot = 30 centimetres
1 mile = 1.6 kilometres
1 ounce = 28 grams
1 pound = 454 grams
1 US quart = 0.947 litre
1 US gallon = 3.8 litres

Metric to US Standard
1 centimetre = 0.4 inch
1 metre = 3 feet 3 inches
1 kilometre = 0.6 miles
1 gram = 0.04 ounce
1 kilogram = 2.2 pounds
1 litre = 1.1 US quarts

RELIGIOUS ORGANIZATIONS

CALIFORNIA, and particularly Northern California, has the reputation of attracting unconventional forms of worship *(see pp424–5)*. Sects, cults and alternative religions seem to thrive in the state as much as the more conventional churches and temples.

The Catholic Church is the largest congregation, with nearly a quarter of its number of Hispanic origin. Los Angeles has the second largest Jewish community in the United States, which worships in a number of beautiful synagogues. Hindu temples, Islamic mosques and a range of more unusual shrines abound throughout the state. Details of venues for every type of worshipper can be found in the telephone book under "Churches".

Self-realization church, an alternative place of worship

DISABLED VISITORS' INFORMATION

California Relay Service
San Francisco
((800) 735-2922.
Los Angeles
((800) 735-2922.

Disability Rights, Education and Defense Fund
2212 6th St, Berkeley, CA 94710.
((510) 644-2555.

STUDENT INFORMATION

Hosteling International-American Youth Hostels
733 15th St NW, Suite 840,
Washington, DC 20005.
((800) 444-6111.

Student Travel Association
51 Grant Ave, San Francisco.
((415) 391-8407.

920 Westwood Blvd, Los Angeles.
((310) 824-1574.

GAY AND LESBIAN

Gay Switchboard
((510) 841-6224.

Out and About
((800) 929-2268.

CONSULATES

Australian Consulate
1 Bush St, 7th Floor, San Francisco.
((415) 362-6160.

British Consulate General
11766 Wilshire Blvd, Suite 850,
Los Angeles.
((310) 477-3322.

Canadian Consulate
300 S Grand Ave, Suite 1000,
Los Angeles.
((213) 346-2701.

French Consulate
540 Bush St, San Francisco.
((415) 397-4330.

German Consulate
1960 Bush St, San Francisco.
((415) 775-1061.

Japanese Consulate
50 Fremont, 23rd Floor,
San Francisco.
((415) 777-3533.

CALIFORNIA TIME

California is in the Pacific Time Zone. Daylight Saving Time begins on the last Sunday in April (at 2am) when clocks are set ahead one hour. It ends on the first Sunday in October (at 2am) when clocks are set back one hour.

City and Country	Hours + or - PT	City and Country	Hours + or - PT
Athens (Greece)	+10	Moscow (Russia)	+11
Auckland (New Zealand)	+20	New York (USA)	+3
Beijing (China)	+16	Paris (France)	+9
Berlin (Germany)	+9	Perth (Australia)	+16
Chicago (USA)	+2	Sydney (Australia)	+18
Kowloon (Hong Kong)	+16	Tokyo (Japan)	+17
London (UK)	+8	Toronto (Canada)	+3
Madrid (Spain)	+9	Washington, DC (USA)	+3

Personal Security and Health

WARNING
YOU ARE ENTERING BEAR COUNTRY
BEARS ARE ACTIVE DAY AND NIGHT
PROPER FOOD STORAGE REQUIRED BY STATE LAW
PROTECT YOUR PROPERTY AND YOURSELF
violators will be subject to a $500 fine

**Bear warning sign in
Northern California**

Like most major cities, the cities of California have some dangerous neighbourhoods. Check with friends or hotel staff which parts of town are considered unwise to visit, either alone or at night. San Francisco is considered one of the safest large cities in the US; unfortunately, problems are more visible in some areas of LA. When travelling in the countryside, always take a good local map, particularly in the deserts and the mountains. It is important to take the advice of the local authorities seriously and in cases of all outdoor pursuits normal safety procedures should be observed.

GUIDELINES ON SAFETY

The notorious gangs of California, particularly in Los Angeles, are rarely seen outside their own areas, and are not necessarily interested in visitors. Visitors are more likely to be the target of theft or car crime. Police officers regularly patrol most of the tourist areas, but it is still advisable to prepare the day's itinerary in advance and to use common sense. Do not allow strangers into your hotel room or give them details of where you are staying.

Lock any valuables away in the hotel safe – do not carry them around with you. Most hotels will not guarantee the security of any belongings kept in your room.

Road safety for pedestrians is also observed by law: jay-walking, or crossing the road anywhere except at an intersection, can result in a fine.

**San Francisco
police officer**

LOST PROPERTY

Although the chances of retrieving property lost in the street are very slim, tele-phone the **Police Non-Emergency Line**. It is important to report all lost or stolen items to the police. If you want to make an insurance claim on your return home, you will need to obtain a copy of the police report to send to the insur-ance company. In case of loss, it is useful to have a list of serial numbers or a photo-copy of all documents kept separately as proof of possession.

If your passport is lost or stolen, get in contact with your embassy or consulate immediately *(see p591)*. For lost or stolen traveller's cheques or credit cards, you should contact the near-est issuing company's office *(see p593)*.

TRAVEL INSURANCE

Travel insurance is not compulsory, but strongly recommended. You should take out cover for emergency medical and dental care while also insuring your personal property. It is also advisable to buy insurance cover for lost or stolen baggage and travel documents, accidental death or injury, trip cancel-lation fees and legal advice.

SAFETY OUTDOORS

The Pacific Ocean is rarely warm, even in high sum-mer. The ocean can also be rough, more suited to surfers than swimmers, with a strong undertow. On the beach, thefts can occur, so always look after your valuables. Take full suntanning precautions. It is important to prepare equipment before hiking in the wilderness. Notify someone of your plans before setting off. Leave the coun-tryside as you found it and be wary of the occasionally dangerous wildlife in many of the parks. As firewood is scarce and forest fires can start quickly, check with the park ranger whether camp fires are allowed.

**National park
ranger**

Local maps are available from the Chamber of Commerce in the near-est town. **The Sierra Club** can advise about excursions. Rock climbing and moun-taineering are becoming increasingly popular in California. In many parks there are services for climbers *(see p579)*. Contact local ranger services for

Patrol motorcycle

Police car

Ambulance

Fire engine

advice on instructors, specific equipment required and current weather conditions.

Precautions in the desert should always be observed. At lower levels, the conditions are usually hot and dry; at high elevations temperatures often drop below freezing at night. Carry extra petrol and water. If your car overheats, do not leave the vehicle to go for help. Keep the engine running and pour water over the radiator. Cool, then refill with water. For further information contact the Death Valley Visitors' Center (see p280).

MEDICAL MATTERS

To visit a doctor's surgery, hospital or pharmacy in the US, it is necessary to have medical insurance. Even with medical cover you may have to pay for the services, then claim reimbursement from your insurance company. If you take medication, bring a back-up prescription with you.

EMERGENCIES

For emergencies that require medical, police or fire services, call 911. Hospital casualty departments are

called emergency rooms; city-owned hospitals, found in the blue pages of the telephone book, are often crowded. Private hospitals can be found in the yellow pages of the telephone book. Hotels will often call a doctor or dentist to visit you in your room. The national organization, **Travellers' Aid Society**, can also provide assistance in many kinds of emergency.

EARTHQUAKES

The expectation and fear of earthquakes should not get in the way of everyday activities. You may experience a tremor, but the most important thing is not to panic. Precautions are important, such as keeping shoes and a torch by the bed when asleep, in case of power cuts or broken glass. Most injuries occur from falling material. If inside, stand in a doorway or crouch under a table. In a car, decrease speed, pull in to the side of the road and stop. When outside, avoid being near trees, power lines or bridges. For further information on earthquake precautions contact **The United States Geological Survey**.

Banking and Currency

SAN FRANCISCO AND LA are major West Coast financial centres – the fine buildings in their financial districts are reflective of their prestige. For the convenience of residents and visitors alike, there are numerous automated teller machines (ATMs) that operate 24 hours a day. In smaller towns, some banks may not exchange foreign currency or traveller's cheques, so it is best to note the bank opening times in advance. Credit cards are very useful, and many situations, such as booking hotels or hiring a car, require them as a form of security.

Bank in San Francisco

TRAVELLER'S CHEQUES

TRAVELLER'S CHEQUES issued by American Express and Thomas Cook in US dollars are accepted at most hotels, restaurants and shops without a fee. It is necessary to show a passport as identification. If you lose your dollar cheques, contact **Thomas Cook Refund Assistance** or the **American Express Helpline**.

Foreign currency traveller's cheques may be cashed at a large bank or at major hotels. Rates of exchange are printed in the newspapers and posted up at banks where exchange services are offered. Personal cheques drawn on foreign banks are rarely accepted.

BUREAUX DE CHANGE

FEES AND COMMISSIONS are charged at bureaux de change. They are usually open on weekdays from 9am to 5pm. The best-known firms are **Thomas Cook Currency Services** and **American Express Travel Service**. Both of these companies have offices throughout California. Alternatively, try a city's main branch of a major bank or look in the yellow pages of the telephone directory.

BANKING

BANK OPENING times vary throughout the state. They are generally open between 10am and 3pm. Banking hours within major cities may be longer: some open as early as 7:30am and close at 6pm, and are often open on Saturday mornings. Credit Unions only serve their own members, so look for banks that offer services to the general public. Always ask about commissions before making a transaction. US dollar traveller's cheques can usually be cashed with a recognized form of photographic identification, such as a passport or an ISIC card. Foreign currency exchange is available in main branches of the larger banks.

CREDIT CARDS

AMERICAN EXPRESS, Diners Club, JCB, MasterCard (Access) and VISA are widely accepted throughout California. As well as the convenience of carrying less cash on your person, credit cards can also occasionally offer insurance on bought merchandise or other benefits. They can be used all over the state to book hotel rooms or hire a car *(see p602)*. Most hotels will ask for a credit card imprint on check-in. The majority of car hire companies often penalize patrons without credit cards by asking for a large cash deposit. Hospitals will accept most credit cards in payment.

AUTOMATED TELLER MACHINES

AUTOMATED teller machines (ATMs) can be found in most bank foyers or on the outside wall near the bank's entrance. They are in operation day and night, so that cash can be accessed outside normal

Foreign currency exchange sign

banking hours. US currency, usually in $5, $10 and $20 notes, can be withdrawn electronically from your bank or credit card account within seconds. Ask your own bank which ATM system your card can access in California and how much each transaction will cost. The more popular systems are **Cirrus** and **Plus**. ATMs also accept various US bank cards, in addition to MasterCard (Access), VISA and other credit cards.

Robberies can occur at ATMs, so it is advisable to use them in the daytime or when there are plenty of people nearby. Withdrawals from ATMs may provide a better foreign currency exchange rate than cash transactions.

Automated teller machine (ATM)

Coins

American coins come in 1, 5, 10 and 25 cent pieces (actual size shown). 50 cents and $1 coins are also minted but are rarely used. Each value of coin has a popular name: 1 cent pieces are called "pennies", 5 cent pieces are "nickels", 10 cent pieces are "dimes" and 25 cent pieces are "quarters".

**25 cent coin
(a quarter)**

**10 cent coin
(a dime)**

**5 cent coin
(a nickel)**

**1 cent coin
(a penny)**

**Reverse of the American
seal on a $1 bill**

Bank Notes

Units of currency in the United States are dollars and cents. There are 100 cents in a dollar. Notes, which are called bills, come in $1, $5, $10, $20, $50 and $100 denominations. The $2 bills are rarely circulated. All dollar bills are the same colour so check the amount carefully before paying. Popular slang for a dollar is a "buck".

DIRECTORY

FINANCIAL SERVICES

Thomas Cook Currency Services
75 Geary St, San Francisco.
Map 5 C4.
📞 *(415) 362-3452.*

Thomas Cook Refund Assistance
📞 *(800) 223-7373.*

American Express Travel Service
455 Market St, San Francisco.
Map 6 D4.
📞 *(415) 536-2600.*

Hilton Center,
901 W 7th St, Los Angeles.
Map 10 C4.
📞 *(213) 627-4800.*

American Express Helpline
📞 *(800) 221-7282.*

Cirrus
📞 *(800) 424-7787.*

Plus
📞 *(800) 843-7587.*

---

1 dollar bill ($1)

5 dollar bill ($5)

20 dollar bill ($20)

50 dollar bill ($50)

100 dollar bill ($100)

Using California's Telephones

PUBLIC TELEPHONES can be found at many street corners, in hotels, restaurants, bars, theatres and department stores. Most are either coin-operated, using 5, 10 and 25 cent pieces, or take phonecards. There are now several, however, that take credit cards.

PUBLIC TELEPHONES

MODERN payphones have a hand receiver and a 12-button key pad. Pacific Bell (PacBell) operate the majority of public payphones. These are marked by a blue and white receiver sign with a bell in a circle. They are mounted on walls, posts or in a booth. Some independent companies also operate payphones, but generally these are not as reliable, and can be more expensive. All charges must be indicated by law. Telephone directories are supplied at most public phones. If there are any complaints about a service, call the operator by dialling 0, the phone company's business office or the **California Public Utilities Commission**.

PAYPHONE CHARGES

THE COST of a local call within the same area code varies with the length of the call, but is always a minimum of 25 cents. After three minutes or more, the operator may interrupt the call to request more money. When calling a number outside the town or city you are in but within the same area code, a recorded message will tell you how much more money to add. Long-distance calls are to numbers with a different area code. These can

Souvenir phonecards

be expensive, but will be less so when dialled direct, without the help of the operator.

Local and long-distance calls are cheaper between 6pm and 8am weekdays and throughout weekends. Hotels charge all calls at premium rate. Telephone numbers that begin with 1-800 are free. To make a reverse charge call, you will need to contact the operator.

Phonecards are available in most towns throughout the state. They are issued by major telephone companies such as AT&T. The cards are convenient if you need to make a call and do not have the correct small change. Phonecards can be used on any telephone by ringing the free number on the back of the card and quoting its pin number. The pin number can also be used to receive instructions in your preferred language. To recharge the card, phone the recharge number on the back and quote both the pin number and your credit card number.

FAX SERVICE

WORLDWIDE FAX SERVICES are readily available throughout California in post offices, hotels and copy bureaux. Fax

USING A COIN-OPERATED PHONE

1 Lift the receiver and listen for the dialling tone.

2 Insert the required coin or coins. The coin drops as soon as you insert it.

3 Dial or press the number.

Coins
Make sure you have plenty of these coins available.

4 If you want to cancel the call before it is answered, or if the call does not connect, press the coin release lever and take your coins from the coin return.

5 cents

10 cents

25 cents

5 If the call is answered and you talk longer than three minutes, the operator will interrupt and tell you how much more money to deposit. Payphones do not give change.

Airport fax machine

charges are usually based on the time of day of the transmission, the destination and the number of pages faxed. Incoming faxes can also be received and will be charged by the page. Look under *Facsimile Transmission Services* in the yellow pages section of the telephone directory for further details. For telegrams, telexes, faxes and electronic mail, you can also contact **Western Union**.

REACHING THE RIGHT NUMBER

• Direct-dial call outside the local area code, but within the USA and Canada: dial **1**.
• International direct-dial call: dial **011** followed by country code (UK: **44**; Australia: **61**; New Zealand: **64**), then the city or area code (omit the first 0) and then the local number.
• International call via the operator: dial **01**, followed by the country code, then the city code (without the first 0), and then the local number.
• International directory enquiries: dial **00**.
• International operator assistance: dial **01**.
• A **1-800** prefix indicates a free call.
• Local directory enquiries: dial **411**.
• From 1997 there will be changes to some California area codes. If you experience difficulties reaching any number, call directory enquiries.
• **For emergency police, fire or ambulance services, dial 911.**

USEFUL NUMBERS

California Public Utilities Commission
📞 *(800) 649-7570.*

Western Union
📞 *(800) 325-6000.*

Directory Enquires within the US
📞 *1-(area code) 555-1212.*

Sending a Letter

Apart from post offices, letters can be sent from hotel concierge desks or posted in letter slots in office reception areas and at air, rail and bus terminals. Street postboxes are painted either blue, or red, white and blue. Weekend mail delivery is limited. Stamps can be purchased at post offices, hotel reception desks or from vending machines in convenience stores and supermarkets. Check international and domestic postal rates.

POSTAL SERVICE

All domestic post is first class and will usually arrive within 1 to 5 days. Letters without the zip (or postal) code will take longer. International airmail to New Zealand, Australia, Canada, Ireland and the United Kingdom takes 5–10 working days. Packages sent overseas by surface parcel rate may take 4–6 weeks for delivery. The Federal post office offers two special services. Priority Mail promises delivery faster than first class mail. The more expensive Express Mail delivers next day within the United States, and within 72 hours to many international destinations. Private Express Mail can be arranged through the Delivery Services listed in the yellow pages of the telephone directory. The two main international express mail companies are **DHL** and **Federal Express**.

US commemorative stamps

POSTE RESTANTE

Larger city post offices have a poste restante service where letters sent c/o General Delivery will be held for 30 days before being returned to the sender. The zip code of the post office and the address of the sender should be clearly marked. The recipient's surname should be underlined so that the letter is filed correctly at the receiving office.

US mail van

San Francisco
c/o General Delivery,
Civic Center, 101 Hyde St,
San Francisco, CA 94142.

Los Angeles
c/o General Delivery,
Los Angeles Main Post Office,
900 N Alameda,
Los Angeles, CA 90086.

San Diego
c/o General Delivery,
San Diego Main Post Office,
San Diego, CA 92110.

POSTAL SERVICES

DHL
📞 *(800) 225-5345.*

Federal Express
📞 *(800) 463-3339.*

United States Postal Service
📞 *(800) 222-1811.*

Standard US postbox

TRAVEL INFORMATION

SAN FRANCISCO AND LA are the two main gateways for visitors travelling to California by air. You can also arrive in the state by car, Amtrak train, long-distance coach or by ocean liner. Despite continuing problems with traffic congestion and environmental pollution, Californians remain devoted to driving.

A passenger jet

Large, comfortable cars, cheap petrol and a comprehensive network of roads make this an efficient and pleasurable way to tour the state. Public transport is a viable and cheap option in the major cities, where historic cable cars and ferries work alongside modern buses and mass transit systems.

Airport arrivals board

TRAVELLING BY AIR

AIR TRAVEL is an integral part of the American lifestyle, and California is no exception. Airports are efficiently designed, with computerized ticketing systems. Competition between airlines has led to a high level of service.

Frequent and reliable connections are offered all over the state. Los Angeles (LAX) and San Francisco (SFO) are the two main airports used by visitors to California. International flights also land at San Diego (SAN), Oakland (OAK) and San Jose (SJC). The state has more than 30 airports handling domestic flights. The major domestic airports include Sacramento and Palm Springs, as well as Santa Barbara, John Wayne/ Orange County and Fresno.

AIR FARES

FARE STRUCTURES are complex, with a variety of passes and bonus systems offered by the numerous airlines flying to and within California. Prices also vary according to season, with the most expensive tickets coinciding with summer months and the holiday periods, such as Christmas and Thanksgiving *(see p35)*. It is always cheaper to travel to or from California on weekdays rather than at weekends. The lowest regular offer is the APEX (Advanced Purchase Excursion Fare), which should be purchased two to three weeks before departure and is non-refundable. A reputable travel agent will be able to supply details on all the latest offers and promotions. They will also be able to point out the advantages and restrictions that accompany the fares and routes available, and tell you whether a visa is required to enter the US.

Most travellers from Europe choose non-stop flights to California, but fares are often cheaper if you fly via another American "hub" city such as Newark or Houston. The

Los Angeles airport control tower

AIRPORT	INFORMATION
Los Angeles (LAX)	(*(310) 646-5252*
San Francisco (SFO)	(*(415) 761-0800*
Oakland (OAK)	(*(510) 577-4000*
San Diego (SAN)	(*(619) 231-2100*
San Jose (SJC)	(*(408) 277-4759*
Sacramento (SMF)	(*(916) 929-5411*
Palm Springs (PSP)	(*(619) 323-8163*

volume of passengers flying, particularly in peak season, is so high that it is best to book as early as possible. If you are touring, a fly-drive package booked before you leave will generally be cheaper than making car hire arrangements in California *(see p602)*.

AT THE AIRPORT

WITH A VAST number of passengers arriving and departing at one time, huge international airports such as Los Angeles and San Francisco can seem bewildering to the jet-lagged, first-time visitor. Queues at immigration and customs points are inevitable at peak times. Dispose of any fresh fruit you may be carrying (a strictly enforced customs regulation) and plan transport from the airport to your destination in advance.

All the major airports have multilingual information booths for the newly arrived. These help with enquiries about the airport, and also give information on the various forms of transport into the city. Car rental desks *(see p602)*, currency exchange facilities *(see pp594–5)* and shuttle bus services can also be found in the airports.

Most car hire companies supply a shuttle bus to the car pick-up points, usually located on the outskirts of the airport. Shuttle buses can also be chartered for a door-to-door service to and from the airport

Baggage check-in desk

and a specific city address. One-way fares vary in price, depending on the distance covered. Journey times given below also vary, according to the number of passengers and their required stops.

All airports have facilities for assisting disabled passengers, although it is advisable to prearrange this through your airline. Smoking is not permitted in any of California's airport terminals.

Car hire shuttle

Door-to-door shuttle bus

CUSTOMS AND DUTY FREE

VISITORS ARRIVING in the US by air and sea are issued with customs declaration forms that must be filled in completely. Adult non-residents are permitted to bring in a limited amount of duty-free items. These include 0.2 gals (1 litre) of alcoholic beverages (beer, wine or spirits), 200 cigarettes, 50 cigars (but not Cuban) or 4.4 lbs (2 kg) of smoking tobacco, and $100 worth of gifts for other people.

AIRLINE CARRIERS (US CONTACT NUMBERS)

All Nippon Airlines
C *(800) 235-9262.*

American Airlines
C *(800) 433-7300.*

British Airways
C *(800) 247-9297.*

Continental Airlines
C *(800) 525-0280.*

Delta Airlines
C *(800) 221-1212.*

Southwest Airlines
C *(800) 435-9792.*

United Airlines
C *(800) 241-6522.*

USAir
C *(800) 428-4322.*

Virgin Atlantic
C *(800) 862-8621.*

ISTANCE FROM CITY	TAXI FARE TO CITY	SHUTTLE BUS
15 miles (24 km) from Downtown	approx $25 to Downtown approx $22 to Beverly Hills	30 mins to Downtown
miles (22 km) from city centre	approx $28-30 to Downtown	25 mins to city centre
miles (12 km) from city centre	approx $22 to Oakland	20 mins to city centre
miles (5 km) from city centre	approx $8 to San Diego	10-15 mins to city centre
miles (12 km) from city centre	approx $8 to San Jose	15 mins to city centre
miles (19 km) from city centre	approx $25 to Sacramento	20 mins to city centre
miles (3 km) from city centre	approx $12 to Palm Springs	no shuttle service

Getting Around California

Authorized taxi licence

Aᴌᴛʜᴏᴜɢʜ ᴏꜰᴛᴇɴ more time-consuming, travelling by train, bus and ferry can be an inexpensive and rewarding way of getting around California. Within the major cities of San Francisco *(see pp380–83)*, Los Angeles *(see pp168–9)* and San Diego *(see pp256–7)*, there are adequate public transport networks, offering buses, trams, Metro trains, ferries and cable cars. They are very busy during the rush hour periods. Taxis and shuttle buses are also useful in the cities. The network of Amtrak railway lines and connecting bus services serves the state's most populous areas and offers some scenic journeys. It is also possible to travel within the state by coach.

Yellow taxi cabs in San Francisco

Coaster train ticket machine

Tʀᴀᴠᴇʟʟɪɴɢ ʙʏ Rᴀɪʟ

Tʜᴇ ᴜsᴇ ᴏꜰ ʀᴀɪʟᴡᴀʏs in the US is dwindling, yet there are still connections between major cities. **Amtrak** runs direct, long-distance routes from LA to Chicago, Seattle, Albuquerque and San Antonio, but no longer offers a direct service to the East Coast.

In California, the rail network is divided into three sections: the San Diegan (linking Santa Barbara and San Diego), the Capitol (between San Jose and Sacramento) and the San Joaquin (connecting Emeryville and Bakersfield). A bus service strikes out in many directions from stops along these lines. Local commuter lines include **Caltrain** (linking San Jose and San Francisco); the Coast Starlight Connection (between San Luis Obispo and Santa Barbara); LA Metrolink; and the Coaster (connecting San Diego and Oceanside).

Lᴏɴɢ-Dɪsᴛᴀɴᴄᴇ Cᴏᴀᴄʜᴇs

Tʜᴇ ɴᴇᴛᴡᴏʀᴋ of coach routes operated by **Greyhound Lines** reaches all parts of the US. In California, services include scenic coastal connections as well as frequent express routes linking major cities such as San Francisco, Sacramento, San Jose, LA and San Diego. Guided tours provide a leisurely way of sightseeing. Several companies offer short package trips in de luxe coaches visiting sights such as Hearst Castle *(see pp202–5)*, Yosemite National Park *(see pp472–5)* and Monterey *(see pp492–5)*. Information about these services can be found in the yellow pages of the telephone book.

For travellers with more time to spare and who wish to get a real feel for the state, the alternative-minded **Green Tortoise** offers leisurely journeys between the major cities of the Pacific Coast. Passengers can break their trip to camp, prepare meals and explore the countryside.

Tᴀxɪs

Tᴀxɪs (more often called "cabs") can usually be found outside main transport termini and major hotels. Elsewhere it is best to order one by telephone – numbers can be found in the yellow pages of the telephone directory. Never stand in a street at night expecting one to pass.

Not all drivers know their way around, so it will help to have your destination marked on a map if it is off the beaten track. All taxi fares are metered according to the distance travelled. Some taxis take credit cards, but it is best to enquire in advance. A tip of 15 per cent is generally expected.

Sʜᴜᴛᴛʟᴇ Vᴀɴs

Cʜᴇᴀᴘᴇʀ ᴛʜᴀɴ taxis and quicker than buses, shuttle vans are a secure and reliable way of travelling within and around California's cities. They provide an efficient transport network, especially between hotels and airports.

Greyhound bus parked along a Californian highway

When calculating your journey time, bear in mind that other passengers will be picked up and dropped off en route. Competition between shuttle bus companies has led to a high standard of service. Their details can be found in the telephone directory. Call several companies to obtain the best quote before booking a long journey. Bus drivers will expect a tip of around $1.

BOATS AND FERRIES

EXPRESS BOAT services provide a fast link from Los Angeles to Santa Catalina Island (see pp232–3), while others sail more leisurely

across San Francisco Bay (see pp288–9). Most ferries carry foot passengers and bicycles, but not motor vehicles.

Despite the building of new bridges, several commuter ferries survive to offer their customers a breezy alternative to the smog of the rush hour traffic. Routes, such as those connecting Oakland, Sausalito and Tiburon with San Francisco, and the San Diego–Coronado ferry, provide a pleasant and reasonably priced way to enjoy a city. To find out about ferry timetables, prices and locations in San Francisco and the Bay Area see page 383, and in San Diego see page 257.

DIRECTORY

TRAIN INFORMATION

Amtrak
(800) 872-7245.

Caltrain
(800) 660-4287.

BUS AND COACH INFORMATION

Greyhound Lines
(800) 231-2222.

The Green Tortoise
494 Broadway,
San Francisco, CA 94133.
(800) 867-8647.

AMTRAK ROUTES

This map shows the main Amtrak routes within California, as well as the bus feeder services to the main stations. Amtrak also has several interstate services to other major cities in the US; the route to Las Vegas is shown below.

Amtrak train

KEY

— San Diegan Amtrak service
— San Joaquin Amtrak service
— Capitol Amtrak service
— Bus feeder service
— Interstate Amtrak service

Travelling by Car

DRIVING is an essential part of the Californian way of life, and for both residents and visitors it is the most convenient way to travel around the state. Roads are well maintained so that they are able to cope with the great volume of rush hour traffic that pours in and out of the main cities every weekday. The state has an efficient network of major roads linking the cities and towns. In remote areas such as in the deserts and mountains, it is sometimes necessary to use a four-wheel drive vehicle.

Traffic on the Harbor Freeway, Los Angeles

RENTING A CAR

IT IS BEST to arrange a fly-drive package before leaving for California. Take note of exactly what is included in the deal and find out whether any extra payments may arise when the car is returned. These additions – which can include optional fuel purchase, extended insurance cover, collision damage waiver, delivery or drop-off charges and vehicle rental tax (a daily city vehicle rental tax) – can double the original pre-paid fee. It is particularly important to find out exactly what is

included in the insurance policy offered by the rental company. Drivers should remember that in California, where litigation is an every-day occurrence, it is sensible to be fully insured.

To rent a car, the driver should be over 25 and have a US or internationally valid driving licence. A major credit card is also important, if not vital, as a guarantee. Some companies will rent to younger drivers, or accept a cash deposit in lieu of a credit card number, but expect higher charges in return. Taking a hire car

across the border into Mexico is not permitted without prior arrangement. The petrol tank should be full when you return the vehicle and you should allow sufficient time to process and check your final bill.

Car hire is generally cheapest at airports *(see p599)* but call the free numbers advertised by rental companies to find out about discounts.

Hire cars in the US generally have automatic transmission. If necessary, spend some time getting familiar with this system. Some companies supply cars with manual transmission ("stick-shift") on request. Classic cars, Harley-Davidson motorcycles and RVs (motor homes) can also be rented from specialist companies.

RULES OF THE ROAD

CALIFORNIANS drive on the right. Seatbelts are compulsory for both driver and passengers. In the US, speed limits are individually set by each state. In California, the maximum speed limit is generally 55 mph (90 km/h) but on selected freeways, 70 mph (110 km/h) limits have now been introduced. In cities, the speed limits are restricted as signposted. These controls are rigorously enforced by the Highway Patrol. Drink-driving is a serious offence and carries very heavy penalties.

Motorways are known as Freeways or Interstate Highways. Bicycles are not permitted on these roads. In rush hours, "high occupancy" lanes, which can only be used by cars carrying more than one passenger, come into force on

TRAFFIC SIGNS

A range of different signs offer warnings and instructions for drivers. Speed limits may vary every few miles, depending on the conditions of the road and the amount of traffic, and should be adhered to. In more remote areas, drivers must be wary of wildlife that may occasionally stray onto the roads. Disregarding traffic signs will result in fines from the Highway Patrol.

Wildlife warning

Traffic flows in a single direction

Entry prohibited

Maximum speed

Give way to all vehicles

Stop at intersection

Kerbing wheels in San Francisco – the kerb acts as a block

PREVENT RUNAWAYS
CURB WHEELS
PARK IN GEAR
SET BRAKE

PARK AT
90 DEGREES

Kerbside parking signs in San Francisco to prevent cars rolling downhill

Time elapsed shown here

Insert coins here

Turn handle to register coins

DIRECTORY

CAR HIRE AGENCIES

Alamo
(800) 327-9633.

Avis
(800) 331-1212.

Budget
(800) 527-7000.

Hertz
(800) 654-3131.

Cruise America Motorhome Rental
(800) 327-7799.

Dubbelju Motorcycle Services
(415) 495-2774.

ROAD CONDITIONS INFORMATION

Statewide
(800) 427-7623.

Northern California
(916) 445-7623.

Southern California
(213) 628-7623.

AUTOMOBILE ASSOCIATIONS

Automobile Association of America
1000 AAA Drive,
Heathrow, FL 32746.
(800) 222-4357.

California State Automobile Association
150 Van Ness Ave,
San Francisco,
CA 94102.
(415) 565-2012.

Automobile Association of Southern California
2601 S Figueroa St,
Los Angeles, CA 90007.
(213) 741-3111.

POLICE DEPARTMENT TOWED VEHICLE INFORMATION

San Francisco
(415) 553-1235.

Los Angeles
(213) 913-4460.

San Diego
(619) 531-2844.

some roads. It is permissible to turn right at red traffic lights if there is nothing coming the other way. The first vehicle to have reached a Stop sign junction has the right of way.

The **Automobile Association of America** (AAA) offers maps, emergency road service and discounts at many hotels and restaurants. The AAA is linked with many automobile clubs abroad so enquire ahead whether they will honour your membership. If not, the annual fee is about $60.

AAA sign

PETROL

Petrol is known as "gas" or "gasoline" and is usually unleaded. It is sold in gallons rather than litres. Cheap by European standards, the price includes a small gasoline tax. Petrol stations are not as widespread as many visitors expect, so be sure to fill up the tank before driving into the mountains, desert or through other remote areas. Many petrol stations have pump attendants. Some pumps take credit cards, and in self-service stations it is common to pay for your petrol prior to putting it into the car.

PARKING

Parking in Californian cities is strictly controlled and can be expensive. Valet parking is obligatory if you pull up outside many up-market hotels and restaurants. Hand the keys to the attendant and pay on departure. Most parking meters accept 25 cent coins, but some systems require dollar notes to be "posted" into the slot relating to the parking space. Car parks have their own set prices. Shopping malls reduce parking fees if you make a purchase there and your till receipt is validated.

Parking restrictions are marked by kerb colourings. If the kerb is painted red, parking is prohibited. A yellow kerb indicates a loading zone. A green kerb allows parking for up to ten minutes, a white kerb only five minutes during business hours. Blue kerbs are for disabled parking only. If parking on the steep hills in San Francisco, you must kerb your wheels into the road if facing uphill, and towards the kerb if facing downhill. If your vehicle is clamped or towed away, contact the local **Police Department Towed Vehicle Information Center**.

General Index

Acknowledgments

DORLING KINDERSLEY would like to thank the following people whose contributions and assistance have made the preparation of this book possible.

MAIN CONTRIBUTORS

Jamie Jensen grew up in LA and now lives in Northern California. He contributed to San Francisco in the Eyewitness series, and his most recent book is *Road Trip USA: Cross-Country Adventures on America's Two-Lane Highways.*

Ellen Payne is Managing Editor of *Los Angeles Magazine* and has worked on numerous travel publications. A poet as well, she frequently writes of Los Angeles in her work.

J Kingston Pierce is a Seattle writer specializing in West Coast history. He is a contributing editor of *San Francisco Focus* and *Seattle* magazines and his book credits include *San Francisco, You're History!*

Rebecca Poole Forée is Editor-in-Chief at Foghorn Press, San Francisco. She has written many travel books, including *Northern California Best Places.*

Nigel Tisdall is the author of several travel guides. He has contributed to *France, Seville and Andalusia* and *Portugal* in the Eyewitness series.

Stanley Young lives in LA. He has written several books including *The Missions of California* and *Paradise Found: The Beautiful Retreats and Sanctuaries of California and the Southwest.*

CONTRIBUTORS AND CONSULTANTS

Virginia Butterfield, Dawn Douglas, Rebecca Renner, Tessa Souter, Shirley Streshinsky, Barbara Tannenbaum, Michael Webb, John Wilcock.

ADDITIONAL PHOTOGRAPHY

Steve Gorton, Gary Grimaud, Kirk Irwin, Neil Lukas, Neil Mersh, Erhard Pfeiffer.

ADDITIONAL ILLUSTRATORS

James A Allington, Arcana Studios, Hugh Dixon, Richard Draper, Dean Entwhistle, Eugene Fleury, Chris Forsey, Andrew Green, Steve Gyapay, Toni Hargreaves, Philip Hockey, John Lawrence, Nick Lipscombe, Mel Pickering, Sallie Alane Reason, Peter Ross, Simon Roulston, John See, Tristan Spaargaren, Ed Stuart, Paul Williams.

CARTOGRAPHY

Lovell Johns Ltd, Oxford, UK; ERA-Maptec Ltd, Dublin, Ireland

PROOF READER

Sam Merrell

INDEXER

Hilary Bird

DESIGN AND EDITORIAL ASSISTANCE

Peter Bennett, Sophie Boyak, Joanna Craig, Cullen Curtiss, Donna Dailey, Stephanie Driver, Michael Ellis, William Gordon, Thomas A Knight, Ciaran McIntyre, Annie McQuitty, Ellen Root, Ingrid Vienings, Marek Walisiewicz.

SPECIAL ASSISTANCE

Marianne Babel, Wells Fargo History Museum, San Francisco; Liz Badras, LA Convention and Visitors' Bureau; Craig Bates, Yosemite Museum; Joyce Bimbo, Hearst Castle, San Simeon; Elizabeth A Borsting and Ron Smith, the *Queen Mary,* Long Beach; Jean Bruce-Poole, El Pueblo de Los Angeles National Monument; Carolyn Cassady; Covent Garden Stamp Shop; Marcia Eymann and Joy Tahan, Oakland Museum of California; Donna Galassi; Mary Jean S Gamble, Salinas Public Library; Mary Haas, California Palace of the Legion of Honor; Nancy Masten, Photophile; Miguel Millar, US National Weather Service, Monterey; Warren Morse, LA County Metropolitan Transportation Authority; Anne North, San Diego Visitors' and Convention Bureau; Donald Schmidt, San Diego Zoo; Vito Sgromo, Sacramento State Capitol Museum; Dawn Stranne and Helen Chang, San Francisco Visitors' and Convention Bureau; Cherise Sun and Richard Ogar, Bancroft Library; Gaynell V Wald, Mission San Juan Capistrano; Chris Wirth, Wine Institute, San Francisco; Cynthia J Wornham and Lori Star, the J Paul Getty Trust.

PHOTOGRAPHY PERMISSIONS

Dorling Kindersley would like to thank the following for their assistance and kind permission to photograph at their establishments: Balboa Park, San Diego; Columbia State Historic Park; Disney Enterprises, Inc.; J Paul Getty Museum, LA; Hearst Castle, San Simeon; Huntington Library, San Marino; Knotts Berry Farm, Buena Park; Los Angeles Children's Museum; Los Angeles County Museum of Art; Museum of Contemporary Art, LA; Museum of Miniatures, LA; Museum of Television and Radio, LA; Museum of Tolerance, LA; Norton Simon Museum, Pasadena; Petersen Automotive Museum, LA; *Queen Mary*, Long Beach; Sacramento State Capitol; San Diego Aerospace Museum; San Diego Automotive Museum; San Diego Museum of Art; San Diego Wild Animal Park; San Diego Zoological Society; Santa Barbara Mission; Southwest Museum, LA; John Steinbeck Library, Salinas; Tao House, Danville; Timken Museum of Art, San Diego; Universal Studios, LA; University of California, Berkeley; University of California, LA; University of Southern California, LA; Wells Fargo History Room, San Francisco; Winchester Mystery House, San Jose; and all other churches, missions, museums, parks, wineries, hotels, restaurants and sights too numerous to thank individually.

PICTURE CREDITS

t = top; tl = top left; tc = top centre; tr = top right; cla = centre left above; ca = centre above; cra = centre right above; cl = centre left; c = centre; cr = centre right; clb = centre left below; cb = centre below; crb = centre right below; bl = bottom left; b = bottom; bc = bottom centre; br = bottom right; bla = bottom left above; bca = bottom centre above; bra = bottom right above; blb = bottom left below; bcb = bottom centre below; brb = bottom right below; d = detail.

Every effort has been made to trace the copyright holders and we apologize in advance for any unintentional omissions. We would be pleased to insert the appropriate acknowledgments in any subsequent edition of this publication.

Works of art have been reproduced with the permission of the following copyright holders:

© AGAGP, Pans and DACS, London 1997: 302tl; © ALAN BOWNESS, Hepworth Estate, *Figure for Landscape*, bronze 1960: 247b; By permission of DARA BIRNBAUM: 308cl; By permission of the Estate of PHILIP GUSTON: 295cr; © DACS, London 1997: 308c; Museum of Contemporary Art, LA, Robert Rauschenberg Coca Cola Plan (1958), The Panza Collection: 121c; © DISNEY ENTERPRISES, INC 222c, 222c, 223, 224t, 224b, 225t, 225b; © MAN RAY TRUST/ADAGP, Paris and DACS, London 1997: 309cra; © EDUARDO PAOLOZZI 1997 ALL RIGHTS RESERVED DACS: 50–51c; SUCCESSION PICASSO/DACS 1997: 152t; By permission of the UNIVERSITY OF CALIFORNIA, BERKELEY: *Within*, 1969, by Alexander Lieberman, gift of the artist, University Art Museum: 405t.

DORLING KINDERSLEY would like to thank the following individuals, companies and picture libraries for permission to reproduce their photographs:

ACE PHOTO AGENCY: T&J Florian 480tl, 480tr, 481b; David Kerwin 13t; Cash Mauritius 598b; Vladimir Pcholkin 96; Laszlo Willinger 159t; Zephyr Pictures/James Blank 18b; ACTION-PLUS PHOTO-GRAPHERS: Chris van Lennep/Keith Maloy 188–9c; Neale Haynes 189br; ALLSPORT: 158tr Stephen Dunn 53br; ANSEL ADAMS CENTER FOR PHOTOGRAPHY: *Monolith, The Face of Half Dome, Yosemite National Park, California 1938*, Ansel Adams, © 1997 the Trustees of the Ansel Adams Publishing Rights Trust, all rights reserved 312b; APPLE COMPUTER INC: 52tr; AQUARIUS LIBRARY: 98cla, 102cr, 103t; *Gone with the Wind*, MGM 102b, *The Jazz Singer*, Warner Bros 103crb; *Jurassic Park*, Spielberg/Universal 142c; ARCAID: Richard Bryant 27c, 69cra; ARCHITECTURAL ASSOCIATION: J Stirling 69tr; ART DIRECTORS PHOTO LIBRARY: 67cra, Craig Aurness 151cr; Spencer Grant 255b; GENE AUTRY WESTERN HERITAGE MUSEUM: 147c.

BANCROFT LIBRARY, UNIVERSITY OF CALIFORNIA, BERKELEY: 40tr, 42crb, 42b, 45tl, 465b, 501c; BARNABY'S PICTURE LIBRARY: 15c, 49t, 50clb, *Giant*, Warner Bros 51br; 52ca, 52br, 53cla, 496cla; BFI STILLS, POSTERS AND DESIGNS: *Mantrap*, Paramount Studios 48–9c, *The War of the Worlds*, Paramount Studios 109b; BISON ARCHIVES: Marc Wanamaker 64bl, *The Sting*, Universal Studios 65cl; MARILYN BLAISDELL COLLECTION: 47t; BRIDGEMAN ART LIBRARY, London: Scottish National Portrait Gallery, Edinburgh 22tr; Kunst-historisches Museum, Vienna 42c; BRITSTOCK IFA: 29c, Bernd Ducke 51bl.

CALIFORNIA ACADEMY OF SCIENCES: 294b, 360tl, 360c, 360b, 361t; Trevor Hill 361cra; Caroline Kopp 357b; CALIFORNIA STATE RAILROAD MUSEUM: 46cla, 46clb, 47cra, 456tl; CALIFORNIA WESTERN RAILROAD: 443t; J ALLAN CASH: 490t; CAROLYN CASSADY: 23c,

330b; CENTER FOR THE ARTS GALLERIES: 295br, 312t; CENTER FOR THE ARTS THEATER/MARGARET JENKINS DANCE COMPANY: 313t; CEPHAS PICTURE LIBRARY: Bruce Fleming 584c; R&K Muschenetz 201t; Mick Rock 446bl, 447c; Ted Stefanski 438; COLORIFIC: J Aaronson 53b; Black Star/Alan Copeland 52cb; David Burnett 53clb; Chuck Nacke 33t; Alon Reiniger 34t, 34cr; Visages/Peter Lessing 16c; Patrick Ward 168b; CORBIS: Beebe Photography/ Morton 30tr; Bettmann/UPI 22c, 51crb, 53clb, 225t, 425cr; Jim Corwin 483; Darrell Gulin 421tr; Conway/W Perry 60c; Robert Holmes 193b, 507b, 580t; Macduff Everton 425b; David Muench 192t, 479b; Everett, *The Maltese Falcon*, Warner Bros 23bl; Galen Rowell/Mountain Light Photography Inc 469b; CROCKER ART MUSEUM: 459c; IMOGEN CUNNINGHAM TRUST: *Two Callas*, 1925, Imogen Cunningham © (1970, 1997) The Imogen Cunningham Trust, 25t.

DEL MAR THOROUGHBRED CLUB: 238cb; Disney characters © DISNEY ENTERPRISES, INC./Used by permission of Disney Enterprises, Inc. 222c, 222b, 224b; Used by permission of DISNEY ENTERPRISES, INC. 223, 224t, 225b; © Disney Enterprises, Inc. 225t.

EMBARCADERO CENTER: 302tr; MARY EVANS PICTURE LIBRARY: 9 (inset), 19bl, 44tr, 47crb, 49b, 50t, 55 (inset), 424t; EXPLORATORIUM: 294t.

THE FINE ARTS MUSEUMS OF SAN FRANCISCO: *Sailboat on the Seine*, c.1874, by Claude Monet, gift of Bruno and Sadie Adrian, 294cla; High chest, gift of Mr & Mrs Robert A Magowan, 356tr; Tall case clock, gift of Willard R Dye in memory of Grace Shelly Dye, 362tl; *Indians Hunting Buffalo*, c.1888, by Albert Bierstadt, gift of Mr & Mrs John D Rockefeller III, 362tr; Standing female bear, jade, Western Han (late 2nd or 1st century BC) China, The Avery Brundage Collection, 362br; *Boatmen on the Missouri*, 1846, George Cales Bingham, oil on canvas, gift of Mr & Mrs John D Rockefeller III, 363t; Burial mask with necklace, museum purchase, Mrs Paul L Wattis Fund, 363c; *Portrait of Orleans*, 1950, Edward Hopper, oil on canvas, partial gift of Mr & Mrs Jerrold Kingsley, 363b; *Old Woman*, c.1618 –9, Georges de La Tour, Roscoe & Margaret Oakes Collection, 75.2.10, 364t; *Virgin and Child*, c.1460, Dieric Bouts Workshop Roscoe & Margaret Oakes Collection, 75.2.14, 364c; *Green*, 1986, Richard Diebenkorn, Achenbach Foundation for Graphic Arts, gift of Crown Point Press, 1991. 28. 1274, 364b; *The Tribute Money*, c.1612, Peter Paul Rubens, purchased with funds from various donors, 44.11, 365t; *The Impresario*, c.1877, Edgar Degas, gift of Mr & Mrs Louis A Benoist, 1956.72, 365cra; *Water Lilies*, c.1914 –7, Claude Monet, Mildred Anna Williams Collection, 1973.3, 365cb; *The Thinker*, c.1880, cast c.1904, Auguste Rodin, gift of Alma de Bretteville Spreckels, 1924.18.1, 365b; FORT MASON MUSEUMS: Museo ItaloAmericano: *Muto*, 1985, Mimmo Paladino, etching, gift of Pasquale Iannetti, 295tl; *Meta III*, 1985, Italo Scanga, oil and lacquer on wood, gift of Alan Shepp, 341bl; Mexican Museum: *Indtos Verdes No 4*, 1980, Manuel Neri, mixed media/paper, 341br.

COLLECTION OF THE J PAUL GETTY MUSEUM, MALIBU, CALIFORNIA: Joseph Nollekens, *Venus* (1773), marble, 124 cm, 56c; Pierre-Auguste Renoir, *La Promenade* (1870), oil on canvas, 81.3 x 65 cm, 66c; Vincent Van Gogh, *Irises* (1889), oil on canvas, 71 x 93 cm, 78t; *Hispano-Moresque Deep Dish* (Valencia, mid-15th century), tin-glazed and lustered earthenware, 10.8 x 49.5 cm, 78b; Attr. André-Charles Boulle, Cabinet on Stand (c.1675–80), veneered oak with gilt bronze mounts , 230 x 151 x 66.7 cm, 79t; Peter Paul Rubens, *Korean Man* (c.1617), black chalk with touches of red chalk in the face, 38.4 x 23.5 cm, 79cra; Claude Monet, *Wheatstacks, Snow Effect, Morning* (1891), oil on canvas, 79crb; Rembrandt, *The Abduction of Europa* (1632), oil on a single oak panel, 79b; Jean-François Millet, *Man with a Hoe* (1860–2), oil on canvas, 80 x 99cm, 80t; Carleton E Watkins, *Cape Horn, Columbia River, Oregon* (negative 1867, print 1881–3), albumen, 40.5 x 52.3 cm, 80b; Sèvres Porcelain Manufactory, Basket (1756), soft paste porcelain, gilding, 22 x 20.1 x 18 cm, 81t; Footed Bowl (Venice, c.1500–50), free-blown calcedonio glass, 12.5 x 19.5 cm, 81c; Gospels (Helmarshausen, c.1120–40), tempera colours, gold and silver on vellum bound between paper boards covered with brown calf, 22.8 x 16.4 cm, 81b; GOLDEN GATE BRIDGE HIGHWAY AND TRANSPORTATION DISTRICT: 51t, 370tl, 370c, 370b, 370–1t, 371c, 371cb; Charles M Hiller 51t; GOLDEN GATE NATIONAL RECREATION AREA, NATIONAL PARK SERVICE: 329blb, 329bc; RONALD GRANT ARCHIVE: 48tl, 98cr, 101cl, 103cl, 583t; Capitol 188tr; *LA Story*, Warner Bros 16t; *Rebel Without A Cause*, Warner Bros 64cra; *The Last Action Hero* Columbia Pictures 64crb; *E.T., The Extra-Terrestrial*, Spielberg/ Universal Studios, 65br; *Gidget*, Columbia Pictures 188c.

ROBERT HARDING PICTURE LIBRARY: 186t, 193c, 288c, 584t; Bildagentur/Schuster 188b; FPG 20cl, 48cla, 49clb, 51cra; Jon Gardey 481t; Tony Gervis 467; Michael J Howell 19tr; Dave Jacobs 421b, 481c; Robert Landau 69crb; Westlight/Bill Ross 10b, 146tr,/Steve Smith 19br 29t; HEARST CASTLE/HEARST SAN SIMEON STATE HISTORICAL MONUMENT: Z Baron 202br; John Blades 202tr, 202clb, 203b, 204c, 205c; V Garagliano 202bc; Ken Raveill 202ca, 203t, 203cra, 204b; Amber Wisdom 203crb; PHOEBE HEARST MUSEUM OF ANTHROPOLOGY: 41crb; HULTON GETTY: 53cr, 101t; HUNTINGTON LIBRARY: 25b, 156b; *Madonna and Child*, Roger van der Weyden 67crb; *Breakfast in Bed*, Mary Cassatt 154c; Gutenberg Bible 155t; *Blue Boy*, Thomas Gainsborough 155crb; *Diana the Huntress*, Houdon 156t; The Wife of Bath from *The Canterbury Tales*, Chaucer (Ellesmere MS), 156c; HUTCHISON LIBRARY: Robert Francis 279t; B Regent 166cl.

THE IMAGE BANK: David Hamilton 19tl; Marvin E Newman 314; Charles C Place 441t; 192clb; Paul Slaughter 496tl; Weinberg-Clark 422tl; THE IMAGE WORKS: Lisa Law 424–5c; IMPACT: Mike McQueen 193t; KIRK IRWIN: 16b, 187t, 208c, 208b, 281b, 429, 586–7.

CATHERINE KARNOW: 190br; KATZ PICTURES: Lamoine 166cr; SABA/Steve Starr 21tl, /Lara Jo Regan 65bl;

ROBERT E KENNEDY LIBRARY: Special Collections, California Polytechnic State University 205t; KOBAL COLLECTION: *Sabrina*, © 1995 Paramount/Brian Hamill 65tr; *LA Story*, Guild Film Distribution 65cla, *The Big Sleep*, Warner Bros 75b; *The Wild One*, Columbia Pictures 190bl.

LA CONVENTION AND VISITORS' BUREAU: Michele & Tom Grimm 169; LA COUNTY MUSEUM OF ART: *La Trahison des Images (Ceci n'est pas une pipe)*, René Magritte, purchased with funds provided by the Mr & Mrs William Preston Harrison Collection, 66t; *In the Woods at Giverny: Blanche Hoschedé at Her Easel with Suzanne Hoschedé Reading*, Claude Monet, Mr & Mrs George Gard De Sylva Collection 110t; *Mother About to Wash Her Sleepy Child*, Mary Cassatt, Mrs Fred Hathaway Bixby Bequest 110cla; *Flower Day*, Diego Rivera, LA County Fund 110c; *Mulholland Drive: The Road to the Studio*, David Hockney, purchased with funds provided by the F Patrick Burnes Bequest 111t; Plate, purchased with funds provided by the Art Museum Council 111cr; Standing Warrior (The King), The Proctor Stafford Collection, purchased with funds provided by Mr and Mrs Allen C Balch 112tl; *Magdalen with the Smoking Flame*, Georges de La Tour, gift of The Ahmanson Foundation 112tr; *Monument to Honoré de Balzac*, Auguste Rodin, gift of B Gerald Cantor; 112c; *The Cotton Pickers*, Winslow Homer, Acquisition made possible by museum trustees 112t; Pair of Officials, China, 618–907, Gift of Leon Lidow 113tr; Dunes, *Oceano*, Edward Weston, © 1981 Center for Creative Photography, Arizona Board of Regents 113b; LA DEPARTMENT OF WATER AND POWER: 48clb, 192b; LA DODGERS INC: 148b; JACK LONDON COLLECTION: California State Parks 22b.

MAGNES MUSEUM PERMANENT COLLECTIONS: 19th-century blue velvet embroidery brocade robe, 403t; MAGNUM PHOTOS: Michael Nichols 53tl; MARINE WORLD AFRICA USA: Charlotte Fiorito 288tr; ANDREW MCKINNEY PHOTOGRAPHY: 43cl, 290tl, 290tr, 291cr, 292tr, 293tr, 293br, 297cr, 297bc, 303crb, 321t, 336c, 359b, 371bl, 398t; METROPOLITAN TRANSIT DEVELOPMENT BOARD, SAN DIEGO: Stephen Simpson 256cla; METROPOLITAN WATER DISTRICT OF SOUTHERN CALIFORNIA: 192c; ROBERT MONDAVI WINERY: 446br; JOHN MUIR NATIONAL HISTORIC SITE: National Park Service 398b; MUSEUM OF TELEVISION AND RADIO: Grant Mudford 86t.

THE NAMES PROJECT: AIDS Memorial Quilt © 1988 Matt Herron 53tr, 350c; THE NATIONAL MOTOR MUSEUM, BEAULIEU: 191bl; PETER NEWARK'S AMERICAN PICTURES: 43br, 44br, 191tl, 293crb; PETER NEWARK'S WESTERN AMERICANA: 44cla, 44bl, 44–5c, 185 (inset), 243br, 285 (inset), 417 (inset), 503 (inset), 587 (inset); NHPA: Joe Blossom 77tr; Rich Kirchner 35t, 444c; Stephen Krasemann 487cra; P McDonald 232b; David Middleton 420t, 432t; Kevin Schafer 420b; John Shaw 209b, 220b, 269t, 420cl, 475c; Roger Tidman 231b; NEW YORK PUBLIC LIBRARY: I N Phelps Stokes Collection, Miriam and Ira D Wallach Division of Art, Prints and Photographs, The New York Public Library, Astor,

Lenox and Tilden Foundations 44clb; THE NORTON SIMON FOUNDATION, PASADENA: *Still Life with Lemons, Oranges and a Rose*, Francisco de Zurbaran (1633) 152b; Buddha Enthroned, Kashmir, India (8th century) 153b; *Woman with a Book*, Pablo Picasso (1832), Estate of Robert Ellis Simon, 1969, 152t; *Saints Paul and Frediano*, Filippino Lippi (1483) 153t; *Self-Portrait*, Rembrandt van Rijn (c.1636–38) 152c; *The Little Fourteen-Year-Old Dancer*, Edgar Degas (1878–81) 153bc.

COURTESY OF THE OAKLAND MUSEUM OF CALIFORNIA: *Yosemite Valley*, Albert Bierstadt (1868) 8–9; *Figure on a Porch*, Richard Diebenkorn (1959) 24cl; *Afternoon in Piedmont*, Xavier Tizoc Martinez (c.1911) 24br; *California Venus*, Rupert Schmid (c.1895) 25c; The Oakland Museum History Department: 20bl, 39b, 40cla, 40–1cb (2), 41cla, 43cr, 45ca, 45crb, 46tl, 48tr, 49cb, 52cla, 52bl, 369br, 408tl, 408tr, 408b, 409t, 425t; The Oakland Museum Kahn Collection 459b; The Oakland Tribune Collection, Gift of Alameda Newspaper Group 50b, 424cl, 424b; OXFORD SCIENTIFIC FILMS: Daniel J Cox 421ca; Michael Fogden 480c; Stan Osolinski 421cr.

PASADENA CONVENTION AND VISITORS' BUREAU: 150b; ERHARD PFEIFFER: 21tr, 26t, 26b, 27b, 59bl, 68t, 69tl, 84, 85, 86b, 87c, 116, 118cl, 128cla, 128b,129t, 129c, 129b, 136, 137, 145t, 539b; PHOTO NETWORK: Mary Messenger 584b; Phyllis Picardi 191br; Woodard 32b; PHOTOPHILE: 30b, 57t, 186c, 234; Jose Carrillo 33b; Scott Crain 14c; Arthur Fox 578t; Mark Gibson 583b; Jim Gray 187b; Michael Hall 64tr, 162t; Matt Lindsay 17b, 33c, 256b, 257b, 600c; Sal Maimone 123bl, 167, 186b, 242br, 418b, 506c; LLT Rhodes 42tl; PHOTO TREK INC: M J Wickham 418cb; PICTOR INTERNATIONAL–LONDON: 54–5, 58t, 58bl, 58br, 190tr, 227t; 276–7, 282b, 289tl, 450, 482, 497t; PICTORIAL PRESS LTD: J Cummings 53cra, 349b; PICTURES COLOUR LIBRARY: 18t, 35bl, 70, 119t; Leo de Wys 577c; POPPERFOTO: 500t.

RETNA PICTURES LTD: LGI Photo Agency/Marco Shark 23br; Steve Granite 65t; REX FEATURES: 350b; RIVERSIDE MUNICIPAL MUSEUM: Chris Moser 40cr.

SALINAS PUBLIC LIBRARY: Courtesy of the Steinbeck Archives, 23t, 501b; SAN FRANCISCO ART INSTITUTE: D Wakely 296c (d), 331t; SAN FRANCISCO CABLE CAR MUSEUM: 293tl, 293bl; SAN FRANCISCO CONVENTION AND VISITORS' BUREAU: 35br, Mark Gibson 292c; Courtesy of Brown, Zukov & Associates 372t; SAN FRANCISCO GIANTS: Martha Jane Stanton 373b; SAN FRANCISCO MUSEUM OF MODERN ART: *Back View*, 1977, Philip Guston, oil on canvas, gift of the artist, 295cr; *Zip-Light*, 1990, Sigmar Willnauer, leather, polyester, zipper, SFMOMA purchase, 308tl; *Aerial Gyrations*, 1953, Charles Sheeler, oil on canvas, Mrs Manfred Bransten Special Fund purchase, 308tr; *Nearly Hit*, 1928, Paul Klee, oil on board, Albert M Bender Bequest Fund purchase 308c; PM Magazine, 1982, Dara Birnbaum, video installation, Accessions Committee Fund and purchased by a gift of Rena Bransten, 308b; *Melodious Double Stops*, 1980,

Richard Shaw, porcelain with decal overglaze, purchased with funds from the National Endowment for the Arts and Frank O Hamilton, Byron Meyer and Mrs Peter Schlesinger, 309tl; *Untitled (Elsa Schiaparelli)* c.1933, by Man Ray, gelatin silver print, The Helen Crocker Family Funds Purchase, 309cra; *The Flower Carrier*, 1935, by Diego Rivera, oil and tempera on masonite, Albert M Bender Collection, gift of Albert M Bender in memory of Caroline Walter, 309crb; *Country Dog Gentlemen*, 1972, by Roy De Forest, polymer on canvas, gift of the Hamilton-Wells Collection, 309b; *Orange Sweater*, 1955, by Elmer Bischoff, oil on canvas, gift of Mr and Mrs Mark Schorer, 313cr; SAN FRANCISCO PUBLIC LIBRARY HISTORY ROOM: 50cla, 329bla, 359c; SAN MATEO COUNTY HISTORICAL ASSOCIATION: 396t; SANTA BARBARA MISSION ARCHIVE LIBRARY: 42cl, 43tl; SANTA BARBARA MUSEUM OF ART: *The Ripened Wheat*, Jules Bastien-Lepage (1884), Museum purchase with funds provided by Suzette and Eugene Davidson and the Davidson Endowment Fund 210cl; SCIENCE PHOTO LIBRARY: NASA 274c; George Bernard 412b; Simon Fraser 14t; David Parker 20t; Peter Menzel 20cr, 489b; SONOMA VALLEY VISITORS' BUREAU: Bob Nixon 449b; SOUTHWEST MUSEUM: ID CT.122, Photo by Don Meyer (491.G.802) 67tr; SPECTRUM COLOUR LIBRARY: 2–3, 190tl, 227cra, 255tl, 456tr, 493t, 576b; D&J Heaton 227crb, 334, 538t; STANFORD UNIVERSITY ARCHIVES: Department of Special Collections, 47b; STEVENSON HOUSE COLLECTION, MONTEREY STATE HISTORIC PARK: Sharon Fong 492t, 493cr, 493b TONY STONE IMAGES: 34b, 397crb, 418t, 468; Jerry Alexander 447t; Glen Allison 354; Ken Biggs 32t, 59tl, 168c; James Blank 139; David Carriere 578b; Jim Corwin 300; Chad Ehlers 59tr; Johan Elzenga 270, 273, 280t, 282t; David R Frazier 426; Roy Giles, 324cla; Lorentz Gullachsen 15t; Gavin Hellier 478t; John Lamb 322; D C Lowe 471t; David Madison 577t; David Maisel 288b; Ed Pritchard 284–5; A&L Sinibaldi 15br, 419cr; Alan Smith 205b; Larry Ulrich 427; John Warden 434–5; LEVI STRAUSS & CO: 333cr, 333b; TIM STREET-PORTER: 28b, 29b, 68bl.

TATE GALLERY LONDON: *It's a Psychological Fact that Pleasure helps your Disposition*, 1948, Eduardo Paolozzi 50–1c; TELEGRAPH COLOUR LIBRARY: 11, 14b; EDWARD THOMAS PHOTOGRAPHY: 28t.

ULSTER MUSEUM, BELFAST: By kind permission of the Trustees 41cl; BY COURTESY OF THE UNITED STATES POSTAL SERVICE: 588t; Stamp Designs © 1995, 307c, 597t.

WELLS FARGO BANK: 45bl, 302b, 304b, 463b; WORLD PICTURES: 12, 13b, 17t, 30c, 64tl, 132–3, 143c, 165, 166b, 189t, 216, 394, 582c, 601.

YOSEMITE MUSEUM: National Park Service 40tl, 40cra, Craig & Jennifer Bates 40cl; Michael Dixon 40clb; YOSEMITE NATIONAL PARK RESEARCH LIBRARY: 47ca.

ZEFA PICTURES: 1, 35c, 422cla, 476–7; Damm 602t; E Silvester 600tr; BILL ZELDIS PHOTOGRAPHY: 38; ZOOLOGICAL SOCIETY OF SAN DIEGO: 249b.

Road Map of California

Inset Map B
SAN FRANCISCO AND THE BAY AREA

Inset Map A
LOS ANGELES